MW01258167

The Unwieldy American State

The Unwieldy American State offers a political and legal history of
the administrative state from the 1940s through the early 1960s. After
Progressive Era reforms and New Deal policies shifted a substantial
amount of power to administrators, the federal government's new
size and shape made one question that much more important: How
should agencies and commissions exercise their enormous authority?
In examining procedural reforms in light of postwar political developments, Joanna L. Grisinger shows how administrative law was shaped
outside the courts. Using the language of administrative law, parties
debated substantive questions about administrative discretion, effective
governance, and national policy and designed reforms accordingly. In
doing so, they legitimated the administrative process as a valid form of
government.

Joanna L. Grisinger is currently a senior continuing lecturer at the
Center for Legal Studies at Northwestern University. She has received
fellowships and research support from the Miller Center of Public
Affairs, the William Nelson Cromwell Foundation, the Harry S. Truman
Library Institute, the Herbert Hoover Presidential Library Association,
Clemson University, and The University of Chicago.

The Unwieldy American State

Administrative Politics Since the New Deal

JOANNA L. GRISINGER
Northwestern University

CAMBRIDGE
UNIVERSITY PRESS

32 Avenue of the Americas, New York NY 10013-2473, USA

Cambridge University Press is part of the University of Cambridge.

It furthers the University's mission by disseminating knowledge in the pursuit of
education, learning and research at the highest international levels of excellence.

www.cambridge.org
Information on this title: www.cambridge.org/9781107671119

First published 2012
First paperback edition 2013

A catalogue record for this publication is available from the British Library

Library of Congress Cataloguing in Publication data
Grisinger, Joanna.
  The Unwieldy American state : administrative politics since the new deal /
Joanna L. Grisinger.
    p.   cm.
  Includes bibliographical references and index.
  ISBN 978-1-107-00432-0 (hardback)
  1. Administrative agencies – United States – History – 20th century.
  2. Administrative law – United States – History – 20th century.
  3. United States – Politics and government – 1945–1989.   I. Title.
  JK411.G75   2011
  352.20973–dc23   2011023044

ISBN 978-1-107-00432-0 Hardback
ISBN 978-1-107-67111-9 Paperback

for my parents
and for Manish

Contents

Acknowledgments   *page* ix
List of Abbreviations   xiii

Introduction   1
1. The War at Home   14
2. A "Bill of Rights" for the Administrative State   59
3. Congress's Watchful Eye   109
4. The Hoover Commission and the 80th Congress   153
5. The Stymied Transformation of Administrative Law   195
Conclusion   251

Works Cited   263
Index   301

Acknowledgments

As an undergraduate at Columbia University, I was fortunate to learn from extraordinary teachers and scholars. Chief among them was Elizabeth Blackmar, who first encouraged me to think seriously about becoming a historian. The University of Chicago was an amazing place to train as a lawyer and a historian; it was there that I learned the importance of asking the right questions and the critical thinking skills needed to answer them. As a law student and then as a graduate student in American history, I was lucky enough to have George Chauncey, Kathleen Neils Conzen, David P. Currie, Neil Harris, Thomas C. Holt, Mae Ngai, William J. Novak, Amy Dru Stanley, David Strauss, and Cass Sunstein as professional models. I also owe a great debt to my fellow graduate students – Lisa Andersen, Emily Brunner, Mike Czaplicki, Scott Lien, Ajay Mehrotra, Steve Porter, Gautham Rao, Laurel Spindel, Michael Stamm, Tracy Steffes, and Kyle Volk – who were generous with moral support, hilarity, and incisive comments on innumerable drafts of dissertation-length dissertation chapters.

As my dissertation advisor, William J. Novak repeatedly encouraged me to believe that my interest in administrative law had enormous relevance for political history. His continuing confidence in the importance of the story I was telling helped restore my enthusiasm whenever I'd been laboring too long in stacks of bureaucratic reports. Mae Ngai offered excellent advice about the scope and limits of my dissertation and pushed me to think broadly in connecting my own story to the multiple political stories of the era. From the beginning of my research, Daniel R. Ernst has been generous with his time and advice, and I have drawn on his encyclopedic knowledge of the administrative state more times than I can count.

I am deeply grateful for the financial support I received for this project from the Miller Center Fellowship in Public Affairs at the University of Virginia, the University of Chicago's Dissertation Teaching and Research Fellowship, the University of Chicago's Harry Barnard Dissertation-Year Fellowship in American History, the William Nelson Cromwell Foundation Grant, and Clemson University's College Research Grant Program. Additional funding from Clemson University, the Herbert Hoover Presidential Library Association Travel Grant, the Harry S. Truman Library Institute Research Grant, and the University of Chicago's Freehling Research Travel Grant and Doolittle Travel Fellowship enabled the research trips and conference travel that made this project possible.

At Clemson University, Thomas J. Kuehn strongly supported my research, and the Department of History offered a wonderful place to work. Stephanie Barczewski, James Burns, Elizabeth Carney, Caroline Dunn Clark, James Jeffries, Steve Marks, Rachel Chico Moore, Megan Taylor Shockley, and Michael Silvestri offered friendship, advice, and pimento cheese in equal measure. Many thanks to Robert L. Nelson and Terence Halliday for allowing me to spend a year at the American Bar Foundation as visiting faculty in 2007–2008, and for hosting me each summer since. The American Bar Foundation provided a quiet place to research and included me within an amazing community of scholars with whom I could discuss the fruits and frustrations of sociolegal scholarship.

In completing this book, I have benefited enormously from the advice and support of friends and colleagues. Susanna Ashton, Felice Batlan, Andrew W. Cohen, Dan Hamilton, Richard Helmholz, Richard John, Laura Kalman, Felicia Kornbluh, Sophia Z. Lee, Kate Masur, Sidney Milkis, Laura Beth Nielsen, Dylan Penningroth, James T. Sparrow, Kristen Stilt, David Tanenhaus, Karen Tani, Allison Brownell Tirres, and Victoria Saker Woeste were generous with time, interest, and conversation. Readers for Cambridge University Press offered excellent advice, and extra credit is due to particularly patient friends and readers – Brian Balogh, Mike Czaplicki, Daniel R. Ernst, Ajay Mehrotra, Steve Porter, Gautham Rao, Reuel Schiller, Christopher W. Schmidt, Michael Stamm, Tracy Steffes, and Kyle Volk – who brought their critical faculties to bear on various drafts of this project as I endeavored to turn a particularly unwieldy dissertation into a book.

Many thanks as well to the librarians and archivists at the University of Chicago, Clemson University, Northwestern University, the University of Virginia, the National Archives and Records Administration, the Herbert Hoover Presidential Library, the Harry S. Truman Presidential Library, and the Dwight D. Eisenhower Presidential Library for their expert assistance. At Cambridge University Press, Eric Crahan was an expert editor, and Abigail Zorbaugh patiently answered my many questions. Anne Kelsey Zibert provided excellent research assistance. Versions of some material appeared in "Law in Action: The Attorney General's Committee on Administrative Procedure," *Journal of Policy History* 20, no. 3 (2008): 379–418; and in "Law and the Administrative State," in Sally Hadden and Alfred L. Brophy, eds., *A Companion to American Legal History* (forthcoming). I am indebted to Suzanne Funk Colburn for permission to use the illustration by Tom Funk featured on the cover.

I am grateful to Brian Balogh, Sidney Milkis, Daniel Carpenter, and the 2002–2003 Fellows of the Miller Center of Public Affairs for valuable conversations about both American political development and American Political

Development; to Lawrence M. Friedman, Robert W. Gordon, Barbara Young Welke, and participants in the 2003 J. Willard Hurst Summer Institute in Legal History for the opportunity to discuss the craft of legal history at length; to participants in the Law and Society Association's 2004 Graduate Student Workshop for conversations about how to engage in sociolegal scholarship; to participants in the Law and Society Association's 2006 Summer Institute at the University of the Witwatersrand in Johannesburg, South Africa, for rich discussions of rights in the regulatory context; and to William J. Novak, James T. Sparrow, and participants in the 2010 Symposium on the State in U.S. History at New York University for fascinating conversations aimed at rethinking the American state. This project was also much improved by the comments and questions posed by participants in the American Bar Foundation Research Seminar; the ABF/Illinois Legal History Seminar; the Law & Society Workshop at Indiana University's Maurer School of Law; and the University of Chicago's Social History, Legal History, and American Political Development Workshops, and by panelists and audience members at the Policy History Conference and meetings of the American Society for Legal History, the American Political Science Association, the Law and Society Association, and the Social Science History Association.

Special thanks to my family and friends for their support, their interest, and often their couches and guest bedrooms during research and conference trips: Carey Bartell and Josh Gilbert, Erika Clowes, Carolyn McKee Greene, Dorothy Grisinger, Steve and Alli Hackney, Samantha and Darren Hardy, Mark Harrison and Kathleen McDavid, Steve and Andrea Hasegawa, Ariel Leifer and Billy Weinberg, Kate Masur and Peter Slevin, Amy Monaghan and Jonathan Beecher Field, Melanie Nordlinger, Kate Pratter Osborne, Kelly and Scott Proudfit, Amy Schulz, Suresh and Dina Shah, Ash and Rebecca Shah, Shauna Toh, Eileen Walsh, Ellen Walsh, Molly Walsh and Chuck Jorgensen, and Kathleen Watford. I could not have done any of this without the love and support of my parents, Pat and John Grisinger; their unwavering encouragement of my legal and historical pursuits means the world to me. Finally, to Manish Shah: thank you, for everything.

Abbreviations

ABA	American Bar Association
ACLU	American Civil Liberties Union
APA	Administrative Procedure Act
APSA	American Political Science Association
CAB	Civil Aeronautics Board
CPSC	Consumer Product Safety Commission
CSC	Civil Service Commission
EPA	Environmental Protection Agency
FAA	Federal Aviation Administration
FCC	Federal Communications Commission
FPC	Federal Power Commission
FSA	Federal Security Agency
FTC	Federal Trade Commission
HUAC	House Un-American Activities Committee
ICC	Interstate Commerce Commission
INS	Immigration and Naturalization Service
IRS	Internal Revenue Service
NLRB	National Labor Relations Board
OPA	Office of Price Administration
PACGO	President's Advisory Committee on Government Organization
RFC	Reconstruction Finance Corporation
SEC	Securities and Exchange Commission
TVA	Tennessee Valley Authority
USDA	Department of Agriculture
WPB	War Production Board

Introduction

By the end of the 1930s, the bureaucrats were in charge. In expanding the federal government's field of play in the preceding decades, Congress and the White House had created dozens of agencies, departments, bureaus, and commissions to handle this new and staggering workload.[1] With the vast growth

---

[1] For more on the early administrative state, see Matthew A. Crenson, *The Federal Machine: Beginnings of Bureaucracy in Jacksonian America* (Baltimore, MD: Johns Hopkins University Press, 1975); Michael Nelson, "A Short, Ironic History of American National Bureaucracy," *Journal of Politics* 44 (1982): 747–78; William E. Nelson, *The Roots of American Bureaucracy, 1830–1900* (Cambridge, MA: Harvard University Press, 1982); William J. Novak, *The People's Welfare: Law and Regulation in Nineteenth-Century America* (Chapel Hill: University of North Carolina Press, 1996); Kimberly S. Johnson, *Governing the American State: Congress and the New Federalism, 1877–1929* (Princeton, NJ: Princeton University Press, 2006); Jerry L. Mashaw, "Recovering American Administrative Law: Federalist Foundations, 1787–1801," *Yale Law Journal* 115 (2006): 1256–344; Jerry L. Mashaw, "Reluctant Nationalists: Federal Administration and Administrative Law in the Republican Era, 1801–1829," *Yale Law Journal* 116 (2007): 1636–740; Jerry L. Mashaw, "Administration and 'The Democracy': Administrative Law from Jackson to Lincoln, 1829–1861," *Yale Law Journal* 117 (2008): 1568–693; Gautham Rao, "The Federal *Posse Comitatus* Doctrine: Slavery, Compulsion, and Statecraft in Mid-Nineteenth-Century America," *Law and History Review* 26 (2008): 1–56; Brian Balogh, *A Government Out of Sight: The Mystery of National Authority in Nineteenth-Century America* (Cambridge: Cambridge University Press, 2009); Jerry L. Mashaw and Avi Perry, "Administrative Statutory Interpretation in the Antebellum Republic," *Michigan State Law Review* (2009): 7–49; Jerry L. Mashaw, "Federal Administration and Administrative Law in the Gilded Age," *Yale Law Journal* 119 (2010): 1362–472. Studies examining the development and expansion of regulatory authority in the late nineteenth century and early twentieth century include Robert E. Cushman, *The Independent Regulatory Commissions* (New York: Oxford University Press, 1941); Samuel P. Hays, *American Political History as Social Analysis: Essays* (Knoxville: University of Tennessee Press, 1980); David B. Tyack, Thomas James, and Aaron Benavot, *Law and the Shaping of Public Education, 1785–1954* (Madison: University of Wisconsin Press, 1987); Martin J. Sklar, *The Corporate Reconstruction of American Capitalism, 1890–1916: The Market, the Law, and Politics* (Cambridge: Cambridge University Press, 1988); Morton Keller, *Regulating a New Economy: Public Policy and Economic Change in America, 1900–1933* (Cambridge, MA: Harvard University Press, 1990); Morton Keller, *Regulating a New Society: Public Policy and Social Change in America, 1900–1933*

of government responsibility during the Great Depression came yet more new agencies that complemented and often overlapped the jurisdictions of older ones.² Individuals claimed benefits from the Social Security Board, the Railroad Retirement Board, and the Veterans Administration at the same time that businessmen defended their companies against claims of unfair competition before the Federal Trade Commission, submitted shipping rates to Interstate Commerce Commission and the Maritime Commission, and asked the Federal Communications Commission and the Federal Alcohol Administration for permission to run radio stations and to sell liquor. Routine matters handled by more than 100 federal agencies and commissions – what Securities and Exchange Commission chairman William O. Douglas called "the shirt-sleeve work of government" – dwarfed the caseload of Congress and the federal courts.³ The National Labor Relations Board, for example, resolved more than 22,500 cases in its first four years of operation, while the Board of Veterans' Appeals held hearings on 46,000 cases in less than six years.⁴ As of 1940, the ICC had received more than 98,000 certificate applications under the Motor Carrier Act of 1935.⁵ If volume is any measure, administrative officials (who themselves became vastly more numerous during the Roosevelt administration) had taken on the lion's share of federal governance.

Americans transformed the political relationships, institutional framework, and legal structure of the federal government as they placed ever more legislative, executive, and judicial authority in executive agencies and departments

(Cambridge, MA: Harvard University Press, 1994); Barbara Young Welke, *Recasting American Liberty: Gender, Race, Law, and the Railroad Revolution, 1865–1920* (Cambridge: Cambridge University Press, 2001); Tracy L. Steffes, "Solving the 'Rural School Problem': New State Aid, Standards, and Supervision of Local Schools, 1900–1933," *History of Education Quarterly* 48 (2008): 181–220.
² See Arthur M. Schlesinger, Jr., *The Age of Roosevelt: The Coming of the New Deal* (Boston: Houghton Mifflin, 1959); Arthur M. Schlesinger Jr., *The Age of Roosevelt: The Politics of Upheaval* (Boston: Houghton Mifflin, 1960); Ellis W. Hawley, *The New Deal and the Problem of Monopoly: A Study in Economic Ambivalence* (Princeton, NJ: Princeton University Press, 1966); Michael E. Parrish, *Securities Regulation and the New Deal* (New Haven, CT: Yale University Press, 1970); Kenneth Finegold and Theda Skocpol, *State and Party in America's New Deal* (Madison: University of Wisconsin Press, 1995); David Plotke, "The Endurance of New Deal Liberalism," *Studies in American Political Development* 10 (1996): 415–20; Nicholas S. Zeppos, "The Legal Profession and the Development of Administrative Law," *Chicago-Kent Law Review* 72 (1997): 1119–57; Karen Orren and Stephen Skowronek, "Regimes and Regime Building in American Government: A Review of Literature on the 1940s," *Political Science Quarterly* 113 (1998): 689–702.
³ William O. Douglas, "Virtues of the Administrative Process," in James Allen, ed., *Democracy and Finance: The Addresses and Public Statements of William O. Douglas as Member and Chairman of the Securities and Exchange Commission*, 243–47 (New Haven, CT: Yale University Press, 1940), 244.
⁴ Attorney General's Committee on Administrative Procedure, *National Labor Relations Board, Monograph No. 18* (Washington, DC: Department of Justice, 1940), 2; Attorney General's Committee on Administrative Procedure, *Final Report* (Washington, DC: Government Printing Office, 1941), Appendix F, 324.
⁵ Attorney General's Committee, *Final Report*, Appendix F, 317.

and in a new "fourth branch" of independent regulatory commissions.[6] The rise of this "administrative state" – a term that I use to describe the whole of the agencies, departments, bureaus, and commissions sprawled awkwardly across the federal landscape – required Americans to replace democratically elected legislatures and politically appointed officials with educated experts removed from patronage and political pressure, in an apparent departure from traditional American governance and constitutional conceptions of the separation of powers. The organizational structures, official rules, specialized expertise, and ostensible independence from the democratic process that characterize administration had become the dominant form of American governance.[7] Indeed, these agencies and commissions offered an alluring alternative to the inherent irrationality and apparent corruption of democratic politics.[8] Even as New Dealers' enthusiasm for expanding the federal government's regulatory commitments waned toward the end of the decade, many of Roosevelt's major programs and agencies endured, operating alongside the fiscal tools and consumption politics on which the federal government would increasingly rely.[9]

---

[6] President's Committee on Administrative Management, *Administrative Management in the Government of the United States* (Washington, DC : Government Printing Office, 1937), 32.

[7] This is the model described in Max Weber, *Economy and Society*, vol. 2, 956–1005 (Berkeley: University of California Press, 1978).

[8] See Robert H. Wiebe, *The Search for Order 1877–1920* (New York: Hill and Wang, 1967); Alfred D. Chandler Jr. and Louis Galambos, "The Development of Large-Scale Economic Organizations in Modern America," *Journal of Economic History* 30 (1970): 201–17; Louis Galambos, "The Emerging Organizational Synthesis in Modern American History," *Business History Review* 44 (1970): 279–90; Alan Trachtenberg, *The Incorporation of America: Culture and Society in the Gilded Age* (New York: Hill and Wang, 1982); Louis Galambos, "Technology, Political Economy, and Professionalization: Central Themes of the Organizational Synthesis," *Business History Review* 57 (1983): 471–93; William R. Brock, *Investigation and Responsibility: Public Responsibility in the United States, 1865–1900* (Cambridge: Cambridge University Press, 1984); John A. Rohr, *To Run a Constitution: The Legitimacy of the Administrative State* (Lawrence: University Press of Kansas, 1986); Ronald A. Cass, "Models of Administrative Action," *Virginia Law Review* 72 (1986): 363–98; Olivier Zunz, *Making America Corporate 1870–1920* (Chicago: University of Chicago Press, 1990); Brian Balogh, "Reorganizing the Organizational Synthesis: Federal-Professional Relations in Modern America," *Studies in American Political Development* 5 (1991): 119–72; Gary Lawson, "The Rise and Rise of the Administrative State," *Harvard Law Review* 107 (1994): 1231–54; Robert L. Rabin, "Federal Regulation in Historical Perspective," *Stanford Law Review* 38 (1986): 1189–326.

[9] John W. Jeffries, "The 'New' New Deal: FDR and American Liberalism, 1937–1945," *Political Science Quarterly* 105 (1990): 397–418; Ira Katznelson and Bruce Pietrykowski, "Rebuilding the American State: Evidence from the 1940s," *Studies in American Political Development* 5 (1991): 301–39; Ira Katznelson, Kim Geiger, and Daniel Kryder, "Limiting Liberalism: The Southern Veto in Congress, 1933–1950," *Political Science Quarterly* 108 (1993): 283–306; John J. Coleman, "State Formation and the Decline of Political Parties: American Parties in the Fiscal State," *Studies in American Political Development* 8 (1994): 195–230; Alan Brinkley, *The End of Reform: New Deal Liberalism in Recession and War* (New York: Alfred A. Knopf, 1995); Michael K. Brown, "State Capacity and Political Choice: Interpreting the Failure of the Third New Deal," *Studies in American Political Development* 9 (1995): 187–212; Bartholomew H. Sparrow, *From the Outside In: World War II and the American State* (Princeton, NJ: Princeton University

ANTLR

This state – less a "New Deal state" than a state that had survived the New Deal – was no longer a hesitant or emergency experiment.

Americans' reaction to their new government included both apprehension about administrative power and new interest in its rules and limits. On the eve of World War II, criticism of the agencies was at a fever pitch. Individual agencies, administrative practices, and the administrative state as a whole were the subject of questions, concerns, and hostility – from conservative members of Congress disturbed by the political activity of bureaucrats, from executive and legislative reformers troubled by the broader shift in policy-making authority, from regulated parties and their lawyers worried about their own economic interests, from Democrats and Republicans concerned about the administration of substantive laws, from law professors and political scientists wondering what this change meant for democracy and for the logic of the constitutional system, and from agency officials and their defenders who repeatedly stressed the legitimacy of administrative action.[10] The further expansion of government during World War II only intensified concerns that the balance between individual rights and public power left regulated parties vulnerable to overly zealous administrators. Given the Office of Price Administration's adoption of methods and procedures common at other agencies, charges of OPA lawlessness implicated the administrative state as a whole. As World War II drew to a close, the political furor surrounding administration pushed members of Congress to address the "problem" of administrative authority.

During the middle of the twentieth century, these political and institutional questions about the proper role of administrative governance in American life played out through battles over administrative procedure and organization – the rules that determined *how* agencies and commissions should exercise their enormous authority. As Americans increasingly eyed government power itself as the thing to be regulated, members of Congress joined prominent lawyers,

Press, 1996); Alan Brinkley, "The Late New Deal and the Idea of the State," in *Liberalism and Its Discontents*, 37–62 (Cambridge, MA: Harvard University Press, 1998); Brian Waddell, *The War against the New Deal: World War II and American Democracy* (DeKalb: Northern Illinois University Press, 2001); Meg Jacobs, *Pocketbook Politics: Economic Citizenship in Twentieth-Century America* (Princeton, NJ: Princeton University Press, 2005).

[10] See "Symposium on Administrative Law," *American Law School Review* 9 (1939): 139–84, 139; Marver H. Bernstein, "The Politics of Adjudication," *Journal of Politics* 16 (1954): 299–323; Jerold S. Auerbach, *Unequal Justice: Lawyers and Social Change in Modern America* (New York: Oxford University Press, 1976); Peter Irons, *The New Deal Lawyers* (Princeton, NJ: Princeton University Press, 1982); Thomas I. Emerson, *Young Lawyer for the New Deal: An Insider's Memoir of the Roosevelt Years*, ed. Joan P. Emerson (Latham, MD: Rowman and Littlefield, 1991); Ronen Shamir, *Managing Legal Uncertainty: Elite Lawyers in the New Deal* (Durham, NC: Duke University Press, 1995); G. Edward White, "The Emergence of Agency Government and the Creation of Administrative Law," in *The Constitution and the New Deal*, 94–127 (Cambridge, MA: Harvard University Press, 2000); Anne Mira Kornhauser, *Saving Liberalism: Political Imagination in the American Century* (PhD dissertation, Columbia University, 2004); Joanna L. Grisinger, "Law and the Administrative State," in Sally Hadden and Alfred L. Brophy, eds., *A Companion to American Legal History* (Hoboken, NJ: Wiley-Blackwell, forthcoming).

academics, and industry groups in criticizing administrators' failure to offer due process to the parties before them. Administrative law offered professional, expert, and nonpartisan language for talking about what the agencies should and should not do. Individuals and institutions across the political spectrum weighed in on the specifics of fair hearings, administrative discretion, secretive decision making, and standards of judicial review, turning an esoteric area of law into an arena of partisan political wrangling and battles for power among competing branches of government. Reformers wrote scathing editorials and supportive articles, formed congressional investigating committees and testified before them, brought together influential Americans for special inquiries and study groups (including the two Hoover Commissions), and drafted far-reaching legal reforms encapsulating their visions of the administrative state (the Administrative Procedure Act of 1946 and the Legislative Reorganization Act of 1946 were among those successfully enacted). Some reforms were addressed to *all* agencies and commissions, some to agencies and commissions with regulatory authority, some to the independent commissions, and still others to individual agencies alone. Through complicated and often arcane discussions of administrative hearings, rule making, and standards of review, proponents and opponents of specific programs and of bureaucracy as a whole struggled to craft rules to ensure the fairness of administrative governance.

In examining these debates, *The Unwieldy State* offers a political history of administrative law reform and a legal history of the administrative politics involved in shaping and legitimating the administrative state in the postwar decades. Arguments locating administrative legitimacy in the reassuringly scientific nature of administration, in administrative expertise and professionalism, or in interest-group liberalism tend to understate the crucial role of law and procedure in making administrative governance acceptable to Americans in the 1940s and 1950s.[11] Legalism and fairness were tightly linked, and parties

---

[11] See James M. Landis, *The Administrative Process* (New Haven: Yale University Press, 1938); Theodore J. Lowi, *The End of Liberalism: The Second Republic of the United States*, 2nd ed. (New York: W. W. Norton & Co., 1979); Brian Balogh, *Chain Reaction: Expert Debate and Public Participation in American Commercial Nuclear Power, 1945–1975* (New York: Cambridge University Press, 1991); Morton J. Horwitz, *The Transformation of American Law, 1870–1960: The Crisis of Legal Orthodoxy* (New York: Oxford University Press, 1992); White, "The Emergence of Agency Government and the Creation of Administrative Law"; Jacobs, *Pocketbook Politics*; Reuel E. Schiller, "Enlarging the Administrative Polity: Administrative Law and the Changing Definition of Pluralism, 1945–1970," *Vanderbilt Law Review* 53 (2000): 1389–453; Daniel Carpenter, *The Forging of Bureaucratic Autonomy: Reputations, Networks, and Policy Innovation in Executive Agencies, 1862–1928* (Princeton, NJ: Princeton University Press, 2001); Reuel E. Schiller, "Reining in the Administrative State: World War II and the Decline of Expert Administration," in Daniel R. Ernst and Victor Jew, eds., *Total War and the Law: The American Home Front in World War II*, 185–206 (Westport, CT: Praeger, 2002); Lizabeth Cohen, *Consumers' Republic: The Politics of Mass Consumption in Postwar America* (New York: Knopf, 2003); Jessica Wang, "Imagining the Administrative State: Legal Pragmatism, Securities Regulation, and New Deal Liberalism," *Journal of Policy History* 17 (2005): 257–93.

inside and outside government turned to administrative rules and procedures to ensure that administrators acted fairly. As one former Justice Department official reminded Attorney General Homer Cummings in 1938, "unless these agencies are fair and the people at large are convinced that they are fair, administrative law will not succeed."[12] Procedural protections for regulated parties and institutional limits on administrators served to reassure Americans that their rights were not in danger from bureaucratic governance.

This pressure for procedural reform indicates more about anti-bureaucratic politics than legal imperatives, as administrative procedure already operated within clearly established legal boundaries. By the late 1930s, in fact, the administrative process *was* legitimate – at least according to judges. Agencies' struggle with reviewing courts had dominated previous decades, during which period many agencies had reassured judges of their trustworthiness by adopting procedures that were more or less quasi-judicial. A rich case law defined the boundaries of administrative due process, and, by 1940, agency officials could defend themselves against claims of administrative lawlessness and "absolutism" by pointing to masses of evidence that administrators were thoroughly bound by existing rules and procedures that judges had repeatedly endorsed.[13] Courts consistently deferred to the agencies' authority and expertise and declined to intervene in any but the most egregious cases.[14]

---

[12] Charles E. Wyzanski to Homer Cummings, Sept. 29, 1938, 3, Cummings Papers, Box 169, UVA.

[13] See A. A. Berle Jr., "The Expansion of American Administrative Law," *Harvard Law Review* 30 (1917): 430–48; Felix Frankfurter, ed., *A Selection of Cases under the Interstate Commerce Act.* 2nd ed. (Cambridge, MA: Harvard University Press, 1922); Ernst Freund et al, *The Growth of American Administrative Law* (St. Louis, MO: Thomas Law Book Co., 1923); Roscoe Pound, "The Growth of Administrative Justice," *Wisconsin Law Review* 2 (1924): 321–39; Gerard C. Henderson, *The Federal Trade Commission: A Study in Administrative Law and Procedure* (New Haven, CT: Yale University Press, 1924); John Dickinson, *Administrative Justice and the Supremacy of Law in the United States* (Cambridge, MA: Harvard University Press, 1927); Felix Frankfurter, "The Task of Administrative Law," *University of Pennsylvania Law Review* 75 (1927): 614–21; I. L. Sharfman, *The Interstate Commerce Commission: A Study in Administrative Law and Procedure*, 4 vols. (New York: Commonwealth Fund, 1931–1937); Board of Investigation and Research, *The Report on Practices and Procedures of Governmental Control*, 78th Cong., 2nd sess., 1944, H. Doc. 678; James M. Landis, *Report on Regulatory Agencies to the President-Elect*, Subcommittee on Administrative Practice and Procedure, Senate Judiciary Committee, 86th Cong., 2nd sess., 1960, Committee Print; see also Rabin, "Federal Regulation in Historical Perspective," 1320; Stephen Skowronek, *Building a New American State: The Expansion of National Administrative Capacities, 1877–1920* (Cambridge: Cambridge University Press, 1982), chap. 8; Schiller, "Enlarging the Administrative Polity: Administrative Law and the Changing Definition of Pluralism, 1945–1970;" Lowi, *End of Liberalism*; Mark Tushnet, "Administrative Law in the 1930s: The Supreme Court's Accommodation of Progressive Legal Theory," *Duke Law Journal* 60 (2011): 1565–637; Thomas W. Merrill, "Article III, Agency Adjudication, and the Origins of the Appellate Review Model of Administrative Law," *Columbia Law Review* 111 (2011): 939–1003.

[14] Daniel R. Ernst has coined the term "procedural Diceyism" to describe the phenomenon in which courts "accorded administrators a great deal of freedom from judicial oversight, as long as they handled disputes in ways that mimicked the courts" (Daniel Ernst, "*Morgan* and the

Although administrators often had the law on their side, critics offered their own definitions of administrative due process, based not in strict adherence to legal definitions but in broader ideas of how government officials ought to behave. Complaints about administrative illegality and excessive zeal offered a language for condemning the administrative state without directly challenging the substance of the regulatory scheme. Public charges of unfair methods and lawless administration not only brought disrepute to the agencies but also threatened to decrease public support for tasks that, practically, were too much for Congress, the White House, or the courts to handle. Scholars focusing on the legal foundations of bureaucratic authority have traced the increasing legalism of the administrative process but have been generally disengaged from the political struggles that shaped administrative law more broadly. However, these political debates about *how* the federal government would intervene called into question the nature of the postwar state and government intervention into American life.[15] Members of Congress, the White House, courts, politicians, lawyers, and businessmen who brought their institutional and political concerns to bear on the question of procedural fairness found procedure and substance inextricably intertwined. Critics questioning the fairness of administrative procedure and the role of bureaucrats were often expressing, through arcane and seemingly apolitical language, concern about the size, cost, and crazy-quilt nature of modern government; conservative antistatism and faith in local control; hostility to labor unions, securities regulation, and government rate-setting; confusion about the role of independent commissions in the constitutional structure; and fears about the potential subversion of federal civil servants.[16] Defining "fairness," then, was no simple task.

Procedural reforms reflected the variety of political incentives at play. Long before claims of "capture" came to dominate discussions of administration, postwar reformers were met with a rich tradition of agencies and commissions

New Dealers," *Journal of Policy History* 20 [2008]: 447–81, 449); see also Daniel R. Ernst, "The Politics of Administrative Law: New York's Anti-Bureaucracy Clause and the O'Brian-Wagner Campaign of 1938," *Law and History Review* 27 (2009): 331–71.

15 Richard B. Stewart, "The Reformation of American Administrative Law," *Harvard Law Review* 88 (1975): 1667–813; Gerald E. Frug, "The Ideology of Bureaucracy in American Law," *Harvard Law Review* 97 (1984): 1276–388; Jerry L. Mashaw, "Explaining Administrative Process: Normative, Positive, and Critical Stories of Legal Development," *Journal of Law, Economics, & Organization* 6 (Special Issue 1990): 267–98.

16 Barry D. Karl, *The Uneasy State: The United States from 1915 to 1945* (Chicago: University of Chicago Press, 1983); Barry D. Karl, "Constitution and Central Planning: The Third New Deal Revisited," *Supreme Court Review* (1988): 163–201; Ellis W. Hawley, "The New Deal State and the Anti-Bureaucratic Tradition," in Robert Eden, ed., *The New Deal and Its Legacy: Critique and Reappraisal*, 77–92 (New York: Greenwood Press, 1989); Jonathan Bell, *The Liberal State on Trial: The Cold War and American Politics in the Truman Years* (New York: Columbia University Press, 2004); David Ciepley, *Liberalism in the Shadow of Totalitarianism* (Cambridge, MA: Harvard University Press, 2006).

carrying out their regulatory tasks while maintaining numerous and widely accepted ties with regulated parties.[17] The growth of the administrative state was notable, in fact, for the expansion of limits on business activity *and* the pervasiveness of government relationships with those businesses. "Fairness" had long included opportunities for interested parties to participate in administrative operations through formal hearings and informal relationships. Regulated parties sought to maintain their existing close and influential relationships with administrative officials, and those officials were well aware that cooperative relationships made their jobs much easier. Federal officials during World War I had established an unprecedented degree of administrative authority over the wartime economy while at the same time making room for the views of powerful economic interests.[18] New Deal-era agencies like the National Recovery Administration, the FCC, and the SEC, and wartime agencies like the OPA

[17] Gabriel Kolko, *The Triumph of Conservatism: A Reinterpretation of American History, 1900–1916* (New York: Free Press, 1963); Gabriel Kolko, *Railroads and Regulation, 1877–1916* (Princeton, NJ: Princeton University Press, 1965); Thomas K. McCraw, "Regulation in America: A Review Article," *Business History Review* 49 (1975): 159–83; Hugh Heclo, "Issue Networks and the Executive Establishment," in Anthony King, ed., *The New American Political System*, 87–124 (Washington, DC: American Enterprise Institute for Public Policy Research, 1978); Ellis W. Hawley, "The Discovery and Study of a 'Corporate Liberalism,'" *Business History Review* 52 (1978): 309–20; Paul J. Quirk, *Industry Influence in Federal Regulatory Agencies* (Princeton, NJ: Princeton University Press, 1981); Daniel T. Rodgers, "In Search of Progressivism," *Reviews in American History* 10 (1982): 113–32; Galambos, "Technology, Political Economy, and Professionalization"; Thomas K. McCraw, *Prophets of Regulation: Charles Francis Adams, Louis D. Brandeis, James M. Landis, Alfred E. Kahn* (Cambridge, MA: Belknap Press of Harvard University, 1984); Mashaw, "Explaining Administrative Process"; Marc Allen Eisner, "Discovering Patterns in Regulatory History: Continuity, Change, and Regulatory Regimes," *Journal of Policy History* 6 (1994): 157–87; Julian E. Zelizer, *Taxing America: Wilbur D. Mills, Congress, and the State, 1945–1975* (Cambridge: Cambridge University Press, 1998); Elizabeth Sanders, *Roots of Reform: Farmers, Workers, and the American State 1877–1917* (Chicago: University of Chicago Press, 1999); Rabin, "Federal Regulation in Historical Perspective."

[18] E. Pendleton Herring, "Politics, Personalities, and the Federal Trade Commission, I," *American Political Science Review* 28 (1934): 1016–29; E. Pendleton Herring, "Politics, Personalities, and the Federal Trade Commission, II," *American Political Science Review* 29 (1935): 21–35; Robert F. Himmelberg, "The War Industries Board and the Antitrust Question in November 1918," *JAH* 52 (1965): 59–74; Robert D. Cuff, "A 'Dollar-a-Year Man' in Government: George N. Peek and the War Industries Board," *Business History Review* 41 (1967): 404–20; Robert F. Himmelberg, "Business, Antitrust Policy, and the Industrial Board of the Department of Commerce, 1919," *Business History Review* 42 (1968): 1–23; Robert D. Cuff, "Woodrow Wilson and Business-Government Relations during World War I," *Review of Politics* 31 (1969): 385–407; Robert D. Cuff, "Bernard Baruch: Symbol and Myth in Industrial Mobilization," *Business History Review* 43 (1969): 115–33; Robert D. Cuff, "The Cooperative Impulse and War: The Origins of the National Defense and Advisory Commission," in Jerry Israel, ed., *Building the Organizational Society: Essays on Associational Activities in Modern America*, 233–46 (New York: Free Press, 1972); Robert D. Cuff, "Herbert Hoover, The Ideology of Voluntarism and War Organization during the Great War," *Journal of American History* 64 (1977): 358–72; Robert Cuff, "Harry Garfield, The Fuel Administration, and the Search for a Cooperative Order during World War I," *American Quarterly* 30 (1978): 39–53.

and the War Production Board similarly embraced relationships among the regulators, the regulated, and the public.[19] Regulated parties and their lawyers accepted regulation with varying levels of enthusiasm, but in doing so wanted quick results in noncontroversial cases, elaborate procedural guarantees in contentious ones, and room for political influence throughout.[20] Their continuing ability to participate in administrative policy making would be protected by administrative law reformers, whose proposals consistently reflected the tensions from combining cooperative and adversarial relationships in the same agency, and by agency officials, who saw this as a useful path to regulatory harmony.[21]

Congress and the White House pursued their own interests in procedural and organizational reform, as reformers inside and outside of government saw opportunities for Congress and the White House to work out their relationships to the administrative state and retain a role in policy making.[22] As the 1930s ended, the White House had limited authority over the agencies and commissions and Congress was in no better shape. Although the legislative branch had been instrumental in creating the administrative state, it could only weakly direct agencies' activities. Several of the regulatory commissions with authority over huge segments of the economy – the NLRB, the SEC, and the FCC, to name just a few – were technically and purposefully independent of each branch of government, and the agencies and departments formally under executive control, such as the Departments of Agriculture, Interior, and Labor, were no less functionally separate. Procedural and organizational reform premised

---

[19] Ellis W. Hawley, *The New Deal and the Problem of Monopoly: A Study in Economic Ambivalence* (Princeton, NJ: Princeton University Press, 1966); Michael E. Parrish, *Securities Regulation and the New Deal* (New Haven, CT: Yale University Press, 1970); Robert M. Collins, "Positive Business Responses to the New Deal: The Roots of the Committee for Economic Development, 1933–1942," *Business History Review* 52 (1978): 369–91; Robert Griffith, "Dwight D. Eisenhower and the Corporate Commonwealth," *American Historical Review* 87 (1982): 87–122; Robert W. McChesney, "Free Speech and Democracy! Louis G. Caldwell, the American Bar Association and the Debate over the Free Speech Implications of Broadcast Regulation, 1928–1938," *American Journal of Legal History* 35 (1991): 351–92; Brinkley, *End of Reform*; Finegold and Skocpol, *State and Party in America's New Deal*; Waddell, *The War against the New Deal*; Cohen, *A Consumers' Republic*; David A. Moss and Michael R. Fein, "Radio Regulation Revisited: Coase, the FCC, and the Public Interest," *Journal of Policy History* 15 (2003): 389–416; Susan L. Brinson, *The Red Scare, Politics, and the Federal Communications Commission, 1941–1960* (Westport, CT: Praeger, 2004); Jacobs, *Pocketbook Politics*; Jason Scott Smith, *Building New Deal Liberalism: The Political Economy of Public Works, 1933–1956* (Cambridge: Cambridge University Press, 2005); Rabin, "Federal Regulation in Historical Perspective."

[20] See Robert A. Kagan, "Do Lawyers Cause Adversarial Legalism? A Preliminary Inquiry," *Law and Social Inquiry* 19 (1994): 1–62; Ernst, "The Politics of Administrative Law."

[21] Hugh Heclo, *A Government of Strangers: Executive Politics in Washington* (Washington, DC: Brookings Institution, 1977).

[22] David H. Rosenbloom, *Building a Legislative-Centered Public Administration: Congress and the Administrative State, 1946–1999* (Tuscaloosa: University of Alabama Press, 2000).

on the idea that leaving decisions to the agencies was unfair offered the political branches the opportunity to improve control and guarantee continuing influence therein.

These various pressures were apparent in a number of different efforts in the late 1940s that purported to offer solutions to the problem of agency zeal. The most famous of these, the Administrative Procedure Act of 1946, articulated minimum standards of fairness for administrative officials and, its sponsor claimed, provided a "bill of rights" for regulated parties in the administrative process.[23] The act demonstrated apprehension about bureaucrats as the primary makers of federal law and policy and quickly came to represent proper standards of due process in the administrative state. That same summer, Congress directed its own members to scrutinize those officials more closely and more systematically. Responding to repeated complaints that Congress was irrelevant, inefficient, and inadequate in light of the enormous bureaucracy that it had helped create, Congress reshaped itself through the Legislative Reorganization Act of 1946 and offered its members the necessary tools for keeping an eye on the administrative state. Soon thereafter, Republicans taking over Congress in 1947 created their own opportunity to engage the administrative state. The first Commission on Organization of the Executive Branch of the Government, which completed its work in 1949, was established by Congress to address the apparent incoherence of the administrative state and to recommend ways to pull the federal government back from the big-government tendencies it had developed during the New Deal and World War II. Following the organizational recommendations of the "Hoover Commission," the White House improved its own management capacities as it expanded presidential control over the executive branch and the independent commissions.

These reforms had much in common. Parties relied on dry and arcane language as they struggled to push decision-making authority into the hands of those most amenable to their own interests. Reformers' professional expertise trumped agency officials' own experience in administrative battlegrounds, as political scientists and public administration scholars offered organizational and structural proposals and lawyers pushed for legal ones. All relied on formal organization and procedures to direct and reduce the discretion of administrators, bringing lawmaking in accord with the rule of law. These reformers shared a common faith that the shape of the state mattered – that is, that top-level reorganization and uniform procedural rules outside politics would actually affect how officials made decisions.[24] At the same time, managing fears

---

[23] Senate Proceedings (statement of Sen. Pat McCarran, Mar. 12, 1946), reprinted in U.S. Senate, *Administrative Procedure Act: Legislative History*, 79th Cong., 1944–46, S. Doc 248 (Washington, DC: Government Printing Office, 1946), 298.

[24] James G. March and Johan P. Olson, "Organizing Political Life: What Administrative Reorganization Tells Us about Government," *American Political Science Review* 77

about administrative governance through discussions of administrative due process meant that the solutions were necessarily limited. Debates over the fate of the administrative state were conducted through discussions of standards of judicial review, the role of hearing examiners in formal hearings, agency rule-making procedures, and the appropriate duties of the agency heads. Not only did these conversations necessarily constrain the potential solutions, but each change rendered the range of options ever narrower.[25]

The result of all this activity was a porous administrative law that allowed multiple parties significant say while reassuring those outside the administrative process that administrative governance was safe. Americans who had resisted bureaucracy became much more comfortable with the agencies and commissions as procedural changes to their unfamiliar form promised to limit apparently unfettered bureaucratic authority.[26] By promising due process, the APA further embedded the administrative process into the federal government and made administrative procedure as a whole harder to attack. At the same time, Congress asserted control over the agencies and commissions in the Legislative Reorganization Act and promised improved oversight. The Hoover Commission's proposals offered tools for the White House to improve its own supervision of the administrative state and offered political support for such reform.

The practical effect, however, was limited by political compromises, congressional limitations, design problems, and sporadic public interest. Many administrators had developed their own informal working relationships with Congress and with regulated parties; by converting many of these informal practices into formal rules and clothing them with public approval, reformers did little to change how agencies conducted themselves. The APA ultimately worked little change in administrative practice, and Congress's promises of improved oversight proved more significant than the actual results. The first Hoover Commission's reforms strengthened the White House's role in supervision, but only when the president chose to exercise that authority. Reforms were also imperfectly tailored to the goals reformers sought to achieve. Uniform solutions that included all the agencies and commissions within their ambit made the enormous and diverse federal government seem both coherent and

(1983): 281–96; Stephen P. Waring, *Taylorism Transformed: Scientific Management Theory since 1945* (Chapel Hill: University of North Carolina Press, 1991); Matthew Holden Jr., *Continuity and Disruption: Essays in Public Administration* (Pittsburgh, PA: University of Pittsburgh Press, 1996); Paul C. Light, *The Tides of Reform: Making Government Work, 1945–1995* (New Haven, CT: Yale University Press, 1997); Harold Seidman, *Politics, Position, and Power: The Dynamics of Federal Organization*, 5th ed. (New York: Oxford University Press, 1998).

25 Reuel Schiller, "'Saint George and the Dragon': Courts and the Development of the Administrative State in Twentieth-Century America," *Journal of Policy History* 17 (2005): 110–24.

26 Karl, *The Uneasy State*; Lucy E. Salyer, *Laws Harsh as Tigers: Chinese Immigrants and the Shaping of Modern Immigration Law* (Chapel Hill: University of North Carolina Press, 1995).

manageable, but were drawn so broadly as to effect few limits on administrative discretion. Creating an administrative state had been a partial and messy process, and sweeping reform proposals that promised to solve the problem of the administrative state writ large fit awkwardly with agencies' distinct institutional and political constraints (as the second Hoover Commission discovered).[27] The result was an administrative law that was neither autonomous nor scientific and that empowered elites in government and in American society to act as they wished.

The rhetorical effect of all of this activity was nonetheless significant. As reformers touted their achievements, claiming that the "rule of law" had been brought to the administrative state, claims of administrative zealotry faded. By the 1950s, it was increasingly difficult to convince Americans that agencies were dangerous or un-American, and it was that much more difficult to discredit their work on that basis. This legitimacy did not mean the end of criticism, however. Agencies increasingly found themselves facing a barrage of complaints about their officials' slowness, intractability, and corrupt tendencies – elements that careful observers had observed in the administrative state for decades. Agencies that had been criticized for being unfair to the parties before them were now charged with failing an inchoate "public interest." The risk-averse strategies agencies had chosen and that outsiders had demanded had backfired, leading to rising backlogs and case-by-case resolution of industrywide problems.[28] At the same time, the same agencies that had long encouraged the participation of regulated parties in the decision-making process found themselves subject to complaints about these relationships. The compromises involved in adopting operating procedures that restricted the discretion of administrators but protected the participation of regulated parties, the White House, and Congress were increasingly untenable, and Americans found themselves dissatisfied with the process they had designed.

James M. Landis's critical report to President-elect John Kennedy in 1960 indicated just how much conversations about the administrative process had shifted and how many long-standing complaints earlier reform efforts had managed to ignore.[29] Attempts by the second Hoover Commission and the American Bar Association in the 1950s to further limit administrative discretion through onerous courtlike procedures and expansive judicial review received a tepid public reception, suggesting that both interested observers and regulated parties were embracing a new model of antibureaucratic politics.

---

[27] Lowi, *End of Liberalism*; Rabin, "Federal Regulation in Historical Perspective"; Carpenter, *The Forging of Bureaucratic Autonomy*; Skowronek, *Building a New American State*; Ajay K. Mehrotra, "Forging Fiscal Reform: Constitutional Change, Public Policy, and the Creation of Administrative Capacity in Wisconsin, 1880–1920," *Journal of Policy History* 20 (2008): 94–112.

[28] See Bernstein, *Regulating Business by Independent Commission*.

[29] Landis, *Report on Regulatory Agencies to the President-Elect*.

Administrative experiments in social regulation in the late 1960s and early 1970s indicated the evolution of administrative politics, as public participation became the new touchstone of reform. The "problem" of the administrative state – once that of powerless citizens against a powerful state – had become quite the reverse.[30]

---

[30] McCraw, *Prophets of Regulation*; Marver H. Bernstein, *Regulating Business by Independent Commission* (Princeton, NJ: Princeton University Press, 1955); Paul R. Verkuil, "The Emerging Concept of Administrative Procedure," *Columbia Law Review* 78 (1978): 258–329; David Vogel, "The 'New' Social Regulation in Historical and Comparative Perspective," in Thomas K. McCraw, ed., *Regulation in Perspective: Historical Essays*, 155–85 (Cambridge, MA: Harvard University Press, 1981); Hugh Heclo, "The Sixties' False Dawn: Awakenings, Movements, and Postmodern Policy-Making," in Brian Balogh, ed., *Integrating the Sixties: The Origins, Structures, and Legitimacy of Public Policy in a Turbulent Decade*, 34–63 (University Park: Pennsylvania State University Press, 1996); Thomas W. Merrill, "Capture Theory and the Courts: 1967–1983," *Chicago-Kent Law Review* 72 (1997): 1039–117; Sidney M. Milkis, "Remaking Government Institutions in the 1970s: Participatory Democracy and the Triumph of Administrative Politics," *Journal of Policy History* 10 (1998): 51–74; Stewart, "The Reformation of American Administrative Law"; Rabin, "Federal Regulation in Historical Perspective"; Schiller, "Enlarging the Administrative Polity"; Reuel E. Schiller, "Rulemaking's Promise: Administrative Law and Legal Culture in the 1960s and 1970s," *Administrative Law Review* 53 (2001): 1139–88.

I

The War at Home

Congressional opposition to the constantly expanding administrative state and to the costs of the programs it administered became increasingly evident during the late 1930s. Many members' own political, ideological, and local concerns trumped their brief enthusiasm for an aggressive response to the economic emergency, and members looked askance at Roosevelt's actions following the landslide Democratic victory in 1936. The president's efforts to reorganize the judicial and executive branches in 1937, his failed attempt to purge several conservative Southern Democrats in the 1938 primaries, and his flirtation with a third term alienated many former allies. Increasingly skeptical conservative Democrats joined Republicans in Congress, forming a coalition that conservative *New York Times* columnist Arthur Krock suggested could be called the "Temporary Committee for Executive Restraint and Correction."[1] Congressional resistance strengthened in subsequent election cycles, as the Democratic party lost a number of Northern liberals in 1938 and 1942. Although Democrats controlled Congress well into the 1940s, leadership became consolidated in the hands of Southern conservatives.

The constitutionality of the New Deal and the agencies that administered it was no longer in question by the late 1930s, but *how* those agencies operated was. Administrative procedure became a subject of partisan politics and a way for parties to talk about bureaucracy. Politicians motivated by anti-New Deal animus, concerns about federal spending and centralized power, and fears of subversion assailed the executive branch and the independent agencies, criticizing the governance of federal programs as an alternative to attacking popular

---

[1] Arthur Krock, "Bi-Partisan Majority Checks the New Deal," *New York Times*, July 23, 1939, E3. For more on the "conservative coalition," see James MacGregor Burns, *Roosevelt: The Lion and the Fox* (New York: Harcourt Brace Jovanovich, 1956); James T. Patterson, *Congressional Conservatism and the New Deal: The Growth of the Conservative Coalition in Congress, 1933–1939* (Lexington: University of Kentucky Press, 1967); David L. Porter, *Congress and the Waning of the New Deal* (Port Washington, NY: Kennikat Press Corp., 1980).

New Deal projects.² As one lawyer plaintively inquired, "Is the Administrative Process a Fifth Column?"³ Congress's own disquiet about the vast and uncontrolled authority of administrative officials was apparent in numerous hostile investigations of agencies that began in the late 1930s and continued through World War II. Among the loudest critics were Rep. Howard W. Smith of Virginia, Rep. Eugene Cox of Georgia, and Rep. Martin Dies Jr. of Texas, Democrats who had survived Roosevelt's attempted purge. Their investigations reflected the increasing political power of conservatives in Congress, but also indicated its limits. Support for new regulatory commitments remained strong in the late 1930s and early 1940s; during these years, Congress expanded the Federal Trade Commission's authority, gave the Federal Power Commission jurisdiction over interstate sales of natural gas, instructed the Food and Drug Administration to evaluate drugs before they entered the marketplace, and significantly enlarged the federal government's authority to regulate air traffic and coordinate transportation.⁴ New Deal programs were also expanded; in 1938, Roosevelt signed the Fair Labor Standards Act and a new Agricultural Adjustment Act, and 1939 amendments to the Social Security Act broadened that program's coverage.

Political hostility to bureaucracy only intensified during World War II, as the Roosevelt administration met wartime challenges with an immense administrative apparatus. As the federal government expanded its reach even further into the marketplace, many complained that the White House was dressing new New Deal programs in wartime garb.⁵ For critics, the Office of Price Administration was a central concern; the OPA was an exceptional wartime experiment that was made possible by models of administration and definitions of administrative due process established much earlier. The OPA's anti-inflationary mission was remarkably popular with the American public,

² See Marver H. Bernstein, "The Politics of Adjudication," *Journal of Politics* 16 (1954): 299–323, 302; Ronald A. Cass, "Models of Administrative Action," *Virginia Law Review* 72 (1986): 363–98, 364; Thomas I. Emerson, *Young Lawyer for the New Deal: An Insider's Memoir of the Roosevelt Years*, ed. Joan P. Emerson (Savage, MD: Rowman & Littlefield Publishers, 1991), 136–42; Daniel R. Ernst, "The Politics of Administrative Law: New York's Anti-Bureaucracy Clause and the O'Brian–Wagner Campaign of 1938," *Law and History Review* 27 (2009): 331–72.
³ Samuel Kaufman, "Is the Administrative Process a Fifth Column?" *John Marshall Law Quarterly* 6 (1940): 1–17.
⁴ Floyd M. Riddick, "Third Session of the Seventy-sixth Congress, January 3, 1940, to January 3, 1941," *American Political Science Review* 35 (1941): 284–303, 299; Susan Wagner, *The Federal Trade Commission* (New York: Praeger, 1971); Ari Arthur Hoogenboom and Olive Hoogenboom, *A History of the ICC: From Panacea to Palliative* (New York: W. W. Norton & Co., 1976); Porter, *Congress and the Waning of the New Deal*; Bradley Behrman, "Civil Aeronautics Board," in James Q. Wilson, ed., *The Politics of Regulation*, 75–120 (New York: Basic Books, 1980); Daniel Carpenter, *Reputation and Power: Organizational Image and Pharmaceutical Regulation at the FDA* (Princeton, NJ: Princeton University Press, 2010).
⁵ John Morton Blum, *V Was for Victory: Politics and American Culture During World War II* (New York: Harcourt Brace Jovanovich, 1976); Lizabeth Cohen, *A Consumers' Republic: The Politics of Mass Consumption in Postwar America* (New York: Knopf, 2003); Meg Jacobs,

and its role in the war effort made it difficult to attack head on. Charges of heedless administrators abusing their powers, however, fit within the wartime narrative of democracy versus autocracy, and members of Congress exploited this tension by accusing the agency of lawlessness to weaken its political viability.[6]

Agency officials responded by demonstrating their legal bona fides and detailing the copious rules and procedures that governed their work. Even as James M. Landis's 1938 lectures offered a view of expert administrators whose very professionalism would prevent their malfeasance, others provided an alternative narrative highlighting the long-established legal limits that circumscribed bureaucratic discretion.[7] Agency officials under attack trotted out their records in court, where judges routinely deferred to administrative decision making, and the Attorney General's Committee on Administrative Procedure, created in 1939, offered copious evidence of the rule-bound nature of administration. Officials at the OPA adopted these strategies, soliciting public support through an enforcement apparatus that drew in thousands of Americans while also seeking public legitimacy through the adoption of firmly legalistic methods.[8] At the same time that the Interstate Commerce Commission, the Securities and Exchange Commission, and the National Labor Relations Board were defending themselves by pointing to years of experience and a record of success in the courts, OPA officials rushed to demonstrate the similarity of their agency to these older ones.

This gulf between how charges of "agency absolutism" were received in the political arena and how they were received in the courts highlighted the division between the administrative state's legal and political legitimacy. By refusing to defer to judicial definitions of administrative due process, members of Congress joined other critics in offering their own definitions of fairness in the administrative state. Theirs was an argument based in the substance as well as the procedures of administration, but, by expressing their concerns in legal language, critics helped frame bureaucracy, and bureaucrats, as illegitimate and lawless on the basis of their procedure. The result of these sustained critiques – many of which lumped the OPA and other wartime agencies together with the

Pocketbook Politics: Economic Citizenship in Twentieth-Century America (Princeton, NJ: Princeton University Press, 2005).

[6] Reuel E. Schiller, "Reining in the Administrative State: World War II and the Decline of Expert Administration," in Daniel R. Ernst and Victor Jew, eds., *Total War and the Law: The American Home Front in World War II*, 185–206 (Westport, CT: Praeger, 2002).

[7] James M. Landis, *The Administrative Process* (New Haven, CT: Yale University Press, 1938); see also Jessica Wang, "Imagining the Administrative State: Legal Pragmatism, Securities Regulation, and New Deal Liberalism," *Journal of Policy History* 17 (2005): 257–93. As Landis argued elsewhere, "Partisanship or zeal on the part of administrative tribunals in behalf of the rights they are created to protect is as much expected of them as zeal on the part of judges in the defense of that body of rights we are pleased to call our liberties" ("Symposium on Administrative Law," *American Law School Review* 9 [1939]: 139–84, 181).

[8] Cohen, *A Consumers' Republic*; Jacobs, *Pocketbook Politics*.

more established domestic agencies – also created the political energy needed for legal reform once the war emergency ended.[9]

As the New Deal waned, the departments, bureaus, agencies, and commissions that populated the complicated federal organizational charts were an easy political target, as the generally opaque nature of the administrative process gave rumors and charges of "administrative absolutism" an opportunity to flourish and made it that much harder for administrative officials to convince Americans that their agencies were trustworthy. Roosevelt's own experience with executive reorganization demonstrated the nature of this resistance. In 1936, the president had established a Committee on Administrative Management to deal with what he called the "higgledy-piggledy patchwork of duplicate responsibilities and overlapping powers" that had come to characterize the administrative state.[10] In their January 1937 report, the three committee members – Louis Brownlow of the Public Administration Clearing House, Charles E. Merriam of the University of Chicago and the Social Science Research Council, and Luther H. Gulick of the Institute of Public Administration – found that "[n]o President can possibly give adequate supervision to the multitude of agencies which have been set up to carry on the work of the Government."[11] Even worse were the independent commissions, which the committee disparaged as "a headless 'fourth branch' of the Government, a haphazard deposit of irresponsible agencies and uncoordinated powers."[12]

The committee thus proposed combining certain agencies and commissions for greater organizational coherence, vesting management authority over *all* of the agencies – the formally independent commissions as well as the executive departments – within the presidency, and improving the White House's ability to keep an eye on things by increasing the president's staff and making the Bureau of the Budget and a new National Resources Planning Board central parts of the president's office. Combined with the judicial reorganization

[9] Blum, *V Was for Victory*; Richard Polenberg, *War and Society: The United States, 1941–1945* (Philadelphia: Lippincott, 1972); Meg Jacobs, "'How About Some Meat?': The Office of Price Administration, Consumption Politics, and State Building from the Bottom Up, 1941–1946," *Journal of American History* 84 (1997): 910–41; Daniel R. Ernst and Victor Jew, eds., *Total War and the Law: The American Home Front in World War II* (Westport, CT: Praeger, 2002).

[10] Franklin D. Roosevelt, "Fireside Chat," Oct. 12, 1937, in Samuel I. Rosenman, ed., *Public Papers and Addresses of Franklin D. Roosevelt*, vol. 1937 (New York: Macmillan Company, 1941), 435. For more on Roosevelt's executive reorganization efforts, see Barry D. Karl, *Executive Reorganization and Reform in the New Deal: The Genesis of Administrative Management, 1900–1939* (Cambridge, MA: Harvard University Press, 1963); Richard Polenberg, *Reorganizing Roosevelt's Government: The Controversy over Executive Reorganization, 1936–1939* (Cambridge, MA: Harvard University Press, 1966); Herbert Emmerich, *Federal Organization and Administrative Management* (University: University of Alabama Press, 1971); Peri E. Arnold, *Making the Managerial Presidency: Comprehensive Reorganization Planning, 1905–1996*, 2nd ed. rev. (Lawrence: University Press of Kansas, 1998).

[11] President's Committee on Administrative Management, *Administrative Management in the Government of the United States* (Washington, DC: Government Printing Office, 1937), 32.

[12] Ibid., 40.

proposal Roosevelt sent to Congress in February, executive reorganization was seen by Congress as a threat to congressional prerogatives and by many Americans as one more attempt to extend White House control over the rest of government. By March 1938, when Roosevelt publicly denied aspirations of dictatorship, it was clear that the plan would not survive.[13] The administrative state remained as unwieldy as ever.

Critics of the New Deal state included conservative Democrat Martin Dies Jr. of Texas, who in May 1938 established a committee to investigate the administrative state as a possible source of contagion.[14] In addition to addressing allegations of Communist influence at the Congress of Industrial Organizations, the American League for Peace and Democracy, and the *New York Times*, witnesses before the House Special Committee to Investigate Un-American Activities testified about Communist infiltration throughout the Roosevelt administration. The Dies Committee questioned the sympathies of employees at the Works Progress Administration, the NLRB, the Tennessee Valley Authority, and the Wages and Hours Administration, called for the resignation of key New Dealers, including Secretary of the Interior Harold Ickes, Labor Secretary Frances Perkins, and WPA administrator Harry Hopkins, and sent names of alleged subversives to the attorney general. It was unclear how the committee distinguished between support for the Roosevelt administration and the endorsement of dangerous ideas from abroad; according to one committee member, "New Dealism" sat alongside Communism, Nazism, and Fascism as one of "the four horsemen of autocracy."[15] This fear of ideological deviance was evident in the 1939 Hatch Act targeting "pernicious political activities"; along with provisions barring federal employees from campaigning (in response to fears that the WPA had created a patronage army for the Democratic Party), the act banned federal workers' "membership in any political party or organization which advocates the overthrow of our constitutional form of government."[16]

Dies extended his quest during wartime, publicizing the political affiliations of employees at the OPA, the War Production Board, the Board of Economic Warfare, and the Office of War Information at the same time he questioned those of employees at peacetime agencies such as at the Treasury Department, the Interior Department, the Federal Works Agency, the National

---

[13] Franklin D. Roosevelt, "The President Refutes Dictatorship Charges Connected with the Pending Reorganization Bill," Mar. 29, 1938, in Samuel I. Rosenman, ed., *Public Papers and Addresses of Franklin D. Roosevelt*, vol. 1938 (New York: Macmillan Company, 1941), 179; Sidney M. Milkis, *The President and the Parties: The Transformation of the American Party System since the New Deal* (New York: Oxford University Press, 1993).

[14] D. A. Saunders, "The Dies Committee: First Phase," *Public Opinion Quarterly* 3 (1939): 223–38; Telford Taylor, *Grand Inquest: The Story of Congressional Investigations* (New York: Simon and Schuster, 1955); David Caute, *The Great Fear: The Anti-Communist Purge under Truman and Eisenhower* (New York: Simon & Schuster, 1978).

[15] Rep. J. Parnell Thomas, quoted in "New Deal Is Held Communist Tool," *New York Times*, Oct. 15, 1938, 3.

[16] Hatch Act, Pub. L. No. 252, § 9(a)(1), 53 Stat. 1147, 1148 (1939); Emerson, *Young Lawyer for the New Deal*.

Youth Administration, the Rural Electrification Administration, the Federal Communications Commission, the SEC, and the FPC.[17] Linking inherently undemocratic administrative forms to the questionable political sympathies of those within was an effective method of questioning administrative action and tainting agency outputs. In one notable example, the FCC drew attention when the commission, under the leadership of Roosevelt appointee James L. Fly, adopted the White House's concerns about monopoly power and embarked on an energetic regulatory effort to diversify broadcast ownership.[18] The FCC's challenge to the existing organization of the industry was met with enormous hostility from broadcast interests and from members of Congress, who, charging that the FCC had no authority to act, quickly launched investigations into the commission.[19] The House Committee on Interstate and Foreign Commerce heard from upset broadcasters as members considered amendments limiting the FCC's authority, and the Dies Committee suggested that certain commission employees – including Dr. Goodwin Watson and Dr. William E. Dodd Jr. of the Foreign Broadcast Intelligence Service – were guilty of subversion. Following an investigation by a subcommittee of the House Appropriations Committee, the removal of Watson and Dodd from government service was recommended, and Congress soon blocked appropriations for the men's salaries.[20] The FCC's support of the men only made the commission that much more vulnerable, and Commissioner Clifford J. Durr's energetic defense of the employees triggered a separate FBI investigation of Durr and his wife.[21]

[17] 89 *Cong. Rec.* 479–84 (statement of Rep. Martin Dies, Feb. 1, 1943).

[18] Henry F. Pringle, "The Controversial Mr. Fly," *Saturday Evening Post*, July 22, 1944.

[19] Erik Barnouw, *The Golden Web: A History of Broadcasting in the United States*, vol. II, *1933 to 1953* (New York: Oxford University Press, 1968); James L. Baughman, *Television's Guardians: The FCC and the Politics of Programming 1958–1967* (Knoxville: University of Tennessee Press, 1985); Joon-Mann Kang, "Franklin D. Roosevelt and James L. Fly: The Politics of Broadcast Regulation, 1941–1944," *Journal of American Culture* 10 (Summer 1987): 23–33; Susan L. Brinson, "War on the Homefront in World War II: The FCC and the House Committee on Un-American Activities," *Historical Journal of Film, Radio and Television* 21 (2001): 63–75; Mickie Edwardson, "James Lawrence Fly's Report on Chain Broadcasting (1941) and the Regulation of Monopoly in America," *Historical Journal of Film, Radio and Television* 22 (2002): 397–423; Susan L. Brinson, *The Red Scare, Politics, and the Federal Communications Commission, 1941–1960* (Westport, CT: Praeger, 2004); Kimberly A. Zarkin and Michael J. Zarkin, *The Federal Communications Commission: Front Line in the Culture and Regulation Wars* (Westport, CT: Greenwood Press, 2006); Michael Stamm, *Sound Business: Newspapers, Radio, and the Politics of New Media* (Philadelphia: University of Pennsylvania Press, 2011), chap. 4.

[20] See Report in the Matter of Goodwin Watson, Frederick L. Schuman, and William E. Dodd Jr., April 26, 1943, File No. 12–12E, "Organizations Cox Investigation," Box 16, General Correspondence 1927–1946, A1, Entry 100A, OED, RG 173, NACP; House Committee on Appropriations, *Report*, 78th Cong., 1st Sess. 1943, H. Rep. 448.

[21] Barnouw, *The Golden Web*; Brinson, *The Red Scare, Politics, and the Federal Communications Commission*; Clement Imhoff, "Clifford J. Durr and the Loyalty Question: 1942–1950," *Journal of American Culture* 12 (1989): 47–54; John A. Salmond, *The Conscience of a Lawyer: Clifford J. Durr and American Civil Liberties, 1899–1975* (Tuscaloosa: University of Alabama Press, 1990).

Although the Supreme Court upheld the FCC's legal authority to regulate and rebuked Congress for its meddling, the political damage to the commission was significant.[22]

Critics also challenged the fairness of administrative decisions by highlighting agencies' deviation from traditional legal methods. The focus of their ire was usually the formal quasi-judicial hearing that occurred in the small number of licensing, rate-making, or enforcement cases not resolved through informal negotiations. These proceedings, in which parties received a personal and adversarial hearing in front of an agency official, were targeted far out of proportion to their frequency. In fact, most administrative enforcement was relatively uncontroversial, conducted through informal proceedings that allowed agency officials to maximize limited resources and spared businesses the cost, delay, and publicity of formal hearings. Parties' willingness to participate in voluntary programs, or to stipulate to their wrongdoing and forgo the formal proceedings and judicial review available to them, suggested at least a certain degree of satisfaction with the informal proceedings.[23] Even at the NLRB, where relations between the regulators and the regulated were consistently contentious, more than 90 percent of the unfair labor claims made against employers were settled, dismissed, or withdrawn before the board could issue a formal complaint.[24]

The formal hearings used in more important or more controversial matters both resembled and sharply diverged from the courtroom model through which property rights were more commonly adjudicated. Hearings were conducted by "hearing examiners," who were generally responsible for hearing testimony, receiving evidence, and drafting nonbinding initial reports containing factual findings and tentative recommendations. Many agencies gave parties an opportunity to respond to the examiners' reports; their arguments, along with the examiner's report and the record developed in the hearing, were used as sources for agency heads issuing final orders.

This model of decision making was designed to maximize the agency's institutional expertise, but it also gave rise to criticism that agencies were incapable of rendering fair decisions since agency officials were exercising their power in improper (and possibly illegal) ways. Notably, examiners lacked the institutional independence and isolation of judges. Practices varied significantly among agencies, but in many instances the examiner was the agency staffer who had handled the case since the initial complaint was filed. In some agencies, due

---

[22] *National Broadcasting Co., Inc. v. United States*, 319 U.S. 190 (1943); *United States v. Lovett*, 328 U.S. 303 (1946); see also Drew Pearson, "Merry-Go-Round," *Washington Post*, April 29, 1943, 11B; Robert E. Cushman, "The Purge of Federal Employees Accused of Disloyalty," *Public Administration Review* 3 (1943): 297–316. For more on Dodd's connections, see John Earl Haynes and Harvey Klehr, *Venona: Decoding Soviet Espionage in America* (New Haven, CT: Yale University Press, 1999), 269–70.

[23] See E. Pendleton Herring, "Special Interests and the Interstate Commerce Commission," *American Political Science Review* 27 (1933): 738–51.

[24] Attorney General's Committee on Administrative Procedure, *National Labor Relations Board, Monograph No. 18* (Washington, DC: Department of Justice, 1940), 17.

to agency preference, the complexity of the case, or budget constraints, a single examiner might conduct the hearing *and* represent the agency's views. Before and after a hearing, examiners might consult with other agency employees about the case in question, and, during the hearing, examiners often questioned parties and witnesses themselves in an effort to improve the record. Defenders of this system argued that this conflation of roles was less problematic than it might seem at first glance; whereas judges played an active role in hearing oral testimony and determining the credibility of witnesses as part of their fact-finding responsibilities, examiners were more typically presented with masses of depositions, statistics, and other documentary evidence about which there was little controversy. Thus, unlike adversarial trials, administrative hearings were an opportunity for parties to discuss the legal and policy implications of uncontested facts with an examiner familiar with the agency's policies. Examiners' role in fact finding nonetheless recalled Chief Justice Charles Evans Hughes's 1931 warning to agency attorneys: "An unscrupulous administrator might be tempted to say 'Let me find the facts for the people of my country, and I care little who lays down the general principles.'"[25] Given examiners' presumed allegiance to their own agencies, examiners were often accused of tilting the proceedings toward their agency and against the private parties before them. One SEC official recalled the "ferocious attacks" on his commission, where critics charged "that all administrators were bent on sacrificing our traditions of decisional fairness and impartiality to the accomplishment of socialistic ends by administrative fiat."[26]

Among the loudest critics was the American Bar Association, the traditionally conservative lawyers' organization whose members opposed the regulatory demands of the New Deal agencies and balked at the combination of investigation, prosecution, and adjudication functions in administrative hearings. The ABA's Special Committee on Administrative Law, established during the heat of Roosevelt's "First Hundred Days," specifically targeted these administrative tribunals, pointing out the ways in which the administrative process failed to require examiners to enforce judicial standards of due process. Esteemed law professor and Special Committee chairman Roscoe Pound famously denounced the lawlessness of the administrative process in the committee's 1938 report, characterizing agency governance as "under complete control of the executive" and at the same time "relieved of judicial review and making its own rules."[27] Such "administrative absolutism," Pound charged, was inconsistent with the rule of law.[28] Taking for granted that the administrative process was deficient and not nearly court-like enough, the ABA proposed to encircle it

---

[25] Charles Evans Hughes, "Important Work of Uncle Sam's Lawyers," *American Bar Association Journal* 17 (1931): 237–39, 238.

[26] Chester T. Lane, review of *Federal Examiners and the Conflict of Law and Administration*, by Lloyd D. Musolf, *Columbia Law Review* 54 (1954): 1008–11, 1008.

[27] "Report of the Special Committee on Administrative Law," *Annual Report of the American Bar Association* 63 (1938): 331–68, 343.

[28] Ibid.

with additional opportunities for both administrators and courts to review administrative decisions.[29]

Revelations about the United States Department of Agriculture's practices provided ammunition for critics already skeptical of agency decision making. In the Supreme Court's 1936 and 1938 decisions in *Morgan v. United States*, Chief Justice Hughes concluded that Secretary of Agriculture Henry A. Wallace, in issuing a 1933 order fixing maximum rates for the sale of livestock in the Kansas City Stock Yards, had not played fair. USDA staffers had enjoyed easy access to the secretary, but, lacking an examiner's report processing some 10,000 pages of testimony and 1,000 pages of exhibits produced during the initial hearing, and without an opportunity for a useful oral argument before the secretary after the initial hearing, the stockmen's agents had been essentially shut out of the decision-making process. The Court rejected the idea that Wallace could adopt "as his own the findings which have been prepared by the active prosecutors for the Government, after an *ex parte* discussion with them and without according any reasonable opportunity to the respondents in the proceeding to know the claims thus presented and to contest them."[30] Such an obvious preference of one side over another failed to provide adequate due process to the regulated parties. The Court's decision shone a light into the USDA's secretive internal operations and illustrated how administrative officials actually reached decisions.[31] It was, the *Wall Street Journal* argued, "a warning to Federal administrative and quasi-judicial agencies to conduct

[29] James E. Brazier, "An Anti-New Dealer Legacy: The Administrative Procedure Act," *Journal of Policy History* 8 (1996): 206–26; George B. Shepherd, "Fierce Compromise: The Administrative Procedure Act Emerges from New Deal Politics," *Northwestern University Law Review* 90 (1996): 1557–683.

[30] *Morgan v. United States*, 304 U.S. 1, 22 (1938); see also Daniel Ernst, "*Morgan* and the New Dealers," *Journal of Policy History* 20 (2008): 447–81; Mark Tushnet, "Administrative Law in the 1930s: The Supreme Court's Accommodation of Progressive Legal Theory," *Duke Law Journal* 60 (2011): 1565–637. The Court excoriated a state public utilities commission for taking the idea of judicial notice too far a year earlier in *Ohio Bell Telephone Co. v. Public Utilities Commission*, 301 U.S. 292 (1937).

[31] Recent Decision, *Columbia Law Review* 36 (1936): 1156–58; Recent Case, *George Washington Law Review* 5 (1936): 119–20; Irving Allan Lore, Recent Case, *Wisconsin Law Review* 12 (1937): 245–47; A. H. Feller, "Prospectus for the Further Study of Federal Administrative Law," *Yale Law Journal* 47 (1938): 647–74; Recent Case, *George Washington Law Review* 7 (1938): 110–15; Note, "Implications of the Second Morgan Decision," *Illinois Law Review* 33 (1938): 227–30; Recent Case Note, *Indiana Law Journal* 14 (1938): 164–66; Recent Decision, *St. John's Law Review* 13 (1938): 138–41; Joseph Wise, Note, "*Morgan v. United States*: Administrative Hearing," *University of Cincinnati Law Review* 12 (1938): 598–605; Frank J. Dugan, Note, "A New Administrative Landmark," *Georgetown Law Journal* 27 (1939): 351–60; Kenneth C. Sears, "The *Morgan* Case and Administrative Procedure," *George Washington Law Review* 7 (1939): 726–39; Note, "Judicial Control of Administrative Procedure: The *Morgan* Cases," *Harvard Law Review* 52 (1939): 509–15; Note, "Aftermath of the *Morgan* Decision," *Iowa Law Review* 25 (1940): 622–38; James Hart, *An Introduction to Administrative Law, with Selected Cases*, 2nd ed. (New York: Appleton-Century-Crofts, 1950); see also Daniel J. Gifford, "The *Morgan* Cases: A Retrospective View," *Administrative Law Review* 30 (1978): 237–88.

their regulatory activities and prosecutions so that businesses may have a fair hearing and a fair decision by an informed tribunal."[32]

Many of the charges of administrative unfairness were lobbed at the NLRB, where, if critics were to be believed, the vast majority of examiners were unfairly biased.[33] The Supreme Court had upheld the NLRB's procedures along with the board's constitutionality in 1937, but more legal claims of unfair hearings were raised against the NLRB than against any other agency (especially once the FCC reorganized its own operations in 1938).[34] That the NLRB reacted to the Supreme Court's warnings in *Morgan* by withdrawing some pending orders to avoid similar trouble in the courts did little to dispel these charges.[35] Explanations based in the peculiar deficiencies of NLRB examiners, the fact that NLRB hearings more frequently involved factual disputes, or the more aggressive approach the NLRB took once it was deemed constitutionally sound were offered by those on different sides of the labor–management divide.[36] The blame, some argued, lay not with the board but with employers hostile to regulation. According to one study by sympathetic scholars, attacks on the NLRB were launched by those who "seek to destroy public confidence in the statute by assailing the methods of its administration."[37] NLRB Chairman J. Warren Madden later characterized the earliest hearings under the Wagner Act as "charged with emotion and bad feeling," with employers' attorneys making "the hearing as unpleasant and as troublesome as it could be."[38] The 1938

[32] "Supreme Court Voids Wallace Order Fixing Stockyard Rates," *Wall Street Journal*, April 26, 1938, 5.

[33] Charles Fahy, "The Preparation and Trial of Cases Before the National Labor Relations Board," *American Bar Association Journal* 25 (1939): 695–99; J. Warren Madden, "Administrative Procedure: National Labor Relations Board," *West Virginia Law Quarterly* 45 (1939): 93–108; Harold W. Davey, "Separation of Functions and the National Labor Relations Board," *University of Chicago Law Review* 7 (1940): 328–46; see also Seymour Scher, "The Politics of Agency Organization," *Western Political Quarterly* 15 (1962): 328–44.

[34] *NLRB v. Jones & Laughlin Steel Corp.*, 301 U.S. 1 (1937); regarding the FCC, see FCC Press release, Nov. 9, 1938, File No. 12–9, "Organization Examiners Division," Box 9, General Correspondence 1927–1946, OED, RG 173, NACP.

[35] *In re NLRB*, 304 U.S. 486 (1938); *Ford Motor Co. v. NLRB*, 99 F.2d 1003 (6th Cir. 1938); *Inland Steel Co. v. NLRB*, 105 F.2d 246 (7th Cir. 1939); see also "'Rudimentary Fair Play,'" *New York Times*, May 2, 1938, 16; "192 Ford Workers Win in NLRB Case," *New York Times*, July 8, 1938, 1; Note, "Aftermath of the Morgan Decision," 636; Dugan, "A New Administrative Landmark," 351–52; Note, "Implications of the Second Morgan Decision," 229.

[36] James A. Gross, *The Making of the National Labor Relations Board: A Study in Economics, Politics, and the Law, 1933–1937* (Albany: State University of New York Press, 1974); James A. Gross, *The Reshaping of the National Labor Relations Board: National Labor Policy in Transition, 1937–1947* (Albany: State University of New York Press, 1981); Peter H. Irons, *The New Deal Lawyers* (Princeton, NJ: Princeton University Press, 1982); Christopher L. Tomlins, *The State and the Unions: Labor Relations, Law, and the Organized Labor Movement in America, 1880–1960* (Cambridge: Cambridge University Press, 1985).

[37] Walter Gellhorn and Seymour L. Linfield, "Politics and Labor Relations: An Appraisal of Criticisms of NLRB Procedure," *Columbia Law Review* 39 (1939): 339–95, 341.

[38] J. Warren Madden, "The National Labor Relations Act and Its Administration," *Tennessee Law Review* 18 (1943): 126–37, 132.

Weirton Steel case illustrated the challenges for NLRB examiners facing hostile employers. The examiner called out the steel company's counsel for his "defiant, contemptuous and contumacious conduct" at the hearing, during which, according to the NLRB, counsel pursued "a calculated attempt to wrest control of the hearing" from the NLRB examiner.[39] When, based on these antics, the examiner expelled the attorney from the hearing, a local crowd in Steubenville, Ohio, organized a demonstration and hung the examiner in effigy.[40]

Some of the loudest attacks on the NLRB came from Congress, where, after his reelection in 1938 over White House opposition, conservative Virginia Democrat Howard W. Smith bypassed the House Labor Committee (then holding its own hearings on the National Labor Relations Act) and launched a new investigation into whether the board was abusing the authority Congress had granted it.[41] Smith had long opposed New Deal programs and the growth of administrative power, and he approached the NLRB with active hostility. During the Smith Committee's hearings in late 1939 and 1940, the committee garnered significant attention from the press and the public as it purported to expose the NLRB's malfeasance. NLRB officials from the board's secretary on down were called out by name for incompetence, unethical behavior, radical political beliefs, and preferring employees to employers and the CIO to the American Federation of Labor. The committee's intermediate report, issued in March 1940, criticized the NLRB's zeal and suggested that "the Board's policies are tinged with a philosophical view of an employer–employee relationship as a class struggle, something foreign to the proper American concept of industrial relations."[42] (Smith's concern with the dangers of subversion was also evident in the Alien Registration Act, signed into law in June 1940.)

NLRB officials were further accused of going beyond their authority to lobby Congress, solicit litigation, blacklist employers, encourage boycotts, and adopt remedies not prescribed in the Wagner Act. The Smith Committee lambasted the NLRB's initial hearing procedures and examiners' practice of conferring with other board employees before, during, and after formal hearings, claiming that NLRB officials played fast and loose with the evidence and that the board's organization "has failed utterly to bring about a proper separation of the judicial and administrative functions."[43] In addition, members

[39] *In re Weirton Steel Co.*, 8 N.L.R.B. 581, 582, 588 (1938).
[40] "NLRB Will Hear Weirton Lawyer," *New York Times*, July 14, 1938, 1; *NLRB v. Weirton Steel Co.*, 135 F.2d 494 (3rd Cir. 1943).
[41] Gross, *The Reshaping of the National Labor Relations Board*; Bruce J. Dierenfield, *Keeper of the Rules: Congressman Howard W. Smith of Virginia* (Charlottesville: University Press of Virginia, 1987).
[42] House Special Committee to Investigate the National Labor Relations Board, *Report on the Investigation of the National Labor Relations Board: Intermediate Report*, 76th Cong., 3rd sess., 1940, H. Rep. 1902, 36.
[43] House Special Committee to Investigate the National Labor Relations Board, *Intermediate Report*, 45; see also "Charges NLRB Exceeded Authority in Steel Case," *Wall Street Journal*,

criticized the NLRB's review attorneys, who essentially served as middlemen (and women) at the board. These "juvenile jurists" (so described by one caustic observer) were responsible for cases once the examiners had completed their work; review attorneys reviewed the hearing transcripts and the examiners' reports and presented cases to the board.[44] This meant, the Smith Committee alleged, that the review attorneys, reputed to be among the most radical at the NLRB, could and did slant cases according to their own questionable political sympathies.[45]

A majority of the committee ultimately recommended a bill that proposed to eliminate the review division and strip the NLRB of its prosecuting functions, thus protecting, Smith argued, "the separation of functions upon which is based our entire concept of democracy."[46] Many protested – Sen. Robert F. Wagner (D-N.Y.) complained that these amendments to his act would be "a feast for a few lawyers, an insuperable problem for the courts, an insurmountable obstacle to any efficient administration of the law, a blessing to those anxious to disobey the law and a merry-go-round for the employers and workers affected by the law" – but while the proposal to break up the NLRB failed, the NLRB was nonetheless weakened.[47] Slashed appropriations led to the end of experts at the Division of Economic Research, where the Smith Committee was particularly troubled by the division head's "strangely exaggerated social consciousness."[48] Board member Edwin Smith, whose "radical sympathies" the Smith Committee had publicized, was among those NLRB officials who stepped down following the Smith Committee's charges, and new Chairman Harry Millis adopted procedural reforms that diminished the role of the review attorneys.[49] The Smith Committee's investigation also succeeded in damaging the NLRB in the public eye, suggesting that it was riddled with Communists and, as one board attorney recalled, "that the board and its staff

Dec. 20, 1939, 3; "NLRB Amendments," *Washington Post*, Mar. 8, 1940, 12. For more on the evidence behind some of these charges, see Ernst, "The Politics of Administrative Law," 361, n. 101.

[44] Willard Edwards, "Juvenile Jurists," *Saturday Evening Post*, Aug. 24, 1940, 29.

[45] House Special Committee to Investigate the National Labor Relations Board, *National Labor Relations Act*, 76th Cong., 3rd sess., 1940, H. Rep. 3109, pt. 1, 141–47; Gross, *The Reshaping of the National Labor Relations Board*.

[46] Howard W. Smith, "NLRA – Abuses in Administrative Procedure," *Virginia Law Review* 27 (1941): 615–32. Dissenting members argued that this amendment, which still required court enforcement of any order, would "introduce all the inefficiency of separation of functions and yet withhold its single most important advantage" (House Special Committee to Investigate the National Labor Relations Board, *Minority Views on the Investigation of the National Labor Relations Board: Intermediate Report*, 76th Cong., 3rd sess., 1940, H. Rept. 1902, pt. 2, 19).

[47] Sen. Robert F. Wagner, quoted in Louis Stark, "Wagner Condemns Revision of NLRA," *New York Times*, Mar. 14, 1940, 1.

[48] House Special Committee to Investigate the National Labor Relations Board, *Intermediate Report*, 34.

[49] House Special Committee to Investigate the National Labor Relations Board, *National Labor Relations Act*, 19.

were a thoroughly one-sided, biased group who were totally oblivious to any canons of fair play or fair procedure."[50]

Defending the board against the unremittingly unsavory picture painted by Smith's committee, supporters argued that these practices were mostly routine and unproblematic examples of the administrative process at work. NLRB chairman Madden asked (rhetorically, one presumes) why the NLRB had been singled out for reform.[51] The *Washington Post* complained that NLRB witnesses describing informal conferences between examiners and prosecutors were "obviously convinced that they had done no wrong"[52] and, indeed, dissenting members of the Smith Committee acknowledged that some of the NLRB's habits were quite common elsewhere (including at the highly formal ICC).[53] The NLRB had adopted legalistic procedures early in its life and continued to revise its procedures in response to judicial review and political attacks.[54] The staff of the Attorney General's Committee on Administrative Procedure reported in 1940 that the NLRB had gone to some trouble to keep their examiners as independent as possible, appointing trial attorneys to represent the NLRB at its hearings and keeping the two groups of attorneys apart.[55] Indeed, they carefully suggested, administrators' "sincere belief in the policies and principles" of the act they administered "cannot be called bias or prejudice, however distasteful such an attitude may be to parties or counsel who believe these policies and principles to be unwise or unfair."[56]

In making this point, the NLRB often had the courts on its side. As Chairman Millis informed the Senate Judiciary Committee in 1941, the NLRB's procedure "has probably received the closest and most intensive scrutiny by the courts of any statute in our history."[57] While the Smith Committee charged that the NLRB was "most deplorably biased" toward employees and parties appealing

[50] Emerson, *Young Lawyer for the New Deal*, 118; see also Gross, *The Reshaping of the National Labor Relations Board*.
[51] Frederick R. Barkley, "Madden Declares NLRB Record Best and Defends Witt," *New York Times*, Feb. 2, 1940, 1.
[52] "NLRB Amendments," *Washington Post*, Mar. 8, 1940, 12.
[53] House Special Committee to Investigate the National Labor Relations Board, *Minority Views on the Investigation of the National Labor Relations Board: Intermediate Report*, 18.
[54] See Walter Galenson, memorandum of interview with Herbert Fuchs, n.d., Folder "Walter Galenson – Chronological," Box 1, Records Relating to the Administration of the Task Force, 1948–1949, NC 115, Entry 52, TF: IRC, RG 264, NACP; *Consolidated Edison Co. v. NLRB*, 305 U.S. 197 (1938); Harry A. Millis and Emily Clark Brown, *From the Wagner Act to Taft-Hartley: A Study of National Labor Policy and Labor Relations* (Chicago: University of Chicago Press, 1950); Gross, *The Making of the National Labor Relations Board*. As of 1939, according to Gellhorn and Linfield, "[i]n only one instance has the Board ordered a new hearing because of what it found to be improper and prejudicial rulings by the presiding Trial Examiner" (Gellhorn and Linfield, "Politics and Labor Relations," 360, n. 57).
[55] Attorney General's Committee, *National Labor Relations Board, Monograph No. 18*, 35.
[56] Ibid., 40; see also Joanna Grisinger, "Law in Action: The Attorney General's Committee on Administrative Procedure," *Journal of Policy History* 20 (2008): 379–418.
[57] Senate Judiciary Committee, Subcommittee on S. 674, S. 675 and S. 918, *Administrative Procedure: Hearings on S. 674, S. 675 and S. 918*, 77th Cong., 1st sess., 1941, pt. 1, 258.

NLRB orders routinely blamed examiners for deviating from judicial norms, federal judges generally disregarded claims that the board's proceedings as a whole were unfair to parties.[58] One appellate court reminded a petitioner that the examiner's examination of a witness resulting in the production of unfavorable evidence "does not necessarily indicate bias,"[59] and another found "that the offender against due and orderly trial procedure" in a particular hearing was the employer's own attorney.[60]

Given that examiners did not control the final decision, judges endorsed NLRB proceedings even when the initial hearing involved practices unlikely to pass muster in the courts. Due process was found to exist in one hearing where an examiner's questions for a witness "were tinged with a sarcasm not appropriate to a judicial officer"[61]; in another, the court upheld the decision even when an examiner had "exceeded all reasonable bounds" in his examination of witnesses.[62] In the latter case, although the examiner's behavior was "justly subject to criticism," the court denied that the hearing "was so unfair as to constitute a denial of due process."[63] Weak performances by examiners were embarrassing for the agency but not necessarily ultimately unfair to the parties, and only in a few cases were board members or examiners so unfair as to convince the reviewing court that the NLRB's decision lacked due process.[64]

Nor were courts less deferential to other agencies. As ICC Commissioner Clyde Aitchison noted in 1940, "our administrative procedure is controlled by 350 Supreme Court decisions."[65] These procedures were no longer novel, and the fact that the courts themselves had established a certain legal legitimacy for administrative procedure was repeatedly made by agency representatives and by others in favor of this shift in authority. The Attorney General's Committee

---

[58] House Special Committee to Investigate the National Labor Relations Board, *National Labor Relations Act*, pt. 1, 149.

[59] *Jefferson Electric Co. v. NLRB*, 102 F.2d 949, 955 (7th Cir. 1939).

[60] *NLRB v. Baldwin Locomotive Works*, 128 F.2d 39, 45 (3rd Cir. 1942).

[61] *NLRB v. Stackpole Carbon Co.*, 105 F.2d 167, 177 (3rd Cir. 1939).

[62] *Cupples Co. Manufacturers v. NLRB*, 106 F.2d 100, 113 (8th Cir. 1939); see also *NLRB v. Ford Motor Co.*, 114 F.2d 905 (6th Cir. 1940).

[63] *Cupples Co. Manufacturers*, 106 F.2d at 113.

[64] See *Montgomery Ward & Co. v. NLRB*, 103 F.2d 147 (8th Cir. 1939); *Inland Steel Co. v. NLRB*, 109 F.2d 9 (7th Cir. 1940); *NLRB v. Washington Dehydrated Food Co.*, 118 F.2d 980 (9th Cir. 1941); *Berkshire Employees Association v. NLRB*, 121 F.2d 235 (3d Cir. 1941); *NLRB v. Phelps*, 136 F.2d 562 (5th Cir. 1943); *Donnelly Garment Co. v. NLRB*, 151 F.2d 854 (8th Cir. 1945). For cases finding that the NLRB had provided a fair hearing, see *Consolidated Edison Co. v. NLRB*, 305 U.S. 197 (1938); *NLRB v. Bradford Dyeing Association*, 310 U.S. 318 (1940); *NLRB v. Remington Rand, Inc.*, 94 F.2d 862 (2d Cir. 1938); *Subin v. NLRB*, 112 F.2d 326 (3rd Cir. 1940); *Consumers Power Co. v. NLRB*, 113 F.2d 38 (6th Cir. 1940); *Continental Box Co., Inc., v. NLRB*, 113 F.2d 93 (5th Cir. 1940); *Press Co., Inc. v. NLRB*, 118 F.2d 937 (D.C. Cir. 1940); *NLRB v. Air Associates, Inc.*, 121 F.2d 586 (2d Cir. 1941). For additional discussion, see Gellhorn and Linfield, "Politics and Labor Relations."

[65] Transcript, Conference of the Attorney General's Committee, June 8, 1940, 4, Folder "Committee Meeting – June 6, 7, and 8," Box 4, A.G. Committee Correspondence, Entry 376, AGCAP, RG 60, NACP.

on Administrative Procedure, in its 1941 final report, issued a sweeping defense of the administrative process as a whole, and current and former administrative officials patiently defended the legality of their procedures before Congress, in speeches to the ABA, and in the pages of law reviews, attempting to dispel some of the mystery and to head off radical procedural reform.[66] NLRB general counsel Charles Fahy, reminding his ABA audience that board hearings were held throughout the country, enthusiastically encouraged the lawyers to come see for themselves how his agency actually operated.[67]

These defenses were supported by a wealth of judicial decisions in which such administrative practices had routinely been deemed fair, or at least held to provide minimum constitutional standards of due process. Although administrators often found themselves defending their hearing procedures against charges that petitioners had been denied due process of law, courts generally dismissed such claims. Many administrative procedures had developed defensively, as agencies and commissions adopted quasi-judicial procedures to demonstrate to reviewing courts that they were not as alien as they might seem.[68] Courts also tended to uphold agency orders when the sufficiency of the facts was in question. The central question of administrative law in earlier decades was whether courts or agencies should have the final say over administrative decision making. Although courts proved initially unwilling to defer to administrators, by the early 1930s courts had developed doctrines allowing them to review agencies' application of law but deferring to their findings of fact.[69]

---

[66] Grisinger, "Law in Action"; Benedict Wolf, "Administrative Procedure before the National Labor Relations Board," *University of Chicago Law Review* 5 (1938): 358–82; Clyde B. Aitchison, "Reforming the Administrative Process," *George Washington Law Review* 7 (1939): 703–25; Fahy, "The Preparation and Trial of Cases before the National Labor Relations Board"; Calvert Magruder, "Administrative Procedures under the Fair Labor Standards Act," *American Bar Association Journal* 25 (1939): 688–95; Madden, "Administrative Procedure: National Labor Relations Board"; Gellhorn and Linfield, "Politics and Labor Relations"; R. E. Freer, "Practice before the Federal Trade Commission," *George Washington Law Review* 7 (1939): 283–303; Robert E. Freer, "Federal Trade Commission Procedure," *American Bar Association Journal* 26 (1940): 342–43 and 370; Chester T. Lane and Robert M. Blair-Smith, "The SEC and the 'Expeditious Settlement of Disputes,'" *Illinois Law Review* 34 (1940): 699–726; Ashley Sellers, "Administrative Procedure – A Suggested Classification of Procedures of Regulatory Agencies in the United States Department of Agriculture," *Washington University Law Quarterly* 25 (1940): 352–84; Madden, "The National Labor Relations Act and Its Administration."

[67] Fahy, "The Preparation and Trial of Cases before the National Labor Relations Board," 698.

[68] See Board of Investigation and Research, *Report on Practices and Procedures of Governmental Control*, 78th Cong., 2nd sess., 1944, H. Doc. 678; Marver H. Bernstein, "The Politics of Adjudication," *Journal of Politics* 16 (1954): 299–323, 317–18; James M. Landis, *Report on Regulatory Agencies to the President-Elect*, Senate Judiciary Committee, Subcommittee on Administrative Practice and Procedure, 86th Cong., 2nd sess., 1960, Committee Print, 50.

[69] Carl McFarland, *Judicial Control of the Federal Trade Commission and the Interstate Commerce Commission, 1920–1930* (Cambridge, MA: Harvard University Press, 1933); Robert E. Cushman, *The Independent Regulatory Commissions* (New York: Oxford University Press, 1941); J. Roland Pennock, *Administration and the Rule of Law* (New York: Farrar and Rinehart

Statutory standards for judicial review varied, but federal courts generally found an agency's factual findings conclusive if "substantial evidence" supported the decision.[70] This was a fairly lenient standard of review, requiring not that the weight of evidence support the decision but that administrators be able to demonstrate that their decisions were not entirely discretionary. As one reviewing court phrased it, the standard "is the dividing line between law and arbitrary power."[71] The requirement of "substantiality" was usually easy enough to meet, given the sheer volume of testimony and documentary evidence involved in any administrative decision. The reviewing court was *not* to sift through the evidence on its own and determine whether it would have made the same decision. Agencies certainly still saw some orders reversed under this standard – which did little to help their reputations – but it nonetheless suggested significant deference to the agencies in sketching out a realm where courts might fear to tread.[72]

1941); Richard B. Stewart, "The Reformation of American Administrative Law," *Harvard Law Review* 88 (1975): 1667–813; Paul R. Verkuil, "The Emerging Concept of Administrative Procedure," *Columbia Law Review* 78 (1978): 258–329; William C. Chase, *The American Law School and the Rise of Administrative Government* (Madison: University of Wisconsin Press, 1982); Robert L. Rabin, "Federal Regulation in Historical Perspective," *Stanford Law Review* 38 (1986): 1189–326; Ann Woolhandler, "Judicial Deference to Administrative Action – A Revisionist History," *Administrative Law Review* 43 (1991): 197–245; Richard D. Stone, *The Interstate Commerce Commission and the Railroad Industry: A History of Regulatory Policy* (New York: Praeger, 1991); Lucy Salyer, *Laws Harsh as Tigers: Chinese Immigrants and the Shaping of Modern Immigration Law* (Chapel Hill: University of North Carolina Press, 1995); G. Edward White, "The Emergence of Agency Government and the Creation of Administrative Law," in *The Constitution and the New Deal*, 94–127 (Cambridge, MA: Harvard University Press, 2000); Hoogenboom and Hoogenboom, *A History of the ICC.*

[70] Federal courts held most agencies to this standard (for example, interpreting language that facts would be conclusive if "supported by evidence" to mean that "substantial evidence" was indeed required); see *FTC v. Curtis Publishing Co.*, 260 U.S. 568 (1923); *Washington, Virginia & Maryland Coach Co. v. NLRB*, 301 U.S. 142 (1937); *Consolidated Edison Co. v. NLRB*, 305 U.S. 197 (1938); *NLRB v. Waterman Steamship Corp.*, 309 U.S. 206 (1940); E. Blythe Stason, "'Substantial Evidence' in Administrative Law," *University of Pennsylvania Law Review* 89 (1941): 1026–51; Robert L. Stern, "Review of Findings of Administrators, Judges and Juries: A Comparative Analysis," *Harvard Law Review* 58 (1944): 70–124.

[71] *NLRB v. Thompson Products, Inc.*, 97 F.2d 13, 15 (6th Cir. 1938); Stason, "'Substantial Evidence' in Administrative Law."

[72] See *NLRB v. Link-Belt Co.*, 311 U.S. 584 (1941). Cases in which courts found inadequate evidence include *NLRB v. Columbian Enameling & Stamping Co.*, 306 U.S. 292 (1939); *NLRB v. Sands Manufacturing Co.*, 306 U.S. 332 (1939); *Appalachian Electric Power Co. v. NLRB*, 93 F.2d 985 (4th Cir. 1938); *NLRB v. Thompson Products, Inc.*; *NLRB v. Lion Shoe Co.*, 97 F.2d 448 (1st Cir. 1938); *Standard Lime & Stone Co. v. NLRB*, 97 F.2d 531 (4th Cir. 1938); *Ballston-Stillwater Knitting Co. v. NLRB*, 98 F.2d 758 (2d Cir. 1938); *NLRB v. Union Pacific Stages, Inc.*, 99 F.2d 153 (9th Cir. 1938); *NLRB v. Empire Furniture Co.*, 107 F.2d 92 (6th Cir. 1939); see also C. Herman Pritchett, "The Supreme Court and Administrative Regulation, 1941–44," *Iowa Law Review* 31 (1945): 103–28. On the effect of these reversals on the NLRB, see Gross, *The Reshaping of the National Labor Relations Board*, 83–84. On the broader question of deference, see Reuel E. Schiller, "The Era of Deference: Courts, Expertise, and the Emergence of New Deal Administrative Law," *Michigan Law Review* 106 (2007): 399–441.

Consistent with these trends, the Supreme Court in the 1940 case of *FCC v. Pottsville Broadcasting Co.* articulated a strong position of respect for the procedure agencies and commissions had designed. When called on to review an FCC order denying a construction permit to a Maryland broadcasting corporation, the Court unanimously declined to concern itself with the specifics of the hearing provided by the FCC. The Court of Appeals, reviewing the initial order, had reprimanded the commission for failing to consider certain factors and demanded that the FCC revisit its denial of the company's application. Rather than simply granting the license, however, the FCC ordered the broadcasting company to begin the applications process anew – thus competing against applicants who had applied in the intervening period. The company protested, but the Supreme Court upheld the FCC's authority. How the FCC should conduct its licensing procedures, was, according to Justice Felix Frankfurter, "explicitly and by implication left to the Commission's own devising, so long, of course, as it observes the basic requirements designed for the protection of private as well as public interest."[73]

Frankfurter went on to reflect on the relative roles of agencies and courts in the post–New Deal era. Expecting the FCC to act as a trial court on remand was inappropriate; the "differences in origin and function preclude wholesale transplantation of the rules of procedure, trial, and review which have evolved from the history and experience of courts."[74] Given the commission's explicit policy-making authority, it would be inappropriate to apply the standard of judicial review intended for lower federal courts to the agencies. As Frankfurter continued, "to assimilate the relation of these administrative bodies and the courts to the relationship between lower and upper courts is to disregard the origin and purposes of the movement for administrative regulation and at the same time to disregard the traditional scope, however far-reaching, of the judicial process."[75] Agencies were *not* courts, and courtroom procedures were not the only fair ones. Judicial recognition of this fact both made the agencies seem more legitimate parts and protected the reified status of courts.

The Court stuck to its defense of administrative government; as Justice Hugo Black remarked in the "Little Steel" case, justices should avoid judicial intervention "into fields hitherto wisely and happily apportioned by the genius of our polity to the administration of another branch of Government."[76] Recognizing that litigation had prevented effective enforcement of the Walsh-Healey Act in the iron and steel industries for more than a year, Black pointed to "the 'confusion and disorder' that can result from the delays necessarily incident to judicial supervision of administrative procedure developed to meet present day needs of Government and capable of operating efficiently and

[73] *FCC v. Pottsville Broadcasting Co.*, 309 U.S. 134, 138 (1940).
[74] Ibid., 143.
[75] Ibid., 144.
[76] *Perkins v. Lukens Steel Co.*, 310 U.S. 113, 128 (1940).

fairly to both private and public interests."[77] The courts were not the right place for such disputes.

Even *Morgan,* in which the Court criticized the USDA's failure to provide the regulated parties with an initial report or a fair hearing, was less an indictment of the existing administrative process than it seemed. Most agencies already provided such reports as a matter of course, and the Court soon established that an examiner's report was not mandatory as long as the issues in the case were clearly defined – a state of affairs usually true of any case in which an initial complaint had been filed.[78] Further, although the Court failed to define exactly what kind of help an agency head could receive from his staff in making the final decision, its apparent acceptance of Secretary Wallace's activities indicated that most agencies were probably within acceptable bounds. Thus, by 1941, defenders of the agencies and commissions could tout their legal legitimacy, pointing to an abundance of cases and studies demonstrating that these bodies had been fully incorporated into the legal system. Political legitimacy did not necessarily follow, however. Although most judges were already convinced that "different" did not necessarily mean "unfair" when it came to administrative procedure, they were not the only ones who needed convincing.

Although a variety of legislative reforms had been proposed in the late 1930s, the United States' entry into World War II meant that opportunities for significant procedural reform of the administrative state waned, even as the growth of new wartime agencies, departments, and commissions made the problem of the administrative state more urgent. In May 1940, President Roosevelt began the process of mobilizing the economy by giving the National Defense Advisory Commission broad authority over industrial and agricultural production, employment, price stabilization, and consumer protection.[79] Roosevelt also invoked his authority to create the Office of Emergency Management in the new Executive Office of the President (created under the reorganization authority Congress had grudgingly provided in 1939), within which he established several new offices focused on the war and firmly under his control. Once the United States entered World War II in December 1941, Congress, through the First War Powers Act, authorized the president to reorganize the functions of the executive branch agencies and commissions. Over the next few

[77] Ibid., 130–31.
[78] *NLRB v. Mackay Radio & Telegraph Co.,* 304 U.S. 333 (1938); Hart, *An Introduction to Administrative Law.* After the Supreme Court in *Commonwealth Edison* (1938) specifically criticized the NLRB's failure to provide some sort of proposed or tentative findings to which the parties could file objections, the NLRB changed its procedures to require such findings. At the FCC, a 1938 reform placed responsibility for drafting the initial report on the parties' attorneys; see also John A. Rohr, *Civil Servants and Their Constitutions* (Lawrence: University Press of Kansas, 2002), 81–82.
[79] Luther Gulick, "War Organization of the Federal Government," *American Political Science Review* 38 (1944): 1166–79, 1169–70.

years, Roosevelt experimented with different arrangements, dividing mobilization authority among new and more specialized executive agencies and bringing in a mix of New Dealers and businessmen to run them.[80]

The tasks of wartime administration were overwhelming, and Roosevelt's
mobilization efforts resembled his response to the economic crisis a decade
earlier. Wartime agencies sprung up as needed, often overlapping or duplicating
work done by existing departments and commissions. Key agencies included
the Office of Production Management, in charge of ensuring that the nation's
industries produced the necessary materials for mobilization (replaced by the
WPB in early 1942), the War Labor Board, to handle wartime labor–management relations, and the OPA, which sought to prevent consumer inflation
through rent control, price control, and rationing programs.[81] As Sen. Harry
S. Truman (D–Mo.) wryly observed in late 1942, "Washington has become a
city where a large proportion of the population makes its living, not by taking
in one another's washing, but by unreeling one another's red tape."[82] Chafing
under the authority of the wartime agencies, businessmen fought for government contracts, contended with materials shortages, and were hamstrung by
production requirements.[83] At the same time, Americans who had grown accustomed to looking to agencies for benefits and pensions now also faced price
caps, consumer goods rationing, and, in some cases, forcible detention.

Even as Americans were still working out what, exactly, agencies and
commissions could be trusted to do, wartime administrative experiments
made the question more pressing. By 1943, the ABA's Special Committee on
Administrative Law was sharply critical of the disarray of methods that accompanied the growth of wartime administration. Charging that there was too
much bureaucracy and too little information about how it worked, the Special
Committee complained that "the citizen often not only does not know where to

---

[80] First War Powers Act, Pub. L. No. 354, 55 Stat. 838 (1941); Stephen Hess, *Organizing the Presidency* (Washington, DC: Brookings Institution, 1976); see also Daniel R. Ernst, "The Ideal and the Actual in the State: Willard Hurst at the Board of Economic Warfare," in Ernst and Jew, eds., *Total War and the Law*.

[81] John Lord O'Brian and Manly Fleishmann, "The War Production Board Administrative Policies and Procedures," *George Washington Law Review* 13 (1944): 1–60; Barton J. Bernstein, "The Removal of War Production Board Controls on Business, 1944–1946," *Business History Review* 39 (1965): 243–60; Barton J. Bernstein, "The Debate on Industrial Reconversion: The Protection of Oligopoly and Military Control of the Economy," *American Journal of Economics and Sociology* 26 (1967): 159–72; Andrew H. Bartels, "The Office of Price Administration and the Legacy of the New Deal, 1939–1946," *Public Historian* 5 (1983): 5–29; Amy Bentley, *Eating for Victory: Food Rationing and the Politics of Domesticity* (Urbana: University of Illinois Press, 1998).

[82] Harry S. Truman, "We Can Lose the War in Washington, Nov. 1942," *American Magazine* (Nov. 1942), reprinted in Arthur M. Schlesinger Jr. and Roger Bruns, eds., *Congress Investigates: A Documented History, 1792–1974*, vol. 4 (New York: Chelsea House Publishers, 1975), 3200.

[83] The Federal Reports Act of 1942 required agencies seeking information from parties to route their requests through the Budget Bureau as a way of easing the burden on businesses. Federal Reports Act of 1942, Pub. L. No. 831, 56 Stat. 1978 (1942); see also Bernard Schwartz, *The Professor and the Commissions* (New York: Alfred A. Knopf, 1959), 208.

go or what to do but, even if he does go some place and do something, the problem of getting an authoritative decision is often appalling and results impossible."[84] This was as true of the older agencies as the newer ones. Comprehensive statutory reform of the agencies and commissions was a low priority during wartime, but individual members of Congress were eager to scrutinize the administrative state from a variety of political positions. Discussing the multiplicity of wartime investigations, Rep. Estes Kefauver (D-Tenn.) recalled WPB head Donald Nelson complaining to the House Small Business Committee, "My coat-tail is literally sticking out running from one committee hearing to the other."[85]

Even before the United States entered the war, its production and mobilization activities attracted congressional interest. One notable investigation emerged from Sen. Truman's concern, early in the government's mobilization effort, that favoritism was prevalent in agencies' awarding of federal defense-related contracts. Big business won the spoils, Truman argued, while "[t]he little manufacturer, the little contractor, and the little machine shop have been left entirely out in the cold."[86] Truman's call for an examination of how defense contracts were distributed led to the Senate Special Committee to Investigate the National Defense Program, created in March 1941; as chairman, Truman had broad authority to investigate military procurement and construction in the national defense context.[87] Within the next few years, the committee's investigations of federal agencies' allocation of war contracts for smaller businesses, army camp construction, rubber production, and aluminum and steel shortages brought many abuses to light. Additional investigations in 1942 and 1943 by other committees probed small businesses' complaints about wartime agencies' substantive policy decisions and their procedures for such decision making.[88]

Another sweeping wartime investigation was led by conservative Democrat Harry F. Byrd of Virginia, who, according to his colleague Paul Douglas, "hated public debt with a holy passion" and who had opposed the New Deal almost from its inception.[89] In September 1941, Byrd proposed a Joint Committee on the Reduction of Nonessential Federal Expenditures, which gathered the Treasury Secretary, the Budget Director, and selected members of the Senate

[84] "Report of the Special Committee on Administrative Law," *Annual Report of the American Bar Association* 68 (1943): 249–53, 250.
[85] Estes Kefauver, "A Code of Conduct for Congressional Investigations," *Arkansas Law Review* 8 (1954): 369–79, 378.
[86] 87 Cong. Rec. 830 (statement of Sen. Harry S. Truman, Feb. 10, 1941).
[87] Wesley McCune and John R. Beal, "The Job that Made Truman President," *Harper's Magazine*, June 1945.
[88] Senate Special Committee to Study Problems of American Small Business, *American Small Business*, 77th Cong., 2nd sess., 1942, S. Rep. 479, pts. 2–4; House Committee on Small Business, *Final Report on the Wartime Problems of Southern Industry*, 78th Cong., 1st sess., 1943, H. Rep. 126.
[89] Paul H. Douglas, *In the Fullness of Time: The Memoirs of Paul H. Douglas* (New York: Harcourt Brace Jovanovich, 1971), 228; see also Ronald L. Heinemann, *Harry Byrd of Virginia* (Charlottesville: University Press of Virginia, 1996).

Committee on Finance, the House Ways and Means Committee, and the House and Senate Committees on Appropriations for the daunting task of examining "all expenditures of the Federal Government" and eliminating those they found "nonessential."[90] The Byrd Committee was established shortly before the war began, as a way of hacking away at the mounting costs of New Deal programs, but committee members – including conservative New Deal proponent Rep. Robert L. Doughton (D–N.C.); hesitant conservative Sen. Carter Glass (D–Va.); Rep. Clifton A. Woodrum (D–Va.), who had been actively involved in an earlier investigation of the WPA; and Sen. Walter F. George (D–Ga.), who had weathered the administration's purge attempt – claimed that the United States' subsequent entry into World War II only made their work more critical.

The picture of administration that emerged from the Byrd Committee's reports, issued with some frequency during 1943 and 1944, was, at best, one of inefficiency and, at worst, one of active impediment to governance (as in the "unintelligible quiz-mania" of paperwork requirements that "actually threatens the war effort itself through a needless diversion of time and effort").[91] It was clear that Roosevelt's transition to "Dr. Win-the-War" and Republican gains in the 1942 midterm elections had left New Deal programs vulnerable to conservative attack. Couching recommended spending cuts as war measures, the committee found many "nonessential" expenditures within the New Deal agencies. Over the objections of Treasury Secretary Henry Morgenthau Jr., Budget Director Harold D. Smith, and Sen. Robert M. La Follette Jr. (R–Wisc.), the Byrd Committee recommended major cuts in several New Deal public works and agriculture programs and the wholesale elimination of the Civilian Conservation Corps and the National Youth Administration.

The Byrd Committee's scrutiny extended beyond the New Deal agencies, as members eyed the entire administrative state with skepticism. The committee blasted agencies for their overstuffed employment registers, their overwhelming and overlapping paperwork requirements, their exorbitant spending on mail, telegrams, and telephone calls, and their failure to comply with the OPA's wartime limits on driving and gas consumption. The Byrd Committee suggested to Americans that agencies were unable to police their own spending; without outside limits imposed on administrators, tax dollars would be wasted and the country weakened.

The OPA came under particular attack for unfair procedures and overzealous enforcement efforts, as members of Congress trotted out by-now familiar arguments against the administrative process.[92] A companion to the WPB,

---

[90] Revenue Act of 1941, Pub. L. No. 250, Title VI, 55 Stat. 687, 726 (1941).

[91] Joint Committee on Reduction of Nonessential Federal Expenditures, *Reduction of Nonessential Federal Expenditures: Additional Report*, 78th Cong., 1st sess., 1943, S. Doc. 4, 4.

[92] For more on the OPA, see David Ginsburg, "Legal Aspects of Price Control in the Defense Program," *American Bar Association Journal* 27 (1941): 527–34; Joseph W. Aidlin, "The Constitutionality of the 1942 Price Control Act," *California Law Review* 30 (1942): 648–54; William R. Bandy, Comment, "Notice and Opportunity to Be Heard in Price Control Proceedings," *Texas Law Review* 20 (1942): 577–89; Samuel D. Estep, George T. Schilling, and

which attempted to coordinate industrial production with government needs (and thus dealt with businesses already accustomed to working with federal bureaucrats), the OPA targeted the retail and consumption decisions that most personally affected Americans. The federal government had been in the business of inflation control since 1940, but officials had only limited authority to act. Fearing inflation at home as war raged in Europe, Roosevelt, in the summer of 1941, had asked Congress to take action. The result was the Emergency Price Control Act of 1942, characterized by Roosevelt as "an important weapon in our armory against the onslaught of the Axis powers," which created the OPA from the Office of Price Administration and Civilian Supply and placed a price administrator at its head.[93]

The act explicitly recognized Americans as consumers and moved to protect them from the horrors of wartime inflation. As the Senate Committee on Banking and Currency declared, with a commendable sense of scale, "of all the consequences of war, except human slaughter, inflation is the most destructive."[94] The act reflected the same determination to police business practices that was evident in a variety of New Deal policies and drew on procedures common throughout the administrative process.[95] A tremendous amount of authority to manage inflationary concerns and direct the daily transactions of Americans was given to a single administrator who could cap sale prices for commodities and prescribe maximum rents for housing; as the Supreme Court later remarked, the agency was in charge of "probably the most comprehensive legal controls over the economy ever attempted."[96] Once the price administrator had determined that inflation was a concern for the commodity or rental area in question (a necessary first step, although not one for which procedures were prescribed), he could issue maximum price or rent orders that were "generally fair and equitable and will effectuate the purposes of this Act."[97] No hearings

James L. McCrystal, Comment, *Michigan Law Review* 41 (1942): 109–49; Elmo B. Hunter, "The Emergency Price Control Act of 1942," *University of Kansas City Law Review* 10 (1942): 129–42; Charles W. Stewart Jr., Note, "The Emergency Court of Appeals: Interpretation of Procedure and Judicial Review under the Price Control Act," *Georgetown Law Journal* 32 (1943): 42–65; Donald D. Holdoegel, "The War Powers and the Emergency Price Control Act of 1942," *Iowa Law Review* 29 (1944): 454–62; Robert A. Sprecher, "Price Control in the Courts," *Columbia Law Review* 44 (1944): 34–64; Joseph E. Goodbar, "Administrative Agency in Action," *Boston University Law Review* 25 (1945): 185–95; John F. McCarthy, "Aspects of Federal Rent Control," *Cornell Law Quarterly* 31 (1945): 68–77.

[93] Franklin D. Roosevelt, "Statement by the President on Signing the Emergency Price Control Act," Jan. 30, 1942, in Samuel I. Rosenman, ed., *Public Papers and Addresses of Franklin D. Roosevelt*, vol. 1942 (New York: Harper & Bros. Publishers, 1950), 67.

[94] Senate Committee on Banking and Currency, *Emergency Price Control Act of 1942*, 77th Cong., 2nd sess., 1942, S. Rep. 931, 2.

[95] Bartels, "The Office of Price Administration and the Legacy of the New Deal"; Alan Brinkley, *The End of Reform: New Deal Liberalism in Recession and War* (New York: Alfred A. Knopf, 1995); Cohen, *A Consumers' Republic*; Jacobs, *Pocketbook Politics*.

[96] *Fleming v. Mohawk Wrecking & Lumber Co.*, 331 U.S. 111, 122 (1947).

[97] Emergency Price Control Act, Pub. L. No. 421, §§ 2(a), 2(b), 56 Stat. 23–25(1942).

were necessary before the order was issued; as some at the OPA's predecessor agency had warned, the "crippling effect" of the resulting delay and confusion "would practically be equivalent to a death warrant for the act."[98]

The price administrator's discretion was not entirely unbounded, however. Congress had declared that the purpose of the act was:

> [T]o stabilize prices and to prevent speculative, unwarranted, and abnormal increases in prices and rents; to eliminate and prevent profiteering, hoarding, manipulation, speculation, and other disruptive practices resulting from abnormal market conditions or scarcities caused by or contributing to the national emergency; to assure that defense appropriations are not dissipated by excessive prices; to protect persons with relatively fixed and limited incomes, consumers, wage earners, investors, and persons dependent on life insurance, annuities, and pensions, from undue impairment of their standard of living; to prevent hardships to persons engaged in business, to schools, universities, and other institutions, and to the Federal, State, and local governments, which would result from abnormal increases in prices; to assist in securing adequate production of commodities and facilities; to prevent a post emergency collapse of values; to stabilize agricultural prices ... and to permit voluntary cooperation between the Government and producers, processors, and others to accomplish the aforesaid purposes.[99]

These admirable but not particularly specific goals were intended to guide the price administrator and to assure reviewing courts that Congress had not run afoul of the nondelegation doctrine. As constitutional law scholar Paul Freund noted, the guidelines were "well within the limits of tolerance" from a legal standpoint but nevertheless "leave much to the judgment of the Administrator."[100] Indeed, one price administrator would later call this statement of purpose "broad enough to justify almost any action taken by the Price Administrator to control prices."[101]

The statutory guidelines alone offered little guidance to the price administrator in determining, say, the price of ladies' hats, but more help was found in the instruction that the price administrator at least "give due consideration" to commodity prices as of early October 1941 and rents as of April 1941 in setting future prices.[102] Once he was ready to issue a price order, the price administrator was obliged to include "a statement of the considerations involved" in making the decision.[103] Requiring the price administrator (or his staff) to

[98] Office of the General Counsel, Office of Price Administration and Civilian Supply, "Emergency Price Control Legislation," July 10, 1941, 9, Folder 4, "Office of Price Administration," Box 21, Nathanson Papers, NU.
[99] Emergency Price Control Act § 1(a).
[100] Paul A. Freund, "The Emergency Price Control Act of 1942: Constitutional Issues," *Law and Contemporary Problems* 9 (1942): 77–88, 87.
[101] Chester Bowles, *Promises to Keep: My Years in Public Life, 1941–1969* (New York: Harper & Row, 1971), 53.
[102] Emergency Price Control Act §§ 2(a), 2(b).
[103] Ibid., § 2(a).

articulate defensible reasons for the regulations was not an especially onerous requirement, but nonetheless served as an additional check on his discretion. An entirely separate set of procedures was required to carry out the OPA's rationing authority, but here, too, the price administrator's authority was not without limits. Because the power to issue orders regarding the allocation of scarce consumer goods came not from the Emergency Price Control Act but from a separate delegation of authority from the WPB (which itself received this power from the president under the Second War Powers Act), the price administrator could only act once another agency had declared a particular good scarce.[104]

Newly appointed Price Administrator Leon Henderson got right to work. Beginning in January 1942, the OPA took over responsibility for the existing tire rationing program, and soon added the rationing of cars, gasoline, bicycles, typewriters, sugar, shoes, meats, and fats. In late April 1942, Henderson designated hundreds of communities as "defense-rental areas" – a first move toward imposing a nationwide "rent ceiling." Henderson also issued a General Maximum Price Regulation (known as "General Max") that brought thousands of consumer goods under the OPA's jurisdiction and ordered their prices be held to the highest price charged during the previous month.[105] As of mid-May, it was unlawful for Americans to sell any of the included items at prices above those established by the price administrator – and, as a *Washington Post* headline blared, "OPA's New Price Ceilings To Cover Nearly Everything."[106] Indeed, listed in the regulations were processed food products (including beef, pork, lard, canned fruits and vegetables, sugar, noodles, rolled oats, coffee, cocoa, fresh milk, ice cream, and baby foods); clothing (including underwear, hats, gloves, and shoes for men, women, and children); and household items (including tobacco, castor oil, soap, razor blades, shaving cream, and toothpaste). As one newspaper article helpfully explained, "Q – What articles are covered by price ceilings? A – Practically every article used in the life and work of America."[107] In September, the OPA was given even broader power over agricultural products, wages, and salaries, and, under Roosevelt's April 1943 "Hold the Line" order, the Administrator would impose stricter price limits in some areas and demand lower prices in others.[108]

In administering the act, the OPA used both formal methods of enforcement and informal methods based on cooperation. As one OPA lawyer suggested, the agency "must convince the public that its action is necessary, informed,

[104] Second War Powers Act, Pub. L. No. 507, 56 Stat. 176 (1942); WPB Directive No. 1, 7 Fed. Reg. 562 (1942); Executive Order No. 9125, 7 Fed. Reg. 2719 (1942); Executive Order No. 9280, 7 Fed. Reg. 10179 (1942); Note, "Rationing of Consumer Goods," *Columbia Law Review* 42 (1942): 1170–81; Note, "Administrative Penalty Regulations," *Columbia Law Review* 43 (1943): 213–18.

[105] General Maximum Price Regulation, 7 Fed. Reg. 3153 (1942).

[106] Alfred Friendly, "OPA's New Price Ceilings to Cover Nearly Everything," *Washington Post*, April 25, 1942, 1.

[107] "Questions and Answers on Price Ceilings," *New York Times*, April 29, 1942, 16.

[108] Jules Backman, "Wartime Price Control," *Annual Survey of American Law* 1943 (1943): 325–42; Executive Order No. 9328, 8 Fed. Reg. 4681 (1943).

and fair. Then and then only can our necessarily limited staffs and resources be concentrated against that minority of chisellers to whom patriotic duty has no significance."[109] Effective enforcement required widespread public endorsement, and wartime agencies stressed the success of their endeavor. Office of War Mobilization staffers offered statistics to demonstrate "that the per capita annual consumption of food has greatly increased" and that World War II had actually "increased the American standard of living so far as food is concerned."[110] The OPA similarly reported that as of 1942, "business, small as well as large, is in better position today than at any previous time."[111] Indeed, "[o]urs is a lusty, vigorous economy, able to meet and to surmount its war problems."[112]

Business cooperation was key. Although the price administrator was nowhere instructed by Congress to hold hearings with affected parties before issuing prices, he was required to "advise and consult with representative members of the industry" whenever possible. By providing opportunities for parties to be heard, Congress offered another set of political constraints, if not legal limits, on the price administrator's decision making. If an industry desired, the price administrator was to establish an "industry advisory committee" with whom he would be required to consult – at least "from time to time."[113] Voluntary agreements with such parties and trade groups were also explicitly permitted and encouraged in both the price control and the rationing contexts, suggesting a continuing belief that agencies should take the opinions of the regulated parties into account. This model was similar to that provided in the National Industrial Recovery Act, which gave businesses a significant role in the federal government's unprecedented intervention into the economy. Chester Bowles, the third price administrator, reported that the participation of more than 600 industry advisory committees had led to "much better policy formulation and compliance" and "a much deeper understanding by industry of price control and rationing problems."[114]

Trade groups were not the only ones brought into the OPA's ambit; Bowles also lauded the work of labor, farm, and consumer groups in the decision-making and enforcement process. Although such involvement somewhat

---

[109] Henry S. Reuss, "The Lawyer in the OPA," *American Law School Review* 10 (1942): 23–29, 26–27.

[110] Walter Brown to James F. Byrnes, memorandum, June 14, 1943, Folder 10, Box 10, Series 4: War Mobilization, Byrnes Papers, CU.

[111] OPA, "Third Quarterly Report for the Period Ended October 31, 1942" (1943), 30, Folder 10, Box 14, Series 4: War Mobilization, Byrnes Papers, CU.

[112] Ibid., 45.

[113] Emergency Price Control Act § 2(a).

[114] Chester Bowles, "OPA Volunteers: Big Democracy in Action," *Public Administration Review* 5 (1945): 350–59, 352; see also Bartels, "The Office of Price Administration and the Legacy of the New Deal"; Carl Henry Monsees, "Industry Advisory Committees in the War Agencies," *Public Administration Review* 3 (1943): 254–62; Harold Leventhal, "Part II: The Role of the Price Lawyers," in Nathaniel L. Nathanson and Harold Leventhal, *Problems in Price Control: Legal Phases*, 49–106 (Washington, DC: Government Printing Office, 1947), 56.

frustrated the efficiency of agency operations, this model sought to improve relations with regulated interests and interested parties by offering them an opportunity to participate in regulation and a place to vent their anger with at least some hope of satisfaction. The use of local volunteers to handle individual rationing decisions was similarly intended to involve citizens themselves in the process, which, Bowles suggested, "enlists public support and enthusiasm as nothing else will."[115] As one study later reported, "unfamiliar, restrictive controls of rationing were much more palatable when local, unpaid citizens stood between them and the community than would have been the case if the controls had been applied by paid officers of the federal government – by 'bureaucrats.'"[116]

The OPA's task of enforcing regulations that applied whenever Americans bought a can of soup or a bar of soap was nonetheless enormous. Given the number of individual transactions involved and the criminalization of previously mundane and legal activities, enforcing the price, rent, and rationing regulations was a tremendous undertaking. One difficulty was the inevitable mismatch in staffing levels. Even though the OPA drew on a large staff – in Washington, in its regional and district offices, and in thousands of local price and rationing boards staffed by hundreds of thousands of volunteers – their numbers were nonetheless dwarfed by the number of retailers, consumers, landlords, and tenants covered by the regulations.[117] As with any criminal statute, the task was hopeless if more than a small minority of the population failed to obey. By December 1942, one journalist suggested that price control was "this country's greatest enforcement problem since prohibition."[118]

Convincing American businessmen to comply without complaint was an uphill battle. As Price Administrator Leon Henderson remarked in late 1942, the Emergency Price Control Act was not directed against "some particular excrescence of private business" but rather "the very normal practice of pricing goods for the greatest gain, a sound, honest and legitimate business policy."[119] Even more difficult than promoting regulations that, in Henderson's words, made "ordinary business policy contrary to the public interest" was encouraging compliance with a multiplicity of legalistic and confusing regulations.[120] In an effort to establish the legal legitimacy of their program, the OPA early on turned to legal tools and borrowed common administrative procedures; according to General Counsel David Ginsburg, the Emergency Price Control

---

[115] Bowles, "OPA Volunteers: Big Democracy in Action," 359; Cohen, *A Consumer's Republic*; Jacobs, *Pocketbook Politics*.

[116] Victor A. Thompson, *The Regulatory Process in OPA Rationing* (New York: King's Crown Press, 1950), 33.

[117] Office of Price Administration, *Rationing, Why and How* (Washington, DC: Government Printing Office, 1942); Reuss, "The Lawyer in the OPA."

[118] Howard Rutledge, "Black Markets," *Wall Street Journal*, Dec. 12, 1942, 1.

[119] Leon Henderson, "A Preface to Price Control," *Law and Contemporary Problems* 9 (1942): 3–5, 4.

[120] Ibid.

Act wore "the peace-time habiliments of administrative law."[121] However, this focus on legality often trumped other concerns. Price Administrator Prentiss Brown, who replaced Henderson, complained to Roosevelt that lawyers "have clogged up OPA."[122] And as one commentator later pointed out, OPA attorneys may have focused on protecting individual rights, but they "did not regard protection against unnecessary trips to a local board as protection of the individual."[123] The number of regulations with which Americans had to contend only increased as the war continued and the price administrator issued additional price control orders targeting specific industries and closing existing loopholes. The difficulties of honest compliance were evident in the case of the Hecht Company department store, which managed to violate the OPA's regulations even as it worked closely with the agency to bring the prices of more than one million items into compliance with the regulations.[124]

To observers, the OPA seemed unconcerned about the burden its legalistic approach placed on businesses. The Truman committee bemoaned "[t]he farmer with a small truck working 12 hours a day to keep body and soul together" who was "suddenly obliged to digest a 32-page pamphlet of instructions and to fill out an elaborate questionnaire requiring detailed data on activities long past from entirely non-existent records."[125] The House Committee on Small Business similarly charged the OPA with either disregarding complaints or resorting to "so many complications of red tape and bureaucratic buck passing as to leave the complainants bewildered."[126] One businessman protested that his industry was "thoroughly in accord with the objective of wartime governmental agencies" but suspected the federal government could achieve its goals "without throwing such a burden of red tape on the wholesale grocers."[127]

Businessmen thus remained skeptical that the OPA was sympathetic to their plight. As Bowles later recalled, the OPA's intransigence "produced a counterreaction among members of the business community, many of whom were still confirmed Roosevelt haters who regarded all government officials as rude, arrogant, power-hungry ideologues."[128] Unlike the WPB, run by executives

[121] David Ginsburg, "The Emergency Price Control Act of 1942: Basic Authority and Sanctions," *Law and Contemporary Problems* 9 (1942): 22–59, 25; see also Harvey C. Mansfield, *A Short History of OPA* (Washington, DC: Government Printing Office, 1948); Thompson, *The Regulatory Process in OPA Rationing*.
[122] Prentiss M. Brown to Franklin D. Roosevelt, memorandum, Mar. 13, 1943, 1, Folder 1, Box 11, Series 4: War Mobilization, Byrnes Papers, CU.
[123] Thompson, *The Regulatory Process in OPA Rationing*, 230.
[124] *Hecht Co. v. Bowles*, 321 U.S. 321 (1944).
[125] Senate Special Committee Investigating the National Defense Program, *Investigation of the National Defense Program*, 77th Cong., 2nd sess., 1942, S. Rep. 480, pt. 13, 1.
[126] House Committee on Small Business, *Final Report on the Wartime Problems of Southern Industry*, Appendix A, 69.
[127] Abner Lichtenstein, quoted in House Committee on Small Businesses, *Final Report on the Wartime Problems of Southern Industry*, 19.
[128] Bowles, *Promises to Keep*, 65.

on leave from General Electric, Goldman Sachs, and Sears, Roebuck, Price Administrator Leon Henderson had come from the National Recovery Administration and seemed to personify New Deal policies.[129] (And worse, according to the Dies Committee, which accused Henderson and several other OPA staffers of Communist sympathies.) As Sen. Robert Taft (R–Ohio) complained in 1941, wartime price control created "exactly the kind of planned economy measure which the New Dealers have been urging for years in time of peace, when there was no justification for it."[130] Persistent attacks on the OPA's failure to sufficiently appreciate business concerns led to Henderson's resignation in December 1942 and to Congress's requirement in August 1943 that OPA policy makers demonstrate "experience in business, industry, or commerce."[131]

Members of Congress wasted no time in charging that the OPA was abusing its authority.[132] A subcommittee of the House Committee on Interstate and Foreign Commerce, looking at the OPA as part of a special investigation of wartime newsprint shortages, assailed the OPA's methods of doing business. Chaired by Rep. Lyle H. Boren (D–Ok.) (who had earlier remarked on Henderson's "dictatorial methods and attacks on the patriotism of opponents" as he led a group of members trying to cut the OPA's appropriations),[133] the subcommittee was characterized by one *New York Times* reporter as "a climax to nation-wide resentment against the autocratic methods of war agencies."[134] The Special Subcommittee also probed what it saw as the OPA's antibusiness bias and its over-the-top efforts "to bring about far-reaching changes in our system of production and distribution."[135]

The subcommittee's hearings turned a spotlight on the tense relationship between businesses and the OPA, focusing in particular on the agency's attempts to establish quality standards in certain industries. Industry officials, trade associations, and retail groups were furious that the OPA had begun issuing grade standards for products, including processed foods and women's hosiery, and argued that the imposition of quality standards was an illegal

[129] O'Brian and Fleishmann, "The War Production Board Administrative Policies and Procedures"; Bernstein, "The Removal of War Production Board Controls on Business"; Bernstein, "The Debate on Industrial Reconversion"; Robert M. Collins, "Positive Business Responses to the New Deal: The Roots of the Committee for Economic Development, 1933–1942," *Business History Review* 52 (1978): 369–91; Bartels, "The Office of Price Administration and the Legacy of the New Deal."

[130] Robert A. Taft, "Price Fixing–A Necessary Evil," *American Bar Association Journal* 27 (1941): 534–38, 536.

[131] National War Agencies Appropriation Act of 1944, Pub. L. No. 139, 57 Stat. 522, 526 (1943).

[132] See Ralph K. Huitt, "The Congressional Committee: A Case Study," *American Political Science Review* 48 (1954): 340–65.

[133] Rep. Lyle H. Boren, quoted in "Gas Ration Foes Out to Bar Funds for Henderson," *Chicago Daily Tribune*, Nov. 29, 1942, 22.

[134] William J. Enright, "Industries Unite to Defend Brands," *New York Times*, May 23, 1943, 8S.

[135] House Committee on Interstate and Foreign Commerce, Special Subcommittee on Investigation of Restrictions on Brand Names and Newsprint, *Brand Names and Newsprint: Interim Report*, 78th Cong., 1st sess., 1943, H. Rep. 808, pt. 1, 16.

assertion of authority that harmed their brands' reputations.[136] Industry representatives claimed that a uniform standard for a particular product would also lead to decreased efficiency and diminished production during wartime, forcing many or all businesses to convert established production lines to make the new product. Price Administrator Prentiss Brown insisted, however, that the power to set quality standards was inherent in the OPA's inflation-fighting powers given the "simple and indisputable fact that *quality deterioration is inflationary.*"[137]

Matters heated up in the contentious case of hosiery regulation, when Brown rejected hosiery manufacturers' protests to the agency's proposed grading and branding of the product that would override differentiations between existing brands. As the president of the National Association of Hosiery Manufacturers quipped, experiences with the OPA's "atmosphere of misunderstanding, suspicion, and even what appears as malice toward the business community" could be described as "'Adventures with Malice in Opaland.'"[138] A representative of the National Retail Drygoods Association agreed, telling the subcommittee that "O.P.A. has achieved more in the creation of confusion, misunderstanding and the unwarranted regimentation of business and the public, than the drafters of the Price Control Act ever could have foreseen – and now, as all observers must know, it is in the act of committing hara-kiri."[139] The subcommittee, sympathetic to those subjected to OPA orders, characterized OPA officials as going well beyond the inflation-fighting goals of the Emergency Price Control Act to impose their own vision of a marketplace.

More was at stake than hosiery, of course, and the subcommittee reported "widespread fears that similar principles might be applied" in many other fields.[140] Members concluded that there was "not the slightest justification for this regulation," and charged that imposing quality standards on goods was an extreme solution to a problem that had not been proven to exist.[141] The OPA, they claimed, had further violated the intent of the Emergency Price Control Act by failing to consult with manufacturers. In the hosiery context, there had been "an almost incredible lack of cooperation between the Office of Price Administration and the affected trade groups," which "clearly was not

---

[136] Maximum Price Regulation No. 306, 8 Fed. Reg. 1114 (1943); Maximum Price Regulation No. 339, 8 Fed. Reg. 2930 (1943).

[137] Prentiss M. Brown, "Price Control: A Communication," *Washington Post*, May 21, 1943, 11 (emphasis in the original).

[138] House Committee on Interstate and Foreign Commerce, Special Subcommittee on Investigation of Restrictions on Brand Names and Newsprint, *Brand Names and Newsprint: Hearings* pt. 1, 78th Cong., 1st Sess., 1943 (statement of Earl Constantine, May 25, 124); "OPA Housecleaning Urged on Congress," *New York Times*, May 26, 1943, 30.

[139] Ibid., 340 (statement of Lew Hahn, May 27, 340); see also "Fine Points of Women's Hosiery Studied in Brand Name Inquiry," *Washington Post*, May 28, 1943, 9.

[140] House Special Subcommittee on Investigation of Restrictions on Brand Names and Newsprint, *Brand Names and Newsprint: Interim Report*, pt. 1, 16.

[141] Ibid., 17.

the industry's fault."[142] As one subcommittee member characterized the hearings, in a speech to the National Wholesale Druggists Association, businessmen "have found themselves frustrated and harassed by executive-branch directives and orders, regulations and ukases."[143] At these same hearings, OPA officials, "when they were asked at what objectives their directives were aimed, broke down and confessed they didn't know."[144] Such experiences convinced subcommittee members that the OPA could not be trusted – a conclusion others in Congress were also reaching.[145]

A similarly hostile approach to the OPA, and to federal regulation as a whole, was adopted by Rep. Howard W. Smith, characterized by one *Washington Post* columnist as "a fanatical believer in 'States' rights' and a fanatical hater of anything that comes under the word 'bureaucracy.'"[146] Following his 1939 investigation of the NLRB's purported lawlessness, the Virginia congressman chaired the House Select Committee to Investigate Acts of Executive Agencies Beyond the Scope of Their Authority, whose formal name signaled what he thought the committee might find. Armed with authority to see whether administrators had gone too far (and assuming that they probably had), the Smith Committee framed the issue as a struggle between bureaucrats and Americans. Smith's focus on whether administrators were acting "beyond the scope of the power or authority" granted by Congress or the president, or were punishing individuals and businesses "without affording those accused of violation an opportunity to present their defense before a fair and impartial tribunal," was not a standard subject of congressional investigations.[147] Determining whether administrative officials had exceeded their statutory authority was both a legal and a political question – one that might be answered one way by courts but another way by members of Congress. Some in Congress had indeed pointed out that this question might be better suited to judicial resolution, but, according to one observer, more "favored 'riding herd' on some of the administrative agencies."[148]

Smith, joined by Rep. Clare Hoffman (R–Mich.), another opponent of New Deal policies and government spending, turned first to the OPA, where they

[142] Ibid., 18.

[143] Charles Halleck, quoted in "Promises Defense of Business Rights," *New York Times*, Oct. 7, 1943, 38.

[144] Ibid.

[145] "Grade Labeling: A Study of Reaction in Action," *Lawyers Guild Review* 3 (Sept.–Oct. 1943): 23–30. Congress limited the OPA's authority to issue grade labeling standards via the Taft Amendment to the Emergency Price Control Act in July 1943 (Pub. L. No. 151, 57 Stat. 566 [1943]).

[146] Marquis Childs, "Washington Calling," *Washington Post*, April 28, 1944, 6; see also Emerson, *Young Lawyer for the New Deal*, 218–23.

[147] H. Res. 102, 78th Cong., 1st sess., 1943. The committee's cumbersome title was soon shortened to the Committee to Investigate Executive Agencies.

[148] John A. Perkins, "American Government and Politics: Congressional Self-Improvement," *American Political Science Review* 38 (1944): 499–511, 504; see also Roland Young, *Congressional Politics in the Second World War* (New York: Columbia University Press, 1956), 107–08.

found much to criticize. The OPA's "illegal, absurd, useless, and conflicting regulations" and the frustration and hostility they engendered would "bring the law into contempt and ridicule" and would result, the committee predicted, in "a complete break-down of the price-control law" that would "necessarily retard the effective prosecution of the war."[149] Overall, the OPA's "complicated and unreasonable regulations" (almost 3,200 rules and orders in less than two years) left Americans "in a constant state of bewilderment."[150] In addition, OPA officials had worked "to stretch as far as possible" the authority granted by Congress and had often gone well beyond it.[151]

The OPA's entire range of activities came under attack in the hearings. One landlady (and Democratic organizer) suggested that the rent control regulations "are unconstitutional because they are against the constitutional rights of citizens" and "were written primarily by persons opposed to individual ownership of property" – some of whom, she pointed out, "are on the Dies list for subversive activities."[152] The Smith Committee found that the decisions of the OPA's Rent Department had led to "hardship and financial loss" to property owners and "unnecessary ill-will" in the landlord–tenant relationship.[153] The OPA's pricing authority was also sharply criticized, as the Smith Committee complained that the price administrator's failure to consult businesses or consider individual circumstances when setting prices led individuals and businesses to suffer. Although the Emergency Price Control Act clearly stated that prices were to be only "generally fair and equitable," rather than fair and equitable for each affected party, the Smith Committee argued that the latter should be adopted as policy. Otherwise, "[t]he individual, if unfortunate, is left to fall by the wayside."[154]

The Smith Committee particularly criticized the enforcement procedures, condemning the OPA's "seizure of judicial and legislative functions" and calling the agency's legalistic tools "a fundamental danger to constitutional government."[155] Under the Emergency Price Control Act, OPA officials, in urging compliance, rooting out violations, and punishing violators, could choose from a variety of methods that included criminal prosecutions by the Justice Department and injunctions issued by federal judges. Most commonly, however, the OPA relied on license suspension proceedings, available once

[149] House Select Committee to Investigate Executive Agencies, *Second Intermediate Report,* 78th Cong., 1st sess., 1943, H. Rep. 862, 20; see also Arthur Vanderbilt, "War Powers and Their Administration," *Annual Survey of American Law* 1943 (1943): 115–79, 153.

[150] House Select Committee to Investigate Executive Agencies, *Second Intermediate Report,* 8.

[151] House Select Committee to Investigate Executive Agencies beyond the Scope of Their Authority, *Investigating Executive Agencies,* 78th Cong., 1st sess., 1943, H. Rep. 699, 3.

[152] House Special Committee to Investigate Executive Agencies, *To Investigate Executive Agencies: Hearings,* pt. 1, 78th Cong., 1st Sess., 1943 (statement of Mary Wright Johnson, May 19), 511.

[153] House Select Committee to Investigate Acts of Executive Agencies beyond the Scope of Their Authority, *Investigating Executive Agencies,* 6.

[154] House Select Committee to Investigate Executive Agencies, *Second Intermediate Report,* 11.

[155] Ibid., 2, 1.

"General Max" licensed everyone selling anything under the OPA's jurisdiction. Once the OPA identified a violation, it could ask a court to suspend the licenses of sellers for up to twelve months (effectively closing their businesses for that period). Many agencies and commissions had long regulated their industries in this manner, requiring that all industry participants have licenses and imposing certain requirements as a condition of keeping the license. Such a solution was less drastic and punitive than criminal proceedings, but, unlike an injunction against future violations, included consequences for past actions.

Rationing authority was less clearly prescribed, although here too the OPA could turn to civil injunctions and criminal prosecutions to force compliance. Most commonly, however, the OPA resorted to a third method that, in its broad outlines, resembled license suspension.[156] Offending sellers were cut off from future allocations for a prescribed time period, significantly disadvantaging them in the marketplace. Indeed, by August 1942, one OPA attorney pointed to more than 100 suspensions for violations of gasoline and tire rationing the agency had already issued, and suggested that such suspension orders – which provided "adequate notice and full administrative hearing" for "every case" – "will be the most effective single means of enforcement of rationing regulations."[157] Unlike judicial license suspensions under the Emergency Price Control Act, however, suspensions for violating ration orders were issued by OPA officials. The Second War Powers Act, on which the rationing power rested, neither provided authority for barring violators from receiving future allocations of rationed goods nor forbade it. To fill in this gap, the OPA promulgated rules spelling out how they would go about issuing suspension orders.

The OPA's assertion of authority to issue its own orders for rationing, when the agency could not do the same under the Emergency Price Control Act, raised eyebrows.[158] According to the Smith Committee, these procedures were rampant violations of individuals' due process rights. By choosing to proceed through administrative suspension orders rather than judicial orders, the OPA had used its rule-making authority to create an entire "pseudo judiciary" system of hearing commissioners and hearings, which served as "mock courts" to police violations and issue suspension orders.[159] Through this "unwarranted and unlawful bureaucratic grab of power," the OPA had established a shadow government that placed "drastic and unconstitutional penalties upon those citizens, depriving them in certain instances of vital rights and liberties without due process of law."[160] In punishing ration violations by banning the use of

---

[156] General Ration Order No. 8, 8 Fed. Reg. 3783 (1943).
[157] Reuss, "The Lawyer in the OPA," 28.
[158] For the details of rationing, see Thompson, *The Regulatory Process in OPA Rationing*.
[159] House Select Committee to Investigate Executive Agencies, *Second Intermediate Report*, 14, 3.
[160] Ibid., 16, 2; see also Vanderbilt, "War Powers and their Administration," 153.

coupon books and cutting off violators' future access to such materials, it had assumed a power "to sentence citizens of the United States to starvation."[161] An OPA order barring Toots Shor's restaurant from using meats, fats, or oils for ninety days was "calculated to completely drive a person out of business."[162] Suspension orders not only constituted unconstitutional takings, the Smith Committee argued, but "invariably require the merchant during the period of the suspension to display his 'guilt' to the public at large in the same fashion as convicts in medieval times were branded or mutilated for the purpose of drawing public ridicule and contempt."[163] The committee specifically complained that such hearings unfairly combined prosecution and judicial powers, and charged that the practice of allowing the government to appeal a hearing commissioner's decision was "closely analogous to the placing of the accused in double jeopardy."[164]

This kind of administrative action was nonetheless standard practice elsewhere. Except for the shortened timelines (described by one observer as "terrifyingly brief"), the OPA's procedures significantly resembled the legalistic formal proceedings well established at other agencies.[165] Administrative hearings were conducted by one of a number of OPA "hearing commissioners," who were kept separate from the enforcement parts of the agency. Following a hearing, the hearing commissioner would draft a report; all parties had five days to respond and to ask for reconsideration. At the OPA, as at other agencies, this report served as a first draft of the agency's final order and a way of sharpening the issues for challenges. If after reconsideration the commissioner was convinced that the allegations of violations were true, he could issue an order suspending a supplier's access to the rationed goods for a stated period of time. This followed steps common elsewhere, although in other agencies the commissioners or agency head would issue the final order. The Attorney General's Committee on Administrative Procedure had recommended moving more authority to these hearing officials, however, and this development was within the bounds of existing proposals. Parties could appeal to the district office, the regional office, and the hearing administrator in Washington, DC,

[161] House Select Committee to Investigate Executive Agencies, *Second Intermediate Report*, 16.
[162] Ibid., 15.
[163] Ibid., 16.
[164] Ibid., 14.
[165] Goodbar, "Administrative Agency in Action," 191; see also OPA Temporary Procedural Regulation No. 4, 7 Fed. Reg. 4296 (1942); OPA Procedural Regulation No. 4, 8 Fed. Reg. 1744 (1943); OPA Procedural Regulation No. 4 Amendment 1, 8 Fed. Reg. 2035 (1943); General Order No. 46, 8 Fed. Reg. 1771 (1943); Rev. Procedural Regulation No. 4, 9 Fed. Reg. 2558 (1944); Arthur L. Brown, "The Office of Administrative Hearings," *Cornell Law Quarterly* 29 (1944): 461–88. As Marver Bernstein noted years later, "clear-cut separation of functions did not gain increased acceptance" for the OPA's suspension orders. "Separation of functions may achieve a higher degree of fairness for the private parties, but it does not necessarily win approval of a regulatory program which is bitterly resented on economic grounds" (Marver H. Bernstein, *Regulating Business by Independent Commission* [Princeton, NJ: Princeton University Press, 1955], 100).

before taking their case to a federal district court.[166] The Smith Committee's rhetoric certainly suggested that members might have opposed the OPA's substantive actions no matter what the procedures for carrying them out, but the committee's sharp attacks on the fairness of fairly traditional quasi-judicial methods for reaching administrative orders raised questions about such methods across the administrative state.

Many jumped on such charges and added their own. The *Washington Post* found reports of the OPA's procedural inventions "really disturbing" and suggested that the agency's "cavalier attitude toward the law" indicated how "democracy may readily degenerate into dictatorial bureaucracy."[167] The San Francisco Bar Association excoriated the rationing procedures in a 1944 report,[168] and the chair of the ABA's committee on administrative law remarked that the fact that courts generally upheld suspension orders was "all the more alarming to citizens who believe in the American doctrine of limited powers under the Constitution."[169] According to Roscoe Pound, the OPA's suspension orders

> belong to a land which believes in government by an omnicompetent superman, with supermen under him, to whom the life, liberty, and property of the citizen is to be subordinated; who are so all-wise as to know offhand what the public interest demands in each case and need no hearings or evidence or arguments to advise them, but are to adjust all relations and order all conduct by the light of their *ex officio* wisdom in a political organization which does not recognize private rights.[170]

Pound, who had previously attacked the administrative state as a whole, found the OPA's suspension order procedures yet "one more illustration of the vice of combining the functions of investigation, prosecuting, and judging in one administrative organization."[171]

Parties soon turned to the courts to vindicate their opposition to the OPA's reckless and lawless activities. As one attorney argued, defending clients charged with stealing gasoline ration coupons, it was "time the courts administered a legal spanking to the OPA and sent it home to Congress for parental guiding."[172] Not everyone agreed, however. OPA officials jumped to their agency's defense, relying not on justifications based on the war emergency but instead on legal claims that the OPA adhered to the best practices of the administrative

[166] Richard H. Field Jr., "Rationing Suspension Orders: A Reply to Dean Pound," *American Bar Association Journal* 30 (1944): 385–90, 386.

[167] "OPA's Powers," *Washington Post*, Nov. 21, 1943, B6.

[168] Bar Association of San Francisco, *Committee Report on Office of Administrative Hearings of the Office of Price Administration* (San Francisco: Bar Association of San Francisco, 1943).

[169] Sylvester C. Smith Jr., "Comment on Mr. Field's Reply for the OPA," *American Bar Association Journal* 30 (1944): 390–92, 390; see also Goodbar, "Administrative Agency in Action."

[170] Roscoe Pound, "The Challenge of the Administrative Process," *American Bar Association Journal* 30 (1944): 121–26, 125.

[171] Ibid., 124.

[172] Leon Lang, quoted in "OPA Regulations Bring Court Tests," *New York Times*, Mar. 9, 1943, 18.

process. Given practices common elsewhere, one official found it "ironic that our efforts to work out the fairest possible procedure have been turned against OPA in the charge that OPA has instituted 'its own system of courts.'"[173] Indeed, the OPA's general counsel argued in 1944, the agency had taken care to clearly separate prosecution and judging. To avoid charges of bias and unfairness (like those levied at agencies with no such division), the price administrator had "set up an entirely separate staff of men, which is independent of the operating and enforcement departments of the agency, to make these decisions for him."[174] As an OPA enforcement attorney in Nashville, Tennessee, argued, the suspension order procedures "measure up well to standards recognized as being essential to a fair and just exercise of the process of administrative adjudication" and included judicial review.[175] These arguments thus linked the OPA's operations to the norms of the administrative process generally, grounding the agency's practices in established principles of due process as articulated by reviewing courts.

The federal courts agreed, as their general deference to administrative operations was broad enough to include the OPA. In contrast with the Smith Committee's accusations that the OPA was vastly exceeding its authority by punishing violators with unfair hearings held by the OPA's own staff, reviewing courts came to see the OPA's operations in a distinctly different light. Reviewing courts accepted the OPA's procedures even when the OPA issued suspension orders to those violating rationing orders – what the *Washington Post* called "the most questionable practice of the OPA."[176] Whether the OPA had the legal authority to respond to violations by suspending violators' access to goods turned on, as the OPA claimed, whether the orders were simply an outgrowth of the allocation and rationing process (for which the Second War Powers Act had provided broad authority), or, as affected businesses claimed, whether the suspension orders were more like criminal sanctions (which the Second War Powers Act did *not* allow the OPA to issue on its own).

An early district court ruling that found the latter and called the hearing commissioner "a modern instance of pure dictatorship" appeared to question the legal authority and legitimacy not just of OPA officials but also of the similar figures who populated the executive branch and the independent commissions.[177] Within a few weeks, another court reviewing a similar violation of gasoline rationing rules upheld the OPA's suspension order and described the agency's "full and fair hearing" for alleged violators.[178] Given

[173] Thomas I. Emerson, letter to the editor, *Washington Post*, Nov. 26, 1943, 10.
[174] Field, "Rationing Suspension Orders," 387.
[175] John M. Cate, "Suspension Order Hearings of the Office of Price Administration in Rationing Cases," *Tennessee Law Review* 18 (1944): 340–46, 346.
[176] "OPA Is Upheld," *Washington Post*, April 2, 1944, B4.
[177] *Wilemon v. Brown*, 51 F. Supp. 978, 982 (N.D. Tex. 1943); see also *Jacobson v. Bowles*, 53 F. Supp. 532 (N.D. Tex. 1944).
[178] *Perkins v. Brown*, 53 F. Supp. 176, 181 (S.D. Ga. 1943); see also *Panteleo v. Brown*, 53 F. Supp. 209 (S.D.N.Y. 1943); *Joliet Oil Corp. v. Brown*, 55 F. Supp. 876 (N.D. Ill. 1943).

that the OPA's procedures resembled procedures at the USDA and the SEC, the court pointed out, the plaintiff's argument against the OPA "is, essentially, an attack upon the accepted procedure of administrative agencies in which the functions of administration and adjudication are sometimes blended. That such blending alone is not sufficient to invalidate a hearing fairly conducted is well established."[179] Reversing the first decision, the Fifth Circuit found that the OPA's action was not punitive. Instead, the dealer's "private interest has merely come into collision with a public interest, and has had to yield."[180] The Supreme Court soon upheld the OPA's authority to issue suspension orders, rejecting the idea that suspension orders in rationing cases were "created by administrative fiat contrary to the Act in question and contrary to constitutional requirements."[181]

Parties who could no longer challenge the suspension order device with any hope of success continued to attack the fairness of the administrative process that had led to the order. Here, too, however, federal courts routinely held the OPA's suspension orders to the same "substantial evidence" standard of review and offered the same deference to administrative judgment as they did when reviewing the orders of older, more established agencies.[182] While the power to allocate goods in the first place required emergency justification, the way in which the OPA did so was deemed thoroughly in line with existing legal traditions. Reviewing courts thus found little difficulty upholding the same assertions of authority in the rationing sphere that Rep. Smith had so loudly decried.

The OPA's most radical challenge to due process was found in the judicial review provisions of the Emergency Price Control Act. These new mechanisms for challenging the OPA's actions were a significant break with existing traditions of administrative procedure. President Roosevelt had suggested upon signing the Emergency Price Control Act that the "broad powers" given to the price administrator required "a responsibility of equal breadth for fair play," and legislative drafters had included clearly prescribed procedures to satisfy those who might complain about the regulations.[183] Regardless of whether the OPA had begun enforcement proceedings, anyone subject to the price administrator's price schedule for a particular commodity could ask the OPA to adjust

---

[179] *Perkins v. Brown*, 53 F. Supp. at 181.

[180] *Brown v. Wilemon*, 139 F.2d 730, 732 (5th Cir. 1944).

[181] *L. P. Steuart & Bro., Inc. v. Bowles*, 322 U.S. 398, 404 (1944).

[182] See *Country Garden Market, Inc. v. Bowles*, 141 F.2d 540 (D.C. Cir. 1944); *La Porte v. Bitker*, 145 F.2d 445 (7th Cir. 1944); *Bowles v. Lee's Ice Cream*, 148 F.2d 113 (D.C. Cir. 1945); *Carter v. Bowles*, 56 F. Supp. 278 (W.D.S.C. 1944);*Williams v. Bowles*, 56 F. Supp. 283 (W.D. Ky. 1944); *Illario v. Bowles*, 57 F. Supp. 404 (D.N.J. 1944); *Di Melia v. Bowles*, 57 F. Supp. 710 (D. Mass. 1944); *In re Rocillo*, 61 F. Supp. 94 (E.D.N.Y. 1945); *Williams v. Bowles*, 61 F. Supp. 275 (S.D. Fla. 1945); *Weinstein v. Bowles*, 62 F. Supp. 455 (D. Mass. 1945). For decisions reversing the OPA, see *Markall v. Bowles*, 58 F. Supp. 463 (N.D. Cal. 1944); *Automobile Sales Co. v. Bowles*, 58 F. Supp. 469 (N.D. Ohio 1944); *Rosenbaum Co. v. Bowles*, 62 F. Supp. 460 (W.D. Pa. 1945); *Cain v. Bowles*, 4 F.R.D. 504 (D. Ore. 1945).

[183] Roosevelt, "Statement by the President on Signing the Emergency Price Control Act," in *Public Papers and Addresses of Franklin D. Roosevelt*, vol. 1942, 67.

prices for a particular commodity; if that request was denied, one could file a written protest with the OPA challenging the validity of that regulation in the sixty days after a price or rent regulation was issued. The price administrator then had thirty days to respond.[184]

If the protest was rejected, the complainant could appeal to the new Emergency Court of Appeals, staffed with three sitting federal judges. Such specialized administrative courts had been established before, with varying success – the ICC's Commerce Court, for example, was short-lived, but the tax and patent courts were quite successful. The Emergency Court, like those courts, offered the twin benefits of speed and expertise. Congress justified the creation of a separate, special court as consistent "with the emergency character of the regulations and orders" in question, and suggested that such a court could "expedite action affecting the validity of such regulations or orders without overburdening the regular courts and judges."[185] Centralizing all challenges in a single court meant that the court could develop a coherent body of law on price and rent control.[186]

The Emergency Court of Appeals would review the price administrator's regulations to determine whether they were either "arbitrary or capricious" or "not in accordance with law."[187] This was a more deferential standard of review than the "substantial evidence" standard typically prescribed for agency adjudication; however, comparing the standards invites confusion, as the Emergency Court was tasked with reviewing rule making, not adjudication. The standard of review alone was not, in fact, a deviation from judicial review of administrative rule making, where due process requirements were lower than in adjudicatory proceedings.[188] As Congress had remarked, it was adopting "the traditional standards for the judicial review of legislation and legislative regulations."[189] This elided the novelty of the procedure, however, for administrative rules were not generally subject to such review before they were enforced in a particular case. The provision for judicial review of regulations independent of any alleged violations essentially created a separate court for declaratory judgments and offered a significant opportunity for parties to challenge the OPA. As OPA attorney Nathaniel Nathanson argued, "the path has been cleared for a speedy and

[184] As OPA attorney Thomas I. Emerson suggested, this hearing was not legally required, but "was of great practical importance" because it allowed the price administrator to forestall a judicial hearing and to "control the admission of evidence and the development of fact, and make his own findings. Then those findings could be subject to review only on the limited basis that they were not supported by substantial evidence" (Emerson, *Young Lawyer for the New Deal*, 154).
[185] Senate Committee on Banking and Currency, *Emergency Price Control Act of 1942*, 23.
[186] See Jacob D. Hyman and Nathaniel L. Nathanson, "Judicial Review of Price Control: The Battle of the Meat Regulations," *Illinois Law Review* 42 (1947): 584–634; Nathaniel L. Nathanson and Harold Leventhal, *Problems in Price Control: Legal Phases* (Washington, DC: Government Printing Office, 1947).
[187] Emergency Price Control Act § 204(b).
[188] *Pacific States Box & Basket Co. v. White*, 296 U.S. 176 (1935); Nathaniel L. Nathanson, "The Emergency Price Control Act of 1942: Administrative Procedure and Judicial Review," *Law and Contemporary Problems* 9 (1942): 60–76.
[189] Senate Committee on Banking and Currency, *Emergency Price Control Act of 1942*, 24.

complete judicial review without any of the risks of disobedience."[190] Another observer found that the cooperative nature of this process created "an atmosphere more of solving a problem than of fighting a battle."[191] Ideally, it was an opportunity for protesting parties to challenge the regulations early on.

Creating a procedure in which parties could challenge the price administrator without first having to break the law could thus be understood as a significant deviation from existing administrative and judicial traditions *and* a distinctive embrace of due process. As an OPA attorney in Atlanta, speaking to the Bar Association of Tennessee in 1943, suggested, "Don't worry your Congressman! Give us the opportunity to help you, and if we are unable to do so, we believe we can show you that our action is proper."[192] Another observer, however, characterized the requirements as "a tortuous procedural tunnel" that would "be exceedingly uninviting" to the disgruntled businessman.[193] One evaluation of the original bill suggested that Congress, well aware that agencies "habitually exceed the powers Congress intended to grant them," was also concerned about its own prerogatives.[194]

At the same time that Congress was putting limits on agency action, however, it was protecting the public policy goals of the Emergency Price Control Act. Allowing parties to challenge regulations before they violated the law compensated for another procedural innovation, requiring challenges to the validity of the regulations to be brought *only* before the Emergency Court. Thus, while the OPA could suspend violators' licenses or demand injunctions against these parties in any court in the country, those facing prosecution could not defend themselves by challenging the regulations in those courts. Under the act, the Emergency Court (and the Supreme Court on appeal) had sole jurisdiction over the validity of the OPA's regulations, prices, and orders.[195] This allowed for broad and rapid enforcement of OPA orders, which would otherwise be confounded by long trials and inconsistent opinions in different courts. While Americans waited for the Supreme Court to act, Nathanson suggested, "price disparities might have caused fundamental economic dislocations, and individual violations might have developed into general price increases whose inflationary tendencies could never be eradicated."[196]

Such provisions were legally novel, because, by limiting judicial review and separating enforcement actions from legal challenges, the act offered the possibility that individuals would be required to obey invalid orders. Even if the Emergency Court declared a regulation invalid, the invalid regulation would

---

[190] Nathanson, "Emergency Price Control Act of 1942," 76.

[191] "Renewal and Amendment of Price Control Legislation," *Lawyers Guild Review* 4 (Jan.–Feb. 1944): 24–39, 27.

[192] T. Nelson Parker, "The Work of the OPA," *Tennessee Law Review* 18 (1943): 6–12, 8.

[193] Edward B. Williams, Note, "OPA, Small Business, and the 'Due Process' Clause – A Study in Relations," *Georgetown Law Journal* 32 (1943): 76–87, 78, 79.

[194] Mark Sullivan, "Emergency Price Control," *Washington Post*, Aug. 13, 1941, 7.

[195] Emergency Price Control Act § 204.

[196] Nathanson, "Emergency Price Control Act of 1942," 75.

remain in effect for thirty days to give the price administrator some breathing room and to ensure that the market category in question would not immediately descend into chaos. As OPA official Harvey Mansfield reflected in his history of the agency, a seller "might have had to choose between conviction for a crime (unrelieved, except perhaps by grace, by a later determination of invalidity) and compliance.... Yet no court anywhere could give him relief for this dilemma."[197] (Mansfield reassured readers that "no case of this sort, with the equities in favor of the seller, is recorded.")[198] Not surprisingly, the Smith Committee extended its criticism to this administrative scheme, complaining that it was "a novelty in our jurisprudence, and if sustained by the courts it should be immediately corrected by amending the act."[199] Another commenter suggested that this arrangement "hardly could be said to meet orthodox requisites of peace time due process,"[200] and the ABA's Special Committee on Administrative Law labeled the promise of judicial review merely "an illusion."[201] The emergency context offered one justification for such provisions; adding a procedure to preemptively challenge the regulations offered another. Someone charged with a crime could be held accountable for forgoing the earlier opportunity to challenge it.

Parties questioned both the constitutional status of the Emergency Price Control Act and the various regulations issued under its authority, but the Emergency Court routinely upheld the price administrator.[202] Reviewing courts endorsed both the constitutionality of the act and the exclusive nature of judicial review provided under it, rejecting arguments that the delegation to the price administrator was too broad or that Congress had violated due process by limiting review.[203] Courts found the act's provisions generally in accord with existing administrative procedure, and found the wartime emergency a compelling argument for any deviations. As a three-judge panel stated in one of the first cases considering the constitutionality of the act, "a nation that may draft its young men into the armed forces to serve at a modest pay most certainly

---

[197] Mansfield, *Short History of OPA*, 276.

[198] Ibid.

[199] House Select Committee to Investigate Executive Agencies, *Second Intermediate Report*, 5.

[200] Comment, "Judicial Review of Price Orders under the Emergency Price Control Act," *Illinois Law Review* 37 (1942): 256–64, 262.

[201] "Report of the Special Committee on Administrative Law," *Annual Report of the American Bar Association* 68, 251.

[202] *Wilson v. Brown*, 137 F.2d 348 (TECA 1943); *Lakemore Co. v. Brown*, 137 F.2d 355 (TECA 1943); *Taylor v. Brown*, 137 F.2d 654 (TECA 1943); Charles W. Stewart Jr., "The Emergency Court of Appeals: Interpretation of Procedure and Judicial Review under the Price Control Act," *Georgetown Law Journal* 32 (1943): 42–65, 64.

[203] For cases upholding the Emergency Price Control Act, see *Henderson v. Kimmel*, 47 F. Supp. 635 (D. Kan. 1942); *Brown v. Wick*, 48 F. Supp. 887 (E.D. Mich. 1943); *United States v. Slobodkin*, 48 F. Supp. 913 (D. Mass. 1943); *United States v. Hark*, 49 F. Supp. 95 (D. Mass. 1943); *United States v. C. Thomas Stores, Inc.*, 49 F. Supp. 111 (D. Minn. 1943); *Brown v. Ayello*, 50 F. Supp. 391 (N.D. Cal. 1943); *United States v. Friedman*, 50 F. Supp. 584 (D. Conn. 1943); *United States v. Sosnowitz & Lotstein, Inc.*, 50 F. Supp. 586 (D. Conn. 1943); *Brown v. Warner Holding Co.*, 50 F. Supp. 593 (D. Minn. 1943); *Brown v. W. T. Grant Co.*, 53 F. Supp. 182 (S.D.N.Y. 1943).

can require its citizens on the home front to make financial and other sacrifices essential to the successful defense of our country."[204] Courts approvingly cited this emergency justification in subsequent cases, while also holding the OPA accountable to traditional doctrines of administrative law.

The Supreme Court soon endorsed the novel review features. In *Lockerty v. Phillips*, a case argued in early May 1943, the Court reviewed a challenge brought by meat wholesalers to protest their prosecution for violating the maximum wholesale prices for beef. When the district court rejected their plea for an injunction, on the grounds that under the exclusive jurisdiction provisions of the Emergency Price Control Act it could not act, they appealed to the Supreme Court.[205] The wholesalers laid out a host of complaints, including that the price administrator was discriminating against them by setting prices for beef but not livestock, that he had ignored important factors in setting such prices, that the delegation of authority to the administrator was unconstitutional, and that the prosecution violated the wholesalers' due process rights. The Court, in a decision handed down only a week after oral argument, affirmed the district court's decision, recognized the sole jurisdiction of the Emergency Court, and suggested that the parties should have availed themselves of the challenge process Congress had so laboriously spelled out.[206]

At least one lower court was not so comfortable with these review provisions, indicating the pervasiveness of the critique. In a case denying a tenant's lawsuit for damages, a federal district court in August 1943 invalidated the Emergency Price Control Act's review provisions on due process grounds, invoked *Morgan*, and used the OPA's example to indict the administrative agencies – "some of which apparently are opposed to any limitation of their powers and are impatient of all constitutional restrictions" – as a whole.[207] As the judge warned darkly, unless courts took action, they may "permit the rights of the people to be destroyed and subject them to control by regulations, which result was never intended by the Constitution, apparently regarded by some agencies as an outmoded instrument."[208] Such ominous language was the exception, not the rule, however, and the Supreme Court proved much more accepting of the administrative experiment.

The Court in *Lockerty* had not determined whether Emergency Price Control Act's bifurcated review system would be acceptable if the parties were defending themselves against the OPA's enforcement of the act; in *Yakus v. United States*, it squarely addressed the question.[209] Reviewing the convictions of parties who had sold wholesale beef for more than the maximum price, the Court rejected the sellers' contention that the delegation of authority to the price administrator was too sweeping. The Court appeared to agree with the

---

[204] *Kimmel*, 47 F. Supp. at 641–42.
[205] *Lockerty v. Phillips*, 49 F. Supp. 513 (D.N.J. 1943).
[206] *Lockerty v. Phillips*, 319 U.S. 182 (1943).
[207] *Payne v. Griffin*, 51 F. Supp. 588, 597 (M.D. Ga. 1943).
[208] Ibid.
[209] *Yakus v. United States*, 321 U.S. 414 (1944).

lower court, which empathized with a price administrator who "had to get out regulations covering great numbers of commodities, affecting a wide range of industries, the full comprehension of each of which is a lifetime study."[210] The scale of this task was enormous, and enforcement proceedings had to be adapted accordingly. Any deviations from administrative norms, the lower court suggested, probably came from exhaustion, not deviousness. Turning to petitioners' due process claims, the Court found that Congress' decision to locate jurisdiction for review exclusively in the Emergency Court, although unusual, was nonetheless constitutional, "so long as it affords to those affected a reasonable opportunity to be heard and present evidence."[211] Comparing the procedures of the OPA to those of the ICC, the Court grounded the former in the broader traditions of the administrative process.

In another decision announced the same day, the Court upheld the price administrator's rent control authority. In *Bowles v. Willingham*, as in *Yakus*, the Court rejected the argument that Congress had improperly delegated authority to the price administrator and upheld the act's judicial review provisions. Justice William O. Douglas, writing for the Court, found that minimum due process standards had been met; "where Congress has provided for judicial review after the regulations or orders have been made effective it has done all that due process under the war emergency requires."[212] Delayed judicial review was judicial review all the same, and such review was not inappropriate for a question of property rights. Here Douglas grounded his decision in the wartime context, emphasizing that "[n]ational security might not be able to afford the luxuries of litigation and the long delays which preliminary hearings traditionally have entailed."[213]

Justice Wiley B. Rutledge, skeptical that Congress could sever enforcement and validity proceedings, had strongly dissented in *Yakus*, describing the review procedures as "short-cut proceedings, trimmed almost to the bone of due process, even for wholly civil purposes, and pared down further by a short statute of limitations."[214] He concurred in *Willingham*, however, where the case at hand was a civil proceeding, for which a hearing before the Emergency Court "approaches the limit of adequacy in the constitutional sense."[215] Justice Owen J. Roberts, dissenting separately, disapproved of the delegations in both. Although he did not object to the overall anti-inflationary provisions of the act, he was troubled by the "remission to an executive official of the function of making and repealing laws applicable to the citizens of the United States."[216] As one observer agreed in the *Wall Street Journal*, the trend toward

---

[210] *Rottenberg v. United States*, 137 F.2d 850, 857 (1st Cir. 1943).
[211] *Yakus*, 321 U.S. at 433.
[212] *Bowles v. Willingham*, 321 U.S. 503, 521 (1944).
[213] Ibid.
[214] *Yakus*, 321 U.S. at 474 (Rutledge, J., dissenting).
[215] *Willingham*, 321 U.S. at 527 (1944) (Rutledge, J., concurring).
[216] Ibid., 537 (Roberts, J., dissenting).

administrative government suggested "something radically wrong at the bottom of our civil society."[217]

Congress amended the Emergency Price Control Act in 1944 to address such concerns about the OPA's procedures, but these decisions represented a significant victory for the OPA and for the legitimacy of such administrative authority.[218] Mansfield commented that, following *Yakus* and *Willingham*, "there was never a sufficient doubt of the basic constitutionality of the act to affect compliance seriously."[219] The Court's deference to OPA officials was clearly linked to the need for swift economic action during wartime. At the same time, it was consistent with the Court's generally broad deference to administrative procedures as long as certain minimum standards of hearing and review were provided. As Director of Stabilization Fred Vinson remarked of OPA operations, "We have done our job without departure from those basic constitutional procedures which even in time of war must ever remain the hallmark of democracy."[220] Judicial decisions signaled that the courts would not noticeably hinder administrative power or intervene in administrative decision making, even without the emergency context, as long as the agency was forthright about its actions.[221] The Court would subsequently draw the line when agencies provided *no* opportunity to be heard, reversing the convictions of Jehovah's Witnesses who refused induction into the military and had no access to the courts to challenge the decisions of local draft boards.[222] However, agencies that complied with basic standards of due process could expect little trouble.

The federal courts' willingness to endorse bureaucratic practices offered a variety of lessons. To some, it signaled that agencies did, in fact, offer due process to parties before them. To others, convinced that the agencies were treating Americans unfairly, it signaled that the courts had abandoned their traditional focus on due process. As one ICC practitioner argued, the Supreme Court's habit of deference offered "the agency full authority to go merrily on its sinful ways" – thus leaving Congress as "our saviour, at least in part, from the arbitrary actions of the administrative agencies."[223] For these critics, the important

---

[217] Thomas F. Woodlock, "Thinking It Over," *Wall Street Journal*, April 17, 1944, 4.

[218] Senate Committee on Banking and Currency, *Extending Price Control Act and Stabilization Act*, 78th Cong., 2nd sess., 1944, S. Rep. 922; Nathaniel L. Nathanson, "Central Issues of American Administrative Law," *American Political Science Review* 45 (1951): 348–85, 370.

[219] Mansfield, *Short History of OPA*, 279.

[220] Vinson, quoted in John H. Crider, "Price Line Held, Vinson Declares," *New York Times*, April 2, 1944, 34.

[221] See *Federal Power Commission v. Natural Gas Pipeline Co.*, 315 U.S. 575 (1942); *NLRB v. Hearst Publications, Inc.*, 322 U.S. 111 (1944).

[222] *Estep v. United States*, 327 U.S. 114 (1946).

[223] C. A. Miller, "Impact of the Federal Administrative Procedure Act on the Procedures of the Interstate Commerce Commission," in George Warren, ed., *The Federal Administrative Procedure Act and the Administrative Agencies*, 305–39 (New York: New York University School of Law, 1947), 309. My thanks to Dan Ernst for the reference.

lesson was that other branches would have to step in to protect Americans. As the ABA's president emphasized in 1944, "*Much of the very legislation we have criticized has already been or would very likely be upheld in the courts as constitutional.* The place to meet constitutional issues is not in the courts, but in the legislatures and in the arena of public opinion."[224] The Smith Committee was one prominent example of such an effort. Members claiming that the OPA was a danger both to individual rights and to the American form of government, full of bureaucrats wholly unrestrained by law, found little encouragement from Supreme Court decisions holding that the OPA's methods and design passed constitutional muster. The agency's judicial review provisions were novel, but much of the rest of the OPA's practice mirrored that routinely approved by the courts. Such legal acceptance was not enough to reassure certain members of Congress, who found that there was still plenty of room for unfairness within constitutional limits. If the courts would not police administration, Congress would have to.

The Smith Committee's investigations of the OPA and the War Labor Board (where they also found evidence of rampant violation of Americans' rights) led committee members in two directions. Neither was particularly inventive; members looking for solutions to the "problem" of administrative authority reached for recommendations already familiar to Congress in the early 1940s. First, following its failure to satisfactorily amend the Emergency Price Control Act, and finding that the administrative procedure bills already before the 78th Congress did not go far enough, the Smith Committee offered its own proposed "Administrative Procedure Act" in August 1944 for *all* agencies (temporary wartime agencies included). Members clearly believed that the problems they had found in the wartime agencies were endemic to administration, and, drawing heavily on the recommendations of the Attorney General's Committee on Administrative Procedure and on other administrative law bills, the committee called for more publicity of agency operations (so as, Smith argued, "to forbid the administration of law by secret processes"), more judicial review (extending to agency rules), an expanded role for interested parties in rule making, and increasingly isolated hearing examiners with more authority.[225] The Smith Committee's bill went further than earlier ones had, however, and added an explicit ban on agencies looking to "implied powers" to enlarge their authority.[226] As the committee stated firmly, without explicit congressional authorization, agencies' "assumption of administrative powers is a usurpation of legislative authority and an infringement upon constitutional government."[227] This provision, apparently meant to target the OPA's rationing

---

[224] Joseph W. Henderson, "Making Secure 'The Blessings of Liberty,'" *Annual Report of the American Bar Association* 69 (1944): 325–43, 341 (emphasis in the original).

[225] Howard W. Smith, "Administrative Law: A Threat to Constitutional Government?" *Virginia Law Review* 31 (1944): 1–8, 6.

[226] House Select Committee to Investigate Executive Agencies, *Sixth Intermediate Report*, 78th Cong., 2nd sess., 1944, H. Rep. 1797, 10.

[227] Ibid., 3.

authority, indicated that the Smith Committee was convinced that *all* administrators would zealously push the boundaries of their power beyond legal limits unless Congress moved to stop them.

Such an analysis was clearly colored by the committee's preconceptions about how administration failed and where the fault lay. Members argued that it was "obviously the duty of Congress" to step in and "to prescribe administrative method as well as administrative jurisdiction."[228] However, Congress's unwillingness to draft clear laws or to amend unclear ones had created the problem in the first place. Congress had intentionally given OPA officials broad discretion, and, as dissenting Smith Committee member Jerry Voorhis (D–Cal.) explained in his memoir, "one major reason why executive agencies sometimes were guilty of exceeding their duly granted authority was because Congress had not specifically set forth what that authority was or the limitations upon it."[229]

Thus, within a few months, the Smith Committee adopted another set of recommendations focused on Congress itself, proposing three new committees aimed at improving Congress's oversight capacities. While remaining skeptical about administrators, the committee now addressed its attention to congressional weakness instead of administrative strength. The problem was not Congress's unwillingness to act, but rather its inability to do so, evidenced by numerous bills providing for congressional reform. Members suggested that Congress was no match for the agencies and commissions, whose staffers were typically better informed and faster to act than members of Congress. As a result, Congress had lost its lawmaking role, becoming "a mere ratifying body of a supreme executive will."[230] This was a problem not just in drafting laws but in supervising their operations; Congress was poorly equipped to keep up with the administrative state. As the *Washington Post* concluded, the Smith Committee was now aiming its fire in the right direction. Because poorly drafted statutes were "an open invitation to 'bureaucrats' to ignore the uncertain will of Congress and follow their own concepts of the public interest," congressional reform was a necessary part of the discussion about abusive agency practices.[231]

These two tracks of administrative change recommended by the Smith Committee indicated the directions reformers would take as the war emergency drew to a close. By the end of the 79th Congress, Congress's efforts to rein in zealous administrators finally took statutory form, as new laws defined the legal procedures through which administrators made decisions and remade the political environment in which they did so. In a two-month period in the summer of 1946, Congress passed and President Truman signed the Administrative

---

[228] Ibid., 1.

[229] Jerry Voorhis, *Confessions of a Congressman* (Garden City, NY: Doubleday, 1947), 313.

[230] House Select Committee to Investigate Executive Agencies, *Seventh Intermediate Report*, 78th Cong., 2nd sess., 1944, H. Rep. 1912, 2.

[231] "Congress Looks Inward," *Washington Post*, Nov. 21, 1944, 8.

Procedure Act and the Legislative Reorganization Act. The former targeted
decision making in the agencies and commissions in the hopes of constraining
bureaucratic discretion, at the same time that the latter pushed Congress to
do a better job supervising administrative officials. Both reflected the diver-
gence between agencies' legal and political legitimacy that many members of
Congress had confronted during wartime. Congress's move toward reform
indicated a rejection of judicial conceptions of due process and an increasing
faith in their own.

2

A "Bill of Rights" for the Administrative State

Political pressure on Congress to do something about the agencies came to a head in the 1940s, a result of the heated political context of the late 1930s and early 1940s in which attacks on Roosevelt's substantive policies were intertwined with attacks on the administrative state that carried them out. Cries of unfairness in the administrative state linked fairness to legality and framed antibureaucratic politics around the need for procedural reform. In 1946, the combination of New Deal debates and World War II–era concerns about the dangers of administrative power were reflected in the Administrative Procedure Act of 1946, the first broad procedural statute for the administrative state. The act allowed reformers to offer a coherent approach to the dozens of agencies and commissions, each of which possessed its own messy and complicated history, institutional structure, and political context. The statute defined minimum standards for agency and commission operations; its key changes, as understood at the time, were those related to the examiners and to the formal hearings they conducted. If the problem of the administrative state was administrative officials who acted recklessly in resolving private parties' property interests, the solution was to provide clear rules for parties challenging agency action and at the same time to preserve parties' opportunities for informal cooperation.

The details of the Administrative Procedure Act owed much to two prewar models for administrative reform: the Walter-Logan bill, drafted by the ABA, passed by Congress, and emphatically vetoed by Roosevelt in December 1940; and recommendations offered by the Attorney General's Committee on Administrative Procedure, established by Roosevelt in 1939 in response to contemporary attacks on the agencies and commissions. Both couched their recommendations in legalistic and apolitical language, and both drew on the professional knowledge of lawyers. These two takes on the administrative process nonetheless offered strikingly different perspectives, suggesting that administrative procedure offered fertile terrain for fighting political battles.

The Walter–Logan bill, which sought to saddle agencies with more proce-dures and surround their actions with more judicial review, reflected the ABA's skepticism about administrators. Lacking any faith in administrators' expertise and fearful of administrative enthusiasm, critics turned to lawyers to draft pro-cedures limiting administrative discretion. The Attorney General's Committee responded with a lengthy defense of the fairness of the administrative process and the officials within it and in doing so changed the debate about the prob-lems of the administrative state. Its recommendations aimed at minimizing the appearance of administrative wrongdoing were focused on winning over Americans skeptical of administration rather than bringing the administrative state into compliance with judicial definitions of due process (which, according to the courts, it largely was).

Parties' understanding of the APA's effect said much about what they believed fairness to mean in the administrative state. Debates about the significance of the APA were, in certain ways, debates over the legitimacy of New Deal reforms and the administrative state as a whole.[1] The bill's drafters consistently argued that the APA was a significant reform that would improve the fairness of administrative governance and bring due process to the administrative state. The suggestion that fairness had heretofore been absent, of course, framed the federal government and those working in it as inherently untrustworthy and discounted their accumulated experience. By this logic, the APA – the "bill of rights" for the administrative state, in the words of Sen. Pat McCarran (R–Nev.) – was the only thing providing adequate constraint on administrative discretion.[2] The bill was needed, Rep. John Jennings Jr. (R–Tenn.) described, since the bureaucrat's "chief indoor sport" was "to evolve out of his own inner consciousness, like a spider spins his web, countless confusing rules and regula-tions which may deprive a man of his property, his liberty, and bedevil the very life out of him."[3] The APA promised to protect parties from biased officials, offering reforms to the hearing examiner system that sought to keep the exam-iners free of agency pressure (and that ABA representatives would attempt to use to remake the hearing examiner in their own image). The act also clarified procedure, offering those confronting the agencies a road map for doing so, according to the Senate Judiciary Committee; it was described by Justice Felix Frankfurter in 1953 "as a far-reaching remedial measure" that ensured a judi-cial check on the administrative process.[4] The ABA and members of Congress

---

[1] See Walter Gellhorn and Kenneth Culp Davis, "Present at the Creation: Regulatory Reform before 1946," *Administrative Law Review* 38 (1986): 511–33; G. Edward White, "The Emergence of Agency Government and the Creation of Administrative Law," in *The Constitution and the New Deal* (Cambridge, MA: Harvard University Press, 2000), 94–127; Robert L. Rabin, "Federal Regulation in Historical Perspective," *Stanford Law Review* 38 (1986): 1189–326.

[2] Senate Proceedings (statement of Sen. Pat. McCarran, Mar. 12, 1946), reprinted in U.S. Senate, *Administrative Procedure Act: Legislative History, 79th Cong., 1944–46, S. Doc 248* (Washington, DC: Government Printing Office, 1946), 298.

[3] House Proceedings (statement of Rep. John Jennings Jr., May 24, 1946) reprinted in *Administrative Procedure Act: Legislative History*, 392.

[4] *Heikkila v. Barber*, 345 U.S. 229, 238 (1953) (Frankfurter, J., dissenting).

used the APA to trumpet the fact that due process had been brought to the administrative state, and to reassure Americans that the agencies and commissions had been brought under control. The Supreme Court's early decisions interpreting the statute indicated the power of this rhetoric; so too did the Truman White House's decision to legitimate its loyalty-security program by surrounding it with procedural protections.

As others pointed out, however, the APA did remarkably little to change the status quo within the agencies themselves.[5] Kenneth Culp Davis, an administrative law professor and active participant in these debates, concluded forty years later that the APA's "considerable accomplishment" was in fact "much more political than legal."[6] As he wrote in his 1951 treatise, the act's accomplishments "were to satisfy the political will for reform, to improve and strengthen the administrative process, and to preserve the basic limits upon judicial review of administrative action."[7] Designed to encompass the vast variation in administrative tasks and methods, the APA's language was intentionally broad and flexible. Although the separation of functions it prescribed was stricter than many contemporary statutes required, provisions reflected existing practice in many agencies and did little more than reaffirm existing judicial standards of due process and judicial review. It also preserved the informal cooperation that parties valued. The ABA touted its success in imposing legal limits on the administrative state, but the APA's content owed more to practices long endorsed by federal courts and recommendations offered by the Attorney General's Committee than to the tight restrictions on administrative discretion the ABA had sought since the 1930s. What is more, these highly touted provisions applied only to a small fraction of administrative operations. As James MacGregor Burns reminded Americans in 1949, the federal government encompassed "a hoof-and-mouth disease inspector in Texas; an economist in Washington; a weather forecaster in New York; a veterans' counselor in Seattle; an expert on Korean affairs in the Pentagon, and thousands of others."[8] The vast majority of administrative action would continue to be handled informally and with much cooperation among parties and agency officials.

---

[5] Paul R. Verkuil, "The Emerging Concept of Administrative Procedure," *Columbia Law Review* 78 (1978): 258–329; Gellhorn and Davis, "Present at the Creation"; Rabin, "Federal Regulation in Historical Perspective"; Martin Shapiro, "APA: Past, Present, Future," *Virginia Law Review* (1986): 447–92; Martin Shapiro, *Who Guards the Guardians? Judicial Control of Administration* (Athens: University of Georgia Press, 1988); Matthew Holden Jr., *Continuity and Disruption: Essays in Public Administration* (Pittsburgh, PA: University of Pittsburgh Press, 1996); White, "The Emergence of Agency Government and the Creation of Administrative Law."

[6] Gellhorn and Davis, "Present at the Creation," 518. Marver Bernstein agreed, remarking in 1954 that the APA was "more important for its political implications than for its specific procedural requirements and definitions." Marver H. Bernstein, "The Politics of Adjudication," *Journal of Politics* 16 (1954): 299–323, 304.

[7] Kenneth Culp Davis, *Administrative Law* (St. Paul, MN: West Publishing, 1951), 9.

[8] James MacGregor Burns, "Our Super-Government – Can We Control It?" *New York Times Magazine*, Apr. 24, 1949, 28.

Once procedural reform had been achieved, antibureaucratic sentiment and the tension between zeal and expertise took new shape as critics turned their attention to administrative personnel. Congressional Republicans who imposed strict limits on NLRB officials in the 1947 Taft-Hartley Act called into question the APA's practical ability to restrain administrators, and separate efforts targeted biased hearing examiners and subversive administrative staffers at all levels. The APA's limits on bureaucratic discretion were not enough for critics who continued to doubt the legitimacy of bureaucratic decision making. However, framing antibureaucratic politics around fairness expressed in terms of legalism provided language that parties on all sides could use. With new (and purportedly significant) procedural rules in place, it was harder to make the case that zealous administrators were something to fear; at the same time, defenders of the administrative process could use this language themselves as they pointed to the deficiencies in programs designed to remove dangerous employees. Going forward, the language of legalism would constrain future reform efforts and make administrative law that much more difficult to challenge.

The ABA – which was among those groups complaining most loudly about administrative misconduct during the 1930s – was a key force pushing for reform that would bring the administrative state to heel. Since its creation in 1933, the ABA's Special Committee on Administrative Law had been hostile to the New Deal administrative state, and alongside Chairman Roscoe Pound's scathing 1938 indictment of "administrative absolutism" in the administrative state, members offered a strict uniform code of procedure with which to bind administrators.[9] This code, introduced into Congress in June 1939 by Rep. Francis Walter (D–Pa.) and Sen. Marvel Mills Logan (D–Ky.), was premised on the idea that agency officials were failing to protect the rule of law in formal administrative hearings, and responded by significantly increasing the opportunities individuals would have to appeal decisions rendered by administrators. Parties could have administrative decisions reviewed by: (1) new review boards to be created within each agency, ensuring some appeal from unfair administrative officials before the agency's decision became final; *and* (2) by federal courts with expanded jurisdiction over administrative action. Rule making was also addressed; public hearings were required before any rule could be made, and ample opportunity was offered for parties to challenge rules in court.[10]

[9] "Report of the Special Committee on Administrative Law," *Annual Report of the American Bar Association* 63 (1938): 331–68, 342; see also Louis L. Jaffe, "Invective and Investigation in Administrative Law," *Harvard Law Review* 52 (1939): 1201–45.

[10] Verkuil, "The Emerging Concept of Administrative Procedure"; Walter Gellhorn, "The Administrative Procedure Act: The Beginnings," *Virginia Law Review* 72 (1986): 219–33; Ronen Shamir, *Managing Legal Uncertainty: Elite Lawyers in the New Deal* (Durham, NC: Duke University Press, 1995); Gellhorn and Davis, "Present at the Creation"; George B. Shepherd, "Fierce Compromise: The Administrative Procedure Act Emerges from New Deal Politics," *Northwestern University Law Review* 90 (1996): 1557–683; James E. Brazier, "An Anti-New Dealer Legacy: The Administrative Procedure Act," *Journal of Policy History* 8 (1996): 206–26;

The agencies feared, however, that the bill would slow down the administrative process by turning all adjudications into formal adjudications, complicating rule making, and adding additional steps to the decision-making process.[11] The ABA also sought to remake judicial review, replacing the variety of existing judicial and statutory requirements with a uniform standard allowing courts to overrule factual findings if they were either "clearly erroneous" or "not supported by substantial evidence." Given that the "substantial evidence" standard of review already applied to much agency action, adding the "clearly erroneous" standard introduced a new element of unpredictability and, according to one observer, "surely makes it possible for reviewing judges bent on broadening the scope of review to go ahead and make these words make a difference."[12]

Committees in each house of Congress reported favorably on the Walter–Logan bill, grounding their support in the broad language of legalism and framing the bill as a return to basic American principles. Members promised to replace "the present situation of indescribable confusion" with uniform rules that would be less bewildering to parties appearing before the agencies.[13] The bill would rein in overzealous bureaucrats who, the House Judiciary Committee warned, "become contemptuous of both the Congress and the courts; disregardful of the rights of the governed; and for lack of sufficient legal control over them a few develop Messiah complexes."[14] Such deviation from constitutional principles was particularly threatening in light of rising totalitarianism abroad. Members of Congress also suggested that the bill could stem the ever-increasing power of the Roosevelt White House. Members avoided specific attacks on the New Deal agencies, but the bill itself exempted many of the older agencies, including the ICC, the FTC, and the Civil Service Commission, while holding newer agencies subject to the stricter procedures. The conservative coalition's support for the bill, on the heels of the Smith Committee's NLRB investigation and Congress's consideration

---

Nicholas S. Zeppos, "The Legal Profession and the Development of Administrative Law," *Chicago-Kent Law Review* 72 (1997): 1119–57; David H. Rosenbloom, "1946: Framing a Lasting Congressional Response to the Administrative State," *Administrative Law Review* 50 (1998): 173–97; Mathew D. McCubbins, Roger G. Noll, and Barry R. Weingast, "The Political Origins of the Administrative Procedure Act," *Journal of Law, Economics, & Organization* 15 (1999): 180–217.

[11] For more on the Walter–Logan bill, see Gellhorn, "Administrative Procedure Act"; Brazier, "An Anti-New Dealer Legacy"; Shepherd, "Fierce Compromise"; Morton J. Horwitz, *The Transformation of American Law, 1870–1960: The Crisis of Legal Orthodoxy* (New York: Oxford University Press, 1992).

[12] Breck P. McAllister, "Administrative Adjudication and Judicial Review," *Illinois Law Review* 34 (1940): 680–98, 691; see also Samuel Kaufman, "Is the Administrative Process a Fifth Column?" *John Marshall Law Quarterly* 6 (1940): 1–17; James M. Landis, "Crucial Issues in Administrative Law: The Walter-Logan Bill," *Harvard Law Review* 53 (1940): 1077–102.

[13] Senate Judiciary Committee, *Providing for the More Expeditious Settlement of Disputes with the United States and for Other Purposes*, 76th Cong., 1st sess., 1939, S. Rep. 442, 10.

[14] House Judiciary Committee, *Providing for the More Expeditious Settlement of Disputes with the United States and for Other Purposes*, 76th Cong., 1st sess., 1939, H. Rep. 1149, 2.

of amendments to weaken the Wages and Hours Act, embroiled the bill in partisan controversy.

Agency officials, pro-administration members of Congress, and the Roosevelt White House joined many outside the government signaling their disapproval. Opponents of the Walter–Logan bill argued in and out of Congress that the bill's procedural provisions were actually intended to hinder the administration of substantive New Deal policies, and a *New York Post* editorial, entitled "A Dull but Dangerous Bill," called the Walter–Logan bill "the most subtle attack yet planned on all the social reforms of the past seven years."[15] The secretary of the liberal National Lawyers Guild charged that the bill was "an attempt to prevent the effective enforcement of the bulk of the New Deal legislation" and, as a way of hiding substantive goals in procedural reforms, "cannot be too strongly indicted as an attack on democratic procedure."[16] As John Foster Dulles, a prominent corporate lawyer and chair of the Special Committee on Administrative Law of the Bar of the City of New York, pointed out, ABA lawyers were also likely to be hostile to the changes in legal practice that the New Deal state represented. As he suggested, shifting lawmaking authority to agencies and commissions was a "flagrant intrusion into the lawyers' preserve" – a development that was "naturally disturbing and upsetting to lawyers and tends to create in them a sullen resentfulness."[17]

Critics also challenged the bill's design, suggesting that its proposed reforms failed to take into account the wildly varying tasks of the agencies and commissions. James M. Landis, dean of Harvard Law School, former FTC and SEC commissioner, and author of *The Administrative Process*, concluded that the bill's reforms would leave "broken and bleeding the processes of administrative law."[18] Comparing the bill's poor draftsmanship to that of the constitutionally inadequate National Industrial Recovery Act, Landis explained: "It would be silly, for example, to build the same structure for a bank as for a railroad station; equally absurd is it to insist that the details of organization and operation of the Federal Communications Commission and the Federal Reserve Board shall be alike."[19]

While Congress considered the Walter–Logan bill, the Roosevelt administration began to consider its own reform of the administrative process aimed at improving the administrative state and defending it from political attacks.

---

[15] Samuel Grafton, "A Dull But Dangerous Bill," *St. Louis Post Dispatch*, Feb. 7, 1940 (reprinted from the *New York Post)*, Folder "Legislation – Administrative Procedure Bills Statements & Articles," Box 8, A.G. Committee Correspondence, Entry 376, AGCAP, RG 60, NACP.

[16] Mortimer Reimer, letter to the editor, *New York Times*, June 14, 1939, 22; see also "Report of the Committee on Administrative Law of the National Lawyers' Guild," approved by the Board of Directors Dec. 16, 1939, Folder "National Lawyers Guild," Box 9, A.G. Committee Correspondence, Entry 376, AGCAP, RG 60, NACP.

[17] John Foster Dulles, "Administrative Law: A Practical Attitude for Lawyers," *American Bar Association Journal* 25 (1939): 275–82 and 352–53, 276.

[18] Landis, "Crucial Issues in Administrative Law," 1102.

[19] Ibid., 1080.

Reform in the executive branch came in reaction to conservative critiques, and to an extended debate critical of the existing system of administrative law. Scholars had long criticized the body of administrative law that federal judges had developed. Administrative law doctrines reflected the law's gradual development and its emphasis on judicial review to protect individual rights, but these values seemed ill-suited to the needs of modern government. Advocates of administration believed that a properly drafted statute, grounded in an understanding of administrative needs, could make administrative law responsive to the public interest *and* to individuals' rights. Further, many saw reform as a way to minimize judicial review of agency decisions. Legal scholars had demonstrated that federal courts gave greater scrutiny to the decisions of agencies they distrusted; improving administrative procedures might ease judicial review.[20]

In light of these arguments, and in a context of continuing political attacks on administration, the Roosevelt administration began its own affirmative defense of the administrative state. In February 1939, President Roosevelt asked Frank Murphy, his new attorney general, to lead a "thorough and comprehensive study" of administrative procedure in federal departments, agencies, and commissions.[21] Such an investigation was welcomed by lawyers worried about the damage that the appearance of impropriety was doing to the administrative state. As attorney Charles Wyzanski had argued to his former boss, Attorney General Homer Cummings, a few months earlier, the Justice Department needed to pay attention to the problem of administrative law; "unless these agencies are fair and the people at large are convinced that they are fair, administrative law will not succeed."[22] The study was promoted as the first serious inquiry into administrative law, implicitly framed as an effort to evaluate the truth of the recent attacks by Congress and the ABA. Staff director Walter Gellhorn suggested that, although there had been "a good deal of talk about administrative procedure," the Attorney General's Committee was in charge of conducting "the first comprehensive survey of the procedures of the particular agencies in their particular tasks, so that we can see with some clarity how far it is safe to apply the generalized comments that have recently become so popular."[23]

[20] See Gerard C. Henderson, *The Federal Trade Commission: A Study in Administrative Law and Procedure* (New Haven, CT: Yale University Press, 1924); I.L. Sharfman, *The Interstate Commerce Commission: A Study in Administrative Law and Procedure*, 4 vols. (New York: Commonwealth Fund, 1931–1937); Carl McFarland, *Judicial Control of the Federal Trade Commission and the Interstate Commerce Commission, 1920–1930* (Cambridge, MA: Harvard University Press, 1933).

[21] Franklin D. Roosevelt to Frank Murphy, Feb. 16, 1939, reprinted in Attorney General's Committee on Administrative Procedure, *Final Report* (Washington, DC: Government Printing Office, 1941), 252.

[22] Charles E. Wyzanski to Homer Cummings, Sept. 29, 1938, 3, Box 169, Cummings Papers, UVA.

[23] "Informal Talk by Walter Gellhorn, delivered August 9, 1939, before the Department of Justice Local, United Federal Workers of America," 13, Folder "Speeches and Articles by Committee

Unlike members of the ABA and the Smith Committee, most of the members of the Attorney General's Committee on Administrative Procedure were presumed to be sympathetic to the Roosevelt administration and to the cause of administrative government. Murphy had staffed his Committee on Administrative Procedure with prominent attorneys, several of whom – including Solicitor General Robert H. Jackson and former Assistant Attorney General Carl McFarland – were appointed directly from Roosevelt's Justice Department. Former Undersecretary of the Treasury Dean Acheson was also named to the committee, as were D. Lawrence Groner, chief judge of the U.S. Court of Appeals for the District of Columbia, and Arthur T. Vanderbilt, a legal reformer and past president of the ABA and the American Judicature Society. Several other members – Lloyd Garrison, dean of the University of Wisconsin Law School, E. Blythe Stason, dean of the University of Michigan School of Law, Henry M. Hart Jr. of Harvard Law School, Harry Shulman of Yale Law School, and Ralph Fuchs of Washington University – came from academe. Some of these members also brought their own government experience to the committee; Hart, for example, had worked with the Justice Department and Garrison had served as the chairman of the first NLRB.[24]

Given the contentious political context, the Attorney General's Committee was immediately seen as the White House's response to the Walter–Logan bill then pending in Congress. Columbia law professor Walter Gellhorn, who directed the committee's research staff, publicly dismissed this claim as "a fairy tale," but members were well aware of such accusations.[25] Most privately opposed the bill; Jackson called it "a damn fool bill," and Hart commented that the bill, if enacted, "would be a major disaster."[26] The committee avoided most controversy, however, by choosing a position of official silence about the bill's substance throughout Congress's deliberations. Roosevelt ultimately vetoed the bill in late 1940, blaming it on "a combination of lawyers who desire to have all processes of Government conducted through lawsuits and

Members," Box 10, A.G. Committee Correspondence, Entry 376, AGCAP, RG 60, NACP; see also Joanna Grisinger, "Law in Action: The Attorney General's Committee on Administrative Procedure," *Journal of Policy History* 20 (2008): 379–418.
[24] James W. Morris recommended to the attorney general in January that the committee should include someone recommended by the ABA president, as long as "such member is of liberal and untrammeled view" (James W. Morris to Frank Murphy, memorandum, Jan. 24, 1939, 2, Folder "Committee, Materials re Formation of – Press Releases, Orders, etc.," Box 3. A.G. Committee Correspondence; Entry 376, AGCAP, RG 60, NACP). Hart was working with the Immigration and Naturalization Service during the committee's work. In October 1939, Golden W. Bell resigned to become legal adviser to the High Commissioner to the Philippines, and Acheson replaced James W. Morris as chairman when Morris was appointed to the federal bench. Attorney General Jackson would be replaced on the committee by his successor, Francis Biddle.
[25] "Informal Talk by Walter Gellhorn, delivered August 9, 1939, before the Department of Justice Local, United Federal Workers of America," question and answer session, 2.
[26] Transcript, Conference of the Attorney General's Committee, Oct. 21, 1939, 2:30 P.M., 15, 7, Folder "Committee Meeting October 21, 1939," Box 3, A.G. Committee Correspondence, Entry 376, AGCAP, RG 60, NACP.

of interests which desire to escape regulation."[27] As he argued, administrative reform was simply political reform cloaked in procedural garb; opponents "rightly see that if they can strike at the heart of modern reform by sterilizing the administrative tribunal which administers them, they will have effectively destroyed the reform itself."[28]

The demise of the bill gave the Attorney General's Committee an opening for its own recommendations regarding the administrative process. The committee and its staff compiled twenty-seven separate monographs, each describing the operations and procedures of individual agencies, bureaus, and departments, and printed a lengthy final report, issued in January 1941, based on the staff's investigations and agencies' responses. (McFarland, Stason, and Vanderbilt issued a separate joint statement, included in the printed report; Judge Groner offered another.) Perhaps influenced by their own government experiences, members of the committee had encouraged agency participation in their investigations; perhaps in reaction to the barrage of criticism agencies faced, administrators were open to the project.

Although the Attorney General's Committee was initially perceived as a political gambit, its final report was seen as a solid investigation and analysis of the inner workings of the administrative process. The committee offered recommendations intended not to strictly limit the agencies but to help them improve their overall operations and gain legitimacy in the public's eyes. The committee's prominent lawyers found scant evidence of wrongdoing in the administrative process and rebuked claims of lawlessness by demonstrating the wealth of multistep procedures for hearings and appeals throughout the administrative process. Indeed, as they argued, "In the best existing practices are embodied the fundamentals of fair administration."[29] Hundreds of pages of studies and citations made their conclusions hard to rebut. The Attorney General's Committee's study thus displaced some of the ABA's critiques and shaped conversations about administrative reform along the lines of their own recommendations.

In considering the question of formal hearings, the committee did not find deviations from the judicial model inherently problematic. Their reports did demonstrate that most "formal" hearings were in fact relatively informal when compared to courts; parties confronted administrative officials not in formal courtrooms but in agencies' own offices, in space borrowed from other agencies, or in the field. Hearings conducted by the War Department's Corps of Engineers were reportedly "more like a New England town meeting than like a judicial trial."[30] At the Federal Alcohol Administration, agency representatives

---

[27] Franklin D. Roosevelt, "The President Vetoes the Bill Regulating Administrative Agencies," Dec. 18, 1940, in Samuel I. Rosenman, ed., *Public Papers and Addresses of Franklin D. Roosevelt*, vol. 1940 (New York: Macmillan Company, 1941), 619.

[28] Ibid.

[29] Attorney General's Committee, *Final Report*, 5.

[30] Attorney General's Committee on Administrative Procedure, *War Department, Monograph No. 15* (Washington, DC: Department of Justice, 1940), 26.

maintained friendly relationships with parties; they "often address each other by their given names when off the record, and frequently indulge in bits of facetious asides."[31] Practices were so informal that the parties and the examiner often smoked during the hearings, and agency officials even "occasionally remove their coats" – weather permitting.[32] Surveying these varying models, the committee suggested that such informality was not ideal but became a problem only when parties lost respect for the examiners and for the hearing process. As the members argued, "fairness does not require a particular form of hearing procedure. It does require an open and fair atmosphere and a receptive presiding officer."[33]

The controversial figure of the hearing examiner was subjected to considerable attention by the Attorney General's Committee. Although the committee had found little evidence of bias or improper influence, implicitly refuting the charges of the Smith Committee and others, members recognized that such charges, however unfounded, were harmful to an agency's reputation. They concluded that formal hearings must be designed with an eye to possible criticism, and thus should "give convincing assurance" to parties before them that the agency's decision "is not motivated by any desire to deal with the parties or their interest otherwise than in the manner which an objective appraisal of the facts and the furtherance of the public duty imposed upon the agency require."[34] Improving the examiner corps was one way of staving off external attack; an examiner should "command public confidence both by his capacity to grasp the matter at issue and by his impartiality in dealing with it."[35]

The Attorney General's Committee was more worried about capacity than bias, as members had found that the ideal of the expert administrator contrasted sharply with the reality of passive and incompetent examiners. The Supreme Court in *Morgan* had frowned at the USDA's failure to provide the parties with an initial report, but the committee turned a spotlight onto the frequent uselessness of such reports. Ideally, the initial report would contain an examiner's factual findings and tentative recommendations. Because the facts themselves were often uncontroverted, potentially more useful for both the parties and the agency were the examiner's conclusions as to their legal and policy implications. However, in some agencies, either by rule or by habit, examiners simply reported the factual findings and avoided any discussion of their significance. Acheson observed to the rest of the committee that "in almost every agency that we have dealt with that had examiners we have run into the decay of

[31] Attorney General's Committee on Administrative Procedure, *Federal Alcohol Administration, Monograph No. 5* (Washington, DC: Department of Justice, 1940), 40.
[32] Ibid.
[33] Attorney General's Committee, *Final Report*, 68.
[34] Ibid., 43.
[35] Ibid.; see also Daniel R. Ernst, "*Morgan* and the New Dealers," *Journal of Policy History* 20 (2008): 447–81.

the examiners"; as a result, the initial report "isn't a report at all, it is just a sort of summary of some of the evidence."[36] At the SEC, for example, parties reportedly complained that examiners' reports were "poorly prepared, poorly reasoned, and of virtually no significance in the ultimate disposition of the case."[37] Even when examiners did reach conclusions, there was no guarantee of their accuracy, for it could be difficult for a low-level examiner to predict the agency's ultimate policy decision. This varied significantly across the administrative state; although the ICC accepted examiners' recommendations in approximately 85 percent of the cases, the FCC decided to abolish examiners' reports entirely once it found that commissioners disagreed with examiners' reasoning or decisions in over half the cases.

The committee thus recommended improving the examiner corps, concluding that once examiners' work could "carry a hallmark of fairness and capacity," then "a great part of the criticisms of administrative agencies will have been met."[38] To attract more capable lawyers, they proposed that examiners should be given higher wages, fixed terms with removal only for cause, and the more impressive title of hearing commissioners. These new hearing commissioners would, members hoped, be able to draft more useful reports and recommendations for agencies; on the basis of these improved reports, the Attorney General's Committee recommended that agency heads defer to hearing commissioners' fact finding unless they found clear error. In this sense, hearing commissioners were to become more like trial judges, although the committee was quick to emphasize that the ultimate decision in any case always remained with the agency heads.

A key question before the committee was the role of examiners in the agencies. The Smith Committee had complained that communication between NLRB examiners and other agency staffers during pending cases influenced examiners' decisions, and other critics charged that examiners across the administrative state were too easily pressured to decide the way their agencies wanted. The Attorney General's Committee reported, in fact, that many of the more controversial and more powerful agencies, including the SEC and the NLRB, already went to some lengths to insulate their personnel in response to such concerns. The Labor Department's Division of Public Contracts, for example, separated its examiners and trial attorneys during travel, even "in places boasting only one reasonably comfortable hostelry."[39] These precautions, the staff

---

[36] Transcript, Conference of the Attorney General's Committee, Feb. 24, 1940, 43, Folder "Committee Meeting Feb. 24 & 25," Box 4, A.G. Committee Correspondence, Entry 376, AGCAP, RG 60, NACP.

[37] Attorney General's Committee on Administrative Procedure, *Securities and Exchange Commission, Monograph No. 26* (Washington, DC: Department of Justice, 1940), 232.

[38] Attorney General's Committee, *Final Report*, 43–44, 44.

[39] Attorney General's Committee on Administrative Procedure, *The Division of Public Contracts, Department of Labor, The Walsh-Healey Act, Monograph No. 1* (Washington, DC: Department of Justice, 1939), 31.

found, "succeeded in surrounding the examiner at the hearing with an aura of judicial respectability."[40]

In other agencies, however, where examiners were fully involved in agency business, the Attorney General's Committee suggested that this was not as problematic as critics had charged. Some agencies, they found, assigned the role of hearing examiner to the staffer who had handled the case from the filing of the initial complaint and allowed examiners to question witnesses; such methods had, at least at the FCC, led to "increasingly intelligent records."[41] As the Attorney General's Committee repeatedly demonstrated, examiners had never been envisioned as neutral arbiters; their function was largely that of accumulating and processing the information agency heads needed to reach a final decision. In addition, the combination of prosecution and judicial functions which may have shocked law review readers made perfect sense for certain proceedings at, say, the USDA's Grain Division. That agency had ended its practice of using one examiner to conduct the hearing and another to represent the division in proceedings regarding grain quality misrepresentation "because of gibes at the Department for using two men where one would suffice."[42] As the Attorney General's Committee staff reported: The "'judge–prosecutor' complex, beloved of lawyers, apparently impresses the grain trade very little if at all."[43] At least some participants in the administrative process, then, also declined to measure fairness by judicial standards.

Nonetheless, to address charges of agency bias and to ensure that such relationships would not become problematic, the majority of the committee suggested that all agencies fully segregate agencies' prosecution and adjudication functions. The examiners in each agency would be barred from performing other administrative tasks, isolated from cases before and after the hearing process, and selected by a new, separate Office of Administrative Procedure. McFarland, Stason, Vanderbilt, and Groner, arguing that these reforms did not go far enough to insulate the examiners from other agency officials, sought to move the process of adjudication – and the examiners themselves – outside the agencies entirely, to an independent board. Examiners would not be fully free to make up their own minds, the dissenters argued, "so long as their appointments, assignments, personnel records, and reputations are

---

[40] Ibid.; see also Nathaniel L. Nathanson, "Separation of Functions within Federal Administrative Agencies," *Illinois Law Review* 35 (1941): 901–37.

[41] Attorney General's Committee on Administrative Procedure, *Federal Communications Commission, Monograph No. 3* (Washington, DC: Department of Justice, 1940), 45. The Federal Communications Bar Association, however, questioned this and other staff observations. (Special Committee of the Federal Communications Bar Association, report to the Executive Committee, May 9, 1940, 8–9, Folder "Attorney General's Committee on Administrative Procedure, 1939–1941: General [2 of 4]," Box 2, Acheson Papers, HSTL.)

[42] Attorney General's Committee, *The Administration of the Grain Standards Act, Department of Agriculture, Monograph No. 7* (Washington, DC: Department of Justice, 1940), 35.

[43] Ibid.

subject to control by an authority which is also engaged in investigating and prosecuting."[44]

By focusing its attention not just on the formal hearings, the Attorney General's Committee also pointed out the extent of cooperation found in the administrative state. Indeed, formal adjudication – the subject of so much lawyerly critique – was a comparatively small part of the administrative process; the great bulk of agency interactions with the regulated parties occurred through less formal methods of licensing, rate making, and investigation. Even in enforcement cases, parties reached informal settlements and stipulated to facts much more frequently than they took advantage of the provisions for formal hearings; this informal decision making was, the committee found, "truly the lifeblood of the administrative process."[45] These informal activities came under less scrutiny because they featured fairly smooth relations between the agency and the parties. Ensuring the appearance of fairness was an easier task where there were few complaints of actual unfairness.

This kind of cooperative relationship between agency officials and the parties they regulated was also evident in the rulemaking process, another key area of operations to which the Attorney General's Committee drew readers' attention. While the committee concluded that formality was poorly suited to agency rulemaking, members found that agencies greatly valued informal consultation with interested parties. Agency officials commonly solicited feedback from regulated industries, trade groups, bar associations, and other parties through telephone calls, written correspondence, and informal conferences. Abe Fortas observed that, at the Bituminous Coal Division,

> we do get tremendous assistance from the industries informally. We turn out a draft in our shop, we then call up the executive secretary and say we are sending over a draft, will they get their people together and go over the rules and when they feel that they have their views in hand that they call us and we will have a joint meeting. He may take a day, two or three days working over these rules and finally when we get the rules out they are something accept[a]ble to the industry and to us.[46]

As Fortas explained, "I think it would be perfectly absurd for a Government agency to try to work it out except in the closest cooperation with the industry."[47] Rather than finding anything problematic about a cozy relationship between agencies, trade groups, and regulated parties, the committee encouraged this model of rulemaking "in order to permit administrative agencies to inform themselves and to afford adequate safeguards to private interests."[48]

---

[44] Attorney General's Committee, *Final Report*, 209.

[45] Ibid., 35.

[46] Transcript, Conference of the Attorney General's Committee, Apr. 27, 1940, 2:30 P.M., 5–6, Folder "Committee Meeting Apr. 27," Box 4, A.G. Committee Correspondence, Entry 376, AGCAP, RG 60, NACP.

[47] Ibid., 6.

[48] Attorney General's Committee, *Final Report*, 103.

Close relationships bolstered agencies' claims to fairness and mollified industry representatives. Parties had significant regulatory input, allowing agency officials to draw on industry research and making the perennially understaffed task of enforcement that much easier.[49]

The courts were the last defense against administrative decisions parties did not like, and here too the Attorney General's Committee took a different approach to the question of judicial review of administrative fact finding than had the ABA. While committee members disagreed among themselves, they shared some central assumptions about the importance of protecting administrative discretion. Most of the committee had declined to wade into the mire of changing existing standards, but McFarland, Stason, and Vanderbilt wanted a new, clear statutory standard to replace the "haphazard, uncertain, and variable results" of existing judicial review.[50] They proposed adding language to the existing "substantial evidence" standard; to make sure that the examiners were appropriately policed, judges would determine whether "substantial evidence" existed based on a review of the "*whole* record" and whether the decision was "*clearly* contrary to the *manifest* weight of the evidence."[51] The minority sought to move toward a clearer and stricter standard of judicial review than was contained in the case law; nonetheless, this standard was far from the judicial control envisioned in the Walter–Logan bill.

The Attorney General's Committee's approach to the administrative process won significant applause on the report's release. The *Columbia Law Review* devoted an issue to the committee's work, in which Felix Frankfurter declared that "[a]nyone who hereafter concerns himself with [administrative] problems without being fully mindful of this *Report* must be either doctrinaire or irresponsible."[52] Although legal observers took exception to individual suggestions, and some found the report overly legalistic and conservative, most applauded the research and recommendations, and the Senate Judiciary Committee quickly scheduled hearings to consider the committee's recommendations.[53] The majority of the committee, fearful of imposing too much uniformity on a decidedly

---

[49] John A. Rohr observes that "the contemporary reader is appalled at the report's nonchalance in regard to the danger that private interests might capture governmental agencies" (John A. Rohr, *To Run a Constitution: The Legitimacy of the Administrative State* [Lawrence: University Press of Kansas, 1986], 168).

[50] Attorney General's Committee, *Final Report*, 210.

[51] Ibid., 211 (emphasis in the original).

[52] Felix Frankfurter, "The Final Report of the Attorney General's Committee on Administrative Procedure: Foreword," *Columbia Law Review* 41 (1941): 585–88, 588.

[53] See John Foster Dulles, "The Effect in Practice of the Report on Administrative Procedure," *Columbia Law Review* 41 (1941): 617–27; J. Forrester Davison, "Administrative Technique – The Report on Administrative Procedure," *Columbia Law Review* 41 (1941): 628–45; A. H. Feller, "Administrative Law Investigation Comes of Age," *Columbia Law Review* 41 (1941): 589–616; Louis L. Jaffe, "The Report of the Attorney General's Committee on Administrative Procedure," *University of Chicago Law Review* 8 (1941): 401–40. For a critical take, see Louis G. Caldwell, "Federal Communications Commission – Comments on the Report of the Staff of the Attorney General's Committee on Administrative Law," *George Washington Law Review* 8 (1940): 749–818.

nonuniform set of processes, offered a legislative proposal containing the broad guidelines of the report's general recommendations, but others argued strongly that the committee needed to turn their recommendations into a more concrete bill. McFarland, Stason, and Vanderbilt provided with their separate statement a comprehensive code of procedure that included their own formal hearing and judicial review proposals but otherwise resembled the committee's substantive recommendations. During the Senate Judiciary Committee's 1941 hearings on various bills based on the Attorney General's Committee proposals, agency representatives lauded the provisions that respected administrative flexibility but cautioned Congress that significant procedural changes, strict separation of functions, and increased judicial review might impede their operations. Although no code resulted in 1941, the work of the Attorney General's Committee proved significant when Congress returned to the question of comprehensive administrative reform after a wartime break.

Within a few years, comprehensive administrative procedure bills were proposed by the ABA and the Smith Committee, among others. The ABA's energy proved crucial to the ultimate enactment of an administrative code, but the content of the ABA's proposals had changed substantially since the Walter–Logan bill's defeat. The Special Committee on Administrative Law – under the new leadership of Carl McFarland – now admitted the flaws of the Walter-Logan bill and recognized that a similar bill would be unlikely to gain support even in the increasingly conservative Congress. Conservative victories in the 1942 elections had significantly slimmed down Democratic majorities and further concentrated Democratic power in Southern hands. This Congress was hostile to bureaucracy, as the Byrd Committee's ongoing investigation of New Deal programs and the Smith Committee's investigation of the OPA demonstrated. On the heels of the abolition of the Civilian Conservation Corps in 1942, the 78th Congress moved to terminate the beleaguered WPA, National Youth Administration, and National Resources Planning Board.

The partisanship that had brought down the Walter-Logan bill meant that subsequent procedural reforms, even those designed by lawyers expert in the field, were no longer presumptively apolitical. The Attorney General's Committee on Administrative Procedure had also refocused the debate about the deficiencies of the administrative process. While the ABA's Special Committee argued in 1945 that "the administrative system must not be permitted to supply an aura of due process and procedural regularity for what are essentially arbitrary and dictatorial methods of government," it would offer bills that moved toward the recommendations of the Attorney General's Committee and away from the Walter–Logan bill's more court-centered approach.[54] No action

---

[54] "Supplemental Report of the Special Committee on Administrative Law," *Annual Report of the American Bar Association* 70 (1945): 272–75, 275; see "Report of the Special Committee on Administrative Law," *Annual Report of the American Bar Association* 69 (1944): 471–73; Frederick F. Blachly and Miriam E. Oatman, "Sabotage of the Administrative Process," *Public Administration Review* 6 (1946): 213–27.

was taken during 1944, but in 1945, a revised version of the ABA's bill joined other administrative procedure bills before a conservative Congress seeking to reform both agencies and itself.

The ABA's bill was significantly more deferential to agency operations than the Walter–Logan bill had been; McFarland described it to Congress as a "skeleton, upon which administrative agencies may adopt their own rules of procedure."[55] It resembled the recommendations of the minority members of the Attorney General's Committee regarding formal hearings and judicial review, and its attention to administrative flexibility and discretion mirrored the consensus of the Attorney General's Committee as a whole. The bill also took into account agencies' concerns about overly rigid procedural requirements, providing, according to the Senate Judiciary Committee, "an outline of minimum basic essentials" rather than a prescriptive code of administrative procedure.[56]

Even as agency representatives wrote plaintive letters to Congress in 1945 professing their support for the idea of improving administrative procedure, most sought to be excused from its provisions – noting politely that the problems addressed by the bills did not exist in their own agency. The agencies and commissions were troubled by the specifics of the reform proposals and by the hostility to the administrative state evidenced therein. The FTC chairman protested the bill's "underlying philosophy" that assumed "the commingling in one agency under long standing Congressional mandates of functions that are quasi-legislative, quasi-executive and quasi-judicial is fundamentally improper and lacking in the fairness usually associated with due process."[57] Officials from military agencies, the ICC, the NLRB, the SEC, the USDA, and others argued that imposing a uniform statute would invite disruptive litigation, slow down their operations, and thus frustrate their work. As Basil Manly of the Federal Power Commission argued, "blanket legislation" would "result in irreparable injury to the Congressional objectives sought to be accomplished in creating such agencies."[58] Requiring agencies to strictly separate their hearing examiners from the rest of their staff would further complicate matters; as the ICC argued, such provisions "if taken literally would deprive the Commission of the expert advice of the members of its staff on technical matters and would tend to obstruct and in a vast number of proceedings would prevent the reaching of a sound decision."[59] Administrators from a number of agencies also

---

[55] House Judiciary Committee, *Administrative Procedure: Hearings on Federal Administrative Procedure* (statement of Carl McFarland, June 21, 1945), reprinted in *Administrative Procedure Act: Legislative History*, 72.

[56] Senate Judiciary Committee, *Administrative Procedure Act*, 79th Cong., 1st sess., 1945, S. Rep. 752, 7.

[57] Ewin L. Davis to Sen. Pat McCarran, June 21, 1945, 2, Folder "S.7 Cont'd" (1), Box 4, S.7 (SEN 79A-E1), 79th Congress, RG 46, NAB.

[58] Basil Manly to Sen. Pat McCarran, Feb. 27, 1945, 1, Folder "S.7 Cont'd" (1), Box 4, S.7 (SEN 79A-E1), 79th Congress, RG 46, NAB.

[59] Walter M. W. Splawn to Rep. Hatton W. Sumners, Sept. 20, 1945, 9, Folder "S.7 (an Act)" (2), S. 7 (H.R. 79A-D21), 79th Congress, RG 233, NAB.

feared the expanded role of the courts; according to the NLRB, "direct judicial review of Board certifications would seriously hamper the peaceful settlement of labor disputes."[60]

In October 1945, Attorney General Tom C. Clark endorsed a revised bill that addressed opposition by exempting several internal functions, observing that the new draft "appears to offer a hopeful prospect of achieving reasonable uniformity and fairness in administrative procedures without at the same time interfering unduly with the efficient and economical operation of the Government."[61] (As one practitioner pointed out, however, Congress had recently revised the ICC's procedures in the Transportation Act of 1940, and it would be a waste of everyone's time to revisit them.[62]) By the spring of 1946, Sen. McCarran pointed both to the amended bill's by-now wide support – from Congress, from the Attorney General, from the ABA, and from the agencies – and hailed the administrative code as "a bill of rights for the hundreds of thousands of Americans whose affairs are controlled or regulated in one way or another by agencies of the Federal Government."[63] McCarran was, perhaps, overstating the enthusiasm of the bill's supporters. Even after the bill had been redrafted to take out its more objectionable aspects, agencies including the ICC, the FTC, and the Labor Department expressed only tepid support, and several others objected to specific provisions.[64] The bill nonetheless gained support from members of Congress, as its broad language allowed supporters to read into it what they liked. Several expressed their belief that the bill would not interfere with agency operations, while others clearly hoped that it would.

The White House was also unenthusiastic. Several agencies pressed the president to reject the bill, but the Budget Bureau decided it was "not bad enough to justify a veto."[65] Acting Budget Director Paul Appleby wondered whether it was advisable to place new rules "stated in broad and general language" on top of agency practices that "are the product of many years of legislation, administrative experience, and judicial review."[66] The bill was, he claimed, "too exclusively the product of legalistic rather than administrative thinking."[67] However,

---

[60] Harry A. Millis to Sen. Pat McCarran, June 28, 1945, 2, Folder "S.7 Cont'd" (1), Box 4, S.7 (SEN 79A-E1), 79th Congress, RG 46, NAB.

[61] Tom C. Clark to Sen. Pat McCarran, Oct. 19, 1945, 2, Folder "S.7 Cont'd" (3), Box 5, S.7 (SEN 79A-E1), 79th Congress, RG 46, NAB; see Shepherd, "Fierce Compromise," 1661–62.

[62] Harry C. Ames, Chairman, Legislative Committee, Association of Interstate Commerce Practitioners, "Memorandum on Procedure Before the Interstate Commerce Commission," Nov. 16, 1945, Folder "S.7 Cont'd" (4), Box 5, S.7 (SEN 79A-E1), 79th Congress, RG 46, NAB.

[63] Senate Proceedings (statement of Sen. McCarran, Mar. 12, 1946), reprinted in *Administrative Procedure Act: Legislative History*, 298.

[64] See Paul H. Appleby to M. C. Latta, June 7, 1946, Folder "Bill File – June 11, 1946 [S. 7]," Box 13, WHBF, HST Papers, HSTL.

[65] Ibid., 3.

[66] Ibid.

[67] Ibid.

Appleby acknowledged the bill's wide support and the political and legal stakes involved. As he suggested, "Greater uniformity of procedures among the agencies, aimed at the essentials of due process, is desirable, and a broadening of judicial review presumably adds to the protection of the citizen."[68] This facile analysis, which declined to go beyond "presumably" in its assessment of the bill's protections, suggested both that the bill had lost most of its controversial features and that the White House was unwilling to come out against a bill that promised to protect due process at the same time it struggled to defend Truman's "Fair Deal" programs and prevent Congress from gutting the OPA, set to expire at the end of June.[69]

Indeed, the code, as ultimately enacted, was a testament to inoffensiveness and did little to change existing administrative practice. Kenneth Culp Davis characterized the statute in his 1951 treatise as "a statement of minimum requirements," with rules "shot through with hortatory provisions and broad grants of discretionary power to deviate from the stated requirements."[70] Concessions made to the agencies and commissions further limited the degree of change. Most agencies and commissions already adhered to judicially defined standards of due process and employed quasi-judicial procedures in their work, a result of agencies scrambling to satisfy reviewing courts and prove their lawfulness to the public in previous years. As one study of the ICC concluded in 1944, "a regulatory body must be especially solicitous that the public should believe it to be competent, careful, and fair, and if this end can be furthered by procedural concessions which to some extent lower efficiency the gain may well be worth the price."[71] Law professor Nathaniel Nathanson similarly argued that "while the administrative laws bills have gradually grown to reflect a more sophisticated conception of the inherent diversity and flexibility of the administrative process, that process has itself been developing some recognizable norms; and so the gap between them has been narrowed from both sides."[72] Not everyone agreed, of course; critics of the act denounced

---

[68] Ibid.

[69] See Richard E. Neustadt, "Congress and the Fair Deal: A Legislative Balance Sheet," *Public Policy* 5 (1954): 351–81; Barton J. Bernstein, "Clash of Interests: The Postwar Battle between the Office of Price Administration and the Department of Agriculture," *Agricultural History* 41 (1967): 45–57; William E. Leuchtenburg, *In the Shadow of FDR: From Harry Truman to Bill Clinton*, 2nd rev. ed. (Ithaca, NY: Cornell University Press, 1993); Meg Jacobs, "'How About Some Meat?': The Office of Price Administration, Consumption Politics, and State Building from the Bottom Up, 1941–1946," *Journal of American History* 84 (1997): 910–41; Lizabeth Cohen, *A Consumers' Republic: The Politics of Mass Consumption in Postwar America* (New York: Knopf, 2003).

[70] Davis, *Administrative Law*, 277; see also Reginald Parker, "The Administrative Procedure Act: A Study in Overestimation," *Yale Law Journal* 60 (1951): 581–99.

[71] Board of Investigation and Research, *Report on Practices and Procedures of Governmental Control*, 78th Cong., 2nd sess., 1944, H. Doc. 678, 64.

[72] Nathaniel L. Nathanson, "Some Comments on the Administrative Procedure Act," *Illinois Law Review* 41 (1946): 368–422, 420; see also Louis L. Jaffe, "Basic Issues: An Analysis," *New York*

its "disastrous" changes that put the administrative process "in a judicialized strait jacket."[73] To the extent that the APA was, in fact, a "judicialized" conception of the administrative state, however, such standards came largely from the existing practices of the agencies and from the doctrines of administrative law created and articulated by the courts over the past six decades, rather than the new law itself.[74]

Thus, the Administrative Procedure Act – passed without a recorded vote, and signed into law on June 11, 1946 (with the ABA's Carl McFarland in attendance) – was an explicit statement of best practices that effectively indicated Congress's approval of much of what the administrative state already did.[75] Shortly after the APA's passage, Sen. McCarran characterized it as "a strongly marked, long sought, and widely heralded advance in democratic government."[76] The act, he argued, provided a "comprehensive charter of private liberty and a solemn undertaking of official fairness."[77] At the same time, however, supporters were reassured by the minimum guidelines and flexibility that allowed agencies and commissions to maintain control over their procedures. In some ways the act served as all things to all people, as its general language allowed some observers to see in the bill provisions that guarded efficiency and administrative discretion and others to see rules protecting individual rights from administrative absolutism and overeager administrators.[78] According to one observer, some parties believed that the APA dealt "a death sentence to all future efficient administrative effort," at the same time that others saw the act as "a gentle slap on the bureaucratic wrist when they would prefer a kick in the bureaucratic buttock."[79]

Some things did change, of course. The APA's information provisions required agencies to make public the details of their decision-making processes, intended, according to the Senate Judiciary Committee, "to take the mystery out of administrative procedure by stating it."[80] These provisions supplemented the requirements of the 1935 Federal Register Act that required publication of final orders, regulations, licenses, and certificates.[81] Under the APA,

---

University Law Review 30 (1955): 1273–96; Verkuil, "The Emerging Concept of Administrative Procedure."

[73] Blachly and Oatman, "Sabotage of the Administrative Process," 213, 226.

[74] See Board of Investigation and Research, *Report on Practices and Procedures of Governmental Control*, 24; Ernst, "*Morgan* and the New Dealers."

[75] Ashley Sellers, "Carl McFarland – The Architect of the Federal Administrative Procedure Act," 16–17.

[76] Pat McCarran, "Foreword," *Administrative Procedure Act: Legislative History*, iii.

[77] Ibid.

[78] Shepherd, "Fierce Compromise."

[79] Alfred Long Scanlan, "Judicial Review under the Administrative Procedure Act – In Which Judicial Offspring Receive a Congressional Confirmation," *Notre Dame Lawyer* 23 (1948): 501–46, 502, 503.

[80] Senate Judiciary Committee, *Administrative Procedure Act*, 12.

[81] Federal Register Act of 1935, Pub. L. No. 220, 49 Stat. 500 (1935).

agencies and commissions were required to publish their opinions, descriptions of their internal organization and operations, and general statements of their official policies.[82] The committee emphasized that "administrative operations and procedures are public property which the general public, rather than a few specialists or lobbyists, is entitled to know or to have the ready means of knowing with definiteness and assurance."[83] The idea that agencies had clear policies that they chose not to share with those appearing before them had clearly irked Congress during its 1941 hearings on administrative procedure; at the same time, however, agencies had expressed their fear that stating their policies on the record would hinder their ability to change their minds. The APA struck a balance, leaving agencies free to make policy determinations on a case-by-case basis while requiring them to make more of their mundane operational details public. One result of these provisions was an immediate and enormous increase in the volume and printing costs of the Federal Register. As the *Washington Post*'s bureaucracy columnist noted in August 1946, "everyone from the President down is reported to be flabbergasted" at the costs of compliance.[84]

The bulk of the APA was devoted to an articulation of broad standards for how the agencies should conduct their business. Certain parts of administrative operation received more attention than others, and formal hearings were central. However, although the statute promised to bring due process to formal administrative adjudication, formal hearings were not imposed where informal ones had previously sufficed. Instead, the APA prescribed procedures that applied only when another statute required the agency to provide a formal hearing, thus limiting its own coverage and leaving agencies free to design informal procedures as they liked.[85] In the comparatively small number of cases where formal adjudication was required and requested by the parties, parties were guaranteed a hearing conducted by the agency head or, more commonly, by an independent hearing examiner. Rulemaking was given its own flexible procedures, intended to preserve the cooperative relationships agencies had already developed with the industries they regulated. The APA required agencies to notify interested parties that they were about to engage in rulemaking and offer them the opportunity to comment either orally or in writing. This largely codified existing practice and guaranteed regulated parties a continuing voice in agency operations. Only where an agency's statute already required rulemaking "on the record after opportunity for an agency hearing" – and most did not – were formal hearing procedures similar to those required for adjudication prescribed.[86]

[82] Administrative Procedure Act, Pub. L. No. 404, §3, 60 Stat. 237 (1946).
[83] Senate Judiciary Committee, *Administrative Procedure Act*, 12.
[84] Jerry Kluttz, "The Federal Diary," *Washington Post*, Aug. 4, 1946, M5.
[85] For details on how this played out in one agency, see Charles F. Wheatley Jr., "A Study of Administrative Procedures – The Department of Interior," *Georgetown Law Journal* 43 (1955): 166–207.
[86] Administrative Procedure Act § 4(b).

Examiners were not renamed hearing commissioners, but their separate role within the agency was clarified. Examiners were to be more isolated from outside influences and from the rest of the agency, shielding them from pressure to decide in a particular manner. Examiners could no longer be supervised by any administrative official "engaged in the performance of investigative or prosecuting functions," and they themselves could "perform no duties inconsistent with their duties and responsibilities as examiners," thus putting an end to examiners wearing many hats in the course of their employment.[87] The statute also called on examiners to avoid conversations with others in their agency about their work. Examiners were barred from consulting "any person or party on any fact in issue" in a particular case without offering *all* parties an opportunity to participate, and were to draft their initial decisions without consultation with others in the agency.[88] Other staffers were similarly warned not to "participate or advise in the decision, recommended decision, or agency review" unless as part of public proceedings.[89]

By defining conversations with fellow agency staffers as improper, the APA appeared to impose a quite strict segregation of functions that would make agencies' operations more like those of courts. The recommendations were similar to those of the Attorney General's Committee, which had recommended a full internal separation of functions; the minority's code called for an end to any conversations between hearing examiners and staffers in the rest of the agency. Thus, the act had the potential to significantly change administrative practice for those agencies that did not already draw clear lines in this area. As Kenneth Culp Davis warned, the combination of functions targeted by the act was "harmless and even affirmatively desirable" at those agencies (such as the Social Security Board and the Veterans Administration) that distributed benefits.[90] The provisions were clearly aimed at regulatory agencies, however, where the greatest harms were seen. The FTC had reportedly revised its own procedures for examiners in March 1946, in light of the Senate bill – an action that a *Washington Post* columnist called "an unexpected plea of guilty as charged by ABA."[91] Agencies had been trying to head off these and similar reforms for years, and Congress and the ABA would take credit for bringing the rule of law to the most controversial area of administrative practice.

These strict requirements were soon watered down, however, as the Justice Department's 1947 *Attorney General's Manual on the Administrative Procedure Act* – an interpretive guide for agencies wondering how to comply

---

[87] Ibid., §§ 5(c), 11.
[88] Ibid., § 5(c).
[89] Ibid.
[90] Kenneth Culp Davis, "Separation of Functions in Administrative Agencies," *Harvard Law Review* 61 (1948): 389–418, 394.
[91] Jerry Kluttz, "The Federal Diary," *Washington Post*, Mar. 6, 1946, 9.

with the APA – suggested that the statute could not logically have meant to keep an examiner away from his agency's collective expertise. According to Attorney General Tom Clark, allowing "an analytical discussion of the record is thoroughly consistent with the purposes of the Act" and would lead to "a more accurate initial or recommended decision and one that better reflects the views of the agency on questions of law and policy."[92] The examiner was barred from communications with the prosecutors, but he was free to request help from staffers "not engaged in investigative or prosecuting functions in that or a factually related case."[93] This interpretation brought the APA in line with much existing agency practice.

Even as some examiners found their position in the agency changed, however, neither the formal hearing as a whole nor the hearing examiners' role in it were transformed. The procedures prescribed in the APA were somewhat less rigid than the Attorney General's Committee had recommended, and certainly less like the courtroom ones for which the ABA had hoped. Instead of new evidentiary requirements, the act merely suggested general principles of relevance to be followed. To be sure, examiners looked a little more like judges under the act. Examiners were given new authority to command the hearing and to respond to objections – making certain, as the Senate Judiciary Committee put it, "that the presiding officer will perform a real function rather than serve merely as a notary or policeman."[94] Once an examiner issued a decision, parties were guaranteed an opportunity to respond (thus addressing any lingering concerns after *Morgan*). The examiners' ability to dictate the agency's final decision remained limited, however. The act adopted the recommendation of the Attorney General's Committee that, to enable faster decision making, the examiner's proposed decision should stand unless the regulated parties or the agency appealed; however, if either party did appeal, the agency would still "have all the powers which it would have in making the initial decision" and could thus take over the case and go through the whole file themselves.[95] The examiners – awkwardly described by the Senate Judiciary Committee as "semi-independent subordinate hearing officers" – thus remained subservient officials in the administrative hierarchy.[96]

The APA's judicial review provisions also allowed the ABA and Congress to take credit for increasing judicial scrutiny of the agencies and commissions, even as the practical effects were likely to be limited. Agencies were instructed to base their decisions on "reliable, probative, and substantial evidence," a provision that itself suggested some common complaints about agency action.[97] Reviewing courts could set aside agency action found to

[92] U.S. Department of Justice, *Attorney General's Manual on the Administrative Procedure Act* (Washington, DC: Government Printing Office, 1947), 55.
[93] Ibid.; see also *NLRB v. Botany Worsted Mills*, 133 F.2d 876 (3rd Cir. 1943).
[94] Senate Judiciary Committee, *Administrative Procedure Act*, 21.
[95] Administrative Procedure Act § 8(a).
[96] Senate Judiciary Committee, *Administrative Procedure Act*, 6.
[97] Administrative Procedure Act § 7(c).

be "arbitrary, capricious, an abuse of discretion, or otherwise not in accordance with law," or, where a formal hearing had been held, "unsupported by substantial evidence" based on the "whole record" created by the agency.[98] Attorney General Clark's suggestion, in the 1947 *Attorney General's Manual*, that this "appears to restate existing law" was partially true.[99] "Substantial evidence" was of course already the default test for judicial review of agency action, and the APA's adoption of this language suggested that judicial review of agency fact finding would remain deferential to agencies that supported their decisions and frustrated with agencies that did not.[100] The "whole record" requirement, while new and undefined, was significant only if one assumed that reviewing judges were not already looking at the whole record.

Congress was at least discontented with certain judicial practices. As the Senate Judiciary Committee suggested, the problem was not with the "substantial evidence" test itself, but with "the practice of agencies to rely upon (and of courts to tacitly approve) something less – to rely upon suspicion, surmise, implications, or plainly incredible evidence."[101] As a result, Congress directed courts to determine "in the exercise of their independent judgment, whether on the whole record the evidence in a given instance is sufficiently substantial to support a finding, conclusion, or other agency action as a matter of law."[102] As one scholar suggested, "the difference in emphasis is not so much over what the Act requires, as over what the Courts have been really doing."[103] It was not at all clear that this problem extended beyond a few prominent cases, but the bill's drafters were able to use this opportunity to provide a new and clearly stated standard of review that asked all courts to reexamine how they reviewed agency decision making. However, by implicitly endorsing what most courts were already doing, Congress blunted the revolutionary impact of the new standard. One contemporary observer predicted that the APA "will not upset the rubric of judicial review which the federal judiciary has fashioned piecemeal, and from which it has no intention of deviating, even though its homemade precepts also now have been expressed, however opaquely, in statutory flapdoodle."[104]

---

[98] Ibid., § 10(e).

[99] Department of Justice, *Attorney General's Manual on the Administrative Procedure Act*, 110.

[100] See *United States v. Carolina Freight Carriers Corp*, 315 U.S. 475 (1942); *NLRB v. Indiana & Michigan Electric Co.*, 318 U.S. 9 (1943); *SEC v. Chenery Corp.*, 318 U.S. 80 (1943); *Eastern-Central Motor Carriers Association v. United States*, 321 U.S. 194 (1944); *NLRB v. Union Pacific Stages, Inc.*, 99 F.2d 153 (9th Cir. 1938); *NLRB v. Columbia Products Corp.*, 141 F.2d 687 (2d Cir. 1944). For a discussion of judicial review prior to the APA, see C. Herman Pritchett, "The Supreme Court and Administrative Regulation, 1941–44," *Iowa Law Review* 31 (1945): 103–28.

[101] Senate Judiciary Committee, *Administrative Procedure Act*, 30.

[102] Ibid.

[103] Nathanson, "Some Comments on the Administrative Procedure Act," 416 n. 112.

[104] Scanlan, "Judicial Review under the Administrative Procedure Act," 503.

Overall, as administrative law professor Bernard Schwartz suggested, the APA "is not revolutionary" but instead "adopts, in large measure, the best existing administrative practice."[105] As one letter writer remarked, the bill effected so little change "that some people wonder what is the point of enacting it."[106] Even under Clark's intentionally generous interpretation, the APA required several agencies to isolate their examiners more than they had previously done; the standard to which all agencies now adhered, however, was not much different from that already adopted by some of the largest and most controversial ones – ones that had proved willing to sacrifice some expertise to protect themselves against political attacks. Thus, the sharp change to legal requirements did not necessarily reflect a similarly sharp change in practice.

Reports from the agencies indicated as much.[107] An attorney from the Federal Security Agency suggested that "no radical changes in the administrative operations" of the Food, Drug and Cosmetic Act were required,[108] and the SEC boasted that its "existing organization and procedures in certain respects afford greater procedural safeguards to all interested persons" than did the APA.[109] A 1955 study of the Interior Department found that "many long-standing procedural vices have continued unchanged" given the department's conclusion that the APA did not require reform of its specific procedures.[110] It depended on the agency, of course; the Federal Power Commission undertook a major revision of its hearing rules, and the FTC, in adapting its own procedure, had, one report suggested, gone "beyond what is required under the Act."[111] The hearing examiner provisions did require some adaptation across the agencies, but the ICC suggested that other parts of the APA were "merely repetitious of what has long been our established procedure."[112] By 1948, the

---

[105] Bernard Schwartz, "Administrative Procedure and the A.P.A.," *New York University Law Quarterly Review* 24 (1949): 514–34, 514; see also Harry A. Millis and Emily Clark Brown, *From the Wagner Act to Taft-Hartley: A Study of National Labor Policy and Labor Relations* (Chicago: University of Chicago Press, 1950), 63–64; Bernstein, "The Politics of Adjudication," 317–18.

[106] J.W.W., letter to the editor, *Washington Post*, Mar. 28, 1946, 8.

[107] See George Warren, ed., *The Federal Administrative Procedure Act and the Administrative Agencies* (New York: New York University School of Law, 1947).

[108] James B. Goding, "The Impact of the Administrative Procedure Act on the Administration of the Federal Food, Drug, and Cosmetic Act," *Food Drug Cosmetic Law Quarterly* 2 (1947): 139–54, 140.

[109] Securities and Exchange Commission, *Twelfth Annual Report of the Securities and Exchange Commission*, 80th Cong., 1st sess., 1947, H. Doc. 26, 128.

[110] Wheatley, "A Study of Administrative Procedures – The Department of Interior," 204.

[111] Irene Till, Committee on Independent Regulatory Commissions, *Staff Report on the Federal Trade Commission* (Commission on Organization of the Executive Branch of the Government, 1948), II-25; see also Federal Power Commission, *Twenty-Sixth Annual Report of the Federal Power Commission*, 80th Cong., 1st sess., 1947, H. Doc. 23, 118; C. Herman Pritchett, Committee on Independent Regulatory Commissions, *Staff Report on the Federal Power Commission* (Commission on Organization of the Executive Branch of the Government, 1948).

[112] Interstate Commerce Commission, *60th Annual Report of the Interstate Commerce Commission*, 80th Cong., 1st sess., 1946, H. Doc. 14, 59.

outgoing president of the ICC Practitioners' Association observed that "everyone interested is still searching in vain for some profound effect it has had upon practice before the Commission."[113]

Those outside the agencies, however, saw the APA's effect as more powerful. One arena for determining what the APA "meant" was the courts, which soon had to decide how much change the statute had wrought. In the immigration context, at least, the Supreme Court viewed the APA as a significant intervention into the administrative process, one that represented a new congressional commitment to fairness in the administrative state. The Immigration and Naturalization Service (and its predecessor, the Bureau of Immigration) joined the rest of the agencies in seeking a balance between efficiency and the appearance of fairness, but this balance was decidedly different in the immigration context. Fewer due process protections were traditionally offered in immigration cases, where the rights of individuals were most clearly at stake. In cases where an immigration officer's decision involved discretionary privileges (as with noncitizens entering the country), courts had long held that due process was satisfied by summary hearings without opportunity for judicial review. In cases where the rights of a citizen were at stake, due process required not more procedures, but judicial review of those summary procedures. As a result, for decades, immigration officers had occupied fluid roles and exercised significant discretion.[114]

In fact, many thought of immigration as a separate part of the administrative process. The Attorney General's Committee had not inquired into the operations of the INS, and most administrative law scholars devoted their attention to economic regulatory commissions, which had much in common with one another but little in common with immigration enforcement. Although immigration officers faced a huge volume of cases, most of which concerned the status of politically weak noncitizens, these cases rarely presented the complex facts or produced the volumes of supporting evidence that ICC and USDA cases, for example, did. As one Justice Department official argued, balking at the INS's inclusion in the administrative procedure bills before Congress in 1941, the bills' concern with hearing commissioners who "pass on complicated rate structures and things of that kind" was inappropriate for an immigration official "who only has to decide a simple little issue as to whether a human being is an alien and whether he entered illegally and should be sent back."[115]

---

[113] Harry C. Ames, 1947–1948 report of the Interstate Commerce Commission Practitioners' Association, excerpted in "I.C.C. View of Procedure Act," *Administrative Law Bulletin* 1 (1949): 2–3, 2.

[114] See Lucy E. Salyer, *Laws Harsh as Tigers: Chinese Immigrants and the Shaping of Modern Immigration Law* (Chapel Hill: University of North Carolina Press, 1995); Gabriel J. Chin, "Regulating Race: Asian Exclusion and the Administrative State," *Harvard Civil Rights-Civil Liberties Law Review* 37 (2002): 1–64.

[115] Senate Judiciary Committee, Subcommittee on S. 674, S. 675 and S. 918, *Administrative Procedure: Hearings on S. 674, S. 675 and S. 918*, pt. 2, 77th Cong., 1st sess., 1941 (statement of Maj. Lemuel B. Schofield, May 2), 574–75.

This distinction continued after the enactment of the APA, which limited examiners to duties "not inconsistent" with their quasi-judicial roles and barred
communications between prosecuting and decision-making staffers in the same
case. INS officials, however, continued to wear both hats during a hearing,
often asking questions and submitting evidence on behalf of the government
while also drafting the proposed decision. Although INS hearing officers did
not handle investigation and prosecution tasks in the same case, they were
responsible for a range of tasks.

Although Congress had not specifically exempted immigration decisions
from the hearing provisions of the APA, many were still surprised when federal courts began holding the INS to the APA's standards. In the summer of
1948, a federal judge in the District of Columbia held that the APA required
immigration officials to provide individuals facing deportation with a formal
hearing conducted by a properly appointed hearing examiner. Although the
Deportation Act itself did not explicitly call for hearings, the court ruled that
reviewing courts had "read due process into the Act, and due process means
a hearing, and that therefore hearing is an integral part of the Deportation
Act."[116] The DC Circuit upheld a subsequent decision suggesting that deportation decisions fell within one of the APA's exemptions, but the Supreme Court
adopted the more expansive view.[117]

In *Wong Yang Sung v. McGrath*, the Court found that the summary procedures used to deport a Chinese citizen arrested in the United States violated the
APA. The statute did not require the INS to provide a hearing under the APA,
but, according to the Court, the Constitution did. The Court looked to the
APA's history, which, read broadly, was grounded in concerns that administrative "power was not sufficiently safeguarded and sometimes was put to arbitrary and biased use."[118] In reaction, Congress had enacted "a new, basic and
comprehensive regulation of procedures"; the APA "represents a long period
of study and strife; it settles long-continued and hard-fought contentions, and
enacts a formula upon which opposing social and political forces have come
to rest."[119] The kinds of unfair hearings about which the APA's drafters were
concerned could occur at the INS as easily as at other agencies. Failing to
impose the APA's standards on the agency would, the Court worried, conflict
with Congress's goal of making administrative procedures more uniform and
disregard its intent to separate prosecution and judicial functions.

Indeed, Justice Robert H. Jackson characterized the combination of functions
in INS hearings as "a perfect exemplification of the practices so unanimously
condemned."[120] Taking the APA's reform seriously, he explained, "It might be
difficult to justify as measuring up to constitutional standards of impartiality

[116] *Eisler v. Clark*, 77 F. Supp. 610, 611 (D.D.C. 1948).
[117] *Wong Yang Sung v. Clark*, 80 F. Supp. 235 (D.D.C. 1948); *aff'd Wong Yang Sung v. Clark*, 174
F.2d 158 (D.C. Cir. 1949); *rev'd Wong Yang Sung v. McGrath*, 339 U.S. 33 (1950).
[118] *Wong Yang Sung*, 339 U.S. at 37.
[119] Ibid., 36, 40.
[120] Ibid., 45.

a hearing tribunal for deportation proceedings the like of which has been condemned by Congress as unfair even where less vital matters of property rights are at stake."[121] Jackson thus found the combination of functions *more* egregious in the deportation context, involving as it did "a voteless class of litigants who not only lack the influence of citizens, but who are strangers to the laws and customs in which they find themselves involved and who often do not even understand the tongue in which they are accused."[122] The APA's requirements would place a greater burden on immigration officials, but "Congress has determined that the price for greater fairness is not too high."[123]

At the same time, however, Congress was free to exempt whatever proceedings it liked from the APA. Members quickly moved to exclude deportation proceedings from the adjudication, hearing, and decision-making provisions of the APA, and the Supreme Court upheld this revision.[124] For some justices, therefore, the APA represented a commitment to fairness in the administrative state, but one that could be easily avoided by subsequent congressional action. Others were less willing to protect due process only on Congress's terms. Justices Hugo Black and Felix Frankfurter strongly objected to Congress's action, arguing that the immigration exemption ran contrary to the commitment to fairness the Court had so recently found in the act. The combinations of functions were, they argued, "wholly inconsistent with our concepts of justice."[125]

Black and Frankfurter also dissented in a subsequent case in which the Court found that the APA's formal hearing procedures covered applications for certificates of public convenience and necessity at the ICC, something that came as a surprise to the commission.[126] The justices argued that the right to a properly appointed hearing examiner could not be waived by a party's failure to raise the issue in a timely manner. Frankfurter found that the APA represented a commitment to a broader conception of fairness that should be present throughout the ICC's operations. The goal of the APA was to remedy "what were believed to be evils in the way in which administrative agencies exercised their authority," and thus it "prohibited

---

[121] Ibid., 50–51.

[122] Ibid., 46.

[123] Ibid., 46–47.

[124] 15 Fed. Reg. 1299–1301 (1950); Supplemental Appropriation Act of 1951, Pub. L. No. 843, 64 Stat. 1044, 1048 (1950). Soon thereafter, Congress passed the 1952 Immigration and Nationality Act, which superseded the 1917 Immigration Act, and the Court allowed the procedures of immigration enforcement to resume along a separate track (*Marcello v. Bonds*, 349 U.S. 302 [1955]). See Note, "The Impact of the Federal Administrative Procedure Act on Deportation Proceedings," *Columbia Law Review* 49 (1949): 73–87; Kelly William Milligan, "*Marcello v. Bonds* and *Escobar-Ruiz v. INS*: Application of the Administrative Procedure Act to Deportation Hearings," *Georgetown Immigration Law Journal* 5 (1991): 339–59, 343.

[125] *Marcello*, 349 U.S. at 318 (Black, J., dissenting).

[126] *United States v. L.A. Tucker Truck Lines, Inc.*, 344 U.S. 33 (1952). This principle was also applied to the Interior Department in *United States v. Libby, McNeil & Libby*, 107 F. Supp. 697 (D. Ala. 1952). For more, see Wheatley, "A Study of Administrative Procedures – The Department of Interior," 181–92.

the commingling of the conflicting functions exercised by these agencies."[127] Justice Douglas agreed, arguing that the act "condemned as unfair a practice which had grown up of allowing one man to be the police officer, the prosecutor, and the judge."[128] Harm occurred whether or not the parties realized they could object.

What the APA "meant," then, was not entirely clear. It required little change at the agencies, but offered courts the opportunity to articulate new rules for judicial review. By interpreting the APA as an important intervention on the side of fairness, courts held agencies and commissions to judicially defined standards of fair practice in keeping with their sense of the spirit of the act. The Supreme Court's willingness to apply the APA in the immigration context indicated the justices' understanding that this was what due process looked like for agencies and commissions – their own numerous decisions notwithstanding. The Court thus vested the APA with a certain symbolic authority, even as it acknowledged Congress's ability to exempt agencies from these requirements as it liked. The statute would not guarantee due process for everyone, nor would it compel procedural fairness beyond its own limited scope.

That some believed the APA had not gone far enough to limit the discretion of certain administrators was evident in the procedural provisions of the 1947 Labor Management Relations (Taft–Hartley) Act.[129] Here the new Republican Congress returned to the question of administrative procedure in the context of long-standing concerns that the Wagner Act had shifted the balance of power too far toward labor and against management. Unions had grown enormously in membership and political strength since 1935, and both employees and employers hoped to direct the outlines of the postwar industrial landscape. In addition, many Americans blamed labor demands for significant postwar inflation that followed the removal of wartime price controls. The massive strike wave beginning in 1945 affected most major industries and did little to win public support for labor unions. Labor unrest and economic instability weakened the Democratic Party, and Republicans asked voters the simple question, "Had Enough?" Once Republicans took control of both houses of Congress following the 1946 midterm elections, conservatives in the 80th Congress were able to enact labor reform that not only indicated hostility to labor but also, according to one study, "gave numerous indications of a basic distrust of the administrative process."[130]

---

[127] *L.A. Tucker Truck Lines, Inc.*, 344 U.S. at 39 (Frankfurter, J., dissenting).

[128] Ibid., 41 (Douglas, J., dissenting).

[129] Labor Management Relations Act of 1947, Pub. L. No. 101, 61 Stat. 136 (1947). See Raymond L. Britton, "Changes in Organization and Procedures of the NLRB," *Southwestern Law Journal* 5 (1951): 226–33; Louis R. Gilbert, Comment, *Marquette Law Review* 35 (1952): 361–64; Seymour Scher, "The Politics of Agency Organization," *Western Political Quarterly* 15 (1962): 328–44.

[130] Millis and Brown, *From the Wagner Act to Taft-Hartley*, 419.

Even as an NLRB official reported confidently in January 1947 that "the Board's customary structure, organization, and practices meet in all really substantial respects the standards of fair administrative procedure" in the APA, employers and conservative politicians repeated now-familiar charges of the NLRB's bias and lawlessness.[131] As the House Committee on Education and Labor agreed, much blame lay with the board, which "seems to have found the temptation to be arrogant, arbitrary, and unfair irresistible."[132] As Congress, through the Taft-Hartley Act, adopted new substantive provisions that gave new rights to employers, weakened the power of unions, and endorsed the politics of anti-Communism, it also imposed new procedural restrictions on NLRB officials. Arguing that "while there are a number of important defects in the National Labor Relations Act itself, there are even more in the way the National Labor Relations Board has administered it,"[133] the House Committee on Education and Labor approved significant revisions to the NLRB's operations, and the Taft-Hartley Act, which Truman called "directly contrary to the spirit and letter" of the APA, passed over his veto.[134]

The act returned to the Smith Committee's idea of splitting the NLRB into two parts, moving the investigation and prosecution of unfair labor practices outside the board entirely.[135] Finding "bias and prejudice to be rampant in the board's staff, and among some members of the board itself," members sought to eliminate the review division and replace the current three-man board with five "fair-minded members" who would focus on quasi-judicial duties.[136] A relatively independent general counsel, appointed by the president and not under the NLRB's authority, was put in charge of the board's investigation and prosecution functions. The NLRB thus became, the first General Counsel (and former NLRB examiner) Robert Denham explained, "a labor relations court" without regulatory responsibilities; board members were essentially treated like hearing examiners.[137] The Taft-Hartley Act thus isolated the NLRB's quasi-judicial functions far more than the board had previously done or than the APA required for other agencies, over the objections of dissenters on the House Committee on Education and Labor who pointed out that this meant "throwing into the

---

[131] David Findling, "NLRB Procedures: Effects of the Administrative Procedure Act," *American Bar Association Journal* 33 (1947): 14–17 and 82–85, 14.

[132] House Committee on Education and Labor, *Labor-Management Relations Act, 1947*, 80th Cong., 1st sess., 1947, H. Rep. 245, 25.

[133] Ibid., 6.

[134] Harry S. Truman, "Veto of the Taft-Hartley Labor Bill," June 20, 1947, in *Public Papers of the Presidents of the United States: Harry S. Truman*, vol. 1947 (Washington, DC: Government Printing Office, 1963), 293.

[135] Millis and Brown, *From the Wagner Act to Taft-Hartley*; James A. Gross, *The Reshaping of the National Labor Relations Board: National Labor Policy in Transition, 1937–1947* (Albany: State University of New York Press, 1981); Christopher L. Tomlins, *The State and the Unions: Labor Relations, Law, and the Organized Labor Movement in America, 1880–1960* (Cambridge: Cambridge University Press, 1985).

[136] House Committee on Education and Labor, *Labor-Management Relations Act*, 26, 5.

[137] Robert N. Denham, "The Taft-Hartley Act," *Tennessee Law Review* 20 (1948): 168–81, 170.

discard the experience gained by the present National Labor Relations Board and its staff over the past 12 years."[138]

Opinions about this procedural reform predictably tracked political opinions about management and labor. The *Washington Post* commended the elimination of the review division and the "intermediate juggling of findings by unnamed employe[e]s working deep within what one investigator called 'the bowels of the agency'" at the same time it embraced the board's shift "from a special prosecutor of employers on behalf of unions to an agency for the suppression of unfair labor practices by both employers and employe[e]s."[139] The fact that the Taft-Hartley Act went further than the APA was, however, met with dismay by unions and NLRB officials, who did not hesitate to point out that the NLRB was being singled out for special treatment. The CIO protested that the NLRB's "structure and operations are to be twisted and ensnarled (unlike any other administrative agency in the entire Government) with provisions which make its own general counsel virtually an agency within an agency."[140] The APA, which seemed to stand for fairness and due process in the administrative state, did not require such radical changes. As one former NLRB counsel complained, the APA had rejected similar proposals "after mature deliberation by the outstanding experts in the field," and the act's "retrogressive and ominous" provisions would "frustrate efficient and informed governmental action."[141]

The Taft-Hartley Act also targeted other aspects of the NLRB's operations, creating stricter standards for how the board was to decide its own cases and tightening standards of judicial review of those decisions. Congress followed the APA and changed the standard of review from a de facto "substantial evidence" standard to one of "substantial evidence on the record considered as a whole,"[142] and members of the House conference committee announced their intention to "very materially broaden the scope of the courts' reviewing power."[143] The House Committee on Education and Labor had condemned the existing standards for "making the Board in effect its own Supreme Court so far as its findings of fact are concerned," and leaving "the courts all but powerless to correct the Board's abuses."[144] The conference committee thus ordered reviewing courts to ensure that the NLRB "does not infer facts that are not supported by evidence or that are not consistent with evidence in the record,

[138] House Committee on Education and Labor, *Labor-Management Relations Act*, 73–74. See James A. Gross, *Broken Promise: The Subversion of U.S. Labor Relations Policy, 1947–1994* (Philadelphia: Temple University Press, 1995).

[139] "Labor Board," *Washington Post*, June 4, 1947, 14.

[140] Nathan E. Cowan, CIO statement, quoted in "Labor Bill Truth Hidden, CIO Holds," *New York Times*, June 5, 1947, 2.

[141] Gerhard P. Van Arkel, "Administrative Law and the Taft-Hartley Act," *Oregon Law Review* 27 (1948): 171–87, 187.

[142] Labor Management Relations Act § 10(e).

[143] House Conference Committee, *Labor-Management Relations Act*, 80th Cong., 1st sess., 1947, H. Rep. 510, 56.

[144] House Committee on Education and Labor, *Labor-Management Relations Act*, 41.

and that it does not concentrate on one element of proof to the exclusion of others without adequate explanation of its reasons for disregarding or discrediting the evidence that is in conflict with its findings."[145] Whatever the board's tendencies in these directions, they would be unlikely to pass muster under traditional "substantial evidence" review. However, the committee inveighed against those cases in which the reviewing court had been overly deferential to the NLRB's presumed expertise, had adopted a relaxed definition of "substantial evidence," or had "in effect 'abdicated' to the Board."[146] Claiming that the APA must have done *something*, and "is generally regarded as having intended to require the courts to examine decisions of administrative agencies far more critically than has been their practice in the past," the committee adopted a similar interpretation for the NLRB.[147]

This interpretation – which would have surprised many observers of the APA, including Attorney General Clark, who, in his sympathetic interpretation of the APA, suggested that the standard "restates the present law" – was confirmed by Supreme Court doctrine.[148] In *Universal Camera v. NLRB*, the Supreme Court declared that the language found in both statutes was indeed meant to do more than simply reaffirm existing judicial practices. The case, involving an NLRB order resting on conflicting evidence, was the Supreme Court's first pass at defining this new standard of judicial review.[149] The appellate court, during its review of the order, saw little difference between the old and new standards of review and decided that "no more was done than to make definite what was already implied."[150] The court acknowledged Congress's concern about the overly pat review provided by some courts, but it suggested that, had Congress meant to change the standard of review entirely, "the matter would not have been left so at large."[151] Other appellate courts adopted this approach, but not everyone agreed; the Sixth Circuit, for example, found the idea that the statutory language represented significant change "inescapable in light of the legislative history."[152]

---

[145] House Conference Committee, *Labor-Management Relations Act, 1947*, 56. For experience under the Taft-Hartley Act, see Joint Committee on Labor-Management Relations, *Labor-Management Relations*, 80th Cong., 2nd sess., 1948, S. Rep. 986, pts. 1–3.

[146] House Conference Committee, *Labor-Management Relations Act*, 55.

[147] Ibid., 56.

[148] Department of Justice, *Attorney General's Manual on the Administrative Procedure Act*, 108.

[149] See Karl J. Howe, "Legislative Changes in Scope of Judicial Review of Administrative Decisions," *Journal of Public Law* 1 (1952): 205–09.

[150] *NLRB v. Universal Camera Corp.*, 179 F.2d 749, 752 (2d Cir. 1950).

[151] Ibid.

[152] *Pittsburgh Steamship Co. v. NLRB*, 180 F.2d 731, 734 (6th Cir. 1950); see also *NLRB v. Caroline Mills, Inc.*, 167 F.2d 212 (5th Cir. 1948); *NLRB v. Tappan Stove Co.*, 174 F.2d 1007 (6th Cir. 1949). For cases arguing that the standard had not significantly changed, see *NLRB v. Austin Co.*, 165 F.2d 592 (7th Cir. 1947); *Eastern Coal Corp. v. NLRB*, 176 F.2d 131 (4th Cir. 1949); *NLRB v. Minnesota Mining & Manufacturing Co.*, 179 F.2d 323 (8th Cir. 1950); *NLRB v. Continental Oil Co.*, 179 F.2d 552 (10th Cir. 1950); *NLRB v. Booker*, 180 F.2d 727 (5th Cir. 1950). See also Note, "Effect of the Taft-Hartley and Administrative Procedure Acts on Scope of Review of Administrative Findings," *Indiana Law Journal* 26 (1951): 406–19.

The Supreme Court adopted the latter approach and declined to find the standard of judicial review "unaltered by recent legislation."[153] Justice Frankfurter, writing for the Court, concluded that the legislative history of administrative reform indicated both a desire to codify "the prevailing 'substantial evidence' test" and "disapproval of the manner in which the courts were applying their own standard."[154] As Frankfurter argued famously (and somewhat vaguely), "in all this Congress expressed a mood."[155] The "mood" of administrative and labor reform reflected "pressures for stricter and more uniform practice, not a reflection of approval of all existing practices."[156] Frankfurter's take resembled that of the Court a year earlier, when it had characterized the APA "as a check upon administrators whose zeal might otherwise have carried them to excesses not contemplated in legislation creating their offices. It created safeguards even narrower than the constitutional ones, against arbitrary official encroachment on private rights."[157]

The Court thus endorsed a view that Congress, in adding the "whole record" requirement to the APA and the Taft-Hartley Act, was essentially trying to wrench courts from their existing lax interpretation and return the standard to that intended by Congress in the first place. Frankfurter remarked that, under each statute, "courts must now assume more responsibility for the reasonableness and fairness of Labor Board decisions than some courts have shown in the past."[158] Directing attention to these unnamed courts, Frankfurter hinted that "enactment of these statutes does not require every Court of Appeals to alter its practice. Some – perhaps a majority – have always applied the attitude reflected in this legislation."[159] Because others, however, had failed to do so, Congress had to intervene to bring all courts in line with the same definition of "substantial evidence." Courts were explicitly directed to take into account "whatever in the record fairly detracts from its weight."[160] Frankfurter denied that such a requirement reduced judicial deference to administrative expertise, although an observer suggested that "there can be little doubt that the findings of the Labor Board in particular, and to some extent of administrative agencies in general, will fare somewhat more roughly than before in the federal courts."[161] Indeed, a study of the substantial evidence test in action between 1951 and 1956 found that challenges to NLRB orders made up a huge percentage of relevant cases (139 NLRB

[153] *Universal Camera Corp. v. NLRB*, 340 U.S. 474, 491 (1951).
[154] Ibid., 483–84.
[155] Ibid., 487; Davis, *Administrative Law*, 925–28.
[156] *Universal Camera Corp.*, 340 U.S. at 489.
[157] *United States v. Morton Salt Co.*, 338 U.S. 632, 644 (1950).
[158] *Universal Camera*, 340 U.S. at 490.
[159] Ibid.
[160] Ibid., 488.
[161] Nathaniel L. Nathanson, "Central Issues of American Administrative Law," *American Political Science Review* 45 (1951): 348–85, 359.

cases to the ICC's 3 and the FCC's 6), and that these challenges resulted in a significant number of reversals.[162]

The legacy of the APA in the Supreme Court suggested that the Court was not itself willing to take on – nor to direct lower courts to take on – the job of policing the administrative process much more than they already did. (Justice Douglas did warn elsewhere, however, that without "strict and demanding" procedural requirements, "*expertise*, the strength of modern government, can become a monster which rules with no practical limits on its discretion."[163]) According to administrative law scholar and Attorney General's Committee staffer Kenneth Culp Davis, courts would find a way to do what they wanted to do; statutory standards "seem unlikely to change the courts' habitual freedom to weigh advantages and disadvantages of reviewing in particular cases."[164]

Courts' and lawyers' deference to the agencies was closely related to how much they trusted career agency officials, evidenced in their treatment of the hearing examiners who had been the subject of so much legal and political interest. Apparently taking for granted that most administrators were agency loyalists, conservative reformers saw the 350 examiner positions as valuable prizes. Part of the APA's solution was getting *better* examiners, thus addressing the findings of the Attorney General's Committee that the sitting hearing examiners were not as competent as one might hope. The improved examiners were to be protected from pressure to decide in favor of the agency, through the APA's requirement that agencies isolate their hearing examiners to reassure parties that the person hearing their side of the story was more like a neutral arbiter than a regular agency staffer. Commentators who emphasized the signal importance of personnel in improving the administrative state consistently equated ability with impartiality. As the *Wall Street Journal* had argued in 1941, those administering administrative law "must be of a relatively higher calibre than the ordinary run of government servants. Above all, they must be impartial concerning the matters with which they deal."[165] In line with these sentiments, the APA explicitly provided for "qualified and competent examiners" to be hired; responsibility for examiners' hiring, firing, and promotion was to rest outside the individual agencies in the Civil Service Commission, in the hopes that examiners might render more objective decisions once freed from the possibility of retaliation.[166] At the same time, following the Attorney General's Committee's recommendations, the APA moved

[162] Frank E. Cooper, "Administrative Law: The 'Substantial Evidence' Rule," *American Bar Association Journal* 44 (1958): 945–49 and 1001–03, 948.
[163] *New York v. United States*, 342 U.S. 882, 884 (1951) (Douglas, J., dissenting) (emphasis in the original).
[164] Davis, *Administrative Law*, 867.
[165] "Review for Board Orders," *Wall Street Journal*, Jan. 28, 1941, 6.
[166] Administrative Procedure Act §11.

to attract such men and women by raising their salaries and giving them a more important role.[167]

Implementing these statutory requirements was another area in which parties battled over what kind of changes the APA required, and in which the link between fairness and legalism became increasingly frayed. The government's efforts to comply with the hearing examiner provisions quickly erupted into controversy over competing notions of expertise. As the CSC began its efforts to hire new hearing examiners, members immediately confronted an obvious question: What should they do with the existing ones? Each of the agencies already employed corps of examiners protected by civil service rules but their roles had changed. The APA gave examiners more responsibility in adjudication, and no responsibility elsewhere. And although examiners were still administrative officers, lacking the life tenure of federal judges, the APA made them more independent than their fellow staffers by barring their firing for any reason other than "good cause" as found by the CSC.

Whether the APA meant these provisions to protect the sitting examiners, or whether Congress had hoped to bring new blood to the administrative process, was not entirely clear. Simply reappointing all of the officials who had served for years would confound the goal of improving staffing; on the other hand, starting fresh with untrained examiners would throw the agencies into chaos. As one observer noted dryly in 1949, the hearing examiner provisions offered "an enticing opportunity for affecting the administrative process," one which "was not disregarded."[168]

The CSC split the difference. Soon after the APA took effect in July 1947, the commission issued regulations setting forth the qualifications for new applicants and for the hearing examiners already in place. It assembled a group of lawyers from outside the CSC to serve on a Board of Examiners in charge of evaluating the hearing examiners; the CSC suggested it would reappoint only those whom their consultants found, as per the APA, to be "qualified and competent" to perform their duties. As the *Washington Post*'s

---

[167] Ibid.; see also Lloyd Musolf, "Administrative Law Judges: A 1948 Snapshot," *Administrative Law Review* 46 (1994): 257–69. The Supreme Court in 1951 stated its understanding "that enhancement of the status and function of the trial examiner was one of the important purposes of the movement for administrative reform" (*Universal Camera Corp.*, 340 U.S. at 494).

[168] Morgan Thomas, "The Selection of Federal Hearing Examiners: Pressure Groups and the Administrative Process," *Yale Law Journal* 59 (1949): 431–75, 433; see also Ralph F. Fuchs, "The Hearing Examiner Fiasco under the Administrative Procedure Act," *Harvard Law Review* 63 (1950): 737–68; Bernstein, "The Politics of Adjudication," 306–08; Chester T. Lane, review of *Federal Examiners and the Conflict of Law and Administration,* by Lloyd D. Musolf *Columbia Law Review* 54 (1954): 1008–11; Note, "Hearing Examiner Status: A Recurrent Problem in Administrative Law," *Indiana Law Journal* 30 (1954): 86–106; Ralph F. Fuchs, "The Hearing Officer Problem – Symptom and Symbol," *Cornell Law Quarterly* 40 (1955): 281–325; Antonin Scalia, "The ALJ Fiasco – A Reprise," *University of Chicago Law Review* 47 (1979): 57–80; Daniel J. Gifford, "Federal Administrative Law Judges: The Relevance of Past Choices to Future Directions," *Administrative Law Review* 49 (1997): 1–60.

bureaucracy columnist later pointed out, this was "one of the few occasions in Civil Service history when career employe[e]s were forced to be reexamined for jobs they had held for years."[169] Given the vagueness of the "qualified and competent" standard, the board would have a great deal of discretion in deciding who to retain and what to consider in making that determination.

Members were determined to use this authority; early in the board's work, Chairman Carl McFarland wrote to select members of Congress wondering "how far we may go – as a practical matter – in weeding out the incompetent and unfit."[170] On the basis of agency records and oral interviews, members looked at the professional experience (generally in the law) and specialized experience (in some area of administration) of those before them. The board also sought to ensure that the examiners and applicants possessed "certain aptitudes and abilities"; members explained that they were looking for "generally apt, able, and temperamentally fitted examiners – not specialists in particular subjects such as radio, railroads, or rates."[171] Or, as McFarland put it, the board's duty was to "make sure that every examiner who is to be retained is mentally and temperamentally equipped to be what federal judges ought to be."[172] As one columnist joked, the APA was "becoming known as the 'full employment act for lawyers.'"[173]

This preference for legal over administrative expertise was not surprising; with the exception of McFarland, few of the board members were experts in administration, but several (McFarland included) had strong connections to the conservative ABA.[174] The board's desire to judge administrative officials by the standards of judicial officers was problematic from the agencies' perspective, however. By discounting the benefits of specialization and ignoring the APA's clear endorsement of noncourtroom methods, the board adopted a different view of "apt" and "able" for the agencies than the agencies had adopted for themselves. Enforcing judicial standards of employment for quasi-judicial examiners (most of whom were, in fact, already trained as lawyers) was one

[169] Jerry Kluttz, "The Federal Diary," *Washington Post*, Apr. 2, 1949, B1.
[170] Carl McFarland to Sen. Pat McCarran, Feb. 2, 1948, Folder "CSC: Congress," Box 5, McFarland Papers, UVA. Similar letters were also sent to Rep. Walter, Rep. John W. Gwynne (R-Iowa), and Sen. Alexander Wiley (R-Wisc.).
[171] "Hearing Examiner Personnel under the Administrative Procedure Act, First Report of the Consultants to the United States Civil Service Commission, Method of Rating Applicants," Jan. 31, 1949, 9, Folder "Administrative Procedure Act, Proposed Legislation – Senatorial," Box 21, McGrath Papers, HSTL; see also Thomas, "The Selection of Federal Hearing Examiners," 462–66.
[172] McFarland to McCarran, Feb. 2, 1948.
[173] Jerry Kluttz, "The Federal Diary," *Washington Post*, Oct. 31, 1946, 7.
[174] As McFarland later remarked to Fuchs, regarding the latter's *Harvard Law Review* article on the matter, "you seem to convict me of 'guilt by Association'!" (Carl McFarland to Ralph Fuchs, Feb. 23, 1950, Folder "CSC: General Correspondence," Box 5, McFarland Papers, UVA.)

concern, but board members were also troubled by the political preferences of the current examiners. Board members evaluated examiners on their "general ability to act independently, objectively, efficiently, and fairly as an administrative judge,"[175] and the CSC noted that the decision to review and set standards for *all* hearing examiners was intended to avoid charges "that hearing examiners are 'hand picked' by the agency and may be biased in favor of the agency."[176] This echoed the ABA's concerns that simply reappointing the examiners to their current posts would entrench the agencies' own positions. Pushing for hearing examiners "free from preconceptions and political motivations or ideologies," the ABA insisted such objectivity was "the core of the distinction between the American system and the Soviet concept of judicial bodies."[177]

Skepticism about this particular group of zealous bureaucrats, which dated back decades, fit nicely into the 80th Congress's concern about possibly disloyal officials. One former ABA president complained that many of the sitting hearing examiners "were 'hatchet men' for Left Wing ideologies or New Deal philosophies against business,"[178] and Senate Judiciary Committee chairman Alexander Wiley (R–Wisc.) asked the CSC to ensure that the new examiners "not be men of leftist thinking, men who don't have complete loyalty to our constitutional system of checks and balances, men who are not devoted to our system of private enterprise; but rather men of outstanding judicial temperament, who are unalterably dedicated to the preservation of the American Way."[179] Such language had the effect of conflating examiners' support for their agency's goals with subversion.

When the board concluded its review in early 1949, the results were striking. Of the 148 incumbent hearing examiners with civil service protection, only 106 were found "qualified for permanent and unconditional appointment."[180] This, the CSC trumpeted in a press release, meant that "70 percent of the hearing examiners" in question were "qualified to continue in

[175] "Hearing Examiner Personnel under the Administrative Procedure Act, First Report of the Consultants to the United States Civil Service Commission, Method of Rating Applicants," 9.

[176] U.S. Civil Service Commission, *65th Annual Report*, 81st Cong., 1st sess., 1948, H. Doc. 13, 31; see also Ralph N. Kleps, review of "First Report of the Consultants to the United States Civil Service Commission, Hearing Examiner Personnel under the Administrative Procedure Act, Method of Rating Applicants," *California Law Review* 37 (1949): 534–37.

[177] "Impartiality Is Essential," *American Bar Association Journal* 33 (1947): 148–49, 148.

[178] William L. Ransom to the Hoover Commission, memorandum, Mar. 18, 1948, 5, Folder "Regulatory Agencies, Correspondence Relating to Task Forces, 1947–49, NC 115, Entry 11, Box 15, OED, RG 264, NACP.

[179] Alexander Wiley to Arthur S. Flemming, April 5, 1947, reprinted in "The 350 Hearing Examiners: Chairman Wiley Asks Open Choices for Fitness," *American Bar Association Journal* 33 (1947): 421–22, 422.

[180] "Hearing Examiner Personnel under the Administrative Procedure Act, First Report of the Consultants to the United States Civil Service Commission, Method of Rating Applicants," 18, Table I.

their positions under the higher standards that became necessary under the Administrative Procedure Act."[181] This also meant, of course, that a substantial number of those who had been serving as examiners were deemed unqualified to continue doing so. Anticipating criticism, the board emphasized that "only a handful" of these low ratings resulted from examiners' "bias, prejudice, or lack of objectively judicial temperament."[182] Most disqualifications, they claimed, were instead attributable to examiners' lack of experience or "abilities indubitably very mediocre at best."[183] Other groups of examiners fared similarly poorly; twelve of the sixty-nine sitting examiners without civil service status were found wholly unqualified, and many of the rest met with only grudging approval.[184]

Examiners, agencies, and the press were skeptical of this argument, pointing out that many of those deemed unqualified had already amassed years of expertise. The wide gulf between the agencies' standards and those of the board was apparent; the Association of Interstate Commerce Commission Practitioners protested that the order was "extremely unfair because certain men have been disqualified whom we all know to be eminently qualified for this position."[185] The NLRB similarly complained that the firings had "eviscerated the hearing examiner staff" and rendered it "unable efficiently to pursue its regular operations without the services of these trained men."[186] The Board of Examiners declined to list its ratings by agency, explaining only that they had found "a wide disparity in the present standards and practices of the several agencies so far as their examiners are concerned."[187] The agencies and the press jumped on the figures, however, demonstrating that certain agencies were particularly affected: twelve of the ICC's forty-eight examiners were deemed unqualified, and the Civil Aeronautics Board had ten of their thirty examiners so designated.[188] The greatest damage occurred at the NLRB, where almost half of the examiners, many of whom were long-time employees, were marked unqualified.[189]

---

[181] CSC Press Release, March 9, 1949 (for release Mar. 11), 1, Folder "CSC: Regulations, Releases, General Statements," Box 5, McFarland Papers, UVA.

[182] "Hearing Examiner Personnel under the Administrative Procedure Act, First Report of the Consultants to the United States Civil Service Commission, Method of Rating Applicants," 17.

[183] Ibid.

[184] Ibid., 18, Table II.

[185] Association of Interstate Commerce Commission Practitioners, quoted in "Public Hearing Asked on Ousted Examiners," New York Times, Mar. 22, 1949, 4.

[186] NRLB letter to the CSC, quoted in "NLRB Says It Needs Rejected Examiners," New York Times, Apr. 2, 1949, 2.

[187] "Hearing Examiner Personnel under the Administrative Procedure Act, First Report of the Consultants to the United States Civil Service Commission, Method of Rating Applicants," 21.

[188] "Appeals Granted 'Unfit' Examiners," New York Times, Mar. 30, 1949, 2.

[189] Joseph A. Loftus, "15 NLRB Examiners Found Unqualified," New York Times, Mar. 13, 1949, 1; see also Thomas, "The Selection of Federal Hearing Examiners," 443.

The disqualified examiners and their agency superiors quickly challenged the board's findings, questioning both the substantive tests the board had used to evaluate them and the procedures by which the board had done so. Through the Federal Trial Examiners' Conference, examiners came together to reject allegations of their inefficiency, arguing that the board should consider the "the importance, complexity and magnitude of each case handled" as part of an examiner's assessment.[190] Examiners also pointed out that the board's cavalier approach violated the very rules the CSC had created to implement the APA's removal provisions – regulations that required notice of the charges against them, opportunity to cross-examine witnesses, and a decision made "on the basis of the record of the hearing."[191] Unfairness permeated the evaluation process, according to critics; one member of the firm of Covington, Burling, Rublee, Acheson & Shorb (which represented several examiners) blasted the board and the CSC for their reliance on confidential sources.[192] The Association of Interstate Commerce Commission Practitioners found the process "subversive of constitutional guarantees and democratic principles and ideals," and complained of the damage to examiners' "professional standing (in the sunset of life devoted to public service), social and professional reputation, and the very livelihood" without procedural protections.[193]

The Civil Service Commission quickly retreated from the findings and rebuked its board, indicating its dismay that examiners "who have apparently performed to the satisfaction of their agencies" were fired under "a rigid interpretation and application of the standards."[194] CSC president Harry Mitchell suggested to McFarland that the board (which had used the standard of "eminently qualified" rather than the APA's "qualified and competent") "should adopt a more liberal view" in its application of the standards when it reconsidered its ratings.[195] Announcing that it would allow the hearing examiners rated ineligible to appeal and to retain their positions while they did so, the CSC also created a separate group of staffers to investigate charges that bias and prejudice had influenced evaluations.[196] And even as the consultants began their reconsideration, the CSC revisited the

---

[190] J. Fred Johnson Jr., Resolution adopted by the Federal Trial Examiners' Conference, Mar. 31, 1949, 2, Folder "CSC: Rating Factors," Box 5, McFarland Papers, UVA.

[191] Appointment, Compensation, and Removal of Hearing Examiners, 12 Fed. Reg. 6321, 6324 (1947); see also Thomas, "The Selection of Federal Hearing Examiners," 445.

[192] Charles A. Horsky to the Chief of the Examining and Placement Division, CSC, April 11, 1949, Folder "CSC: NLRB," Box 5, McFarland Papers, UVA.

[193] Association of Interstate Commerce Commission Practitioners to Congress, quoted in Jerry Kluttz, "The Federal Diary," *Washington Post*, May 23, 1949, B1.

[194] Harry B. Mitchell to Carl McFarland, May 4, 1949, Folder "CSC: Rating Factors," Box 5, McFarland Papers, UVA.

[195] Ibid.

[196] The CSC's committee found "no evidence in any of the files that race, religion, economic or political consideration entered into the decisions rendered by the Board." Harry B. Mitchell to William J. Houston, Feb. 14, 1950, 5, Folder "CSC: General Correspondence," Box 5, McFarland Papers, UVA.

ratings on its own, and by June found many of the disqualified examiners (including all of those at the ICC and most at the NLRB) eligible to retain their jobs.

Bad feelings lingered, however; the ICC, in their annual report, noted the "unfortunate and discouraging effect upon the morale" of the staff stemming from the "long-continued delay and uncertainty" of the evaluation process.[197] This feeling was shared by the Board of Examiners themselves, most of whom resigned in July arguing that it was *they* who had been poorly treated. The board suggested that the ad hominem attacks launched against them were a "perverted result" that served as "a warning to people who are importuned, and tempted, to participate in federal personnel administration."[198] Board members blamed the contretemps on the agencies, specifically the "organized clamor" of the examiners, the NLRB's "wide and skillful dissemination of irresponsible and absurd charges of bias and prejudice," and the "intemperate attack on the validity of the system" by the ICC.[199] The CSC came in for its own share of blame for failing to defend the board.

By late 1949 the CSC had capitulated entirely, permanently reappointing almost all of the sitting examiners and starting from scratch to promulgate regulations for hiring and firing the examiners in accordance with the APA.[200] Only one incumbent examiner with civil service status was ultimately let go.[201] In fact, the CSC did not propose new regulations for hiring and firing examiners until the fall of 1951, a state of affairs that led McCarran, chair of the Senate Judiciary Committee, to charge that the CSC "is either incapable of properly administering the law, or is unwilling to do so."[202] Nor were these new regulations uncontroversial. When the commission had taken responsibility for promoting, as well as hiring and firing, examiners, it had also adopted the practice of sorting examiners into different grades, each with their own responsibilities and salaries. This practice, in which examiners were assigned cases based on their difficulty, had been common at the agencies, but came in for significant heat from those who feared an agency could rig the system to ensure certain cases went to certain examiners. McCarran criticized this provision, arguing that under the APA, "all examiners should be superior," and suggesting that the CSC had created "a nefarious promotion scheme" that "leaves

---

[197] Interstate Commerce Commission, *63rd Annual Report*, 81st Cong., 2nd sess., 1949, H. Doc. 400, 58.

[198] Carl McFarland to Harry B. Mitchell, July 25, 1949, 6, Folder "CSC: Second Report and Resignation," Box 5, McFarland Papers, UVA.

[199] Ibid.

[200] 16 Fed. Reg. 9623 (1951).

[201] President's Conference on Administrative Procedure, Committee on Hearing Officers, *Appointment and Status of Federal Hearing Officers* (Lester Report) (Washington, DC: President's Conference on Administrative Procedure, 1954), 14.

[202] Sen. Pat McCarran to Robert C. Ramspeck, Sept. 6, 1951, reprinted in Senate Judiciary Committee, *Hearing Examiner Regulations Promulgated under Section 11 of the Administrative Procedure Act*, 82nd Cong., 1st sess., 1951, S. Doc. 82, 10; see also Bernstein, "The Politics of Adjudication," 308–12.

to the agency the initiative and the control."[203] Such regulations were contrary to McCarran's vision of functionally independent examiners who were to "be very nearly the equivalent of judges even though operating within the Federal system of administrative justice."[204]

The Federal Trial Examiners Conference contested the regulations in court, on the grounds that the provisions for promotion, removal, and rotation of cases would stymie examiners' independence and thwart the APA. The lower courts agreed that examiners' independence deserved protection, but the Supreme Court adopted the approach of Judge David Bazelon's dissent in the appellate court. Bazelon argued that courts should not overstate the importance of examiner independence; after all, in framing the APA, Congress "did not adopt any of the extreme proposals to isolate hearing examiners from the agencies or insulate them completely from expressions of the agencies' views."[205] The Court similarly resisted the urge to adopt a highly judicialized conception of the examiner's role, recognizing that agencies should take examiners' skill and expertise into account in assigning cases. As Bazelon argued, treating all examiners alike "would go a long way toward dissipating the administrative expertise upon which courts now rely in giving deference to administrative judgments."[206] The majority of the Court found that regulations did not conflict with the history of administrative reform generally, or the APA specifically, a history in which Congress intended to make hearing examiners at least "semi-" or "partially" independent of the agencies in which they heard cases. Dissenting Justices Black, Frankfurter, and Douglas warned that the provisions assigning cases by rank "are so nebulous that the head of an agency is left practically free to select any examiner he chooses for any case he chooses," but the majority found such claims unconvincing.[207]

Although the CSC's regulations were ultimately upheld, some seven years after the APA's enactment, the commission's efforts to fit examiners into the administrative process demonstrated the multiple ways parties could use legalistic arguments for their own purposes. Some parties, fighting to realize their vision of the administrative state, saw in the examiners ideological bias and agency influence. Others, however, saw experienced staffers following the leads of the agency heads. Without consensus about what made a good hearing examiner, political considerations inevitably came into play. At the end of this controversy, examiners were still decisively agency employees rather than judges on loan to the administrative process. Indeed, the Court in *Universal Camera* had concluded that even under review on the "whole record," the examiner's

---

[203] Ibid.

[204] Ibid., 9.

[205] *Ramspeck v. Federal Trial Examiners Conference*, 202 F.2d 312, 314 (D.C. Cir. 1952) (Bazelon, J., dissenting).

[206] Ibid., 315.

[207] *Ramspeck v. Federal Trial Examiners Conference*, 345 U.S. 128, 145 (1953) (Black, J., dissenting); see also Bernard Schwartz, "Administrative Law," *New York University Law Review* 29 (1954): 101–24, 108–12; Bernstein, "The Politics of Adjudication," 311–12.

report was only one part of the record.[208] McCarran's subsequent proposal to have the president appoint the examiners and to subject them "to the canons and standards applicable to members of the Federal Judiciary" failed to catch on, reflecting some limits of this path of reform.[209]

Examiners were *not* the only administrative officials Congress and the White House worried about, of course. The APA's status as a "bill of rights" for the administrative state was problematic once the federal government began applying the tools of bureaucracy to questions of domestic subversion with rather less concern for procedural niceties than those under investigation might have liked.[210] Indeed, defining due process for the administrative state became a very different problem once administrators were asked to turn their attention from collective bargaining, railroad rates, and broadcast licenses to hunting for subversive employees within their own departments. While those skeptical of administrators pointed to the harm that disloyal officials could cause, bureaucratic supporters used the language of lawfulness and due process to criticize methods of removal.

Building on charges going back to the Dies Committee, as well as more recent events including the *Amerasia* affair, Republicans during the 1946 election season repeatedly claimed that New Deal Democrats had allowed

---

[208] *Universal Camera*, 340 U.S. at 496; see also *FCC v. Allentown Broadcasting Corp.*, 349 U.S. 358 (1955).

[209] Senate Judiciary Committee, *Presidential Appointment of Trial Examiners*, 83rd Cong., 2nd sess., 1954, S. Rep. 2199, 4; Fuchs, "The Hearing Officer Problem – Symptom and Symbol."

[210] For contemporary analyses, see Robert E. Cushman, "The Purge of Federal Employees Accused of Disloyalty," *Public Administration Review* 3 (1943): 297–316; Roger S. Abbott, "The Federal Loyalty Program: Background and Problems," *American Political Science Review* 42 (1948): 486–99; H. Eliot Kaplan, "Loyalty Review of Federal Employees," *New York University Law Quarterly Review* 23 (1948): 437–48; John Lord O'Brian, "Loyalty Tests and Guilt by Association," *Harvard Law Review* 61 (1948): 592–611; J. Edgar Hoover, "Role of the FBI in the Federal Employee Security Program," *Northwestern University Law Review* 49 (1954): 333–47; Association of the Bar of the City of New York, *Report of the Special Committee on the Federal Loyalty-Security Program* (New York: Dodd, Mead & Co., 1956); Murray Seasongood and Richard L. Strecker, "The Loyalty Review Board," *University of Cincinnati Law Review* 25 (1956): 1–42; Robert Horn, "The Protection of Internal Security," *Public Administration Review* 16 (1956): 40–52; Harry S. Truman, *Memoirs* (Garden City, NY: Doubleday & Co., 1956); Robert J. Morgan, "Federal Loyalty-Security Removals, 1946–1956," *Nebraska Law Review* 36 (1957): 412–46; Joseph L. Rauh Jr., "Nonconfrontation in Security Cases: The *Greene* Decision," *Virginia Law Review* 45 (1959): 1175–90; Michael C. Slotnick, "The Anathema of the Security Risk: Arbitrary Dismissals of Federal Government Civilian Employees and Civilian Employees of Private Contractors Doing Business with the Federal Government," *University of Miami Law Review* 17 (1962): 10–50. For scholarly assessments, see Alan D. Harper, *The Politics of Loyalty: The White House and the Communist Issue, 1946–1952* (Westport, CT: Greenwood Publishing, 1969); David Caute, *The Great Fear: The Anti-Communist Purge under Truman and Eisenhower* (New York: Simon and Schuster, 1978); Francis H. Thompson, *The Frustration of Politics: Truman, Congress, and the Loyalty Issue 1945–1953* (London: Associated University Presses, 1979); Stanley I. Kutler, *The American Inquisition: Justice and Injustice in the Cold War* (New York: Hill and Wang, 1982); Ellen Schrecker, *Many Are the Crimes: McCarthyism in America* (Boston: Little, Brown, 1998).

Communists to infiltrate the federal government. Questioning the loyalty of all federal employees proved a remarkable political tool for those attacking the decisions of agencies, commissions, departments, and bureaus. At the FCC, for example, commissioners' efforts to improve the quality of broadcast programming were met with enormous hostility. The FCC's investigation into station programming, culminating in a March 1946 report known as the "Blue Book," revealed a dearth of public service and noncommercial programs. The report, along with the commission's announcement that it planned to take programming into account in renewing licenses in the future, caused an uproar in the broadcasting industry. Broadcasters, offended at the FCC's assertion of authority in this area, charged that the FCC in fact had no authority to act, that it was censoring the broadcasters, and that the policy (in the so-called Pink Book) was a product of Communists at the commission.[211] Their ire pushed the FCC to retreat from its policy by the end of 1946.

A broader effort was launched after Republican victories in the 1946 elections put the White House on the defensive. In late 1946, Truman appointed a Temporary Commission on Employee Loyalty, staffed with representatives from a number of agencies, and in March 1947, on their recommendation, he established a comprehensive program to investigate the loyalty of employees across the administrative state. Agencies and commissions had become accustomed to dealing with allegedly disloyal employees – the FCC, for example, established a Committee on Loyalty Investigations in 1943 to investigate such charges, and the State Department in early 1947 made public the firings of some forty workers on the basis of their foreign ties – but Truman's program replaced the variety of statutes and executive orders with a clear set of rules that applied with equal force to all employees. Under Executive Order 9835, an agency was to dismiss an employee from government employment if "on all the evidence, reasonable grounds exist for belief that the person involved is disloyal to the Government of the United States."[212] Several of the criteria for determining disloyalty – including sabotage, espionage, treason, revolutionary advocacy, and disclosing confidential information – involved activities that were already illegal; added to these, however, was a broad provision that employees could be fired for "[m]embership in, affiliation with or sympathetic association with" any group the Attorney General deemed "totalitarian, fascist, communist, or subversive."[213] The conservative *Chicago Tribune* hailed Truman's move "to drive

[211] Erik Barnouw, *The Golden Web: A History of Broadcasting in the United States*, vol. II, *1933 to 1953* (New York: Oxford University Press, 1968); "The Fortieth Anniversary of the Federal Communications Commission," *Federal Communications Bar Journal* 27 (1974): 109–60, 131; James L. Baughman, *Television's Guardians: The FCC and the Politics of Programming, 1958–1967* (Knoxville: University of Tennessee Press, 1985); Susan L. Brinson, *The Red Scare, Politics, and the Federal Communications Commission, 1941–1960* (Westport, CT: Praeger, 2004); Kimberly A. Zarkin and Michael J. Zarkin, *The Federal Communications Commission: Front Line in the Culture and Regulation Wars* (Westport, CT: Greenwood Press, 2006).
[212] Executive Order No. 9835, 12 Fed. Reg. 1935, 1938 (1947).
[213] Ibid; see also *Joint Anti-Fascist Refugee Committee v. McGrath*, 341 U.S. 123 (1951).

Communists, fellow travelers, and parlor pinks from the pay rolls of New Deal agencies and governmental departments" and delighted in his rejection of "the New Deal policy of bending over backward in favor of pinkos."[214]

The executive order backed up this proscription by giving the agencies and commissions clear directions for enforcing it. Indeed, according to one contemporary observer, the "shrill and spasmodic attacks" on employee loyalty soon became "a rather respectable program of personnel administration."[215] An employee accused of disloyalty as the result of such investigations was given several opportunities to defend himself. The first step was an administrative hearing before a loyalty board assembled from staffers within the employee's own agency; here the employee was entitled to have an attorney, to present evidence (although not the power to subpoena unwilling witnesses), and to use rules of evidence that resembled those used elsewhere in the administrative process. If removal was recommended, the employee could appeal his case to the agency head(s), and then to a Loyalty Review Board established within the CSC. Three separate hearings were afforded the accused employee, including one by government officials outside the employee's agency and presumably unknown to him. The program thus appeared to bring due process protections like those required for administrative action in other areas to the project of rooting out potentially disloyal employees within the administrative state.

These procedures, which went far beyond what was legally required in the civil service context, were intended to reassure Americans concerned about the program's potential for unfairness. The administration was under no legal obligation to provide multiple hearings, as courts had clearly established that government employment did not constitute the "life, liberty, or property" protected by the Fifth Amendment's due process clause. Under civil service rules, federal employees were only entitled to notice of their impending removal and a written opportunity to respond. Given the national security concerns that underlay the loyalty investigations, the White House might have been able to defend even more limited procedures. Instead, however, the administration rooted the loyalty program firmly in administrative ideas of procedural due process. The same kinds of procedural protections that reassured Americans about the fairness of economic regulation were called into service as the White House asked the bureaucrats who handled such regulation to take on a new and very different task.

Defending his program in November, Truman stated emphatically that the federal government "must be the model of a fair employer."[216] The parallel was

[214] "Truman Orders Bureau Chiefs to Purge Reds," *Chicago Daily Tribune*, Mar. 23, 1947, 1; see Athan Theoharis, "The Escalation of the Loyalty Program," in Barton J. Bernstein, ed., *Politics and Policies of the Truman Administration*, 242–68 (Chicago: Quadrangle Books, 1970).

[215] Egbert S. Wengert, review of *The Federal Loyalty-Security Program,* by Eleanor Bontecou, *American Political Science Review* 48 (1954): 225–26, 225.

[216] Harry S. Truman, "Statement by the President on the Government's Employee Loyalty Program," Nov. 14, 1947, in *Public Papers of the Presidents of the United States: Harry S. Truman*, vol. 1947, 491.

clear: Democratic governments protected individual rights, and Communist ones did not. Reassuring Americans that the loyalty boards were "definitely not 'kangaroo' courts," he pledged that "every effort has been made to guarantee full protection to those who are suspected of disloyalty."[217] The president also attempted to bolster the public's confidence in the government officials tasked with making loyalty determinations. Truman touted the fact that the Loyalty Review Board was staffed with "outstanding citizens of the United States" who "have no ax to grind. They will not be concerned with personalities. Their judgment will be as detached as is humanly possible."[218] Observers echoed these arguments; the *Los Angeles Times,* reviewing the program in 1948, suggested that the procedures "would convince a reasonable person that the government is not setting forth on a 'witch hunt.'"[219] Almost two years later, *Washington Post* bureaucracy columnist Jerry Kluttz optimistically concluded that the Loyalty Review Board's frequent reversal of agencies' removal recommendations was "conclusive proof that employe[e]s are protected by the appeals system."[220]

Others, however, were less convinced. As former Attorney General Francis Biddle reflected some years later: "Certain shadowy paper rights were given the employee, who sometimes got a fair hearing, sometimes did not."[221] While the loyalty program's procedures resembled those developed by administrative officials in their broad design, observant attorneys quickly noticed the differences. In a joint letter to the *New York Times,* Zechariah Chafee Jr. and Erwin Griswold were among the Harvard Law School professors who expressed their concern about "the misty procedure so indistinctly sketched" by President Truman.[222] As they argued, the loyalty program "fails to draw upon the cumulative experience of courts and administrative agencies" while also ignoring "the conception of sound administrative procedure reflected in the very recently enacted Administrative Procedure Act."[223] They pointed out that Truman's program very much resembled licensing, an activity for which agencies had clear and long-established procedures.

However, a comparison between the existing standards of administrative procedure and those of the loyalty program indicated substantial deviations. As two Yale Law School scholars (one with significant past experience at the NLRB and the OPA) concluded, the loyalty program "falls far short of providing the safeguards established by the Administrative Procedure Act for other types of

[217] Ibid., 490.
[218] Ibid.
[219] "Government Loyalty Check Procedure," *Los Angeles Times,* Jan. 2, 1948, 4.
[220] Jerry Kluttz, "The Federal Diary," *Washington Post,* Dec. 12, 1949, B1.
[221] Francis Biddle, "Subversives in Government," *Annals of the American Academy of Political and Social Science* 300 (1955): 51–61, 56.
[222] Zechariah Chafee Jr., Erwin N. Griswold, Milton Katz, and Austin W. Scott, letter to the editor, *New York Times,* Apr. 13, 1947, 8E.
[223] Ibid.

administrative proceedings."[224] An allegedly disloyal employee had fewer rights than a broadcast station facing a revocation of its permit by the FCC or a USDA poultry inspector whose license was threatened. In addition, the program left administrators on the loyalty boards with tremendous discretion. Political scientist Marver Bernstein, criticizing the government's overly broad standard of disloyalty, suggested that "[a]dministration is often called upon to deal with questions too exact and nice for the law, but it has never been supposed that it could handle satisfactorily concepts too broad for the law."[225]

For sitting bureaucrats, the contrast between the formal procedures they followed in regulating private parties and those they used in judging one another must have been striking. First, instead of creating a new agency specializing in loyalty investigations or placing the program under the authority of the CSC's personnel experts, the Truman administration essentially asked staffers in the agencies and commissions to judge one another. Not only were members of agency loyalty boards not expert in this area (they received only brief training and materials for guidance), but the program diverted their attention from the duties for which they did possess specialized expertise.[226]

Second, although the FBI was responsible for the initial investigation, these agency officials appeared to combine the very functions that the agencies, the ABA, and the APA had spent so much energy separating. A critical Senate committee examining the operation of the program in 1948 suggested that "the fact that the loyalty boards both prepare and hear the charges against an allegedly disloyal employee subjects the impartiality of the hearings to grave doubt."[227] As Lloyd Garrison, the chairman of the first Labor Board and a member of the Attorney General's Committee, complained: "If in the field of labor relations we have thought it necessary to separate the prosecutor from the judge, how much the more so should we do this in the field of security cases, which

---

[224] Thomas I. Emerson and David M. Helfeld, "Loyalty among Government Employees," *Yale Law Journal* 58 (1948): 1–143, 35. For the ensuing discussion, see J. Edgar Hoover, "A Comment on the Article 'Loyalty among Government Employees,'" *Yale Law Journal* 58 (1949): 401–11; Thomas I. Emerson and David M. Helfeld, "Reply by the Authors," *Yale Law Journal* 58 (1948): 412–21; J. Edgar Hoover, "Rejoinder by Mr. Hoover," *Yale Law Journal* 58 (1949): 422–25.

[225] Marver H. Bernstein, "The Loyalty of Federal Employees," *Western Political Quarterly* 2 (1949): 254–64, 260.

[226] As attorney John Lord O'Brian argued in 1955, "[t]he creation of administrative commissions and agencies was originally justified by the assertion that the members would possess a certain *expertise* in dealing with business and economic problems. But there is no expertise in the field of ideas. This is an excellent illustration of the way in which principles and procedures applicable to the regulation of property rights are thoughtlessly and by some false analogy extended to impose limitations on human liberty" (John Lord O'Brian, *National Security and Individual Freedom* [Cambridge, MA: Harvard University Press, 1955], 32–33 n. 18 [emphasis in the original]).

[227] Senate Committee on Expenditures in the Executive Departments, Subcommittee on Investigations, *Investigation of Federal Employees Loyalty Program: Interim Report*, 80th Cong., 2nd sess., 1948, S. Rep. 1775, 18.

affect the lives, the fortunes, and the honor of the individuals involved?"[228] Even worse, here agency officials were in charge of judging not recalcitrant businesses but their own colleagues. FCC Commissioner Clifford Durr, who declined reappointment to the FCC in 1948 at least in part over the loyalty program, protested both the unfairness of the rules in general and of this aspect in particular. Attaching his dissent to the FCC's proposed rules in June 1948, Durr argued that the combination of functions was particularly problematic for these officials, who "are assigned the role of judges but are accountable as prosecutors."[229] Overall, he concluded, the hearing "makes a mockery not only of 'due process' but of elementary standards of fairness."[230]

In addition, although the executive order emphasized that an employee would receive notice of the specific charges against him, the source of these charges remained confidential from *both* the employee *and* those evaluating his loyalty if the FBI found that security concerns required it.[231] In such cases, an employee would have no opportunity to cross-examine his accuser or prepare a successful defense, and the agency board (as well as the agency head and the Loyalty Review Board) would be similarly unable to evaluate the credibility of the charges. In response, the CSC instructed agency loyalty boards to "take into consideration the fact that the employee may have been handicapped in his defense" by this lack of information.[232] Biddle described "two records" in the cases, "one which went to the employee and to the court" and one that was "the *real* record on which the action hinged."[233] Such secrecy was certainly unusual in the administrative process, and agencies' internal reforms following

[228] Lloyd K. Garrison, "Some Observations on the Loyalty-Security Program," *University of Chicago Law Review* 23 (1955): 1–11, 10–11. Eleanor Bontecou would later note that some (unnamed) agencies had in fact created their own internal separation of functions (Eleanor Bontecou, *The Federal Loyalty-Security Program* [Ithaca, NY: Cornell University Press, 1953], 245).

[229] Dissenting Views of Commissioner Clifford J. Durr re Proposed Rules Governing FCC Loyalty Procedure, n.d., 2, Folder "Federal Communications Commission," Box 20, Records Relating to Loyalty Review Boards, 1947–1952, A1, Entry 1011, LRB, RG 146, NACP. Durr repeated his objections in a subsequent article (Clifford J. Durr, "The Loyalty Order's Challenge to the Constitution," *University of Chicago Law Review* 16 [1949]: 298–306, 303). For more on Durr, see Clement Imhoff, "Clifford J. Durr and the Loyalty Question: 1942–1950," *Journal of American Culture* 12 (1989): 47–54; John A. Salmond, *The Conscience of a Lawyer: Clifford J. Durr and American Civil Liberties, 1899–1975* (Tuscaloosa: University of Alabama Press, 1990); Barnouw, *The Golden Web*; Sarah Hart Brown, *Standing Against Dragons: Three Southern Lawyers in an Era of Fear* (Baton Rouge: Louisiana State University Press, 1998).

[230] Dissenting Views of Commissioner Durr re Proposed Rules Governing FCC Loyalty Procedure, 2; see also Durr, "The Loyalty Order's Challenge to the Constitution," 303.

[231] Executive Order No. 9835, 12 Fed. Reg. 1935 (1947).

[232] Directive III, Manner of Conducting Hearings before Agency Loyalty Boards (part of Dec. 23, 1947 press release), Folder "Executive Order 9835 (5 of 5)," Box 24; see also National Labor Relations Board Loyalty Board Rules and Regulations, Feb. 17, 1948, 9, Folder "National Labor Relations Board," Box 22, both in Records Relating to Loyalty Review Boards, 1947–52, A1, Entry 1011, LRB, RG 146, NACP.

[233] Biddle, "Subversives in Government," 56.

the *Morgan* decision and the APA's adoption of these protections had largely rendered such complaints moot. Eleanor Bontecou, a critical observer of the loyalty program, noted the White House's "great pride" in "the strict legality of the procedures" it had provided.[234]

Truman downplayed the potential for harm in the loyalty program's secrecy provisions, suggesting that only "[i]n some unusual" circumstances would an employee not receive all of the information underlying the charges against him.[235] Loyalty Review Board Chairman Seth W. Richardson similarly insisted that his board had designed its procedures "to minimize to the fullest degree possible, any possible injustice" from FBI confidentiality, even as he acknowledged that in most cases, the ability of the employee to see and challenge the sources of the evidence against him "will probably not be practicable."[236] In 1948, the Loyalty Review Board moved toward even more procedural protections, requiring that all agency boards "invite identified adverse witnesses to attend the hearing, testify in the individual's presence, and subject themselves to cross-examination."[237] Without subpoena power, however, it was not clear that "invited" witnesses would actually attend.

Anyway, Richardson suggested, the hearing procedures compensated for this secrecy; "if, after three impartial examinations as to the fact, it is finally determined that reasonable grounds do exist for the belief that the employee is disloyal, the Government ought not to be required to permit the continuance of such an employee in its service."[238] However, multiple layers of review based on limited information would do little to check the government's power of removal and ensure that employees' rights were being protected. Abe Fortas, one of the few prominent attorneys who defended employees accused of disloyalty, described the program as one where "appeal is loaded upon appeal, almost to the point of exhaustion of the individual accused and the Government officials concerned."[239] However, "nowhere in the elaborate labyrinth of procedure, devised by the board is there opportunity for the accused employe[e] to come to grips with the real evidence against him."[240] Even Richardson would

---

[234] Bontecou, *The Federal Loyalty-Security Program*, 206.

[235] Truman, "Statement by the President on the Government's Employee Loyalty Program," Nov. 14, 1947, in *Public Papers of the Presidents of the United States: Harry S. Truman*, vol. 1947, 490.

[236] Seth W. Richardson statement, Dec. 23, 1947, 7, 6, Folder "Executive Order 9835 (5 of 5)," Box 24, Records Relating to Loyalty Review Boards, 1947–1952, A1, Entry 1011, LRB, RG 146, NACP; reprinted in "Aims and Procedures Are Outlined by Loyalty Board," *New York Times*, Dec. 28, 1947, 28.

[237] U.S. Civil Service Commission, *66th Annual Report*, 81st Cong., 2nd Sess., H. Doc. 401, 1950, 33.

[238] Richardson statement, Dec. 23, 1947, 10.

[239] Abe Fortas, letter to the editor, *Washington Post*, Jan. 17, 1948, 7; see also Louis Cassels, "Arnold, Fortas, Porter & Prosperity," *Harper's Magazine*, Nov. 1951; Laura Kalman, *Abe Fortas: A Biography* (New Haven, CT: Yale University Press, 1990).

[240] Fortas, letter to the editor.

later concede that the nondisclosure of sources "could not and should not be sustained with regard to a citizen *non*-employee in controversy with the Government. Such practice certainly smacks of unfairness and does not jibe with what is usually done in court."[241]

The secrecy provisions tainted the hearings. If both the employee and the agency loyalty board lacked full information about the charges, the record of the initial hearing would be incomplete and largely worthless in subsequent proceedings. And as critics pointed out, "[t]here is no requirement that the findings of the loyalty board must be supported by the evidence. In fact, there is no requirement that the loyalty board make any findings whatever."[242] Nor did Truman require agencies to provide a proposed decision with a discussion of the evidence once the hearing had concluded. Instead, the employee would receive only a written determination stating whether he should be allowed to keep his job. Although fuller decisions were likely impracticable for agency loyalty boards, their absence was striking in the context of administrative law. The Supreme Court and the Attorney General's Committee had both sharply criticized nonexistent and inadequate proposed decisions, and most agencies had chosen to require more complete reports for parties' guidance. In an ironic turn, provisions protecting examiners from retribution by their agencies made them harder to remove on grounds of disloyalty. The APA required that the CSC fire examiners only on the basis of "good cause," after a hearing and full disclosure of evidence; to the CSC's consternation, this conflicted with the loyalty-security program's less rigorous standards and, given the evidentiary requirements, it would be much more difficult to remove subversive examiners than to remove other bureaucrats with less authority and discretion.[243]

Finally, judicial review was not explicitly provided. Employees who had exhausted their administrative appeals and faced removal by the Loyalty Review Board could ask federal courts to enjoin their removal, but Truman's executive order neither provided for review as a matter of right nor made clear what the standard of review would be. Federal courts were not granted a supervisory role over the loyalty program, and the courts did not demand one. Indeed, the procedures of the loyalty program faced little resistance from the federal courts, which saw no reason to impose strict due process standards in this context.

In the 1950 case of *Bailey v. Richardson*, in which Dorothy Bailey, a labor leader who had fought against racial and gender discrimination in federal

---

[241] Seth W. Richardson, "The Federal Employee Loyalty Program," *Columbia Law Review* 51 (1951): 546–63, 549 (emphasis in the original).

[242] Chafee et al., letter to the editor, *New York Times*, Apr. 13, 1947, 8E.

[243] Bernstein, "The Politics of Adjudication," 313–14, 317; John D. Morris, "U.S. Examiner Held Immune to Ouster," *New York Times,* Dec. 21, 1951, 14. The CSC worked out separate procedures early on (see Seth Richardson to All Departments and Agencies, Memorandum No. 15, July 23, 1948, Folder "Memoranda to All Executive Departments and Agencies, No. 1–No. 57," Box 10, Records Relating to Loyalty Review Boards, 1947–52, A1, Entry 1011, LRB, RG 146, NACP).

hiring, challenged her removal from the U.S. Employment Service, the court of appeals stated that, without a property right in her federal job, Bailey was not entitled to due process when removed from it.[244] The court went further, however, and rejected the due process arguments that the law firm of Arnold, Fortas, and Porter made on her behalf. Bailey had received notice of the specific charges against her, had access to an attorney, and was given the opportunity to engage in oral argument and to present her own evidence. Rejecting the argument that firing an employee required the government to provide "specificity in charges equivalent to that of valid criminal charges, confrontation by witnesses, cross examination … and hearing upon evidence openly submitted," the court found, "[e]ven if the due process clause applies, we would think it does not require so much."[245] Thus reducing to a minimum the procedural protections a federal employee could expect, the court drew no parallels to the standards of adjudication that applied across the rest of the administrative state. Thurmond Arnold, however, saw the decision as more evidence that bureaucrats were "a class apart who may be tried by the Gestapo procedures denounced at Nuremberg."[246]

Even though the law may not have required much in the way of fair procedures, political realities demanded it. The Truman administration chose to equate fairness with procedural protections, even as procedures that had been carefully worked out in the economic context proved to be an awkward fit in testing employee loyalty. However, the APA's clear statement of administrative norms – some of which exceeded constitutional requirements – gave American lawyers a yardstick against which to measure the procedures of the loyalty program.[247] Those comparing the APA to the loyalty program would find the latter wanting, weakening the government's attempts to legitimize the program as a whole. Procedures far from the courtroom model could be justified by the stated urgency of the determinations; those deviating from the administrative model were more problematic, given that the administrative process was designed expressly for efficient operation. Evident in these discussions, however, was the speed with which the APA had come to represent a standard of due process against which other government procedures might struggle to be justified.

The APA's legacy as a "bill of rights" for the administrative process was thus more complicated than that hopeful language suggested. Comparing the

---

[244] *Bailey v. Richardson*, 182 F.2d 46 (D.C. Cir. 1950), *aff'd by an equally divided court*, 341 U.S. 918 (1951); see also Margaret C. Rung, *Servants of the State: Managing Diversity & Democracy in the Federal Workforce, 1933–1953* (Athens: University of Georgia Press, 2002).

[245] *Bailey*, 182 F.2d at 59.

[246] Senate Committee on Labor and Public Welfare, Special Subcommittee on the Establishment of Commission of Ethics in Government, *Establishment of a Commission on Ethics in Government: Hearings*, 82nd Cong., 1st Sess., 1951 (statement of Thurmond Arnold, July 6), 373. My thanks to Dan Ernst for the reference.

[247] See Bontecou, *The Federal Loyalty-Security Program*, 212.

rhetoric that surrounded the APA with its practical effects suggests that the act did more to change opinions about the administrative process than to change the inner workings of the agencies. The act protected existing informal procedures, thus allowing cooperative relationships between regulated parties and agency officials to continue. At the same time, it made sure that those same parties had formal tools to challenge administrative action they opposed. As the Taft-Hartley Act made clear, the APA did not resolve questions about how to separate functions in the agencies and commissions. Nor did it end questions over who should be included in the hearing examiner corps or the appropriate level of judicial review for administrative action.

Triumphalist language surrounding the APA did serve to insulate subsequent administrative activity and administrative reform from attack. As Kenneth Culp Davis famously argued in 1951, "[t]he battle over fundamentals had ceased. The federal administrative process was secure."[248] The act could also be used to attack the administrative process elsewhere. Attorneys skeptical of Truman's loyalty-security program used the act's terms to illustrate the procedural deficiencies of the loyalty boards, and in the immigration context, parties used the idea of procedural protections to extend the procedural rights of businesses to more vulnerable parties. Prolabor interests similarly compared the provisions of the APA to those of the Taft-Hartley Act to point out the degree to which the NLRB was singled out for special scrutiny and highlight the political motives at play. The act nonetheless signaled that procedural due process was now available in the administrative state.

[248] Davis, *Administrative Law*, 9.

3

Congress's Watchful Eye

Less than two months after the Administrative Procedure Act was enacted, President Truman signed into law another bill aimed at fixing the administrative state. Like the APA, the Legislative Reorganization Act of 1946 reflected Congress's fundamental uneasiness that bureaucrats had become the primary makers of law and policy in the modern state.[1] Both statutes were motivated

---

[1] Literature on the Legislative Reorganization Act and Congress includes: George B. Galloway, "Development of the Committee System in the House of Representatives," *American Historical Review* 65 (1959): 17–30; MacAlister Brown, "The Demise of State Department Public Opinion Polls: A Study in Legislative Oversight," *Midwest Journal of Political Science* 5 (1961): 1–17; John F. Bibby, "Committee Characteristics and Legislative Oversight of Administration," *Midwest Journal of Political Science* 10 (1966): 78–98; Nelson W. Polsby, "The Institutionalization of the U.S. House of Representatives," *American Political Science Review* 62 (1968): 144–68; Walter Kravitz, "Evolution of the Senate's Committee System," *Annals of the American Academy of Political and Social Science* 411 (1974): 27–38; Morris S. Ogul, *Congress Oversees the Bureaucracy* (Pittsburgh, PA: University of Pittsburgh Press, 1976); Congressional Quarterly, *Origins and Development of Congress*, 2nd ed. (Washington, DC: CQ Press, 1982); Mathew D. McCubbins and Thomas Schwartz, "Congressional Oversight Overlooked: Police Patrols versus Fire Alarms," *American Journal of Political Science* 28 (1984): 165–79; Joel D. Aberbach, *Keeping a Watchful Eye: The Politics of Congressional Oversight* (Washington, DC: Brookings Institution, 1990); Roger H. Davidson, "The Advent of the Modern Congress: The Legislative Reorganization Act of 1946," *Legislative Studies Quarterly* 15 (1990): 357–73; Walter Kravitz, "The Advent of the Modern Congress: The Legislative Reorganization Act of 1970," *Legislative Studies Quarterly* 15 (1990): 375–99; John Roos, "Thinking about Reform: The World View of Congressional Reformers," *Polity* 25 (1993): 329–54; John J. Coleman, "State Formation and the Decline of Political Parties: American Parties in the Fiscal State," *Studies in American Political Development* 8 (1994): 195–230; Diana Evans, "Congressional Oversight and the Diversity of Members' Goals," *Political Science Quarterly* 109 (1994): 669–87; Paul C. Milazzo, "'An Oxcart in the Age of the Atom': Legislative Reorganization and the Quest for a Modern Congress" (Master's Thesis, University of Virginia, 1994); David H. Rosenbloom, *Building a Legislative-Centered Public Administration: Congress and the Administrative State, 1946–1999* (Tuscaloosa: University of Alabama Press, 2000); David H. Rosenbloom, "1946: Framing a Lasting Congressional Response to the Administrative State," *Administrative Law Review* 50 (1998): 173–97; E. Scott Adler, *Why Congressional Reforms Fail: Reelection and the House Committee System* (Chicago: University of Chicago Press, 2002); Julian E. Zelizer, *On Capitol Hill: The Struggle to Reform Congress and Its Consequences, 1948–2000* (Cambridge:

by a concern about the combination of legislative, executive, and judicial functions in individual agencies *and* by a fundamental distrust of bureaucrats themselves. Congressional reformers described the "widespread congressional and public belief that a grave constitutional crisis exists in which the fate of representative government itself is at stake."[2] This "constitutional crisis"? The fact that "[p]ublic affairs are now handled by a host of administrative agencies headed by nonelected officials with only casual oversight by Congress."[3] Assuming that the agencies and commissions required constant attention (not unlike the industrial conditions administrators were themselves supposed to be supervising), members recognized that they were failing to keep an eye on the administration of the laws that granted agencies and commissions enormous discretion. Nor were other practical checks available; the Roosevelt administration was sympathetic to its agencies, and courts could do little to police administrators acting within their broad statutory authority. For members of Congress hostile to the administrative state, this was the equivalent of no check at all.

Fearing that it was being overshadowed by the White House and by the massive bureaucracies it had spent the past several decades helping construct, and worried about what the bureaucrats were up to, Congress sought to push members toward greater scrutiny of the administrative state. Doing so, however, required a new legislative approach. As Rep. Mike Monroney (D–Ok.) argued, Congress was "the board of directors of the world's largest enterprise," but remained wedded to traditional methods of operation that offered little staff support and few resources for research.[4] The federal government was "a hundred times larger than General Motors, Ford Motor Co., A. T. & T., the Pennsylvania Railroad System, and General Electric all rolled into one," but Congress was "trying to do this work sitting on an old-fashioned high bookkeeper's stool with a slant-top desk, a Civil War ledger, and a quill pen."[5]

Congress thus took a hard look at its own institutional structure. While Congress had, during the past decade, allowed Roosevelt to reorganize the executive branch, empowered the federal courts to create their own rules of procedure, considered judicial reorganization, and authorized multiple investigations

Cambridge University Press, 2004). For studies of Congress more generally, see Roland Young, *The American Congress* (New York: Harper, 1958); Eric Schickler, *Disjointed Pluralism: Institutional Innovation and the Development of the U.S. Congress* (Princeton, NJ: Princeton University Press, 2001); Aaron Wildavsky and Naomi Caiden, *The New Politics of the Budgetary Process*, 4th ed. (New York: Addison Wesley Longman, 2001); Nelson W. Polsby, *How Congress Evolves: Social Bases of Institutional Change* (Oxford: Oxford University Press, 2004); Lewis L. Gould, *The Most Exclusive Club: A History of the Modern United States Senate* (New York: Basic Books, 2005); David R. Mayhew, *Divided We Govern: Party Control, Lawmaking, and Investigations, 1946–2002*, 2nd ed. (New Haven, CT: Yale University Press, 2005).

[2] Joint Committee on the Organization of Congress, *Organization of the Congress*, 79th Cong., 2nd sess., 1946, S. Rep. 1011, 1.

[3] Ibid.

[4] 92 *Cong. Rec.* 10039 (statement of Rep. Mike Monroney, July 25, 1946).

[5] Ibid.

of the administrative state, it had, historian Charles Beard observed in 1942, "never made a thorough inquiry into its own record, into its own weaknesses, and into ways and means of bringing its own organization and procedure into line with modern needs and of raising its standing and competence as a principal branch of National Government."[6] Once Congress finally turned its attention in this direction, it drafted a set of institutional reforms that promised to end administrative abuses of authority by restoring Congress to its rightful place of primacy over the administrative state.[7] The Legislative Reorganization Act of 1946, rooted in a belief that organizational reform could change behavior, revamped the congressional committee structure, combining multiple committees in each house into new standing committees with functionally defined authority mirroring that of the agencies and commissions. These newly specialized committees were affirmatively instructed to engage in "continuous watchfulness" of the agencies and commissions within their jurisdiction; in doing so, they could draw on the expertise of new expert staffers and expanded subpoena power.[8] After 1946, congressional committees would be in a considerably better position to engage in oversight.

This potential for improved oversight was, however, not necessarily translated into actual performance, as it was up to members of Congress to decide how to use their new tools. The act established some necessary preconditions for congressional oversight, but its vague language, lack of enforcement incentives, and failure to grapple with seniority power and the filibuster meant that it did not significantly increase committee surveillance of all agencies' day-to-day operations, end duplication, or overcome partisan motives. While the legal reforms signaled Congress's interest in the fairness of the administrative state, they worked little change in agencies' already legalistic procedures that protected informal access and formal challenges by private interests. Much as Kenneth Culp Davis had observed about the APA, the Legislative Reorganization Act was more of a political achievement than a legal one, signaling the danger of the administrative state and affirming Congress's role in protecting Americans from bureaucrats.[9] At the same time, political imperatives did more than the Legislative Reorganization Act to place agencies under significant scrutiny.

The antibureaucratic sentiments that gave rise to the Legislative Reorganization Act continued after its passage, as oversight continued to

[6] Charles Beard, "In Defense of Congress," *American Mercury*, Nov. 1942, reprinted in *The Organization of Congress – Symposium on Congress by Members of Congress and Others*, 79th Cong., 1st sess., 1945, Joint Committee Print, 5.

[7] See Matthew A. Crenson and Francis E. Rourke, "By Way of Conclusion: American Bureaucracy since World War II," in Louis Galambos, ed., *The New American State: Bureaucracies and Policies since World War II*, 137–77 (Baltimore, MD: Johns Hopkins University Press, 1987); Rosenbloom, *Building a Legislative-Centered Public Administration*.

[8] Legislative Reorganization Act, Pub. L. No. 601, §136, 60 Stat. 812, 832 (1946).

[9] See David H. Rosenbloom, "Retrofitting the Administrative State to the Constitution: Congress and the Judiciary's Twentieth-Century Progress," *Public Administrative Review* 60 (2000): 39–46.

involve significant scrutiny of certain kinds of administrative behavior. This
attention was not necessarily the type of "continuous watchfulness" that the
Joint Committee had envisioned. And in the legal realm as in the administrative one, future efforts to restrict the agencies through statutory reform
were less likely once Congress already had the power to do what it wanted to
do. This was apparent during the late 1940s and early 1950s, as allegations
of corruption and subversion merged to create suspicion around all federal
employees.[10] Although complaints about the unfairness of agency procedures
were less prevalent in the years after the APA, complaints about subversive employees, evidenced in an increasing number of congressional investigations as well as Truman's loyalty-security program, followed naturally
from charges of overly zealous administrators made in earlier years. In this
environment, it was easy for members of Congress to question bureaucrats'
motives and score points off bureaucracy. (The hearings to reappoint ardent
New Dealer Leland Olds as chairman of the Federal Power Commission in
1949, over industry opposition and congressional charges of Communist
influence, offer one example of this tendency.[11]) Concerns about the fairness
of the administrative process gave way to concerns about the fairness of congressional investigations, however, as investigators' own methods diverged
from the kind of due process embodied in the APA. At the same time, charges
of corruption became increasingly common, seemingly at odds with charges
that officials were motivated by radical political beliefs. Over time, questions
of corruption would come to dominate public understanding, and self-serving
behavior would replace administrative zeal as the "problem" to be solved.

By the early 1940s, the idea of fixing Congress in order to fix the agencies
had already become popular among members of Congress and others thinking
seriously about the institution. Complaints about Congress's habit of looking
at the agencies and commissions only once their problems were impossible to
ignore dated back years, and suggestions that Congress should take a more
affirmative role were commonplace.[12] As public administration scholar Arthur
Macmahon observed in 1943, Congress "seeks to be continuously a participant in guiding administrative conduct and the exercise of discretion."[13] By
most accounts, however, Congress was unable to do so.

[10] See David K. Johnson, *The Lavender Scare: The Cold War Persecution of Gays and Lesbians in
the Federal Government* (Chicago: University of Chicago Press, 2004).
[11] Joseph P. Harris, "The Senatorial Rejection of Leland Olds: A Case Study," *American Political
Science Review* 45 (1951): 674–92; Robert A. Caro, *Master of the Senate* (New York: Alfred A.
Knopf, 2002).
[12] Such complaints were evident in the Brookings Institution's 1937 report prepared for Sen. Harry
F. Byrd's investigating committee (Senate Select Committee to Investigate the Executive Agencies
of the Government, "Investigation of Executive Agencies of the Government," 75th Cong., 1st
sess., 1937, S. Rep. 1275); see also Roos, "Thinking about Reform."
[13] Arthur W. Macmahon, "Congressional Oversight of Administration: The Power of the Purse-I,"
Political Science Quarterly 58 (1943): 161–90, 162.

During the early 1940s, members of Congress publicly bemoaned their inability to manage the growth of administrative authority. Reaching out to Americans tired of price controls and wartime bureaucracy, members of all political stripes voiced their concerns that the executive agencies and independent commissions would expand indefinitely, using authority that Congress had given them but could not police. Articles in the popular press – like Sen. Robert La Follette Jr.'s (R–Wisc.) "What's the Matter with Congress?" – pointed to the institution's deficiencies,[14] and Oklahoma Democrat Mike Monroney warned radio listeners that the "monumental problems of supervising the administration of our Government" had "outstripped the machinery of Congress to do an effective job of control."[15] Members of Congress, eager to protest the lawlessness and unfairness of agencies and commissions, could do little about those problems on a day-to-day basis.

Specifically, observers inside and outside Congress claimed that the institution's antiquated structure hindered members' ability to rein in the bureaucrats exercising quasi-legislative and quasi-judicial authority without limits. Charles Beard, writing in *American Mercury*, found that Congress "has stubbornly continued organization forms and methods adapted to an age of handicrafts and small farms," which were "today utterly inadequate for a complete discharge of its constitutional duties."[16] Congress had delegated enormous authority to executive agencies and independent commissions to handle the work it could not do itself; now it appeared Congress could not even handle the job of looking to see what those agencies and commissions were doing. Indeed, Monroney reminded radio listeners, "the job [Congress's] machinery was designed to control was only three one-hundredths of 1 percent the size of the task it has today."[17] The effect of all this, according to the *Washington Post*, was that "Congress is losing face with the American people."[18]

Members who found themselves outmatched by bureaucrats shaped their solutions to match their frustration. During the 78th Congress alone, members introduced more than forty bills targeting their institution's organization and administrative capacity.[19] Many of these proposals, introduced by members ranging from Minnesota Republican William Pittenger to former Socialist Jerry Voorhis of California, sought to replace ad hoc investigating committees

[14] Sen. Robert La Follette Jr., "What's the Matter with Congress?" *The Progressive and La Follette's Magazine*, April 16, 1945, reprinted in *The Organization of Congress – Symposium*, 140.

[15] Rep. Mike Monroney, "Streamlining Congress," radio address, Sept. 13, 1944, reprinted in *The Organization of Congress – Symposium*, 144–45.

[16] Beard, *The Organization of Congress – Symposium*, 4.

[17] Monroney, "Streamlining Congress," *The Organization of Congress – Symposium*, 145.

[18] "Study of Congress," *Washington Post*, June 27, 1944, 6.

[19] See Marshall E. Dimock, "Administrative Efficiency within a Democratic Polity," from *New Horizons in Public Administration* (University: University of Alabama Press, 1945), reprinted in *The Organization of Congress – Symposium*, 29; for a more detailed discussion, see John A. Perkins, "American Government and Politics: Congressional Self-Improvement," *American Political Science Review* 38 (1944): 499–511.

with strong permanent ones engaging in consistent scrutiny of the administrative state. These proposals varied widely in form; the Smith Committee had proposed a single Joint Committee on Executive Agencies and Procedures to engage in such scrutiny, while Rep. Everett Dirksen (R–Ill.) recommended a new Joint Committee on Administrative Review to scrutinize all agency-made rules and regulations before they took effect.[20] Rep. Pittenger recommended that joint committees should collect information about the agencies and commissions, and Rep. Voorhis suggested instead that oversight be placed in the existing standing committees. Additional bills moved to improve congressional staffing and address the lack of information members had about what was going on inside agencies and commissions. The latter was of particular concern; Rep. Estes Kefauver (D–Tenn.) proposed giving House members an opportunity to question agency officials on a regular basis,[21] and Rep. Monroney suggested "that a 'house dick,' empowered to knock on the doors of the agencies and say, 'Who are you, what have you got in there and what are you doing?' would do the most good."[22] Once modern tools were in hand, members anticipated, Congress could take charge of bureaucrats run amok.

In place of these immediate reforms, however, members of the 78th Congress adopted the resolution offered by Rep. Monroney and Sen. Francis Maloney (D–Conn.) to first conduct an in-depth study of Congress by Congress – its committee system, its staffing, and, crucially, its relationship with the executive branch. While the specifics of administrative procedure had been debated in agency offices and in the pages of law journals for decades, little background material comparable to the studies of the Attorney General's Committee on Administrative Procedure existed to help congressional reformers. Members thus embarked on their own investigation of the topic, headed by Monroney and Maloney (the latter replaced after his death in January 1945 by Sen. Robert M. La Follette Jr., a Republican progressive whose sympathetic investigation of civil liberties in the late 1930s had illuminated growing pains at the NLRB).[23] The Joint Committee on the Organization of Congress, established in December 1944, included many with strong views about the proper relationship between Congress and the agencies. Members included Florida New Dealer Sen. Claude Pepper (D–Fla.), Sen. Richard Russell (D–Ga.), who had broken with the New Deal over Roosevelt's court-packing plan, ardent anti-New Dealer Rep. Eugene Cox (D–Ga.), Sen. Wayland Brooks (R–Ill.), a conservative opponent of wartime bureaucracy, and Rep. Dirksen, a Republican critical of excessive government spending.

---

[20] See House Select Committee to Investigate Executive Agencies, *Seventh Intermediate Report*, 78th Cong., 2nd sess., 1944, H. Rep. 1912.

[21] Estes Kefauver, "The Need for Better Executive-Legislative Teamwork in the National Government," *American Political Science Review* 38 (1944): 317–25.

[22] Rep. Mike Monroney, quoted in Robert C. Albright, "Reorganizing Congress This Session Depends on Luck o' the Irish," *Washington Post*, Sept. 3, 1944, B6.

[23] Jerold S. Auerbach, "The La Follette Committee: Labor and Civil Liberties in the New Deal," *Journal of American History* 51 (1964): 435–59.

The Joint Committee drew from the testimony and written statements of members of Congress, congressional staffers, agency representatives, lawyers, and political scientists; members also looked to editorials, articles, and formal studies conducted by the American Political Science Association's Committee on Congress and by Robert Heller for the National Planning Association.[24] With encouragement from the Senate Rules Committee, which complained that Congress was "severely handicapped" in keeping up with the administrative agencies, the problem of bureaucratic power became a major focus of Congress.[25]

Opinions and suggestions ranged widely, but most parties agreed that too much power had shifted away from Congress to the executive agencies and independent commissions. Witnesses repeated now familiar concerns about Congress's inability to do anything about it. Conservative anti-New Dealer Rep. Homer Capehart (R–Ind.) complained about the "superduper-superduper" federal government,[26] while Georgia Democrat and civil service expert Robert Ramspeck reflected that Congress's relationship to the executive branch "reminds me of a little colt trying to keep up with a race horse."[27] Joint Committee member Rep. Eugene Cox – who two years earlier had remarked on the House floor that "we are living under a government of dictatorship by bureaucrats"[28] – criticized the idea of a "browbeaten and feather-legged Congress" that did nothing more than follow the lead of the executive branch.[29]

Certainly much of this concern stemmed from the tensions between the legislative and executive branches that had been growing since during the Roosevelt administration. Congress had rebuffed President Roosevelt's 1937 executive reorganization proposal, based in part on his expert committee's assumption that the president, not Congress, should be in charge of the independent commissions; members viewed this as an attempt to strengthen the

[24] George B. Galloway et al, "Congress – Problems, Diagnosis, Proposals: Second Progress Report of the American Political Science Association's Committee on Congress," *American Political Science Review* 36 (1942): 1091–102; American Political Science Association, Committee on Congress, *The Reorganization of Congress* (Washington, DC: Public Affairs Press, 1945); Robert Heller, *Strengthening the Congress*, Planning Pamphlet No. 39 (Washington, DC: National Planning Association, 1945); see also Lawrence H. Chamberlain, "Congress – Diagnosis and Prescription," *Political Science Quarterly* 60 (1945): 437–45; Donald R. Matthews, "American Political Science and Congressional Reform: The American Political Science Association's Committee on Congress (1941–1945) and Study of Congress (1965–1973)," *Social Science History* 5 (1981): 91–120.

[25] Senate Rules Committee, *Establishing a Joint Committee on the Organization of the Congress*, 78th Cong., 2nd sess., 1944, S. Rep. 1034, 2.

[26] Joint Committee on the Organization of Congress, *Organization of Congress: Hearings*, pt. 2, 79th Cong., 1st sess., 1945 (statement of Rep. Homer E. Capehart, April 6), 260.

[27] Joint Committee on the Organization of Congress, *Organization of Congress: Hearings*, pt. 2 (statement of Rep. Robert Ramspeck, April 17), 304.

[28] 89 *Cong. Rec.* 185 (statement of Rep. Eugene Cox, Jan. 14, 1943).

[29] Joint Committee on the Organization of Congress, *Organization of Congress: Hearings*, pt. 1, (statement of Rep. Cox, March 15), 31.

executive branch at Congress's expense. Several sitting members of Congress, including Cox, also had stinging memories of the White House's intervention in the 1938 Democratic primaries. And as more and more legislation origi-nated in the White House and in the agencies, members feared what a *Los Angeles Times* reporter called the "grave danger" that Congress would "turn itself into a mere rubber stamp for the President."[30] House members in 1944, concerned that the United States was "becoming more and more a government by directive rather than a government of laws," even launched a study into the use of executive orders, many of which "appear to have neither statutory nor constitutional justification."[31]

Members framed their efforts as part of a broader ideological choice between democracy and bureaucracy. The problem was not that Congress had ceded power to the White House, members argued, but rather that policy-making authority had shifted out of the hands of democratically elected officials into the hands of unaccountable bureaucrats. Cox described the "little fellows put in charge of the administration of the law setting up rules and regulations having all the force and effect of law and they come down upon the people and simply strip them of all of their rights."[32] Congressional control was an essential part of preserving democratic values, political scientist Leonard White suggested, "since an uncontrolled body of permanent officials and employees would almost certainly degenerate into a bureaucracy, with all the unpleasant connotations of that word."[33] Some sort of democratic check was imperative.

The strength of Congress mattered, then, not just for Congress but for American democracy. Here antibureaucratic politics emerged in full force. As La Follette had earlier reasoned, congressional reform was necessary if "control of governmental policy is to remain with the people's elected representatives" rather than "drift into the hands of a relatively irresponsible bureaucracy."[34] More than just congressional power was at stake; as Rep. Martin Dies derided the "irresponsible, unrepresentative, crackpot, radical bureaucrats" working in wartime and civilian agencies in 1943, he argued that "we are rapidly approach-ing a period in America when the real power and function of government will not be exercised in this Chamber, but it will be exercised by bureaucracy."[35]

---

[30] E. C. Krauss, "Congress Needs a Change, Too," *Los Angeles Times*, Oct. 28, 1944, A4.

[31] Senate Judiciary Committee, *Continuing the Authority for a Study into the Legal and Constitutional Authority for the Issuance of Executive Orders of the President and of Departmental Regulations, and Increasing the Limit of Expenditures*, 79th Cong., 1st sess., 1945, S. Rep. 7, 2; on executive dominance, see Schickler, *Disjointed Pluralism*; Joseph Cooper, "The Twentieth-Century Congress," in Lawrence C. Dodd and Bruce I. Oppenheimer, eds., *Congress Reconsidered*, 7th ed., 335–66 (Washington, DC: CQ Press, 2001).

[32] Joint Committee on the Organization of Congress, *Organization of Congress: Hearings* pt. 1 (statement of Rep. Eugene Cox, March 22), 122.

[33] Leonard D. White, "Congressional Control of the Public Service," *American Political Science Review* 39 (1945): 1–11, 11.

[34] Robert M. La Follette Jr., "A Senator Looks at Congress," *Atlantic Monthly*, July 1943, reprinted in *The Organization of Congress – Symposium*, 135.

[35] 89 *Cong. Rec.* 479, 477 (statement of Rep. Martin Dies, Feb. 1, 1943).

Calling bureaucracy "as deadly and poisonous as any form of fascism there is," Dies suggested America was on the path to totalitarian government.[36]

The solution, Congress found, was to improve itself. As George Galloway, a public administration scholar and the chairman of the APSA's Committee on Congress, suggested, "[a] stronger and more representative legislature" was "the antidote to bureaucracy."[37] Rep. Voorhis complained that Congress had resorted to defending its relevance "merely by voting against proposals of the Executive, without putting forward any alternative constructive program of its own."[38] A variety of proposals thus aimed to restore Congress's primacy in setting the national policy agenda and drafting its own laws. Finding congressional policy making "splintered and uncoordinated," the Joint Committee recommended that majority and minority policy committees be created in each house.[39] Heller had suggested this reform, hoping it "could furnish an effective mechanism for the exercise of party leadership and a focus for party responsibility and accountability."[40] The emphasis was on bringing members together to discuss these issues; members assumed that these structural changes could solve more intractable substantive problems. What kind of policy such committees might make as a result was left unaddressed.

Administrative oversight was a trickier problem, involving as it did dozens of agencies and thousands of bureaucrats. The APSA's Committee on Congress found the job of overseeing administrative work to be "probably the most important function of Congress,"[41] and Heller's report similarly suggested that one of Congress's primary functions was to "[h]old the executive branch accountable."[42] This accountability required Congress to "continuously review administrative interpretations, rules, and procedures in order to make certain that they conform with the intent of Congressional legislation."[43] However, the APSA's committee found that existing congressional oversight tools "proved inadequate as legislative checks on administrative action," and witnesses before the Joint Committee repeatedly emphasized that Congress was failing to meet its responsibilities in this area.[44]

Congress blamed its own short attention span, evident in its tendency to pass broad legislation and then abdicate the field. Rep. Voorhis reminded members: "We do a lazy sort of job, we just say 'Here is a big problem,' and, therefore,

---

[36] Ibid., 479.
[37] George B. Galloway, "On Reforming Congress," *Free World*, June 1944, reprinted in *The Organization of Congress – Symposium*, 64.
[38] Joint Committee on the Organization of Congress, *Organization of Congress: Hearings*, pt. 1 (statement of Rep. Jerry Voorhis, March 15), 29.
[39] Special Committee on the Organization of Congress, *Legislative Reorganization Act of 1946*, 79th Cong., 2nd sess., 1946, S. Rep. 1400, 4.
[40] Heller, *Strengthening the Congress*, 14 (emphasis removed from the original).
[41] APSA Committee on Congress, *The Reorganization of Congress*, 14.
[42] Heller, *Strengthening the Congress*, 4.
[43] Ibid.
[44] APSA Committee on Congress, *The Reorganization of Congress*, 55.

we empower so-and-so to solve the problem, and appropriate so much money to enable him to do it."[45] Any resulting oversight of an agency's operations depended more on the whims of individual members than on institutional forces. The House Committee for Expenditures in the Executive Departments was among the standing committees that were supposed to keep an eye on the executive agencies, but, as the *Chicago Tribune* reported with disappointment, "The New Dealers saw the threat it held over their wild expenditures and packed it with docile Democrats."[46]

Picking up the slack were special committees, like those chaired by Rep. Howard W. Smith (D–Va.) and Sen. Harry Truman (D-Mo.), created explicitly to investigate agency operations. As a form of oversight, however, these ad hoc investigating committees were spotty at best and negligent at worst. Because heading a powerful special investigation was widely considered a path to political prominence, members flocked to high-profile issues and left more mundane matters to fester. As Voorhis reminisced some years later, "many congressional investigations are launched because some member who is not unpopular with his colleagues simply wants to be chairman of an investigation committee."[47] Members of such a committee had the incentive to justify their existence (and expenses) by finding something to criticize. As one study group put it, aggressive action by an agency whose "existence depends upon retaining the confidence of the legislature" was thus discouraged.[48]

Committee duplication and inefficiency were significant concerns, as there was no limit to the number of committees that could operate at any one time. By one senator's count, during the 79th Congress alone, there were more than 30 existing and proposed special and select investigating committees in the Senate, and more than 100 in the House.[49] Not surprisingly, these committees often duplicated the work of the standing committees and each another, wasting the time of members of Congress and agency officials alike. Moreover, because special committees often lacked the authority to introduce bills, any legislative reforms they proposed still had to go through a standing committee. Having members' own political orientations, aspirations, and personal vendettas, rather than their expertise in a particular area, drive the investigations was widely recognized as a poor path to systematic oversight.

The embarrassment of Rep. Eugene "Goober" Cox's 1943 investigation of the FCC – during which Cox pulled the hair of another representative on the floor of the House – was only the most recent reminder of this

[45] Joint Committee on the Organization of Congress, *Organization of Congress: Hearings*, pt. 1 (statement of Rep. Voorhis, Mar. 15), 39.
[46] "How to Get Things Done," *Chicago Daily Tribune*, Dec. 6, 1943, 16.
[47] Jerry Voorhis, "Congressional Investigations: Inner Workings," *University of Chicago Law Review* 18 (1951): 455–63, 456.
[48] Board of Investigation and Research, *Report on Practices and Procedures of Governmental Control*, 78th Cong., 2nd sess., 1944, H. Doc. 678, 10.
[49] Joint Committee on the Organization of Congress, *Organization of Congress: Hearings*, pt. 3 (written statement of Sen. John L. McClellan, May 25), 657–67.

tendency.[50] In 1943, the FCC and its chairman, James L. Fly, were already under fire from broadcasting interests and from members of Congress for their activist definition of the FCC's "public interest" standard, evidenced in the Dies Committee's charges about the loyalty of certain FCC staffers.[51] Cox, a strident opponent of Fly's leadership, had in 1942 accused Fly of "a monstrous abuse of power" and suggested he was "rapidly becoming the most dangerous man in the Government."[52] Cox became even angrier in early 1943, when FCC officials, upon learning that Cox had accepted $2,500 from a radio station in Albany, Georgia, in exchange for his help in obtaining a broadcast license, asked the Justice Department to investigate this apparent violation of federal law.

Once the FCC began license renewal proceedings for the station in January 1943, Cox convinced House members to create a Select Committee to Investigate the Federal Communications Commission, chaired by Cox himself. Defending his own investigation, Cox painted an unsavory picture of the FCC as "a nest of 'reds'" and "the nastiest nest of rats to be found in this entire country."[53] Cox also reported what he said were widespread complaints that Fly "was undertaking to set up a despotic dictatorship over all media of communication."[54] His investigation would help Americans fight back, Cox argued on the floor of the House, and "will operate as a depressant upon the bureaucrats seeking to swallow up all legislative power which belongs alone to Congress and should be of like concern to you."[55]

The Cox Committee was met with skepticism from its inception, given the chairman's obvious conflict of interest. Echoing complaints about agency unfairness, one Wisconsin newspaper asked for Cox's resignation on the grounds that one "cannot be judge, prosecutor and defendant at the same time."[56] As columnist Drew Pearson suggested, by allowing Cox's self-interested investigation, Congress was "conducting a unique exhibition of how to lose the confidence of the Nation."[57] In May, before the committee began its hearings but

---

[50] Robert De Vore, "Cox, Irked by Radio Talk, Pulls Rogers' Hair on House Floor," *Washington Post*, May 19, 1943, 1; H. H. Wilson, *Congress: Corruption and Compromise* (New York: Rinehart & Company, 1951), chap. 4.

[51] Erik Barnouw, *The Golden Web: A History of Broadcasting in the United States*, vol. II, *1933 to 1953* (New York: Oxford University Press, 1968); Susan L. Brinson, *The Red Scare, Politics, and the Federal Communications Commission, 1941–1960* (Westport, CT: Praeger, 2004).

[52] 88 *Cong. Rec.* 794 (statement of Rep. Eugene Cox, Jan. 28, 1942).

[53] 89 *Cong. Rec.* 235 (statement of Rep. Eugene Cox, Jan. 19, 1943); see also "House Orders Investigation of FCC Setup," *Washington Post*, Jan. 20, 1943, 1; Robert D. Leigh, "Politicians v. Bureaucrats," *Harper's Magazine*, Jan. 1945.

[54] 89 *Cong. Rec.* 235 (statement of Rep. Cox, Jan. 19. 1943).

[55] Ibid., 234.

[56] Editorial in *Capital Times*, Madison, WI, Jan. 24, 1943, reprinted in ACLU, "Memorandum in support of the Memorial to the House of Representatives for Fair Play to the Federal Communications Commission," 29, File No. 12-12e, Organizations Cox Committee Protests & Endorsements, Box 16, General Correspondence 1927–1946, A1, Entry 100A, OED, RG 173, NACP.

[57] Drew Pearson, "The Washington Merry-Go-Round," *Washington Post*, Apr. 10, 1943, B9.

well after a flurry of subpoenas for FCC records, FCC Commissioner Clifford J. Durr asked Speaker Sam Rayburn (D-Tex.) to remove Cox from the committee given his apparent prejudice against the commission. The *Washington Post*, leaked the information by Durr, agreed that "it is not the reputation and prestige of the FCC that is at stake in this instance but that of the House itself."[58] Once hearings began in July, the commission's fears were realized. House committee members demanded FCC commissioners' personal financial records, probed the FCC's reluctance to turn the fingerprints of licensees over to the FBI, looked into whether the FCC had demanded too many draft exemptions for its staff, and held hearings on whether the FCC had hurt the war effort by failing to transfer authority over illegal and unlicensed broadcasts and interference to the War and Navy Departments. Certain members of the committee would later conclude that the FCC had engaged in political chicanery in licensing proceedings and that it had at various times "employed its powers to reward its political friends," had "sought to punish newspapers politically opposed to the administration" through its rules regarding newspaper ownership of broadcast stations, had "endangered the national security and interfered with the prosecution of the war," and had been "in part responsible for the disaster at Pearl Harbor."[59]

Cox was hammered by the press for months over his investigation, which appeared to adopt the same kinds of secretive and unfair procedures he and others had criticized in the agencies. Once the hearings began, FCC officials had no opportunity to defend themselves, even as evidence damaging to the FCC was welcomed. Early on, Fly publicized a memo purportedly sent by the committee's counsel to its members, with suggested strategies to "keep the commission's side of the case from reaching the public."[60] A *Washington Post* editorial characterized Cox's investigation as "deliberate harassment" and complained that Cox had adopted "the most flagrant star chamber proceedings."[61] Hearings began during the summer recess, only after one of the Democrats on the committee had left Washington for the summer.[62] Fly himself embarked on a counterattack, writing letters and holding press conferences to rebut the Cox Committee's specific charges and trumpeting the insincerity of the investigation. Claiming that Congress's investigatory power was "too essential an instrument for maintaining the health of our body politic to permit it to be prostituted for personal vengeance," Fly argued that "the committee has sought the headlines by twisting and distorting meager evidence carefully calculated to do injury to the commission and its personnel."[63] He excoriated the staff's practice of

[58] "Biased Investigation," *Washington Post*, May 14, 1943, 10.
[59] House Select Committee to Investigate the Federal Communications Commission, *Investigation of the Federal Communications Commission: Final Report*, 78th Cong., 2nd sess., 1945, H. Rep. 2095, 54, 55.
[60] "Fly Charges Cox with Plan to Seize Headlines," *Los Angeles Times*, July 16, 1943, 17.
[61] "Box and Cox," *Washington Post*, July 7, 1943, 14.
[62] Edward Ryan, "Rep. Magnuson to Force FCC Showdown," *Washington Post*, Sept. 28, 1943, 1.
[63] James L. Fly, letter to the editor, *New York Times*, Aug. 22, 1943, 8E.

eliciting testimony without committee members present, so that the most damaging parts could be extracted and read into the public record.[64]

Many were sympathetic to Fly and to the FCC; Rep. Samuel Weiss (D–Pa.) wrote to Fly that Americans "were losing respect for Congress when Congress by its action permitted an accused – in a serious case – to become the judge, prosecutor and jury against the prosecuting agency."[65] American Civil Liberties Union director Roger Baldwin condemned the committee's methods, "so plainly violative of the most elementary rules of fair play,"[66] and the ACLU published a pamphlet protesting the unfairness of proceedings driven by "the interests of the personal grievances of the chairman and of powerful forces determined to discredit governmental regulation of radio."[67] The pamphlet also gathered negative editorials from around the country, giving readers a sense of nationwide opposition; according to the *Austin American*, Congress's "palpably unfair action further discredits a body which already has an uneasy hold on the average citizen's confidence."[68]

Fed up with the House Judiciary Committee's refusal to remove Cox as chair, the publisher of the *Washington Post* printed an open letter to Speaker Rayburn asking for Cox's removal and suggesting that the Cox Committee was "a mockery of basic American traditions of fair play. It has been a star chamber; it has been black with bias; it has sought to terrorize those who exposed the chairman's own corrupt practices."[69] Pressured by Congress, Cox resigned from the Select Committee in what the *Washington Post* called "a clearcut victory for constructive journalism."[70] The FCC probe continued under a new, more judicious chairman, and the committee concluded its work with a report questioning the legitimacy of its own investigation and noting the "innumerable bitter conflicts largely based on personal interests and animosities," which had interfered with actual oversight.[71] Overall, it concluded that Fly, who was no longer at the FCC, left the commission "better than he found it" and suggested that the committee rather than the FCC, had been guilty of excess zeal.[72]

---

[64] Ibid.

[65] Samuel A. Weiss to James L. Fly, Oct. 5, 1943, File No. 12-12E, Organization Cox Investigation, Box 16, General Correspondence 1927–1946, A1, Entry 100A, OED, RG 173, NACP.

[66] Roger N. Baldwin to James L. Fly, Sept. 3, 1943, File No. 12-12E, Organization Cox Investigation, Box 16, General Correspondence 1927–1946, A1, Entry 100A, OED, RG 173, NACP.

[67] ACLU, "Memorandum in support of the Memorial to the House of Representatives for Fair Play to the Federal Communications Commission," Sept. 1943, 6, File No. 12-12e, Organizations Cox Committee Protests & Endorsements, Box 16, General Correspondence 1927–1946, A1, Entry 100A, OED, RG 173, NACP.

[68] *American*, Austin, TX, July 5, 1943, reprinted in ACLU, "Memorandum in support of the Memorial to the House of Representatives for Fair Play to the Federal Communications Commission," 29.

[69] Eugene Meyer, "A Public Letter to Speaker Rayburn," *Washington Post*, Sept. 27, 1943, 1.

[70] Ernest Lindley, "Editorial Victory," *Washington Post*, Oct. 4, 1943, 11.

[71] House Select Committee to Investigate the Federal Communications Commission, *Investigation of the Federal Communications Commission: Final Report*, 51.

[72] Ibid., 52.

Two different conclusions from the Cox Committee's work were possible: either the FCC was entirely lawless, or the Cox Committee had been. Many in Congress and in the news media assumed the latter; columnist Merlo Pusey looked at the Cox, Dies, and Kerr Committees as evidence that "Congress is angry and is striking out at 'bureaucrats' with any weapon that seems to be handy."[73] Both conclusions led to the same result, however: Congress needed to find a better way of dealing with the agencies and commissions. As Pusey continued, Congress "has reason to be perturbed by the vast gangling bureaucracy" but should "be thinking about the infinitely bigger job of enacting legislation to regulate the quasi-judicial and regulatory agencies."[74]

Although such events made it clear that the oversight process needed reform, they did not offer obvious solutions. The bills to reform administrative procedure pending before the judiciary committees in the 78th and 79th Congresses targeted administrators' discretion but did little to improve Congress's own authority. Limiting administrative power while increasing congressional power could have been accomplished in a variety of ways, most particularly by amending the substantive laws for each agency and commission. Rep. Voorhis called on Congress to stop giving agencies broad grants of power and instead pass specific legislation – for example "a real, honest-to-goodness law about the thing which would not have to place any great degree of discretion in anybody's hands but which would outline in the law itself just how the thing is to work."[75] However, this assumed Congress was willing or able to do this work. New statutes would still demand institutional knowledge and expertise before greater specificity would be possible, and revising existing statutes would require Congress to grapple with the industries and interest groups that had built up in each area. Nor was it clear that members of Congress had gone so far as to agree on what specific changes they wanted to see in, for example, the Federal Power Commission or the Maritime Commission.

Instead, assuming that the institution itself was to blame for the oversight problem, witnesses proposed several solutions targeting Congress's existing organization and committee structure. Rep. Estes Kefauver, a liberal Democratic reformer from Tennessee, repeated his earlier suggestion that requiring administrative officers to report to the House for questioning on a regular basis would encourage them to be more scrupulous.[76] Other proposals that had found little success in previous sessions of Congress, including those to give standing committees additional responsibility for oversight and to create new committees to shoulder some of the burden, were also offered to the Joint Committee for their consideration. Rep. Smith reiterated his suggestion of a permanent joint committee to keep on top of administrative decisions and orders instead of

---

[73] Merlo Pusey, "Wartime Washington," *Washington Post*, May 19, 1943, 11.
[74] Ibid.
[75] Joint Committee on the Organization of Congress, *Organization of Congress: Hearings*, pt. 1 (statement of Rep. Voorhis, Mar. 15), 39.
[76] Joint Committee on the Organization of Congress, *Organization of Congress: Hearings*, pt. 1 (statement of Rep. Estes Kefauver, Mar. 16), 79–80.

waiting until "somebody comes to your office or mine and complains that this agency has done so-and-so."[77] Sen. John McClellan (D–Ark.) proposed a permanent Joint Committee on Administrative Practices and Efficiency, remarking that agencies would be deterred from mischief knowing "that there existed a permanent investigating committee ready, willing, and able to investigate and supervise their conduct."[78]

This proactive structural approach was adopted, with some tweaks, by the Joint Committee as it attempted to move Congress away from the special-committee model of investigation and oversight. The Legislative Reorganization Act placed authority squarely in the standing committees "to carry on continuing review and oversight of legislation and agencies within their jurisdiction"[79] – a vision consistent with Robert Heller's advice that Congress should use its oversight authority "in a systematic, thorough, and regular manner, not in a sporadic, hit-or-miss, disorganized fashion."[80] Oversight authority – the duty of engaging in "continuous watchfulness" of the agencies and commissions – was handed to those committees presumed to have the most expertise about the area being regulated and the greatest interest in keeping an eye on the regulators.[81] Monroney expressed his hope that oversight would become "fully half the work" of the standing committees.[82] As he explained to his committee, Congress's responsibility "is not finished when we pass legislation. It is also to see how that legislation works" once the agency administered it.[83] "If that policy is not in line with what the standing committee had in mind when it passed the legislation," he suggested, "we should have each month a chance to bring that policy into line with what the committee intended because, after all, they know more about it than the rest of Congress because they had hearings on it."[84] The Joint Committee expressed its hope that this reform would foster better relations between Congress and the agencies, creating "an open channel of complaints of agency shortcomings or abuses of authority."[85]

Eliminating special and select investigating committees could give the standing committees room to adopt a more judicious approach. Administrative law scholar Nathaniel Nathanson was optimistic that these congressional committees could take "an over-all point of view" toward regulation that could give rise to "a healthy, mutual respect between the committee and administrator,

[77] Joint Committee on the Organization of Congress, *Organization of Congress: Hearings*, pt. 1 (statement of Rep. Howard W. Smith, Mar. 28), 194.

[78] Joint Committee on the Organization of Congress, *Organization of Congress: Hearings*, pt. 3 (written statement of Sen. John L. McClellan, May 25), 655.

[79] Joint Committee on the Organization of Congress, *Organization of the Congress*, 5.

[80] Heller, *Strengthening the Congress*, 4.

[81] Legislative Reorganization Act § 136.

[82] Mike Monroney, "Congress' Slender New Shoes Will Pinch Some Toes at First," *Washington Post*, Aug. 4, 1946, B3.

[83] Joint Committee on the Organization of Congress, *Organization of Congress: Hearings*, pt. 4 (statement of Rep. Mike Monroney, June 1), 735.

[84] Ibid.

[85] Joint Committee on the Organization of Congress, *Organization of the Congress*, 6.

both of whom have a common objective and, in substantial measure, a common fund of information."[86] Price Administrator Chester Bowles, who reminded the Joint Committee of the "atmosphere of suspicion, charges, and misunderstanding" that developed when Congress and agency representatives met only during times of crisis, similarly suggested that discussions between the OPA and congressional committees "would result in improvement in our own operation and I am sure that it would result in an improvement in the understanding of Congress of the problems."[87]

For this to happen, however, major reorganization was needed, as the Joint Committee agreed that Congress's existing committee structure was inadequate to handle the newly defined task of oversight. Congress's organization had developed unevenly over time, and the jurisdiction of the standing committees was sometimes illogical and often redundant. Nor were the special and select committees the only sources of duplication; membership on many different standing committees added to the existing workload of members of Congress (which the Joint Committee found "too heavy to bear") and multiplied that of agency officials testifying before them.[88] As the head of the National Housing Agency reflected, "the task of the administrator would be eased if he had more continuous contact with the Congress through a simplified committee structure requiring fewer points of contact."[89] Fewer committees would help both Congress and the agencies.

The Legislative Reorganization Act thus completely overhauled the existing committee structure in light of Congress's oversight responsibilities. Each major policy area was placed under the jurisdiction of a single standing committee in each house, and the number of such committees was dramatically reduced: from 33 to 15 in the Senate, and from 48 to 19 in the House. Acknowledging the need to adjust congressional organization to that of the administrative state, the Joint Committee organized the committees by the content of regulatory policy; the committees thus largely mirrored each other (with the notable exception of the House Committee on Un-American Activities, which had no official Senate counterpart).[90] In several cases, this led to significant consolidation. The Senate Committee on Interior, Natural Resources, and Public Works, for example, absorbed nine committees: Commerce, Indian Affairs, Interoceanic Canals, Irrigation and Reclamation, Mines and Mining, Public Buildings and Grounds, Public Lands and Surveys, and Territories and Insular Affairs. This also meant, however, that the task of oversight was not evenly

---

[86] Nathaniel L. Nathanson, "Some Comments on the Administrative Procedure Act," *Illinois Law Review* 41 (1946): 368–422, 421, 422.

[87] Joint Committee on the Organization of Congress, *Organization of Congress: Hearings*, pt. 4, (statement of Chester Bowles, June 1), 729, 733–34.

[88] Special Committee on the Organization of Congress, *Legislative Reorganization Act of 1946*, 3; see also APSA Committee on Congress, *The Reorganization of Congress*, 37–46.

[89] Joint Committee on the Organization of Congress, *Organization of Congress: Hearings*, pt. 3 (statement of John B. Blandford Jr., May 14), 513.

[90] See Rosenbloom, *Building a Legislative-Centered Public Administration*.

distributed; the Senate Committee on Interstate and Foreign Commerce, which had the same number of members as the Senate Committee on the District of Columbia, had responsibility for, among other things, six of the most powerful independent commissions (the ICC, the SEC, the FTC, the FCC, the Civil Aeronautics Board, and the Federal Power Commission).[91]

The Joint Committee's conception of oversight extended beyond the duty of "continuous watchfulness" given to the standing committees. Additional checks on agency spending were to come from the Committees on Appropriations and the Committees on Expenditures in the Executive Departments in each house. Although Congress was legally responsible for supervising agencies' spending, the Joint Committee concluded that, under Congress's present setup, there was little it could do. At the same time that agencies had "ample funds to collect and present evidence to support their appeal" for funds, Congress lacked "adequate facilities for scrutinizing these justifications" and was unable "to resist the pressure of departments and agencies in behalf of larger expenditures."[92] To address this problem, the Legislative Reorganization Act gave the two committees on Expenditures in the Executive Departments explicit authority over budgeting, accounting, and, most broadly, "studying the operation of Government activities at all levels" to determine the "economy and efficiency" of federal activities.[93] At the same time, the four committees with jurisdiction over spending – the House Ways and Means and Appropriations committees and the Senate Finance and Appropriations committees – were instructed to develop a yearly "legislative budget" – a single resolution containing all anticipated federal spending for the next fiscal year that would allow Congress to plan overall appropriations for the year rather than reacting to individual budget requests.

The combination of topical standing committees, appropriations committees, and expenditures committees was, George Galloway later explained, intended to create a "three-way division of labor in the performance of the oversight function."[94] This also meant, of course, that between the two houses, each agency would be responsible to six committees. Two of these – the Committees on Expenditures in the Executive Departments – had roving authority to inquire into the operations of the administrative state that appeared to purposely duplicate that of the standing committees. The division of oversight authority was tidy on paper, but it contained clear areas of overlap.[95]

[91] For summaries of the Legislative Reorganization Act's provisions, see Aaron L. Ford, "The Legislative Reorganization Act of 1946," *American Bar Association Journal* 32 (1946): 741–44 and 808–09; Charles W. Shull, "The Legislative Reorganization Act of 1946," *Temple Law Quarterly* 20 (1947): 375–95.

[92] Joint Committee on the Organization of Congress, *Organization of the Congress*, 19.

[93] Legislative Reorganization Act §§ 102 (g)(2)(B), 121(h)(2)(B).

[94] Senate Committee on Expenditures in the Executive Departments, *Legislative Reorganization Act of 1946: Hearings on Evaluation of Legislative Reorganization Act of 1946*, 80th Cong., 2nd sess., 1948 (statement of George B. Galloway, Feb. 18), 121.

[95] See Joseph P. Harris, "The Reorganization of Congress," *Public Administration Review* 6 (1946): 267–82, 279.

Responding to complaints from members and other witnesses, the Joint Committee also took steps to address additional aspects of congressional operation that noticeably hindered Congress's ability to keep up with the agencies and commissions. In response to members' grumbling about their daunting workloads, new explicit limitations on members' committee assignments were imposed to reduce some of these obligations.[96] Title IV of the Legislative Reorganization Act (better known as the Federal Tort Claims Act), and Title V (the General Bridge Act), moved responsibility for bridge issues and small personal claims against the government out of Congress, thus significantly reducing the amount of time members were required to devote to these minor but numerous matters.

Another impediment was members' and committees' limited staff assistance. Like the president, Congress needed help; as Heller argued, members "*should not spend one working minute on anything that somebody else can do just as well.*"[97] Lacking their own research staff, members depended on the executive branch for information. Rep. Dirksen joined many of his colleagues in his annoyance with officials who "have all the facts at their finger tips, but all they need to tell us is what they want us to know."[98] Frustrated, he continued, "We don't even know enough to ask the right questions. It's a sort of combination quiz program and fishing expedition."[99] If administrative experts were untrustworthy, the only way to counter the agencies was for members to develop their own sources of expertise. The Joint Committee heard numerous complaints from members about Congress's own lack of expertise; conservative Democrat Rep. E. C. Gathings of Arkansas was shocked to observe that a recent congressional investigation of the USDA featured "employees paid by the executive branch of the Government investigating themselves."[100] Rep. Edward H. Rees (R–Kan.), an opponent of "big government," similarly found that members' dependence on agency staff meant that "we don't have any authority who has given the question unbiased study from the viewpoint of Congress and who can furnish such information to its members."[101] Echoing these complaints, the Joint Committee condemned the "shocking lack of adequate congressional fact-finding services and skilled staffs" and moved to equip standing committees with the tools to perform their oversight functions with both efficiency and expertise.[102]

The Legislative Reorganization Act authorized each standing committee to appoint four professional staff members and up to six clerical staffers on

[96] Senators could sit on two standing committees; representatives were limited to one.

[97] Heller, *Strengthening the Congress*, 18 (emphasis in the original).

[98] Dirksen, quoted in "Congressman: A Case History," *Fortune*, April 1943, reprinted in *The Organization of Congress – Symposium*, 56.

[99] Ibid.

[100] Joint Committee on the Organization of Congress, *Organization of Congress: Hearings*, pt. 2 (statement of Rep. E. C. Gathings, Apr. 6), 263.

[101] Joint Committee on the Organization of Congress, *Organization of Congress: Hearings*, pt. 2 (statement of Rep. Edward H. Rees, Apr. 20), 326–27.

[102] Joint Committee on the Organization of Congress, *Organization of the Congress*, 9.

a permanent, nonpartisan basis. These employees, who might easily have a longer tenure with a single committee than individual members of Congress, would be able to specialize and compete with agency experts. (As one Senate staff member cautioned, however, Congress should not attempt to duplicate levels of staffing in the agencies for fear that committees "may easily become as bureaucratic as the agencies Congress wishes to supervise."[103]) Additional informational assistance would be available from the Legislative Reference Service in the Library of Congress. The act also explicitly forbade committees from relying on "experts or other personnel detailed or assigned from any department or agency of the Government" without written permission.[104] Taken together, these reforms were aimed at improving congressional expertise to help committees keep a better eye on the execution of the laws, and, going forward, to help members of Congress draft more specific laws.

The act had the active support of many members of Congress already hostile to the bureaucratic state, as well as significant bipartisan support.[105] The idea of strengthening congressional authority against the executive branch was appealing to most members, and all would benefit from improved staff expertise. Specific provisions improving members' pay and pensions proved a substantial additional lure.[106] Reform-minded members also recognized the importance of moving quickly, given the widespread expectation of a Republican victory in the 1946 midterm elections. Because fewer committees meant fewer chairman positions, and fewer opportunities to exercise power, many believed that reform would be harder to achieve once the Democrats lost control of Congress. (As Galloway, the Joint Committee's staff director, pointed out in April, the Republicans' "appetite for all the powers, privileges, and perquisites that go with the present system will probably be overpowering."[107]) The White House was also enthusiastic, and President Truman quickly wrote to La Follette that the Joint Committee's report was "tops."[108] As the former senator predicted, with the new organization in place, "the business of the Congress would be very much expedited and its efficiency would be greatly improved."[109]

The bill also held some attraction for those outside the institution. Since the early 1940s, members had been playing to the public, accompanying their resolutions and reform proposals with articles and editorials in popular magazines and newspapers bemoaning the state of Congress and urging reform. In

---

[103] Joint Committee on the Organization of Congress, *Organization of Congress: Hearings*, pt. 2 (statement of George H. E. Smith, Apr. 24), 375.

[104] Legislative Reorganization Act § 202(f).

[105] Schickler, *Disjointed Pluralism*, 141.

[106] Davidson, "Advent of the Modern Congress."

[107] George B. Galloway to Rep. Mike Monroney, Apr. 22, 1946, Folder 4, Box 321, On the Reorganization of Congress, 79th Congress (Senate), RG 128, NAB.

[108] Harry S. Truman to Sen. Robert M. La Follette Jr., Mar. 11, 1946, Folder 3, Box 321, On the Reorganization of Congress, 79th Congress (Senate), RG 128, NAB.

[109] Ibid.

late 1945, Galloway reported to Joint Committee members on the successful penetration of this campaign into American consciousness:

> During recent weeks millions of Americans have seen the motion picture – Spotlight on Congress – which featured efforts to strengthen our great institution. More than 80,000 copies of the Heller Report on Congress have been sold. The Town Meeting of the Air and the American Forum of the Air are arranging radio debates this fall on Congressional reconstruction.
>
> Millions of readers of *Life* magazine saw and pondered the twelve pages of pictures about Congress and our Committee which appeared last June. The three great pressure groups – industry, labor, agriculture – have endorsed a comprehensive program for revitalizing Congress. Five million members of the National League of Women Voters have put Congressional reorganization at the top of their agenda for 1945–46. And scores of Senators and Representatives have gone for it.
>
> No committee could hope for greater public and legislative interest and support than we have received.[110]

The press was enthusiastic. Columnist Merlo Pusey emphasized that without reform, "our chance of retaining representative government will be lost,"[111] and the *Washington Post* argued that the bill's provisions were each "a significant step toward modernization of our democratic system."[112] The editor of the *Wall Street Journal*, in a congratulatory letter to La Follette following the Joint Committee's report, offered the paper's help "in keeping the matter before the public and in securing action."[113] Having convinced Americans that the administrative state was dangerous, that there was a problem with Congress, and that a weak Congress was a threat to democracy, Congress was able to win support for a reform bill based in detailed study and expert input.

Erwin Griswold wrote from Harvard Law School to congratulate Sen. La Follette on the bill's Senate passage: "Although procedural matters of this sort are always more or less unspectacular, I can think of few bills of greater importance so far as the domestic welfare of the country is concerned."[114] Much support was, however, shallow; as with the APA, Americans may have been willing to support proposals that promised to cut off "bureaucrats" at the knees, but they were unlikely to be feel strongly about the specifics of committee consolidation. The APSA's Committee on Congress pushed for publicity regarding the broad need for reform, but most of the technical revisions did not win much interest from the press or the public.[115] Thus, last-minute changes to the bill,

[110] George B. Galloway to Rep. Eugene Cox, Oct. 23, 1945, 1, Folder 3, Box 321, On the Reorganization of Congress, 79th Congress (Senate), RG 128, NAB. (Similar letters were sent to other members of Congress.)

[111] Merlo Pusey, "Overworked Congress," *Washington Post*, Dec. 18, 1945, 6.

[112] "For a Modern Congress," *Washington Post*, June 10, 1946, 6.

[113] W. H. Grimes to Sen. Robert M. La Follette Jr., Mar. 5, 1946, Folder 1, Box 321, On the Reorganization of Congress, 79th Congress (Senate), RG 128, NAB.

[114] Erwin Griswold to Sen. Robert M. La Follette Jr., June 12, 1946, Folder 1, Box 321, On the Reorganization of Congress, 79th Congress (Senate), RG 128, NAB.

[115] See Matthews, "American Political Science and Congressional Reform."

pushed by certain members of Congress shoring up their own political positions, did not disrupt the larger message of reform.

Indeed, the bill languished in the House during the summer of 1946, passing only after amendments eliminated provisions creating majority and minority policy committees and establishing a council to foster cooperation between the legislative and executive branches.[116] As a result, a large portion of the bill's provisions that would have allowed Congress to compete with the executive branch in policy formulation fell away. The oversight provisions survived largely unscathed, with one significant exception – the Joint Committee's recommended ban on special and select investigating committees was not included in the Legislative Reorganization Act. While the standing committees were still empowered to take on oversight tasks, Congress also remained free to continue its ad hoc habits.

Although the Budget Bureau warned of "the possibility that the expanded Congressional staff in its dealings with the departments and agencies might tend to give instructions or solicit direct recommendations, to the detriment of control by the President,"[117] Truman signed the Legislative Reorganization Act into law in August 1946, predicting that the act "should permit easier and closer relations between the executive agencies of the Government and the Congress."[118] Congressional supporters touted the act, claiming that it would improve Congress, control the agencies and commissions, and save American democracy. George Galloway argued that the "legislative miracle" of the Legislative Reorganization Act would "go far to renew popular faith in the capacity of our representative democracy to handle the problems of the postwar world."[119] Sen. La Follette similarly anticipated that it might "increase the efficiency of Congress, clear the legislative log-jam, and renew popular faith in American democracy."[120] As the Joint Committee had earlier reminded the rest of Congress, the rise of totalitarianism abroad "had its beginnings in the decline and final break-down of their national legislatures which were either suppressed by the dictators or converted into mere pawns of power politics."[121] The act promised great things; by August 1946, La Follette could assure readers of the *New York Times Magazine* – aware "that two conflicting ideologies are striving for power and favor in the world today" – that through "an

---

[116] See D. B. Hardeman and Donald C. Bacon, *Rayburn: A Biography* (Austin: Texas Monthly Press, 1987), 319; Coleman, "State Formation and the Decline of Political Parties."

[117] James E. Webb to Maurice C. Latta, Aug 1, 1946; Folder "Bill File August 2, 1946 [S. 1880–S. 2349]," Box 20, WHBF, HST Papers, HSTL.

[118] Harry S. Truman, "Statement by the President Upon Signing the Legislative Reorganization Act," Aug. 2, 1946, in *Public Papers of the Presidents of the United States: Harry S. Truman*, vol. 1946 (Washington, DC: Government Printing Office, 1962), 373.

[119] George B. Galloway, "Communication: Reorganization Achievement," *Washington Post*, July 30, 1946, 4.

[120] Robert M. La Follette Jr., "Congress Wins a Victory Over Congress," *New York Times Magazine*, Aug. 4, 1946, 46.

[121] Joint Committee on the Organization of Congress, *Organization of the Congress: First Progress Report*, 79th Cong., 1st sess., 1945, S. Doc. 36, 2.

efficient and responsive National Legislature that will truly meet the needs of the people, we will help to preserve our own democracy, liberties and form of government."[122]

The Legislative Reorganization Act took effect at the beginning of the 80th Congress, at the same time Republicans found themselves in control of both houses of Congress for the first time since the Hoover administration.[123] In the 1946 midterm elections, best known for the Democrats' bungling of the inflation issue and the Republicans' charges about Communism abroad and subversion at home, Joseph McCarthy won Robert La Follette's Wisconsin Senate seat, and conservative California Republican Richard Nixon replaced New Deal supporter and former Socialist Jerry Voorhis in the House. At the same time they had accused Roosevelt and Truman of harboring Communists in the executive branch, Republican candidates had trumpeted their plans to bring to order the perceived excesses of the New Deal and the World War II state.[124] The Legislative Reorganization Act, as a reassertion of congressional authority over the administrative state, appeared to offer a useful way of doing just that.

What oversight meant in practice depended on the individual committees, however, because proposals targeting the strength of Congress and its tools of administrative oversight had not gone further to imagine what properly supervised agencies would look like.[125] Certain characteristics of oversight, such as congressional consistency, knowledge, and thoroughness, were emphasized before the Joint Committee, but the flip side of oversight – agency performance – was not. Administrators lacked any clear guidelines for how they could avoid members of Congress looking askance at their activities, a state of affairs that encouraged administrative passivity and defensive behavior. As one political scientist mused in 1951, "Getting along with Congress is a motto so plainly inscribed above administrative portals that being 'good' in the eyes of the most immediately influential lawmakers becomes almost second nature."[126]

---

[122] La Follette, "Congress Wins a Victory Over Congress," 92.

[123] The act authorized each standing committee and subcommittee in the Senate to "make investigations into any matter within its jurisdiction" (§ 134[a]); lacking similar authority, House standing committees at the beginning of each Congress requested authority and funds for such investigations as a matter of course (House Committee on Interstate and Foreign Commerce, Subcommittee on Legislative Oversight, *Federal Communications Commission: Interim Report*, 85th Cong., 2nd sess., 1958, H. Rep. 1602, 3).

[124] See Susan M. Hartmann, *Truman and the 80th Congress* (Columbia: University of Missouri Press, 1971).

[125] Harris, "The Reorganization of Congress," 278–79; Seymour Scher, "Congressional Committee Members as Independent Agency Overseers: A Case Study," *American Political Science Review* 54 (1960): 911–20; John F. Bibby, "Committee Characteristics and Legislative Oversight of Administration," *Midwest Journal of Political Science* 10 (1966): 78–98; John F. Bibby, "Congress' Neglected Function," in Melvin R. Laird, ed., *Republican Papers*, 476–88 (New York: Frederick A. Praeger, 1968).

[126] Fritz Morstein Marx, "Congressional Investigations: Significance for the Administrative Process," *University of Chicago Law Review* 18 (1951): 503–20, 508.

Experience had taught the agencies that bold regulatory moves would likely be met skeptically by some member of Congress, who could draw on language of due process and administrative absolutism in response. Members of Congress who embraced antibureaucratic approaches were thus able to signal their commitment to government reform and to the goals of the Legislative Reorganization Act without actually agreeing among themselves what agency officials were doing wrong.

While placing oversight in the standing committees assigned responsibility for scrutiny and created additional opportunities for scrutiny to occur, it did little to change the incentives of those who worked within it. The Legislative Reorganization Act included neither strong inducements for committees to act nor clear penalties for failure to do so.[127] Members would be politically accountable for agency failures on their watch, but how this represented a change from the pre-1946 regime was unclear. Indeed, one observer commented that it was "hardly more than a beginning of the needed reform of Congress, and not a very good beginning at that."[128] Like the APA, the Legislative Reorganization Act would come to represent more rhetorical than real change.

In first few years after the act went into effect, its accomplishments were mixed. Committee members certainly appreciated the Legislative Reorganization Act's staffing provisions; in 1950, more than 85 percent of members in each house ranked this aspect of the bill "successful" or "moderately successful."[129] George Galloway reported, four years after the act went into effect, that approximately half of the new committees had "well-trained and competent experts"; such assistance translated into "improved performance of their committees, more adequate records, better hearings and reports, more effective liaison between committees and the corresponding administrative agencies, and general improvement in efficiency."[130] Overall, however, the act's effect was somewhat limited. As another observer remarked of Congress after its reorganization, "Some chromium and a couple of bug-eye headlights may have been superimposed, but it is still the same old Model-T rattletrap."[131]

The committee organization devised by the Joint Committee did not last long, as a new standing committee on Astronautics and Space Exploration and new joint committees on Atomic Energy, Foreign Economic Cooperation, and Labor–Management Relations were created by Congress in the course of new legislation.[132] In addition, even as the history (if not the text) of the act

---

[127] Seymour Scher, "Conditions for Legislative Control," *Journal of Politics* 25 (1963): 526–51.

[128] Harris, "The Reorganization of Congress," 268.

[129] Senate Committee on Expenditures in the Executive Departments, *Organization and Operation of Congress: Hearings on Evaluation of the Effects of Laws Enacted to Reorganize the Legislative Branch of the Government*, 79th Cong., 1st sess., 1951, 7.

[130] George B. Galloway, "The Operation of the Legislative Reorganization Act of 1946," *American Political Science Review* 45 (1951): 41–68, 55.

[131] Albert L. Warner, "The Chaos of Congress," *Harper's Magazine*, Mar. 1950, 60.

[132] Harry W. Jones, "Department of Legislation," *American Bar Association Journal* 34 (1948): 726–27.

disfavored special and select investigating committees, a number of existing committees (such as the Senate Special Committee to Study the Problems of American Small Business Enterprises and Sen. Byrd's Joint Committee on Non-essential Expenditures) were continued in the 80th Congress and were soon joined by others (such as the House Select Committee to Investigate Newsprint, and additional committees investigating Organized Crime and Undesirable Books), further diluting the structure established by the act.[133] Reducing the number of standing committees also led directly to a rise in the number of subcommittees, and members who had earlier found themselves overwhelmed with committee obligations now owed allegiance to multiple subcommittees. Only a few months into the 80th Congress, the *New York Times* reported that 146 subcommittees were operating in Congress. The Senate and House Appropriations Committees and the House Armed Services Committee were the worst offenders, with twelve subcommittees each.[134]

Even with new authority, consistent oversight remained a problem in many areas. In most cases, committees continued with the same commitment to oversight (or lack thereof) that they had demonstrated under the earlier model. The Joint Committee on Labor–Management Relations was criticized for its enthusiastic scrutiny of the NLRB's individual decisions, but it was an outlier.[135] Rep. Monroney reported in 1948 that the oversight requirement "has met with only partial success" given the difficulties "of reorganizing the committees, of extending emergency legislation, and the general heavy work load" that committees faced.[136] Sen. McClellan would suggest, after observing the act in operation, that it might still be a good idea to create a separate, permanent joint committee focused on administrative procedure; "when reports of some administrative procedure come in that is not according to law or that is questionable in any way, you can call up in that committee the chief of the department involved and often lock the door before the horse is stolen."[137] Such recommendations indicated that oversight by the standing committees was not living up to initial expectations.

[133] See V. Stanley Vardys, "Select Committees of the House of Representatives," *Midwest Journal of Political Science* 6 (1962): 247–65.

[134] "Congress Sprouts 146 Subcommittees in Reorganization," *New York Times*, Apr. 14, 1947, 1; "19 House Committees Include 115 Groups," *New York Times*, Mar. 20, 1947, 23.

[135] See Association of the Bar of the City of New York, "Congressional Oversight of Administrative Agencies: A Report of the Committee on Administrative Law," *Record of the Association of the Bar of the City of New York* 5 (1950): 11–29; Beryl Harold Levy, "Congressional Oversight of Administrative Agencies," *American Bar Association Journal* 36 (1950): 236–37; James A. Gross, *Broken Promise: The Subversion of U.S. Labor Relations Policy, 1947–1994* (Philadelphia: Temple University Press, 1995).

[136] Senate Committee on Expenditures in the Executive Departments, *Legislative Reorganization Act of 1946: Hearings* (statement of Rep. Monroney, Feb. 17), 84; see also Harry W. Jones, "Department of Legislation," *American Bar Association Journal* 34 (1948): 1018–19.

[137] Senate Committee on Expenditures in the Executive Departments, *Legislative Reorganization Act of 1946: Hearings* (statement of Sen. McClellan, Feb. 2), 54.

Other observers agreed that Congress's legislative work was getting in the way of oversight, as standing committees were still "too heavily burdened" with making laws "to keep very close watch upon the executive agencies coming under their jurisdiction."[138] Contrary to expectations, Congress passed more private bills in the 81st Congress than it had in any Congress in the past forty years.[139] Also blamed were "inadequate committee personnel, lack of clarity as to specific committee jurisdiction, and general inertia."[140] Failure to abolish the tradition of seniority further complicated committee initiative. The *Washington Post* complained that Republicans in the 80th Congress were "critically handicapped" by the rule that appointed as committee chairmen "misfits and reactionaries" along with "doddering old men who are no longer able to keep pace with the exacting demands of the age in which we are living."[141] Such individuals were unlikely to make the most of their new authority.

When other members embraced their new responsibilities, however, problems of duplication quickly returned. Multiple investigations of the Reconstruction Finance Corporation, export controls, and military procurement were launched, and several Republicans in the 80th Congress seized the opportunity to look into the operations of the FCC yet again, on an issue that combined the political allure of anti-Communism with traditional concerns about the combination of functions in administrative agencies. Following the FCC's grant of multiple radio licenses to alleged subversive Edward Lamb of Ohio, the House Un-American Activities Committee moved to examine whether the commission habitually granted valuable broadcast licenses to Communists and fellow travelers.[142] Soon thereafter, the Senate Interstate and Foreign Commerce Committee, which had recently criticized the FCC's case-by-case methods of policy making as slow and "contrary to every concept of American jurisprudence," created a new subcommittee to investigate the FCC's licensing practices.[143] At the same time, the House approved yet another investigation of how the FCC was treating license applications from questionable applicants and what it was doing about subversive programming by existing licensees.[144] Instead of giving this investigation to the standing commission with authority over the FCC, the investigation was conducted by a new Select Committee to

[138] Elbert D. Thomas, "How Congress Functions Under Its Reorganization Act," *American Political Science Review* 43 (1949): 1179–89, 1186; see also Galloway, "Operation of the Legislative Reorganization Act," 59 (for almost identical language).

[139] Floyd M. Riddick, "The Eighty-First Congress: First and Second Sessions," *Western Political Quarterly* 4 (1951): 48–66, 52.

[140] George E. Outland, "Congress Still Needs Reorganization," *Western Political Quarterly* 1 (1948): 154–64, 161.

[141] "Unfinished Business," *Washington Post*, Feb. 23, 1948, 8.

[142] "FCC Under Probe by House Un-American Activities Group," *Washington Post*, May 8, 1948, 7; see also Brinson, *The Red Scare, Politics, and the Federal Communications Commission*.

[143] Senate Committee on Interstate and Foreign Commerce, *Communication Act Amendments of 1948*, 80th Cong., 2nd sess., 1948, S. Rep. 1567, 17.

[144] H. Res. 691, 80th Cong., 2nd sess., 1948.

Investigate the Federal Communications Commission, created specifically for that purpose. Although the House Rules Committee had been generally intractable during the 80th Congress, the *Washington Post* remarked, its members approved this special investigation "with the speed of electricity."[145] Thus, only a few years after the passage of an act intended to end such practices, FCC officials again faced multiple investigations from both standing and special committees.

Nor did these committees appear to represent the best in continuous watchfulness. Incentives for publicity seekers remained the same, and the House Select Committee, chaired by Rep. Forest A. Harness (R–Ind.), did nothing to challenge sociologist Edward Shils's observation that "the congressional investigation is often just the instrument which the legislator needs in order to remind his constituents of his existence."[146] Harness, who had proposed the special committee in the first place, had been labeled "something of a Congressional nonentity of Kokomo, Ind.," in the *Washington Post*, and was joined on the committee by Rep. Cox, an unapologetic enemy of the FCC.[147] Overall, the *Post* characterized the new committee as "another star chamber, conceived in politics and dedicated to the proposition that a Federal agency can do no right."[148] Indeed, the Harness special committee ultimately resembled some of the pre-1946 investigations, diving with enthusiasm into charges of Communism, atheism, and excessive power. The committee excoriated the commission for failing to investigate the backgrounds of potential licensees. Members also accused lawyers in the commission's "omnipresent and omnipotent" law department of usurping the lawmaking functions of the commissioners, and suggested that the FCC was exceeding its statutory authority in its day-to-day operations.[149] Overall, the committee concluded, the FCC "offers an example of the danger of merging the legislative, the executive, and the judicial branches of our Government," illustrating how the executive branch could "dominate and control, in as autocratic a manner as any other form of government, the lives of the citizens."[150]

Similar criticisms were offered by the subcommittee of the Senate Committee on Interstate and Foreign Commerce a month later. The FCC, this committee charged, acts slowly, "frequently ignores and bypasses its own rules in arriving at decisions," and "arrogates to itself powers and authority" beyond those granted in the statute.[151] The committee suggested a number of organizational

[145] "Like Lightning," *Washington Post*, June 19, 1948, 6.
[146] Edward A. Shils, "Congressional Investigations: The Legislator and His Environment," *University of Chicago Law Review* 18 (1951): 571–84, 573.
[147] John Crosby, "Radio in Review," *Washington Post*, Sept. 25, 1948, 7.
[148] "Like Lightning," *Washington Post*, 6.
[149] House Select Committee to Investigate the Federal Communications Commission, *Final Report*, 80th Cong., 2nd sess., 1949, H. Rep. 2479, 4.
[150] Ibid., 8.
[151] Senate Committee on Interstate and Foreign Commerce, *Communications Study*, 81st Cong., 1st sess., 1949, S. Rep. 49, 2.

and procedural reforms that would further separate prosecution and judicial functions for greater efficiency and greater fairness. Complaining about the FCC's use of its hearing examiners, the subcommittee suggested that the FCC move toward the review–attorney method reviled and recently abolished at the NLRB.[152] That these studies were evidence of improved oversight was not at all clear.

In a number of additional investigations, conservative members of Congress used their oversight authority to reveal malfeasance in the Truman administration and the administrative state.[153] Much energy came from the Senate Committee on Expenditures in the Executive Departments, which began to flex its muscles as a standing investigatory committee guarding against inefficiency and corruption.[154] Members soon established a subcommittee, seen as an heir to Truman's illustrious Senate War Investigating Committee (and Sen. Owen Brewster's [R-Maine] somewhat less illustrious one), devoted entirely to investigations of "economy and efficiency" in the federal government. In 1948, at the same time Truman was deriding Congress for failing to enact his "Fair Deal" proposals, this Permanent Investigations Subcommittee, which the *New York Times* called "[t]he most powerful Senate investigating committee in history," focused its attention squarely on the Truman administration.[155] Led by Sen. Homer Ferguson (R–Mich.) during the 80th Congress, members used their authority to investigate, among other things, charges of political patronage by Truman's political machine, the Justice Department's handling of allegations of election fraud in Kansas City, Missouri, and defects in Truman's loyalty program.[156]

Once leadership returned to the Democrats, the Permanent Investigations Subcommittee launched investigations of fraud and security with equal vigor.

[152] Ibid., 3.
[153] Jones, "Department of Legislation"; Floyd M. Riddick, "American Government and Politics: The First Session of the Eightieth Congress," *American Political Science Review* 42 (1948): 677–93; James MacGregor Burns, *Congress on Trial: The Legislative Process and the Administrative State* (New York: Gordian Press, 1966 [originally 1949]); Floyd M. Riddick, "The Eighty-First Congress: First and Second Sessions," 62–63; Earl Latham, *The Communist Controversy in Washington: From the New Deal to McCarthy* (Cambridge, MA: Harvard University Press, 1966).
[154] See Senate Committee on Government Operations, *50th Anniversary, History 1921–1971*, 92nd Cong., 1st sess., 1971, S. Doc. 92–31; Robert David Johnson, "The Government Operations Committee and Foreign Policy during the Cold War," *Political Science Quarterly* 113 (1998): 645–71; Walter J. Oleszek, *Congressional Procedures and the Policy Process*, 5th ed. (Washington, DC: CQ Press, 2001), chap. 9.
[155] William S. White, "Senators Chosen for Wide Scrutiny of Truman Regime," *New York Times*, Feb. 27, 1948, 1; see also "New Investigating Committee Is Half GOP, Half Southern," *Washington Post*, Feb. 27, 1948, 21.
[156] See Senate Committee on Expenditures in the Executive Departments, Subcommittee on Investigations, *Investigation of Federal Employees Loyalty Program: Interim Report*, 80th Cong., 2nd sess., 1948, S. Rep. 1775; Senate Committee on Expenditures in the Executive Departments, Subcommittee on Investigations, *First Annual Report*, 81st Cong., 1st sess., 1949, S. Rep. 5.

In 1949, under the leadership of conservative Senator Clyde R. Hoey (D–N.C.), certain members of the Senate Committee on Expenditures in the Executive Departments began inquiring into allegations of misconduct in the awarding of government contracts, especially regarding what columnist Arthur Krock referred to as "the five percenters and their venial, venal or just damfool friends and damfoolisher clients."[157] The Hoey subcommittee found "an unsavory fraternity" of those who swindled businessmen by offering to trade on their (often fictitious) personal relationships with agency officials in exchange for 5 percent of the value of the resulting government contract.[158] The subcommittee's report warned of the shady creature "who suddenly appears from a hotel lobby or emerges from a cocktail lounge in answer to the businessman's prayer, and then with equal alacrity disappears with his cash payment in hand when the deal is completed."[159] Individual agency officials were doing nothing wrong; the "five percenters" either took credit for a decision the agency would have made anyway or blamed their failure on others more corrupt than they. The subcommittee condemned these unscrupulous middlemen, who, "with a certain amusement, will refer to some person still naïve enough to believe that decisions are ever honestly made by Government officials."[160]

However, the agencies were not entirely blameless; poor information about the government's contracting process, "combined with a lackadaisical and often abrupt attitude on the part of some Government employees," created a market for the fraudulent services of these influence men.[161] The problem here was too little administrative enthusiasm, not too much; the administrative process operated so slowly that businessmen naturally sought a faster path. As the House Select Committee on Lobbying Activities argued in 1950, "pressures thrive on Government when it becomes too complex for ordinary citizens to understand."[162] The problem was not just the harm to the victimized businessmen; the alleged corruption placed the legitimacy of the administrative process at stake. As the Hoey subcommittee reflected ruefully: "Businessmen who would prefer to be honest, in their anxiety to get business, are lulled into the easy belief that everybody is cheating and soon conclude that as long as it involves no risk on their part they are willing to pay someone to do a little on their behalf."[163] This reflected poorly on everyone.

---

[157] Arthur Krock, "In the Nation," *New York Times*, Aug. 11, 1949, 22.

[158] Senate Committee on Expenditures in the Executive Departments, Subcommittee on Investigations, *The 5-Percenter Investigation: Interim Report*, 81st Cong., 2nd sess., 1950, S. Rep. 1232, 1.

[159] Ibid., 3.

[160] Ibid., 5.

[161] Ibid., 22.

[162] House Select Committee on Lobbying Activities, *General Interim Report*, 81st Cong., 2nd sess., 1950, H. Rep. 3138, 66; see Note, "Investigations in Operation: House Select Committee on Lobbying Activities," *University of Chicago Law Review* 18 (1951): 647–57.

[163] Senate Committee on Expenditures in the Executive Departments, Subcommittee on Investigations, *The 5-Percenter Investigation: Interim Report*, 1.

While few government officials were implicated in the inquiry (with the notable exception of Major General Harry Vaughan, the Truman aide whose receipt of a deep freezer won much attention), the subcommittee suggested that it might be time to develop official standards of conduct for agency officials. For government to work, Hoey argued, "It is important not only that we have good government but that the public have confidence in the integrity and the decency of its Government."[164] Such standards could send a message to citizens that government business was being performed honestly, and might also remind a wavering official "that probably he is not getting the gift because the donor likes the color of his eyes or is genuinely concerned with his household needs."[165] Administrative integrity and transparency was becoming at least as important as administrative fairness.

The ethics of government employees became an increasingly significant matter of public interest in the early 1950s.[166] At the same time the Hoey subcommittee was investigating the illegal activities of "five-percenters," a subcommittee of the Senate Committee on Banking and Currency began looking into questionable behavior at the Reconstruction Finance Corporation.[167] This investigation, headed by Sen. J. William Fulbright (D–Ark.), examined how the RFC – a Depression-era institution created to loan money to interests unable to qualify for private loans – disbursed its valuable benefits. The subcommittee was particularly troubled by the frequency with which departing RFC officials would take jobs at private companies that had earlier received RFC loans. Such close relationships between those granting the loans and those accepting them suggested questionable motives at play and called into question the value of close ties between the regulators and the regulated.

---

[164] Hoey, quoted in Senate Committee on Expenditures in the Executive Departments, Subcommittee on Investigations, *The 5-Percenter Investigation: Interim Report*, 2.

[165] Senate Committee on Expenditures in the Executive Departments, Subcommittee on Investigations, *The 5-Percenter Investigation: Interim Report*, 22.

[166] Jules Abels, *The Truman Scandals* (Chicago: Henry Regnery, 1956); Cabell B. H. Phillips, *The Truman Presidency: The History of a Triumphant Succession* (New York: Macmillan, 1966); Andrew J. Dunar, *The Truman Scandals and the Politics of Morality* (Columbia: University of Missouri Press, 1984).

[167] See Senate Committee on Banking and Currency, *Operations of the Reconstruction Finance Corporation*, 80th Cong., 2nd sess., 1948, S. Rep. 974; Senate Committee on Banking and Currency, *Study of Reconstruction Finance Corporation: Interim Report, Texmass Petroleum Co. Loan*, 81st Cong., 2nd sess., 1950, S. Rep. 1689; Senate Committee on Banking and Currency, Subcommittee on Reconstruction Finance Corporation, *Study of Reconstruction Finance Corporation: Interim Report, Lustron Corp. – Transportation Contract*, 81st Cong., 2nd sess., 1950, S. Rep. 1689, pt. 2; Senate Committee on Banking and Currency, *Study of Reconstruction Finance Corporation: Interim Report, Favoritism and Influence*, 82nd Cong., 1st sess., 1951, S. Rep. 76; Senate Committee on Banking and Currency, *Study of Reconstruction Finance Corporation and Proposed Amendment of RFC Act*, 82nd Cong., 1st sess., 1951, S. Rep. 649; see also Senate Committee on Expenditures in the Executive Departments, Permanent Subcommittee on Investigations, *American Lithofold Corp., William M. Boyle, Jr., Guy George Gabrielson: Interim Report*, 82nd Cong., 2nd sess., 1952, S. Rep. 1142; Russell Baker, "An Ozark 'Professor' Studies Wall Street," *New York Times Magazine*, Mar. 6, 1955, 17.

The subcommittee focused its ire on the RFC's board members for taking friendship and political connections into account when approving loans. In several instances, board members had influenced examiners' decisions and approved loans over examiners' recommendations to the contrary, making such decisions "without any apparent affirmative reason" and even "notwithstanding the existence of persuasive reasons why loans should not be made."[168] In addition, at least one White House aide had been involved in making loan recommendations. The charges – which included evidence about one loan recipient giving a mink coat to the wife of a former RFC official – grabbed public attention. The *Chicago Tribune* – finding that the investigation demonstrated "countless instances showing that money could be shoveled out of the treasury by a crew of roustabouts with less cost and at least as much prudence as the RFC brings to the task of lending" – concluded that the RFC "is tainted with politics, scandal, and graft. Congress should stop the stalling and put it out of existence before it goes deeper into the hole."[169]

Truman, who had long disliked Fulbright, dismissed the subcommittee's report as "asinine," but the RFC disclosures, on the heels of the five-percenter investigation and with additional revelations emerging about questionable decision making in the Maritime Commission (where the *Washington Post* was shocked at "a record of incompetence, procrastination and evasion rarely equaled in a Government agency") and in the SEC, the ethics of the Truman White House and of federal employees as a whole were called into question.[170] The *Washington Post* suggested that the scandals were evidence of "machine government in operation" and suggested that if Truman "fails to arrest the moral erosion now all too evident, the consequences will have to be laid at his own door."[171] Columnist Stewart Alsop agreed that "[t]he moral mildew which has been attacking the American political fabric needs holding up to the light."[172]

---

[168] Senate Committee on Banking and Currency, *Study of Reconstruction Finance Corporation: Interim Report, Favoritism and Influence*, 5.

[169] "Fold It Up," *Chicago Daily Tribune*, July 9, 1950, 18.

[170] Harry S. Truman, "The President's News Conference of February 8, 1951," in *Public Papers of the Presidents of the United States: Harry S. Truman*, vol. 1951 (Washington, DC: Government Printing Office, 1965), 145; "Maritime Scandal," *Washington Post*, May 23, 1950, 10. Regarding the Maritime Commission, see House Committee on Expenditures in the Executive Departments, *Inquiry into the Operations of the Maritime Commission: Fourth Intermediate Report*, 81st Cong., 1st sess., 1949, H. Rep. 1423. The House Committee on Expenditures in the Executive Departments noted "the deplorable situation generally existing from top to bottom within the Maritime Commission" and pointed to "instances of inordinate delays, extreme administrative lassitude, and indecisiveness" (House Committee on Expenditures in the Executive Departments, *Further Inquiry into the Operations of the Maritime Commission: Sixth Intermediate Report*, 81st Cong., 2nd sess., 1950, H. Rep. 2104, 4, 30). Regarding the SEC, see House Committee on Interstate and Foreign Commerce, *Study of the Securities and Exchange Commission*, 82nd Cong., 2nd sess., 1952, H. Rep. 2508.

[171] "Scandals of 1951," *Washington Post*, Mar. 29, 1951, 10.

[172] Stewart Alsop, "Matter of Fact," *Washington Post*, Apr. 1, 1951, B5.

Truman responded to evidence of corruption by replacing the RFC's five-man board with a single administrator, as Fulbright had recommended, to concentrate responsibility and accountability for the RFC's loans.[173] Other agencies adopted internal reform, but these piecemeal efforts failed to entirely reassure Congress.[174] Thus, following subsequent embarrassing hearings on the RFC, Sen. Fulbright recommended that a commission be established to devise a code of ethics to govern the behavior of federal employees. Sen. Paul H. Douglas (D–Ill.), a member of the Fulbright subcommittee who had himself suggested amending the APA to add a code of ethics, made this cause his own and led a subcommittee of the Senate Labor and Public Welfare Committee in a study of how government employees and individuals appearing before the government should conduct themselves to protect the public interest.[175]

Witnesses before the subcommittee in its hearings during the summer of 1951 included agency officials, members of Congress, and such prominent Americans as Louis Brownlow, Reinhold Niebuhr, Robert Jackson, Learned Hand, Thurman Arnold, and David Lilienthal. The subcommittee noted the breadth of agencies' discretion over matters of tremendous value, and, echoing older critiques, suggested that agencies were "usurping legislative functions" through their aggressive use of administrative authority.[176] The subcommittee found, however, that administrators were not entirely to blame. Determining the limits of their power was a more difficult task than it might seem, for "in addition to the language of substantive acts of Congress," administrators "receive instructions from the appropriation acts, the two Appropriations Committees and at least two legislative committees in each House, and sometimes also from individual committee members."[177] Unfortunately for agency officials, "these instructions are not always consistent."[178] Arnold raised another concern, suggesting that government employment "is becoming so harassed, restricted, preached against, distrusted, and generally kicked around that brilliant young men with other opportunities pass it by."[179]

---

[173] Reorganization Plan No. 1 of 1951, 65 Stat. 773 (1951).

[174] Senate Committee on Expenditures in the Executive Departments, *Activities of the Senate Committee on Expenditures in the Executive Departments*, 82nd Cong., 1st sess., 1951, S. Rep. 1, 50.

[175] See "Code of Proper Conduct," *Washington Post*, Mar. 17, 1951, 8; Paul H. Douglas, *In the Fullness of Time: The Memoirs of Paul H. Douglas* (New York: Harcourt Brace Jovanovich, 1972).

[176] Senate Committee on Labor and Public Welfare, Special Subcommittee on the Establishment of a Commission of Ethics in Government, *Ethical Standards in Government*, 82nd Cong., 1st sess., 1951, Committee Print, 32.

[177] Ibid.

[178] Ibid.

[179] Senate Committee on Labor and Public Welfare, Special Subcommittee on the Establishment of a Commission on Ethics in Government, *Establishment of a Commission on Ethics in Government: Hearings*, 82nd Cong., 1st sess., 1951 (statement of Thurmond Arnold, July 6), 374.

At the same time, however, complaints about administrators' ethics were legion. The Douglas subcommittee did not point fingers at specific individuals or agencies, but it did condemn particular practices stemming from cozy relationships between administrators and select regulated parties. Douglas himself denounced the use of favors, kickbacks, and promises of lucrative employment to influence government officials, and declared that "[g]overnment work should not be settled at cocktail bars or around dinner tables in hotels."[180] Most witnesses supported some sort of code of ethics directed at administrators' selfish motives, and the subcommittee proposed immediate amendments to the APA to prevent government employees from profiting from their government positions, disclosing confidential information, accepting gifts or hospitality, talking about job opportunities, or becoming otherwise "unduly involved" socially with anyone involved in business before the government.[181] Under this code, federal employees who entered the private sector were not to represent the other side before their former agency in matters in which they had been involved, and were further to wait out a two-year "cooling-off" period before appearing before their former agencies on any matter. Finally, the subcommittee offered a separate bill requiring that federal officials above a certain rank make public their income – which members suggested might "deter individuals from accepting any income, holding any assets, or making any transactions which they believe are questionable."[182]

In addition, although a few witnesses joined Commerce Secretary Charles Sawyer, who blasted the idea that "the solution of every problem lies in the organization of another alphabetical agency,"[183] most strongly favored – and the committee ultimately recommended – the creation of a new ethics commission to examine the problem and to suggest "moral standards of official conduct."[184] The proposal indicated discomfort with the current state of government ethics, but also suggested that figuring out additional ethical standards required more time and political capital than Congress could spare. The committee argued that a commission, with members drawn from both private life and public service, could spend time "to mature its recommendations"; such a commission also might "be less subject to a charge of bias" against the agencies.[185]

The subcommittee also reflected on the role that public interest groups, churches, and individuals played in encouraging (or discouraging) government ethics. As members commented, "A society which produces only

---

[180] Douglas, quoted in "Senator Lists Aim of 'Ethics' Inquiry," *New York Times*, Apr. 9, 1951, 25.
[181] Senate Committee on Labor and Public Welfare, Special Subcommittee on the Establishment of a Commission of Ethics in Government, *Ethical Standards in Government*, 2.
[182] Ibid., 3.
[183] Charles Sawyer, quoted in Senate Committee on Labor and Public Welfare, *Commission on Ethics in Government*, 82nd Cong., 1st sess., 1951, S. Rep. 933, 3.
[184] Senate Committee on Labor and Public Welfare, *Commission on Ethics in Government*, 6.
[185] Ibid., 4.

unrestrained pressures on government cannot for long produce officials who will be able to resist those pressures."[186] Evidence of malfeasance in government procurement at the Maritime Commission, at the RFC, and at the Bureau of Internal Revenue had "caused genuine distress among thoughtful people" and had "fostered cynicism among many others."[187] Overall, Americans had bad feelings about public employees, who by now were "stereotyped in popular opinion as both lazily bureaucratic and unduly zealous," although the "prestige of the public service" was "certainly lower when considered as an abstraction than when particular groups of public servants are considered."[188] The subcommittee offered a range of explanations including low pay, lack of challenging positions, and "frequent attacks made upon public employees, both individually and as a class," and suggested the matter was ripe for further study.[189] Some solution was needed, for "there is no justifiable reason for attaching a stigma to any group or any vocation which performs an essential service to society."[190]

The *Washington Post* opined that the subcommittee had "put their fingers on one of the great weaknesses of our present political life" – that is, "whether a sense of justice and impartial administration of public affairs can survive in the operations of modern government."[191] The *Chicago Tribune* approvingly reprinted an editorial arguing that the solution was not legal reform "but officials with a little more decency and honor and honesty – elements of character that are developed by right thinking and right living, and not by the kind commonly found among cheap political hacks recruited from the underworld machines of the big cities."[192] Douglas soon published a collection of his lectures on the same topic, in which he continued to press for a code of ethics to apply to everyone involved in the administrative process that could serve as "a guide to the perplexed" and could limit "both the corrupters and the corrupted, the seducers and the seduced."[193]

Although Douglas's investigation had little immediate effect, it brought attention to a problem that would only worsen in years to come.[194] The points he made were further confirmed by revelations that employees at the Bureau of Internal Revenue had accepted money, furniture, and fur coats in exchange

[186] Senate Committee on Labor and Public Welfare, Special Subcommittee on Establishment of Commission of Ethics in Government, *Ethical Standards in Government*, 64.

[187] Ibid., 15.

[188] Ibid., 10–11, 32.

[189] Ibid., 33.

[190] Ibid.

[191] "Ethics in Government," *Washington Post*, Oct. 25, 1951, 12.

[192] "To the Grafters Belong the Spoils," reprinted from the Ontario (CA) *Daily Report*, in *Chicago Daily Tribune*, Jan. 4, 1952, 14.

[193] Paul H. Douglas, *Ethics in Government* (Cambridge, MA: Harvard University Press, 1952), 63.

[194] Paul H. Douglas, "Improvement of Ethical Standards in the Federal Government: Problems and Proposals," *Annals of the American Academy of Political and Social Science* 280 (1952): 149–57.

for special treatment for certain taxpayers.[195] Dozens of employees resigned, and Truman reorganized the bureau to decrease political influence and increase institutional scrutiny, but neither this reform nor Truman's appointment of a Special Assistant to the Attorney General in early 1952 to investigate corruption addressed the broader problem of ethics in an administrative state now seen as untrustworthy.[196]

Oversight also included concerns about subversion, as Cold War rhetoric meant that agencies found themselves defending the loyalty of their employees to congressional committees as well as to the CSC. Complaints about individual agency employees often provided a distraction from judicious examination of the more tedious details of agency operations. In this new political climate, even the expert staffers of the Legislative Reference Service were called into question in late 1946. Allegations of researchers' Communist ties were retracted, but rumors about the staff lingered.[197] Additional charges against federal employees were soon leveled by the House Un-American Activities Committee, a standing committee newly invigorated under the leadership of Rep. J. Parnell Thomas (R–N.J.) in the 80th Congress.[198] In the summer of 1948, a few months before the November elections, HUAC heard testimony about the continuing presence of Communists throughout the federal government, including within the Office of Strategic Services and the State Department. Explosive charges made against State Department official Alger Hiss, a seemingly prototypical New Dealer, threatened to tar administrative officials and the Roosevelt White House with the stain of disloyalty.[199] As James Reston of the *New York Times* reported in 1949, Hiss had become a symbol of the New Deal; for liberals to accept Hiss's guilt "would be to cast a reflection on the Administration he served and the policy that Administration has followed."[200]

[195] House Committee on Ways and Means, *Internal Revenue Investigation*, 82nd Cong., 2nd sess., 1953, H. Rep. 2518; House Committee on Ways and Means, Subcommittee on Administration of the Internal Revenue Laws, *Internal Revenue Investigation: Report by Mr. King*, 82nd Cong., 2nd sess., 1952, Subcommittee Print; House Committee on Ways and Means, Subcommittee on Administration of the Internal Revenue Laws, *Internal Revenue Investigation: Report by Mr. Kean*, 82nd Cong., 2nd sess., 1953, Subcommittee Print; see also Abels, *The Truman Scandals*.

[196] Reorganization Plan No. 1 of 1952, 66 Stat. 823; for more on the IRS scandals, see W. H. Lawrence, "Truman Revamps Tax Set-up to Eliminate 64 Collectors; Civil Service for New Heads," *New York Times*, Jan. 3, 1952, 1; John W. Snyder, "The Reorganization of the Bureau of Internal Revenue," *Public Administration Review* 12 (1952): 221–33; Arthur Krock, "In the Nation," *New York Times*, Feb. 5, 1952, 28.

[197] Walter Trohan, "New Congress' Pink 'Advisers' Face G.O.P. Ax," *Chicago Daily Tribune*, Dec. 26, 1946, 1.

[198] Robert K. Carr, *The House Committee on Un-American Activities, 1945–1950* (Ithaca, NY: Cornell University Press, 1952).

[199] See G. Edward White, *Alger Hiss's Looking-Glass Wars: The Covert Life of a Soviet Spy* (New York: Oxford University Press, 2004).

[200] James Reston, "Partisan Opinions Expressed on Hiss," *New York Times*, June 9, 1949, 4.

More than twenty separate investigations were launched into Communist activities in each of the 80th, 81st, and 82nd Congresses – the number increasing as the United States became involved in the Korean conflict – and members of the 83rd Congress conducted more than fifty such investigations.[201] Along with HUAC, prominent investigating committees taking on the subject of subversive bureaucrats included the Permanent Investigations Subcommittee of the Senate Committee on Expenditures in the Executive Departments, whose investigation of the security risks involved in the government employment of "sex perverts" pushed many gay and lesbian workers out of federal employment, the Senate Foreign Relations Committee, which in 1950 investigated Sen. Joseph McCarthy's charges about Communist influences at the State Department, and the Senate Judiciary Committee's Internal Security Subcommittee, established in 1951 for additional investigations.[202]

When Sen. McCarthy took over as chairman of the Permanent Investigations Subcommittee in 1953, he put matters of subversion at the forefront of the subcommittee's mission. Hearings revealed the existence of a "secret Communist underground" in the federal government through which Communists were "guiding research and preparing memoranda on which basic American policies were set, writing speeches for Cabinet officers, influencing congressional investigations, drafting laws, manipulating administrative reorganizations – always serving the interest of their Soviet superiors."[203] Congress's attention to oversight was critical; combining prominent instances of ethical lapses and espionage, McCarthy argued that "the treason of Alger Hiss and William Remington; the scandals in the Reconstruction Finance Corporation; the activities of 5-percenters; the corruption in the Gen. Bennett Meyers case; the role of the underworld in operations affecting interstate commerce" – all were the result of effective

---

[201] David Caute, *The Great Fear: The Anti-Communist Purge under Truman and Eisenhower* (New York: Simon & Schuster, 1978), 85.

[202] Senate Committee on Expenditures in the Executive Departments, Subcommittee on Investigations, *Employment of Homosexuals and Other Sex Perverts in Government: Interim Report*, 81st Cong., 2nd sess., 1950, S. Rep. 241; Johnson, *The Lavender Scare*; Caute, *The Great Fear*; Alan D. Harper, *The Politics of Loyalty: The White House and the Communist Issue, 1946–1952* (Westport, CT: Greenwood Publishing, 1969); Francis H. Thompson, *The Frustration of Politics: Truman, Congress, and the Loyalty Issue 1945–1953* (London: Associated University Presses, 1979); Stanley I. Kutler, *The American Inquisition: Justice and Injustice in the Cold War* (New York: Hill and Wang, 1982); Gregory B. Lewis, "Lifting the Ban on Gays in the Civil Service: Federal Policy Toward Gay and Lesbian Employees since the Cold War," *Public Administration Review* 57 (1997): 387–95; Ellen Schrecker, *Many Are the Crimes: McCarthyism in America* (Boston: Little, Brown, 1998); Randolph W. Baxter, "'Homo-Hunting' in the Early Cold War: Senator Kenneth Wherry and the Homophobic Side of McCarthyism," *Nebraska History* 84 (2003): 118–32.

[203] Senate Judiciary Committee, Subcommittee to Investigate the Administration of the Internal Security Act and Other Internal Security Laws, *Interlocking Subversion in Government Departments*, 83rd Cong., 1st sess., 1953, Committee Print, 5, 49.

congressional oversight.[204] His subcommittee trumpeted its own achievements in ridding the federal government of security risks, corruption, and
inefficiency. During the 83rd Congress alone, the subcommittee investigated
security risks in the Government Printing Office and subversive materials
distributed by the US Information Service Centers abroad, at the same time
that they examined "inefficiency and incompetence" in the Federal Security
Agency's audit programs and, at the Voice of America, "waste and mismanagement of such magnitude as to suggest deliberate sabotage as a possible
alternative to hopeless incompetence."[205]

Increasingly, however, the behavior of these investigating committees gave
rise to criticism on the grounds of fairness, often along the lines of the criticisms
that agencies themselves faced.[206] The push to bring due process to congressional investigations focused not on administrative oversight but on how the reorganized committees and subcommittees conducted themselves. Much of this,
of course, came from the activities of those congressional committees actively
seeking out Communists, fellow travelers, and garden-variety subversives, and
the dominance of the inquisitorial model shaped perceptions of congressional
investigations for some time. By 1951, George Galloway reported, congressional investigations, formerly solely a matter of academic concern, were increasingly being attacked by "bar associations, newspaper editors, leaders of civic
groups, and members of Congress."[207] Many members objected to practices
that allowed the committee chairman or committee majority to marginalize

---

[204] Senate Committee on Government Operations, Permanent Investigations Subcommittee,
Annual Report of the Committee on Government Operations, 83rd Cong., 2nd sess., 1954,
S. Rep. 881, 2.

[205] Ibid., 42, 18.

[206] Walter Gellhorn, "Report on a Report of the House Committee on Un-American Activities,"
Harvard Law Review 60 (1947): 1193–234; Note, "Constitutional Limitations on the
Un-American Activities Committee," *Columbia Law Review* 47 (1947): 416–31; Robert K.
Carr, "Investigations in Operation: The Un-American Activities Committee," *University of
Chicago Law Review* 18 (1951): 598–633; J. W. Fulbright, "Congressional Investigations:
Significance for the Legislative Process," *University of Chicago Law Review* 18 (1951): 440–
48; "Investigations in Operation: House Subcommittee on Monopoly Power," *University of
Chicago Law Review* 18 (1951): 658–61; George Meader, "Congressional Investigations:
Importance of the Fact-Finding Process," *University of Chicago Law Review* 18 (1951): 449–
54; Voorhis, "Inner Workings"; Shils, "The Legislator and His Environment"; Ray Forrester,
"History and Function of Congressional Investigations," *Arkansas Law Review* 8 (1954): 352–
59; Lloyd K. Garrison, "Congressional Investigations: Are They a Threat to Civil Liberties?"
American Bar Association Journal 40 (1954): 125–28; Telford Taylor, *Grand Inquest: The
Story of Congressional Investigations* (New York: Simon and Schuster, 1955); Alan Barth,
Government by Investigation (Clifton, NJ: Augustus M. Kelley Publishers, 1973, reprint ed.
[originally 1955]); Joseph P. Harris, *Congressional Control of Administration* (Washington, DC:
Brookings Institution, 1964); James Hamilton, *The Power to Probe: A Study of Congressional
Investigations* (New York: Random House, 1976); see also Terence C. Halliday, "The Idiom
of Legalism in Bar Politics: Lawyers, McCarthyism, and the Civil Rights Era," *American Bar
Foundation Research Journal* 1982 (1982): 911–88.

[207] George B. Galloway, "Congressional Investigations: Proposed Reforms," *University of Chicago
Law Review* 18 (1951): 478–502, 480.

them or, worse, to ignore them altogether. Chairmen were criticized for issuing subpoenas without a majority vote, or for releasing reports bearing the committee's imprimatur but without the consent (or even the knowledge) of the entire committee.

Other practices harmed the subjects of the investigation and the witnesses called by the committee. In a 1948 series of editorials in the *Washington Post* pointing out deficiencies in Congress's own behavior, the paper remarked on committees' "vicious practice" of taking witness testimony in executive session and then having the witness repeat only portions selected by the committee in an open hearing.[208] "Such screening of testimony," the *Post* argued, "is more in line with totalitarian methods than with democracy."[209] Also under fire was the use of confidential information as the basis of public charges, which was "so utterly out of keeping with the democratic concept of fair play that no rule against it should be necessary."[210] Additional complaints included issuing charges without hearings to back them up, leaking confidential information to the press, failing to give individuals a chance to respond to public charges against them or to derogatory information supplied by other witnesses, depriving those who did appear of an attorney, and examining individuals in executive sessions, far from prying eyes and often with only one member (or, worse, only one staffer) present.[211]

Such practices were not new, of course; parties complaining of Congress run amok could point to the Dies Committee, the Smith Committee's investigation of the NLRB, the Cox Committee's FCC inquiry, the Senate War Investigating Committee under Sen. Brewster, and Sen. Kefauver's investigation into organized crime, among many others, as evidence, and Sen. Douglas's subcommittee had expressed its own concerns.[212] Few committees committed all of these offenses, and many committees of Congress committed none, but the most public and visible committees in Congress were charged with quite a few. The multiplication of subcommittees further complicated matters, as dividing, for example, the twenty-one members of the Senate Appropriations Committee among twelve subcommittees meant (even with members serving on more than one subcommittee) that many fewer members were exercising the committee's lawmaking and investigating power. This carried its own perils, Rep. Hugh Scott (R–Pa.) pointed out, for "power comes to be centered in the hands of

[208] "Turning on the Light," *Washington Post*, Feb. 20, 1948, 20.

[209] Ibid.

[210] Ibid.

[211] On the Dies Committee, see Jerry Voorhis, *Confessions of a Congressman* (Garden City, NY: Doubleday & Co., 1947), chap. 15.

[212] See Thomas I. Emerson, *Young Lawyer for the New Deal: An Insider's Memoir of the Roosevelt Years*, ed. Joan P. Emerson (Savage, MD: Rowman & Littlefield Publishers, 1991); see also *Marcello v. United States*, 196 F.2d 437 (5th Cir. 1952); *Aiuppa v. United States*, 201 F.2d 287 (6th Cir. 1952); Senate Special Committee to Investigate Organized Crime in Interstate Commerce, *Organized Crime in Interstate Commerce: Final Report*, 82nd Cong., 1st sess., 1951, S. Rep. 725.

very small groups of men whose only common background is success in the arena of partisan politics."[213] McCarthy's four-man Permanent Investigations Subcommittee in the early 1950s, famous for anonymous charges, executive sessions, and hostility to witnesses and their lawyers, exemplified this problem. The Senate Judiciary Committee's Internal Security Subcommittee had itself held more than 400 "one-man hearings" over three years – well more than half of all the hearings held during that time.[214]

Kefauver subsequently pushed to require a special approval process for sub-committees of only one or two members; investigating authority, he argued, was "just too much power to be put in the hands of one man."[215] As the *Washington Post* reflected in 1954, in light of the recent anti-Communist investigations, "an irresponsible investigator with standing authority and no time limit upon his operations can continue his rampage indefinitely with little direction or interference from the Senate."[216] All things considered, the *Post* concluded that these subcommittees were "a worse evil than the proliferation of special investigating committees," which at least had more members and more clearly defined responsibilities.[217] The idea that subcommittees were doing too much, rather than too little, became the next subject of congressional self-scrutiny, as Americans' concern about how Congress hunted for subversives turned into demands for reform.

Pressure on Congress to bring its own behavior into line with that of the courts and the agencies mounted inside and outside of Congress. Complicating matters, however, was that there was no model for what congressional com-mittees should, or should not, do. Committees had enormous leeway to act; members of Congress and scholars of the institution repeatedly emphasized that committees were not courts, should not be held to the standards of courts, and, in fact, were bound by few legal (and, thus, no practical) restrictions on what they could do.[218] The Legislative Reorganization Act had done little to address this problem, leaving it to each committee to determine its governing

---

[213] Hugh Scott and Rufus King, "Rules for Congressional Committees: An Analysis of House Resolution 447," *Virginia Law Review* 40 (1954): 249–72, 51.

[214] Senate Committee on Rules and Administration, Subcommittee on Rules, *Rules of Procedure for Senate Investigating Committees*, 83rd Cong., 2nd sess., 1954, Subcommittee Print, 17.

[215] Estes Kefauver, "A Code of Conduct for Congressional Investigations," *Arkansas Law Review* 8 (1954): 369–79, 374.

[216] "Check on Investigators," *Washington Post*, Sept. 3, 1954, 18.

[217] Ibid.

[218] James M. Landis, "Constitutional Limitations on the Congressional Power of Investigation," *Harvard Law Review* 40 (1926): 153–221; George B. Galloway, "The Investigative Function of Congress," *American Political Science Review* 21 (1927): 47–70; Senate Judiciary Committee, *Memorandum on Proceedings Involving Contempt of Congress and its Committees*, 80th Cong., 2nd sess., 1948, Committee Print; M. Nelson McGeary, "Congressional Investigations: Historical Development," *University of Chicago Law Review* 18 (1951): 425–39; John W. Gilligan, "Congressional Investigations," *Journal of Criminal Law and Criminology* 41 (1951): 618–38; Joseph F. Dolan, "The Investigating Power of Congress: Its Scope and Limitations," *Dicta* 31 (1954): 285–304.

rules and procedures. Its provisions encouraging open hearings and transparency in operations were often disregarded. However, as antisubversion investigators turned from large industries and public policies to individuals, their departure from judicial methods so recently emphasized by Congress in regard to the administrative agencies became clearer. As one author charged, congressional committees were "a notorious exception" to the rule of law.[219] Without any minimum standards of procedure, individual committees were in charge of making their own rules. HUAC and the Senate Committee on Government Operations were actually among those committees that had adopted specific procedural requirements, requiring majority approval for most actions and acknowledging the right of individuals to defend themselves against charges of subversion.[220] (HUAC did not require majority action for everything, however, as evidenced by Rep. Harold H. Velde's [R–Ill.] subpoena of former President Truman and Justice Tom Clark without his committee's assent.[221]) More to the point, however, when committee members entirely ignored their own rules of procedure, no enforcement mechanism existed to protect witnesses.

Congressional investigations thus became a popular punching bag, dominating discussions of Congress in the media and in scholarly articles much as the need for administrative fairness and congressional reorganization had done earlier in the decade. One letter writer in 1953, identifying himself only as "Bureaucrat," complained to the *Washington Post* about the inadequacy of legislation regarding "those publicity seekers and political mountebanks who now sit in the seat of inquisition."[222] As the *Post* itself remarked, "Congress is falling in the esteem of the people, and that decline is likely to continue until it curbs the misuse of its vast investigative power to serve petty, mean and partisan ends."[223] Scholars and members of Congress offered a host of solutions, including moving authority for congressional investigations to independent commissions outside Congress and holding anyone lying to congressional investigators liable for civil and criminal penalties.[224]

By far the most common proposal was a code of fair procedure to hold congressional committees and subcommittees to commonly accepted standards of due process.[225] As Sen. Scott Lucas (D–Ill.) argued in 1948, "a code embodying the traditional American ideal of fair play" was necessary to avoid

---

[219] Will Maslow, "Fair Procedure in Congressional Investigations: A Proposed Code," *Columbia Law Review* 54 (1954): 839–92, 885.

[220] C. P. Trussell, "Code of Rights for Witnesses Offered by Mundt and Nixon," *New York Times*, Dec. 28, 1948; Maslow, "Fair Procedure in Congressional Investigations," 857.

[221] James Reston, "All Lose in White Case," *New York Times*, Nov. 13, 1953, 13.

[222] "Bureaucrat," letter to the editor, *Washington Post*, Mar. 3, 1953, 14.

[223] "For Want of a Code," *Washington Post*, Mar. 22, 1950, 12; see also Trussell, "Code of Rights for Witnesses Offered by Mundt and Nixon."

[224] On independent investigating commissions, see Lindsay Rogers, "Congressional Investigations: The Problem and Its Solution," *University of Chicago Law Review* 18 (1951): 464–77. On civil penalties, see Lloyd N. Cutler, letter to the editor, *New York Times*, Sept. 5, 1948, 6E.

[225] See Maslow, "Fair Procedure in Congressional Investigations," 842 n. 15; George B. Galloway, "Congress in Action," *Nebraska Law Review* 28 (1949): 493–505, 505.

"the shooting-from-the-hip so characteristic of the House Committee on un-American Activities."[226] Congress was inundated with such proposals beginning in 1945 and continuing into the early 1950s, and in the 83rd Congress alone, twenty-four separate bills and resolutions were offered by members ranging from Rep. Dies to Sen. Kefauver to Sen. Prescott Bush (R–Conn.) to Rep. Jacob Javits (R–NY). Proposed codes generally included the right of a witness to be accompanied by an attorney, the right of witnesses to offer their own written or oral statement to the committee to be placed in the record, the right of individuals discussed in committee proceedings to respond to defamatory or derogatory information, the right of parties and others to cross-examine witnesses, the duty of committees to make transcripts available, the requirement of majority approval to issue subpoenas and committee reports, a ban on "one-man" investigating committees, and, following Kefauver's 1951 organized crime investigation, the right to be free from television and radio cameras while testifying.[227] Many members emphasized the obvious logic of due process protections common elsewhere in the federal government. As Kefauver described the code he and a number of other senators had drafted, the provisions "seek only to guarantee basic rights which are just as important before a Congressional investigation as they are before a court or a judicial tribunal."[228] The idea of such a code won wide support from members of Congress, bar associations (including the New York City Bar Association and the American Bar Association, each of whom offered their own versions), public groups such as the American Jewish Congress, and editorial writers at the *New York Times*, the *Wall Street Journal*, and the *Washington Post*. As the *Post* emphasized, such practices were "nothing more or less than the good old concept of justice."[229]

Calls for a congressional code of fair procedure were framed around procedural abuse as an overarching problem with uniform, procedural reform as the single appropriate solution, similar to the design of the Legislative Reorganization Act and the APA. This was true even though most Americans could easily have named the worst offenders. Few readers of the 1951 *University of Chicago Law Review* issue devoted to the problem would have been surprised when Lindsay Rogers, then a professor of law at Columbia, named certain members of Congress who had "terrorized our hired men in Washington" and had "misused investigations to wreak personal vengeance and to publicize their unattractive figures in headlines, newsreels, and on the wireless."[230] However, as the *Post* had argued years earlier, "To avoid confusion and subject all congressional inquiries to standards that the best committees adhere to by custom," a single code was necessary.[231]

[226] Scott W. Lucas, "Curbing the Capitol 'Cannibals,'" *Washington Post*, July 4, 1948, 2B.
[227] William J. O'Connor Jr., "Investigatory Powers of the House Un-American Activities Committee," *Cornell Law Quarterly* 33 (1948): 565–71.
[228] Kefauver, "A Code of Conduct for Congressional Investigations," 376.
[229] "Turning on the Light," *Washington Post*, Feb. 20, 1948, 20.
[230] Rogers, "The Problem and Its Solution," 465.
[231] "Code of Fair Inquiry," *Washington Post*, Apr. 8, 1948, 10.

The APA in fact served as a useful model for reformers seeking to protect individuals from the state. Lindsay Rogers had suggested that Congress apply the APA to itself, making clear that "members of investigating committees were to be judges and not inquisitors; that each committee must have counsel charged with the responsibility of preparing and presenting the evidence on the matters to be inquired into; and that the committee members should not participate in the examination or cross-examination of witnesses."[232] Kefauver complained that Congress had created a set of guidelines for government officials with the APA, but it was, as McCarthy's conduct indicated, "unwilling to do the same thing for itself."[233]

Some, however, voiced skepticism. The former assistant counsel of the Truman Committee suggested that a committee "cannot effectively discharge its investigative and policy-making duties operating as a court, with pleadings, motions, arguments and rules of evidence."[234] Such safeguards "would render investigations and legislation worse – not better."[235] University of Chicago Law School dean Edward Levi suggested that the variety of things congressional investigations did made it "not at all clear that one workable definition of proper procedure or one workable definition of proper subject matter can be set forth."[236] More were doubtful that new rules would change the behavior of publicity hounds who already ignored existing rules. As Rogers reminded readers, "there will always be congressional inquisitors who will allow their consciences to be subservient to their cravings for headlines and to disregard the obligations of procedures prescribed by law."[237] The *Washington Post* pointed out that such a law "would outlaw most of the abuses of power in which Senator McCarthy indulges," but noted that McCarthy's Permanent Investigations Subcommittee was already bound by similar rules.[238]

At best, then, a code of fair procedure might simply serve to illustrate how far deviants had strayed from the path of acceptable behavior. Rules could not, one observer noted, "guarantee the cessation of hit-and-run smears, of sensational accusations not based on evidence, on bullying inquisitors, of deliberate efforts to distort, mislead or confuse, of judgments handed down without hearing the individual condemned, of committee chairmen who ride roughshod over their fellow committee members."[239] They could, however, put "stumbling blocks in the path of the demagogue" and "create a climate of opinion that by frowning upon abuses may make them politically unprofitable."[240]

---

232 Rogers, "The Problem and Its Solution," 467.
233 Kefauver, "A Code of Conduct for Congressional Investigations," 370.
234 George Meader, "Limitations on Congressional Investigation," *Michigan Law Review* 47 (1949): 775–86, 780.
235 Ibid., 781.
236 Edward H. Levi, "Congressional Investigations: Foreword," *University of Chicago Law Review* 18 (1951): 421–22, 421.
237 Rogers, "The Problem and Its Solution," 466.
238 "Rules that Would Help," *Washington Post*, Feb. 27, 1954, 10.
239 Maslow, "Fair Procedure in Congressional Investigations," 847.
240 Ibid., 847, 848.

Support for these proposals was broad, but getting the proposals through Congress was tricky. The bills had to make their way through the notoriously recalcitrant House Rules Committee and the Senate Committee on Rules and Administration, chaired during the 83rd Congress by McCarthy's ally (and new chairman of the Senate Judiciary Committee's Internal Security Subcommittee), Sen. William E. Jenner (R–Ind.). HUAC, now led by Rep. Velde, strongly opposed such reform, as did former chairmen McCarran and Dies. (As Velde pointed out, the committees themselves needed protection from "some of the most vitriolic, disrespectful, unethical, and belligerent witnesses and counsel for witnesses who have ever appeared before any committee of Congress."[241]) Past bills and resolutions had repeatedly disappeared into committee, but in 1954 the Senate Subcommittee on Rules held hearings on three of the proposals to reform Senate procedures.[242] Alongside members of Congress, those testifying in favor of the Kefauver bill included representatives from religious and public interest organizations concerned about the hunt for subversives, including the Federal Bar Association, the American Jewish Congress, Veterans of Foreign Wars, the National Council of the Churches of Christ, the Anti-Defamation League of B'nai B'rith, Americans for Democratic Action, and the ACLU.

Following these hearings, however, the subcommittee remained skeptical that a problem existed and recommended minimum standards in place of new procedural requirements. Finding that "[n]o case has been made out that one-man hearings are by their very nature productive of unfairness or abuse," they instead pointed to McCarran's testimony that otherwise, the Senate Internal Security Subcommittee "would not have been able to function."[243] In the manner of agencies seeking exemption from procedural rules, members argued that ensuring witnesses' access to counsel "would encourage dilatory and obstructive tactics by unwilling witnesses."[244] In addition, investigations diverged so widely "that it is by no means clear that one workable procedural code can be set forth to apply uniformly to all investigations."[245] In 1955, the House Rules Committee ultimately approved a weaker resolution (one more amenable to HUAC members, and drafted with their support) setting out flexible minimum

---

[241] Senate Committee on Rules and Administration, Subcommittee on Rules, *Rules of Procedure for Senate Investigating Committees: Hearings on S. Res. 65, S. Res. 146, S. Res. 233, S. Res. 249, S. Res. 253, S. Res. 256, S. Con. Res. 11, and S. Con. Res. 86*, pt. 5, 83rd Cong., 2nd sess. 1954 (statement of Rep. Harold H. Velde, July 13), 270; "The Other Side," *Chicago Daily Tribune*, July 26, 1954, 22.

[242] See Senate Committee on Rules and Administration, Subcommittee on Rules, *Rules of Procedure for Senate Investigating Committees*.

[243] Senate Committee on Rules and Administration, Subcommittee on Rules, *Rules of Procedure for Senate Investigating Committees*, 17. Instead of a strict ban on small subcommittees, subcommittee members pointed out pragmatically that "[c]ommittees know the dispositions of their individual members" and recommended that each "adjust its quorum" as necessary (17).

[244] Senate Committee on Rules and Administration, Subcommittee on Rules, *Rules of Procedure for Senate Investigating Committees*, 23.

[245] Ibid., 11.

standards for House committees.[246] The practice of establishing one-man committee hearings was banned, and counsel was to be provided, but various provisions ensuring majority control were struck.

Ultimately, Congress continued to lack any overall code of fair procedure,
even in the years following the Senate's formal censure of Sen. McCarthy.
Although this censure might have relieved the need for immediate reform, a
Washington Post editorial pointed out that condemning McCarthy's actions
would hardly avoid such problems in the future. "If the abuses associated with
McCarthyism are to be corrected, regulations that will prevent one-man inqui-
sitions and protect witnesses must be written into the rules of the House and
Senate, with adequate provision for their enforcement."[247] At the end of the
day, however, no general code of procedure was adopted, and Congress turned
its attention to other things.

By the mid-1950s, the two major administrative procedure acts of 1946 had
proven little match for the politics of the administrative process. In a context
where evidence of bad behavior in any agency acted to justify reform aimed at
every agency, the APA and the Legislative Reorganization Act both promised
to bring both law and politics to bear on the heretofore unrestrained agencies and commissions. Both statutes sought to protect the regulated parties
from the agencies, through resort to courts under the APA and congressional
committees under the Legislative Reorganization Act. Both statutes sought to
protect the regulated parties from the agencies and both prescribed a single
overarching solution to the problem at hand. Both demonstrated a persistent
commitment to using uniform structures and formal legal authority to monitor
how administrators exercised the discretion and legal authority that Congress
had given them in the first place. At the same time, both provided the illusion
of fairness without actual change. The Legislative Reorganization Act did, of
course, rearrange the committee structure of Congress on the model of the
executive agencies and independent commissions and give those committees
better tools to oversee administrative activities. The APA similarly established
new minimum standards for administrative behavior. However, the influence
of each on the administrative state was at best fragmented and was heavily
influenced by postwar political imperatives.

Given how little change they effected in practice (and how predictable this
outcome was), it is useful to consider the presence of the acts themselves, rather
than any particular outcomes, as the intended solution to the problem at hand.
In an environment where Congress was under fire, members used investigations

[246] See Edward J. Heubel, "Committee Resistance to Reform: The House Adopts a Code for
Investigating Committees," *Midwest Journal of Political Science* 1 (1957): 313–29, 325–27;
Floyd M. Riddick, "The Eighty-Fourth Congress: First Session," *Western Political Quarterly*
8 (1955): 612–29, 624; Congressional Quarterly, *Congress and the Nation 1945–1964: A
Review of Government and Politics in the Postwar Years* (Washington, DC: CQ Press, 1965),
1683–85.

[247] "Rules for Investigators," *Washington Post*, Jan. 9, 1955, E4.

and statutory reform to assert their right to define what "fairness" meant in the administrative state. The Legislative Reorganization Act, then, served as proof that Congress had managed to address both its own shortcomings and those of the agencies through expert analysis of the problems and shared consensus on the solutions. Members accepted the presence of agency governance, but suggested that administrators could not be left on their own. Instead, there was an important role for Congress to play. As members continued to exercise their oversight authority, a new set of administrative problems appeared, based more in administrators' selfishness than in their zeal for government action.

4

The Hoover Commission and the 80th Congress

The Republicans who took control of Congress in 1947 did so not just by campaigning on their ability to better protect the security of the United States. Throughout the campaign season, candidates had also touted their plans to reduce the cost, size, and scope of the federal government. The latter did not happen smoothly, of course. Defense spending and employment skyrocketed in the postwar years, and the National Security Act of 1947, which unified the War and Navy Departments and established the Central Intelligence Agency and the National Security Council, created massive new bureaucratic strongholds.[1] In the domestic sphere, however, as one observer recalled, Republicans came to Congress "with a determination to see if it would be possible to roll back the New Deal."[2] The *Chicago Tribune* reported in January that Republicans "solemnly pledged a return to government by the people instead of by burocracy," and their enthusiasm for this project was evident as they cut bureaucratic budgets, launched offensives against individual agencies, and challenged the legitimacy of the administrative state as a whole.[3] The Taft-Hartley Act, passed in June 1947, was one part of this project; the Commission on Organization of the Executive Branch of Government, established a month later, was another.

The "Hoover Commission," named after its chairman, Herbert Hoover, was the 80th Congress's attempt to harness the expertise of those outside the administrative state in support of explicitly conservative goals. By focusing attention on the overall size and shape of government rather than on specific policies and programs, members of the Hoover Commission who looked forward to making major cuts in government functions and offices framed their efforts as

[1] For a discussion of defense organization, see Michael J. Hogan, *A Cross of Iron: Harry S. Truman and the Origins of the National Security State, 1945–1954* (Cambridge: Cambridge University Press, 1998).
[2] Jarold Kieffer oral history interview, Oct. 10, 1979, HHL, 1.
[3] Laurence Burd, "House Majority Pledges to Pull U.S. 'Out of Bog,'" *Chicago Daily Tribune*, Jan. 4, 1947, 2; see also Vermont Royster, "Payroll Propaganda," *Wall Street Journal*, April 7, 1947, 1; Gale E. Peterson, *President Harry S. Truman and the Independent Regulatory Commissions, 1945–1952* (New York: Garland Publishing, 1985).

"good government" reforms rather than partisan attacks on New Deal programs. The commission's recommendations were based on the findings of eminent academics, businessmen, and government officials, in a further effort to elevate political issues above partisanship. Expertise was in the hands of those observing the administrative agencies, not the bureaucrats themselves. In certain ways, then, the Hoover Commission had much in common with President Roosevelt's Committee on Administrative Management, which had addressed administrative disorder with solutions intended to entrench and strengthen it.

The Hoover Commission's ability to enact major changes to federal policy was significantly curtailed when the predicted Republican administration failed to materialize. In the new political context of 1949, where Democrats controlled the White House and both houses of Congress, Hoover and his commission grudgingly accepted the government's existing policy commitments but not their form. Members focused on presenting Congress with managerial and organizational solutions that would improve presidential supervision of administrative officials while preserving Congress's authority over the independent commissions. The Hoover Commission thus became synonymous with ideas of strict hierarchical structures, improved presidential supervision, powerful agency heads, and more professional staffers. Willing to seize the high-profile political opportunity the Hoover Commission offered, the Truman White House embraced many of the Hoover Commission's recommendations and added their own.[4] The ultimate legacy of the Hoover Commission was, in fact, to further legitimize administrative governance, carving out a place for the agencies and commissions in the federal government, expanding the president's role therein, and putting the weight of the Hoover Commission's reputation behind its operations.[5]

Unlike previous examinations of bureaucracy during the 1940s, fairness was not the key issue. Efficiency was. The commission did not provide new fodder to support claims of "administrative absolutism"; instead, through a strikingly effective marketing campaign, it directed attention to a different set of administrative problems and tapped a new vein of antibureaucratic politics.

---

[4] For studies of reorganization during the Truman administration, see Herbert Emmerich, *Essays on Federal Reorganization* (University: University of Alabama Press, 1950); Harvey C. Mansfield, "Reorganizing the Federal Executive Branch: The Limits of Institutionalization," *Law and Contemporary Problems* 35 (1970): 461–95; Herbert Emmerich, *Federal Organization and Administrative Management* (University: University of Alabama Press, 1971); Stephen Hess, *Organizing the Presidency* (Washington, DC: The Brookings Institution, 1976); Ronald C. Moe, *Executive Branch Reorganization: An Overview* (Washington, DC: Government Printing Office, 1978); William E. Pemberton, *Bureaucratic Politics: Executive Reorganization during the Truman Administration* (Columbia: University of Missouri Press, 1979); Ronald C. Moe, *The Hoover Commissions Revisited* (Boulder, CO: Westview Press, 1982); Peri E. Arnold, *Making the Managerial Presidency: Comprehensive Reorganization Planning, 1905–1996*, 2nd ed. (Lawrence: University Press of Kansas, 1998).

[5] See Matthew A. Crenson and Francis E. Rourke, "By Way of Conclusion: American Bureaucracy since World War II," in Louis Galambos, ed., *The New American State: Bureaucracies and Policies since World War II*, 137–77 (Baltimore: Johns Hopkins University Press, 1987), 140.

Administrative governance was slow and plodding, not tyrannical, and the administrators populating the ommission's many reports were neither subversive nor overly zealous. Unfortunately for Americans, nor were they demonstrating their alleged expertise. Instead, the commission told stories of bureaucrats protecting themselves but uninterested in working efficiently or well. The Hoover Commission popularized a new way of thinking about the administrative state, one that foreshadowed claims of administrative capture and administrative indolence that became increasingly widespread in the 1950s. Administration was plagued by delays and backlogs resulting from legalistic proceduralism, and independent commissions in particular were criticized for failure to engage in the type of broad, long-term planning for which they had been given independence in the first place. The "problem" of the administrative state, then, was its failure to deliver good government at a reasonable price. The idea that administrators were simply looking out for themselves was coming to replace the idea that they were defending their own conception of the public interest. This new vision of how agencies operated fed the Hoover Commission's focus on formal authority rather than the political contexts in which each agency and commission struggled to operate.

Early in the 80th Congress, at the same time members of each house were familiarizing themselves with their oversight authority under the Legislative Reorganization Act, the new Republican leadership began planning new inquiries into the administrative state. In creating the Commission on Organization of the Executive Branch of the Government in July 1947, Congress gathered together a group of prominent Americans and assigned them the task of investigating and eliminating the inefficiencies and high costs of federal governance. Language allowing the commission to determine which government services and functions were "not necessary to the efficient conduct of government" and to recommend their wholesale abolition suggested that Congress had given the commission a sweeping mandate.[6] No agencies or commissions were exempted from the inquiry, so the federal government as a whole was fair game. As one participant recalled, the commission's "intent was to examine not only how the Federal Government conducted programs – that is from a management point of view – but *why*."[7]

Although Republicans in Congress were the chief supporters of this investigation, the statute required balance in the commission's membership. The twelve members – four each appointed by the White House, the House, and the Senate – were equally split between Democrats and Republicans and between those in the public and private sector. Half of the commission's members – former president Herbert Hoover, former Undersecretary of State Dean Acheson, Secretary of Defense James V. Forrestal, Civil Service Commissioner Arthur S. Flemming, former SEC and Maritime Commission chairman Joseph

---

[6] Pub. L. No. 162, § 1, 61 Stat. 246 (1947).
[7] Kieffer oral history interview, Oct. 10, 1979, 1.

P. Kennedy, and former Roosevelt assistant James H. Rowe Jr. – were experienced administrators, and three more – Sen. George Aiken (R–Vt.), Sen. John L. McClellan (D–Ark.), and Rep. Carter Manasco (D–Ala.) – were familiar with problems of government spending as present or past members of the Senate or House Committees on Expenditures in the Executive Departments. This study group staffed, at least in part, with prominent men from the private sector loosely resembled Roosevelt's Brownlow Committee, which had examined the similarly complicated federal landscape in 1937, and the Attorney General's Committee on Administrative Procedure, which explored its inner workings a few years later. As with those committees, the prominence of the Hoover Commission's members would go far in bolstering their ultimate recommendations.

Hoover, who was quickly elected chairman by the group, took this idea further and organized twenty-four separate task forces, each with its own project director and research staff, to investigate particular subjects and report their findings to the commission. Relying on experts in each field offered Hoover a way to strengthen the commission's own authority in the areas under investigation while at the same time giving well-known Americans a stake in the project's success or failure. This approach was one that the Budget Bureau had previously suggested to President Truman, who had struggled to win support for his own reorganization proposals in 1946 and 1947.[8] One option "for reducing the purely partisan Congressional treatment" of the president's reorganization proposals, the bureau suggested, would be turn to an advisory committee that would call together "distinguished citizens from varied walks of life" to study government organization.[9] This was the method the Hoover Commission would choose for itself. According to one staffer, commission members hoped that the task force method "could induce outstanding individuals to serve the Commission, that it could speed up the work, and that the various supporting studies would provide a expert foundation for the Commission's own recommendations."[10] Expertise about the government's problems was to be found outside the government; bringing in new voices would legitimate the commission's findings.

Some task forces focused on a specific industry or policy area, such as Veterans Affairs, Public Works, and Federal Business Enterprises; others focused on problems common to multiple areas, such as those on Personnel Management and Budgeting and Accounting, or broader relationships, such as Regulatory Agencies and Federal-State Relations. Consistent with his belief in bringing the public and private sectors together, Hoover drew widely from

[8] For more on Truman's reorganization goals, see Pemberton, *Bureaucratic Politics*.
[9] "Use of an Advisory Committee in Preparing Reorganization Plans for Presentation to the Congress in Early 1947," Aug. 12, 1946, 1, Folder "Bureau of the Budget: Reorganization," Box 19, Webb Papers, HSTL.
[10] Ferrel Heady, "The Operation of a Mixed Commission," *American Political Science Review* 43 (1949): 940–52, 943.

business, government, and academia, selecting task force members including Lewis Meriam of the Brookings Institution, former War Production Board vice chairman Ferdinand Eberstadt, former War Secretary and Secretary of State Henry L. Stimson, and New York City planner Robert Moses. Certain studies, such as the task force reports on the Post Office, Lending Agencies, and Business Enterprises, were contracted out to private management consulting firms; others, including those on Transportation and Public Welfare, were assigned to research institutions such as the Brookings Institution and the Institute of Public Administration. At the same time, Hoover reached for men and women he felt would support his own conception of the commission's goals. As one Hoover assistant later remarked, the task forces "all seemed to have a fairly considerable conservative element in them." [11]

Indeed, the political preferences of the Hoover Commission's personnel were evident early on. Although the *Washington Post* lauded the "unimpeachable integrity" of the commission's members, the inclusion of such figures as Hoover, Kennedy, and Rowe suggested that old New Deal battles might take new form within the commission. [12] One former Commerce Department colleague, in a terse telegram congratulating Hoover on his appointment, remarked that the "[v]estigial New Deal bureaucratic units" were "much alarmed judging from my continuous incoming phone calls." [13] These partisan lines were apparent in an initial disagreement over the scope of the project itself. Consistent with his longtime approach to government, Hoover was interested in using the commission to reduce the size of government and to chip away at the profusion of administrative agencies. Throughout his career, Hoover had resisted significant government intervention in the marketplace. During his tenure as U.S. Food Administrator during World War I, as Secretary of Commerce during the Harding and Coolidge administration, and as president, Hoover had been enthusiastic about the benefits of business-government cooperation but markedly hostile to government activity that competed with private businesses or exercised significant coercive authority. [14]

[11] Don K. Price oral history interview, HHL, 18.
[12] "Reorganization," *Washington Post*, Nov. 14, 1948, 4B.
[13] Julius Klein to Herbert Hoover, telegram, July 18, 1947, Folder "General Management of the Executive Branch Correspondence – Dr. Julius Klein," Box 12, HC I, HHPPP, HHL.
[14] For more on Hoover, see Herbert Hoover, *The Challenge to Liberty* (New York: Charles Scribner's Sons, 1934); see also Carl N. Degler, "The Ordeal of Herbert Hoover," *Yale Review* 52 (June 1963): 563–83; Ellis W. Hawley, "Herbert Hoover, the Commerce Secretariat, and the Vision of an 'Associative State,' 1921–1928," *Journal of American History* 61 (1974): 116–40; Robert D. Cuff, "Herbert Hoover, the Ideology of Voluntarism and War Organization during the Great War," *Journal of American History* 64 (1977): 358–72; Joan Hoff Wilson, "Hoover's Agricultural Policies 1921–1928," *Agricultural History* 51 (1977): 335–61; Kim McQuaid, "Corporate Liberalism in the American Business Community, 1920–1940," *Business History Review* 52 (1978): 342–68; Robert D. Cuff, "The Dilemmas of Voluntarism: Hoover and the Pork-Packing Agreement of 1917–1919," *Agricultural History* 53 (1979): 727–47; Ellis W. Hawley, "Three Facets of Hooverian Associationalism: Lumber, Aviation, and Movies, 1921–30," in Thomas K. McCraw, ed., *Regulation in Perspective: Historical Essays*, 95–123

The commission that came to bear his name offered Hoover an enormous opportunity to articulate his view of proper governance and demonstrate it in practice. Addressing his fellow commissioners at their first meeting, Hoover echoed the concerns of Roosevelt and his Brownlow Committee as he charged that the supervisory burden on the president "is intolerable. It is impossible, physically, for him to have sufficient contact with those agencies to supervise them."[15] Nor was this the only problem. Government had grown so large, Hoover informed the commission, that "I have a rough estimate that there are more people now employed in the United States advising how to get on with the Government than there are employed by the Government itself."[16] This, he suggested, "must be a tremendous burden on the productivity of the country."[17]

Budget Director James Webb later recalled that Hoover began with the thought that "he should tell the country and the Congress all the things that were being done that were wrong and ought to be changed."[18] Commissioner Rowe similarly claimed that "Hoover definitely thought he was going to use the Commission as a vehicle to overturn the New Deal in substance."[19] Rowe and Acheson forcefully protested this broad interpretation of the commission's powers, and, as Acheson argued to Hoover before the 1948 elections, "both as a matter of practicality and of law, I don't believe that twelve men selected to get all views on organization can in a year review the substantive legislation of the United States and recommend what should be retained and what scrapped."[20] Such a job, he argued, "would involve the highest legislative policy on some of the most controversial matters before the country on which opinion is divided geographically, politically, and on the basis of economic groups. To achieve any sort of agreement here would be a miracle."[21]

Most of the commissioners adopted Hoover's expansive understanding of their role, however, and adopted a policy statement confirming their belief that the commission had been "clearly directed" by Congress to investigate "the boundaries of government functions in the light of their cost, their usefulness,

(Cambridge, MA: Harvard University Press, 1981); David D. Lee, "Herbert Hoover and the Development of Commercial Aviation, 1921–1926," *Business History Review* 58 (1984): 78–102; David E. Hamilton, "Building the Associative State: The Department of Agriculture and American State-Building," *Agricultural History* 64 (1990): 207–18.

[15] Transcript of meeting, Sept. 29, 1947, 2–3, Folder "Francis P. Brassor, 1947–50," Box 32, HC I, HHPPP, HHL.

[16] Ibid., 2.

[17] Ibid.

[18] Truman White House oral history interview, HSTL, 42.

[19] James H. Rowe Jr. oral history interview, HSTL, 82.

[20] Dean Acheson to Herbert Hoover, Aug. 27, 1948, 2, Folder "COEBG 47–49: Correspondence (3)," Box 64, Flemming Papers, DDEL; see also James H. Rowe to Francis P. Brassor, memorandum, Oct. 11, 1948, 1, Folder "Minutes and Agenda of Meetings, 1947–1949," Box 19, Acheson Papers, HSTL.

[21] Acheson to Hoover, Aug. 27, 1948, 2.

their limitations, and their curtailment or elimination."[22] Such a task was what the public wanted and what the 80th Congress had pledged to achieve; "at no time has there been such a public desire for a complete reconsideration of the province of the Federal government and overhaul of the business methods of Federal administration and their relationship to the citizen."[23] Press coverage of the commission during 1948 indicated similar enthusiasm about scaling back government. The *Chicago Tribune* criticized the federal government for having "no organization, no unity, anywhere," and the *Los Angeles Times* compared the "uncontrolled and illogical" growth of government to "the multiplication of cells in a cancer."[24] As the paper complained, "Congressmen find it almost impossible to hack purposefully at this bureaucratic jungle."[25]

Even though administrative officials came in for their share of the blame, these were not the bureaucratic zealots of Congress's wartime charges or the ABA's nightmares. Instead, the press attacked administrators who took government salaries but provided no value to Americans. Suggesting that "bureaucrats are not above deception and intimidation" to keep their jobs, the *Los Angeles Times* reported that "[t]he conniving bureaucrats of the depression agencies created 15 years ago are still hanging on in the boom, their payrolls scarcely diminished."[26] Deriding what the paper routinely (and efficiently) called "burocracy," the *Chicago Tribune* similarly claimed "The New Deal makes a virtue of duplication and disorder because that is the way to put more burocrats on the pay roll to support the machine."[27] Democrats were to blame, the paper reported; the New Deal growth in federal workers was considerable, and "Truman, with an election coming, has been adding an average of 482 new payrollers each day."[28] It was not only subversive government employees, then, that Republican presidential candidate Thomas Dewey referenced in 1948 as he promised Americans "the biggest, fanciest housecleaning in the history of the Federal Government."[29]

Even as Hoover stacked his task forces with like-minded individuals, his commission stayed out of electoral politics during the 1948 election season to reinforce the nonpartisan image of the commission. Hoover tried to prevent the early public release of task force materials, noting that "I have a horror

[22] Policy Statement, Oct. 20, 1947, 2, Folder "Sidney A. Mitchell, Oct. 1947 – June 1948," Box 36, HC I, HHPPP, HHL. Commissioner Rep. Clarence J. Brown (R-Ohio) confirmed that he had intended to give the commission the authority to investigate policy questions (See Minutes of Official Proceedings, Oct. 7 and 8, 1948, 2, Folder "Minutes and Agenda of Meetings, 1947–1949," Box 19, Acheson Papers, HSTL).

[23] Policy Statement, Oct. 20, 1947, 2.

[24] "The Maze," *Chicago Daily Tribune*, Sept. 18, 1948, 10; "The Disease of Big Government," *Los Angeles Times*, Oct. 6, 1948, B4.

[25] "The Disease of Big Government," *Los Angeles Times*, B4.

[26] Ibid.

[27] "The Maze," *Chicago Daily Tribune*, 10.

[28] Ibid.; see Arnold, *Making the Managerial Presidency*, 127–28.

[29] Dewey, quoted in "Dewey Promises Biggest Federal Housecleaning," *Washington Post*, June 11, 1948, 14.

of getting anything out to the public that could be used in the campaign."[30] There was, however, a widespread understanding that the Hoover Commission was preparing its recommendations for implementation by a Republican White House following Dewey's predicted victory. As the *Chicago Tribune* commented, "it is to be hoped that there will be a new President" by the time the Hoover Commission completed its studies; "Mr. Dewey is often acclaimed as a competent administrator, but no one can competently administer a lunatic asylum."[31] Congress had instructed the Hoover Commission to report its findings and recommendations in January 1949; the postelection date was selected, one Hoover correspondent noted, "very deliberately so as to lay the groundwork for the expected complete housecleaning that will be necessary at that time."[32] During the campaign, Hoover designated his assistant as a liaison to Dewey's staff, and, as the Hoover Commission's public relations director later recalled, members assumed that "after election day had come and gone there would be Mr. Dewey with a green light, smiling and bowing, while the Commission unveiled its report and sailed down a clear track."[33]

Given that Truman's own approach to state building included significant expansion of the federal government's responsibilities in areas including housing, education, employment, social welfare, health insurance, public works, and race relations, the Hoover Commission's silence shielded Truman from the commission's possible criticism.[34] During his 1948 campaign, Truman had his hands full with challenges from Republicans (who objected to his attempts to expand the New Deal state), Dixiecrats (who found Truman and the Democratic Party far too sympathetic to civil rights), and the Progressive Party (which was concerned about Truman's foreign policy choices and wanted to push the Democratic Party further left).[35] Additional attacks from an allegedly apolitical assembly of experts were not what the beleaguered White House needed.

The Democratic sweep in the 1948 elections significantly changed the political environment for the Hoover Commission's work. Hoover's assistant Don K. Price later recalled "a terribly frigid atmosphere" the next morning, as much depended on Truman's support of the project.[36] As Charles B. Coates, the Hoover Commission's Director of Public Relations, pointed out, Truman "had it in his

[30] Transcript, Hoover Commission Meeting, Mar. 22, 1948, 18, Folder "Volume I – originals Transcripts of Commission Meetings, Meetings 1 through 9," Box 27, Transcripts of Meetings of the Commission, Sept. 29, 1947–May 26, 1949, NC115, Entry 2, SO, RG 264, NACP.

[31] "The Maze," *Chicago Daily Tribune*, 10.

[32] Julius Klein to Herbert Hoover, July 18, 1947, 1, Folder "General Management of the Executive Branch Correspondence – Dr. Julius Klein," Box 12, HC I, HHPPP, HHL. (Klein forwarded this message from Rep. Brown.)

[33] Charles B. Coates oral history interview, HHL, 2.

[34] Richard E. Neustadt, "Congress and the Fair Deal: A Legislative Balance Sheet," *Public Policy* 5 (1954): 351–81.

[35] For more on Truman and the 1948 elections, see Susan M. Hartmann, *Truman and the 80th Congress* (Columbia: University of Missouri Press, 1971).

[36] Price oral history interview, 29.

power to abolish it if he chose – to ignore it. He was President. He could have squashed it like a bug, really."[37] After some hasty maneuvering, the commission obtained Truman's public support. As Rowe recalled, Hoover "could read the election returns."[38] The project of entirely remaking the New Deal state became unrealistic; as the *Washington Post* bureaucracy columnist suggested, Americans "voted, in effect, for more housing, more social security, and more New Deal measures in general."[39] Thus the Hoover Commission shifted focus. One Hoover Commission staffer recollected Hoover and Truman striking an explicit agreement: if the Hoover Commission kept to questions of "management improvement – how better to do the things the Federal Government was doing," the Truman administration would stand behind "the Commission's recommendations for strengthening the basic apparatus of government."[40]

This arrangement benefited everyone. Hoover no longer had to fear throwing out a year's work, and Truman had much to gain by allying himself with the Hoover Commission. As columnist Drew Pearson reported in late November, Truman "plans to use Hoover's name to wrest from Congress powers which they refused give to Franklin Roosevelt."[41] At stake was formal reorganization authority that would allow Truman to send reorganization plans to Congress for approval. The reorganization plan process placed the burden on Congress to react; if Congress failed to reject the plans within a short period, they became law. Truman's earlier reorganization proposals had met with resistance in Congress, and, following the expiration of reorganization authority in 1948, the White House's requests for extension had fallen on deaf ears in Congress. As Truman's Budget Director James Webb advised a few days after the election, the White House "ought not to miss the chance to make this fundamental reform in the way the Constitution works, and make your leadership more effective and your job easier."[42]

Webb clearly had in mind Roosevelt's difficulty in securing reorganization authority from a hesitant Congress. With Hoover's support, however, Truman might be given even more authority than Roosevelt. The latter's Brownlow Committee had recommended combining *all* executive agencies and independent commissions within one of twelve departments (which included two new departments, devoted to Social Welfare and Public Works) under the president's control, but Congress, reluctant to cede power to Roosevelt, had first excluded the independent commissions from his authority in the reorganization bills, and then refused to grant such authority at all.[43] The Reorganization Act that

[37] Coates oral history interview, 4.
[38] Rowe oral history interview, 83.
[39] Jerry Kluttz, "The Federal Diary," *Washington Post*, Nov. 8, 1948, B1.
[40] Kieffer oral history interview, Oct. 10, 1979, 2.
[41] Drew Pearson, "Merry-Go-Round," *Washington Post*, Nov. 19, 1948, 13C.
[42] James Webb to Harry S. Truman, memorandum, Nov. 5, 1948, 2, Folder "285-E 1948," Box 919, WHCF: OF 285, HST Papers, HSTL.
[43] Joseph P. Harris, "The Progress of Administrative Reorganization in the Seventy-Fifth Congress," *American Political Science Review* 31 (1937): 862–70; Lindsay Rogers, "Reorganization: Post Mortem Notes," *Political Science Quarterly* 53 (1938): 161–72.

Congress passed in 1939 was significantly weaker than that proposed by the White House two years earlier, allowing the president to combine executive agencies but barring him from creating new executive departments or entirely abolishing old ones. He was also prevented from any interference with agencies and commissions about which Congress felt proprietary, including the General Accounting Office, the Civil Service Commission, and the independent regulatory commissions.[44] As Webb told Truman, congressional opposition was to be expected, but "there is now a possibility of getting the last Republican President to urge you to accept an implementation of and organization for executive responsibility that the Republican Party has historically denied to Presidents."[45]

Even before the commission's research was complete, Hoover took additional steps to prevent his work from falling into obscurity. He was well aware that once the reports were released, the commission's work was only half done; actually implementing the commission's recommendations would require strong action by Truman, by Congress, and by officials in the affected executive agencies and independent commissions. Truman had promised to support the project, and could be relied on to support at least those recommendations that furthered his own goals, but Hoover anticipated significant opposition from the agencies and commissions subject to such reforms. This was the point at which previous reorganization efforts had been thwarted, through a combination of active opposition from administrators, Congress, and interest groups, on the one hand, and Americans' general apathy, on the other. Roosevelt's own executive reorganization effort had been opposed not just by members of Congress but by his own administrative officials and by regulated interests who feared change. During the Brownlow Committee's conversations with Henry Wallace, Harold Ickes, and other officials, Louis Brownlow later recalled, "each Cabinet member thought that the ideal reorganization plan would leave his department intact but bring into it, and thus under his control, a bunch of the bureaus now unfortunately misplaced and badly managed under the direction of other members of the Cabinet."[46] The Budget Bureau had similarly cautioned Truman in 1946 that reorganization proposals had to be kept secret, "or they will be sabotaged by employees, officials, congressmen, and private interest groups."[47] Comptroller General Lindsay Warren warned the House Committee on Expenditures in the Executive Departments in 1947 that the creation of yet another commission to make recommendations, without legal authority to implement those recommendations, was "a waste of public

[44] Reorganization Act of 1939, Pub. L. No. 19, 53 Stat. 561 (1939).
[45] Webb to Truman, memorandum, Nov. 5, 1948, 1–2, Folder "285-E 1948," Box 919, WHCF: OF 285, HST Papers, HSTL; see also Hess, *Organizing the Presidency.*
[46] Louis Brownlow, *A Passion for Anonymity: The Autobiography of Louis Brownlow* (Chicago: University of Chicago Press, 1958), 372–73.
[47] "Use of an Advisory Committee in Preparing Reorganization Plans for Presentation to the Congress in Early 1947," 4.

funds."[48] And as the Hoover Commission's work neared completion, observers spoke darkly of administrators' wiles, suggesting that the relative success or failure of the Hoover Commission's recommendations "will depend upon the discipline which the Administration leaders can enforce upon the lower echelons of Government officials and their Congressional patrons."[49] Indeed, one reporter warned that, even before any reports had been issued, "the labor and left-wing allies of the administration are putting out adverse propaganda."[50]

Hoover, clearly concerned that his commission would fall victim to such forces, moved to create countervailing pressure in favor of reorganization. As Commissioner Arthur Flemming recalled, Hoover "said, 'If we stop now, and just file this report, it will gather dust and nothing will happen.' He said, 'We've got to take some steps to rally public opinion back of these recommendations.'"[51] Even before the reports were completed, Hoover developed a strategy to get the public interested in the commission and the hundreds of recommendations it planned to offer. He recruited Charles Coates, an executive at General Foods, to serve as the Hoover Commission's Director of Public Relations and to develop a strategy to "sell" the reports to the public. This was a daunting task; Coates recalled that, when he was hired in late 1948, "I had never heard of the Hoover Commission; nobody else had."[52] From this inauspicious beginning came an enormous publicity campaign intended to drum up significant public support for the reorganization project as a whole, and to provide a counterbalance to the anticipated opposition by portraying them as power-hungry administrators and selfish private interests.

Crucial to this effort was the Citizens Committee for the Hoover Report, a nonpartisan interest group established by the Hoover Commission in early 1949. The committee sought to create enough support among the public to overcome the anticipated opposition. Members of the Hoover Commission's lobbying group included Columbia University President Dwight D. Eisenhower, Harvard University President James B. Conant, former Supreme Court Justice Owen Roberts, former Vice Presidents John Nance Garner and Charles G. Dawes, former Commerce Secretary Jesse Jones, General Electric President Charles W. Wilson, Studio Executive Louis B. Mayer, and Management Engineer Lillian Gilbreth.[53] Such an august set of participants would, it was hoped, elevate the Hoover Commission out of the realm of base politics in the public mind and indicate that consensus between public and private interests was possible.

---

[48] Lindsay C. Warren to Rep. Clare E. Hoffman, May 21, 1947, 11, Folder "285-A 1947," Box 917, WHCF: OF 285, HST Papers, HSTL.

[49] Cabell Phillips, "Hoover Board Plans Affected by Election," *New York Times*, Nov. 14, 1948, E7.

[50] Frank R. Kent, "Labor, Left-Wingers Gun for Hoover Report," *Los Angeles Times*, Nov. 24, 1948, A4.

[51] Arthur S. Flemming oral history interview, HSTL, 24.

[52] Coates oral history interview, 1.

[53] "Group to Push Hoover Reform Plan Organized," *Chicago Daily Tribune*, Mar. 30, 1949, 5.

Temple University president and former vice president of *Time* magazine Robert L. Johnson headed the project; with Hoover's help, he argued, "we can bring enough of the right kind of pressure to bear to make it difficult for anyone in Congress to oppose the program."[54] Rather than attacking Congress, Johnson suggested, "let's try to make the Congressmen feel that we are endeavoring to give them the necessary ammunition to defeat any selfish groups that might take the warpath against us."[55] This approach proved remarkably successful in overcoming interest group and bureaucratic opposition and in keeping pressure on Congress and on the Truman administration to adopt the reforms. By portraying the project as a nonpartisan effort to protect American democratic government, the Hoover Commission was able to accuse its opponents of being self-interested and potentially anti-American.

The commission's February 1949 report on General Management in the Executive Branch, the first report sent to Congress, addressed the president's role in managing the executive branch (which, the Hoover Commission had decided, included the formally independent regulatory commissions) and set the tone for the reports that would follow. This report reflected Hoover's broad concern about the president's relationship to the administrative state and attempted to complement the more functional task force studies. Rather than creating a separate task force for this project, Hoover, with the help of Don Price, a former Budget Bureau employee working at the Public Administration Clearing House, relied on assistants from academia and government, existing research, and his own experience. As Herbert Emmerich recalled Hoover commenting, "Who is there who ought to know more about it?"[56]

The main thrust of Hoover's report on general management was the need for more presidential control over the various agencies and commissions, so that the executive branch would have "the simplicity of structure, the unity of purpose, and the clear line of executive authority that was originally intended under the Constitution."[57] The report envisioned the president at the top of an enormous pyramidal organizational chart, with all authority flowing from him to department heads, and from these department heads to subordinate officials. Hoover himself took to the radio to describe "a great need for a definite line of command running from the President to the office-boy, and back up from the office-boy to the President."[58] Thus, rather than shrinking the

---

[54] Robert L. Johnson to Herbert Hoover, Feb. 21, 1949, Folder "Robert L. Johnson, Feb.–Apr. 1949," Box 34, HHPPP, HCI, HHL.

[55] Ibid.

[56] Herbert Hoover, quoted in Emmerich, *Federal Organization and Administrative Management*, 86; see also Arnold, *Making the Managerial Presidency*, chap. 5.

[57] Commission on Organization of the Executive Branch of the Government (Hoover Commission I), *General Management of the Executive Branch* (Washington, DC: Government Printing Office, 1949), viii.

[58] Herbert Hoover, quoted in "Hoover Urges Cut in U.S. Employe[e]s," *New York Times*, Apr. 19, 1949, 20.

administrative state to lessen the burdens on the president – a proposal that would have been politically difficult before the 1948 elections and impossible thereafter – Hoover moved to enlarge the powers of the president to manage the administrative state, something he had been thinking about even before the election.[59]

Implicit in both the Hoover Commission's earlier approach and this one was a sense that administrators and their institutions had too much political power and too much legal independence. As Hoover argued, "the United States is paying heavily for a lack of order, a lack of clear lines of authority and responsibility, and a lack of effective organization in the executive branch."[60] The organizational proposals of the Hoover Commission sought to bring all bureaucrats in line and make clear who was responsible when work did not get done. This model of supervision – strictly defining the jurisdiction of each administrative official and embedding him in a hierarchical organization – resembled the most formal conception of bureaucracy, which, by limiting administrative discretion by rules and organization, ensured that bureaucrats ignored their own personal motives and followed their supervisor's lead. Bureaucrats in this system were thus envisioned not as zealous policy makers but as jealous staffers seeking to maintain their personal fiefdoms. Too little, rather than too much, regulatory energy was a new complaint about the administrators in light of the charges of subversion Congress and the Truman White House were busy investigating.

One key to improved presidential oversight was the reduction of the president's workload to a manageable level. Hoover found that more than seventy-five agencies and commissions reported directly to the president. These included the independent commissions, such as the ICC and FTC; offices in the Executive Office of the President, such as the Budget Bureau and the Council of Economic Advisers; executive departments, such as Interior, Agriculture, Justice, and State; and other permanent agencies, ranging from the Atomic Energy Commission to the CSC to the Smithsonian Institution. As a result, Hoover argued, it would be "manifestly impossible for the President to give adequate supervision to so many agencies."[61] He thus recommended cutting the number of executive agencies by two-thirds – not abolishing them, but grouping them into larger departments "by major purposes" so that each department would have "a coherent mission."[62] Including all the agencies in this new organizational scheme would also simplify lines of supervision, "cutting through the barriers which have in many cases made bureaus and agencies partially independent of the Chief Executive."[63] Simply moving the agencies and departments would not reduce the work of the federal government; it would, however,

---

[59] See Fordyce W. Luikart to Arthur S. Flemming, memorandum, July 28, 1948, 3, Folder "COEBG 47–49: Commissioners' Assistants – Meeting Minutes," Box 61, Flemming Papers, DDEL.

[60] Hoover Commission I, *General Management of the Executive Branch*, ix.

[61] Ibid., 35–36.

[62] Ibid., 34.

[63] Ibid., 7.

reduce the work of the president and, as the *Washington Post* described, "bring these floating ribs into an orderly organizational pattern."[64] Formal authority and clear organization charts to replace the "chaos of bureaus and subdivisions" were thus central to the Hoover Commission's project.[65]

In addition, each department was to be internally reorganized so that it would operate more efficiently in its own right. As one senator had complained a few years earlier in hearings on legislative reorganization, the federal government was "being run by deputy administrators down through the departments, because there aren't enough hours in the day for those at the top to do much about it except sign orders."[66] This point recalled the problems described by the Attorney General's Committee, which had complained that agency heads were overwhelmed with rote and trivial tasks they were either unwilling or legally unable to delegate. In important cases, they were often forced to adopt the recommendations of lower-level staffers who were more familiar with the materials in question. Dean Acheson had commented during one committee conference that "many of the commissions try to do far more than any human can possibly do."[67] He singled out the SEC and the NLRB, where "the commissioners themselves try to do an amount of work which would take twice as many men working 24 hours a day to do it. Some of the division chiefs have nervous breakdowns."[68]

Following the Attorney General's Committee's final report, many agencies and commissions had tried to delegate more of their routine work away from the agency heads and commissioners. The Hoover Commission found, however, that the "unduly detailed and rigid" rules that dictated administrative operations still slowed them down.[69] In many cases, agencies and commissions were powerless to change their internal organization or wrest away power Congress had expressly given to lower-level officials. One researcher described the NLRB as "caught between the upper millstone of a workload over which it has little control, and the nether millstone of Congressional hostility to the delegation of decision-making authority to subordinates."[70] In reaction, the Hoover Commission recommended that any legal authority vested in subordinate officers be transferred (by statute, if necessary) to the department head, who could then delegate that authority back to staffers at his discretion. The

[64] "Simplified Government," *Washington Post*, Feb. 8, 1949, 12.
[65] Hoover Commission I, *General Management of the Executive Branch*, 31.
[66] Joint Committee on the Organization of Congress, *Organization of Congress: Hearings*, pt. 2, 79th Cong., 1st sess., 1945 (statement of Sen. Homer E. Capehart, Apr. 6), 260.
[67] Transcript, Conference of the Attorney General's Committee, June 8, 1940, 2, Folder "Committee Meeting – June 6, 7, and 8," Box 4, A.G. Committee Correspondence, Entry 376, AGCAP, RG 60, NACP.
[68] Ibid., 2.
[69] Hoover Commission I, *General Management of the Executive Branch*, 5.
[70] Walter Galenson, Committee on Independent Regulatory Commissions, *Staff Report on the National Labor Relations Board* (Commission on Organization of the Executive Branch of the Government, 1948), II-8.

clarity of operations would also make it easier for the president – in whom, Hoover insisted, final legal authority always rested – to intervene.

These ideas echoed many of the themes articulated by Roosevelt's Brownlow Committee in 1937 about presidential responsibility and authority. The Brownlow Committee had proposed consolidating the huge number of agencies and commissions into a few better-organized ones and locating all authority over the executive branch in the president, who they envisioned as "a responsible and effective chief executive as the center of energy, direction, and administrative management."[71] The president was to be responsible for the nonjudicial functions of the independent regulatory commissions – commissions that, members observed dryly, should be called "the 'irresponsible' regulatory commissions" as "Congress has found no effective way of supervising them, they cannot be controlled by the President, and they are answerable to the courts only in respect to the legality of their activities."[72] Presidential control, bolstered by strong staff support within the White House, would facilitate cooperation and coordination across the administrative state and provide some democratic accountability over the officials therein. As Don Price recalled, Hoover "had great sympathy" for some of Roosevelt's reorganization proposals; Hoover's own presidential attempts at reorganization had included similar solutions, and it was hardly surprising that he returned to such ideas given the opportunity.[73]

The General Management report was well received, not least because of its apparently nonpartisan suggestions. The *Wall Street Journal* characterized it as "an outstanding public service,"[74] and the *Chicago Tribune* remarked pointedly that it was "a sharp attack on the sprawling burocracy and overlapping jurisdictions, with their accompanying inefficiency and waste, that have developed under the New Deal."[75] The *Tribune* nonetheless expressed its dismay that "nothing is said about the sacrifice by the government of any function which it now exercises."[76] At the same time, the *Washington Post* suggested the report was "a candid recognition of the fact that big Government is here to stay and a well-reasoned plea that Government be given the straight lines of authority and simplified organization it will need to serve the people in accord with their demands."[77] Even the executive departments and agencies to be reorganized were in favor of these proposals, which, after all, only

[71] President's Committee on Administrative Management, *Administrative Management in the Government of the United States* (Washington, DC: Government Printing Office, 1937), 3.
[72] Ibid., 40.
[73] Price oral history interview, 14; see Lawrence Sullivan, "Hoover Urges Speed on U.S. Reorganizing," *Washington Post*, Feb. 18, 1932, 1; Hess, *Organizing the Presidency*.
[74] "Mr. Hoover's First Report," *Wall Street Journal*, Feb. 8, 1949, 6.
[75] "Rules for a Madhouse," *Chicago Daily Tribune*, Feb. 11, 1949, 16.
[76] Ibid.
[77] "Simplified Government," *Washington Post*, 12.

increased the authority of the department heads. Congress was also supportive, although, one congressional committee later reflected ruefully, Hoover
was so convincing in arguing for presidential control over the independent
commissions "that no one seemed to remember that they were creatures and
arms of the Congress."[78]

The Hoover Commission issued numerous additional reports in the first
half of 1949 on topics including the Post Office, the Labor Department, personnel, transportation, and the defense establishment. Hoover's choice of the
task force method meant that the commission was swamped with reports from
its task forces in late 1948, each with its own findings, recommendations, and
tone. Even where the jurisdiction of several task forces overlapped, the groups
were only fitfully coordinated; members of the Task Force on Federal Medical
Services reportedly threatened to quit, complaining about the irony of "duplication by an agency established to end duplication."[79] Given the number of
task force reports and the wealth of information and variety of approaches
they contained, the commission, under Hoover's leadership, had a lot of work
to do to quickly pull together their own coherent reports for Congress.

Hoover had a significant role in drafting the reports, and his approach to government management was evident throughout. The problems of the administrative state were, for the Hoover Commission, simply parts of the central problem
of inadequate presidential authority and inefficient distribution of functions. With
"too many separate agencies to permit adequate attention and direction from the
President," policy coordination was extremely difficult.[80] Troublingly, "in certain
fields such as labor, transportation, or medical services no one is charged with
considering the problem as a whole."[81] At the same time, "many agencies contain
functions which are totally unrelated to each other, if not inconsistent; creating
a lack of central purpose and greatly increasing the problem of internal coordination."[82] Thus, in its topical reports, the Hoover Commission detailed what
recommendations grouping agencies by "major purpose" or "major function"
would look like in practice. Reorganization of the Department of Agriculture
would consolidate forestry issues under one head, the Federal Security
Agency would be replaced with a new Department of Health, Education, and
Welfare, and many of the dozens of federal agencies handling medical functions
would be combined into this cabinet-level department with authority over social
security services, education, and the Bureau of Indian Affairs.

[78] House Select Committee on Small Business, Subcommittee No. 1 on Regulatory Agencies and
Commissions, *The Organization and Procedures of the Federal Regulatory Commissions and
Agencies and their Effect on Small Business*, 84th Cong., 2nd sess., 1956, H. Rep. 2967, 18.
[79] Charles Aikin to Dean Acheson, memorandum, July 12, 1948, 1, Folder "Memoranda to Dean
Acheson from Charles Aikin and James Rowe, 1948," Box 19, Acheson Papers, HSTL; see also
Charles Aikin, "Task Force: Methodology," *Public Administration Review* 9 (1949): 241–51.
[80] Commission on Organization of the Executive Branch of the Government (Hoover Commission I), *Concluding Report* (Washington, DC: Government Printing Office, 1949), 41.
[81] Ibid.
[82] Ibid.

Transportation regulation was a particular concern. A critical 1944 report had found transportation regulation "often slow, sometimes exceedingly slow, and frequently expensive" and "not invariably immune from partisan influences."[83] Drawing on both the task force report on Independent Regulatory Commissions and a separate report on transportation policy prepared by the Brookings Institution, the Hoover Commission criticized both the individual commissions' dearth of planning and the failure of the federal government to develop an overall transportation policy. With the ICC in charge of rails and roads, the Maritime Commission in charge of the seas, and the Civil Aeronautics Board in charge of the air, "[n]o single Government agency is in a position to evaluate the total needs in transportation, the total service provided, or the net results of all Federal transportation undertakings."[84] Combining at least the nonregulatory transportation functions of the ICC, the CAB, and the Maritime Commission into the Commerce Department, along with the Public Roads Administration and the Coast Guard, as the Hoover Commission recommended, would consolidate in a single agency responsibility for railroad, motor carrier, and aircraft safety, railroad consolidation plans, ship construction, operation, and sales, and responsibility for promoting transportation and considering new routes and new services in a single agency. With its new authority, the Commerce Department could take a comprehensive approach to transportation policy that considered existing railroad, highway, water, *and* air routes and capacities in designing routes and capacities for the future. The *New York Times* approved, suggesting that the affected commissions could then "exercise the genuine functions of regulation with fewer outside diversions," even as it involved "some stepping on bureaucratic toes and some shock to bureaucratic lethargies."[85] Officials at the commissions, however, were more hostile, resisting the transfer of responsibilities and suggesting that the ease with which the Hoover Commission had classified certain functions as "regulatory" and others as "nonregulatory" ignored the complicated and interrelated nature of their work.[86] Although the Hoover Commission saw the commissions' resistance as inherently self-serving, administrators would have slightly more luck convincing members of Congress to oppose these changes.

Another consistent problem was personnel, for without competent staffers at all levels, the Hoover Commission's other proposals could not succeed. However, as Hoover charged in the General Management report, the federal government had not done enough "to build a corps of administrators of the highest level of ability with an interest in the program of the Government

---

[83] Board of Investigation and Research, *The Report on Practices and Procedures of Governmental Control*, 78th Cong., 2nd sess., 1944, H. Doc. 678, 3.

[84] Commission on Organization of the Executive Branch of the Government (Hoover Commission I), *Department of Commerce* (Washington, DC: Government Printing Office, 1949), 15.

[85] "A New Commerce Department," *New York Times*, Mar. 8, 1949, 24.

[86] See Senate Committee on Expenditures in the Executive Departments, *Progress on Hoover Commission Recommendations*, 81st Cong., 1st sess., 1949, S. Rep. 1158, 261–62.

as a whole."[87] The commission's report on Personnel Management urged significant reforms in government hiring and firing; these "sweeping changes," the *Washington Post* opined, "may well prove to be the most important of its recommendations."[88] The report, based on a report from a task force that included political scientist and former CSC commissioner Leonard D. White, longtime foe of government spending Sen. Harry F. Byrd (D–W.Va.), Atomic Energy Commission Chairman David Lilienthal, and representatives from the American Management Association, Westinghouse Electric Company, and Penn Mutual Life Insurance Company, found significant inefficiencies in the current system and argued that the recent 300 percent growth in federal civilian employment had clearly strained the capabilities of the personnel machinery.

The Hoover Commission described "slow and cumbersome" hiring procedures, too much "red tape" in firing procedures, too many "inefficient and unnecessary employees," and high turnover rates suggesting "low morale."[89] The central problem here was how to employ "men and women of the highest intelligence and whose devotion to duty and whose competence is commensurate with the needs of our Government."[90] One observer suggested that this task was made more difficult by antibureaucratic politics, including "the curious, contradictory way in which Americans respect a Federal job and its title, but brand public servants as 'bureaucrats' and 'tax-eaters.'"[91] At the same time, officials' "spirits rebel at loose, careless questioning of their loyalty."[92] The Hoover Commission report, however, reflected little concern about employee loyalty, instead focusing on making sure that "unnecessary employees are constantly weeded out."[93] Competency was the crucial element; as the Hoover Commission emphasized, "We cannot entrust the Government of today to second-rate men and women."[94] Contrary to public belief, then, bureaucrats *could* be capable; the trick was finding the ones who were.

Standing in the way of ensuring competent employees was the red tape involved in firing the incompetent ones. One researcher described the damage that aging and even a few actively obstructionist employees were doing at the FTC; she found, however, that "the difficulties in proving incompetence to the Civil Service Commission are virtually insurmountable."[95] Incentives were also poorly structured. The Hoover Commission acknowledged the

[87] Hoover Commission I, *General Management of the Executive Branch*, 5.

[88] "Experts for Government," *Washington Post*, Feb. 13, 1949, B4.

[89] Commission on Organization of the Executive Branch of the Government (Hoover Commission I) *Personnel Management* (Washington, DC: Government Printing Office, 1949), 3, 5.

[90] Ibid., 2.

[91] John J. Corson, "To Get Better Men for a Better Government," *New York Times Magazine*, Mar. 27, 1949, 44.

[92] Ibid.

[93] Hoover Commission I, *Personnel Management*, 9.

[94] Ibid., 43.

[95] Irene Till, Committee on Independent Regulatory Commissions, *Staff Report on the Federal Trade Commission* (Commission on Organization of the Executive Branch of Government, 1948), II-40.

phenomenon of "empire building" by bureaucrats, who believed that their pay was based on the number of employees they supervised.[96] At the same time, low pay led talented people to avoid or leave government service. Without skilled employees leading the government, "danger to the welfare and security of the country, as well as immense financial losses" would follow."[97]

The Hoover Commission's approach here resembled its approach elsewhere – members recommended reorganizing the CSC, streamlining its personnel process, and removing overly rigid rules. Much of the work of hiring, promoting, and firing employees (excepting, of course, the hearing examiners) would reside in the departments, agencies, and commissions where officials knew best what kind of employees they needed. The CSC would take more of a leadership position by "setting standards for the handling of personnel programs by the agencies" and by keeping an eye on how administrators handled their personnel programs.[98] The standards would ideally be geared to allow agencies to focus on getting and retaining the best people while firing the rest more easily. Thus, along with higher pay for those in all branches of government, the Hoover Commission recommended incentives to administrators for reducing the number of employees. As the *Washington Post* suggested, the recommendations were "a daring but fundamentally sound break" from past practice; "[t]he time is overdue for a switchover from negative guarding of Federal jobs from the spoilsmen to positive, selective recruitment for a higher type of public service."[99]

The excessively procedural nature of the administrative process, the Hoover Commission found, led to sloth instead of speed in other areas. Their analysis was thus a far cry from the tone of previous congressional investigations, which consistently recommended ever more scrutiny and additional procedural limits. According to the Hoover Commission, the federal government was hamstrung by "excessive and necessary paper work" as a result of "detailed statutes, rules, regulations, failure to use modern mechanical methods and insufficient attention to the problems of internal administrative management."[100] This was true in the independent commissions as well, where, three years after the APA promised to bring due process to administrative procedure, "cumbersome and costly administrative procedures" prevailed.[101] "All of this detail," the commission found, was hardly "essential for fair and full solution of the various problems."[102] The Hoover Commission declined to revisit the APA so soon after it took effect, but it suggested that the Budget Bureau work out recommendations "to improve

---

[96] Hoover Commission I, *Personnel Management*, 4.
[97] Ibid., 20.
[98] Ibid., 9.
[99] "Experts for Government," *Washington Post*, 4B.
[100] Hoover Commission I, *Concluding Report*, 35.
[101] Commission on Organization of the Executive Branch of the Government (Hoover Commission I), *The Independent Regulatory Commissions* (Washington, DC: Government Printing Office, 1949), 10.
[102] Ibid.

and thereby reduce the cost of disposing of business before administrative agencies."[103] Such recommendations were welcomed by agencies and commissions; as one department argued to the Senate Committee on Expenditures in the Executive Departments, "We must avoid at all costs the tendency to develop restrictive controls growing out of a few isolated cases of malpractice."[104]

Concerns about petty proceduralism were especially present at the independent regulatory commissions, which the Hoover Commission singled out for special study. Hoover expressed his concern early on about the results of "failure in the past to pay full regard to the separation of legislative, executive and judicial powers" and the "transgression over our fundamental concept of single-headed responsibility of several minds in legislative or judicial agencies."[105] Assisted by Executive Director Harold Leventhal, three men (Harvard Law School Professor Robert R. Bowie, former General Electric Executive Owen D. Young, and former Senator Robert La Follette Jr.) were asked to determine whether the independent commission was a useful method of regulation. Bowie and La Follette were already well aware of the problem of business-government relationships; so too was Young, who had been involved with the Commerce Department's Business Advisory Council in the 1930s and had chaired the National Resources Planning Board's advisory committee on transportation in the 1940s. The multiheaded independent commissions, characterized by Hoover as "between wind and water" given their peculiar location in the federal government, posed a unique management challenge.[106] The task force intentionally modeled their research on that of the Attorney General's Committee, relying on individual studies of nine major independent regulatory commissions (the ICC, the FTC, the FCC, the SEC, the NLRB, the CAB, the Maritime Commission, the Federal Power Commission, and the Federal Reserve Board). These reports, each drafted by a lawyer or professor of law, political science, or economics after observation of agency proceedings and consultation with officials, administrative practitioners, and regulated parties, focused on certain common issues: how the commissions were organized and operated, how the commissions made (or failed to make) broad policies, and how they related to the White House, to Congress, and to the major industries they regulated.[107] Task force members drew from these studies in writing

[103] Ibid., 11.
[104] Department of Commerce, quoted in Senate Committee on Expenditures in the Executive Departments, *Progress on Hoover Commission Recommendations*, 21.
[105] "Memorandum of the Chairman as to the Program of the Commission," Oct. 20, 1947, 2, Folder "Minutes Commission Meetings 9-27-47 through 5-26-49," Box 27, Minutes of Meetings of the Commission, Sept. 29, 1947–May 26, 1949, NC-115, Entry 1, SO, RG 264, NACP.
[106] Transcript, Hoover Commission Meeting, Jan. 12, 1948, 23, Folder "Volume I – originals Transcripts of Commission Meetings, Meetings 1 through 9," Box 27, Transcripts of Meetings of the Commission, Sept. 29, 1947–May 26, 1949, NC-115, Entry 2, SO, RG 264, NACP.
[107] See C. Herman Pritchett, "The Regulatory Commissions Revisited," *American Political Science Review* 43 (1949): 978–89.

their own report, and, with all of these reports in hand, much of the Hoover Commission's own report was drafted by administrative expert James Landis, who served as Joseph Kennedy's assistant on the Hoover Commission.[108]

The commission's final report on the regulatory commissions answered the ultimate question – should the independent commissions remain independent? – in the qualified affirmative. Although the Hoover Commission here and elsewhere recommended moving commissions' executive and administrative functions to executive agencies, it recognized the benefits of multiple commissioners contemplating regulatory problems and engaging in quasi-judicial decision making while insulated from outside pressures. One observer pointed out that the Hoover Commission, unlike the Brownlow Committee, "is not overly exercised by any 'threat' to presidential powers implied in the existence of independent regulatory commissions."[109] This may have owed something to the Hoover Commission's close relationship to Congress and Congress's desire to protect its prerogatives, but it was in seeming contrast to the commission's focus on presidential responsibility elsewhere. As acting FCC chairman Rosel H. Hyde noted to the Budget Bureau, the Hoover Commission "has made a considerable contribution toward good government by simply recognizing that the independent regulatory commissions do have a definite place in the Federal system."[110] Some commissions were weak, while others were performing well; the Hoover Commission's task force singled the SEC out for praise as "an outstanding example of the independent commission at its best."[111] Overall, the staff reports cast the individual commissions and the commission form in a generally positive light. "Despite the cost of the method of consultation and deliberation," the task force suggested, "we are convinced that it is a valuable process for arriving at wise policies and decisions in areas allowing so wide a choice."[112]

It was clear from the staff reports that formal independence caused fewer problems than the organization charts suggested. On paper, no clear mechanisms existed to coordinate policy among the commissions or with the executive branch. However, as the task force reported, "the varied pressures or influences on the independent commissions" have avoided "most of the theoretical difficulties implicit in independence."[113] In practice, only a small minority

---

[108] See Pritchett, "The Regulatory Commissions Revisited."

[109] G. Homer Durham, "An Appraisal of the Hoover Commission Approach to Administrative Reorganization in the National Government," *Western Political Quarterly* 2 (1949): 615–23, 615.

[110] Rosel Hyde to Frank Pace Jr., June 2, 1949, 1, File No. 12–12, Organization Federal Communications Commission, Jan. 1, 1947–Nov. 30, 1951, Box 8, General Correspondence 1947–1956, OED, RG 173, NACP.

[111] Commission on Organization of the Executive Branch of the Government (Hoover Commission I), Committee on Independent Regulatory Commissions, *Task Force Report on Regulatory Commissions* (Washington, DC: Government Printing Office, 1949), 144.

[112] Ibid., 22.

[113] Ibid., 26.

of a commission's work actually conflicted with that of another commission or executive agency. Where overlap did exist, agency officials had generally worked out methods of effective informal policy coordination. Transportation specialist Ernest Williams reported that, at the ICC, "scarcely a single solid instance of a conflict of substance appears,"[114] and, the Hoover Commission task force concluded, "conflict and inadequate coordination between the commissions and other agencies is limited in extent and generally avoided by cooperation."[115] In this area, they concluded, "the actual experience is far more convincing than theory."[116]

Nor were independent commissions all that independent in practice. As Bowie reported after a meeting with commissioners from different agencies: "All recognized that the extent of independence was greater on paper than in fact. The pressure of public opinion, Executive influence, Congressional influence, and the industry, all tend to temper the statutory independence of these Commissions."[117] Contacts with the White House were frequent, although they rarely resulted in presidential influence on commission policy. In some cases, the president was not particularly interested in the policy areas; in others, he felt that little was to be gained. (Writing about the NLRB, economist and labor expert Walter Galenson remarked that any "advantages accruing to the President from closer policy control of the Board would have been far outweighed by the corresponding necessity of assuming responsibility for its actions."[118]) The task force members and the Hoover Commission as a whole recommended that the president exert more control than he currently did and suggested internal reforms to that end. Consistent with their recommendations elsewhere, the Hoover Commission proposed keeping the multiheaded commissions intact and centralizing power in a single individual to establish the clear lines of formal authority they favored. The chairman would take over full authority for administrative tasks, thus reducing the workload of the other commissioners; in addition, the increased transparency of authority within the commission would enable the president to keep tabs on the chairman's activities. Although not directly subject to presidential authority, the chairman would be chosen by the president and would be "the commission's principal spokesman" to both the White House and Congress.[119] This solution addressed the "often loose and casual and sometimes nonexistent" policy coordination,

---

[114] Ernest W. Williams, Committee on Independent Regulatory Commissions, *Staff Report on the Interstate Commerce Commission*, (Commission on Organization of the Executive Branch of the Government, 1948), IV-2.

[115] Hoover Commission I, Committee on Independent Regulatory Commissions, *Task Force Report on Regulatory Commissions*, viii.

[116] Ibid., 28.

[117] Robert R. Bowie, memorandum of June 1 meeting, June 3, 1948, 6, Folder "Dr. Robert R. Bowie – Chronological," Box 1, Records Relating to the Administration of the Task Force, 1948–1949, NC-115, Entry 52, TF: IRC, RG 264, NACP.

[118] Galenson, *Staff Report on the National Labor Relations Board*, III-5.

[119] Hoover Commission I, *The Independent Regulatory Commissions*, 6.

and satisfied the Hoover Commission's passion for organizational coherence while nodding to the commissions' independence.[120]

One of the most pronounced defects of the independent commissions, according to the Hoover Commission, was their failure to engage in the kind of broad and deliberate policy planning for which they had been created. The commissions were "too engrossed in case-by-case activities and thus fail to plan their roles and to promote the enterprises entrusted to their care."[121] According to the staff reports, this problem was endemic. The CAB, for example, assigned air routes through "case-by-case judicial procedure" – something the task force suggested "leaves much to be desired as a method for directing the growth of a Nation-wide route pattern."[122] The Maritime Commission's focus on "a thousand matters of minor policy and implementation of policy" meant that it failed to develop "well thought out programs and relatively precise policies."[123] Concerns about this behavior were not new. A 1944 study of the ICC had acknowledged the inefficiencies of this method but found they were balanced by "the maintenance of public confidence in its purposes and its methods"[124]; by contrast, the Senate Committee on Interstate and Foreign Commerce argued in 1948 that the FCC's practice of changing policies through adjudication "is a thoroughly bad and indefensible procedure" that "smacks of cunning and clever legal subterfuge."[125] Although the case method itself was highly reactive as a form of policy planning, agencies' right to select between adjudication and rule making based on their own evaluation of the situation had been upheld by the Supreme Court.[126] However, as the Hoover Commission demonstrated, commissions were not using this power wisely.

---

[120] Ibid., 4.

[121] Ibid., 15.

[122] Hoover Commission I, Committee on Independent Regulatory Commissions, *Task Force Report on Regulatory Commissions*, 78. James M. Landis, commenting on the CAB report, suggested that the board "suffers from an overdose of legalistic attitudes and procedures," which "may be due in part to accidents of personality in its early and present history. Poor lawyers and timorous people usually retreat to procedures of this type in the hope that somehow they will obviate the difficulties of decision and minimize the need for assuming responsibility. But also, if judicial procedures don't fit a particular problem, the tendency is to apply more rather than less of these same procedures." James M. Landis to Robert R. Bowie, Sept. 23, 1948, 1, Folder "Comments on Preliminary Report," Box 4, Task Force Studies, 1948–49, NC-115, Entry 54, TF: IRC, RG 264.

[123] James MacGregor Burns, Committee on Independent Regulatory Commissions, *Staff Report on the United States Maritime Commission* (Commission on Organization of the Executive Branch of the Government, 1948), II-19.

[124] Board of Investigation and Research, *The Report on Practices and Procedures of Governmental Control*, 78th Cong., 2nd sess., 1944, H. Doc. 678, 64.

[125] Senate Committee on Interstate and Foreign Commerce, *Communication Act Amendments of 1948*, 80th Cong., 2nd sess., 1948, S. Rep. 1567, 17.

[126] *SEC v. Chenery Corp.*, 332 U.S. 194 (1947); for more, see Robert L. Rabin, "Federal Regulation in Historical Perspective," *Stanford Law Review* 38 (1986): 1189–326, 1270; Nicholas S. Zeppos, "The Legal Profession and the Development of Administrative Law," *Chicago-Kent Law Review* 72 (1997): 1119–57, 1145–51.

In relying on the case method, commissions lurched from decision to decision without developing clearly articulated standards, thus making it more difficult for themselves, for staffers handling cases in their early stages, and for parties trying to predict what the commission would do. The CAB's decisions, for instance, demonstrated "an amazing degree of vacillation and inconsistency" that made it almost impossible for observers to figure out on what grounds it was making decisions.[127] The SEC and ICC at least did a fairly good job honoring the precedents they had developed through case-by-case adjudication, but other commissions were less reliable. Irene Till described any policy at the FTC as "lost in a maze of individual cease and desist orders," each of which "seems to exist in its own vacuum" and was often "wholly unrelated to any other work of the Commission."[128] The FCC, which had "adopted some high-sounding principles" to govern applications for broadcasting licenses, "could not or would not apply these principles."[129] Instead, FCC commissioners ruled on applications on the basis of "hunch, snap judgment, or call it what you may."[130] The problem was circular, as the task force pointed out; the FCC had no time to plan or develop broad rules, but would never find that time "unless the Commission defines its regulatory program, formulates the policies needed for its achievement, and organizes its resources so as to dispose of its business in the most efficient and expeditious manner."[131]

The task force emphasized that, ideally, a regulatory commission "should be constantly engaged in seeking to define its standards; in reviewing the regulatory program as a whole; and in anticipating emerging problems and planning for their solution."[132] Members recommended that commissions move away from formal hearings wherever possible and otherwise adopt methods to hasten decisions. Indeed, Landis, who was particularly annoyed by planning failures, suggested in an early draft of the Hoover Commission's report that reform could "emphasize the significance of reducing planning from a plane of casual speculation to that of intense and studied application."[133]

The Hoover Commission's response was to address the commissioners' workload. The deliberative nature of decision making by a group was useful but slow, the task force reported, and "should be used only where its special

---

[127] Edward C. Sweeney, Committee on Independent Regulatory Commissions, *Staff Report on the Civil Aeronautics Board* (Commission on Organization of the Executive Branch of the Government, 1948), II-22.

[128] Till, *Staff Report on the Federal Trade Commission*, IV-31.

[129] William W. Golub, Committee on Independent Regulatory Commissions, *Staff Report on the Federal Communications Commission* (Commission on Organization of the Executive Branch of the Government, 1948), II-41.

[130] Ibid., II-42.

[131] Hoover Commission I, Committee on Independent Regulatory Commissions, *Task Force Report on Regulatory Commissions*, 96.

[132] Ibid., 39–40.

[133] James M. Landis, "Tentative Draft of the Commission's Report on Independent Regulatory Agencies," Jan. 26, 1949, 17, Folder "Regulatory Commissions Report of Commission – Drafts," Box 27, HC I, HHPPP, HHL.

advantages are necessary."[134] The Hoover Commission recommended moving as much executive work as possible to the executive branch, hiring an executive director (responsible to the chairman) to perform the commission's administrative and personnel work, and increasing the delegation of rote work to staffers. With more time, commissioners would be free to develop clear standards, which in turn would improve policy making throughout the commission.[135]

These organizational solutions only went so far, however. Lacking from the Hoover Commission's final report was a solution to the external pressures that also shaped commission action. Commission deficiencies were often less a failure of organizational design or administrative will than a defensive strategy for managing a highly contested political context. As long as Congress and the Budget Bureau measured the efficiency of a commission by the number of cases it handled, commissions had little incentive to take on large questions and time-consuming investigations. And, as the staff studies demonstrated, even clear official policies might well give way to more powerful pressures from Congress or the executive branch. The task force criticized Congress for its attempts to interfere in administrative decision making.[136] The staff was skeptical about the value of congressional supervision; researchers described members of Congress approaching the commissions on behalf of their constituents at the same time that Congress's exercise of its oversight duties veered into the realm of harassment. The NLRB and the Maritime Commission had been the unwelcome recipients of this congressional attention, and the FCC, under near-constant scrutiny during the 1940s, found itself cowed by these investigations. Attorney William W. Golub's report on the FCC described members of Congress expressing their displeasure with the commission through both formal investigations (like the Cox Committee's notorious investigation) and appropriations hearings

---

[134] Hoover Commission I, Committee on Independent Regulatory Commissions, *Task Force Report on Regulatory Commissions*, 22.

[135] The enormous workload generated by wartime pressures and normal administrative ones was apparent in the Court's 1947 reading of the Emergency Price Control Act to allow the price administrator to delegate his power to issue subpoenas to lower-level officers. Recognizing administrative realities, the Court suggested that "[t]o tempt the Administrator to solve the problem by supplying all his offices with subpoenas signed in blank would not further the development of orderly and responsible administration" (*Fleming v. Mohawk Wrecking & Lumber Co.*, 331 U.S. 111, 123 [1947]. Justice Jackson, concurring, followed up on this point, reminiscent of the decision in *Morgan* a decade earlier. Without the power to delegate authority to sign subpoenas, "one of two practices would be certain to result. He might sign large batches of blank subpoenas and turn them over to subordinates to be filled in over his signature. Or he might sign batches of subpoenas already made out by subordinates, probably without reading them and certainly without examining the causes for their issuance or the scope of the information required" (Ibid., 123–24 [Jackson, J., concurring]. Either way, he concluded, "The personal signature of the Administrator on the subpoena under those circumstances is no protection to individual rights" (ibid., 124).

[136] See William W. Golub, memorandum of interview with William J. Dempsey, March 25, 1948, 1, Folder "FCC Reports of Interview," Box 5, Task Force Studies, 1948–49, NC-115, Entry 54, TF: IRC, RG 264.

that turned into "brief investigations of any phase of the Commission's activities which are prominent at the moment."[137] As a result, Golub argued, the FCC had become defensive, acting "with an awareness of Congressional attitudes and the distinct possibility that it will be called to account for its judgments."[138]

The regulated parties added to this pressure, significantly influencing commissions' priorities and specific regulatory policies. At the NLRB, members were "subjected to unremitting pressure by interest groups, which combined with a work load of unmanageable proportions has not been conducive to a philosophical examination of problems and policies."[139] The FCC responded to the heavy demand for broadcast licenses by directing most of its energy thusly, while "[a]ny real regulation of the mammoth telephone industry continues to remain a matter of statutory hope."[140] The task force noted that the "combination of wide discretion on the part of officials, and strong motives for influencing the officials on the part of the regulated industry, involve serious risks of corruption and unfairness."[141] They credited the commissions' independence and their multiheaded leadership for keeping the commissions mostly "above suspicion of favoritism or partiality."[142] The individual reports made clear, however, the difficulty of drawing the line between useful cooperation on broad policy questions and improper influence on particular cases.

Keeping officials entirely apart from the regulated interests was impractical. The most successful agencies, such as the ICC and the SEC, had cultivated good working relations with their industries, and the SEC had adopted strategies and methods that "enabled it to get a great deal of help in working out its program of regulation without running the risk of excessive influence on the part of the industry."[143] However, some commissions were perhaps *too* close to those they regulated. The CAB was "frequently criticized for being saturated with the aviation industry's point of view,"[144] and the Maritime Commission, which had both regulatory and promotional responsibilities, "in some official circles" was "referred to as the 'kept woman of the shipping industry.'"[145] Members of the broadcasting industry similarly attempted to bend the FCC commissioners to their will through "conferences with individual Commissioners or staff members; government-industry committees; luncheons and other social activities;

[137] Golub, *Staff Report on the Federal Communications Commission*, III-38.
[138] Ibid., III-35.
[139] Galenson, *Staff Report on the National Labor Relations Board*, II-31.
[140] Golub, *Staff Report on the Federal Communications Commission*, IV-31.
[141] Hoover Commission I, Committee on Independent Regulatory Commissions, *Task Force Report on Regulatory Commissions*, 20.
[142] Ibid.
[143] Carl F. Farbach, Committee on Independent Regulatory Commissions, *Staff Report on the Securities and Exchange Commission* (Commission on Organization of the Executive Branch of the Government, 1948), II-36; see also E. S. Redford, "The Value of the Hoover Commission Reports to the Educator," *American Political Science Review* 44 (1950): 283–98, 291–93.
[144] Sweeney, *Staff Report on the Civil Aeronautics Board*, II-45.
[145] Burns, *Staff Report on the United States Maritime Commission*, III-28.

invitations to industry conventions; and the arrangement of demonstrations of developments in the act."[146] Agencies at odds with those they regulated were in a different and even more awkward position. The FTC had no organized constituent group, representing as it did "the inchoate, unorganized mass of ordinary citizens engaged in the serious business of earning a living."[147] Thus, little affirmative support existed for the FTC's antitrust mission, causing problems as the commission went up against those who were "well organized, well financed, and experienced in the tactics of fending off legislative action in this field."[148]

The problems of congressional and industry pressure, however, were not problems the Hoover Commission took on, even as administrators made clear the extent of the problem. Indeed, here the general antibureaucratic (or at least antibureaucrat) tenor of the Hoover Commission's project was apparent. The staff's detailed studies, completed shortly before the 1948 elections, reflected well on the individual commissions and generally garnered approval from administrators past and present.[149] Other observers, however, questioned the reports' bias in favor of the agencies. Staff assistant and former Republican National Committee research director Harold Metz complained that investigators were too critical of Congress, inappropriately so in the context of a commission created by members of Congress suspicious of the administrative state. At the same time, he charged, investigators were insufficiently critical of the administrative officials they had consulted. Noting that Columbia professor Walter Galenson "has long been an active supporter of organized labor, and especially of the CIO," Metz complained that in the NLRB report itself, his "pro-labor proclivities are fairly well concealed but they nevertheless appear from time to time."[150] Although Galenson was a Harvard Business School professor who had previously worked for the War Labor Board, the chief counsel of the Joint Committee on Labor-Management Relations complained of "the impossibility of the job being performed by a non-lawyer who has had no previous experience with the agency he is studying in the short time allotted."[151]

Critical of Galenson's complaints about the Smith Committee's investigation of the NLRB, Metz similarly questioned Golub's FCC report for failing to take into account the Cox Committee's charges against FCC commissioner James L. Fly and the political activities of former FCC commissioner Clifford J. Durr

[146] Golub, *Staff Report on the Federal Communications Commission*, III-56.

[147] Till, *Staff Report on the Federal Trade Commission*, III-22.

[148] Ibid.

[149] See James L. Fly to Robert R. Bowie, Dec. 8, 1948, 2, Folder "FCC Comments," Box 5, Task Force Studies, 1948–49; James M. Landis to Bowie, Sept. 23, 1948, Folder "Comments on Preliminary Report," Box 4, Task Force Studies, 1948–49, both in NC-115, Entry 54, TF: IRC, RG 264.

[150] Harold Metz to Sidney A. Mitchell, memorandum, Sept. 2, 1948, 6, Folder "Regulatory Agencies," Box 15, Correspondence Relating to Task Forces, 1947–49, NC-115, Entry 11, OED, RG 264, NACP.

[151] Thomas E. Shroyer to Sen. Joseph H. Ball, memorandum, June 5, 1948, 2, Folder "Regulatory Agencies," Box 15, Correspondence Relating to Task Forces, 1947–49, NC-115, Entry 11, OED, RG 264, NACP.

and his wife, Virginia.[152] Former Cox Committee counsel Eugene Garey complained to Hoover about early reports that the FCC report "puts a halo on the
head of every Commissioner and official, past and present," while "Congress is
given hell in not too polite language for otherwise meddling in things not concerning it."[153] Hoover himself was somewhat skeptical; as he replied to Garey,
"From what I hear, no doubt that was a fool report."[154]

These internal differences notwithstanding, the overall public picture of
administration that emerged from the Hoover Commission reports was very
different from that depicted by earlier congressional investigations and editorial
rants. Although the *Los Angeles Times* suggested that "there is no more important task" than "overhauling the nine regulatory commissions" – a task that
included "setting boundaries to their activities and bounds to their ambition" –
the Hoover Commission did not claim that administrators were exercising too
much power or abusing their discretion.[155] Nor did it spend time discussing the
loyalty of these officials. Agencies could not be left to their own devices – that
much was clear – but the reasons had changed. Members described administrative officials trapped within organizational structures that limited their ability to
perform their tasks efficiently and well. The Hoover Commission responded by
applying their own ideal design for the administrative state that relied on external controls. Such reforms were structural and uniform, based on the assumption
that a single theory could prescribe the ideal design for all agencies, regardless
of the political context or the work involved. These assumptions allowed the
commission to dismiss administrative officials' opinions of their proposals, limiting the degree to which the commission would take practical considerations
into effect. As Hoover suggested dismissively to a radio audience, "Bureaucracy
believes in holding on to its jobs, and each bureaucrat believes that his organization is perfect."[156] The expertise that counted came from external observers.

Some observers were skeptical of the Hoover Commission's optimistic approach to organizational problems. One *Wall Street Journal* columnist
compared the recommendations to "Chinese checkers" and suggested that the
Hoover Commission wanted "to shuffle the little squares, each representing an
office, into pleasing arrangements."[157] Overall, he complained, "The nature of
bureaucracy, which is the root of the evil, is not changed by changing a bureau's
name or its office space."[158] Political scientists and public administration scholars were similarly critical. One remarked that the reports "exhibit concern only

[152] Harold Metz to Sidney A. Mitchell, memorandum, Nov. 2, 1948, Folder "Regulatory Agencies,"
Box 15, Correspondence Relating to Task Forces, 1947–49, NC-115, Entry 11, OED, RG 264,
NACP.
[153] Eugene Garey to Herbert Hoover, Oct. 26, 1948, 1, Folder "GAD-GAZ," Box 34, HC I, HHPPP,
HHL. (Garey was quoting "one of my Washington friends.")
[154] Herbert Hoover to Eugene Garey, Oct. 27, 1948, Folder "GAD-GAZ," Box 34, HC I, HHPPP,
HHL.
[155] "Overhauling Regulatory Commissions," *Los Angeles Times*, May 24, 1949, A4.
[156] Hoover, quoted in "Hoover Urges Cut in U.S. Employe[e]s," *New York Times*, 20.
[157] Vermont Royster, "Chinese Checkers," *Wall Street Journal*, May 9, 1949, 4.
[158] Ibid.

for economy and efficiency in an imaginary world where propaganda, power politics, selfish motives, human frailties, are non-existent; or where these facts of political life lie prostrate before the gods of authority, chain of command, economy, order, and efficiency – with the word 'responsibility' thrown in."[159] In 1947, Maxwell School dean and former Budget Bureau official Paul Appleby had cautioned that "political" factors were not simply hurdles to overcome but were part and parcel of the administrative process. Appleby suggested that reformers understand the importance of "giving due regard to political efficiency as well as to operating efficiency."[160] As administrators were well aware, politics did not go away simply because the commissions were independent. Thus Appleby offered another vision of reorganization, one that acknowledged its role as a political and democratic, if not necessarily partisan, reform. Political scientist Emmette Redford similarly characterized administration as "myriad complexities – not neat contrasts" and suggested, "the real research which is needed is on the relationships of men at various levels in a hierarchy and particularly on the relationships between political and permanent officials."[161] The Hoover Commission avoided these lessons, however, and left little room for actual policy disagreement in the debates about implementation.

For the most part, however, newspapers, public administration scholars, and political scientists were quite enthusiastic about the Hoover Commission's reports. One reporter suggested it was "the most thorough job in history in a study of this Government,"[162] and the *Wall Street Journal* applauded the Hoover Commission's "fine service in showing us what a cancer bureaucracy has become."[163] The *New York Times* called it "a big job done with spectacular thoroughness,"[164] and, six weeks later, "a spectacularly good job."[165] In a 1949 symposium of the *American Political Science Review* devoted to the Hoover Commission reports, Charles Aikin (Acheson's assistant on the Hoover Commission) and Louis Koenig observed, "it has become something of a mode to favor the Hoover reports, just as one opposes sin."[166] Indeed, an April 1949 poll suggested that Americans who had heard about the Hoover Commission's pursuit of efficiency and economy supported its recommendations by the outsized margin of twenty-to-one.[167]

Commentators commended both the commission's critique of the size of government and the apparent unwillingness to slash at it more purposefully.

[159] Durham, "Appraisal of the Hoover Commission Approach," 620.
[160] Paul H. Appleby, "Toward Better Public Administration," *Public Administration Review* 7 (1947): 93–99, 94.
[161] Redford, "The Value of the Hoover Commission Reports to the Educator," 288.
[162] James E. Warner, "Hoover Shakeups Face Tough Sledding," *Washington Post*, Apr. 17, 1949, 3B.
[163] "The Will and the Way," *Wall Street Journal*, May 13, 1949, 4.
[164] "Big-Business Government," *New York Times*, Feb. 15, 1949, 22.
[165] "Reform in Washington," *New York Times*, Mar. 30, 1949, 24.
[166] Charles Aikin and Louis W. Koenig, "Introduction," in "The Hoover Commission: A Symposium," *American Political Science Review* 43 (1949): 933–40, 933.
[167] George Gallup, "Sentiment 20–1 for Adopting Proposals of Hoover Group," *Washington Post*, May 6, 1949, 25.

The *New York Times* applauded the Hoover Commission for having "accepted the fundamental fact that" the duties of government had "grown far beyond anything that may have been contemplated by the Founding Fathers, and therefore require an enormously expanded governmental apparatus."[168] The Hoover Commission attempted "to cut through the vast jungle of governmental departments and agencies which have grown up with these functions and have made government by far the biggest business in the country" and end "the curse of bureaucracy."[169]At the same time, however, James MacGregor Burns, a political scientist involved in the independent regulatory commissions, described the Hoover Commission's "latest excursion into the Dark Continent of the national bureaucracy" as producing "the most convincing evidence we have yet had that our super-Government is here to stay."[170] The master of the National Grange worried that the Hoover Commission's early proposals were "merely delegations of power to do whatever the official might want" and "would make it possible to build up a dictatorship most difficult to overthrow."[171] However, many endorsed the recommendations that clearly echoed those of Roosevelt's Brownlow Committee. One scholar agreed that "[p]erhaps the most important idea" was that the president "should have not less power but more power over administration."[172] Aikin and Koenig agreed that this approach might be "the Hoover Commission's most valuable work."[173]

As Hoover was well aware, publishing the reports and recommendations was only a start. Indeed, the commission in its concluding report warned Congress about the craven, self-interested individuals and groups "who would seek to escape reorganization" and who had foiled similar efforts in the past.[174] Emphasizing the interrelated nature of its recommendations, members cautioned, "Once the practice of exempting certain agencies and excepting particular functions has begun, the chances of achieving substantial improvements in the efficiency of the Government will speedily diminish."[175] Fortunately for the Hoover Commission, its Citizens Committee was waiting in the wings to frame both the recommendations and its own efforts as above partisan squabbling.

The Hoover Commission's image of nonpartisanship, carefully cultivated by Hoover and the Citizens Committee, glossed over internal battles during the commission's deliberations. Although the 1948 elections had rendered moot

---

[168] "A Monumental Task Ends," *New York Times*, Mar. 3, 1949, 24.

[169] Ibid.

[170] James MacGregor Burns, "Our Super-Government – Can We Control It?" *New York Times Magazine*, Apr. 24, 1949, 7.

[171] Albert S. Goss to Herbert Hoover, Oct. 4, 1950, 1, Folder "GER-GUS," Box 34, HC I, HHPPP, HHL.

[172] John W. Lederle, "The Hoover Commission Reports on Federal Reorganization," *Marquette Law Review* 33 (1949): 89–98, 95.

[173] Aikin and Koenig, "Introduction," 937.

[174] Hoover Commission I, *Concluding Report*, 47.

[175] Ibid., 48.

early disputes about the commission's authority to make policy recommendations, debates over the direction of the reports, specific recommendations, and Hoover's methods of operation persisted. James K. Pollock, Rowe, and Acheson in particular were frustrated by the efforts of Hoover and others to guide the commission toward conservative results and offered numerous dissents. The report on Federal Business Enterprises, according to the *Washington Post*, caused "internecine strife" as "the inevitable result of the commission's unwise action in proposing policy changes of a highly controversial nature."[176] As Rowe argued to Hoover, the report, which offered policy suggestions alongside organizational ones, was "wrong as a matter of governmental organization"; such an approach "has in it the possibility of wrecking all the good work which the Commission has done in its other fourteen reports."[177] Hoover and the conservatives were similarly frustrated with Rowe and Acheson; as Coates recollected, "I think their general strategy was to try to torpedo the report if they could."[178]

Nonetheless, the public face of the Hoover Commission as constructed by its public relations efforts was one of bipartisan amity. Hoover, in a 1949 article for *Fortune* describing the reports, suggested that the general agreement of "twelve tough-minded individuals of different political and ideological views" – with only "a few minor dissents" – demonstrated "how exhaustive has been the determination of facts."[179] Citizens Committee chairman Robert L. Johnson described commissioners toiling outside the political spotlight "in almost complete obscurity" and modestly speculated that "[t]here must have been times when they felt as lonely as the little band of men who met long ago to frame an unheard-of document called the Constitution of the United States."[180] The collection of reports published by McGraw-Hill was issued without any of the dissenting statements, further reinforcing the appearance of consensus.

It was also crucial to the campaign that the Citizens Committee be perceived as an interest group fighting for the *public* interest. The Citizens Committee intentionally positioned itself as nonpartisan; according to Coates, the committee was "a national civic cause" and "the furthest thing from a 'special interest' group that has come together in America for many years."[181] Johnson portrayed the public support for the Hoover Commission as organic; "Somewhere deep

---

[176] "Government in Business," *Washington Post*, Apr. 7, 1949, 10.

[177] James Rowe to Herbert Hoover, Feb. 24, 1949, Folder "James Rowe Jr., 1949–50," Box 38, HC I, HHPPP, HHL.

[178] Coates oral history interview, 9.

[179] Herbert Hoover, "The Reform of Government," *Fortune*, May 1949, 1, Folder "Publicity – *Fortune* article, May 1949," Box 40, HCI, HHPPP, HHL.

[180] Robert L. Johnson, address before the Massachusetts Federation of Taxpayers Associations, Inc., May 7, 1949, 3, Folder "Hoover Report 1949, Folder 1, Proposed Legislation – Senatorial," Box 27, McGrath Papers, HSTL.

[181] Charles B. Coates to Louis N. Brockway, Apr. 14, 1949, 2, Folder "Charles B. Coates, 1948–49," Box 33, HC I, HHPPP HHL.

down in the hearts of the American people a responsive chord was struck."[182] However, the Citizens Committee actively developed strategies to build support for the commission reports. In creating "a real grass roots movement," one public relations professional advised the Citizens Committee, "the most important single consideration is packaging the story in such a way that it will incite the average person to take an active interest in whether or not Mr. Hoover's project is successful."[183] As he stressed, "*The gap between what you have to sell, and what the people want to buy must be bridged.*"[184] Materials were designed to do just that. One list of "do's and don'ts" for the Citizen Committee's speeches and written material instructed members to "[s]tress *bipartisanship* of Commission and *nonpartisanship* of Committee" and "[m]ention President Truman frequently to balance necessarily frequent mention of Mr. Hoover."[185] Members were to avoid the use of "terms with political overtones," including "New Deal" or "American system of fair enterprise."[186] At the same time, they were encouraged to adopt "warm, friendly, constructive words" like "streamline" and "modernize" in place of "rip-snorting words such as 'slash,' 'abolish,' 'taxeater,' 'bureaucrat,' 'living at the public teat,' etc."[187] The intended effect of such a campaign was to make the Hoover Commission and Citizens Committee look good, and the bureaucrats, by implication, look bad.

This image of the commission's project made it easier to sell to the public, as did its confident approach and its preference for simplicity. For both political and public relations purposes, Hoover had demanded clarity and brevity in the final reports – specifically, that they be short enough to fit on a single page of the *New York Times*.[188] While political scientist Emmette Redford had criticized the reports for offering "a tone of certainty and an impression of conclusiveness" without "sufficient analysis of basic assumptions, of the various facets of problems, and of the alternative approaches in their solution," the commission saw these as positive characteristics in trying to reach the American public.[189] Key to the success of the Citizens Committee was its decision to "sell" the recommendations as a single issue. Rather than attempting to garner separate support for individual recommendations concerning, say, budgeting and accounting or the Labor Department, the Citizens Committee packaged the commission's 277 recommendations as a unified set

---

[182] Johnson, address before the Massachusetts Federation of Taxpayers Associations, Inc., 4.

[183] Fred Smith to Robert L. Johnson, Mar. 3, 1949, 1, Folder "Robert L. Johnson, Feb.–Apr. 1949," Box 34, HCI, HHPPP, HHL.

[184] Ibid. (emphasis in the original).

[185] Citizens Committee for the Hoover Report, "'DO'S AND DON'TS' on Preparing Material about the Hoover Report," n.d., 1 (emphasis in the original), Folder "285-E Citizens Committee for Reorganization of the Executive Branch of the Government," Box 927, WHCF: OF 285, HST Papers, HSTL.

[186] Ibid., 3.

[187] Ibid., 1.

[188] Price oral history interview, 12.

[189] Redford, "The Value of the Hoover Commission Reports to the Educator," 284.

that, taken together, promised more economical and efficient government. This approach sought to make it difficult for opponents to find some middle ground, as one was either for the Hoover Reports in their entirety or against them.

Evidence of government waste anywhere thus became support for reform everywhere, and the Citizens Committee publicized egregious examples of waste and profligate spending as evidence of systematic decay throughout the federal government. This publicity was crucial to the battle for implementation; as Coates explained to one correspondent at the advertising firm Young & Rubicam, "Fighting bureaucratic fire with fire, our first-line weapon will be the 'smoking mimeograph machine.'"[190] Johnson asked one interested audience: "Do you realize it costs the Post Office 2½ cents to print and deliver a penny postcard?" He pressed further: "Is it not ridiculous that 47 federal agents representing seven different agricultural field services should be devoted to the service of 1500 farmers in a single county in Georgia?"[191] Speaking to an audience at the National Exchange Club, Coates made a similar point by describing the "16 agencies concerned in wild life preservation, 28 administering welfare projects, 29 making loans, and 50 compiling statistics that often disagreed" that the Hoover Commission had unearthed.[192] Each of the specific examples proved the need for broad reform. "If it were any laughing matter," Coates remarked, "federal business procedure would be simply hilarious."[193]

The Citizens Committee – with its slogan "Better Government for a Better Price" – also repeatedly trumpeted the savings that would result from implementation of the Hoover Commission's recommendations. Although members of the Hoover Commission did not put too much emphasis on this point, the Citizens Committee guessed that more than $5.5 billion of the government's money could be saved. Publicizing these large numbers as potential savings for taxpayers proved to be an effective way of getting attention from the public and the press. These figures were not always well supported, however. The commission's report on regulatory commissions, for example, had predicted that eliminating procedural hoops and delays could result in some savings for the regulated interests, but little for the government. The *Los Angeles Times* agreed, suggesting that improving coordination "will not, directly, save the taxpayers much money" but could "save business and industry so much money as to cause a substantial decrease in the cost of living."[194] Truman himself, required to address likely savings in his reorganization plans, emphasized the

[190] Coates to Brockway, Apr. 14, 1949, 2, Folder "Charles B. Coates, 1948–49," Box 33, HC I, HHPPP, HHL.
[191] Johnson, address before the Massachusetts Federation of Taxpayers Associations, Inc., 9.
[192] Charles B. Coates, "Freedom's War on Waste," speech to the National Exchange Club, 32nd Annual Convention, Washington, DC, Sept. 3, 1950, 3, Folder "Charles B. Coates, 1950," Box 33, HC I, HHPPP, HHL.
[193] Ibid.
[194] "Overhauling Regulatory Commissions," *Los Angeles Times*, 4.

general efficiency of the plan but declined to issue specific predictions about economy. The Citizens Committee, however, estimated a possible $15 million in government savings from these recommendations alone. "If the red tape is cut, the savings to the economy will be far greater than that within the government itself."[195] These estimates raised eyebrows even among some Hoover Commission staffers, and the Citizens Committee's rhetoric, while popular with the public, eventually weakened the committee's credibility when the savings failed to materialize.

The Citizens Committee also explicitly appealed to citizens' patriotism. The Hoover Commission's concluding report had emphasized the importance of immediate reform, given the link between democracy and efficiency; as members claimed, "the highest aims and ideals of democracy can be thwarted through excessive administrative costs and through waste, disunity, apathy, irresponsibility, and other byproducts of inefficient government."[196] Hoover had taken the occasion of his seventy-fifth birthday to warn that the "welfare state" was "a disguise for the totalitarian state by the route of spending."[197] Coates similarly warned an audience that "[t]he Russians can profit from our inefficiencies; only we can correct them."[198] He celebrated the commission's democratic task:

> One wonders today how Moscow evaluated the first news of the Hoover Commission. The whole idea must have been utterly beyond Russian comprehension. Imagine a government investigating itself! Imagine both political parties cooperating in the project! (Imagine *having* two political parties, for that matter!) Imagine empowering citizens to question the actions of officials! Imagine the officials gladly answering the questions! And imagine publishing the results to the people and to the whole wide world! In the enlightened land of barbed wire and firing squads, no such nonsense would be tolerated.[199]

Nods to patriotism and national security allowed the Citizens Committee to claim that opposition to any of the reforms was not just self-serving but actively harmful. Emphasizing that the Korean War only increased the need for greater government efficiency and economy, Robert Johnson argued to members of Congress that "[e]very dollar we waste is a gift to the enemies of freedom."[200]

These arguments proved remarkably successful for the Citizens Committee in winning public opinion and bringing pressure to bear on the White House

[195] Citizens Committee for the Hoover Report, memorandum, n.d., 2, Folder "Citizens' Committee for the Hoover Report," Box 39, HC I, HHPPP, HHL.
[196] Hoover Commission I, *Concluding Report*, 3.
[197] Herbert Hoover, quoted in "On 'Last Mile to Collectivism,' Hoover, at 75, Warns Country," *Washington Post*, Aug. 11, 1949, 14.
[198] Coates, "Freedom's War on Waste," 12.
[199] Ibid., 1–2 (emphasis in the original).
[200] Robert L. Johnson, quoted in "We're in for the Duration," *Los Angeles Times*, July 26, 1950, A4.

and Congress. The committee actively encouraged the formation of state Citizens Committees and established relationships with state taxpayers associations, local Chambers of Commerce, Jaycees, and women's clubs to encourage them to express support. Coates claimed triumphantly that "[n]o less than 50,000 speeches, possibly twice that many, were made in one year to service clubs, women's groups – in church basements, union halls, farm meetings and college campuses."[201] The Citizens Committee also sought out newspaper coverage, sponsored television shows, and encouraged citizens to write letters of support; Hoover himself appeared on a CBS radio program to discuss "You and the Hoover Commission." Citizens Committee members gave speeches at their clubs and schools, wrote to their congressmen and local newspapers, and marched in parades. Meadville, Pennsylvania, declared a "Hoover Report Week" during January 1950.[202] Newspapers applauded the Citizens' Committee project, seeing it as a way of keeping reorganization recommendations alive. Johnson, pointing to the wide support the Citizens Committee had received from individuals from all backgrounds, asked, "Isn't it just about the most heartening thing that has happened in America in years?"[203]

In response to this aggressive campaign, individuals across the country expressed overwhelming support for the Hoover program, inundating Congress and the White House with tens of thousands of letters, petitions, and signed forms expressing their support and demanding to know why the commission's recommendations had not been immediately adopted.[204] One enthusiastic correspondent recommended "an organization of 'Hoover-izers' aimed to force governmental economy by creating a movement of people who, like Thoreau, announce their willingness to go to jail, in protest against waste, rather than pay their federal income taxes!"[205] As he carefully explained, "the humor of the idea is what might make it popular!"[206] (Not all Americans agreed, of course. As one correspondent reminded the president, "Mr. Hoover streamlined us into bread lines.")[207]

The Citizens Committee's public relations strategy thus placed opponents in a tricky position. As the *Los Angeles Times* reported, "[a]lmost everybody" supported lowering the costs and the size of the federal government, "except

---

[201] Coates, "Freedom's War on Waste," 6.

[202] Louis T. Benezet to Herbert Hoover, Jan. 6, 1950, Folder "Charles B. Coates, 1951–52," Box 33, HCI, HHPPP, HHL.

[203] Johnson, address before the Massachusetts Federation of Taxpayers Associations, Inc., 8.

[204] A memo from the White House mailroom in September 1950 reported that "[a]pproximately 45,600 newspaper clippings and petitions re[:] Favorable Action on the Hoover Commission Report, have been dispatched to the Bureau of the Budget today" (G.L. Clark, memorandum to the File Room, Sept. 21, 1950, Folder "285-E (1950–53)," Box 920, WHCF: OF 285, HST Papers, HSTL).

[205] Jack Hardy to Herbert Hoover, Jan. 17, 1950, 1, Folder "HAI-HAR," Box 34, HC I, HHPPP, HHL.

[206] Ibid.

[207] A. P. Gremean to Harry S. Truman, Feb. 9, 1949, 3, Folder "285-E-Misc. CON," Box 927, WHCF: OF 285, HST Papers, HSTL.

the labor union bosses, the extreme left wingers, the Federal jobholders and their sponsoring members of Congress."²⁰⁸ Indeed, the *Times* argued, "Opposition can hardly be defended except on the lowest political and patronage planes."²⁰⁹ Agencies and commissions that expressed mixed support for the recommendations, as many did, risked being tagged as the "bureaucrats" who were part of the problem, and their defenders were seen to have a similar conflict of interest. As Sen. Robert A. Taft (R-Ohio) informed the Citizens Committee's research director, agencies "have endorsed recommendations which involve higher salaries, additional personnel, or increased powers" while opposing "virtually every recommendation which would dismember to some extent their own bureaucratic empire."²¹⁰ Even veterans' groups and their defenders were not immune from criticism; as one of Hoover's assistants emphasized to Hoover, parties *"do not want anything removed from the Veterans' Administration because it is their private preserve and they are able to exercise leverage when it is separate."*²¹¹ Coates complained to one public audience that some "15 big, powerful national organizations lined up in opposition to one section or another of the Hoover Report" favored the overall project but "just wanted an exception made for some agency or bureau with which they happened to have a well-developed working relationship or from which they received some form of patronage, subsidy, or beneficent regulation."²¹²

As the Citizens Committee defined the terms of the public debate and stirred up public enthusiasm for an issue the *Los Angeles Times* acknowledged had "no sex appeal," the Truman administration was happy to capitalize on the strong support for the Hoover Commission to pursue a program of reorganization and management improvement in the executive branch that adapted the Hoover Commission's recommendations to its own preferences.²¹³ Truman clearly relished the opportunity to return to reorganization, and the Hoover Commission's principles of management accorded with those Truman had brought to the presidency.²¹⁴ The White House thus stood behind several of the Hoover Commission's proposals, including a more efficient Executive Office of the President, centralized purchasing and supply for the federal government, better personnel management by the president, and improved management capacities within the agencies. Such reforms had only recently been politically

²⁰⁸ Frank R. Kent, "With the President Pointing in Both Directions at Once …," *Los Angeles Times,* May 6, 1949, 4.
²⁰⁹ Ibid.
²¹⁰ Robert A. Taft to Robert L. L. McCormick, Sept. 1, 1949, 2, Folder "Robert L. L. McCormick, July–September 1949," Box 35, HCI, HHPPP, HHL.
²¹¹ Robert L. L. McCormick to Herbert Hoover, Dec. 20, 1949, 1 (emphasis in the original), Folder "Robert L. L. McCormick, Oct.–Dec. 1949," Box 36, HC I, HHPPP, HHL.
²¹² Coates, "Freedom's War on Waste," 8.
²¹³ "President Truman Kicks Off," *Los Angeles Times,* June 22, 1949, 4.
²¹⁴ See Harry S. Truman, "Statement by the President Upon Receiving Final Report of the Hoover Commission," May 26, 1949, in *Public Papers of the Presidents of the United States: Harry S. Truman,* vol. 1949 (Washington, DC: Government Printing Office, 1964), 264–66; John Fischer, "Mr. Truman Reorganizes," *Harper's Magazine,* Jan. 1946.

impossible, but as budget director Frank Pace commented, the White House could now reap the benefits of "a new Presidential term, a generally favorable political climate, and the support – at least on this issue – of the Commission on the Organization of the Executive Branch."[215] Pace suggested that "the present opportunity to create and staff an improved organization for central management activities is one which has not been equaled for many years and which may not be equaled for many years to come."[216]

Several of the Hoover Commission's recommendations were enacted by Congress with support and pressure from the Truman administration, including the creation of a General Services Administration for centralized purchasing, the reorganization of the State Department (with the help of Dean Acheson, who had since become Truman's secretary of state), and the amendment of the National Security Act of 1947 to replace the National Military Establishment with a single Department of Defense. Truman also directed the executive agencies and independent commissions to review the "effectiveness and economy" of the programs they administered, and placed continuing responsibility for management improvement in an Advisory Committee on Management Improvement, created in July 1949 with members drawn from executive agencies, academia, and the private sector.[217]

Rather than adopting the rest of the Hoover Commission's specific recommendations wholesale, Truman, with the help of his advisory committee, developed plans for management improvement in the various agencies. Implementation of such proposals required presidential reorganization authority; with the Hoover Commission's encouragement, Congress passed a broad Reorganization Act in June 1949 that allowed the president to submit reorganization plans through April 1953.[218] Against the influence of what the *Los Angeles Times* suggested were "Washington bureaucrats who flourish under the existing setup and profit from confusion and inefficiency," the act contained no exemptions for individual agencies or commissions (as the 1945 statute had).[219] Nor did it bar Truman from abolishing or moving executive departments

[215] Frank Pace to Harry S. Truman, memorandum, Feb. 14, 1949, 1, Folder "285-E (Feb. 1949)," Box 919, WHCF: OF 285, HST Papers, HSTL.

[216] Ibid., 4.

[217] Executive Order No. 10072, 14 Fed. Reg. 4797 (1949); see President's Advisory Committee on Management Improvement, *Report to the President*, Nov. 3, 1950, and President's Advisory Committee on Management Improvement, *Second Annual Report*, Aug. 7, 1951, both in Folder "285-H Advisory Committee on Management Improvement," Box 927, WHCF: OF 285, HST Papers, HSTL; President's Advisory Committee on Management, "Improvement of Management in the Federal Government," *Public Administration Review* 13 (1953): 38–49; Emmerich, *Federal Reorganization and Administrative Management*.

[218] House Committee on Expenditures in the Executive Departments, *Reorganization Act of 1949*, 81st Cong., 1st sess., 1949, H. Rep. 23; Reorganization Act of 1949, Pub. L. No. 109, 63 Stat. 203 (1949).

[219] "Public Has Stake in Reorganization," *Los Angeles Times*, Apr. 12, 1949, 4; see also Robert de Roos and Arthur A. Maass, "The Lobby that Can't Be Licked: Congress and the Army Engineers," *Harper's Magazine*, Aug. 1949.

or establishing new ones (although, as Hoover pointed out to Congress, "It does not give him new timber to build anything with; no new functions in the Government.").[220] The act did give more authority to Congress than past ones had; the president's reorganization plans, once submitted to Congress, would automatically take effect unless *either* house of Congress vetoed it within sixty days (in contrast to earlier grants of authority requiring a concurrent resolution). Although columnist Joseph Alsop warned darkly that this provision drove "a dagger" through the president's authority "to bring order out of the chaos of the whole executive branch," Truman had significant success with this set of reorganization plans.[221]

Most of the reorganization plans Truman proposed in 1949 and 1950 at least generally paralleled Hoover Commission recommendations. To the consternation of the Citizens Committee, however, they rarely mirrored the recommendations exactly. Certain House members criticized Truman's use of the "Hoover Commission" mantle, accusing the administration of "foist[ing] upon an unsuspecting public, legislation bearing the Hoover label, but never designed to accomplish the purposes of the Hoover Commission."[222] Certain reorganization plans attempted to organize the executive branch by government function, as in the successful plan to consolidate federal labor functions in the Labor Department and the unsuccessful proposal to locate federal welfare activities in a Department of Welfare or the Federal Security Agency. Others attempted to strengthen the presidency, moving the National Security Council and the National Security Resources Board into the Executive Office of the President. Still others sought to strengthen the legal authority of department heads at the Post Office and the departments of Treasury, Justice, Interior, Commerce, and Labor, and of new chairmen at the SEC, the FTC, the CAB, the CSC, and the Federal Power Commission (over the objections of commissioners).[223]

In several controversial areas, however, failed reorganization plans demonstrated the limits of the commission's uniform approach. Multiple plans

---

[220] House Committee on Expenditures in the Executive Departments, *Reorganization of Government Agencies: Hearings on H.R. 1569*, 81st Cong., 1st Sess., 1949 (statement of Herbert Hoover, Jan. 31), 141.

[221] Joseph Alsop, "Matter of Fact," *Washington Post*, May 11, 1949, 11. (The provision was added by Sen. McClellan, apparently to protect the Army Corps of Engineers.)

[222] House Committee on Expenditures in the Executive Departments, *Reorganization Plan No. 2 of 1949*, 81st Cong., 1st sess., 1949, H. Rep. 1204, 18. For more on the Hoover Commission in the 80th Congress, see Senate Committee on Expenditures in the Executive Departments, *Progress on Hoover Commission Recommendations*; Senate Committee on Expenditures in the Executive Departments, *Action on Hoover Commission Reports*, 81st Cong., 2nd sess., 1950, S. Rep. 2581; Senate Committee on Expenditures in the Executive Departments, *Reorganizations in the Executive Branch of the Government*, 81st Cong., 2nd sess., 1950, S. Rep. 2680.

[223] Within a year, and in part due to ongoing congressional investigations, the Maritime Commission was reorganized. Reorganization Plan No. 21 of 1950 split the Maritime Commission into a Federal Maritime Board (in charge of regulatory functions) and a Maritime Administration (in charge of promotional functions), both within the Commerce Department (64 Stat. 1273 [1950]).

broke the recommendations apart, allowing interest groups and agencies to organize in opposition. Among the defeated plans were those providing for a stronger USDA secretary, presidential appointment of a "strong chairman" at the ICC (which was vehemently opposed by the railroad interests and by some in Congress as "an entering wedge for further encroachments upon the independence of the Commission"), and the same for the FCC (where the plan was strongly opposed by broadcasters and their attorneys).[224] In addition, reorganization plans that would have moved the Federal Security Agency into a new Department of Welfare and created a new Department of Health, Education, and Security (a proposal the Citizens Committee opposed) were disapproved, as were plans to reorganize the USDA and the Treasury Department and to move the Reconstruction Finance Corporation to the Commerce Department.

The Truman administration's 1950 effort to use a reorganization plan to undo the Taft-Hartley Act's reorganization of the NLRB also failed. By placing all agency authority in the board, the proposal to eliminate the general counsel position (and get rid of Robert Denham, the much-disliked general counsel) was entirely consistent with the Hoover Commission's overall ethos. As Walter Galenson had pointed out in his report, "the housing of two agencies under one roof is hardly conducive to efficiency."[225] The task force had made recommendations in this area (although it did not go so far as to move the general counsel's functions back to the board), but the Hoover Commission had avoided the issue. The Citizens Committee refused to support a plan they saw as a policy question and that many others saw as Truman's attempt to undo part of the act he had unsuccessfully vetoed in 1947 and had campaigned against since.[226] Here Truman appeared to be engaging in the bureaucratic gamesmanship the Citizens Committee had deplored, and the conservative *Chicago Tribune* attacked the president for using the Hoover Commission reports to support "petty moves of personal or political advantage to himself."[227]

Over the next few years, the Citizens Committee continued to press the White House and Congress for additional action. While the committee sent twenty draft bills to Congress and fifty-one additional proposed reorganization plans to Truman in 1951, the administration's enthusiasm waned, especially once the Korean War began in June 1950 and Truman shifted the focus of his Advisory

[224] House Committee on Expenditures in the Executive Departments, *Reorganization Plan No. 7 of 1950*, 81st Cong., 2nd sess., 1950, H. Rep. 1971, 14. Regarding the FCC, see House Select Committee on Small Business, Subcommittee No. 1 on Regulatory Agencies and Commissions, *The Organization and Procedures of the Federal Regulatory Commissions and Agencies and their Effect on Small Business*, 18–19.

[225] Galenson, *Staff Report on the National Labor Relations Board*, II-29.

[226] See James A. Gross, *Broken Promise: The Subversion of U.S. Labor Relations Policy, 1947–1994* (Philadelphia: Temple University Press, 1995), chap. 5.

[227] "4 Billions Not Saved," *Chicago Daily Tribune*, Apr. 14, 1950, 20; see also Louis Stark, "Board's Power Is Crux of Dispute Over N.L.R.B.," *New York Times*, Mar. 26, 1950, E7; Nathaniel L. Nathanson, "Central Issues of American Administrative Law," *American Political Science Review* 45 (1951): 348–85, 352.

Committee on Management Improvement toward issues of mobilization.[228]
The Hoover Commission had nonetheless succeeded where previous reorganization efforts had failed, employing new tactics to win support for – and
ultimately implementation of – its organizational and management reforms.
Of the more than 270 recommendations offered by the Hoover Commission,
approximately 70 percent were ultimately implemented, making the Hoover
Commission the most successful executive reorganization effort yet.[229] Out of
the Hoover Commission came the General Services Administration, the Budget
and Accounting Procedures Act of 1950, and the origins of the Department
of Health, Education, and Welfare, established in 1953. A 1956 evaluation
suggested that spending on the Korean War had swallowed up the Hoover
Commission's true savings, but "[t]here is no doubt, however, that the savings
were large."[230]

By all accounts, those on both sides of the partisan divide saw the Hoover
Commission as a success. Administrative governance had been evaluated by
panels of experts, agencies were put on notice for their profligate tendencies,
and recommendations promising efficiency were adopted throughout the
federal government. In late 1950, Citizens Committee staffers bragged that
"[f]or the first time," the United States could meet wartime "without cook-
ing up an 'alphabet soup' of temporary, autonomous, duplicatory, and often
headless agencies."[231] The Hoover Commission's recommendations embodied
a clear faith that formal organization could solve administrative problems.
The Hoover Commission's report on General Management of the Executive
Branch, which fully embraced Hoover's theory of government organization,
articulated an approach to federal organization based in a top-down, presidentially centered theory of government control and coordination that relied
on clear authority, uniform design, and new organizational charts. It was this
vision that, through its association with the 80th Congress and with Hoover,
came to stand for a particular strain of conservatism.

   Nonetheless, the reforms resulting from the Hoover Commission's recommendations were, outside the defense context, rather minimal; as the

---

[228] For more on the reorganization plans, see Robert L. L. Johnson to Harry S. Truman, May 8,
     1951, 1–2, Folder "285-A 1951," Box 918, WHCF: OF 285, HST Papers, HSTL.
[229] The Citizens Committee for the Hoover Report estimated that, as of 1955, "seventy-two per
     cent of the recommendations of the First Hoover Commission have been adopted" (Ray Harvey,
     Louis W. Koenig, and Albert Somit, *Achievements in Federal Reorganization: The Contribution
     of the First and New Hoover Commissions* [New York: Citizens Committee for the Hoover
     Report, 1955], 16); see also House Committee on Government Operations, *Summary of the
     Objectives, Operations, and Results of the Commissions on Organization of the Executive
     Branch of the Government*, 88th Cong., 1st sess., 1963, Committee Print.
[230] Neil MacNeil and Harold W. Metz, *The Hoover Report 1953–1955: What It Means to You as
     Citizen and Taxpayer* (New York: Macmillan Company, 1956), 10.
[231] "Products of the Hoover Commission Report," Nov. 15, 1950, Folder "Charles B. Coates,
     1950," Box 33, HC I, HHPPP, HHL.

Washington Post suggested, the 1949 reorganization plans "do not entail any sweeping changes in the organizational set-up."[232] The *New York Times* similarly reported in August that the numerous plans "took effect today without noticeable impact on the 217,237 Federal employe[e]s here."[233] Even though the agencies had been reorganized, "it is not likely that the changes can be detected easily at first except on the charts of the bureaus and departments involved."[234] The *Wall Street Journal* suggested more critically – but along the same lines – that the 1949 plans "do not enforce either simplification of the federal establishment or reduction of its expenditures."[235] *Harper's Magazine*, noting that the agencies were "lapsing into a soggy bureaucratic routine," suggested that "[e]ven the Hoover Commission apparently was astonished to discover how hard it is to accomplish anything within the moldering labyrinths of our patchwork bureaucracy."[236] The most significant reforms improved the president's ability to deal with the existing organization of the administrative state and guaranteed him a role in administrative governance. This role was likely to be partial and sporadic, however. One skeptical observer of the Hoover Commission's reports found that the commission had inadvertently demonstrated "the incompetence of the presidency for more than an 'off the cuff' Yes or No or Maybe. One man can hardly do anything other than stand above the battle."[237]

More significant was the new way of thinking about administrative governance that resulted. The very fact that such incremental reforms had been adopted, in the name of a broad and highly publicized Republican initiative, suggested that such reforms might be sufficient to fix the agencies' problems. As presidential supervision was brought to the administrative state, through rhetoric if not through daily practice, claims of administrative lawlessness declined in power. The commission and the Truman administration thus further insulated the agencies from attack. What replaced earlier complaints were increasingly common ones about administrators' slowness and intractability. In place of rhetoric that suggested government agencies operated with reckless abandon, the Hoover Commission made the case that Americans were not getting *enough* service for their money. By the 1950s, agencies that had sought to legitimate their institutions in the public eye through procedural reforms found themselves facing complaints about those very issues. Agencies pointed to ever-smaller appropriations that imperiled their ability to keep up with rapidly expanding industries. In its 1951 annual report, the ICC accused Congress of "deregulation" via "the gradual but steady reduction of the appropriations,"

---

[232] "Reorganization," *Washington Post*, Aug. 19, 1949, 20.
[233] "Six Truman Plans Shuffle Agencies," *New York Times*, Aug. 21, 1949, 32.
[234] Ibid.
[235] "Streamlining Government?" *Wall Street Journal*, Sept. 8, 1949, 4.
[236] John Fischer, "Truman & Co., Limited," *Harper's Magazine*, July 1949, 22.
[237] Herman Finer, "The Hoover Commission Reports: Part I," *Political Science Quarterly* 64 (1949): 405–19, 416.

which resulted in "an impairment of efficient administration, a growing inability to perform the functions and duties required by the statute, and a weakening of the commission's regulatory authority which has already assumed serious proportions."[238] At the same time, the careful strategies agencies had chosen to legitimate themselves to the public were themselves in question. As one self-proclaimed "bureaucrat" wearily explained to Americans, "you protect the purity of public business by legal red tape," to the detriment of "competent staffs struggling for several years to try to cut away needless and costly strictures in administrative channels" that "were created by your fear of me and fellow bureaucrats."[239] At the same time, however, another line of criticism was developing. Although the Hoover Commission had largely ignored administrators' close relationships with those outside the commissions, observers soon looked at these relationships with a more cynical eye.

[238] Interstate Commerce Commission, *65th Annual Report*, 82nd Cong., 2nd sess., 1951, H. Doc. 280, 132; see also Peterson, *President Harry S. Truman and the Independent Regulatory Commissions*.

[239] Wycliffe Allen, "I Am a Bureaucrat," *Public Administration Review* 11 (1951): 116–18, 117.

5

The Stymied Transformation of Administrative Law

As the 1952 elections placed the presidency and both houses of Congress under Republican control for the first time in two decades, the problem of the administrative process became one for the new administration to solve. In the years following the passage of the Administrative Procedure Act and the Legislative Reorganization Act, an increasing number of Americans had become convinced that the Hoover Commission's criticisms of rule-bound and indolent administration lay closer to the truth than did the ABA's charges of recklessness and zeal. Contrary to the hopes of many conservatives, Dwight D. Eisenhower's interest in federal reform extended neither to significant cuts in existing programs nor to major changes in the administrative process. Eisenhower's initiatives in reforming the administrative process were incremental at best, addressing agencies' practical problems of delay and resources while largely staying away from questions of fairness. Proposals to address administrative speed and expense essentially accepted the role of administrative governance in American life.

That the public debate had shifted was evident in politicians' tepid reception for new plans to hamstring the administrative process. When the new Republican Congress succeeded in creating a second Hoover Commission in the summer of 1953, many expected great things. Eisenhower's organizational thinking, his focus on voluntarism, and his preference for private management over public control seemed a good fit with Hoover's own brand of conservatism. (So, too, did Eisenhower's involvement with the first Hoover Commission.) However, declining to allow Hoover and his commission to dictate the White House's goals, Eisenhower offered them a cool reception. This was particularly true of the proposals offered by members of the second Hoover Commission's Task Force on Legal Services and Procedure, who proposed a complete remaking of the administrative process in the image of the federal courts. The task force's report articulated a strikingly oppositionist tone to the administrative process and demonstrated little faith in administrators. Suggesting that the administrative process still failed to provide regulated parties with fair hearings, the task force recommended vesting even less discretion in administrative officials and shifting as much administrative work as possible to the federal courts, moving government functions out of the hands of bureaucrats and into the hands of judges. While members indicted the administrative state for the burdensome and unjust demands agencies placed on regulated parties and for the cost incurred by the government of doing so, the Hoover Commission task force's solutions – described by one observer "as a blitzkrieg effort at total victory" for fans of judicial control of the administrative state – would have slowed down the regulatory process enormously, and were at best an awkward alternate route to getting government out of business.[1] By the late 1950s, the last thing anyone wanted was slower administration.

Another problem had also emerged: corruption by administrators too close to the agencies they regulated. By the late 1950s, outside observers and agency officials agreed that the regulatory agencies were in trouble. One law professor suggested that "the prestige and authority of administrative agencies are again, as in the late thirties, in a declining state" – due in part to "recurrent charges of political influence at work in high places in administrative agencies."[2] The "corruption" critique focused on the powerful influence of regulated parties and outside interests on the administrative process. Anecdotal evidence of questionable behavior was found in a number of agencies, in episodes such as the resignation of ICC chairman Hugh Cross based on claims that he had pressed railroad officials to offer a Chicago baggage transportation contract to a private company that had already made Cross an offer of employment.[3] By 1957, Harvard Law School professor Louis Jaffe was suggesting, in an article for *Harper's Magazine*, that "the air in Washington, New York, and Boston has been thick with rumors of political favoritism in the Federal Communications Commission."[4] These close ties were not a new development; indeed, the Attorney General's Committee on Administrative Procedure and the APA actively encouraged agencies and commissions to develop working relationships with the parties they regulated. What *was* new was the apparently belated realization by outside observers that such influence might be more than a counterweight to agency power. The egregious episodes that garnered headlines in the daily papers were not exceptional; they were common relationships simply carried too far past the point of propriety. Students of administration were increasingly realizing that the combination of promotional responsibilities and regulatory authority placed administrators in a difficult position. And given that many agencies awarded valuable benefits, there were enormous incentives for the regulated parties to try to influence the regulators. The House Special Subcommittee on Legislative Oversight's revelations about conflicts of

[1] Ferrel Heady, "The New Reform Movement in Regulatory Administration," *Public Administration Review* 19 (1959): 89–100, 93.

[2] J. Forrester Davison, "An Administrative Court of the United States," *George Washington Law Review* 24 (1956): 613–18, 617.

[3] See Senate Committee on Government Operations, Permanent Subcommittee on Investigations, *Annual Report*, 84th Cong., 2nd sess., 1956, S. Rep. 1444, 28–34; David A. Frier, *Conflict of Interest in the Eisenhower Administration* (Ames: Iowa State University Press, 1969).

[4] Louis L. Jaffe, "The Scandal in TV Licensing," *Harper's Magazine*, Sept. 1957, 77.

interest at the FCC illuminated issues raised late in the Truman administration and created significant pressure for reform.

Hostility to bureaucrats was a major theme of the 1952 campaign season, apparent in the Republicans' platform targeting Democrats who had "arrogantly deprived our citizens of precious liberties by seizing powers never granted" and who "work unceasingly to achieve their goal of national socialism."[5] Emphasizing Korea, Communism, and corruption, Republicans suggested that Democrats had been poor stewards of government.[6] Democrats had countenanced government corruption, "shielded traitors to the Nation in high places," and (in a nod to the Declaration of Independence) "violated our liberties by turning loose upon the country a swarm of arrogant bureaucrats and their agents who meddle intolerably in the lives and occupations of our citizens."[7] Eisenhower's campaign targeted Truman's failure to eradicate internal subversion and root out corruption in the federal government, and the president-elect's advisory committee suggested that the new president needed to make clear "his intention to rid Government of the incompetent, dishonest, disloyal and the political hanger-on."[8] In his February 1953 State of the Union speech, the new president addressed these concerns as he promised that "dedication to these basic precepts of security and efficiency, integrity, and economy can and will produce an administration deserving of the trust the people have placed in it."[9] Soon thereafter, Eisenhower tightened loyalty standards for federal hiring and retention and, with the help of Attorney General Herbert Brownell, moved to clean out the Internal Revenue Service and the Justice Department after the Truman administration's scandals.[10] As

[5] Republican Party Platform of 1952, *New York Times*, July 11, 1952, 8.

[6] See James T. Patterson, *Grand Expectations: The United States, 1945–1974* (New York: Oxford University Press, 1996), 256.

[7] Republican Party Platform of 1952 , *New York Times*, 8.

[8] Special Committee on Government Organization to Dwight D. Eisenhower, Memorandum No. 3, Dec. 31, 1952, 15, Folder "Executive Office – Reorganization (3)," Box 14, Name Series, DDE Papers, AWF, DDEL.

[9] Dwight D. Eisenhower, "Annual Message to Congress on the State of the Union," Feb. 2, 1953, in *Public Papers of the United States: Dwight D. Eisenhower*, vol. 1953 (Washington, DC: Government Printing Office, 1960), 26; see also Herman Miles Somers, "The Federal Bureaucracy and the Change of Administration," *American Political Science Review* 48 (1954): 131–51.

[10] Regarding the loyalty program, see Executive Order No. 10450, 18 Fed. Reg. 2489 (1953). The program abolished the Loyalty Review Board and placed final authority with the department head; individual agency review boards were replaced by a "security officer" inside the agency. Procedures were also put in place for organizations to appeal their inclusion on the Attorney General's List of Subversive Organizations. This, of course, required that federal employees in sensitive positions (and all new applicants) be re-reviewed. According to the *Washington Post*, "the new program indulges in what appears almost to be sadism in reopening all cases which involved an FBI investigation under the old procedure" ("Two-Way Security Program," *Washington Post*, Apr. 30, 1953, 8). On IRS reform, see Herbert Brownell, *Advising Ike: The Memoirs of Attorney General Herbert Brownell* (Lawrence: University Press of Kansas, 1993),

Eisenhower assured Americans in January 1954, his ideal for government service was "men and women of brains, conscience, heart, and integrity" and with
"an intellectual grasp of the problems before them that is matched by their
devotion to what is just and humane. Such people are true public servants; not
bureaucrats."[11] What, then, defined "bureaucrats" was not explained.

Nonetheless, Eisenhower, who during the campaign had expressed his preference for some sort of "middle way" between New Deal programs and traditionally conservative Republican approaches, did not declare all-out war on
the federal programs established in previous years.[12] James Reston of the *New
York Times*, evaluating Eisenhower's first term in 1956, suggested that it was
"surely one of the great paradoxes of recent American political history" that
Republicans had "swallowed the basic tinkering techniques of the past and
not even attempted to repeal a single New Deal measure."[13] Hardly a fan of
Roosevelt's New Deal or Truman's Fair Deal programs, Eisenhower recognized
that these regulatory and social welfare innovations were politically unassail-
able. Even Herbert Hoover had advised Eisenhower soon after his election that
little could be done to reverse the trend toward government regulation of the
private sector. The best the new president could do, Hoover suggested, would
be to tamp down further growth.[14] Although Eisenhower declined to propose
major new programs, his administration supported the limited expansion of
Social Security, unemployment insurance, and the federal minimum wage.[15]

150; House Judiciary Committee, Subcommittee to Investigate the Department of Justice,
Investigation of the Department of Justice, 83rd Cong., 1st sess., 1953, H. Rep. 1079; Andrew
J. Dunar, *The Truman Scandals and the Politics of Morality* (Columbia: University of Missouri
Press, 1984).

[11] Dwight D. Eisenhower, "Radio and Television Address to the American People on the Administration's
Purposes and Accomplishments," Jan. 4, 1954, in *Public Papers of the United States: Dwight D.
Eisenhower*, vol. 1954 (Washington, DC: Government Printing Office, 1960), 3.

[12] Text of Dwight D. Eisenhower's speech on "Middle Way" in Boise, Idaho, *New York Times*, Aug.
21, 1952, 12.

[13] James Reston, "Eisenhower's Four Years: An Evaluation of the Republican Administration in a
Complex World," *New York Times*, July 22, 1956, 42.

[14] Robert H. Ferrell, ed., *The Eisenhower Diaries* (New York: W. W. Norton & Co., 1981), 365.

[15] For discussion of Eisenhower's domestic policies, see Edward Berkowitz and Kim McQuaid,
"Welfare Reform in the 1950s," *Social Service Review* 54 (1980): 45–58; Fred I. Greenstein,
The Hidden-Hand Presidency: Eisenhower as Leader (New York: Basic Books, 1982); Douglas
B. Harris, "Dwight Eisenhower and the New Deal: The Politics of Preemption," *Presidential
Studies Quarterly* 27 (1997): 333–42. For more on the Eisenhower White House, see Robert
J. Donovan, *Eisenhower: The Inside Story* (New York: Harper & Brothers, 1956); Edward
H. Hobbs, "The President and Administration – Eisenhower," *Public Administration Review*
18 (1958): 306–13; Charles C. Alexander, *Holding the Line: The Eisenhower Era, 1952–
1961* (Bloomington: Indiana University Press, 1975); Vincent P. De Santis, "Eisenhower
Revisionism," *Review of Politics* 38 (1976): 190–207; Robert Griffith, "Dwight D. Eisenhower
and the Corporate Commonwealth," *American Historical Review* 87 (1982): 87–122; Alan
Brinkley, "A President for Certain Seasons," *Wilson Quarterly* 14 (1990): 110–19; William E.
Leuchtenburg, *In the Shadow of FDR: From Harry Truman to Bill Clinton* (Ithaca, NY: Cornell
University Press, 1993); Francis H. Heller, "The Eisenhower White House," *Presidential Studies
Quarterly* 23 (1993): 509–17; Robert Maranto, "The Administrative Strategies of Republican

Eisenhower's willingness to accept a social safety net and his hesitation about rolling back popular programs did not translate into enthusiasm for bureaucrats or government control. Eisenhower was skeptical of government-by-administration, questioning the constitutionality of the administrative state and suggesting that governance through independent regulatory commissions was "threatening the individual liberties and the entire system of free government" in America.[16] Eisenhower's brand of conservatism acknowledged a role for the federal government in fiscal policy but objected to excessive government meddling in the marketplace.[17] As he carefully explained in his 1955 State of the Union address, his administration's "two simple rules" were that "the Federal Government should perform an essential task only when it cannot otherwise be adequately performed" and that, in doing so, "our government must not impair the self-respect, freedom and incentive of the individual."[18] Following these principles, he argued, "the government can fully meet its obligation without creating a dependent population or a domineering bureaucracy."[19]

Along these lines, Eisenhower sought to return authority to state governments wherever possible, convincing Congress to create a commission on intergovernmental affairs dedicated to evaluating what the federal government was doing that the states could do instead. He also attempted to take government out of competition with private interests, as was evident in his approach to public power. This was an area where, during his campaign, Eisenhower had complained of the "zealots" behind a "whole-hog Federal Government" that "believes that it must own and control just as many of our resources as it can lay its hands on – by fair means or foul."[20] In a controversial episode during Eisenhower's first term, the White House, seeing an opportunity to limit the TVA's responsibilities, lower the federal deficit, and encourage private enterprise, targeted a proposed new Tennessee Valley Authority steam plant near Paducah, Kentucky.[21] The Truman administration had put funds in its final budget for the new plant, through which the TVA would supply power to the Atomic Energy Commission. However, as Sherman Adams, Eisenhower's

Presidents From Eisenhower to Reagan," *Presidential Studies Quarterly* 23 (1993): 683–97; Henry Z. Scheele, "President Dwight D. Eisenhower and U.S. House Leader Charles A. Halleck: An Examination of an Executive-Legislative Relationship," *Presidential Studies Quarterly* 23 (1993): 289–99; Patterson, *Grand Expectations*.

16 Dwight D. Eisenhower, quoted in Arthur Krock, "In the Nation," *New York Times*, Jan. 18, 1952, 26; on his constitutional views, see Ferrell, ed., *The Eisenhower Diaries*, 229–30.

17 See Iwan W. Morgan, *Eisenhower versus 'The Spenders': The Eisenhower Administration, the Democrats, and the Budget, 1953–1960* (New York: St. Martin's Press, 1990), 16; see also Reston, "Eisenhower's Four Years."

18 Dwight D. Eisenhower, "Annual Message to the Congress on the State of the Union," Jan. 6, 1955, in *Public Papers of the United States: Dwight D. Eisenhower*, vol. 1955 (Washington, DC: Government Printing Office, 1959), 22.

19 Ibid.

20 "Text of Eisenhower's Seattle speech on Power Projects," *New York Times*, Oct. 7, 1952, 22.

21 Ferrell, ed., *The Eisenhower Diaries*, 297–300.

chief of staff, later recalled, the president thought "the TVA was big enough already."[22] The White House thus moved to place the proposed plant in private hands, and the Atomic Energy Commission signed a contract with local power company owners Messrs. Dixon and Yates. The plan – which offered highly favorable terms to the private power companies involved – was approved by the attorney general, the comptroller general, the SEC, the Federal Power Commission, and the Joint Committee on Atomic Energy.

By the summer of 1955, however, the deal had fallen apart, victim to charges of conflict of interest on the part of one of the businessmen involved. Evidence that Adams had put pressure on the SEC to postpone a key hearing further called the propriety of the deal into question. As the Senate Judiciary Committee's Subcommittee on Antitrust and Monopoly concluded, the Dixon-Yates controversy "provides a dramatic case study of the waste, disorder, and confusion which inevitably surround governmental action which is calculated to serve big business interests rather than the public generally."[23] Overall, the deal, which seemed to be premised more on deference to private business interests than on actual economy or efficiency, failed to validate Eisenhower's approach to governance.

Eisenhower's preference for business interests over loosely defined ideas of the "public interest" was also evident in his handling of the regulatory agencies. Although Eisenhower did little to cut the powers of the agencies and commissions – rejecting, for instance, pressure from the National Association of Manufacturers to transfer some of the NLRB's jurisdiction to the federal courts – he used his appointment power to appoint bureaucrats who shared his point of view.[24] Eisenhower's cabinet officials (famously "eight millionaires and a plumber"), commissioners, and appointees to government advisory commissions reflected his desire to bring businessmen and their corporate approaches into federal policy making.[25] Under new leadership, agencies including the

[22] Sherman Adams, *Firsthand Report: The Story of the Eisenhower Administration* (New York: Harper & Brothers, 1961), 312. For more on the Dixon-Yates controversy, see A. J. G. Priest, "Dixon-Yates and the Public Interest," *Virginia Law Review* 41 (1955): 289–309; Aaron B. Wildavsky, *Dixon-Yates: A Study in Power Politics* (New Haven, CT: Yale University Press, 1962); Donovan, *Eisenhower: The Inside Story*; Frier, *Conflict of Interest in the Eisenhower Administration*, chap. 5.

[23] Senate Judiciary Committee, *Power Policy Dixon Yates Contract: Staff Report of the Subcommittee on Antitrust and Monopoly on Investigation Concerning the Charges of Monopolistic Influences in the Power Industry*, 84th Cong., 2nd sess., 1956, Committee Print, xxix.

[24] See Mozart G. Ratner, "Policy-making by the New 'Quasi-Judicial' NLRB," *University of Chicago Law Review* 23 (1955): 12–35; Seymour Scher, "Regulatory Agency Control Through Appointment: The Case of the Eisenhower Administration and the NLRB," *Journal of Politics* 23 (1961): 667–88.

[25] T.R.B., "Washington Wire," *New Republic*, Dec. 15, 1952, 3; T.R.B., "Washington Wire," *New Republic*, Feb. 2, 1953, 3; William Safire, *Safire's Political Dictionary* (New York: Oxford University Press, 2008), 209–10; see also Griffith, "Dwight D. Eisenhower and the Corporate Commonwealth"; "Republicans Reshape the FTC," *Business Week*, June 5, 1954; Bernard Schwartz, *The Professor and the Commissions* (New York: Alfred A. Knopf, 1959); David M.

NLRB and the FCC became notably more sympathetic to the private interests before them.[26]

Eisenhower's budget policy also influenced his approach to the agencies and commissions he supervised. Along with his "New Look" at defense priorities, Eisenhower proposed few new regulatory commitments and attempted to reduce the costs of existing ones wherever possible. Having taken office burdened with a multibillion-dollar deficit, Eisenhower was committed to balancing the nation's budget (which he managed to do twice in his first term), largely through spending cuts in federal expenditures and staffing that, on top of the Truman administration's cuts, notably limited administrative capacities.[27] The new administration immediately called on agencies to make cuts, slicing the budget proposals in Truman's 1954 budget by billions of dollars; Eisenhower would seek to keep appropriations low throughout his administration.[28] As the FCC would complain in December 1957, the commission "is trying to handle an administrative load which has more than doubled in volume and complexities since World War II with little change in amount of appropriations or number of personnel."[29] As many agencies and commissions had already discovered during the Truman administration, budget cuts or even simply lack of increases in appropriations to keep up with inflation (combined with congressional pay raises for civil servants) meant staffing cuts that hampered the performance of their regulatory tasks.[30]

Welborn, "Presidents, Regulatory Commissioners and Regulatory Policy," *Journal of Public Law* 15 (1966): 3–29.

[26] For more on agency policy, see Cabell Phillips, "The Business Invasion of Washington," *Harper's Magazine*, Oct. 1953; Joseph A. Loftus, "Eisenhower's Four Years: An Evaluation of Administration Policy Toward Labor and the Union Leaders," *New York Times*, July 25, 1956, 1; Scher, "Regulatory Agency Control through Appointment"; Erik Barnouw, *The Image Empire: A History of Broadcasting in the United States*, vol. III – *from 1953* (New York: Oxford University Press, 1970); Alexander, *Holding the Line*; Erwin G. Krasnow and Lawrence D. Longley, *The Politics of Broadcast Regulation*, 2nd ed. (New York: St. Martin's Press, 1978); Terry M. Moe, "Regulatory Performance and Presidential Administration," *American Journal of Political Science* 26 (1982): 197–224; James L. Baughman, *Television's Guardians: The FCC and the Politics of Programming, 1958–1967* (Knoxville: University of Tennessee Press, 1985); Maranto, "The Administrative Strategies of Republican Presidents From Eisenhower to Reagan"; James A. Gross, *Broken Promise: The Subversion of U.S. Labor Relations Policy, 1947–1994* (Philadelphia: Temple University Press, 1995).

[27] See Louis L. Jaffe, "The Effective Limits of the Administrative Process: A Reevaluation," *Harvard Law Review* 67 (1954): 1105–35, 1130–32; J. Sinclair Armstrong, "Congress and the Securities and Exchange Commission," *Virginia Law Review* 45 (1959): 795–816; Adams, *Firsthand Report*; Morgan, *Eisenhower versus 'The Spenders.'*

[28] Donovan, *Eisenhower: The Inside Story*, chap. 4; see also Eisenhower, "Annual Message to the Congress on the State of the Union," Jan. 6, 1955, in *Public Papers of the United States: Dwight D. Eisenhower*, vol. 1955, 17.

[29] John C. Doerfer, "1957 and the FCC," Dec. 31, 1957, 5, File No. 12-12, "Organization – Federal Communications Commission," Box 4, General Correspondence 1957–1966, A1, Entry 100C, OED, RG 173, NACP.

[30] Joel Seligman, *The Transformation of Wall Street: A History of the Securities and Exchange Commission and Modern Corporate Finance*, 3rd ed. (New York: Aspen Publishers, 2003).

Eisenhower also took up the issue of government organization early in his administration, calling in February 1953 for a reorganization effort aimed at "discovering and removing outmoded functions and eliminating duplication."[31] Coming into office with a military background, Eisenhower wanted his own office to run with a similar efficiency.[32] Shortly after his 1952 victory, the president-elect assembled his brother Milton, Nelson Rockefeller, and Civil Service Commissioner Arthur Flemming and asked them to help his incoming administration get a handle on organizational issues, especially in light of mobilization for the Korean War. Eisenhower had his own interest in reorganization; as Milton Eisenhower recalled, his brother believed "many of the national programs were wasteful and inefficient," and it was time "to consolidate gains, improve the federal structure, and obtain full value for the billions of dollars spent on fairly new social programs."[33]

His approach to administration had much in common with that of the Hoover Commission, and Hoover himself ultimately applauded many of the president's early reforms. The president-elect had directed his committee to focus on "[s]trengthening the executive authority of the President and of the heads of Departments and Agencies" as well as "[e]liminating functions which have outlived their usefulness, and curtailing activities which are extended beyond present need."[34] Hoping that his committee could wrap up earlier efforts at reorganization, Eisenhower instructed it to review existing studies and the remaining Hoover Commission recommendations for guidance on how to proceed.[35] Supporters of the Hoover Commission were enthusiastic; the 1952 Republican platform had promised "a thorough reorganization of the Federal Government in accordance with the principles set forth in the report of the Hoover Commission," and members of the Hoover Commission and its Citizens Committee for the Hoover Report, who saw Republican control of both branches as an opportunity to finish the commission's work, immediately began pressing the new administration for reform.[36]

Eisenhower was less enthusiastic about major renovation of federal governance than many Republicans, however, and he was also less eager to enact the

---

[31] Eisenhower, "Annual Message to the Congress on the State of the Union," Feb. 2, 1953, in *Public Papers of the United States: Dwight D. Eisenhower*, vol. 1953, 25.

[32] See Charles J. V. Murphy, "Eisenhower's White House," *Fortune*, July 1953; Stephen Hess, *Organizing the Presidency* (Washington, DC: Brookings Institution, 1976).

[33] Milton S. Eisenhower, *The President Is Calling* (Garden City, NY: Doubleday & Co., 1974), 255.

[34] "Special Committee on Government Organization," Jan. 13, 1953, 1, Folder "Rockefeller, Nelson 1952–55 (6)," Box 31, Administration Series, DDE Papers, AWF, DDEL.

[35] The President's Committee was also presented with the Temple University Survey of Federal Reorganization, a report organized by Robert L. Johnson, chairman of the Citizens Committee for the Hoover Report, before the election and issued early in 1953, to provide the new administration with information on the Commission's reports (Robert L. Johnson et al., *The Temple University Survey of Federal Reorganization*, 2 vols. [Philadelphia: Temple University Press, 1953]).

[36] Republican Party Platform of 1952, *New York Times*, July 11, 1952, 8.

remaining Hoover Commission recommendations than the Citizens Committee would have liked. Eisenhower's own three-man committee, which became the President's Advisory Committee on Government Organization once Eisenhower took office, resisted pressure from Hoover Commission boosters and made clear that the administration would chart its own course.[37] PACGO focused on broad questions of management authority and organizational placement, and Eisenhower's reorganization efforts during his first year in office demonstrated his receptiveness to the possibility of good administration and competent administrators. PACGO members met frequently, worked quickly, and closely consulted with the Budget Bureau, with members of Congress, and with new administrators at the agencies and commissions to make sure everyone involved approved the proposed reforms (a step the congressionally driven Hoover Commission had chosen to omit). With the help of the Budget Bureau and the support of department heads, PACGO transmitted 20 separate reports to Eisenhower by the end of April, containing approximately 140 recommendations on a variety of topics.

Based on these recommendations, and with new reorganization authority in hand, the president sent nine reorganization plans to Congress in the first half of 1953; all were approved. As was evident from these plans, the Eisenhower White House was clearly amenable to hierarchical administrative organization as a path to better operation and control, indicating how mainstream the Brownlow Committee's and Hoover Commission's approach had become. PACGO members distanced themselves, however, from those "trying to fit all the agencies of Government to a set of 'management principles.'"[38] Instead, members suggested, they sought "a digging down-to-earth approach of studying what is expected of any particular agency and then trying to find the simplest administrative means for carrying out these specific tasks."[39] For example, finding that the Federal Security Agency was inadequate to serve the coordinating task it had been given, owing in part to the fact that it was "developed by transferring under the FSA tent strong, almost autonomous bureaus" that "in most cases have maintained their original status, prestige, and authority," PACGO recommended that it become a cabinet-level Department of Health, Education and Welfare – a proposal that both the Brownlow Committee and the Hoover Commission had put forth and that the Eisenhower administration successfully implemented in 1953.[40] Also consistent with earlier recommendations, the administration adopted several reforms to strengthen the Executive Office of the President, including improvements to the Civil Service Commission, the Council of Economic Advisers, and the creation of a new Office of Defense

---

[37] Executive Order No. 10432, 18 Fed. Reg. 617 (1953).
[38] Preface, Recommendations of the President's Advisory Committee on Government Organization, Apr. 1953, 4 Folder "PACGO Recommendations Apr. 1953 (1)," Box 4, Miscellaneous Series, DDE Papers, AWF, DDEL.
[39] Ibid.
[40] PACGO to Dwight D. Eisenhower, Memorandum No. 4, Feb. 10, 1953, 1, Folder "Legislative Meetings – 1953 (1)," Box 1, Legislative Meeting Series, DDE Papers, AWF, DDEL.

Mobilization in which civil defense coordination was consolidated. Following up on an earlier promise to improve the civil service system, Eisenhower issued an executive order to improve his control over executive branch personnel and to push the CSC chairman to take a larger role. PACGO also recommended that the president submit to the new Congress previously rejected Hoover Commission reorganization plans to create a presidentially appointed "strong chairman" in the independent commissions without one; given continued resistance from the commissions, however, this proposal met with little success.

Eisenhower's approach was evident as well in defense reorganization, in which he was especially engaged. At the same time that PACGO was wrapping up its initial work on the civilian government, another group – chaired, like PACGO, by Nelson Rockefeller – was looking into duplication, management, and waste at the Defense Department. The Committee on Department of Defense Organization focused on the kinds of improvements in efficiency and centralized control in the Defense Department that the Hoover Commission and PACGO had sought in the civilian agencies. The model was, in fact, largely civilian. Secretary of Defense Charles ("Engine Charlie") Wilson, the former head of General Motors, provided the president with an organization chart of that company as a model, suggesting that given "the size and diversification of interests in General Motors," the company "had essentially the same problem of organization that exists in the Defense Department."[41] Reorganization Plan No. 6 of 1953, which gave the Defense Secretary additional staff assistance and created "clear lines of responsibility and authority" throughout the Defense Department, was thus much in line with Eisenhower's approach.[42]

An attempt to address administrative procedures across the government was also launched in the spring of 1953, following the complaints of federal judges that, reported Chief Justice Fred Vinson, "unnecessary delay, expense and volume of record" in certain administrative cases were causing "a serious problem in the administration of justice" for federal courts.[43] Following the Judicial Conference's recommendation for a study of the problem, in April the president called together representatives from 56 agencies and departments, members of the judiciary, members of the bar, and federal hearing examiners to

[41] Charles E. Wilson to Dwight D. Eisenhower, Feb. 13, 1953, Folder "Legislative Meetings – 1953 (3)" Box 1, Legislative Meeting Series, DDE Papers, AWF, DDEL.
[42] Dwight D. Eisenhower, "Special Message to the Congress Transmitting Reorganization Plan 6 of 1953 Concerning the Department of Defense," April 30, 1953, in *Public Papers of the Presidents of the United States: Dwight D. Eisenhower*, vol. 1960–1961 (Washington, DC: Government Printing Office, 1960), 227.
[43] Fred Vinson to Dwight D. Eisenhower, Mar. 24, 1953, Folder "103-D-2 Conference on Administrative Procedure (1)," Official File Series, DDE Papers, Central Files, DDEL; see Advisory Committee on Procedure before Administrative Agencies, "Judicial Conference Study of Administrative Procedure," *I.C.C. Practitioners' Journal* 19 (Oct. 1951): 3–13.

share their expertise and develop recommendations so "that the administrative process may be improved to the benefit of all."[44]

The findings and recommendations of the President's Conference on Administrative Procedure, directed to the president, to the Judicial Conference, and to the agencies themselves, provided a snapshot of the administrative process, much as the Attorney General's Committee had twelve years earlier.[45] The narrow scope of the problems addressed, however, were a far cry from the claims of "administrative absolutism" to which the Attorney General's Committee had responded. Conference members defined their project narrowly, aiming their recommendations at the specific and mundane problems faced by agency officials and the parties before them. Overwhelmingly voluminous records and backlogs of cases plagued everyone, and, as Judge E. Barrett Prettyman, the conference's chairman, described, "the time-honored processes of the judiciary and the administrative agencies alike creak and groan and all but stop entirely."[46] Committees were established to examine several narrow problems of administration, including questions of prehearing procedure, pleadings, evidence, hearing officers, and the creation of an Office of Federal Administrative Procedure. These were not dramatic questions of administrative discretion or judicial control, but were instead practical issues with which administrators themselves were struggling.

The recommendations issued by the conference indicated members' pragmatic approach, grounded in administrative ease of operations. Members targeted the "unnecessary delay, expense, and volume of records in adjudicatory and rule-making proceedings," which, they determined, were "detrimental to the public interest."[47] Indeed, members noted the conference's "underlying philosophical declaration" that tied the public interest to "the public importance of efficiency in the administrative process."[48] The work of the conference offered insight into administrators' concerns about problems of delay and cost, and suggested that external observers should be more concerned about problems of inefficiency than those of administrative discretion.

First, the conference recommended that agencies and commissions consider additional uniformity in their procedure, particularly in regard to service of process, subpoenas, depositions and interrogatories, official notice, stipulations,

---

[44] Press Release, Apr. 29, 1953, 1, Folder "103-D-2 Conference on Administrative Procedure (1)," Official File Series, DDE Papers, WHCF, DDEL.

[45] See Bernard Schwartz, "Administrative Law," *New York University Law Review* 29 (1954): 101–24; Patricia H. Collins, "Administrative Procedure: The Conference Submits Its Final Report," *American Bar Association Journal* 41 (1955): 311–14 and 371–73; E. Barrett Prettyman, *Trial by Agency* (Charlottesville: Virginia Law Review Association, 1959).

[46] E. Barrett Prettyman, "Reducing the Delay in Administrative Hearings: Suggestions for Officers and Counsel," *American Bar Association Journal* 39 (1953): 966–70, 966.

[47] President's Conference on Administrative Procedure, *Report of the Conference on Administrative Procedure* (Washington, DC: Government Printing Office, 1955), 13.

[48] Ibid., 66.

and the form and content of decisions. The conference's Committee on Uniform Rules proposed that the Federal Rules of Civil Procedure, promulgated in 1938, serve as a model for such uniform procedures. This was less an attempt to "judicialize" the administrative state than it was to draw on existing procedures and the practical lessons of administrative experience as a rough guide to possible action. The committee recognized the limits of uniform rules, but argued that uniformity was at least a worthy goal since "unnecessary or accidental variations in agency procedures simply clutter up an already complicated legal system."[49]

This reform project was to be handed to a proposed Office of Federal Administrative Procedure to be created within the Justice Department. As the conference's Committee on Uniform Rules suggested, any new rules "must be preceded by thorough spade work," should come from "close cooperation with the agencies and the bar," and should allow "for continuous study and revision" instead of "a one-shot operation."[50] A permanent office would be well situated to engage in the kinds of research and follow-up required. The idea of a centralized agency aimed at studying existing administrative practice, amassing information and statistics about the administrative process, and working toward improvement was, members of the conference wearily reported, "not a new idea."[51] In fact, the creation of such an office had been enthusiastically recommended by the Attorney General's Committee and the Hoover Commission, and the Administrative Office of the United States Courts was already serving such a function for the federal courts.

The conference also offered a variety of suggestions targeting the overall cost and delay of the administrative process and the volume of records with which parties and reviewing courts had to contend. Participants pointed to "the marked influence of judicial criticism upon the attitude of hearing officers in admitting evidence," and suggested that courts commend examiners who excluded irrelevant evidence.[52] To allow administrative hearings to proceed both more fairly and more efficiently, members recommended that agencies require issues to be made clear before administrative hearings, that documentary evidence and the written testimony of expert witnesses should be provided prior to administrative hearings, that hearing examiners should be permitted to hold pretrial hearings and to exclude irrelevant information, and that agencies should offer practice manuals and attorneys' manuals for those practicing before them. So that parties could better cope with the massive size of administrative records, the conference recommended that agencies be encouraged to adopt uniform rules regarding the certification and filing of briefs and records,

[49] President's Conference on Administrative Procedure, Committee on Uniform Rules, *Report of the Committee on Uniform Rules* (Washington, DC: President's Conference on Administrative Procedure, 1954), 10.
[50] Ibid., 31.
[51] President's Conference on Administrative Procedure, *Report of the Conference on Administrative Procedure*, 46.
[52] Ibid., 54.

and that Congress allow parties to file abbreviated records on appeal from agency decisions.

Overall, the conference focused on the increasingly common problem of delay and inefficiency within the administrative process rather than concern about the lawless discretion of hearing examiners. Although one committee split on where hearing examiners should be placed, the conference declined to make significant changes to the existing hearing examiner system, finding the hearing examiners "generally competent" and the administration of current system "essentially sound."[53] Members reaffirmed their commitment to the examiner removal procedures provided by the APA, noting that even though complaints against the examiners were legion, no hearing examiners had been removed under the statute. Nor did the conference seek to impose additional judicial controls on administrative action; the conference's Committee on Judicial Review limited its recommendations to mundane ones regarding uniform rules for filing documents with appellate courts. Thus, for the agencies at least, the problem of lawless discretion was not one of significant concern.

The Eisenhower administration's efforts in the areas of administration and reorganization were not enough, however, for Republicans considering another Hoover Commission-type inquiry. Even as PACGO in early 1953 offered reorganization plans borrowed from the first Hoover Commission, congressional Republicans saw their party's control of the executive and legislative branches as an opportunity to begin a new investigation of executive branch administration aimed toward more clearly conservative goals. The tools were available; the Citizens Committee for the Hoover Reports had remained active during the Truman administration, and Hoover himself had called for a second commission even before the election as a way to return Americans' attention to questions of reorganization. More was at stake, of course; as one aide observed, Hoover in his first attempt "hadn't been able to do what he really set out to do, which was to change the whole character of the Federal Government and strip it down, and put more authority back into the states, localities, and private sector."[54] Given his former unpopularity, Hoover also clearly appreciated the opportunity to reenter public life and to redefine his public image. Reorganization had become his issue. Speaking at the Bohemian Grove in 1952, Hoover's lighter side emerged as he described other areas of life needing reorganization attention. "The wedding service" he surmised, "could save

[53] Ibid., 59; see also President's Conference on Administrative Procedure, Committee on Hearing Officers, *Appointment and Status of Federal Hearing Officers* (Kintner report) (Washington, DC: President's Conference on Administrative Procedure, 1954); President's Conference on Administrative Procedure, Committee on Hearing Officers, *Appointment and Status of Federal Hearing Officers* (Lester report) (Washington, DC: President's Conference on Administrative Procedure, 1954); Note, "Hearing Examiner Status: A Recurrent Problem in Administrative Law," *Indiana Law Journal* 30 (1954): 86–106; Ralph F. Fuchs, "The Hearing Officer Problem – Symptom and Symbol," *Cornell Law Quarterly* 40 (1955): 281–325.
[54] Jarold Kieffer oral history interview, Oct. 10, 1979, HHL, 4.

much time if it omitted the advice to the young. Their minds are concentrated on the honeymoon – and they need no advice about it."[55]

The creation of a second Commission on Organization of the Executive Branch in July 1953, over Eisenhower's resistance, indicated that conservatives and reorganization enthusiasts did not feel that the White House was doing enough on its own against bureaucracy and the bureaucrats. The second Hoover Commission was to go further than the first, evidenced by the additional legal authority Congress gave to the second. Along with responsibility for rooting out duplication and inefficiency and recommending abolition of government activities members found "not necessary to the efficient conduct of government" – powers that the first commission had possessed – Congress gave the second Commission new authority to recommend the elimination of "nonessential services, functions, and activities which are competitive with private enterprise."[56] As one of the commissioners put it, they could "go one step further and inquire, 'Should the Government be performing these functions, and, if so, to what extent?'"[57] The commission took seriously the assumption that private businesses should be preferred over government operations, something about which Hoover had felt strongly for years.[58] Indeed, given his experience a few years earlier, Hoover had explicitly encouraged members of Congress to draft the statute to avoid dispute over the commission's authority in this area. And as Jarold Kieffer later recalled, "Hoover at the very first meeting announced, 'This time we will not be deflected from our purpose.'"[59]

The new commission's composition reflected its conservative project, and Hoover likely anticipated few surprises from the group. Five of the twelve commissioners (Arthur Flemming, Sen. John McClellan [D–Ark.], Rep. Clarence J. Brown [R–Ohio], Joseph P. Kennedy, and Sidney A. Mitchell) had been involved with the first Hoover Commission, and William Hallam Tuck, the second commission's executive director, had worked with Hoover on several previous war and food aid efforts. This Hoover Commission, unlike the first,

[55] Herbert Hoover, Remarks at the Bohemian Grove, Aug. 2, 1952, 4, Folder "Subject Series Speeches and Statements Hoover, Herbert 1940–55," Box 4, MacNeil Papers, HHL.

[56] An Act for the Establishment of a Commision on Governmental Operations, Pub. L. No. 108, § 1, 67 Stat. 142 (1953). For more on the second Hoover Commission, see Harvey C. Mansfield, "Reorganizing the Federal Executive Branch: The Limits of Institutionalization," *Law and Contemporary Problems* 35 (1970): 461–95; Herbert Emmerich, *Federal Organization and Administrative Management*; Ronald C. Moe, *Executive Branch Reorganization: An Overview* (Tuscaloosa: University of Alabama Press, 1971); Ronald C. Moe, *The Hoover Commissions Revisited* (Boulder, CO: Westview Press, 1982); Peri E. Arnold, *Making the Managerial Presidency: Comprehensive Reorganization Planning, 1905–1996*, 2nd ed. (Lawrence: University Press of Kansas, 1998).

[57] Robert G. Storey, "The Second Hoover Commission: Its Legal Task Force," *American Bar Association Journal* 40 (1954): 483–86 and 536–39, 485.

[58] See Herbert Hoover, *The Challenge to Liberty* (New York: Charles Scribner's Sons, 1934).

[59] Kieffer oral history interview, May 21, 1980, 25.

did not require that members be evenly split along party lines; as a result, Republicans held a slight majority over Democrats (a group that included Rep. Chet Holifield [D-Cal.] and James A. Farley, the former chairman of the Democratic National Committee and cabinet member during the Roosevelt administration). President Eisenhower, who found Hoover's conservatism "a trifle on the motheaten side," attempted to dilute the commission with more moderate Republicans from his administration, including PACGO member Arthur Flemming and Attorney General Brownell, and also instructed PACGO to keep an eye on the commission.[60]

Once again in the role of chairman, Hoover made clear that this commission would take on new areas of investigation, moving beyond the first commission's focus on the internal organization of particular departments and agencies to assess the broader government functions (such as budgeting, accounting, and procurement) that affected all agencies. As he had in the first commission, Hoover created a number of task forces staffed with well-known Americans to perform the actual research. Some of the task forces, such as those on Federal Activities Competitive with Private Enterprise and Legal Services and Procedures, took up new topics, whereas others, including those on Budget and Accounting, Medical Services, Personnel, and Transportation, returned to areas examined by the first Hoover Commission. Drawing on its task forces' research, the commission issued nineteen separate reports highlighting redundancy, waste, and inefficiency throughout the federal government. Drawing from these reports, the Citizens Committee trumpeted the fact that seven separate civil service programs existed for federal employees, that paperwork alone cost the federal government $4 billion a year, a sum equivalent to the entire federal budget before 1933, and that twenty-six departments and agencies provided federal medical services.[61] The reports were also stuffed with evidence of mismanagement and failures in communication and coordination. Given the enormous percentage of federal expenditures devoted to military spending, the military was a particularly enticing target. The Hoover Commission described the international shipment of ping-pong balls, the inefficiency of transporting an Air Force band from Massachusetts to Bermuda for monthly concerts, and the Army's efforts to transport canned tomatoes from California to the East Coast while the Navy was busy moving canned tomatoes from the East Coast to California.[62] Among the most publicized examples of excess was the

---

[60] Ferrell, ed., *The Eisenhower Diaries*, 247; see also Brownell, *Advising Ike*, 305–07.

[61] Citizens Committee for the Hoover Report, *Digests and Analyses of the Nineteen Hoover Commission Reports* (Washington, DC: Citizens Committee for the Hoover Report, 1955), 2, 14, 241.

[62] Commission on Organization of the Executive Branch of the Government (Hoover Commission II), *Transportation* (Washington, DC: Government Printing Office, 1955), 7, 52; Citizens Committee for the Hoover Report, *Digests and Analyses of the Nineteen Hoover Commission Reports*, 104.

revelation that Navy warehouses contained a 719-month supply of canned hamburger – a product with a shelf life of 24 months.[63]

Following up on the Hoover Commission's recommendations was the commission's own public-pressure machinery. The Citizens Committee for the Hoover Report, so persuasive after the first Hoover Commission, was already in place and ready to press for 100 percent implementation of the commission's recommendations. To ensure wider consumption by the public and the media, the Citizens Committee actively repackaged the commission's recommendations in a number of different forms. CBS Public Affairs produced a documentary – "Waste Not, Want Not" – for the committee, and Hoover appeared on the National Association of Manufacturers radio program "It's YOUR Business!"[64] One Citizens Committee pamphlet provided a list of suggested projects for those interested in reorganization, inviting college students to "[a]nalyze the propaganda and opinion forming techniques used by any selected pressure group" and to "[p]lan and carry out a campaign (personal letters, petition, visit, etc.) designed to influence the votes of local Congressmen on legislation dealing with the Hoover Commission recommendations."[65] A 1958 campaign called for a "Teapot Tempest"; the flier, to which a teabag was attached, called women to the support of government reform. "'We've simmered long enough – Let's Come to a Boil!' Join the 'Teapot Tempest' and make yourself heard!"[66] Through these efforts, the Citizens Committee revived the narrative of a nonpartisan Hoover Commission interested only in government efficiency and savings. In addition, characterizing itself as "a pressure group against pressure groups," the Citizens Committee again placed itself in contrast to the interest groups, politicians, and bureaucrats who opposed reform based on their own selfish interests.[67] Members would continue to push the White House for action well after the reports were issued.

The Hoover Commission ultimately offered 314 separate targeted recommendations, most of which relied on business principles and privatization of government services. In several reports, including those on Surplus Property and Business Organization of the Department of Defense, the commission suggested that the federal government should conduct itself in accordance with the management precepts of private enterprise in which, it was implied,

[63] Commission on Organization of the Executive Branch of the Government (Hoover Commission II), *Food and Clothing in the Government* (Washington, DC: Government Printing Office, 1955), 19–20; see also Citizens Committee for the Hoover Report, *Digests and Analyses of the Nineteen Hoover Commission Reports*, 103.

[64] Transcript, "It's YOUR Business!," n.d., Folder "Subject File Research Memorandum – Specials and Miscellanous TO Citizens Committee for the Hoover Report Series Editorials on Commission Work 1955 March – May," Box 52, HCII, HHPPP, HHL.

[65] Ray Harvey, Louis W. Koenig, and Albert Somit, *Achievements in Federal Reorganization: The Contribution of the First and New Hoover Commissions* (New York: Citizens Committee for the Hoover Report, 1955), 26–27.

[66] Citizens Committee for the Hoover Report promotion, March 1958, 1, Folder "General File Teapot Tempest 1958," Box 67, HC II, HHPPP, HHL.

[67] Harvey, Koenig and Somit, *Achievements in Federal Reorganization*, 25.

mismanagement was anathema. Other reports more pointedly suggested ways for the federal government to excuse itself from activities that overlapped with private enterprise. The report on Business Enterprises, for example, described the wide variety of government businesses (including helium production by the Interior Department and military bakeries, dry cleaners, and meat-cutting plants) that were competitive only because of government benefits and subsidies. These advantages made it harder for private businesses to compete against them and resulted in higher taxes for everyone.[68] Answering the question "Is this 'creeping socialism?'" with a resounding yes, the Citizens' Committee suggested, "the rate is such as to suggest that 'running' is a more apt description than 'creeping.'"[69] Similar themes appeared in several of the commission's other reports, including those on Transportation and Water Resources and Power. The report on Lending, Guaranteeing, and Insurance Agencies found 104 separate administrative units were engaged in lending activities, a task, it argued, private businesses were well equipped to handle.[70] Throughout these reports, Hoover trumpeted the potential savings that would result from removing government involvement. The federal budget could be balanced, he argued, taxes cut, and money returned to the Treasury without any ill effect on the nation. As before, failure to achieve these goals was blamed on Congress and on bureaucrats, who "resist all attempts to cut down their personal empires."[71]

The Hoover Commission's focus on specific policy areas and tasks performed by agencies and commissions, rather than the organizational efficiency of the administrative state as a whole, was illustrated in its approach to the independent regulatory commissions. Even as the Hoover Commission planned significant reductions in federal commitments and regulatory authority, it stopped short of recommending a full restructuring of these commissions. The second commission was much less enthusiastic than the first about changing the ways in which the independent agencies operated, indicating its willingness to sacrifice organizational tidiness for political ease. The first Hoover Commission had had varied success with similar proposals, and staff revisiting the question quickly concluded that approximately half of these agencies – including the cabinet departments, most of the independent commissions, and other agencies such as the Atomic Energy Commission, the Civil Services Commission, and the Veterans Administration – had "roots lying so deep in history" or had "assumed functions of such great national importance" that there was no good reason to change their independent

[68] Commission on Organization of the Executive Branch of the Government (Hoover Commission II), *Business Enterprises* (Washington, DC: Government Printing Office, 1955).

[69] Citizens Committee for the Hoover Report, *Digests and Analyses of the Nineteen Hoover Commission Reports*, 123.

[70] Commission on Organization of the Executive Branch of the Government (Hoover Commission II), *Lending, Guaranteeing, and Insurance Activities* (Washington, DC: Government Printing Office, 1955), 1.

[71] Citizens Committee for the Hoover Report, Special Research Memorandum No. 9, 1, Folder "Research Memorandum (1–19)," Box 51, HC II, HHPPP, HHL.

status. [72] Many of the rest were deemed "very modest in size or importance or both."[73] Thus, the second Hoover Commission, with its expressed intention to scale back government, bring down costs, and simplify the administrative state, immediately ran up against thirty agencies with enough status to bar reorganization or movement, and an additional thirty-two for which political pressures and potential costs made action difficult or impossible to achieve.

The commission ultimately chose not to push hard for the reorganization of these agencies; commissioners themselves opposed several of the proposed transfers, and most also likely recalled agencies' resistance to similar recommendations by the first Hoover Commission. Experience had also illustrated the difficulties of keeping order in a reorganized state. Eleven independent agencies had been abolished or relocated in light of the first Hoover Commission's recommendations, but twelve new ones had been created in the intervening years. Administrative organization had proven much less amenable to reform in reality than in theory, and the commission declined to expend much effort in this area.[74]

One part of the Hoover Commission, however, was *very* interested in the inner workings of the administrative process. The second Hoover Commission's Task Force on Legal Services and Procedure was in some ways a natural outgrowth of the Hoover Commission's project and in others an awkward fit. To the extent that members looked at the distribution of authority within each agency and commission and criticized duplication therein, the task force's recommendations were consistent with the commission's efforts to minimize federal functions, reduce expenditures, and lower taxes. However, the task force, established to take up questions of administrative law and procedure in the executive agencies and the independent commissions, was not focused on the excessive costs or disorganization of the executive branch. The work of the members ranged much further afield.[75]

---

[72] Staff on Independent Agencies, "Independent Agencies of the United States Government," Feb. 10, 1954, 2, Folder "Task Force on Independent Agencies Report of Task Force Drafts, 1954," Box 3, HC II, HHPPP, HHL.

[73] Ibid., 5.

[74] Moe, *The Hoover Commissions Revisited*.

[75] For discussion of the studies on Legal Services and Procedure, see Storey, "The Second Hoover Commission," 483; Kenneth Culp Davis, "Evidence," *New York University Law Review* 30 (1955): 1309–41; Whitney R. Harris, "The Hoover Commission Report: Improvement of Legal Services and Procedure," *American Bar Association Journal* 41 (1955): 497–500 and 558–62; Whitney R. Harris, "The Hoover Commission Report: Improvement of Legal Services and Procedure," *American Bar Association Journal* 41 (1955): 713–17; Guy Farmer, "An Administrative Labor Court: Some Observations on the Hoover Commission Report," *George Washington Law Review* 24 (1956): 656–71; Robert E. Freer, "The Case against the Trade Regulation Section of the Proposed Administrative Court," *George Washington Law Review* 24 (1956): 637–55; Anthony F. Arpaia, "The Independent Agency – A Necessary Instrument of Democratic Government," *Harvard Law Review* 69 (1956): 483–506; Clarence A. Davis, "Government Legal Services, Procedures, and Representation: A Discussion of the Hoover Report and the Administration of the Department of the Interior," *Northwestern University Law Review* 50 (1956): 726–38; Davison, "An Administrative Court of the United States"; Robert S. Pasley, "Legal Services in the Government: Some Thoughts on the Hoover Commission Report," *Journal of Public Law* 6 (1957): 163–93.

The first Hoover Commission's studies of executive agencies and independent commissions (begun shortly after the APA took effect) had stayed away from procedural questions, but Hoover commissioner Robert G. Storey, dean of the Southern Methodist University School of Law and a participant in the CSC's ill-fated hearing examiner evaluations, assembled a task force of lawyers to consider the problem.[76] The task force comprised several practicing lawyers, many with administrative experience, including Ross L. Malone Jr. of New Mexico (a former deputy attorney general of the United States) and San Francisco lawyer (and former special assistant to the attorney general) Herbert Watson Clark. Several judges also served on the task force: James Marsh Douglas, former chief justice of the Missouri Supreme Court (the task force's chairman), Elbert Parr Tuttle of the Fifth Circuit Court of Appeals (a former general counsel for the Treasury Department), and Judge Harold R. Medina of the Second Circuit Court of Appeals, who as a trial court judge had presided over the trial of Communist leaders in *Dennis v. United States*. They were joined by Montana State University president Carl McFarland (a former assistant to the attorney general), University of Michigan Law School dean E. Blythe Stason, and former Harvard law dean and experienced administrator James M. Landis. Arthur Vanderbilt, chief justice of the New Jersey Supreme Court, and Justice Robert H. Jackson were included as consultants to the task force.

Few of the members were strangers to one another; McFarland, Stason, and Vanderbilt had joined together in dissent twelve years earlier on the Attorney General's Committee, and several other members had worked with one another through the ABA. Six of those attached to the task force were past or future presidents of the ABA, and four others were also active in the association. The Hoover Commission's selection of these lawyers quickly gave rise to concerns that the task force's conclusions would be too heavily weighted in favor of lawyers. (The task force's subsequent recommendation that the practice of law before the agencies should be restricted to lawyers did nothing to discredit these allegations.) Many were also concerned that the task force would adopt the conservative approach to administrative law traditionally favored by the ABA. Much as some nonlawyers had feared, task force members approached the administrative state with a shared assumption that due process was at least as important as efficiency in the administrative process.

At the task force's first meeting in February 1954, Hoover greeted the lawyers by observing that there existed "no field in the whole government that so sorely needs remedies" as that of administration.[77] He advised task force members that "the whole field is open to you" and, directing members' attention to "the confusion of powers of review" and the "many overlaps, duplications, and waste of public money" involved in legal services, made it clear

---

[76] See Hoover Commission II, minutes, Nov. 16, 1953, 5, Folder "Minutes of Meetings – Commission 1954," Box 49, HC II, HHPPP, HHL.

[77] Herbert Hoover, remarks to Task Force on Legal Services and Procedure, Feb. 5, 1954, 1, Folder "Task Force on Legal Services and Procedure Misc. Correspondence Folder #2 2/2/54 – 9/9/55," Box 3, HC II, HHPPP, HHL.

that he envisioned a wide-ranging investigation.[78] Hoover also reminded members that they were free to recommend substantive policy changes alongside procedural reforms, "even to the extent of recommending amendments to the Constitution."[79] After eleven months of research and study, during which task force members divided themselves into groups to handle specific questions, submitted questionnaires to the agencies, and consulted with agency officials and associations of administrative practitioners, the task force sent its report and recommendations covering legal services, representation, and procedures to the commission in January 1955. Not surprisingly, the task force's recommendations would reflect the breadth of their investigation.

Parts of the task force's criticisms and recommendations targeted the disorganization of the administrative process and echoed the Hoover Commission's concerns. Members found significant gaps and overlaps in the jurisdiction of agencies and commissions that led to conflict and unnecessary duplication. Administrative development, the task force charged, had been "haphazard and uncoordinated" and "frequently without sufficient regard for the jurisdiction and power of other agencies and departments."[80] Regulation of food, for example, was accomplished by the USDA, the Food and Drug Administration, and the IRS; banking issues fell under the control of the Treasury Department, the Federal Deposit Insurance Corporation, and the Federal Reserve Board at the same time. Because the exercise of executive power was both a potential threat to private parties and a costly enterprise for government, the task force called on Congress to eliminate such duplication and suggested that state and local authority be recognized. Such reform would save the government money and "relieve citizens from the burden of complying with the requirements of more than a single agency in any given regulatory area."[81] Specific statutory language would also limit administrators' discretion, return authority to Congress, and improve judicial review by making the judge's task easier. The Hoover Commission itself agreed with this critique of duplication, arguing "it violates common sense that two or more agencies should exercise the same type of authority over the same matter."[82] Along the same lines, members adopted the task force's recommendations regarding legal services and further recommended that standard and uniform procedures for admission to practice before agencies and commissions replace the multiple standards currently in force.

Members also found problems in the federal government's methods of organizing government lawyers. Some 5,300 civilian attorney positions spread throughout the executive branch were uncoordinated, resulting in "a fragmentation of legal services within the executive branch, with diversity of legal

---

[78] Ibid., 2, 1.

[79] Ibid., 2.

[80] Commission on Organization of the Executive Branch of the Government (Hoover Commission II), Task Force on Legal Services and Procedure, *Report on Legal Services and Procedure* (Washington, DC: Government Printing Office, 1955), 113, 21.

[81] Ibid., 21.

[82] Hoover Commission II, *Legal Services and Procedure*, 48.

opinions and jurisdictional conflicts based upon inconsistent statutory inter-pretations."[83] Immediate assumption of coordination responsibilities by the Justice Department (for civilian agencies) and by the Defense Department (for the military) was recommended, as was a civil service system for attorneys to be located in a new Office of Legal Services and Procedure in the Justice Department.

Although these recommendations regarding the proper organization of the administrative state had much in common with the Hoover Commission's other studies and overall ethos, the recommendations regarding administrative procedure took a very different approach. Here the task force's recommendations were significantly informed by the legal training and political preferences of its members, who feared administrative discretion and moved to judicialize administrative procedure far beyond the flexible measures established in the Administrative Procedure Act. Articulating one of the task force's guiding assumptions, task force members emphasized: "*The more closely that administrative procedures can be made to conform to judicial procedures, the greater the probability that justice will be attained in the administrative process.*"[84] Overall, the task force appeared wistful for the administrative proposals of years past, where judicial control seemed both a politically feasible and operationally functional way of limiting administrative discretion.

The task force did attempt to tie economy and efficiency concerns to individual rights and due process. However, even as members claimed that the "*[f]ormalization of administrative procedures along judicial lines is consistent with efficiency and simplification of the administrative process,*" their recommendations would have significantly enlarged administrative staffs (and in some areas duplicated functions), slowed down administrative decision making, and vastly increased the work of the federal courts.[85] The efficiency concerns of the Hoover Commission thus took a back seat to the task force's concerns that individual rights were being lost in the administrative process.

Much of the task force's critique centered, as so many earlier ones had, on agencies' formal hearings. The APA had separated investigation, prosecution, and adjudication functions within each agency and commission, and kept the hearing examiners relatively insulated from other officials. Congress had subsequently imposed even stricter separation at the NLRB in the 1947 Taft-Hartley Act and at the FCC in the 1952 Communications Act Amendments, changes the task force noted approvingly.[86] Eight years after the APA, however, the task force found that major revision of the APA was needed "to strengthen it as the charter of due process of law in administrative proceedings."[87] Abandoning

[83] Hoover Commission II, Task Force on Legal Services and Procedure, *Report on Legal Services and Procedure*, 8.
[84] Ibid., 138 (emphasis in the original).
[85] Ibid.
[86] Ibid., 180.
[87] Ibid. 2.

the APA's guiding principles of flexibility and deference to agency decision making, members proposed a new administrative code that would remake the administrative process in the image of the federal trial courts, adopting the pretrial procedures, discovery rules, and rules of evidence used in civil trials. At the same time, examiners – again to be renamed "hearing commissioners" to make their quasi-judicial status clear – were to be of a higher caliber and to be further isolated from the agencies in which they worked. (Under the APA, agencies still had some authority over their removal.) Finding that the CSC's experience in evaluating executive officers translated poorly to evaluations of legal and quasi-judicial personnel, the task force recommended that responsibility for hiring and firing be transferred from the CSC to a Chief Hearing Commissioner, under the authority of a new administrative court.

Additional proposals sought to apply judicial standards of independence to a huge amount of administrative action. The separation of investigation, prosecution, and judicial functions provided in initial formal hearings was to be extended into areas of agency business including licensing, rate making, rulemaking, informal hearings, and the final decisions of the agency – all areas in which the interplay of expert administrative staffers was intentionally designed to improve cooperation and to lead to better regulation overall. As hearing commissioners mastered their newly judicialized role, the task force proposed that they become more powerful. The decisions of hearing commissioners were thus to have as much authority as the decisions of trial courts when reviewed by federal appellate courts. Hearing commissioners' findings of fact would be final unless the agency on review determined that the findings were clearly erroneous. This echoed the Attorney General's Committee but was a significant change from contemporary practice, as the APA had left it to each agency to determine how much weight to give hearing examiners' initial decisions. The Supreme Court in *Universal Camera* had emphasized that, under the APA, agencies were obliged to consider an examiner's decision as part of the evidence but did not need to give it primacy.[88] The task force recommended that agency heads and commissioners should still have a free hand regarding "policy" decisions, but their failure to clarify what this meant suggested that the limits of the examiners' authority would be newly broad and undefined.

These proposals legitimating agency decision making only insofar as it looked like judicial decision making were just a beginning. Clearly uncomfortable with the quasi-judicial authority Congress had repeatedly vested in agencies, the task force further recommended moving such functions out of the agencies and into "a superior instrumentality for the protection of private rights" – that is, a new and independent Administrative Court in which the existing Tax Court and the quasi-judicial authority of the ICC, the FTC, the FCC, the CAB, the FPC, the Federal Reserve Board, the Tariff Commission, the

[88] *Universal Camera*, 340 U.S. 474, 496; *FCC v. Allentown Broadcasting Corp.*, 349 U.S. 358 (1955). Reviewing courts nonetheless took the examiner's views seriously; see Frank E. Cooper, "Administrative Law: The 'Substantial Evidence' Rule," *American Bar Association Journal* 44 (1958): 945–49 and 1001–03, 1002.

Interior Department and the USDA would be placed.[89] This proposal echoed decades of similar proposals, including, most recently, plans offered by Sen. McCarran following the passage of the APA. The task force's vision was of a federal district court, subject to the Federal Rules of Civil Procedure and to judicial review by federal appellate courts. This proposal to remove the agencies' power to make policy through case-by-case adjudication reflected a strong distrust of administrators as well as a striking departure from decades of practice. The task force emphasized that the proposed shift was "not a criticism" but rather "a recognition that the governmental function has attained sufficient maturity and stability to warrant its future treatment in accordance with the more traditional concept of the separation of powers."[90] In other words, they argued, the agencies had developed a body of precedents that could be applied by judges. At the same time, the arrangement stripped administrators of the authority to make new law for new situations in individual cases.

Finally, additional proposals sought to greatly extend judicial control, arguing that "[a] plain, simple, and prompt judicial remedy should be available for every legal wrong because of agency action or failure to act."[91] De novo review would be used where there had been no formal hearing before the agency. In the APA, Congress had chosen not to bind administrators with judicial review requirements above and beyond those already provided by individual statutes or by case law. Agency action was not subject to review where it was precluded by existing statutes or where agency actions were committed to agency discretion. The task force, however, found that "no sound reason exists" for such congressional exemptions. "Whether or not a person has suffered a legal wrong for which he should have a judicial remedy should be left to the courts to decide."[92] Members thus proposed to vastly extend both the kinds of agency actions that courts could review and their opportunities for challenging administration even before administrative action was final. Whenever agencies went to court to exercise their investigatory and subpoena authority, judges were to take it upon themselves to "consider the jurisdictional question" underlying the agency action.[93] Administrative decisions would be voidable if the agency had not adequately separated its prosecution and adjudication functions, and courts could "enjoin, at any stage of an agency proceeding, agency action in excess of constitutional or statutory authority."[94] Courts could even police administrative delay (which the task force found was an ongoing problem), with the authority to review "any legal wrong resulting from a failure by an agency to act with reasonable dispatch."[95]

---

[89] Hoover Commission II, Task Force on Legal Services and Procedure, *Report on Legal Services and Procedure*, 248. The task force indicated that additional jurisdiction over labor and immigration questions might added at a later time.

[90] Ibid., 242.

[91] Ibid., 28.

[92] Ibid., 207, 29.

[93] Ibid., 174.

[94] Ibid., 230.

[95] Ibid., 186.

The standards of judicial review were also to be broadened, and the APA's abuse of discretion standard clarified to include "a clearly unwarranted exercise of discretion."[96] Rather than upholding decisions supported by "substantial evidence on the whole record" – the standard articulated in the APA and in the Taft-Hartley Act – judges would be empowered to scrutinize the evidence themselves to determine whether the agency's decisions were "clearly erroneous in view of the reliable, probative, and substantial evidence on the whole record."[97]

Claiming that the "substantial evidence" test had developed out of necessity, by judges presented with "an administrative record which frequently was made by persons who were not legally trained, which often contained irrelevant and incompetent evidence, and which could not practicably be examined or evaluated as an appellate court customarily examines and evaluates the findings of fact of trial courts against a trial transcript on appeal," the task force suggested that such conditions no longer applied.[98] As administrative decision making became more like judicial decision making (which the task force found it had), and as examiners became more like judges, the records of administrative proceedings could now be reviewed "in substantially the same way that trial transcripts are reviewed."[99]

The task force's pervasive hostility to administrative decision making and its disdain for administrative expertise were not received with tremendous enthusiasm by the twelve members of the Hoover Commission. Commissioners accepted the recommendations aimed at eliminating duplication but were notably resistant to the proposed administrative code. When in March 1955 the commission issued its own recommendations in the area of legal services and procedure (contrary to some commissioners' suggestion that the commission simply forward the task force's recommendations to Congress without endorsement), members downplayed the controversial procedural recommendations. Commissioners were concerned about the political consequences of endorsing the task force's recommendations, in part because of their anti-bureaucratic stance and in part because the specialized nature of the recommendations could be seen as bolstering the professional interests of private lawyers. Acknowledging that the APA needed significant revisions, the Hoover Commission claimed that it "served, and should continue to serve, as the basic charter of Federal administrative law," and declined to replace it entirely or adopt many of the task force's recommendations.[100]

[96] Ibid., 29.
[97] Ibid. The task force staff director acknowledged that this was "a radical departure" from present standards; "to abolish the substantial evidence rule will be as pleasing to the Bar as it may be displeasing to the judiciary" (Whitney R. Harris to E. Blythe Stason, Carl McFarland, and Bernard Schwartz, memorandum, Oct. 8, 1954, 2, Folder "Task Group 3," Box 7, Records of Task Group 3, Miscellaneous Records, 1953–54, NC 116, Entry 44, TF: LSP, RG 264, NACP).
[98] Ibid.
[99] Ibid.
[100] Hoover Commission II, *Legal Services and Procedure*, 50.

The commission nonetheless proposed some radical changes to the administrative process, in a report that appeared to share the task force's skepticism about administrators. The commission recommended extending the separation of functions beyond anything required in the APA and providing new "special review staffs or assistants" to aid officials separated from their staff, such as were already found in certain boards and commissions.[101] The commission also agreed that formal agency adjudication should be as much like adjudication in the federal courts as possible, through the use of increasingly judicialized hearings and professionalized hearing commissioners, and that, in addition, agencies' judicial functions should be transferred to the courts "wherever it may be done without harm to the regulatory process" or to the proposed administrative court (with a labor section).[102] Exemptions from the APA were discouraged, and statutory preclusions of judicial review were to be extended to questions and functions previously exempt under the APA.

The commission further agreed with the proposal that "[a] plain, simple, and prompt judicial remedy should be made available for every legal wrong resulting from agency action or inaction, except where Congress expressly precludes judicial review."[103] The authority to select cases for enforcement was integral to an agency's policy-making authority; this provision, however, would have established federal courts, not administrators, as the final arbiters of administrative law. Also significant was the commission's recommendation that reviewing courts should begin to interpret congressional delegations of authority to ban all activity not specifically permitted. As they suggested, "Agency action shall not be deemed to be within the statutory authority and jurisdiction of the agency merely because such action is not contrary to the specific provisions of a statute."[104] This recommendation had the potential to dramatically limit the activities of agencies and commissions that had been operating under presumed statutory authority for decades.

The Hoover Commission thus appeared to endorse a drastic makeover of the administrative state. However, because nine of the twelve commissioners declined to support some or all of the recommendations regarding administrative procedure, it is hard to know exactly what to make of their report. Six commissioners – Hoover, Brownell, Flemming, Kennedy, Mitchell, and Solomon C. Hollister – joined in a brief statement indicating that, while they supported proposals to establish an independent Administrative Court and to turn hearing examiners into hearing commissioners, they did not support the remaining proposals concerning administrative procedure given "their possible consequences and possible increase in the expenditures of the Government."[105]

---

[101] Ibid., 62.
[102] Ibid., 85.
[103] Ibid., 75
[104] Ibid., 79.
[105] Ibid., 95.

As Flemming's assistant warned him, the recommendations requiring full separation of functions in adjudication "completely neglects the environment in which an agency head works" and "makes nothing out of political realities; it would try to make him like a judge and even that isn't realistic."[106] Putting almost final decision-making authority in hearing examiners "assumes vast powers of intelligence and comprehension" in staffers who "could be the most irresponsible class of officials in the Government."[107] Formal separation of functions for formal rulemaking was "unreasonable and defies human nature and requirements."[108] As Kennedy remarked to the Hoover Commission's executive director, "I assure you that, as Chairman of the Securities and Exchange Commission, I didn't conceive of my job to be to accept the decisions of any hearing examiner or to review his work for major errors. His responsibility was to dig out the facts; it was my responsibility to use those facts in the manner in which I believed Congress wanted them used."[109] And Kieffer informed Flemming that the agencies' responses "were uniformly adverse."[110] (Commissioners did, however, find that "in view of the searching investigation and the eminence at the Bar of the members of the task force," the recommendations should be sent to Congress outside the Hoover Commission's aegis. Bills introducing several of these recommendations would be introduced by members of Congress.) Kennedy warned that the commission should "go slow in letting the courts interfere with agency action before it has been completed."[111] Although Kennedy was himself a lawyer and experienced administrator, many on the commission were not; as a result, Kennedy was "leery of jumping into a technical and highly controversial field, which really seems to me to be beyond the scope of our ability."[112]

Farley and Holifield filed more elaborate dissents; like Kennedy, Holifield objected that the report was "too 'legalistic' in its approach to problems of Government organization and management."[113] He accused the task force – in its rush to separate the legislative, executive, and judicial functions in the agencies – of subverting Congress, which had combined the functions in the first place. Several commissioners were additionally concerned that the task force's recommendations appeared designed to allow regulated parties to either inhibit the administrative process or bring it to a full stop.

This significant disagreement among the commissioners on the question of administrative procedure did not bode well for the report's reception or for the

---

[106] Jarold Kieffer to Arthur S. Flemming, Mar. 9, 1955, 4, Folder "COEBG, 53–55: Legal Services and Procedure (1)," Box 86, Flemming Papers, DDEL.

[107] Ibid., 6, 9.

[108] Ibid., 3.

[109] Joseph P. Kennedy to John B. Hollister, Mar. 11, 1955, 2, Folder "Task Force on Legal Services and Procedure Misc. Correspondence Folder #1 10/17/53–1/12/54," Box 3, HC II, HHPPP, HHL.

[110] Jarold Kieffer to Arthur S. Flemming, memorandum, Mar. 9, 1955, Folder "COEBG, 53–55: Legal Services and Procedure (1)," Box 86, Flemming Papers, DDEL.

[111] Kennedy to Hollister, Mar. 11, 1955, 1.

[112] Ibid., 1.

[113] Hoover Commission II, *Legal Services and Procedure*, 97–98.

commission's nonpartisan image, and Hoover sought to mute any public disagreement among the commissioners. Storey reassured Hoover that the report could be released as "a unanimous report by a distinguished Task Force" – and pointed out that "the Commission is unanimous on *every* recommendation" excepting the administrative code ones.[114] The subsequent press release indeed emphasized the commissioners' unanimous approval for the legal services and representation recommendations, and attempted to minimize the rest as "highly technical modifications of the Administrative Procedure Act."[115]

Some of the proposals, such as the administrative court, were applauded by the press; the *New York Times* called it "[b]y far the most important proposal in the commission's exhaustive and detailed report,"[116] and the *Wall Street Journal* commended the fact that an agency or commission "would no longer function as investigator, prosecutor, judge and law enforcer all rolled into one."[117] Such reform, the *Journal* argued, "would give businessmen more assurance of a fair shake in their dealings with these agencies."[118] The *Los Angeles Times* similarly suggested that the proposed court could "do away with 'push-button lawyers'" who "find legal excuses for what the agency wants to do."[119] It might also "produce an orderly uniformity where now there is jangling confusion."[120]

Others, however, widely criticized the idea that the rule of law required so much change. Even as law professor Bernard Schwartz argued that agencies had already turned into courts "[i]n all but name,"[121] Ralph Fuchs argued that the task force recommendations adopted by the commission attempted "to out-judicialize the courts,"[125] and Louis Jaffe similarly suggested that the report "so insists on the judicialization of the administrative process that it ends by refusing to recognize its existence."[126] Fuchs sharply criticized the commission's proposals regarding internal separation of functions, arguing that to deprive hearing commissioner of accumulated agency expertise would "cut the heart out of administrative processes."[127] Many found the practical task of separating adjudication and policy-making functions so cleanly to be impossible, and one Interior Department official

---

[114] Robert G. Storey to Herbert Hoover, Mar. 22, 1955, 2, Folder "General File Correspondence: Storey, Robert 1955–1956," Box 59, HC II, HHPPP, HHL (emphasis in the original).

[115] Press Release, Apr. 11, 1955, 1, Folder "Second Hoover Commission Legal Services and Procedure Task Force Press Releases 1954 – Mar. 1955," Oulahan Papers, HHL.

[116] "Hoover Group Would Limit Judicial Powers of Agencies, Set Up a Court," *Wall Street Journal*, Apr. 11, 1955, 8.

[117] "Administrative Courts," *New York Times*, Apr. 14, 1955, 28.

[118] "Hoover Group Would Limit Judicial Powers of Agencies, Set Up a Court," 8.

[119] "Reform of Administrative Regulation," *Los Angeles Times*, Apr. 21, 1955, 4.

[120] Ibid.

[121] Bernard Schwartz, "Administrative Justice and Its Place in the Legal Order," *New York University Law Review* 30 (1955): 1390–417, 1416.

[125] Ralph F. Fuchs, "Hearing Commissioners," *New York University Law Review* 30 (1955): 1342–74, 1373.

[126] Louis L. Jaffe, "Basic Issues: An Analysis," *New York University Law Review* 30 (1955): 1273–96, 1296.

[127] Ralph F. Fuchs, "The Hoover Commission and Task Force Reports on Legal Services and Procedure," *Indiana Law Journal* 31 (1955): 1–44, 30.

suggested that the proposed administrative court thus "should be regarded, to say the least, with polite skepticism."[125] Agency representatives joined others taking to the pages of law reviews to display their hostility. One former FTC chairman argued that stripping away so much authority from the FTC "would virtually destroy" it; the task force's "assumption that all unfair methods of competition are presently known and catalogued" did not account for "the highly ingenious and inventive mind of the American business huckster."[126] Ending existing statutory exemptions, the Interior Department official suggested, would impose "the practical difficulties of having to seek several million dollars of additional money for administration from the Congress, of employing a large number of additional people, and in spite of that, of probably creating a backlog of cases where the delays might be more serious than the occasional miscarriages of justice resulting from failure to comply with the Act."[127]

Nor had the task force or the commission proved that such reforms were actually necessary.[128] Kenneth Culp Davis noted that the reports offer the "probably unintended" impression that the Hoover Commission "assumes its own wisdom to be so overpowering that reasons need not be given, that experience need not be canvassed, and that sources need not be revealed."[129] Jaffe suggested that the whole project was unnecessary: "Large and important settlements of the great political and legal issues" – like the APA – "should not be disturbed on the ground that they do not completely realize abstract and doctrinaire propositions."[130] Agency heads were similarly dubious. As the ICC chairman claimed, the task force's recommendations "were hastily conceived and were urged without reference to the careful and exhaustive studies of administrative agencies made in the recent past by informed experts" – including those of the first Hoover Commission.[131]

Agency officials also recognized the broader challenge lurking in the recommendations. One former NLRB chairman argued that the "revolutionary objective" of the Hoover Commission was "to liquidate the formidable array of powerful administrative agencies,"[132] while the chairman of the ICC similarly found the recommendations "the latest in a series of persistent efforts to weaken the quasi-legislative regulatory agencies."[133] This pervasive criticism from academics and administrators, combined with disagreement among the

---

[125] Charles B. Nutting, "The Administrative Court," *New York University Law Review* 30 (1955): 1384–89, 1389.

[126] Freer, "The Case against the Trade Regulation Section of the Proposed Administrative Court," 653.

[127] Davis, "Government Legal Services, Procedures, and Representation," 728.

[128] See Freer, "The Case against the Trade Regulation Section of the Proposed Administrative Court"; Farmer, "An Administrative Labor Court."

[129] Davis, "Evidence," 1339.

[130] Jaffe, "Basic Issues," 1275; see also Freer, "The Case against the Trade Regulation Section of the Proposed Administrative Court," 643.

[131] Arpaia, "The Independent Agency," 494.

[132] Farmer, "An Administrative Labor Court," 658.

[133] Arpaia, "The Independent Agency," 492.

commissioners themselves, suggested that the administrative procedure recommendations would not be easily implemented.

Given this opposition and the absence of enthusiastic public support, the Eisenhower administration determined that it would take no action to modify administrative procedure or create an administrative court. Little was to be gained by challenging the legitimacy of administrative operations. For the most part, in fact, the Eisenhower administration took a largely defensive approach to the second Hoover Commission and its Citizens Committee for the Hoover Report. The second Hoover Commission and the Eisenhower White House had few overlapping goals, and Eisenhower continued to fear that Hoover and his supporters, who had already demonstrated their ability to pressure politicians and publicize what they perceived as recalcitrance, would usurp the White House's control over reorganization. PACGO members had been monitoring the second Hoover Commission since November 1953, but remained quiet about its work. Nelson Rockefeller's feeling, expressed to his fellow PACGO members in the fall of 1954, was that the administration had "[b]etter leave this hornet's nest alone now."[134]

In the fall of 1955, a few months after the Hoover Commission had finished its work, Eisenhower placed Meyer Kestnbaum, head of his Commission on Intergovernmental Relations (and president of the Chicago men's clothing concern Hart Schaffner & Marx) in charge of coordinating the administration's response to the commission. Kestnbaum, supported by certain other members of Eisenhower's cabinet, walked a fine line. He encouraged executive branch agencies to adopt proposals with which the White House agreed, in order to combat charges that the White House was uncooperative; at the same time, he recommended deferring more problematic ones to the newly Democratic Congress and to the commission's own initiative. As of February 1958, Kestnbaum was able to report that, of the 497 separate recommendations the administration had identified within the 314 numbered recommendations, the administration had accepted 383 (77.1 percent) in full or in part and had implemented (or was in the process of implementing) 291 (76 percent) of those.[135]

The recommendations regarding Legal Services and Procedure were among the more contentious ones. After soliciting the views of departments, agencies, and commissions on the proposed code, Attorney General Brownell reported in August 1955 that officials were "almost unanimously" alarmed by what such radical revisions would do and "demonstrated with considerable

---

[134] Notes of Committee Meeting, Oct. 4, 1954, 3, Folder "18 Minutes and notes for PACGO meetings, FYs. 1953–54," Box 2, PACGO Papers, DDEL.

[135] Kestnbaum to Eisenhower, memorandum, Feb. 10, 1958, Folder "General File Kestnbaum Report – Progress Report on 2nd Hoover Commission 1957–1957 & undated," Box 61, HC II, HHPPP, HHL. Congress's accounting was somewhat less generous, as members found that 53 percent of the recommendations had been implemented as of 1958 (Senate Committee on Government Operations, Subcommittee on Reorganization, *Action by the Congress and the Executive Branch of the Government on the Second Hoover Commission Reports, 1955–57*, 85th Cong., 2nd sess., 1958, S. Rep. 1289).

persuasiveness that the proposals would so drastically affect and restrict agency operations that it would be impossible for them to protect the public interest effectively."[136] Brownell himself agreed that "these proposals are unsound, unworkable, and so costly that they should be rejected."[137]

The proposed administrative code engendered significant opposition from within the administration, and the Budget Bureau was hostile to the judicialization it prescribed. Most agencies and commissions remained resistant to the idea of increasing the administrative separation of functions; Treasury described the effects as "both staggering and incomprehensible," and the Budget Bureau described the strategy as "utter folly!"[138] The latter condemned the assumption that only through such methods "can individual rights be adequately safeguarded (even though it may force more cumbersome administrative practices). It assumes arbitrariness on the part of administrators."[139] Bureau staff was similarly critical of the various proposals to expand judicial review and thus delay administrative activity; providing a judicial remedy for "every legal wrong resulting from agency action or inaction," as proposed, "would upset the balance of power among the great constitutional branches of government by letting the courts instead of the Congress decide what executive actions should be subject to judicial review."[140]

The administrative court proposal came under particular fire from the agencies. The FTC, which had recently reorganized itself, found the idea "most objectionable," and the FPC saw it as part of a broader goal "to weaken the administrative process by not only stifling it with legal formality but by increasing the time and expense for carrying out these administrative functions."[141] As the Budget Bureau fumed,

> This is turning the clock back with a vengeance! This recommendation (1) attacks the theory of specialization underlying the establishment of all regulatory commissions; (2) would mean the loss of capacity to program enforcement efforts through case selection; (3) would mean a serious loss of political responsibility; (4) is based on the false notion that the fields covered by these regulatory commissions have become so stabilized that the policies can be written into law in such rigid, specific terms that they can be enforced by the judiciary.
>
> *AND ALL OF THIS WITHOUT CITING A SINGLE SPECIFIC WRONG THAT THESE STEPS WOULD CORRECT!!*[142]

[136] Herbert Brownell to Ashley Sellers, Aug. 2, 1955, 3, Folder "133 Legal Services Report (1955) (Hoover Commission)," Box 23, Kestnbaum Papers, DDEL.
[137] Ibid.
[138] Budget Bureau, "Staff Analysis of Hoover Commission Recommendations on Legal Services and Procedure," n.d., Tab 37, 2, 5, Folder "48 Hoover Commission Legal Services and Procedure, 1955 (2)," Box 9, PACGO Papers, DDEL.
[139] Ibid., 4.
[140] Ibid., Tab 43, 2.
[141] Budget Bureau, "Report on Legal Services and Procedure," Sept. 21, 1955, 1, Folder "133 Legal Services Report (1955) (Hoover Commission)," Box 23, Kestnbaum Papers; DDEL.
[142] Budget Bureau, "Staff Analysis of Hoover Commission Recommendations on Legal Services and Procedure," n.d., Tab 51 (emphasis in the original).

Members of PACGO generally agreed, rejecting the assumption that "the regulatory fields covered by the agencies involved have become stabilized and thus susceptible to guidance by occasional judicial decisions."[143] Instead, they found, "the case is quite the reverse," and thus such a proposal "could well thwart enforcement of the present regulatory laws."[144] Kestnbaum himself argued that "[t]o subject the regulatory processes to the kind of delay which is regarded as a normal aspect of the judicial system would, in many cases, render it virtually ineffective."[145] This motive, he suspected, was exactly what the Hoover Commission hoped for. When, in late 1956, Kestnbaum prepared to meet with Hoover Commission supporters to discuss the Legal Services and Procedure recommendations, his message for the assembled men was: "The Administration does not support this at all. It might be embarrassing."[146]

The one significant accomplishment in this area was the creation of an Office of Federal Administrative Procedure, which had been recommended by the Attorney General's Committee, the two Hoover Commissions, the President's Conference on Administrative Procedure, and the ABA. The office was established within the Justice Department in 1957, largely as a result of the Eisenhower administration's action. Initiative for administrative reform was placed in this office, where officials would work with agencies, lawyers, bar associations, and other interested parties to study administrative procedures across agencies, coordinate procedures among agencies, maintain information on administrative process, and evaluate the usefulness of reforms and uniform rules.[147]

Further reform to administrative procedure was not a high priority for the Hoover Commission's revamped public relations efforts. The Citizens Committee remained responsible for publicity and grassroots efforts, but the group's overblown rhetoric about savings that had never materialized and its earlier pressure to enact reform only tangentially related to the first Hoover Commission's recommendations had injured its reputation with Congress. In response, Hoover created a new group, the Committee of Hoover Commission Task Force Members, to reach out to Congress and help the Citizens Committee provide information to congressional committees and executive departments. The business community was heavily represented on this committee, much as

---

[143] PACGO, "Staff Paper on Report on Legal Services and Procedures, Recommendation No. 51," Sept. 30, 1955, 1, Folder "133 Legal Services Report (1955) (Hoover Commission)," Box 23, Kestnbaum Papers, DDEL.

[144] Ibid.

[145] Close-out memorandum re Recommendation No. 51, June 11, 1956, Folder "37 Hoover Commission (Kestnbaum analysis) Final Recommendation (close-out memoranda) 1956–57 (1)," Box 6, PACGO Papers, DDEL.

[146] "Notes for discussion with Mr. Hook and members of his committee," 11/14/56 meeting, 3, Folder "104 Hoover Commission – Task Force Members," Box 18, Kestnbaum Papers, DDEL.

[147] Department of Justice, *Annual Report of the Office of Administrative Procedure* (Washington, DC: Office of Administrative Procedure, 1957), v.

it had been on the task forces; Armco Steel Corporation chairman Charles R. Hook led a group that included the chairman of Jones & Laughlin Steel Corporation, the president of the Delaware, Lackawanna & Western Railroad, and the chairman of the board of Sears, Roebuck & Company. Financial contributions arrived from major companies including the U.S. Steel Corporation, General Electric, Procter & Gamble, and Chrysler.[148] However, the group did not include members of the Legal Services task force and did not unduly exert itself in pressing for their reforms.

The ABA picked up the slack on the rest of the recommendations through its own Special Committee on Legal Services and Procedure. The ABA had sought greater uniformity and increased judicialization since the APA, and, headed by former USDA official Ashley Sellers, the new committee worked alongside the Citizens Committee for the Hoover Report as it attempted to implement its own versions of the Hoover Commission's recommendations (and some of the task force's recommendations that the commission had rejected). The ABA's Special Committee obtained (to the Hoover Commission's delight) the ABA House of Delegates' support for "a comprehensive re-examination" of administrative procedure and soon drafted legislative proposals in multiple areas, including a Code of Administrative Procedure that closely resembled the Hoover Commission's code.[149] By adding additional formal procedures to the administrative process, the ABA sought to further isolate examiners and make their decisions harder for the agency to overrule. Separate administrative courts with original jurisdiction over trade and labor were proposed; although the details and jurisdiction differed from the Hoover Commission's proposals, the ultimate goal of moving quasi-judicial functions out of the regulatory agencies was the same. The codes' judicial review provisions similarly recalled older proposals to expand judicial control, as the ABA sought to increased judicial review – requiring review of all agency action or inaction unless *explicitly* precluded by Congress, extending review to statutory interpretation and to any action found to be an "abuse or clearly unwarranted exercise of discretion," and authorizing courts to enjoin agency action "clearly in excess of constitutional or statutory authority."[150]

Although the ABA spent the next several years drafting bills and pressing for reform, strong opposition from agencies and commissions, administrative practitioners, and the attorney general meant little was accomplished. The Legal Services and Procedure recommendations were, at their core, calling for a vast reconstruction of the administrative state. Whatever jurisdiction

---

[148] Committee of Hoover Commission Task Force Members, Annual Report, 1960, Folder "Subject Series Hoover Commission Committee of Task Force Members 1960–62 and undated," Box 3, MacNeil Papers, HHL.

[149] "Proceedings of the House of Delegates," *ABA Annual Report* 81 (1956): 369–423, 383; see also Dante B. Fascell, "The Problem of Complexities and Delays in Administrative Proceedings and Practice," *Administrative Law Bulletin* 12 (1959): 6–11.

[150] "Report of the Special Committee on Legal Services and Procedure," *ABA Annual Report* 81 (1956): 491–535, 493.

could not be transferred to the courts would be so hemmed in by procedure, so subject to judicial scrutiny, and so isolated from that of other administrators as to be virtually unrecognizable to someone whose understanding of the administrative process came from James Landis's blushing 1938 tribute to expert administrators. As observers increasingly pointed out, the last thing the administrative process needed was *more* formality.[151] By the early 1960s, the Senate Subcommittee on Administrative Practice and Procedure concluded that, regardless of the "[a]cademic niceties and literary perfection" the ABA appeared to be pursuing, the proposed code appeared "inconsistent with any real attempt to reduce delay and expense."[152] No groundswell of congressional or public support appeared, no new administrative code was enacted, and no administrative court was created. Consistent opposition from the agencies and a lack of strong pressure in Congress left the bills adrift. By the early 1970s, the ABA gave up its pursuit of a replacement code and moved instead to target specific parts of the APA for amendment.[153] Further judicializing the administrative state had become a losing battle.

Increasing pessimism about the effectiveness of procedures came from a variety of sources. As academic observers increasingly complained, the agencies and commissions were not regulating *enough*. Independent commissions in particular were using their enormous legal authority in ways that failed to address the problems the regulated parties wanted addressed, leading to unpredictability and frustration for all. According to former CAB member Louis J. Hector, this groundswell of criticism bore "little relation to the old antiadministrative crusade."[154] Indeed, these were not attacks on agencies' zealous and lawless methods. Instead, as scholars including Samuel Huntington, Marver Bernstein, Ernest Williams, and Louis Jaffe argued during the 1950s, administrative failures could be blamed on the structure and procedures of the agencies themselves. This was not, however, simply a repetition of the first Hoover Commission, for critics pointed both to organizational capacity and supervision and to administrators' own incentives to act.

The procedures and habits eagerly adopted by agencies and commissions in previous years to secure their place in the administrative process had hamstrung their work, and the touted independence of commissions, intended to

---

[151] Ralph F. Fuchs, "The Proposed New Code of Administrative Procedure," *Ohio State Law Journal* 19 (1958): 423–31; "Pending Proposals to Amend the Federal Administrative Procedure Act: An Analysis of S. 518," *Administrative Law Review* 20 (1968): 185–236, 218 (Clark Byse comments).

[152] Senate Judiciary Committee, Subcommittee on Administrative Practice and Procedure, *Administrative Practice and Procedure*, 87th Cong., 1st sess., 1961, S. Rep. 168, 11.

[153] "The 12 ABA Recommendations for Improved Procedures for Federal Agencies," *Administrative Law Review* 24 (1972): 389–411; Cornelius B. Kennedy, "Foreword: A Personal Perspective," *Administrative Law Review* 24 (1972): 371–88.

[154] Louis J. Hector, "The New Critique of the Regulatory Agency," speech before the ABA's Section on Administrative Law, Aug. 25, 1959, 8, Folder "167 Regulatory Agencies – General," Box 20, PACGO Papers, DDEL.

help officials make decisions free of political pressures, had cut officials off from sources of political support that might have counterbalanced the pressures of the regulated groups. Agencies and commissions shaped policy to compromise with the interests they regulated and adopted risk-averse strategies – such as restricting policy development to case-by-case adjudication – that limited the breadth of such determinations. Stuck in old organizational schemes and tied to judicialized procedures, commissions were slow to act, quick to acquiesce, and ill-equipped to adapt to new conditions.

This critique was not entirely new, of course. Researchers for the Hoover Commission had pointed out similar flaws in the late 1940s, and Sen. Douglas's subcommittee on ethics, following its 1951 investigation, had commented on how, over time, agencies and commissions "surrender their regulatory zeal," becoming "more and more the protagonists of a clientele industry, and less and less the vigilant defenders of the welfare of consumers or the general public."[155] Douglas himself had concluded that aging agencies inevitably succumbed to "administrativistis" as "the once virile agency loses its crusading spirit and becomes both lethargic and indifferent to the public interest."[156] Such a reorientation of the agency's interests toward those of the regulated parties was, the Douglas subcommittee opined, "apparently institutional rather than personal," which made its solution more difficult.[157] In a series of essays and books in the 1950s, critics laid bare the failures of the aging agencies, and, by the late 1950s, Hector could point to a growing belief "that the combination of rule-making, policy formulation, planning, administration, adjudication, investigation and prosecution in one agency simply does not work."[158]

Ineffective regulation of transportation was a particular concern. Political scientist Samuel P. Huntington, in an influential 1952 essay on the ICC, pointed to evidence that the traditionally respected commission was slipping in legal, political, and public opinion. The ICC was not unfair to the railroads it regulated; instead, Huntington called out the commission for the unfair bias it

---

[155] Senate Committee on Labor and Public Welfare, Special Subcommittee on Establishment of a Commission on Ethics in Government, *Ethical Standards in Government*, 82nd Cong., 1st sess., 1951, Committee Print, 31.

[156] Paul H. Douglas, *Ethics in Government* (Cambridge, MA: Harvard University Press, 1952), 30.

[157] Senate Committee on Labor and Public Welfare, Special Subcommittee on Establishment of Commission of Ethics in Government, *Ethical Standards in Government*, 60.

[158] Hector, "The New Critique of the Regulatory Agency," 7. For contemporary scholarship on the "capture critique," see Richard B. Stewart, "The Reformation of American Administrative Law," *Harvard Law Review* 88 (1975): 1667–813; Paul R. Verkuil, "The Emerging Concept of Administrative Procedure," *Columbia Law Review* 78 (1978): 258–329; Robert L. Rabin, "Federal Regulation in Historical Perspective," *Stanford Law Review* 38 (1986): 1189–326; Thomas W. Merrill, "Capture Theory and the Courts: 1967–1983," *Chicago-Kent Law Review* 72 (1997): 1039–117; Reuel E. Schiller, "Rulemaking's Promise: Administrative Law and Legal Culture in the 1960s and 1970s," *Administrative Law Review* 53 (2001): 1139–88.

demonstrated in *favor* of railroad interests. Early in its life, he argued, the ICC had realized that its own success required the support of the railroads and their clients and had designed its regulatory policies accordingly. In exchange for this favorable working relationship, "the railroads have made the Commission the beneficiary of what has been their not inconsiderable political power."[159] This relationship worked well enough for a while, but reliance on railroad support meant that the ICC's ability to evaluate what policies were in the public interest became warped. Arguing that "adaptation to changing environmental circumstances" was necessary "for administrative as well as biological organisms," Huntington concluded that the ICC had not successfully adapted.[160] Even as the railroads' preeminence in transportation had weakened over time, the ICC had continued to protect the railroad industry against competition from water, air, and motor carriers and had thus estranged itself from those industries. Nor had it developed any clear transportation policy, other than "giving the railroads what they want."[161] Huntington's solution promised more vigorous regulation by reassigning functions; he proposed breaking up the ICC and moving its functions to three new agencies located in the Commerce Department to be focused on railroad, water, and highway transportation. Huntington's conclusions about the ICC and transportation policy were quickly called into question by those in and outside the ICC, but his institutional critique of the ICC, and its implications for commission governance more broadly, lingered.[162]

The railroad industry's grim financial state was a major concern for the White House as well. As Eisenhower's Cabinet Committee on Transport Policy and Organization reported in 1956, ICC policies had failed to keep up with the massive changes in transportation technologies and economics that had occurred during the ICC's lifetime. "Paradoxically," the committee remarked, transportation regulation was "based on the historic assumption that transportation is monopolistic, despite the fact that the power of individual transportation enterprises to exercise monopoly control has been rapidly eliminated by the growth of pervasive competition."[163] The committee, which comprised

---

[159] Samuel P. Huntington, "The Marasmus of the ICC: The Commission, the Railroads, and the Public Interest," *Yale Law Journal* 61 (1952): 467–509, 481.

[160] Ibid., 470.

[161] Ibid., 508.

[162] Charles S. Morgan, "A Critique of 'The Marasmus of the ICC: The Commission, the Railroads, and the Public Interest,'" *Yale Law Journal* 62 (1953): 171–225; C. Dickerman Williams, "Transportation Regulation and the Department of Commerce," *Yale Law Journal* 62 (1953): 563–74; Samuel P. Huntington, C. Dickerman Williams, and Charles S. Morgan, "The ICC Re-Examined: A Colloquy," *Yale Law Journal* 63 (1953): 44–63; Jaffe, "The Effective Limits of the Administrative Process."

[163] Department of Commerce, *Modern Transport Policy* (Washington, DC: U.S. Department of Commerce, 1956), 2; see also James C. Nelson, "Revision of National Transport Regulatory Policy: A Review Article," *American Economic Review* 45 (1955): 910–18; Robert W. Harbeson, "New Perspectives in Transport Regulation: The Cabinet Committee Report," *Northwestern University Law Review* 52 (1957): 490–513.

Commerce Secretary Sinclair Weeks, Office of Defense Mobilization Director (and PACGO member) Arthur Flemming, and Defense Secretary Charles Wilson, with help from additional department heads, therefore recommended that – to save Americans "billions of dollars per year" – federal transportation policy should "endorse greater reliance on competitive forces in transportation pricing" appropriate for the competitive context in which it operated.[164] Ultimately, Congress in the 1958 Transportation Act moved to avert catastrophe in the railroad sector by empowering the ICC to do more to help the railroads with their financial problems.[165]

Aviation was another concern. Former CAB chairman Harold A. Jones offered a sharp critique of his own agency in 1953, noting that the establishing act gave "greatly more power and wider discretion than ever before given to a regulatory agency; and great expectations were held for this 'new deal' in regulatory commissions."[166] The CAB, like other agencies, had failed to develop expertise or evolve clear policies and standards; at the same time, these regulatory gaps opened the way for pernicious influence. The board also suffered constant delays, not least because of the requirement that the president himself approve CAB route decisions. Attempts to manage aviation responsibilities across the government further complicated the issue; one study found "over 75 committees, subcommittees, and special working groups" regarding aviation facilities.[167] The House Government Operations Committee, responding to a litany of complaints about the CAB, criticized the board's poor operation, its "preoccupation with relatively small problems," and its failure to investigate the thorny problem of passenger fares.[168] Congress ultimately responded with the Federal Aviation Act of 1958, which consolidated many aviation functions in a Federal Aviation Administration but kept the CAB as the regulatory arm.[169] Much like the 1958 Transportation Act, and Eisenhower's creation of a national interstate highway system in 1956, however, this approach

---

[164] Department of Commerce, *Modern Transport Policy*, 2, 4; see also Congressional Quarterly. *Congress and the Nation 1945–1964: A Review of Government and Politics in the Postwar Years* (Washington, DC: CQ Press, 1965).

[165] See Senate Committee on Interstate and Foreign Commerce, *Transportation Act of 1958*, 85th Cong., 2nd sess., 1958, S. Rep. 1647; Robert A. Smith, "Administrative Law – Powers of Agencies – The Interstate Commerce Commission and Discontinuance of Railroads under the Transportation Act of 1958," *Michigan Law Review* 57 (1959): 1258–60.

[166] Harold A. Jones, "The Anomaly of the Civil Aeronautics Board in American Government," *Journal of Air Law and Commerce* 20 (1953): 140–57, 141.

[167] "Report of Aviation Facilities Study Group to the Budget Bureau, December 31, 1955," *Journal of Air Law and Commerce* 22 (1955): 475–83, 481; see also House Committee on Government Operations, *Federal Role in Aviation*, 84th Cong., 2nd sess., 1956, H. Rep. 2949; Congressional Quarterly, *Congress and the Nation*.

[168] House Judiciary Committee, Subcommittee on Antitrust, *The Airlines Industry*, 85th Cong., 2nd sess., 1956, H. Rep. 1328, 56.

[169] Sherman O. Morris, "The Federal Aviation Act of 1958," *University of Kansas City Law Review* 28 (1959–1960): 35–40.

did little to consider railroad, aviation, maritime, and ground transportation as a concerted whole.[170]

As the first Hoover Commission had emphasized, topics like transportation called for a comprehensive government approach, and, given the intentionally limited jurisdictions of the executive agencies and independent commissions, the White House was, for all practical purposes, the only place where such coordination would be possible. Even after the first Hoover Commission's reforms and Commerce Secretary Charles Sawyer's own recommendations, however, much transportation regulation remained scattered among the ICC, the CAB, and the Commerce Department. Although the federal government spent enormous amounts of money promoting and regulating transportation and building and supporting its infrastructure, it continued to give little thought to how the systems worked together.[171] Reviving the idea of a single department for transportation (considered but rejected by the first Hoover Commission), in September 1959 PACGO recommended to Eisenhower that he ask Congress to move certain transportation-related agencies and functions (including the FAA, the Coast Guard, and various executive functions of the ICC and the CAB) into a new Department of Transportation. As Arthur Flemming and Budget Director Maurice Stans pointed out to Eisenhower, transportation implicated questions of "national defense, development of foreign and domestic commerce, and postal needs" best supervised by the president.[172] Eisenhower's interest was trumped by his concern about the costs of creating a new department given the growing federal deficit, however, and he did little more than recommend the proposal to Congress in his final budget message.

As critiques of the regulatory commissions accumulated, the Eisenhower administration also sought solutions based on expanded presidential authority. As Flemming pointed out at one PACGO meeting, "while the regulatory agencies operate with considerable independence they are located in the Executive Branch and the President bears at least public responsibility for their success and failures."[173] Although this understanding of the federal organization chart might have surprised Congress, reorganization plans adopting the first Hoover Commission's proposals had already given the president more authority over several (but not all) of the independent commissions. During Eisenhower's administration, PACGO and the Budget Bureau sought to extend presidential control over the executive agencies and the independent commissions. PACGO played with a variety of possible organizational arrangements that would place responsibility for policy coordination in the White House while keeping the

[170] Alexander, *Holding the Line.*
[171] David I. Mackie, "The Necessity for a Federal Department of Transportation," *Journal of Public Law* 8 (1959): 1–46.
[172] Arthur S. Flemming and Maurice Stans to Dwight D. Eisenhower, Sept. 23, 1959, 6, Folder "President's Advisory Committee on Government Organization (1)," Box 29, Administration Series, DDE Papers, AWF, DDEL.
[173] PACGO meeting minutes, Aug. 17, 1956, 3, Folder "20 Minutes and notes for PACGO meetings, FY. 1956," Box 3, PACGO Papers, DDEL.

president's workload manageable. Members floated the idea of seeking legislation to create an executive branch official with special responsibility for the
administrative state – for example, an "Administrative Vice President" who
could serve as "the business manager of the government" in charge of approving regulations, making findings committed by statute to presidential authority
(such as approving airline routes and fishery regulations), and coordinating policy among the independent commissions.[174] Recognizing the difficulty of creating such a position, members offered proposals for a new presidential assistant
in the Executive Office of the President with authority over personnel and
management functions. PACGO subsequently suggested a "First Secretary" for
national security and foreign policy, organizationally superior to the cabinet,
and, by 1959, recommended strengthening presidential coordination within the
Executive Office by creating a new Office of Executive Management to replace
the various "temporary staff arrangements" used "to deal promptly with many
troublesome or potentially troublesome matters."[175]

Political scientist Emmette Redford, asked by PACGO late in Eisenhower's
second term to prepare a study of the president's relationship with the independent commissions, repeated claims that the commissions were unable to
coordinate their own work among themselves. Redford asserted the president's
broad "extra-legal and political responsibility for leadership which extends to
all gaps in policy which affect the great interests of the national public."[176] He
thus recommended that the president should "supply policy guidance, consistent with law, to the commissions, bringing to their attention urgent public
needs, relevant facts, and policy considerations. This he should do openly so as
to establish firmly his unquestioned right of leadership."[177] Here, too, little in
the way of permanent reform was adopted, but Eisenhower in his final budget
message called for an Office of Executive Management and a First Secretary
of the Government, recommended strong chairmen plans at the commissions, and informed Congress that presidential responsibility "to control and
supervise the exercise of executive functions by all Federal regulatory bodies
should be clarified."[178]

---

[174] PACGO to Eisenhower, Oct. 10, 1957, 1, Folder "69 Director of Adm., Bureau of the Budget
Management, Special Asst. to the Pres. for Management, Administrative Vice-President
(Business Mgt) 1956–57"; PACGO to Eisenhower, Mar. 21, 1956, Folder "64 The Presidency
Proposal to Delegate certain duties to the elected Vice-President and to an Administrative Vice-
President (Feb.-Apr. 1956)," both in Box 11, PACGO Papers, DDEL.
[175] PACGO to Eisenhower, memorandum, Dec. 6, 1958, Folder "PACGO (2)," Box 29,
Administration Series; Cabinet Paper, Jan. 13, 1959, 1, Folder "Cabinet Meeting of January
23, 1959," Box 12, Cabinet Series, both in DDE Papers, AWF, DDEL.
[176] Emmette S. Redford, *The President and the Regulatory Commissions* (A Report Prepared for
the President's Advisory Committee on Government Organization, 1960), 16.
[177] Ibid., 3 of summary.
[178] Dwight D. Eisenhower, "Annual Budget Message to the Congress," fy. 1962 (Jan. 16, 1961),
in *Public Papers of the Presidents of the United States: Dwight D. Eisenhower*, vol. 1960–1961,
946.

Increased presidential control and coordination was only one of the many solutions proposed during the second half of the 1950s. Agencies were not simply failing to coordinate policies among themselves, they were also failing to make clear policies at all. In a number of academic critiques of administrative governance, observers painted a picture of tortoise-like regulatory agencies hamstrung by procedural requirements, moving very slowly in their own work and quick to retract into their shells to avoid conflict. These critiques appeared in academic books and articles, in congressional reports, in studies prepared for the White House, and, perhaps most famously, in the scathing memo Louis J. Hector sent Eisenhower about practices at the CAB as he resigned from that board in 1959. Disappointment with the independent commissions permeated these critiques. As Marver Bernstein suggested in his influential 1955 book, the same commissions that had been suspected of "excessive zeal and lack of concern with individual property rights" were now "characterized by their apathetic approach to the public interest in regulation of economic life."[179] According to one *New York Times* reporter, the Hector memo "reflects the opinion of a growing number of liberal lawyers that the very concept of regulation that liberal lawyers helped to develop in years past has now turned sour."[180]

Under this increasingly widespread critique, commissioners leaned toward the interests they regulated not necessarily because of quid pro quo relationships with individual industry leaders but because of the broader incentive structures in which they operated. To protect themselves from attack, Bernstein argued, administrators chose the safest and most judicialized procedures for their decision-making process, namely case-by-case adjudication. This was not the courts' fault; judges had repeatedly endorsed flexible procedural due process standards for administration, and the Supreme Court acknowledged that it was up to agencies to make the choice between rule making and adjudication. Nor did Bernstein blame the APA, which had preserved administrative discretion and adopted existing procedures as a model. Instead, he pointed to the commissions themselves, where commissioners attempted "to acquire the respectability and social acceptability achieved by the courts" by adopting procedures mimicking judicial ones.[181]

Administrative formality, unfortunately, slowed down the administrative process, established enormous backlogs, and left important policy areas untouched.[182] Ernest Williams, a transportation specialist at Columbia

---

[179] Marver H. Bernstein, *Regulating Business by Independent Commission* (Princeton, NJ: Princeton University Press, 1955), 95.

[180] Richard E. Mooney, "White House Eyes Role of Agencies," *New York Times*, Sept. 21, 1959, 23.

[181] Bernstein, *Regulating Business by Independent Commission*, 99; see also John B. Gage, "Chairman's Page," *Administrative Law Bulletin* 11 (1959): 203–10.

[182] See Warren E. Baker, "Policy by Rule or *Ad Hoc* Approach – Which Should It Be?" *Law and Contemporary Problems* 22 (1957): 658–71; Henry J. Friendly, "A Look at the Federal Administrative Agencies," *Columbia Law Review* 60 (1960): 429–46, 435. The second Hoover Commission's Task Force on Legal Services and Procedure had also questioned the practice,

University, complained in a 1956 report on regulatory issues for PACGO that "the great issues presented to commissions are not to be decided by a coldly neutral weighing of the facts presented in an adversary proceeding."[183] Hector's pessimistic memorandum similarly pointed out that formality was enormously inefficient as a form of policy making since it forced investigations into quasi-judicial clothing, bound by all of the APA's procedural rules. One complex CAB investigation into air service in the Midwest was conducted by a hearing examiner entirely isolated from the rest of the agency. "There was no machinery for him to seek out actively the information which he thought he needed; instead, he just sat and took what the interested towns and airlines brought him."[184] When the board found itself dissatisfied by his work, they had to start over again. Developing a route plan took three years, "almost entirely because of the inefficient procedures by which it was handled."[185]

Scholars outdid one another in reaching for metaphors of sloth. As law professor Nathaniel Nathanson observed in 1956, "the virtues of full hearing in most types of economic regulation have been so enthusiastically embraced that" such hearings, "instead of operating with the secrecy and dispatch supposedly characteristic of Star Chamber proceedings, now moves with the mammoth gradualness of cinemascope in slow motion."[186] Another scholar, observing the NLRB, concluded that the natural result of case-by-case policy making was that "the caldron of litigation becomes a nightmare version of that magic soup-producing pot of nursery tales which flooded the streets of the town."[187] One former SEC general counsel found that the SEC's initial "spirit of administrative expedition" in adjudication had given way to "a type of modern ordeal by administrative process."[188] Nor did Congress refrain from comment. The House Committee on Interstate and Foreign Commerce, examining the FCC, argued that the separation of functions only made things worse, as the FCC "is provided with a staff of experts, with whom it cannot consult without reopening the record, allowing the interested parties to be present, giving opportunity for reply, and needlessly adding to the size

encouraging sanctions only for behavior "proscribed or restricted by generally applicable rule of the agency." Hoover Commission II, Task Force on Legal Services and Procedure, *Report on Legal Services and Procedure*, 222.

[183] Ernest Williams to PACGO, Sept. 14, 1956, 8, Folder "167 Regulatory Agencies – General," Box 20, PACGO Papers, DDEL.

[184] Louis J. Hector, "Problems of the CAB and the Independent Regulatory Commissions," *Yale Law Journal* 69 (1960): 931–64, 933.

[185] Ibid., 932. For a dissenting view, see Carl A. Auerbach, "Some Thoughts on the Hector Memorandum," *Wisconsin Law Review* 1960 (1960): 183–96.

[186] Nathaniel L. Nathanson, "Law and the Future: Administrative Law," *Northwestern University Law Review* 51 (1956): 174–86, 174.

[187] Cornelius J. Peck, "The Atrophied Rule-Making Powers of the National Labor Relations Board," *Yale Law Journal* 70 (1961): 729–61, 753.

[188] William H. Timbers and Barry H. Garfinkel, "Examination of the Commission's Adjudicatory Process: Some Suggestions," *Virginia Law Review* 45 (1959): 817–30, 822.

and volume of testimony which, in all probability, in the more difficult cases, already extends to thousands of pages." Thus, members concluded, "[t]he judicial imputation of expertise to Commission decisions under these circumstances is in effect a legal fiction."[189]

Nor was it clear that due process was preserved by these procedures. As Hector charged, agencies "are long on judicial form and short on judicial substance."[190] In some cases, no decision rule existed; in others, officials' authority to make new policy through cases (and thus to disregard precedents) meant that future litigants could never be entirely confident what the commission would do in the future.[191] Meanwhile, Hector argued, although judicial trappings were provided in the initial hearing, examiners' reports often mattered little in practice. The actual decision was made later, based on "fact, policy, and legal questions" and by commissioners who had "little personal familiarity with the record."[192] Bernstein similarly suggested that decades of procedural reforms aimed at improving the initial hearing were all for show, as the ultimate decision lay with commissioners themselves, whose decision-making processes were "rather casual and frequently unsystematic."[193] The disconnect between examiners, who observed procedural niceties but had little idea what the commissioners would do, and commissioners, who played fast and loose with procedure but had the ultimate authority to decide, called into question the amount of expertise involved in the actual decision. As Hector argued, "any resemblance between an examiner's recommended decision and the final decision of the Board in a significant case is almost coincidental."[194] Another observer pointed out that commissions were practically begging parties to engage in improprieties; without "consistent criteria" to which to respond, "in order to assure a favorable decision when valuable economic interests are involved, parties may feel compelled to rely upon more than precedent and rational persuasion formally submitted."[195]

Given the disadvantages in time, cost, and frustration, why did commissions persist in making policy through formal procedures? Case-by-case adjudication was, of course, useful for certain complicated questions.[196] In actuality,

---

[189] House Committee on Interstate and Foreign Commerce, *Regulation of Broadcasting: Half a Century of Government Regulation of Broadcasting and the Need for Further Legislative Action*, 85th Cong., 2nd sess., 1958, Subcommittee Print, 158.

[190] Hector, "Problems of the CAB and the Independent Regulatory Commissions," 931.

[191] See *NLRB v. Guy F. Atkinson Co.*, 195 F.2d 141 (9th Cir. 1952).

[192] Hector, "Problems of the CAB and the Independent Regulatory Commissions," 944.

[193] Marver H. Bernstein, "The Politics of Adjudication," *Journal of Politics* 16 (1954): 299–323, 319; see also Schwartz, *The Professor and the Commissions*.

[194] Hector, "Problems of the CAB and the Independent Regulatory Commissions," 945.

[195] Note, "Ex Parte Contacts with the Federal Communications Commission," *Harvard Law Review* 73 (1960): 1178–99, 1179.

[196] See Auerbach, "Some Thoughts on the Hector Memorandum," 188; Baker, "Policy by Rule or Ad Hoc Approach."

however, commissions had little to gain from bold action, and case-by-case policy making was a risk-averse strategy for managing the difficult political contexts in which the commissions operated. Echoing Samuel J. Huntington's attack on the ICC, Bernstein argued that the problem of "administrative arteriosclerosis" was due less to commissioners' failure to adapt to new political forces than to the commissions' original design.[197] By making the commissions legally independent of any branch – what Carl McFarland described as "a form of orphanage" – Congress had also separated them from political support in the White House, Congress, and the public.[198] Thus, Bernstein argued, independence "removes the commission from the public spotlight and allows public support for regulation to wither and die."[199] Administrators were always a convenient scapegoat for politicians and regulated parties, but neither the White House nor Congress was likely to receive political benefit from backing the commissions. Thus, facing little political support and likely legal challenge for any action, commissions adopted what they saw as the safest path. They declined to act unless necessary, and then accumulated mountains of evidence and proceeded through judicialized methods that would stand up in court. Case-by-case action was conservative, incremental, easily reversible, and unlikely to offend the entire industry at once.

Thus, it was hardly surprising that, abandoned by Congress and the executive branch, and with no incentive to work with other agencies and commissions, a commission naturally turned to regulated parties themselves when it did make policy. Indeed, the first Hoover Commission's research had shown just that. According to Bernstein, agencies facing criticism became "extraordinarily sensitive to the demands of regulated groups" while paying little attention to other aspects of regulation.[200] Because administrators had constant contact with the entities they regulated and little contact with others representing alternate views, commissions developed "a myopic view of the public interest which rationalizes the regulatory *status quo*."[201] In addition, Louis Jaffe pointed out, agency budget cuts made the agencies *more* dependent on the parties they regulated.[202] As Jaffe noted elsewhere, while it was "a stereotype of political wisdom that the bureaucrat is ever ready to exercise authority arbitrarily," Congress and the public should be concerned about officials who "become uncomfortable at having to exercise authority and will anxiously seek to placate as many interests as possible. This fear to offend, complaisance, and readiness to listen and be 'fair' and 'reasonable' clog the muscles of the will, and what begins in amiability can end in corruption."[203]

[197] Bernstein, *Regulating Business by Independent Commission*, 101.
[198] Carl McFarland, "Landis' Report: The Voice of One Crying In the Wilderness," *Virginia Law Review* 47 (1961): 373–438, 402.
[199] Bernstein, *Regulating Business by Independent Commission*, 73.
[200] Ibid., 100.
[201] Ibid., 89.
[202] Jaffe, "The Effective Limits of the Administrative Process."
[203] Jaffe, "The Scandal in TV Licensing," 77.

In addition, Hector remarked, several of the commissions had conflicting missions; a commission "whose duty it is to look after the economic well-being of an industry cannot be expected at the same time to enforce vigorously penalty provisions when these would work economic hardship on members of the industry."[204] Commissioners were supposed to mingle with the parties they regulated to maintain their knowledge of the industry, but at the same time were to remain neutral and innocent observers. Ethical problems naturally followed, as "members of regulatory agencies are in reality trying to live in two worlds with two separate sets of standards."[205] Indeed, as Bernstein argued, a commission "discovers that its administrative career can be more convenient, less hazardous, and less exhilarating when its activities do not interfere with managerial freedom except as affirmative governmental action is requested by regulated groups."[206] The commissions had little reason to change this state of affairs, and the regulated parties had even less; as Bernstein argued, "the myth of commission independence" was "a conscious effort by regulated groups to confine regulatory authority to an agency that is somewhat more susceptible than an executive department to influence, persuasion, and, eventually, capture and control."[207]

Although most observers agreed on the outlines of the new problem of the administrative state, they disagreed about the solutions. Many observers agreed that the commissions had to become *less* independent, although what this would look like was not clear. The White House preferred proposals expanding presidential control over the independent commissions; according to Bernstein, injecting more representative democracy into the administrative process might counterbalance the regulated interests and offer a richer perspective on the public interest. As he suggested, commissions "must undertake to win friends and influence legislators in order to obtain the authority and sanctions necessary to regulatory success."[208] Others suggested that more judicial guidance was needed, given agencies' notable lack of the expert policy making that had earned them deference.[209] Louis Jaffe, who found that the problem with the agencies was "the expectable consequence of their broad and ill-defined regulatory power," shied away from judicial solutions and suggested instead that improvements to the administrative process were needed.[210]

By contrast, others, like Hector at the CAB and Newton Minow at the FCC, sought to divide the independent commissions into their parts. Hector's conclusion – "that an independent regulatory commission is not competent in these

---

[204] Hector, "Problems of the CAB and the Independent Regulatory Commissions," 957.
[205] Ibid., 958.
[206] Bernstein, *Regulating Business by Independent Commission*, 99.
[207] Ibid., 146.
[208] Ibid., 261.
[209] Louis B. Schwartz, "Legal Restriction of Competition in the Regulated Industries: An Abdication of Judicial Responsibility," *Harvard Law Review* 67 (1954): 436–75.
[210] Jaffe, "The Effective Limits of the Administrative Process," 1134.

days to regulate a vital national industry in the public interest" – extended to all of the independent commissions and placed the blame on the commissions' inherently contradictory functions.[211] Bernard Schwartz argued in 1955 that a commission with both executive and judicial tasks did both poorly,[212] and Hector remarked in a 1959 speech that this "institutional schizophrenia" resulted "in a sort of amorphous procedural mish-mash which gets neither the administrative, the policy-making nor the judicial job done properly."[213] Thus, he proposed moving the CAB's policy-making and administrative functions to an executive branch department focused on transportation, its judicial functions to an administrative court, and its investigation and prosecution functions to the Justice Department or a similar agency, so that policies "made and enunciated by an executive agency" could be "then applied to specific cases by an independent administrative court or set of courts."[214] FCC commissioner Newton Minow offered a similar solution to President John F. Kennedy as he stepped down in 1963, recommending that the FCC be divided between an administrative court for adjudication functions, and a single administrator for administrative functions.[215]

Hector's suggestions met with significant opposition, however. Members of the CAB defended themselves against Hector's attack in their own memo to Eisenhower, and the chairman of the FTC suggested that "[t]he forty-five years of precedent contained in the *Federal Trade Commission Reports*" already served as "a valuable exposition of policy."[216] The Budget Bureau was similarly skeptical, and University of Texas professor Emmette Redford criticized the proposal in a report to PACGO, suggesting it was "based on the doubtful assumption that the regulatory scrambled egg can be cleanly separated into an executive-policy determining yellow and a quasi-judicial white."[217] Judge Henry J. Friendly, a former general counsel of Pan American World Airways, also rejected Hector's proposal to separate the commissions, condemning those engaged "in carping criticism and in chasing reorganizational rainbows."[218] Rejecting recent decades of congressional, presidential, and judicial solutions,

---

[211] Hector, "Problems of the CAB and the Independent Regulatory Commissions," 931.

[212] Schwartz, "Administrative Justice and Its Place in the Legal Order".

[213] Hector, "The New Critique of the Regulatory Agency," 9.

[214] Hector, "Problems of the CAB and the Independent Regulatory Commissions," 945. Barring this, "the least that comports with fair procedure is that a regulatory commission, when it disagrees with the policy decisions of an examiner, announce clearly what the policy is and then send the case back to the man who knows the facts" (Ibid.; see also Schwartz, *The Professor and the Commissions*, 273–75).

[215] Newton N. Minow, "Suggestions for Improvement of the Administrative Process," *Administrative Law Review* 15 (1963): 146–53.

[216] Earl W. Kintner, "The Current Ordeal of the Administrative Process: In Reply to Mr. Hector," *Yale Law Journal* 69 (1960): 965–77, 971; see also "C.A.B. Denounces Plan for Reform," *New York Times*, Mar. 31, 1960, 64.

[217] Redford, *The President and the Regulatory Commissions*, 2 (summary).

[218] Friendly, "A Look at the Federal Administrative Agencies," 446.

Friendly suggested, "there is only one answer, albeit a trite one – get better men as members of the commissions and keep them there."[219]

At the same time agency heads were apparently doing little to further the public interest, they were revealed elsewhere to be grabbing for gifts and dispensing favors to their friends. The propriety of contacts between those inside and outside the agency became a contested question in the late 1950s as highly publicized evidence of preferential treatment called the idea of public interest regulation into question. Lawyers and reformers who had long been concerned with preventing agency staffers from talking to each other outside the presence of the regulated parties had generally seen the problem as the presence of an environment (as in *Morgan*) in which regulated parties could not participate. The ABA, pushing for enactment of a new administrative code, continued to argue that the more isolated agency officials were from other agency staffers during adjudication, the fairer the proceedings would be for those being regulated.

This focus on the harm of internal communications prevented lower-level employees from imposing their own views on agency heads but ignored the possibility that external communications could do the same thing. The parties themselves valued opportunities to influence decision makers, and agencies believed such contacts encouraged compliance and garnered the goodwill of the regulated interests. Contributions from regulated parties had been intentionally built into agency policy making at all levels, as evidenced in the APA's protection of such involvement in nonadjudicatory proceedings. As one contemporary observer pointed out, economic regulation "*requires* that the agency properly influence industry and that industry properly influence the agency. This premise is a foundation stone of our system of federal administrative law."[220] Such contacts were increasingly seen as problematic when they bled from rule making into adjudication.[221] Indeed, one analysis of the FCC's stricter separation of functions argued that the 1952 amendments "*have insulated the Commission from its own staff and established elaborate hearing procedures, but the amendments have not insulated the Commission in adjudicatory proceedings from Congress, the executive, or the public.* Lack of fairness – if by what we mean pressures brought to bear *dehors* the record – still persists."[222]

The question of unethical behavior flared into public controversy in 1957, as one highly publicized congressional investigation revealed just how

---

[219] Ibid., 444.

[220] Leo A. Huard, "Influence in Federal Agency Law-Making and Adjudicatory Proceedings – Should We Adopt a Code of Agency Ethics?" *Administrative Law Bulletin* 11 (1958): 22–26, 23 (emphasis in the original).

[221] Note, "Ex Parte Contacts with the Federal Communications Commission."

[222] Ben C. Fisher, "Communications Act Amendments, 1952 – An Attempt to Legislate Administrative Fairness," *Law and Contemporary Problems* 22 (1957): 672–96, 679 (emphasis in the original); see also Jaffe, "The Effective Limits of the Administrative Process," 1135; House Committee on Interstate and Foreign Commerce, *Regulation of Broadcasting*.

commonplace it was.[223] The investigation in question was conducted by the House Interstate and Foreign Commerce Committee's Special Subcommittee on Legislative Oversight, established in April 1957 to look into the affairs of the numerous agencies within the committee's scope. Given the subcommittee's jurisdiction, its oversight authority was broad: six of the major independent commissions (the SEC, the ICC, the CAB, the FCC, the FTC, and the FPC), along with smaller but important agencies including the Railroad Retirement Board and the Food and Drug Administration. In light of emerging critiques, the subcommittee was broadly directed to examine how the agencies were executing the laws and whether the agencies were doing things they should not have been doing – whether congressional statutes were "being faithfully executed by the agency in the public interest," whether agencies were influenced by outside pressures, and whether congressional statutes were being interpreted in such a way as "to enlarge the area of regulation" or to use "procedures not intended by the Congress."[224] The overall project was intended to answer Speaker Sam Rayburn's question "whether or not the law, as we intended it, is being carried out or whether a great many of these laws are being repealed or revamped by those who administer them."[225] As one *Wall Street Journal* reporter predicted, "at least some agencies will get a spanking on charges of succumbing to political and industry pressure."[226]

Rather quickly, however, the "dull routine inquiry" many had predicted became something more.[227] The subcommittee, with administrative law scholar Bernard Schwartz as chief counsel, began its probe with an immediately unpopular move, asking the commissioners at the "big six" commissions to report any gifts, favors, or hospitality they had received from the businesses they regulated.[228] Agency employees and attorneys for the regulated industries were similarly unenthusiastic when asked by the subcommittee to report any incidents of impropriety they had witnessed. Embarrassment followed when, in January

[223] See Schwartz, *The Professor and the Commissions*; Frank C. Newman, "The Supreme Court, Congressional Investigations, and Influence Peddling," *New York University Law Review* 33 (1958): 796–810; R. W. Lishman, "'Independence' in the Independent Regulatory Agencies," *Administrative Law Review* 13 (1961): 133–40; Frier, *Conflicts of Interest in the Eisenhower Administration*.

[224] Subcommittee statement of policy, quoted in House Committee on Interstate and Foreign Commerce, Subcommittee on Legislative Oversight, *Federal Communications Commission: Interim Report*, 85th Cong., 2nd sess., 1958, H. Rep. 1602, 7; see also McFarland, "Landis' Report: The Voice of One Crying In the Wilderness."

[225] Rep. Sam Rayburn, quoted in Subcommittee on Legislative Oversight, House Committee on Interstate and Foreign Commerce, *Interim Report*, 4.

[226] Ted Lewis Jr., "Congress May Take Offspring Agencies On Trip to Woodshed," *Wall Street Journal*, Oct. 28, 1957, 1.

[227] John Fisher, "Stage Set for 'Countdown' in TV Probe," *Chicago Daily Tribune*, Feb. 16, 1958, 2.

[228] Rep. Morgan M. Moulder to John C. Doerfer, Oct. 3, 1957, Folder "Organization – Federal Communications Commission Investigation by Legislative Oversight Committee," File No. 12–12g, Box 4, General Correspondence 1957–1966, A1, Entry 100C, OED, RG 173, NACP.

1958, the *New York Times* printed a confidential memo Schwartz had prepared about unsavory activities at the FCC. Schwartz alleged that FCC commissioners routinely engaged in less than judicious behavior, accepting gifts of televisions, drinks, meals, and golf fees from the businesses they regulated, allowing businesses to pay their travel expenses (while in some cases also "double-dipping" and accepting the government's per diem), engaging in ex parte contacts with applicants, and, as a *Wall Street Journal* reporter sniffed, "generally carrying on in a manner not fitting people in a quasi-judicial position."[229] These charges, along with allegations that Chairman Oren Harris – who had his own financial interest in an Arkansas television station – was attempting to stymie the investigation, encouraged interest in what the investigation would show, and put pressure on the subcommittee to continue, if only, the *Washington Post* suggested, "to allay suspicion of an attempted whitewash."[230]

At least some members of Congress were already worried that major players in the broadcasting industry received preferential treatment, as evidenced by hearings held by the House Select Committee on Small Business in 1956 to get to the bottom of "disturbing reports" that the FCC "has become responsive to, or under the influence and control of, the White House and the industry which the Commission is empowered to regulate."[231] Hearings in early 1958 by the House Interstate and Foreign Commerce Committee's Special Subcommittee on Legislative Oversight questioned the Eisenhower administration's anticorruption bona fides and focused on whether commissioners were using their government positions to enrich themselves. Witnesses including FCC commissioners (and Eisenhower appointees) John C. Doerfer and Richard A. Mack sketched an environment where benefits flowed from the communications industry to FCC commissioners and their wives in the form of gifts, entertainment, travel to industry conferences, and state-of-the-art radios and televisions installed in commissioners' homes at the industry's expense. These activities, while of dubious ethical propriety, were in keeping with the FCC's habitual deference to the broadcasting industry. The importance of personal relationships had become that much more important with the boom in television broadcasting in the 1950s; the end of the FCC's freeze on television broadcasting licenses created a rush for these opportunities.[232]

[229] Ted Lewis Jr., "House Unit Inquiry on Federal Regulatory Agencies Opens Today," *Wall Street Journal*, Jan. 27, 1958, 2.

[230] "Pox on Both Houses," *Washington Post*, Feb. 11, 1958, A18. Regarding Harris, see Barnouw, *The Image Empire*, 65.

[231] House Select Committee on Small Business, Subcommittee No. 1, *The Organization and Procedures of the Federal Regulatory Commissions and Agencies and Their Effect on Small Business: Hearings Part III: Federal Communications Commission*, 84th Cong., 2nd Sess., 1956, 692; see also House Select Committee on Small Business, Subcommittee No. 1 on Regulatory Agencies and Commission, *The Organization and Procedures of the Federal Regulatory Commissions and Agencies and their Effect on Small Business*, 84th Cong., 2nd sess., 1956, H. Rep. 2967.

[232] Erik Barnouw, *The Golden Web: A History of Broadcasting in the United States,* vol. II, 1933 to 1955 (New York: Oxford University Press, 1968); Barnouw, *The Image Empire*.

Given commissioners' isolation from the advice of their staff, fewer internal checks existed to manage these pressures.[233]

Embarrassing as these revelations of commissioners' compromised objectivity were, even more damaging were reports of decisions made outside the procedural channels and tainted by friendship and favors. In one highly publicized incident, the FCC's award of a license for Channel 10 Miami, following weeks of formal hearings and months of FCC decision making, was called into question once it was known that the applicants' attorney was a long-time friend of Commissioner Mack.[234] The matter ultimately resulted in Mack's resignation and the subsequent indictments of both men. Channel 4 Pittsburgh had similarly been awarded after meetings between the applicants, Mack, and former FCC Chairman George McConnaughey; rumors that McConnaughey had taken money from the applicants in exchange for a license were never proven.[235] In yet another high-profile episode, evidence emerged that FCC members had received personal letters, phone calls, and gifts from the successful applicant for Sangamon Valley Channel 2 in Springfield, Illinois, and had failed to follow the FCC's own procedural requirements in awarding the license. When these allegations of impropriety reached the Supreme Court, justices questioned the validity of the station award and remanded the case.[236] Based on similar evidence arising from the congressional investigation, circuit courts soon sent several other FCC licensing decisions back to the commission.[237]

Although the subcommittee eventually broadened its inquiry to include the other independent commissions, its most publicized findings related to individual misbehavior. Chief among them was that of powerful White House chief of staff Sherman Adams, who had contacted both the SEC and the FTC on behalf of his friend Bernard Goldfine.[238] The commissions had been proceeding

---

[233] Baughman, *Television's Guardians*.

[234] Schwartz, *The Professor and the Commissions*, 167–69.

[235] FCC Chairman John C. Doerfer, who left the commission in 1960 when his own relationship with a broadcasting concern came under fire, protested in his resignation letter that close ties to regulated parties "despite appearances, do not imperil the integrity of either the government official or the member of industry." John C. Doerfer to Dwight D. Eisenhower, March 10, 1960, Folder "Federal Communications Commission," Box 14, Administration Series, DDE Papers, AWF, DDEL.

[236] *Sangamon Valley Television Corp. v. United States*, 358 U.S. 49 (1958) [per curiam]; *WIRL Television Corp. v. United States*, 358 U.S. 51 (1958) [per curiam]; *Sangamon Valley Television Corp. v. United States*, 269 F.2d 221 (D.C. Cir. 1959); *Sangamon Valley Television Corp. v. United States*, 294 F.2d 742 (D.C. Cir. 1961); *Fort Harrison Television Corp. v. FCC*, 324 F.2d 379 (D.C. Cir. 1963). The original license assignment was ultimately upheld.

[237] *WKAT, Inc. v. FCC*, 258 F.2d 418 (D.C. Cir. 1958); *Massachusetts Bay Telecasters, Inc. v. FCC*, 261 F.2d 55 (D.C. Cir. 1958); *WORZ, Inc. v. FCC*, 268 F.2d 889 (D.C. Cir. 1959); House Committee on Interstate and Foreign Commerce, Special Subcommittee on Legislative Oversight, *Independent Regulatory Commissions*, 86th Cong., 2nd sess., 1961, H. Rep. 2238.

[238] See Adams, *Firsthand Report*, chap. 21; Susan Wagner, *The Federal Trade Commission* (New York: Praeger Publishers, 1971).

against Goldfine's textile companies for what the subcommittee described as "obviously improper corporate financial practices" and "long continued and flagrant violation of the Wool Products Labeling Act"; while Adams denied that he had intended to influence either commission, he admitted that he had, at various times, enjoyed Goldfine's hospitality and had accepted from him an Oriental rug and a vicuña coat.[239] At best, Adams (who resigned over the revelations) was guilty of a striking naïveté. The *Washington Post* commented on "the sheer boneheadedness of his having allowed Mr. Goldfine to buy $2000 worth of hotel rooms for him,"[240] and the *Chicago Tribune* suggested that Adams certainly should have realized that any contact from the White House chief of staff "was bound to have an effect upon lesser lights in the burocracy, and that a feather in these circumstances might be equal to a baseball bat in others."[241]

In the subcommittee's final report on these matters (released in January 1959), members focused not just on these individual cases of misconduct (some of which the subcommittee had sent to the Justice Department for possible prosecution), but on the broader damage the revelations had done to "the widespread confidence of the public in the fairness and integrity of the operations of governmental institutions."[242] In Goldfine's case, for example, the SEC's own failures were on clear display. Increased access to judicial review was recommended to reassure Americans, as the subcommittee recognized that "[a] backlog of disgruntled citizens with solid ground for complaints going unredressed may be almost as injurious to the body politic as a backlog of unfinished administrative or judicial business."[243] Actual changes to avoid these conflicts in the future were also recommended, with a particular focus on personnel. The subcommittee proposed that administrative officials should be "men of unquestioned ability and character," and commissioners should do more of their own work, with "less reliance upon information derived from the regulated industry ... and more reliance upon the independent investigatory results of the commissions themselves."[244]

In addition, the subcommittee encouraged immediate legislative action to bar conflicts and to strengthen existing conflict of interest rules so that the independent commissions would become neither "Washington branch offices of the regulated industry" nor "instruments of overaggressive seekers of special privileges."[245] As one observer pointed out, the subcommittee had "added

---

[239] House Committee on Interstate and Foreign Commerce, Special Subcommittee on Legislative Oversight, *Independent Regulatory Commissions*, 85th Cong., 2nd sess., 1959, H. Rep. 2711, 43, 44.

[240] "Sauce for the Goose," *Washington Post*, June 14, 1958, A10.

[241] "The Same Mr. Adams," *Chicago Daily Tribune*, June 14, 1958, 12.

[242] House Special Subcommittee on Legislative Oversight, *Independent Regulatory Commissions*, H. Rep. 2711, 60.

[243] Ibid., 62.

[244] Ibid., 61, 14.

[245] Ibid., 61.

impressively to the mountains of data that demonstrate our immense need for laws designed to curb influence peddling."[246] The subcommittee optimistically anticipated that a code of ethics "may well serve as a deterrent to the bad and a source of reassurance to the good as to the propriety of their conduct in doubtful situations."[247]

Indicating the variety of available solutions, Congress in July 1960 combined one of the ABA's bills, with its focus on pernicious internal influence, with the Harris subcommittee's bill, which looked to the corruption of outside influence. This proposed "Independent Regulatory Agencies Act" was ethics legislation directed at the six commissions that would apply to *everyone* involved in the decision-making process – parties, lawyers, agency employees, and members of Congress alike. While the bill, endorsed by lawyers at the ABA's Special Committee on the Federal Administrative Practice Act and the District of Columbia Bar Association, was ultimately unsuccessful, it was an interesting effort to bridge old and new concerns about the administrative process.

The bill attempted an awkward blend of the Harris subcommittee's code of ethics and the ABA's code of administrative procedure. The initial draft aimed "to strengthen the independence and effectiveness" of the commissions and "to increase the confidence of the public" in their "efficient, fair and independent operation."[248] While conflict-of-interest laws banned certain behaviors, and a number of agencies had rules governing conduct, there was no comprehensive code of ethical behavior for administrative officials or those appearing before them. Congress had moved in this direction in June 1958, adopting a nonbinding "Code of Ethics for Government Service" for *all* federal employees, which urged them to avoid favoritism or profiting by their offices.[249] Still missing, however, were enforceable rules that clearly spelled out the line between permissible and impermissible contacts with regulated parties.

The new code thus attempted to strike a balance between insulating administrators from improper influence and preventing them from gathering the information they needed to do their jobs. The commissions were to develop regulations to protect the independence of agency officials and to limit communications outside of proper channels of procedure. In proceedings that the APA required to be "on the record" – generally matters involving formal adjudication where officials made their decisions based on material developed during a hearing and placed on the record – ex parte communications with agency officials involved in the "decisional process" were banned. Behind-the-scenes

---

[246] Newman, "The Supreme Court, Congressional Investigations, and Influence Peddling," 810.

[247] House Special Subcommittee on Legislative Oversight, *Independent Regulatory Commissions*, H. Rep. 2711, 22.

[248] H.R. 4800, 86th Cong., 2nd sess., 1960.

[249] H. Con. Res. 175 (85th Cong., 2nd sess.) (1958); see also Senate Committee on Post Office and Civil Service, *Code of Ethics for Government Service*, 85th Cong., 2nd sess., 1958, S. Rep. 1812; House Committee on Post Office and Civil Service, *Code of Ethics for Government Service*, 85th Cong., 2nd sess., 1958, H. Rep. 1208.

interactions, notes, and other communications, impossible to eliminate entirely, were to become matters of public record.

At the same time, the bill proposed to revoke the APA's exemptions that excluded rate making and licensing from the category of "on-the-record" hearings, thus handing more work to examiners and placing more barriers between examiners, agency heads, and others in the agency. "Ex parte" was now a term of opprobrium for internal as well as external matters, and, as the House Committee on Interstate and Foreign Commerce argued, in on-the-record proceedings, "[b]asic fairness requires" that those "staff members who are likely to become advocates of a point of view" due to their involvement with the case at an earlier stage "should not communicate ex parte with the members of the Commission or the hearing officers or employees involved in the decisional process with respect to such proceeding."[250] The committee thus combined the earlier threat with a newly realized one, ensuring that individuals in the agency "are placed on a substantially equal footing with outside parties and their representatives," from whom a similar threat was expected.[251]

Not surprisingly, agency representatives were unenthusiastic. As one ICC representative wrote to Chairman Harris, the commission found it "absolutely essential" that ICC staffers "remain free to obtain the completely frank views of our senior staff members without any obligation to make such views a part of the public record."[252] Outside contacts were also useful in speeding matters along, reinforced in the House subcommittee's inquiry into the propriety of communications between the FPC and prominent Democratic lobbyist Thomas Corcoran on behalf of a gas concern in May 1960. Here, the matter at hand was covered by the rates and public utilities exemption in the APA; in addition, given the FPC's huge backlog and "intolerable delays," the subcommittee suggested that the commission "is acting in the public interest by having cooperative ex parte contacts with industry representatives."[253] Such contacts made it possible "that gas could be supplied to Michigan and Wisconsin consumers for the winter of 1960."[254] Friendly sponsors in Congress introduced several of the ABA's bills during the 1960s, and, while the ABA continued to solicit feedback from agency officials and lawyers, certain provisions remained relatively consistent. In multiple versions of the bill, the ABA sought to expand

[250] House Committee on Interstate and Foreign Commerce, *Independent Regulatory Agencies Act of 1960*, 86th Cong., 2nd sess., 1960, H. Rep. 2070, 15.
[251] Ibid.
[252] John H. Winchell to Rep. Oren Harris, June 10, 1960, reprinted in House Committee on Interstate and Foreign Commerce, *Independent Regulatory Agencies Act of 1960*, 30.
[253] House Committee on Interstate and Foreign Commerce, Special Subcommittee on Legislative Oversight, *Independent Regulatory Commissions*, H. Rep. 2238, 23; Charles D. Ablard, "Ex Parte Contacts with Federal Administrative Agencies," *American Bar Association Journal* 47 (1961): 473–76.
[254] House Committee on Interstate and Foreign Commerce, Subcommittee on Legislative Oversight *Independent Regulatory Commissions*, H. Rep. 2238, 23.

internal separation of functions requirements to more agency actions, limiting discussion among agency staffers as they handled these matters. However, these proposals, seen as overly complicated given existing administrative problems, gained little traction and suggested the limits of additional procedural reform.

In January 1961, in Eisenhower's final budget message, the president trumpeted his administration's organizational accomplishments. Chief among them were the new Department of Health, Education, and Welfare, the reorganization of the Defense Department, and the creation of the National Aeronautics and Space Administration and the FAA. He also offered some final remarks about the problem of the regulatory agencies, waiting until he was leaving office, as Flemming had recommended a few years earlier, to "obviate the political problem."[255] Eisenhower recommended that Congress grant future presidents permanent reorganization authority and more control over the organization and staffing of the president's own Executive Office. In addition, reacting to budget cuts in the 1940s and 1950s that had exacerbated backlogs and hampered enforcement, Eisenhower included in his final budget significant increases for the ICC, the FTC, the FCC, the SEC, and the CAB that would allow them to supplement their dwindling numbers of staffers. However, the problem seemed larger than these solutions.[256] As Ralph Fuchs observed in 1960, "doubt has arisen whether the public interest entrusted to the agencies is being served at all adequately."[257]

When John F. Kennedy took office later that month, backed by strong Democratic majorities in Congress, many anticipated an immediate push to fix the problem. Both major parties during the 1960 campaign had addressed the problems of administrative corruption and administrative indolence that had come into clear relief during the Eisenhower administration, and the new president moved to energize the regulatory process by requesting more money for the inadequately funded agencies and commissions, demanding monthly status reports from the major independent commissions, and appointing men who promised a more vigorous approach to regulation.[258]

Kennedy also drew heavily on a review of the major independent commissions conducted by James M. Landis, the administrative expert then serving as a Kennedy family attorney. Landis, who had observed the agencies from

---

[255] PACGO meeting minutes, Mar. 26, 1957, 1, Folder "21 Minutes and notes for PACGO meetings FY. 1957 (2)," Box 3, PACGO Papers, DDEL.

[256] J. Howard Rossbach, letter to the editor, *New York Times*, Apr. 22, 1954, 28.

[257] Ralph F. Fuchs, "Fairness and Effectiveness in Administrative Agency Organization and Procedures," *Indiana Law Journal* 36 (1960): 1–50, 1.

[258] See Bernard D. Nossiter, *The Mythmakers: An Essay on Power and Wealth* (Boston: Houghton Mifflin Co., 1964); Welborn, "Presidents, Regulatory Commissioners and Regulatory Policy"; William L. Cary, *Politics and the Regulatory Agencies* (New York: McGraw-Hill Book Co., 1967); Barnouw, *The Image Empire*; Krasnow and Longley, *The Politics of Broadcast Regulation*; Baughman, *Television's Guardians*; Gross, *Broken Promise*; Patterson, *Grand Expectations*.

inside (as a commissioner at the FTC, the SEC, and the CAB) and out (as dean of the Harvard Law School), in December 1960 presented Kennedy with a *Report on Regulatory Agencies to the President Elect*, summarizing the rising tide of complaints and criticism and suggesting that immediate reforms were necessary for the independent commissions to function properly.[259] Drawing on existing critiques and on his own experience at the CAB, Landis made clear that the problem of the independent commissions was more a management problem than a legal one. Kennedy would echo Landis's complaints in his April 1961 speech on the administrative process, remarking that "the *absence* of a firm and comprehensive policy as to what role, if any, existing methods should play in our national economy actually is a policy in itself" – that is, according to a Senate subcommittee, one "of unrestrained and destructive competition guided by private interests rather than that of the public as a whole."[260]

Landis had blamed both the APA and the agencies and commissions for the fact that administrators relied too heavily on formal adjudication while spending far too little effort on policy making. He called for more coordination among the agencies, singling out transportation, energy, and communications policies in particular as areas that should be "welded into an integrated whole" by the White House.[261] Instead, however, he found that relying on quasi-judicial methods at lower levels and then requiring commissioners to pass on the results placed an enormous burden on everyone involved. The NLRB, given its full separation of prosecution and judicial functions, often served as an example of too much formality, and several additional contemporary studies described how the Taft-Hartley Act had crippled the board. An advisory committee headed by Archibald Cox, in its 1960 report to the Senate Committee on Labor and Public Welfare, lambasted the conditions at the board and concluded that "justice delayed is often justice denied."[262] A separate investigation

---

[259] James M. Landis, *Report on Regulatory Agencies to the President-Elect*, Senate Judiciary Committee, 86th Cong., 2nd sess., 1960, Committee Print; Memo to Sen. John F. Kennedy, Oct. 30, 1960, in Charles O. Jones, ed., *Preparing to Be President: The Memos of Richard E. Neustadt* (Washington, DC: AEI Press, 2000), 50; see also Milton M. Carrow, "Dean Landis and the Regulatory Process," *George Washington Law Review* 29 (1961): 718–38; McFarland, "Landis' Report"; Note, "The Progress of Federal Agency Reorganization under the Kennedy Administration," *Virginia Law Review* 48 (1962): 300–77; Louis L. Jaffe, "James Landis and the Administrative Process," *Harvard Law Review* 78 (1964): 319–28; Donald A. Ritchie, *James M. Landis: Dean of the Regulators* (Cambridge, MA: Harvard University Press, 1980); Donald A. Ritchie, "Reforming the Regulatory Process: Why James Landis Changed His Mind," *Business History Review* 54 (1980): 283–302.

[260] John F. Kennedy, "Special Message to the Congress on Regulatory Agencies," Apr. 13, 1961, in *Public Papers of the Presidents: John F. Kennedy*, vol. 1961 (Washington, DC: Government Printing Office, 1962), 270 (emphasis in the original).

[261] Landis, *Report on Regulatory Agencies*, 74.

[262] Advisory Panel on Labor-Management Relations Law, *Organization and Procedure of the National Labor Relations Board*, Senate Committee on Labor and Public Welfare, 86th Cong., 2nd sess., 1960, S. Doc. 81, 2.

of the Eisenhower-era NLRB by the House Education and Labor Committee found that employees' legal rights were threatened by the board's slowness in election matters, and that the board's "unconscionable delay" in unfair practice cases made the results "almost nugatory and futile."[263] A McKinsey and Company study of the NLRB offered, subcommittee members found, additional "glaring examples of how an agency can become involved in 'bureaucratic procedures' to the extent that the basic usefulness of the agency is most seriously impaired."[264]

Soon after giving a speech in April 1961 devoted to the problem of the regulatory commissions, Kennedy called for a new administrative conference (something the major commissions had asked Eisenhower for a year earlier) and sent Congress a number of reorganization plans based on Landis's recommendations. Several of these plans targeted the problem of the commissioners' workloads by allowing commissions to delegate their final decisions to lower-level staff members. This reform, which had also been recommended by those studying the NLRB and by the Senate Judiciary Committee's Subcommittee on Administrative Practice and Procedure, largely formalized many existing practices.[265] Given the huge volume of cases each commission faced, commissioners could do little more than sign off on decisions reached by their staff. As Landis had remarked, "members of administrative commissions do not do their own work. The fact is that they simply cannot do it."[266] One commissioner "had to make a decision during his work-day every five minutes," and another one "made 18,000 decisions in five years."[267] Officially delegating more routine tasks to lower-level staffers and making hearing examiners' decisions final, unless the commission chose to grant review, meant, Kennedy argued, agency heads could "conserve their time for the consideration of major matters of policy and planning."[268] The White House succeeded in obtaining reorganization plans providing for delegation by presidentially appointed chairman at the CAB and the FTC, and within a few months Congress provided for a similar delegation of authority at the FCC, the SEC, and the ICC.[269] By 1962, the Senate Judiciary Committee's

[263] House Committee on Education and Labor, Subcommittee on National Labor Relations Board, *Administration of the Labor-Management Relations Act by the NLRB*, 87th Cong., 1st sess., 1961, Committee Print, 1.

[264] Ibid., 73; see also Gross, *Broken Promise*, 156–59.

[265] Senate Judiciary Committee, Subcommittee on Administrative Practice and Procedure, *Administrative Practice and Procedure*.

[266] Landis, *Report on Regulatory Agencies*, 19.

[267] Ibid., 20.

[268] John F. Kennedy, "Special Message to Congress Transmitting Reorganization Plan 1 of 1961," Apr. 27, 1961, in *Public Papers of the Presidents: John F. Kennedy*, vol. 1961, 324.

[269] Communication Act of 1952 Amendments, Pub. L. No. 87-192, 75 Stat, 420; Interstate Commerce Act Amendments, Pub. L. No. 87-247, 75 Stat. 517; see also Krasnow and Longley, *The Politics of Broadcast Regulation*, 64 n. 17; Note, "The Progress of Federal Agency Reorganization under the Kennedy Administration"; Congressional Quarterly, *Congress and the Nation*.

Subcommittee on Administrative Practice and Procedure attributed part of the "significant improvements" in the agencies and commissions to these successful reorganization plans.[270]

Little more was achieved during the Kennedy administration, however. Kennedy followed up his address on the regulatory agencies with another targeting the ethical questions the agencies faced. Drawing on Landis's analysis of administrative misbehavior as "[c]ancers" that "sweep through the entire process dulling the sense of public service and destroying the confidence that the public must repose in public servants," Kennedy emphasized the need to balance fairness and expertise.[271] Restricting officials' ex parte interactions entirely was impractical, as it would "restrict their means of gathering that very expertise that was the reason for the creation of the agency" and "keep them away from a grass roots exploration of what the ends of any segment of the public are."[272] At the same time, of course, such interactions could have insidious effects. Landis's solution was to improve agency personnel, but Kennedy placed the burden of solving the problem on the agencies themselves. Along with a subsequent executive order spelling out appropriate behavior for many federal employees, Kennedy asked Congress to require each agency and commission to develop their own set of standards for ex parte contact.[273] Appearance was key, "[f]or the basis of effective government is public confidence, and that confidence is endangered when ethical standards falter or appear to falter."[274]

Developments in administrative procedure during the Eisenhower and Kennedy administrations suggest how much the context for discussing administrative law had changed. Administrators' enthusiasm was less of a concern than administrators' *lack* of enthusiasm. The Senate Subcommittee on Administrative Practice and Procedure, following extensive hearings in early 1960, was troubled by the "widespread lack of public confidence in the fairness of agency decisions."[275] The problem they identified – one with which agency representatives agreed – was not immorality but the heavy-handed procedural requirements that led to significant delay and enormous backlogs and forced participants needing action into illegitimate channels. Nor were supporters and opponents of Kennedy's reorganization plans the usual suspects; administrators who had

---

[270] Senate Judiciary Committee, Subcommittee on Administrative Practice and Procedure, *Administrative Practice and Procedure*, 87th Cong., 2nd sess., 1962, S. Rep. 1480, 1. One observer did question whether the reorganization plan for the FTC had really done much to improve the situation (Daniel J. Baum, "Reorganization, Delay and the Federal Trade Commission," *Administrative Law Review* 15 [1963]: 92–110).

[271] Landis, *Report on Regulatory Agencies*, 36.

[272] Ibid., 15.

[273] Executive Order No. 10939, 26 Fed. Reg. 3951 (1961).

[274] John F. Kennedy, "Special Message to the Congress on Conflict-of-Interest Legislation and on Problems of Ethics in Government," Apr. 27, 1961, in *Public Papers of the Presidents: John F. Kennedy*, vol. 1961, 326.

[275] Senate Judiciary Committee, Subcommittee on Administrative Practice and Procedure, *Administrative Practice and Procedure*, 86th Cong., 2nd sess., 1960, S. Rep. 1484, 8.

strenuously opposed similar proposals to finalize examiners' decisions made by
the conservative ABA in the past had become more receptive to the idea, given
the ever-increasing demands on their time. (To be fair, similarities between the
ABA's proposals and those of the White House only went so far. The reorganization plans allowed the chairman of each commission to decide when and
where to delegate authority, and allowed the commissions to decide when to
review examiners' decisions.[276] The ABA's, by contrast, would have left the
commissions little discretion.[277]) Even so, FCC chairman Newton Minow suggested that through such reform, the commission might avoid "frozen procedural concepts developed over a quarter of a century ago."[278]

The contrast between the reception of the kinds of proposals offered in
the late 1930s and those offered in the late 1950s suggest the gradual consolidation and acceptance of the administrative state in the post–New Deal era.
Plans to improve administrative workloads were accepted by administrators,
but proposals to move administrative authority to the courts met with a hostile reception. The idea of "bureaucrats run amok" was no longer the terrifying
idea that it had been even a decade earlier. By 1955, administrative agencies
and independent regulatory commissions were more familiar features of the
federal landscape, and the ABA's feverish visions of "administrative absolutism" had given way to new concerns about slow administration and unethical
administrators. Proposals to further judicialize the administrative state did not
get far in the 1960s; in addition, efforts to create a third Hoover Commission
failed, and the Legislative Reorganization Act of 1970 did little to change
oversight requirements. Deregulation debates in coming years would focus on
the economic inefficiency of administrative regulation rather than its inherent
unfairness.[279] The APA had gone far in addressing concerns about the excesses
of the administrative state, and few were willing to suffer the chaos of creating
a new administrative system from scratch.

[276] Frank W. McCulloch, "The NLRB and Techniques for Expediting the Administrative Process,"
Administrative Law Review 14 (1961): 97–104.

[277] Note, "The Progress of Federal Agency Reorganization under the Kennedy Administration";
Robert M. Benjamin, "A Lawyer's View of Administrative Procedure – The American Bar
Association Program," *Law and Contemporary Problems* 26 (1961): 203–37; "Pending
Proposals to Amend the Federal Administrative Procedure Act."

[278] Newton N. Minow to William L. Dawson, May 11, 1961, 1, File No. 12-12, Organization –
Federal Communications Commission, Box 4, General Correspondence 1957–1966, A1, Entry
100C, OED, RG 173, NACP.

[279] See Martha Derthick and Paul J. Quirk, *The Politics of Deregulation* (Washington, DC: Brookings
Institution, 1985); Joseph D. Kearney and Thomas W. Merrill, "The Great Transformation
of Regulated Industries Law," *Columbia Law Review* 98 (1998): 1323–409; Rabin, "Federal
Regulation in Historical Perspective"; Thomas McCraw, *Prophets of Regulation: Charles
Francis Adams, Louis D. Brandeis, James M. Landis, Alfred E. Kahn* (Cambridge, MA: Harvard
University Press, 1984).

Conclusion

The political history of administrative law in the 1940s and 1950s suggests a need to study the state even when the more obvious markers of state building are absent. In place of the disillusionment narrative contained in the public interest–capture dichotomy, the postwar years demonstrate a shift in the criticisms of agencies and indicate that the seeds for many of the administrative habits found offensive in the late 1960s and 1970s were present much earlier.[1] This period of administrative development has received comparatively little attention, sandwiched as it is between the New Deal programs of the 1930s and the explosion of health and environmental regulation in the late 1960s and early 1970s. Both moments have garnered much attention from scholars, but the decades in between were a crucial period during which each branch of government struggled to come to grips with the location of massive amounts of federal power in administrative forms.[2] Focusing only on the creation of new agencies misses the significant transformation in administrative potential and in political rhetoric that resulted. The administrative state remained a problem to be solved, but the "problem" itself had changed. The twin strands of proceduralism and cooperation that dominated administrative law throughout this period were no longer considered a positive good. By 1960, as older critiques of administrative absolutism had been put to rest by active reformers and by procedural reforms that allayed such fears, administrators came under attack less for what they did (adjudicate private rights) than what they failed

---

[1] Thomas W. Merrill, "Capture Theory and the Courts: 1967–1983," *Chicago-Kent Law Review* 72 (1997): 1039–117; Alan B. Morrison, "The Administrative Procedure Act: A Living and Responsive Law," *Virginia Law Review* 72 (1986): 253–70.

[2] David Vogel, "The 'New' Social Regulation in Historical and Comparative Perspective," in Thomas K. McCraw, ed., *Regulation in Perspective: Historical Essays*, 155–85 (Cambridge, MA: Harvard University Press, 1981); Robert L. Rabin, "Federal Regulation in Historical Perspective," *Stanford Law Review* 38 (1986): 1189–326; Marc Allen Eisner, "Discovering Patterns in Regulatory History: Continuity, Change, and Regulatory Regimes," *Journal of Policy History* 6 (1994): 157–87; Daniel B. Rodriguez, "Jaffe's Law: An Essay on the Intellectual Underpinnings of Modern Administrative Law Theory," *Chicago-Kent Law Review* 72 (1997): 1159–86.

to do (think broadly, articulate sweeping policy statements, or work effectively with other agencies). Claims of indolence, sloth, capture, and corruption were not new but had new salience. The administrative narrative had changed more than the administrative process.

Developments in the administrative process described in previous chapters significantly informed state building in the subsequent era, as concerns about interagency coordination, case-by-case decision making, and agency ethics persisted and shaped Congress's approach to the administrative state in the coming decades. During the late 1960s and early 1970s, Americans saw an outpouring of new regulatory statutes that matched the Progressive era and the New Deal era in regulatory enthusiasm but reflected a new focus on protecting their health, welfare, and safety. More was to be protected than a fair and competitive marketplace. A partial list of congressional activity includes the Civil Rights Act (1964), the Federal Metal and Nonmetallic Mine Safety Act (1966), the National Highway Transportation Safety Act (1966), the National Environmental Policy Act (1969), the Endangered Species Conservation Act (1969), the Clean Air Act Amendments (1970), the Occupational Safety and Health Act (1970), the Consumer Product Safety Act (1972), and the Endangered Species Act (1973).

When Congress and the White House placed these federal responsibilities in new administrative bodies including the Environmental Protection Agency, the Consumer Product Safety Commission, and the National Highway Transportation Safety Administration, organizational coherence remained important.[3] Agencies with similar tasks were brought together when possible, evident in the Department of Transportation, finally created in 1966, and in the 1970 reorganization plan that created the Environmental Protection Agency by bringing together agency functions from various bureaus and offices within the Department of the Interior, the Department of Agriculture, the Department of Health, Education and Welfare, the Council on Environmental Quality, the Atomic Energy Commission, and the

---

[3] William F. Pedersen Jr., "Formal Records and Informal Rulemaking," *Yale Law Journal* 85 (1975): 38–88; Vogel, "The 'New' Social Regulation in Historical and Comparative Perspective"; Cass R. Sunstein, *After the Rights Revolution: Reconceiving the Regulatory State* (Cambridge, MA: Harvard University Press, 1990); Jerry L. Mashaw and David L. Harfst, *The Struggle for Auto Safety* (Cambridge, MA: Harvard University Press, 1990); Richard A. Harris and Sidney M. Milkis, *The Politics of Regulatory Change: A Tale of Two Agencies*, 2nd ed. (New York: Oxford University Press, 1996); Hugh Davis Graham, "Legacies of the 1960s: The American 'Rights Revolution' in an Era of Divided Governance," *Journal of Policy History* 10 (1998): 267–88; Hugh Davis Graham, "Since 1964: The Paradox of American Civil Rights Regulation," in Morton Keller and R. Shep Melnick, eds., *Taking Stock: American Government in the Twentieth Century*, 187–218 (Cambridge: Cambridge University Press, 1999); Robert A. Kagan, "Adversarial Legalism and American Government," in Marc K. Landy and Martin A. Levin, eds., *The New Politics of Public Policy*, 88–118 (Baltimore: The Johns Hopkins University Press, 1995); Morrison, "The Administrative Procedure Act: A Living and Responsive Law"; Reuel E. Schiller, "Rulemaking's Promise: Administrative Law and Legal Culture in the 1960s and 1970s," *Administrative Law Review* 53 (2001): 1139–88.

Federal Radiation Council.[4] Given the plight of the independent commissions in previous decades, Congress generally avoided both independence and the multiheaded commission form. Most new agencies were headed by an administrator placed somewhere within the executive branch to enable presidential supervision and coordination. And responding to continuing concerns about the separation of powers, Congress kept the adjudication functions of agencies entirely separate from the investigation and rulemaking ones.[5]

In response to decades of complaints about agencies' failure to state broad principles of policy and their preference for adjudication, many of the statutes explicitly instructed the new agencies to make policy through rulemaking instead of case-by-case adjudication.[6] As Judge Henry J. Friendly argued in an influential 1962 book, "the basic deficiency" of the administrative process was its "failure to 'make law'."[7] Reiterating familiar claims that commissions lacked clear standards, Friendly called on agencies to use their rulemaking authority whenever possible. The failure to state broad rules and the failure to engage

[4] Emmette S. Redford and Marlan Blissett, *Organizing the Executive Branch: The Johnson Presidency* (Chicago: University of Chicago Press, 1981), chap. 3; Marc K. Landy, Marc J. Roberts, and Stephen R. Thomas, *The Environmental Protection Agency: Asking the Wrong Questions from Nixon to Clinton,* exp. ed. (New York: Oxford University Press, 1994).

[5] OSHA's powers were divided between the Labor Department and a separate Occupational Safety and Health Review Commission. A similar division was adopted in the Federal Mine Safety and Health Act. See Marshall J. Breger, "The APA: An Administrative Conference Perspective," *Virginia Law Review* 72 (1986): 337–61.

[6] For discussion of the choice between rulemaking and adjudication, see Warren E. Baker, "Policy by Rule or *Ad Hoc* Approach – Which Should It Be?," *Law and Contemporary Problems* 22 (1957): 658–71; C. Roger Nelson, "Chairman's Page," *Administrative Law Review* 16 (1964): 77–79; Ben C. Fisher, "Rule Making Activities in Federal Administrative Agencies," *Administrative Law Review* 17 (1965): 252–61; Ralph F. Fuchs, "Agency Development of Policy through Rule-Making," *Northwestern University Law Review* 59 (1965): 781–807; Bernie R. Burrus and Harry Teter, "Antitrust: Rulemaking v. Adjudication in the FTC," *Georgetown Law Journal* 54 (1966): 1106–30; Cornelius J. Peck, "A Critique of the National Labor Relations Board's Performance in Policy Formulation: Adjudication and Rule-Making," *University of Pennsylvania Law Review* 117 (1968): 254–75; Merton C. Bernstein, "The NLRB's Adjudication-Rule Making Dilemma under the Administrative Procedure Act," *Yale Law Journal* 79 (1970): 571–622; Daniel J. Gifford, "The New Deal Regulatory Model: A History of Criticisms and Refinements," *Minnesota Law Review* 68 (1983): 299–332; Eisner, "Discovering Patterns in Regulatory History"; Glen O. Robinson, "The Making of Administrative Policy: Another Look at Rulemaking and Adjudication and Administrative Procedure Reform," *University of Pennsylvania Law Review* 118 (1970): 485–539; Note, "Substantive Rulemaking and the FTC," *Fordham Law Review* 42 (1973): 178–96; Melvin G. Dakin, "Ratemaking as Rulemaking – The New Approach at the FPC: Ad Hoc Rulemaking in the Ratemaking Process," *Duke Law Journal* 1973 (1973): 41–88; George W. Chesrow, Comment, "NLRB Policymaking: The Rulemaking – Adjudication Dilemma Revisited in *NLRB v. Bell Aerospace Co.*," *University of Miami Law Review* 29 (1975): 559–83; Ronald A. Cass, "Models of Administrative Action," *Virginia Law Review* 72 (1986): 363–98, 382–83; Richard J. Pierce Jr., "Rulemaking and the Administrative Procedure Act," *Tulsa Law Journal* 32 (1996): 185–201.

[7] Henry J. Friendly, *The Federal Administrative Agencies: The Need for Better Definition of Standards* (Cambridge, MA: Harvard University Press, 1962), viii.

in rulemaking were not necessarily the same problem, however.[8] The National Labor Relations Board, for one, was often criticized for having never engaged in substantive rulemaking, but, as one observer later remarked, "the Board's notoriously settled habits make the rulemaking issue academic in all but the most dramatic cases."[9] Indeed, as more than one person pointed out, Friendly's own examples of successful policy articulation came from adjudication.

The problem, then, was less agencies' failure to state clear rules than their insistence on doing so through the Administrative Procedure Act's adjudication procedures. This method was not only time-consuming, but unfair to the parties involved; at the NLRB, one scholar charged, some "individual cases have been manipulated or at least distorted for the ulterior ends of rulemaking."[10] Cornelius J. Peck, in a 1961 critique, explained that the NLRB's habits meant that fewer people received notice when the board was contemplating a policy change, and fewer people were able to participate in what was essentially a rulemaking process. Overall, Peck argued, this rejection of rulemaking methods "has produced grossly unsatisfactory results."[11] The Senate Judiciary Committee included additional rulemaking provisions in its 1966 bill to amend the APA, and courts also jumped into the fray, citing Friendly and Peck as they pushed agencies to use the APA's rulemaking provisions.[12] Recognizing that Congress had given the agencies a choice of methods for making policy, courts repeatedly hinted that officials were making the wrong choice. In 1969, the Supreme Court weighed in, expressing in *NLRB v. Wyman-Gordon Co.* both deference to the NLRB and displeasure about its reliance on a prospective "rule" it had made through an earlier adjudication.[13] A plurality of the Court upheld the NLRB's policy even as justices criticized the board's dependence on "a rule-making procedure of its own invention."[14] Justice Douglas, dissenting, was even more critical, suggesting that the Court "let the Board 'have its cake and eat it too.'"[15] Rulemaking had advantages that adjudication did not, pushing "important issues into full public display," thus leading to "more responsible administrative action."[16]

---

[8] David L. Shapiro, "The Choice of Rulemaking or Adjudication in the Development of Administrative Policy," *Harvard Law Review* 78 (1965): 921–72.

[9] M. Beth Troiano, Note, "Rulemaking or Adjudication in Administrative Policy Formation: Rock versus Hard Place?" *Duquesne Law Review* 13 (1975): 967–82, 981.

[10] Robinson, "The Making of Administrative Policy," 512.

[11] Cornelius J. Peck, "The Atrophied Rule-Making Powers of the National Labor Relations Board," *Yale Law Journal* 70 (1961): 729–61, 761.

[12] Senate Judiciary Committee, *Amending the Administrative Procedure Act*, 89th Cong., 2nd sess., 1966, S. Rep. 1234, 10; *NLRB v. E&B Brewing Co., Inc.*, 276 F.2d 594 (6th Cir. 1960); *NLRB v. A.P.W. Products Co.*, 316 F.2d 899 (2d Cir. 1963); *NLRB v. Majestic Weaving Co., Inc.*, 355 F.2d 854 (2d Cir. 1966); *NLRB v. Penn Cork & Closures, Inc.*, 376 F.2d 52 (2d Cir. 1967); see also Peck, "A Critique of the National Labor Relations Board's Performance in Policy Formulation," 260.

[13] *NLRB v. Wyman-Gordon Co.*, 394 U.S. 759 (1969).

[14] *Id.* at 764.

[15] *Id.* at 776 (Douglas, J., dissenting).

[16] *Id.* at 779 (Douglas, J., dissenting).

These admonitions were increasingly heeded by existing agencies, which moved toward rulemaking as they clarified their authority in this area.[17] Congress also forcibly imposed the rulemaking model on health and environmental regulations as it drafted new legislation.[18] The Occupational Safety and Health Act, for instance, required the Secretary of Labor to promulgate standards for workplace safety and health, while the Endangered Species Act instructed the Secretary of the Interior to determine which species were threatened and then promulgate protective regulations accordingly.[19] Congress also provided more specific instructions to agencies than it had traditionally done; the Consumer Product Safety Commission was specifically instructed to consider certain factors, and the 1970 Clean Air Act amendments made explicit the reductions in emissions the EPA was to achieve and the time frame within which the EPA Administrator was to promulgate such standards.[20] Over time, as more agencies moved to rulemaking, reviewing courts began working out what procedure should look like in this area.[21]

In addition, in response to "capture" critiques, the public as a whole became part of the regulatory process. Americans no longer wanted to bind and weaken the administrative process; they wanted it to work better, and they wanted a part in it.[22] Thus, at the same time Congress protected interested parties' ability to participate by moving agencies toward the APA's existing rulemaking procedures, it expanded parties' ability to weigh in on agency policy.[23] Reflecting

[17] See Burrus and Teter, "Antitrust"; J. Skelly Wright, "The Courts and the Rulemaking Process: The Limits of Judicial Review," *Cornell Law Review* 59 (1974): 375–97; Schiller, "Rulemaking's Promise"; Pierce, "Rulemaking and the Administrative Procedure Act"; Morrison, "The Administrative Procedure Act"; *Permian Basin Area Rate Cases*, 390 U.S. 747 (1968); Merrill, "Capture Theory and the Courts."

[18] Sidney A. Shapiro and Robert L. Glicksman, "Congress, the Supreme Court, and the Quiet Revolution in Administrative Law," *Duke Law Journal* 1988 (1988): 819–78; Vogel, "The 'New' Social Regulation."

[19] See Lloyd Meeds, "A Legislative History of OSHA," *Gonzaga Law Review* 9 (1974): 327–48; George Cameron Coggins, "Conserving Wildlife Resources: An Overview of the Endangered Species Act of 1973," *North Dakota Law Review* 51 (1974): 315–40; Note, "Due Process and Employee Safety: Conflict in OSHA Enforcement Procedures," *Yale Law Journal* 84 (1975): 1380–93.

[20] Clean Air Amendments of 1970, Pub. L. No. 91–604, 84 Stat. 1676 (1970). See Sidney Edelman, "Air Pollution Abatement Procedures under the Clean Air Act," *Arizona Law Review* 10 (1968): 30–36; Note, "Clean Air Act Amendments of 1970: A Congressional Cosmetic," *Georgetown Law Journal* 61 (1972): 153–87; Roger D. Blair, "Problem of Pollution Standards: The Clean Air Act of 1970," *Land Economics* 49 (1973): 260–68; Rabin, "Federal Regulation in Historical Perspective"; Eisner, "Discovering Patterns in Regulatory History."

[21] *United States v. Florida East Railway Co.*, 410 U.S. 224 (1973); Antonin Scalia, "Vermont Yankee: The APA, the D.C. Circuit, and the Supreme Court," *Supreme Court Review* 1978 (1978): 345–409; Rabin, "Federal Regulation in Historical Perspective."

[22] Richard B. Stewart, "The Reformation of American Administrative Law," *Harvard Law Review* 88 (1975): 1667–813; Theodore J. Lowi, *The End of Liberalism: The Second Republic of the United States*, 2nd ed. (New York: W. W. Norton, 1979); Reuel E. Schiller, "Enlarging the Administrative Polity: Administrative Law and the Changing Definition of Pluralism, 1945–1970," *Vanderbilt Law Review* 53 (2000): 1389–453.

[23] Eisner, "Discovering Patterns in Regulatory History."

critiques of the closed nature of administrative decision making, these procedures sought to involve many more people in drafting and enforcing administrative policy. Statutory provisions allowed the public to compel agencies to
act – something officials inside the agencies had apparently been unable to
do. Several statutes included "citizen suit" provisions under which individuals could bring their own actions for enforcement. The 1970 Clean Air Act
amendments, for example, allowed individuals to sue someone for violating
an administrative standard or order, and even to sue the administrator "where
there is alleged a failure of the Administrator to perform any act or duty" that
he was required to perform.[24] The public was also included in a new form
of rulemaking at the Consumer Product Safety Commission, where Congress
called for rules to be formulated *outside* of the commission.[25] Once the CPSC
determined there was reason to consider a product dangerous, it was to give
notice in the Federal Register and to "include an invitation for any person" (at
least, anyone "technically competent") to draft a standard (at the commission's
expense, if necessary).[26] Once submitted to the CPSC, this proposed rule would
become the basis for proposed rulemaking, with another round of opportunity
for public comment.

More transparency across the administrative state was offered in the 1965
Freedom of Information Act, which the American Bar Assocation drafted in
response to frustration from the public, the press, and Congress. As the House
Special Subcommittee on Government Information reported, since the 1930s,
"a paper curtain has descended over the Federal Government" – based in "an
attitude which says that we, the officials, not you, the people, will determine
how much you are to be told about your own Government."[27] As the counsel
of the House Foreign Operations and Government Information subcommittee
wrote to the subcommittee's chairman, the relevant section of the APA "has
been turned into a vehicle to withhold information from the public." [28]

The Freedom of Information Act, which amended the APA's public information provisions, was signed by President Lyndon B. Johnson on July 4, 1966,
over agency resistance.[29] The act added significant new provisions to the APA,

---

[24] Clean Air Amendments of 1970, § 304(a).

[25] See Antonin Scalia and Frank Goodman, "Procedural Aspects of the Consumer Product Safety
Act," *UCLA Law Review* 20 (1973): 899–982; Judith A. Hermanson, "Regulatory Reform by
Statute: The Implications of the Consumer Product Safety Commission's 'Offeror System,'"
Public Administration Review 38 (1978): 151–55; Cathy Marie Johnson, "New Wine in New
Bottles: The Case of the Consumer Product Safety Commission," *Public Administration Review*
50 (1990): 74–81.

[26] Consumer Product Safety Act, Pub. L. No. 92–573, §§ 7(b), 7(d), 86 Stat. 1207, 1213.

[27] House Committee on Government Operations, *Availability of Information from Federal
Departments and Agencies: Twenty-Fifth Intermediate Report*, 84th Cong., 2nd sess., 1956, H.
Rep. 2947, 81.

[28] Benny L. Kass to Rep. John E. Moss, memorandum, Feb. 1, 1965, 1, Folder "Revision of APA
(Board of Consultants) [1964–67]," Box 3, McFarland Papers, UVA.

[29] See House Committee on Government Operations, *Clarifying and Protecting the Right of the
Public to Information*, 89th Cong., 2nd sess., 1966, H. Rep. 1497; Senate Judiciary Committee,

which already required agencies to publish their orders, opinions, rules, procedures, and organizational design in the Federal Register. Under the Freedom of Information Act, agencies were additionally required to open to the public their internal "statements of policy and interpretations" and their "administrative staff manuals and instructions to staff" – documents that, the House Committee on Government Operations noted, possessed "the force and effect of law in most cases" but had "been kept secret from the members of the public affected by the decisions."[30] Agencies also had to make their votes and parts of their records available to the public to read and copy. Whereas "matters of official record" had previously only been available "to persons properly and directly concerned," the amendment widened this category to "any person." In addition, where agencies had previously been able to keep material private "for good cause," the burden was now on an agency to defend its preference for secrecy. Most crucially, the act added a powerful enforcement mechanism, allowing citizens to present their case for access to a district court on an expedited basis. Although the Freedom of Information Act was not a wholesale reform of the APA along the lines proposed in earlier years, it signaled a new shift granting many more people access to the administrative process than the comparatively small group of businessmen and lawyers who had traditionally operated within it.[31]

Courts got into the act as well, allowing new challenges to agency action by broadening legal definitions of who constituted an "interested party."[32] Although judges had consistently required that parties seeking to participate in administrative action demonstrate an economic interest in the proceedings, this definition was broadened in the late 1960s to allow public interest groups to bring a wider array of views to bear on the agencies. In one notable case, a civil rights group was permitted to challenge the Federal Communications Commission's award of a broadcasting license to a Mississippi television station on the basis of its hostility to African Americans; in another, environmental values were recognized as an interest the Federal Power Commission could be obliged to consider.[33] Within a few years, the Supreme Court agreed

Subcommittee on Administrative Practice and Procedure, *Administrative Practice and Procedure*, 88th Cong., 2nd sess., 1964, S. Rep. 929, 5.

[30] Freedom of Information Act, Pub. L. No. 89–487, §§3(b)(B), 3(b)(C), 80 Stat. 250 (1966); House Committee on Government Operations, *Clarifying and Protecting the Right of the Public to Information*, 7.

[31] Hugh Heclo, "The Sixties' False Dawn"; Sidney M. Milkis, "Remaking Government Institutions in the 1970s: Participatory Democracy and the Triumph of Administrative Politics," in David Brian Robertson, ed., *Loss of Confidence: Politics and Policy in the 1970s*, 51–74 (University Park: Pennsylvania State University Press, 1998).

[32] *Greater Boston Television Corp. v. FCC*, 444 F.2d 841 (D.C. Cir. 1970); see also Schiller, "Enlarging the Administrative Polity"; Stewart, "The Reformation of Administrative Law"; Daniel J. Gifford, "The *Morgan* Cases: A Retrospective View," *Administrative Law Review* 30 (1978): 237–88.

[33] *Office of Communications of the United Church of Christ v. FCC*, 359 F.2d 994 (D.C. Cir. 1966); *Scenic Hudson Preservation Conference v. FPC*, 354 F.2d 608 (2d Cir. 1965); see also

that interests need not be solely economic; depending on the statute in question, aesthetic, conservational, and spiritual interests could also confer standing.[34] Outspoken former FCC Commissioner Nicholas Johnson, in *How to
Talk Back to Your Television Set* (1967), informed Americans that "you can,
and should, have a voice" and urged members of the public to get involved
in licensing renewals.[35] Through these new doctrines, public involvement
increased significantly.

Transparency and participation eventually joined with ethics in the
Government in the Sunshine Act of 1976, where Congress finally addressed
the problem of ex parte communications. President John F. Kennedy had discussed the issue in an April 1961 speech on the conflict-of-interest problem
that drew on James Landis's analysis of administrative misbehavior as "[c]anc-
ers" that "sweep through the entire process dulling the sense of public service
and destroying the confidence that the public must repose in public servants."[36]
Restricting officials' ex parte interactions entirely was impractical, as it would
"restrict their means of gathering that very expertise that was the reason for
the creation of the agency"; at the same time, of course, such interactions could
have insidious effects.[37] Kennedy emphasized the need to balance fairness and
expertise, asked Congress to require each agency and commission to develop
their own set of standards for ex parte contact, and subsequently issued an executive order spelling out appropriate behavior for many federal employees.[38]

Congress had similarly found the balance between useful communications
and unethical behavior difficult to strike. In 1961, the Senate Subcommittee
on Administrative Practice and Procedure found itself unable to articulate
exactly "where and how the line should be drawn" but concluded that something had to be done to combat the "belief that in many of the most fiercely
fought controversies the ultimate decision turned on matters not in the record
and against which the losing party could not defend himself."[39] At the same
time, Sen. Everett Dirksen (R–Ill.) argued, dissenting from the subcommittee's
report, "any attempt to properly influence a decision is salutary" given that the

Erwin G. Krasnow and Lawrence D. Longley, *The Politics of Broadcast Regulation*, 2nd ed.
(New York: St. Martin's Press, 1978); Steven D. Classen, *Watching Jim Crow: The Struggles over
Mississippi TV, 1955–1969* (Durham, NC: Duke University Press, 2004); Kay Mills, *Changing
Channels: The Civil Rights Case that Transformed Television* (Jackson: University Press of
Mississippi, 2004); Rabin, "Federal Regulation in Historical Perspective."

[34] See *Association of Data Processing Service Organizations, Inc. v. Camp*, 397 U.S. 150 (1970);
Sierra Club v. Morton, 405 U.S. 727 (1972).

[35] Nicholas Johnson, *How to Talk Back to Your Television Set* (Boston: Little, Brown & Co.,
1970), 205–06.

[36] James M. Landis, *Report on Regulatory Agencies to the President-Elect*, Senate Judiciary
Committee, Subcommittee on Administrative Practice and Procedure, 86th Cong., 2nd sess.,
1960, Committee Print, 36.

[37] Ibid., 15.

[38] Executive Order No. 10939, 26 Fed. Reg. 3951 (1961).

[39] Senate Judiciary Committee, Subcommittee on Administrative Practice and Procedure,
Administrative Practice and Procedure, 87th Cong., 1st Sess., 1961, S. Rep. 168, 4.

federal government's expansive role did "not guarantee that it will operate efficiently or fairly without a good bit of prodding."[40] The subcommittee resisted a broad legislative solution, suggesting instead that the president be authorized to promulgate an ethical code. Focusing on full disclosure as the key, members recommended criminal sanctions for nondisclosure and argued that "if such communications be made at all, they be made openly, so that all the parties to the case and the public can intelligently assess the considerations likely to govern the decision."[41]

The Administrative Conference took up the question of ex parte contacts with interested parties and in 1962 similarly recommended that each agency move to adopt a code.[42] Over the years, several agencies and commissions had developed their own ethical standards, and by 1962, most of the major regulatory agencies had established rules regarding ex parte contacts. However, no single overall standard existed.[43] By the end of the decade, pressure existed for better rules, aided by scathing reports offered by members of Ralph Nader's investigatory project that turned the spotlight on the clubbiness and ineffectiveness of multiple commissions and congressional committees.[44]

The 1976 Government in the Sunshine Act was a concession to these concerns. The statute called for a record of contacts between agency officials and outside parties in both adjudicatory and nonadjudicatory matters to be made public, and further moved toward transparency by opening up meetings at multiheaded agencies to the public and requiring agencies to retain transcripts, recordings, or minutes of closed meetings for public examination. The hearing examiner (by now an "administrative law judge") was empowered to challenge the neutrality of parties who had engaged in ex parte communications, and agencies were authorized to consider ex parte communications "sufficient grounds for a decision adverse to a party who has knowingly committed such violation or knowingly caused such violation to occur."[45]

[40] Ibid., 24.
[41] Ibid., 4.
[42] Administrative Conference of the United States, Committee on Internal Organization and Procedure, *Report on Recommendations for the Prohibition of Ex Parte Communications Between Persons Inside and Persons Outside the Agency* (Washington, DC: Government Printing Office, 1962).
[43] See Senate Committee on Labor and Public Welfare, Special Subcommittee on Establishment of Commission of Ethics in Government, *Ethical Standards in Government*, 82nd Cong., 1st sess., 1951, Committee Print, 51; "Report of Special Ad Hoc Committee on Code for Agency Conduct," *Administrative Law Bulletin* 11 (1958): 5–14.
[44] Edward F. Cox, Robert C. Fellmeth, and John E. Schulz, *The Nader Report On the Federal Trade Commission* (New York: Richard W. Baron Publishing Co., 1969); Robert C. Fellmeth, *The Interstate Commerce Omission: The Public Interest and the ICC* (New York: Grossman Publishers, 1970); David E. Price, *The Commerce Committees: A Study of the House and Senate Commerce Committees* (New York: Grossman Publishers, 1975).
[45] Government in the Sunshine Act, Pub. L. No. 94–409, § 4(c), 90 Stat. 1241, 1247 (1976); see also Robert W. Sloat, "Government in the Sunshine Act: A Danger of Overexposure," *Harvard Journal on Legislation* 14 (1977): 620–50; Note, "The Government in the Sunshine Act – An Overview," *Duke Law Journal* 1977 (1977): 565–92; Sherry Iris Brandt-Rauf, "Ex Parte

The concerns of the post–New Deal era thus continued to shape administrative law decades later, even as ideas of "public power" and the "public interest" came to include welfare and benefit programs and society-wide health, safety, and environmental protection. At the same time, experience changed the way in which participants talked about the administrative state and the kinds of reforms to which they gravitated. The administrative state would remain a key arena of policymaking, and the rules and regulations governing how administrators acted continued to serve as a battleground for parties who knew just how much was at stake.

The development of administrative governance in the 1940s, 1950s, and 1960s, during which time administrative procedures and organizational plans were battlegrounds for a variety of interested parties who sought to push and pull the administrative process in ways that would produce the results they desired, offers some useful lessons for scholars seeking to understand administrative law and the postwar era. First, as this political history demonstrates throughout, administrative law is not exclusively the creation of courts. In a period of judicial deference to administrative activity, administrative law underwent significant change as a result of pressure from other directions. Thus the administrative process cannot be understood independent of politics and historical context. However arcane and specialized they may appear from the outside, the rules and procedures guiding agencies' actions are of much practical interest for actors within the administrative arena. Nor do conceptions of "public power" and "private rights" exist in a vacuum; conversations about how to balance the two are loaded with parties' specific and shifting meanings about what the government is doing at any given time and whose rights are in danger as a result. The same is true, of course, for the organizational structures of agencies, where "efficiency" and "economy" are hardly neutral terms.[46]

This study thus suggests the need to bring together subjects commonly studied in isolation. The specifics of administrative law doctrines – usually discussed in law reviews – and the detailed organizational design of institutions – typically an area of public administration scholarship – need to be studied together, alongside historical and political science scholarship on congressional evolution, iron triangles, and political culture. Agencies are subject to the same democratic and interest group pressures as Congress, the White House, and the courts, *and* to novel pressures emerging from their independence, organizational design, and statutory authority. Never as strong or as independent as their opponents claimed, agencies and commissions after the New Deal formed

Contacts Under the Constitution and Administrative Procedure Act," *Columbia Law Review* 80 (1980): 379–94; William H. Allen, "The Durability of the Administrative Procedure Act," *Virginia Law Review* 72 (1986): 235–52; Morrison, "The Administrative Procedure Act: A Living and Responsive Law."
[46] Martin Shapiro, "APA: Past, Present, Future," *Virginia Law Review* 72 (1986): 447–92.

a partial, "hollow-core" state, reliant on democratic pressures and powerful friends to accomplish their statutory tasks.[47] Taking these varied influences seriously requires understanding each in its historical context, as the interests of congressional committees, White House reformers, judges, lawyers, and regulated interests changed over time and with experience.[48]

Moving beyond the standard narratives adds further complexity to our understanding of the administrative state. Agencies were certainly affected by regulated interests, but to argue that they were "captured" entirely misses the complicated role of multiple additional influences.[49] Discussions of "iron triangles," "iron rectangles," and "issue networks" bring in Congress and additional interest groups but still exclude the broader role of political culture, where, in this period, New Deal, wartime, and Cold War imperatives were at play.[50] In addition, models of administrative life cycles predicting inevitable decline suggest there is nothing historically specific about administrative weakness – a claim that historians should find immediately suspect.[51] Such confined models also fail to capture how agencies learned from one another (for good and for ill), and how outsiders learned about agencies (often as scandals at one agency caused problems at others).

Second, it is equally important to include administrative procedure in our understanding of political history. As the federal government took responsibility for more and more areas of American life and assigned this responsibility to departments, bureaus, agencies, and commissions, the procedures through which administrative officials made policy and the discretion they exercised in doing so became ever more important subjects of historical inquiry. Discussing the political economy of the postwar era without discussing the administrative agencies is an impossible task, and analysis of the law that governs these agencies cannot be left to the rarified pages of law reviews.[52] Debates over postwar administrative procedure were political debates over what role the regulated

---

[47] Ellis Hawley, "The New Deal State and the Anti-Bureaucratic Tradition," in Robert Eden, ed., *The New Deal and Its Legacy: Critique and Reappraisal*, 77–92 (New York: Greenwood Press, 1989), 87; see also Barry D. Karl, *The Uneasy State: The United States from 1915 to 1945* (Chicago: University of Chicago Press, 1983); Barry D. Karl, "Constitution and Central Planning: The Third New Deal Revisited," *Supreme Court Review* 1988 (1988): 163–201.

[48] Joanna L. Grisinger, "Law and the Administrative State," in Sally Hadden and Alfred L. Brophy, eds., *A Companion to American Legal History* (Hoboken, NJ: Wiley-Blackwell, forthcoming).

[49] Thomas K. McCraw, "Regulation in America: A Review Article," *Business History Review* 49 (1975): 159–83.

[50] See Hugh Heclo, "Issue Networks and the Executive Establishment," in Anthony King, ed., *The New American Political System*, 87–124 (Washington, DC: American Enterprise Institute for Public Policy Research, 1978); R. Shep Melnick, "The Politics of Partnership," *Public Administration Review* (1985): 653–60, 658.

[51] See, i.e., Marver H. Bernstein, *Regulating Business by Independent Commission* (Princeton, NJ: Princeton University Press, 1955).

[52] Schiller, "Enlarging the Administrative Polity"; Reuel E. Schiller, "The Administrative State, Front and Center: Studying Law and Administration in Postwar America," *Law and History Review* 26 (2008): 415–27; Karen M. Tani, "*Flemming v. Nestor*: Anticommunism, the Welfare State, and the Making of 'New Property,'" *Law and History Review* 26 (2008): 379–414.

parties and the political branches of the federal government would play in administrative governance, which has much to do with what the government would (and would not) do. At the same time, scholars also need to take seriously the powerful role of legalism, as rule-of-law thinking came to the agencies through legal language.[53]

In particular, in light of the strong hostility to bureaucracy in the post–New Deal era, the administrative process is a useful site to understand and complicate understandings of American anti-statism.[54] Opposition to bureaucratic governance and to statist control has multiple and conflicting characteristics, which include resistance to "bigness," high costs, aggressive governing, passivity, inefficiency, too much power, and too little transparency. Certainly the nature of resistance to the New Deal state differed in some important ways from hostility to Cold War bureaucracies, even as many of the same administrative tools were in use.[55] Identifying the qualities of anti-statism at any given point and examining how these qualities changed over time helps us understand what, exactly, Americans found objectionable about government control and what this suggests about their understanding of the state.

[53] William J. Novak, "The Legal Origins of the Modern American State," in Austin Sarat, Bryant Garth, and Robert A. Kagan, eds., *Looking Back at Law's Century*, 249–86 (Ithaca, NY: Cornell University Press, 2002); Schiller, "Enlarging the Administrative Polity"; Daniel Ernst, "*Morgan* and the New Dealers," *Journal of Policy History* 20 (2008): 447–81; William J. Novak, "The Myth of the 'Weak' American State," *American Historical Review* 113 (2008): 752–72; Daniel R. Ernst, "The Politics of Administrative Law: New York's Anti-Bureaucracy Clause and the O'Brian-Wagner Campaign of 1938," *Law and History Review* 27 (2009): 331–72.

[54] Novak, "The Myth of the 'Weak' American State."

[55] Hugh Heclo, "The Sixties' False Dawn: Awakenings, Movements, and Postmodern Policy-Making," in Brian Balogh, ed., *Integrating the Sixties: The Origins, Structures, and Legitimacy of Public Policy in a Turbulent Decade*, 34–63 (University Park: Pennsylvania State University Press, 1996); Horwitz, *Transformation of American Law*, chap. 8.

Works Cited

Manuscript Collections

National Archives, Washington, DC (NAB)

Records of the U.S. Senate, Record Group 46 (RG 46)
Records of Joint Committees of Congress, Record Group 128 (RG 128)
Records of the U.S. House of Representatives, Record Group 233 (RG 233)

National Archives, College Park, MD (NACP)

General Records of the Department of Justice, Record Group 60 (RG 60)
  Records of the Attorney General's Committee on Administrative Procedure (AGCAP)
Records of the Civil Service Commission, Record Group 146 (RG 146)
  Records of the Loyalty Review Board (LRB)
Records of the Federal Communications Commission, Record Group 173 (RG 173)
  Office of the Executive Director (OED)
Records of the Commission on Organization of the Executive Branch of Government,
    Record Group 264 (RG 264)
  Records of the Secretary's Office (SO)
  Records of the Office of the Executive Director (OED)
  Records of the Task Force on Independent Regulatory Commissions, 1948–49
    (TF: IRC)
  Records of the Task Force on Legal Services and Procedure, 1953–55 (TF: LSP)

Herbert Hoover Presidential Library, West Branch, IA (HHL)

Papers of Herbert Hoover, Post-Presidential Papers (HHPPP)
  Commission on Organization of the Executive Branch of the Government, 1947–49
    (HCI)
  Commissions on Organization of the Executive Branch of the Government, 1953–55
    (HCII)
Theodore G. Klumpp Papers (Klumpp Papers)
Neil MacNeil Papers (MacNeil Papers)
Courts Oulahan Papers (Oulahan Papers)

Charles B. Coates Oral History Interview, Nov. 14, 1967
Jarold Kieffer Oral History Interview, Oct. 10, 1979 and May 21, 1980
Don K. Price Oral History Interview, July 20, 1970

Harry S. Truman Presidential Library, Independence, MO (HSTL)

Papers of Harry S. Truman (HST Papers)
   White House Central Files: Official File (WHCF: OF)
   White House Bill File (WHBF)
Dean G. Acheson Papers (Acheson Papers)
J. Howard McGrath Papers (McGrath Papers)
James Webb Papers (Webb Papers)
Arthur S. Flemming Oral History Interview, June 19, 1989
James H. Rowe Jr. Oral History Interview, Jan. 15, 1970
Truman White House Oral History Interview, Feb. 20, 1980

Dwight D. Eisenhower Presidential Library, Abilene, KS (DDEL)

Dwight D. Eisenhower: Papers as President of the United States, 1953–1961 Ann
   Whitman File DDE Papers, AWF)
Dwight D. Eisenhower: Records as President, White House Central Files, 1953–61
   (DDE Papers, WHCF)
Papers of the U.S. President's Advisory Committee on Government Organization
   (PACGO Papers)
Arthur Flemming Papers (Flemming Papers)
Meyer Kestnbaum Papers (Kestnblaum Papers)

University of Virginia, Charlottesville, VA (UVA)

Homer Stille Cummings Papers, Mss. No. 9973, Special Collections, University of
   Virginia (Cummings Papers)
Carl McFarland Papers, Mss. No. 85–3, Special Collections, University of Virginia Law
   Library (McFarland Papers)

Northwestern University, Evanston, IL (NU)

Nathaniel L. Nathanson Files, Series 17/1, Northwestern University Archives (Nathanson
   Papers)

Clemson University, Clemson, SC (CU)

James F. Byrnes Papers, Mss. 90, Special Collections, Clemson University Libraries
   (Byrnes Papers)

Newspapers and Magazines

New York Times
Washington Post
Wall Street Journal
Chicago Daily Tribune

Los Angeles Times
Business Week
Fortune
Saturday Evening Post
Harper's Magazine
The New Republic

Reports and Government Publications

Advisory Panel on Labor-Management Relations Law. *Organization and Procedure of the National Labor Relations Board.* Senate Committee on Labor and Public Welfare. 86th Cong. 2nd sess. 1960. S. Doc. 81.

Administrative Conference of the United States. Committee on Internal Organization and Procedure. *Report on Recommendations for the Prohibition of Ex Parte Communications Between Persons Inside and Persons Outside the Agency.* Washington, DC: Government Printing Office, 1962.

American Bar Association. "Report of the Special Committee on Administrative Law." *Annual Report of the American Bar Association* 63 (1938): 331–68.

"Report of the Special Committee on Administrative Law." *Annual Report of the American Bar Association* 68 (1943): 249–53.

"Report of the Special Committee on Administrative Law." *Annual Report of the American Bar Association* 69 (1944): 471–73.

"Supplemental Report of the Special Committee on Administrative Law." *Annual Report of the American Bar Association* 70 (1945): 272–75.

"Proceedings of the House of Delegates." *Annual Report of the American Bar Association* 81 (1956): 369–423.

"Report of the Special Committee on Legal Services and Procedure." *Annual Report of the American Bar Association* 81 (1956): 491–534.

Attorney General's Committee on Administrative Procedure. *The Division of Public Contracts. Department of Labor. The Walsh–Healey Act. Monograph No. 1.* Washington, DC: Department of Justice, 1939.

Federal Communications Commission. Monograph No. 3. Washington, DC: Department of Justice, 1940.

Federal Alcohol Administration. Monograph No. 5. Washington, DC: Department of Justice, 1940.

The Administration of the Grain Standards Act. Department of Agriculture. Monograph No. 7. Washington, DC: Department of Justice, 1940.

War Department. Monograph No. 15. Washington, DC: Department of Justice, 1940.

National Labor Relations Board. Monograph No. 18. Washington, DC: Department of Justice, 1940.

Securities and Exchange Commission. Monograph No. 26. Washington, DC: Department of Justice, 1940.

Final Report. Washington, DC: Government Printing Office, 1941.

Board of Investigation and Research. *Report on Practices and Procedures of Governmental Control.* 78th Cong. 2nd sess. 1944. H. Doc. 678.

Commission on Organization of the Executive Branch of the Government (Hoover Commission I). *General Management of the Executive Branch.* Washington, DC: Government Printing Office, 1949.

Department of Commerce. Washington, DC: Government Printing Office, 1949.

The Independent Regulatory Commissions. Washington, DC: Government Printing Office, 1949.

Personnel Management. Washington, DC: Government Printing Office, 1949.

Concluding Report. Washington. DC: Government Printing Office, 1949.

Commission on Organization of the Executive Branch of the Government (Hoover Commission I). Committee on Independent Regulatory Commissions. *Task Force Report on Regulatory Commissions.* Washington, DC: Government Printing Office, 1949.

Burns, James MacGregor. *Staff Report on the United States Maritime Commission.* Washington, DC: Commission on Organization of the Executive Branch of the Government, 1948.

Farbach, Carl F. *Staff Report on the Securities and Exchange Commission.* Washington, DC: Commission on Organization of the Executive Branch of the Government, 1948.

Galenson, Walter. *Staff Report on the National Labor Relations Board.* Washington, DC: Commission on Organization of the Executive Branch of the Government, 1948.

Golub, William W. *Staff Report on the Federal Communications Commission.* Washington, DC: Commission on Organization of the Executive Branch of the Government, 1948.

Pritchett, C. Herman. *Staff Report on the Federal Power Commission.* Washington, DC: Commission on Organization of the Executive Branch of the Government, 1948.

Sweeney, Edward C. *Staff Report on the Civil Aeronautics Board.* Washington, DC: Commission on Organization of the Executive Branch of the Government, 1948.

Till, Irene. *Staff Report on the Federal Trade Commission.* Washington, DC: Commission on Organization of the Executive Branch of the Government, 1948.

Williams, Ernest W. *Staff Report on the Interstate Commerce Commission.* Washington, DC: Commission on Organization of the Executive Branch of the Government, 1948.

Commission on Organization of the Executive Branch of the Government (Hoover Commission II).

Business Enterprises. Washington, DC: Government Printing Office, 1955.

Food and Clothing in the Government. Washington, DC: Government Printing Office, 1955.

Legal Services and Procedure. Washington, DC: Government Printing Office, 1955.

Lending, Guaranteeing, and Insurance Activities. Washington, DC: Government Printing Office, 1955.

Transportation. Washington, DC: Government Printing Office, March 1955.

Commission on Organization of the Executive Branch of the Government (Hoover Commission II). Task Force on Legal Services and Procedure. *Report on Legal Services and Procedure.* Washington, DC: Government Printing Office, 1955.

President's Committee on Administrative Management. *Administrative Management in the Government of the United States.* Washington, DC: Government Printing Office, 1937.

President's Conference on Administrative Procedure. *Report of the Conference on Administrative Procedure.* Washington, DC: Government Printing Office, 1955.

President's Conference on Administrative Procedure. Committee on Uniform Rules. *Report of the Committee on Uniform Rules.* Washington, DC: President's Conference on Administrative Procedure, 1954.

President's Conference on Administrative Procedure. Committee on Hearing Officers. *Appointment and Status of Federal Hearing Officers* (Kintner Report). Washington, DC: President's Conference on Administrative Procedure, 1954.

Appointment and Status of Federal Hearing Officers (Lester Report). Washington, DC: President's Conference on Administrative Procedure, 1954.

U.S. Congress. House. Committee on Appropriations. *Report.* 78th Cong. 1st sess. 1943. H. Rep. 448.

U.S. Congress. House. Conference Committee. *Labor-Management Relations Act.* 80th Cong. 1st sess. 1947. H. Rep. 510.

U.S. Congress. House. Committee on Education and Labor. *Labor-Management Relations Act.* 80th Cong. 1st sess. 1947. H. Rep. 245.

U.S. Congress. House. Committee on Education and Labor. Subcommittee on National Labor Relations Board. *Administration of the Labor-Management Relations Act by the NLRB.* 87th Cong. 1st sess. 1961. Committee Print.

U.S. Congress. House. Committee on Expenditures in the Executive Departments. *Reorganization Act of 1949.* 81st Cong. 1st sess. 1949. H. Rep. 23.

Inquiry into the Operations of the Maritime Commission: Fourth Intermediate Report. 81st Cong. 1st sess. 1949. H. Rep. 1423.

Reorganization Plan No. 2 of 1949. 81st Cong. 1st sess. 1949. H. Rep. 1204.

Reorganization of Government Agencies: Hearings on H.R. 1569. 81st Cong. 1st sess. 1949.

Reorganization Plan No. 7 of 1950. 81st Cong. 2nd sess. 1950. H. Rep. 1971.

Further Inquiry into the Operations of the Maritime Commission: Sixth Intermediate Report. 81st Cong. 2nd sess. 1950. H. Rep. 2104.

U.S. Congress. House. Committee on Government Operations. *Availability of Information from Federal Departments and Agencies: Twenty-Fifth Intermediate Report.* 84th Cong. 2nd sess. 1956. H. Rep. 2947.

Federal Role in Aviation. 84th Cong. 2nd sess. 1956. H. Rep. 2949.

Summary of the Objectives, Operations, and Results of the Commissions on Organization of the Executive Branch of the Government. 88th Cong. 1st sess. 1963. Committee Print.

Clarifying and Protecting the Right of the Public to Information. 89th Cong. 2nd sess. 1966. H. Rep. 1497.

U.S. Congress. House. Committee on Interstate and Foreign Commerce. *Study of the Securities and Exchange Commission.* 82nd Cong. 2nd sess. 1952. H. Rep. 2508.

Regulation of Broadcasting: Half a Century of Government Regulation of Broadcasting and the Need for Further Legislative Action. 85th Cong. 2nd sess. 1958. Subcommittee Print.

Independent Regulatory Agencies Act of 1960. 86th Cong. 2nd sess. 1960. H. Rep. 2070.

U.S. Congress. House. Committee on Interstate and Foreign Commerce. Special Subcommittee on Investigation of Restrictions on Brand Names and Newsprint.

Brand Names and Newsprint: Interim Report. 78th Cong. 1st sess. 1943. H. Rep. 808. Pt. 1.

Brand Names and Newsprint: Hearings. Pt. 1. 78th Cong. 1st Sess. 1943.

U.S. Congress. House. Committee on Interstate and Foreign Commerce. Special Subcommittee on Legislative Oversight. *Independent Regulatory Commissions.* 85th Cong. 2nd sess. 1959. H. Rep. 2711.

Independent Regulatory Commissions. 86th Cong. 2nd sess. 1961. H. Rep. 2238.

U.S. Congress. House. Committee on Interstate and Foreign Commerce. Subcommittee on Legislative Oversight. *Federal Communications Commission: Interim Report* 85th Cong. 2nd sess. 1958. H. Rep. 1602.

U.S. Congress. House. Committee on the Judiciary. *Providing for the More Expeditious Settlement of Disputes with the United States and for Other Purposes.* 76th Cong. 1st sess. 1939. H. Rep. 1149.

U.S. Congress. House. Committee on the Judiciary. Subcommittee to Investigate the Department of Justice. *Investigation of the Department of Justice.* 83rd Cong. 1st sess. 1953. H. Rep. 1079.

U.S. Congress. House. Committee on the Judiciary. Subcommittee on Antitrust. *The Airlines Industry.* 85th Cong. 2nd sess. 1956. H. Rep. 1328.

U.S. Congress. House. Committee on Post Office and Civil Service. *Code of Ethics for Government Service.* 85th Cong. 2nd sess. 1958. H. Rep. 1208.

U.S. Congress. House. Committee on Small Businesses. *Final Report on the Wartime Problems of Southern Industry.* 78th Cong. 1st sess. 1943. H. Rep. 126.

U.S. Congress. House. Committee on Ways and Means. *Internal Revenue Investigation.* 82nd Cong. 2d Sess. 1953. H. Rep. 2518.

U.S. Congress. House. Committee on Ways and Means. Subcommittee on the Administration of the Internal Revenue Laws. *Internal Revenue Investigation: Report by Mr. King.* 82nd Cong. 2nd sess. 1952. Subcommittee Print.

Internal Revenue Investigation: Report by Mr. Kean. 82nd Cong. 2nd sess. 1953. Subcommittee Print.

U.S. Congress. House. Select Committee to Investigate the Federal Communications Commission. *Investigation of the Federal Communications Commission: Final Report.* 78th Cong. 2nd sess. 1945. H. Rep. 2095.

U.S. Congress. House. Select Committee to Investigate the Federal Communications Commission. *Final Report.* 80th Cong. 2nd sess. 1949. H. Rep. 2479.

U.S. Congress. House. Select Committee to Investigate Acts of Executive Agencies Beyond the Scope of Their Authority. *To Investigate Executive Agencies.* 78th Cong. 1st sess. 1943. H. Rep. 699. Pt. 1.

U.S. Congress. House. Select Committee to Investigate Executive Agencies. *Second Intermediate Report.* 78th Cong. 1st sess. 1943. H. Rep. 862.

Sixth Intermediate Report. 78th Cong. 2nd sess. 1944. H. Rep. 1797.

Seventh Intermediate Report. 78th Cong. 2nd sess. 1944. H. Rep. 1912.

U.S. Congress. House. Select Committee on Lobbying Activities. *General Interim Report.* 81st Cong. 2nd sess. 1950. H. Rep. 3138.

U.S. Congress. House. Select Committee on Small Business. Subcommittee No. 1 on Regulatory Agencies and Commissions. *The Organization and Procedures of the Federal Regulatory Commissions and Agencies and their Effect on Small Business.* 84th Cong. 2nd sess. 1956. H. Rep. 2967. Pts. 1–4.

U.S. Congress. House. Special Committee to Investigate Executive Agencies. *To Investigate Executive Agencies: Hearings.* pt. 1. 78th Cong. 1st Sess. 1943.

U.S. Congress. House. Special Committee to Investigate the National Labor Relations Board. *Report on the Investigation of the National Labor Relations Board: Intermediate Report.* 76th Cong. 3rd sess. 1940. H. Rep. 1902. Pt. 1.

Minority Views on the Investigation of the National Labor Relations Board: Intermediate Report. 76th Cong. 3rd sess. 1940. H. Rep. 1902. Pt. 2.

National Labor Relations Act. 76th Cong. 3rd sess. 1940. H. Rep. 3109. Pt. 1.

U.S. Congress. Joint Committee on Labor-Management Relations. *Labor-Management Relations.* 80th Cong. 2nd sess. 1948. S. Rep. 986 and S. Rep. 986, Pt. 3.

U.S. Congress. Joint Committee on the Organization of Congress. *The Organization of Congress – Symposium on Congress by Members of Congress and Others.* 79th Cong. 1st sess. 1945. Committee Print.

Organization of Congress: Hearings. 79th Cong. 1st sess. 1945.

Organization of the Congress: First Progress Report. 79th Cong. 1st sess. 1945. S. Doc. 36.

Organization of the Congress. 79th Cong. 2nd sess. 1946. S. Rep. 1011.

U.S. Congress. Special Committee on the Organization of Congress. *Legislative Reorganization Act of 1946.* 79th Cong. 2nd Sess. 1946. S. Rep. 1400.

U.S. Congress. Joint Committee on Reduction of Nonessential Federal Expenditures. *Reduction of Nonessential Federal Expenditures. Additional Report.* 78th Cong. 1st sess. 1943. S. Doc. 4.

U.S. Congress. Senate. Committee on Banking and Currency. *Emergency Price Control Act of 1942.* 77th Cong. 2nd sess. 1942. S. Rep. 931.

Extending Price Control Act and Stabilization Act. 78th Cong. 2nd sess. 1944. S. Rep. 922.

Operations of the Reconstruction Finance Corporation. 80th Cong. 2nd Sess. 1948. S. Rep. 974.

Study of Reconstruction Finance Corporation: Interim Report, Texmass Petroleum Co. Loan. 81st Cong. 2nd sess. 1950. S. Rep. 1689. Pt. 1.

Study of Reconstruction Finance Corporation: Interim Report, Lustron Corp. – Transportation Contract. 81st Cong. 2nd sess. 1950. S. Rep. 1689. Pt. 2.

Study of Reconstruction Finance Corporation: Interim Report. Favoritism and Influence. 82nd Cong. 1st sess. 1951. S. Rep. 76.

Study of Reconstruction Finance Corporation and Proposed Amendment of RFC Act. 82nd Cong. 1st sess. 1951. S. Rep. 649.

U.S. Congress. Senate. Committee on Expenditures in the Executive Departments. *Legislative Reorganization Act of 1946: Hearings on Evaluation of Legislative Reorganization Act of 1946.* 80th Cong. 2nd sess. 1948.

Progress on Hoover Commission Recommendations. 81st Cong. 1st sess. 1949. S. Rep. 1158.

Action on Hoover Commission Reports. 81st Cong. 2nd sess. 1950. S. Rep. 2581.

Reorganizations in the Executive Branch of the Government. 81st Cong. 2nd sess. 1950. S. Rep. 2680.

Activities of the Senate Committee on Expenditures in the Executive Departments. 82nd Cong. 1st sess. 1951. S. Rep. 1.

Organization and Operation of Congress: Hearings on Evaluation of the Effects of Laws Enacted to Reorganize the Legislative Branch of the Government. 82nd Cong. 1st sess. 1951.

U.S. Congress. Senate. Committee on Expenditures in the Executive Departments. Subcommittee on Investigations. *Investigation of Federal Employees Loyalty Program: Interim Report.* 80th Cong. 2nd sess. 1948. S. Rep. 1775.

First Annual Report. 81st Cong. 1st sess. 1949. S. Rep. 5.

Employment of Homosexuals and Other Sex Perverts in Government: Interim Report. 81st Cong. 2nd sess. 1950. S. Rep. 241.

The 5-Percenter Investigation: Interim Report. 81st Cong. 2nd sess. 1950. S. Rep. 1232.

American Lithofold Corp. William M. Boyle Jr. Guy George Gabrielson: Interim Report. 82nd Cong. 2nd sess. 1952. S. Rep. 1142.

U.S. Congress. Senate. Committee on Government Operations. *50th Anniversary: History 1921–1971.* 92nd Cong. 1st sess. 1971. S. Doc. 92–31.

U.S. Congress. Senate. Committee on Government Operations. Permanent Subcommittee on Investigations. *Annual Report of the Committee on Government Operations.* 83rd Cong. 2nd sess. 1954. S. Rep. 881.

Annual Report. 84th Cong. 2nd sess. 1956. S. Rep. 1444.

U.S. Congress. Senate. Committee on Government Operations. Subcommittee on Reorganization. *Action by the Congress and the Executive Branch of the Government on the Second Hoover Commission Reports, 1955–57.* 85th Cong. 2nd sess. 1958. S. Rep. 1289.

U.S. Congress. Senate. Committee on Interstate and Foreign Commerce. *Communication Act Amendments of 1948.* 80th Cong. 2nd sess. 1948. S. Rep. 1567.

Communications Study. 81st Cong. 1st sess. 1949. S. Rep. 49.

Transportation Act of 1958. 85th Cong. 2nd sess. 1958. S. Rep. 1647.

U.S. Congress. Senate. Committee on the Judiciary. *Report on S. 915: Providing for the More Expeditious Settlement of Disputes with the United States and for Other Purposes.* 76th Cong. 1st sess. 1939. S. Rep. 442.

Continuing the Authority for a Study into the Legal and Constitutional Authority for the Issuance of Executive Orders of the President and of Departmental Regulations, and Increasing the Limit of Expenditures. 79th Cong. 1st sess. 1945. S. Rep. 7.

Report on S.7. A Bill to Improve the Administration of Justice by Prescribing Fair Administrative Procedure. 79th Cong. 1st sess. 1945. S. Rep. 752.

Administrative Procedure Act: Legislative History. 79th Cong. 2nd sess. 1946. S. Doc. 248.

Memorandum on Proceedings Involving Contempt of Congress and Its Committees. 80th Cong. 2nd Sess. 1948. Committee Print.

Hearing Examiner Regulations Promulgated under Section 11 of the Administrative Procedure Act. 82nd Cong. 1st sess. 1951. S. Doc. 82.

Presidential Appointment of Trial Examiners. 83rd Cong. 2nd sess. 1954. S. Rep. 2199.

Power Policy Dixon Yates Contract: Staff Report of the Subcommittee on Antitrust and Monopoly on Investigation Concerning the Charges of Monopolistic Influences in the Power Industry. 84th Cong. 2nd sess. 1956. Committee Print.

Amending the Administrative Procedure Act. 89th Cong. 2nd sess. 1966. S. Rep. 1234.

U.S. Congress. Senate. Committee on the Judiciary. Subcommittee on S. 674, S. 675 and S. 918. *Administrative Procedure: Hearings on S. 674, S. 675, and S. 918.* 77th Cong. 1st sess. 1941. Pts. 1 and 2.

U.S. Congress. Senate. Committee on the Judiciary. Subcommittee on Administrative Practice and Procedure. *Administrative Practice and Procedure.* 86th Cong. 2nd sess. 1960. S. Rep. 1484.

Administrative Practice and Procedure. 87th Cong. 2nd sess. 1962. S. Rep. 1480.

Administrative Practice and Procedure. 88th Cong. 2nd sess. 1964. S. Rep. 929.

U.S. Congress. Senate. Committee on the Judiciary. Subcommittee to Investigate the Administration of the Internal Security Act and Other Internal Security Laws. *Interlocking Subversion in Government Departments.* 83rd Cong. 1st sess. 1953. Committee Print.

U.S. Congress. Senate. Committee on the Judiciary. Subcommittee on Administrative Practice and Procedure. *Commission on Ethics in Government.* 82nd Cong. 1st Sess. 1951. S. Rep. 933.

Administrative Practice and Procedure. 87th Cong. 1st sess. 1961. S. Rep. 168.

U.S. Congress. Senate. Committee on Labor and Public Welfare. Special Subcommittee on the Establishment of a Commission of Ethics in Government. *Ethical Standards in Government.* 82nd Cong. 1st sess. 1951. Committee Print.

Establishment of a Commission on Ethics in Government: Hearings. 82nd Cong. 1st Sess. 1951.

U.S. Congress. Senate. Committee on Post Office and Civil Service. *Code of Ethics for Government Service.* 85th Cong. 2nd sess. 1958. S. Rep. 1812.

U.S. Congress. Senate. Committee on Rules. *Establishing a Joint Committee on the Organization of the Congress.* 78th Cong. 2nd sess. 1944. S. Rep. 1034.

U.S. Congress. Senate. Committee on Rules and Administration. Subcommittee on Rules. *Rules of Procedure for Senate Investigating Committees.* 83rd Cong. 2nd sess. 1954. Subcommittee Print.

U.S. Congress. Senate. *Rules of Procedure for Senate Investigating Committees: Hearings Hearings on S. Res. 65, S. Res. 146, S. Res. 233, S. Res. 249, S. Res. 253, S. Res. 256, S. Con. Res. 11, and S. Con. Res. 86.* Pt. 5. 83rd Cong. 2nd Sess. 1954.

U.S. Congress. Senate. Select Committee to Investigate the Executive Agencies of the Government. "Investigation of Executive Agencies of the Government." 75th Cong. 1st Sess. S. Rep. 1275.

U.S. Congress. Senate. Special Committee Investigating the National Defense Program. *Investigation of the National Defense Program.* 77th Cong. 2nd sess. 1942. Sen. Rep. 480. Pt. 13.

U.S. Congress. Senate. Special Committee to Investigate Organized Crime in Interstate Commerce. *Organized Crime in Interstate Commerce: Final Report.* 82nd Cong. 1st sess. 1951. S. Rep. 725.

U.S. Congress. Senate. Special Committee to Study Problems of American Small Business. *American Small Business.* 77th Cong. 2nd sess. 1942. S. Rep. 479. Pts. 2–4.

U.S. Department of Commerce. *Modern Transport Policy.* Washington, DC: U.S. Department of Commerce, 1956.

U.S. Department of Justice. *Attorney General's Manual on the Administrative Procedure Act.* Washington, DC: Government Printing Office, 1947.

Annual Report of the Office of Administrative Procedure. Washington, DC: Office of Administrative Procedure, 1957.

U.S. Civil Service Commission. *65th Annual Report.* 81st Cong. 1st sess. 1948. H. Doc. 13.

Federal Power Commission. *Twenty-Sixth Annual Report of the Federal Power Commission.* 80th Cong. 1st sess. 1947. H. Doc. 23.

Interstate Commerce Commission. *60th Annual Report of the Interstate Commerce Commission.* 80th Cong. 1st sess. 1946. H. Doc. 14.
  63rd Annual Report. 81st Cong. 2nd sess. 1949. H. Doc. 400.
  65th Annual Report. 82nd Cong. 2nd sess. 1951. H. Doc. 280.
Office of Price Administration. *Rationing, Why and How.* Washington, DC: Government Printing Office, 1942.
Securities and Exchange Commission. *12th Annual Report of the Securities and Exchange Commission.* 80th Cong. 1st sess. 1947. H. Doc. 26.

Books and Articles

"Grade Labeling: A Study of Reaction in Action." *Lawyers Guild Review* 3 (Sept.–Oct. 1943): 23–30.
"I.C.C. View of Procedure Act." *Administrative Law Bulletin* 1 (1949): 2–3.
"Impartiality Is Essential." *American Bar Association Journal* 33 (1947): 148–49.
"Investigations in Operation: House Subcommittee on Monopoly Power." *University of Chicago Law Review* 18 (1951): 658–61.
Note. "Administrative Penalty Regulations." *Columbia Law Review* 43 (1943): 213–18.
Note. "Aftermath of the *Morgan* Decision." *Iowa Law Review* 25 (1940): 622–38.
Note. "Clean Air Act Amendments of 1970: A Congressional Cosmetic." *Georgetown Law Journal* 61 (1972): 153–87.
Note. "Constitutional Limitations on the Un-American Activities Committee." *Columbia Law Review* 47 (1947): 416–31.
Note. "Due Process and Employee Safety: Conflict in OSHA Enforcement Procedures." *Yale Law Journal* 84 (1975): 1380–93.
Note. "Effect of the Taft-Hartley and Administrative Procedure Acts on Scope of Review of Administrative Findings." *Indiana Law Journal* 26 (1951): 406–19.
Note. "Ex Parte Contacts With the Federal Communications Commission." *Harvard Law Review* 73 (1960): 1178–99.
Note. "The Government in the Sunshine Act – An Overview." *Duke Law Journal* (1977): 565–92.
Note. "Hearing Examiner Status: A Recurrent Problem in Administrative Law." *Indiana Law Journal* 30 (1954): 86–106.
Note. "The Impact of the Federal Administrative Procedure Act on Deportation Proceedings." *Columbia Law Review* 49 (1949): 73–87.
Note. "Implications of the Second Morgan Decision." *Illinois Law Review* 33 (1938): 227–30.
Note. "Investigations in Operation: House Select Committee on Lobbying Activities." *University of Chicago Law Review* 18 (1951): 647–57.
Note. "Investigations in Operation: House Subcommittee on Monopoly Power." *University of Chicago Law Review* 18 (1951): 658–61.
Note. "Judicial Control of Administrative Procedure: The *Morgan* Cases." *Harvard Law Review* 52 (1939): 509–15.
Note. "The Progress of Federal Agency Reorganization under the Kennedy Administration." *Virginia Law Review* 48 (1962): 300–77.
Note. "Rationing of Consumer Goods." *Columbia Law Review* 42 (1942): 1170–81.
Note. "Substantive Rulemaking and the FTC." *Fordham Law Review* 42 (1973): 178–96.

"Pending Proposals to Amend the Federal Administrative Procedure Act: An Analysis of S. 518." *Administrative Law Review* 20 (1968): 185–236.

"Renewal and Amendment of Price Control Legislation." *Lawyers Guild Review* 4 (Jan.-Feb. 1944): 24–39.

Recent Case. *George Washington Law Review* 5 (1936): 119–20.

Recent Case. *George Washington Law Review* 7 (1938): 110–15.

Recent Case Note. *Indiana Law Journal* 14 (1938): 164–66.

Recent Case Note. *St. John's Law Review* 13 (1938): 138–41.

Recent Decision. *Columbia Law Review* 36 (1936): 1156–58.

"Report of Special Ad Hoc Committee on Code for Agency Conduct." *Administrative Law Bulletin* 11 (1958): 5–14.

"Report of Aviation Facilities Study Group to the Budget Bureau, December 31, 1955." *Journal of Air Law and Commerce* 22 (1955): 475–83.

"Symposium on Administrative Law." *American Law School Review* 9 (1939): 139–84.

"The 12 ABA Recommendations for Improved Procedures for Federal Agencies." *Administrative Law Review* 24 (1972): 389–411.

"The 350 Hearing Examiners: Chairman Wiley Asks Open Choices for Fitness." *American Bar Association Journal* 33 (1947): 421–22.

Abbott, Roger S. "The Federal Loyalty Program: Background and Problems." *American Political Science Review* 42 (1948): 486–99.

Abels, Jules. *The Truman Scandals*. Chicago: Henry Regnery, 1956.

Aberbach, Joel D. *Keeping a Watchful Eye: The Politics of Congressional Oversight*. Washington, DC: Brookings Institution, 1990.

Ablard, Charles D. "Ex Parte Contacts with Federal Administrative Agencies." *American Bar Association Journal* 47 (1961): 473–76.

Adams, Sherman. *Firsthand Report: The Story of the Eisenhower Administration*. New York: Harper & Brothers, 1961.

Adler, E. Scott. *Why Congressional Reforms Fail: Reelection and the House Committee System*. Chicago: University of Chicago Press, 2002.

Advisory Committee on Procedure before Administrative Agencies. "Judicial Conference Study of Administrative Procedure." *I.C.C. Practitioners' Journal* 19 (Oct. 1951): 3–13.

Aikin, Charles. "Task Force: Methodology." *Public Administration Review* 9 (1949): 241–51.

Aikin, Charles, and Louis W. Koenig. "Introduction." *American Political Science Review* 43 (1949): 933–40.

Aidlin, Joseph W. "The Constitutionality of the 1942 Price Control Act." *California Law Review* 30 (1942): 648–54.

Aitchison, Clyde B. "Reforming the Administrative Process." *George Washington Law Review* 7 (1939): 703–25.

Alexander, Charles C. *Holding the Line: The Eisenhower Era, 1952–1961*. Bloomington: Indiana University Press, 1975.

Allen, William H. "The Durability of the Administrative Procedure Act." *Virginia Law Review* 72 (1986): 235–52.

Allen, Wycliffe. "I Am a Bureaucrat." *Public Administration Review* 11 (1951): 116–18.

American Political Science Association. Committee on Congress. *The Reorganization of Congress*. Washington, DC: Public Affairs Press, 1945.

Appleby, Paul H. "Toward Better Public Administration." *Public Administration Review* 7 (1947): 93–99.

Armstrong, J. Sinclair. "Congress and the Securities and Exchange Commission." *Virginia Law Review* 45 (1959): 795–816.

Arnold, Peri E. *Making the Managerial Presidency: Comprehensive Reorganization Planning, 1905–1996.* 2nd ed. Lawrence: University Press of Kansas, 1998.

Arpaia, Anthony F. "The Independent Agency – A Necessary Instrument of Democratic Government." *Harvard Law Review* 69 (1956): 483–506.

Association of the Bar of the City of New York. *Report of the Special Committee on the Federal Loyalty-Security Program.* New York: Dodd, Mead & Co., 1956.

Association of the Bar of the City of New York. "Congressional Oversight of Administrative Agencies: A Report of the Committee on Administrative Law." *Record of the Association of the Bar of the City of New York* 5 (1950): 11–29.

Auerbach, Carl A. "Some Thoughts on the Hector Memorandum." *Wisconsin Law Review* 1960 (1960): 183–96.

Auerbach, Jerold S. "The La Follette Committee: Labor and Civil Liberties in the New Deal." *Journal of American History* 51 (1964): 435–459.

Unequal Justice: Lawyers and Social Change in Modern America. New York: Oxford University Press, 1976.

Backman, Jules. "Wartime Price Control." *Annual Survey of American Law* 1943 (1943): 325–42.

Baker, Warren E. "Policy by Rule or Ad Hoc Approach – Which Should It Be?" *Law and Contemporary Problems* 22 (1957): 658–71.

Balogh, Brian. "Reorganizing the Organizational Synthesis: Federal-Professional Relations in Modern America." *Studies in American Political Development* 5 (1991): 119–72.

Chain Reaction: Expert Debate and Public Participation in American Commercial Nuclear Power, 1945–1975. New York: Cambridge University Press, 1991.

A Government Out of Sight: The Mystery of National Authority in Nineteenth-Century America. Cambridge: Cambridge University Press, 2009.

Bandy, William R. Comment. "Notice and Opportunity to Be Heard in Price Control Proceedings." *Texas Law Review* 20 (1942): 577–89.

Bar Association of San Francisco. *Committee Report on Office of Administrative Hearings of the Office of Price Administration.* San Francisco: Bar Association of San Francisco, 1943.

Barnouw, Erik. *The Golden Web: A History of Broadcasting in the United States,* vol. II, *1933 to 1953.* New York: Oxford University Press, 1968.

The Image Empire: A History of Broadcasting in the United States, vol. III – *from 1953.* New York: Oxford University Press, 1970.

Bartels, Andrew H. "The Office of Price Administration and the Legacy of the New Deal, 1939–1946." *Public Historian* 5 (1983): 5–29.

Barth, Alan. *Government by Investigation.* reprint ed. Clifton, NJ: Augustus M. Kelley Publishers, 1973 (originally 1955).

Baughman, James L. *Television's Guardians: The FCC and the Politics of Programming, 1958–1967.* Knoxville: University of Tennessee Press, 1985.

Baum, Daniel J. "Reorganization, Delay and the Federal Trade Commission." *Administrative Law Review* 15 (1963): 92–110.

Baxter, Randolph W. "'Homo-Hunting' in the Early Cold War: Senator Kenneth Wherry and the Homophobic Side of McCarthyism." *Nebraska History* 84 (2003): 118–32.

Behrman, Bradley. "Civil Aeronautics Board." In James Q. Wilson, ed., *The Politics of Regulation* (75–120). New York: Basic Books, 1980.

Bell, Jonathan. *The Liberal State on Trial: The Cold War and American Politics in the Truman Years*. New York: Columbia University Press, 2004.

Benjamin, Robert M. "A Lawyer's View of Administrative Procedure – The American Bar Association Program." *Law and Contemporary Problems* 26 (1961): 203–37.

Bentley, Amy. *Eating for Victory: Food Rationing and the Politics of Domesticity*. Urbana: University of Illinois Press, 1998.

Berkowitz, Edward, and Kim McQuaid. "Welfare Reform in the 1950s." *Social Service Review* 54 (1980): 45–58.

Berle, A. A. Jr. "The Expansion of American Administrative Law." *Harvard Law Review* 30 (1917): 430–48.

Bernstein, Barton J. "The Removal of War Production Board Controls on Business, 1944–1946." *Business History Review* 39 (1965): 243–60.

"Clash of Interests: The Postwar Battle between the Office of Price Administration and the Department of Agriculture." *Agricultural History* 41 (1967): 45–57.

"The Debate on Industrial Reconversion: The Protection of Oligopoly and Military Control of the Economy." *American Journal of Economics and Sociology* 26 (1967): 159–72.

Bernstein, Marver H. "The Loyalty of Federal Employees." *Western Political Quarterly* 2 (1949): 254–64.

"The Politics of Adjudication." *Journal of Politics* 16 (1954): 299–323.

Regulating Business by Independent Commission. Princeton, NJ: Princeton University Press, 1955.

Bernstein, Merton C. "The NLRB's Adjudication-Rule Making Dilemma under the Administrative Procedure Act." *Yale Law Journal* 79 (1970): 571–622.

Bibby, John F. "Committee Characteristics and Legislative Oversight of Administration." *Midwest Journal of Political Science* 10 (1966): 78–98.

"Oversight and the Need for Congressional Reform." In Melvin R. Laird, ed., *Republican Papers* (476–88). New York: Frederick A. Praeger, 1968.

Biddle, Francis. "Subversives in Government." *Annals of the American Academy of Political and Social Science* (1955): 51–61.

Blachly, Frederick F. and Miriam E. Oatman. "Sabotage of the Administrative Process." *Public Administration Review* 6 (1946): 213–27.

Blair, Roger D. " Problem of Pollution Standards: The Clean Air Act of 1970." *Land Economics* 49 (1973): 260–68.

Blum, John Morton. *V Was for Victory: Politics and American Culture During World War II*. New York: Harcourt Brace Jovanovich, 1976.

Bontecou, Eleanor. *The Federal Loyalty-Security Program*. Ithaca, NY: Cornell University Press, 1953.

Bowles, Chester. "OPA Volunteers: Big Democracy in Action." *Public Administration Review* 5 (1945): 350–59.

Promises to Keep: My Years in Public Life, 1941–1969. New York: Harper & Row, 1971.

Brandt-Rauf, Sherry Iris. "Ex Parte Contacts under the Constitution and Administrative Procedure Act." *Columbia Law Review* 80 (1980): 379–94.

Brazier, James E. "An Anti-New Dealer Legacy: The Administrative Procedure Act." *Journal of Policy History* 8 (1996): 206–26.

Breger, Marshall J. "The APA: An Administrative Conference Perspective." *Virginia Law Review* 72 (1986): 337–61.

Brinkley, Alan. "A President for Certain Seasons." *Wilson Quarterly* 14 (1990): 110–19.

   The End of Reform: New Deal Liberalism in Recession and War. New York: Alfred A. Knopf, 1995.

   "The Late New Deal and the Idea of the State." In *Liberalism and Its Discontents* (37–62). Cambridge, MA: Harvard University Press, 1998.

Brinson, Susan L. "War on the Homefront in World War II: The FCC and the House Committee on Un-American Activities." *Historical Journal of Film, Radio and Television* 21 (2001): 63–75.

   The Red Scare, Politics, and the Federal Communications Commission, 1941–1960. Westport, CT: Praeger, 2004.

Britton, Raymond L. "Changes in Organization and Procedures of the NLRB." *Southwestern Law Journal* 5 (1951): 226–33.

Brock, William R. *Investigation and Responsibility: Public Responsibility in the United States, 1865–1900*. Cambridge: Cambridge University Press, 1984.

Brown, Arthur L. "The Office of Administrative Hearings." *Cornell Law Quarterly* 29 (1944): 461–88.

Brown, MacAlister. "The Demise of State Department Public Opinion Polls: A Study in Legislative Oversight." *Midwest Journal of Political Science* 5 (1961): 1–17.

Brown, Michael K. "State Building and Political Choice: Interpreting the Failure of the Third New Deal." *Studies in American Political Development* 9 (1995): 187–212.

Brown, Sarah Hart. *Standing against Dragons: Three Southern Lawyers in an Era of Fear*. Baton Rouge: Louisiana State University Press, 1998.

Brownell, Herbert. *Advising Ike: The Memoirs of Attorney General Herbert Brownell*. Lawrence: University Press of Kansas, 1993.

Brownlow, Louis. *A Passion for Anonymity: The Autobiography of Louis Brownlow*. Chicago: University of Chicago Press, 1958.

Burns, James MacGregor. *Roosevelt: The Lion and the Fox*. New York: Harcourt Brace Jovanovich, 1956.

   Congress on Trial: The Legislative Process and the Administrative State. New York: Gordian Press, 1966 (originally 1949).

Burrus, Bernie R., and Harry Teter. "Antitrust: Rulemaking v. Adjudication in the FTC." *Georgetown Law Journal* 54 (1966): 1106–30.

Caldwell, Louis G. "Federal Communications Commission – Comments on the Report of the Staff of the Attorney General's Committee on Administrative Law." *George Washington Law Review* 8 (1940): 749–818.

Caro, Robert A. *Master of the Senate*. New York: Alfred A. Knopf, 2002.

Carpenter, Daniel. *The Forging of Bureaucratic Autonomy: Reputations, Networks, and Policy Innovation in Executive Agencies, 1862–1928*. Princeton, NJ: Princeton University Press, 2001.

   Reputation and Power: Organizational Image and Pharmaceutical Regulation at the FDA. Princeton, NJ: Princeton University Press, 2010.

Carr, Robert K. "Investigations in Operation: The Un-American Activities Committee." *University of Chicago Law Review* 18 (1951): 598–633.

   The House Committee on Un-American Activities, 1945–1950. Ithaca, NY: Cornell University Press, 1952.

Carrow, Milton M. "Dean Landis and the Regulatory Process." *George Washington Law Review* 29 (1961): 718–38.

Cary, William L. *Politics and the Regulatory Agencies.* New York: McGraw-Hill Book Co., 1967.

Cass, Ronald A. "Models of Administrative Action." *Virginia Law Review* 72 (1986): 363–98.

Cate, John M. "Suspension Order Hearings of the Office of Price Administration in Rationing Cases." *University of Tennessee Law Review* 18 (1944): 340–46.

Caute, David. *The Great Fear: The Anti-Communist Purge under Truman and Eisenhower.* New York: Simon & Schuster, 1978.

Chamberlain, Lawrence H. "Congress – Diagnosis and Prescription." *Political Science Quarterly* 60 (1945): 437–45.

Chandler, Alfred D., and Louis Galambos. "The Development of Large-Scale Economic Organizations in Modern America." *Journal of Economic History* 30 (1970): 201–17.

Chase, William C. *The American Law School and the Rise of Administrative Government.* Madison: University of Wisconsin Press, 1982.

Chesrow, George W. "NLRB Policymaking: The Rulemaking – Adjudication Dilemma Revisited in *NLRB v. Bell Aerospace Co.*" *University of Miami Law Review* 29 (1975): 559–83.

Chin, Gabriel J. "Regulating Race: Asian Exclusion and the Administrative State." *Harvard Civil Rights-Civil Liberties Law Review* 37 (2002): 1–64.

Ciepley, David. *Liberalism in the Shadow of Totalitarianism.* Cambridge, MA: Harvard University Press, 2006.

Citizens Committee for the Hoover Report. *Digests and Analyses of the Nineteen Hoover Commission Reports.* Washington, DC: Citizens Committee for the Hoover Report, 1955.

Classen, Steven D. *Watching Jim Crow: The Struggles over Mississippi TV, 1955–1969.* Durham, NC: Duke University Press, 2004.

Coggins, George Cameron. "Conserving Wildlife Resources: An Overview of the Endangered Species Act of 1973." *North Dakota Law Review* 51 (1974): 315–40.

Cohen, Lizabeth. *A Consumers' Republic: The Politics of Mass Consumption in Postwar America.* New York: Knopf, 2003.

Coleman, John J. "State Formation and the Decline of Political Parties: American Parties in the Fiscal State." *Studies in American Political Development* 8 (1994): 195–230.

Collins, Patricia H. "Administrative Procedure: The Conference Submits Its Final Report." *American Bar Association Journal* 41 (1955): 311–14 and 371–73.

Collins, Robert M. "Positive Business Responses to the New Deal: The Roots of the Committee for Economic Development, 1933–1942." *Business History Review* 52 (1978): 369–91.

Comment. "Judicial Review of Price Orders under the Emergency Price Control Act." *Illinois Law Review* 37 (1942): 256–64.

Committee on Congress. "Congress – Problems, Diagnosis, Proposals: Second Progress Report of the American Political Science Association's Committee on Congress." *American Political Science Review* 36 (1942): 1091–102.

The Reorganization of Congress. Washington, DC: American Political Science Association, 1945.

Congressional Quarterly. *Congress and the Nation 1945–1964: A Review of Government and Politics in the Postwar Years.* Washington, DC: CQ Press, 1965.

Origins and Development of Congress, 2nd ed. Washington, DC: CQ Press, 1982.

Cook, Donald C. "Investigations in Operation: Senate Preparedness Subcommittee." *University of Chicago Law Review* 18 (1951): 634–46.

Cooper, Frank E. "Administrative Law: The 'Substantial Evidence' Rule." *American Bar Association Journal* 44 (1958): 945–49 and 1001–03.

Cooper, Joseph. "The Twentieth-Century Congress." In Lawrence C. Dodd and Bruce I. Oppenheimer, eds., *Congress Reconsidered*, 7th ed. (335–66) Washington, DC: CQ Press, 2001.

Cox, Edward F., Robert C. Fellmeth, and John E. Schulz. *The Nader Report On the Federal Trade Commission*. New York: Richard W. Baron Publishing Co., 1969.

Crenson, Matthew A. *The Federal Machine: Beginnings of Bureaucracy in Jacksonian America*. Baltimore: Johns Hopkins University Press, 1975.

Crenson, Matthew A., and Francis E. Rourke. "By Way of Conclusion: American Bureaucracy since World War II." In Louis Galambos, ed., *The New American State: Bureaucracies and Policies since World War II* (137–77). Baltimore: Johns Hopkins University Press, 1987.

Cuff, Robert D. "A 'Dollar-a-Year Man' in Government: George N. Peek and the War Industries Board." *Business History Review* 41 (1967): 404–20.

"Bernard Baruch: Symbol and Myth in Industrial Mobilization." *Business History Review* 43 (1969): 115–33.

"Woodrow Wilson and Business-Government Relations during World War I." *Review of Politics* 31 (1969): 385–407.

"The Cooperative Impulse and War: The Origins of the National Defense and Advisory Commission." In Jerry Israel, ed., *Building the Organizational Society: Essays on Associational Activities in Modern America* (233–46). New York: Free Press, 1972.

"Herbert Hoover, The Ideology of Voluntarism and War Organization during the Great War." *Journal of American History* 64 (1977): 358–72.

"Harry Garfield, The Fuel Administration, and the Search for a Cooperative Order during World War I." *American Quarterly* 30 (1978): 39–53.

"The Dilemmas of Voluntarism: Hoover and the Pork-Packing Agreement of 1917– 1919." *Agricultural History* 53 (1979): 727–47.

Cushman, Robert E. *The Independent Regulatory Commissions*. New York: Oxford University Press, 1941.

"The Purge of Federal Employees Accused of Disloyalty." *Public Administration Review* 3 (1943): 297–316.

Dakin, Melvin G. "Ratemaking as Rulemaking – The New Approach at the FPC: Ad Hoc Rulemaking in the Ratemaking Process." *Duke Law Journal* 1973 (1973): 41–88.

Davey, Harold W. "Separation of Functions and the National Labor Relations Board." *University of Chicago Law Review* 7 (1940): 328–46.

Davidson, Roger H. "The Advent of the Modern Congress: The Legislative Reorganization Act of 1946." *Legislative Studies Quarterly* 15 (1990): 357–73.

Davis, Clarence A. "Government Legal Services, Procedures, and Representations: A Discussion of the Hoover Report and the Administration of the Department of the Interior." *Northwestern University Law Review* 50 (1956): 726–38.

Davis, Kenneth Culp. "Separation of Functions in Administrative Agencies." *Harvard Law Review* 61 (1948): 389–418.

Administrative Law. St. Paul, MN: West Publishing Co., 1951.

"Evidence." *New York University Law Review* 30 (1955): 1309–41.

Davison, J. Forrester. "Administrative Technique – The Report on Administrative Procedure." *Columbia Law Review* 41 (1941): 628–45.

"An Administrative Court of the United States." *George Washington Law Review* 24 (1956): 613–18.

De Santis, Vincent P. "Eisenhower Revisionism." *Review of Politics* 38 (1976): 190–207.

Degler, Carl N. "The Ordeal of Herbert Hoover." *Yale Review* 52 (1963): 563–83.

Denham, Robert N. "The Taft-Hartley Act." *Tennessee Law Review* 20 (1948): 168–81.

Derthick, Martha and Paul Quirk. *The Politics of Deregulation*. Washington, DC: Brookings Institution, 1985.

Dickinson, John. *Administrative Justice and the Supremacy of Law in the United States.* Cambridge, MA: Harvard University Press, 1927.

Dierenfield, Bruce J. *Keeper of the Rules: Congressman Howard W. Smith of Virginia.* Charlottesville: University Press of Virginia, 1987.

Dolan, Joseph F. "The Investigating Power of Congress: Its Scope and Limitations." *Dicta* 31 (1954): 285–304.

Donovan, Robert J. *Eisenhower: The Inside Story.* New York: Harper & Brothers, 1956.

Douglas, Paul H. *Ethics in Government*. Cambridge, MA: Harvard University Press, 1952.

"Improvement of Ethical Standards in the Federal Government: Problems and Proposals." *Annals of the American Academy of Political and Social Science* 280 (1952): 149–57.

In the Fullness of Time: The Memoirs of Paul H. Douglas. New York: Harcourt Brace Jovanovich, 1972.

Douglas, William O. "Virtues of the Administrative Process." In James Allen, ed., *Democracy and Finance: The Addresses and Public Statements of William O. Douglas as Member and Chairman of the Securities and Exchange Commission.* New Haven, CT: Yale University Press, 1940.

Dugan, Frank J. Note. "A New Administrative Landmark." *Georgetown Law Journal* 27 (1939): 351–60.

Dulles, John Foster. "Administrative Law: A Practical Attitude for Lawyers." *American Bar Association Journal* 25 (1939): 275–82 and 352–53.

"The Effect in Practice of the Report on Administrative Procedure." *Columbia Law Review* 41 (1941): 617–27.

Dunar, Andrew J. *The Truman Scandals and the Politics of Morality*. Columbia: University of Missouri Press, 1984.

Durham, G. Homer. "An Appraisal of the Hoover Commission Approach to Administrative Reorganization in the National Government." *Western Political Quarterly* 2 (1949): 615–23.

Durr, Clifford J. "The Loyalty Order's Challenge to the Constitution." *University of Chicago Law Review* 16 (1949): 298–306.

Edelman, Sidney. "Air Pollution Abatement Procedures under the Clean Air Act." *Arizona Law Review* 10 (1968): 30–36.

Edwardson, Mickie. "James Lawrence Fly's Report on Chain Broadcasting (1941) and the Regulation of Monopoly in America." *Historical Journal of Film, Radio, and Television* 22 (2002): 397–423.

Eisenhower, Dwight D. *Public Papers of the Presidents of the United States: Dwight D. Eisenhower*. Vol. 1955. Washington, DC: Government Printing Office, 1959.

Public Papers of the Presidents of the United States: Dwight D. Eisenhower. Vol. 1953. Washington, DC: Government Printing Office, 1960.

Public Papers of the Presidents of the United States: Dwight D. Eisenhower. Vol. 1954. Washington, DC: Government Printing Office, 1960.

Public Papers of the Presidents of the United States, Dwight D. Eisenhower. Vol. 1960–1961. Washington, DC: Government Printing Office, 1961.

Eisenhower, Milton S. *The President Is Calling*. Garden City, NY: Doubleday & Co., 1974.

Eisner, Marc Allen. "Discovering Patterns in Regulatory History: Continuity, Change, and Regulatory Regimes." *Journal of Policy History* 6 (1994): 157–87.

Emerson, Thomas I. *Young Lawyer for the New Deal: An Insider's Memoir of the Roosevelt Years*, Joan P. Emerson, ed. Latham, MD: Rowman and Littlefield, 1991.

Emerson, Thomas I., and David M. Helfeld. "Loyalty among Government Employees." *Yale Law Journal* 58 (1948): 1–143.

"Reply by the Authors." *Yale Law Journal* 58 (1948): 412–21.

Emmerich, Herbert. *Essays on Federal Reorganization*. University: University of Alabama Press, 1950.

Federal Organization and Administrative Management. University: University of Alabama Press, 1971.

Ernst, Daniel R. "The Ideal and the Actual in the State: Willard Hurst at the Board of Economic Welfare." In Daniel R. Ernst and Victor Jew, eds., *Total War and the Law: The American Home Front in World War II* (149–83). Westport, CT: Praeger, 2002.

"*Morgan* and the New Dealers." *Journal of Policy History* 20 (2008): 447–81.

"The Politics of Administrative Law: New York's Anti-Bureaucracy Clause and the O'Brian-Wagner Campaign of 1938." *Law and History Review* 27 (2009): 331–72.

Estep, Samuel D., George T. Schilling, James L. McCrystal. Comment. *Michigan Law Review* 41 (1942): 109–49.

Evans, Diana. "Congressional Oversight and the Diversity of Members' Goals." *Political Science Quarterly* 109 (1994): 669–87.

Fahy, Charles. "The Preparation and Trial of Cases before the National Labor Relations Board." *American Bar Association Journal* 25 (1939): 695–99.

Farmer, Guy. "An Administrative Labor Court: Some Observations on the Hoover Commission Report." *George Washington Law Review* 24 (1956): 656–71.

Fascell, Dante B. "The Problem of Complexities and Delays in Administrative Proceedings and Practice." *Administrative Law Bulletin* 12 (1959): 6–11.

Feller, A. H. "Prospectus for the Further Study of Federal Administrative Law." *Yale Law Journal* 47 (1938): 647–74.

"Administrative Law Investigation Comes of Age." *Columbia Law Review* 41 (1941): 589–616.

Fellmeth, Robert C. *The Interstate Commerce Omission: The Public Interest and the ICC*. New York: Grossman Publishers, 1970.

Ferrell, Robert H., ed. *The Eisenhower Diaries*. New York: W. W. Norton & Co., 1981.

Field, Richard H., Jr. "Rationing Suspension Orders: A Reply to Dean Pound." *American Bar Association Journal* 30 (1944): 385–90.

Findling, David. "NLRB Procedures: Effects of the Administrative Procedure Act." *American Bar Association Journal* 33 (1947): 14–17 and 82–85.

Finegold, Kenneth, and Theda Skocpol. *State and Party in America's New Deal.* Madison: University of Wisconsin Press, 1995.

Finer, Herman. "The Hoover Commission Reports, Part I." *Political Science Quarterly* 64 (1949): 405–19.

Fisher, Ben C. "Communications Act Amendments, 1952 – An Attempt to Legislate Administrative Fairness." *Law and Contemporary Problems* 22 (1957): 672–96.

"Rule Making Activities in Federal Administrative Agencies." *Administrative Law Review* 17 (1965): 252–61.

Ford, Aaron L. "The Legislative Reorganization Act of 1946." *American Bar Association Journal* 32 (1946): 741.

Forrester, Ray. "History and Function of Congressional Investigations." *Arkansas Law Review* 9 (1954): 352–59.

Frankfurter, Felix. ed. *A Selection of Cases under the Interstate Commerce Act.* 2nd ed. Cambridge, MA: Harvard University Press, 1922.

"The Task of Administrative Law." *University of Pennsylvania Law Review* 75 (1927): 614–21.

"The Final Report of the Attorney General's Committee on Administrative Procedure: Foreword." *Columbia Law Review* 41 (1941): 585–88.

Freer, R. E. "Practice before the Federal Trade Commission," *George Washington Law Review* 7 (1939): 283–303.

Freer, Robert E. "Federal Trade Commission Procedure," *American Bar Association Journal* 26 (1940): 342–43 and 370.

"The Case against the Trade Regulation Section of the Proposed Administrative Court." *George Washington Law Review* 24 (1956): 637–55.

Freund, Ernst, Robert V. Fletcher, Joseph E. Davies, Cuthbert W. Pound, John A. Kurtz and Charles Nagel. *The Growth of American Administrative Law.* St. Louis, MO: Thomas Law Book Co., 1923.

Freund, Paul A. "The Emergency Price Control Act of 1942: Constitutional Issues." *Law and Contemporary Problems* 9 (1942): 77–88.

Friendly, Henry J. "A Look at the Federal Administrative Agencies." *Columbia Law Review* 60 (1960): 429–46.

The Federal Administrative Agencies: The Need for Better Definition of Standards. Cambridge, MA: Harvard University Press, 1962.

Frier, David A. *Conflict of Interest in the Eisenhower Administration.* Ames: Iowa State University Press, 1969.

Frug, Gerald E. "The Ideology of Bureaucracy in American Law." *Harvard Law Review* 97 (1984): 1276–388.

Fuchs, Ralph F. "The Hearing Examiner Fiasco under the Administrative Procedure Act." *Harvard Law Review* 63 (1950): 737–68.

"Hearing Commissioners." *New York University Law Review* 30 (1955): 1342–74.

"The Hoover Commission and Task Force Reports on Legal Services and Procedure." *Indiana Law Journal* 31 (1955): 1–44.

"The Hearing Officer Problem – Symptom and Symbol." *Cornell Law Quarterly* 40 (1955): 281–325.

"The Proposed New Code of Administrative Procedure." *Ohio State Law Journal* 19 (1958): 423–31.

"Fairness and Effectiveness in Administrative Agency Organization and Procedures." *Indiana Law Journal* 36 (1960): 1–50.

"Agency Development of Policy through Rule-Making." *Northwestern University Law Review* 59 (1965): 781–807.

Fulbright, J. W. " Congressional Investigations: Significance for the Legislative Process." *University of Chicago Law Review* 18 (1951): 440–48.

Gage, John B. "Chairman's Page." *Administrative Law Bulletin* 11 (1959): 203–10.

Galambos, Louis. "The Emerging Organizational Synthesis in Modern American History." *Business History Review* 44 (1970): 279–90.

"Technology, Political Economy, and Professionalization: Central Themes of the Organizational Synthesis." *Business History Review* 57 (1983): 471–93.

Galloway, George B. "The Investigative Function of Congress." *American Political Science Review* 21 (1927): 47–70.

"Congress in Action." *Nebraska Law Review* 28 (1949): 493–505.

"Congressional Investigations: Proposed Reforms." *University of Chicago Law Review* 18 (1951): 478–502.

"The Operation of the Legislative Reorganization Act of 1946." *American Political Science Review* 45 (1951): 41–68.

"Development of the Committee System in the House of Representatives." *American Historical Review* 65 (1959): 17–30.

Galloway, George B., et al. "Congress – Problems, Diagnosis, Proposals: Second Progress Report of the American Political Science Association's Committee on Congress." *American Political Science Review* 36 (1942): 1091–102.

Garrison, Lloyd K. "Congressional Investigations: Are They a Threat to Civil Liberties?" *American Bar Association Journal* 40 (1954): 125–28.

"Some Observations on the Loyalty-Security Program." *University of Chicago Law Review* 23 (1955): 1–11.

Gellhorn, Walter. "Report on a Report of the House Committee on Un-American Activities." *Harvard Law Review* 60 (1947): 1193–234.

"The Administrative Procedure Act: The Beginnings." *Virginia Law Review* 72 (1986): 219–33.

Gellhorn, Walter, and Kenneth Culp Davis. "Present at the Creation: Regulatory Reform before 1946." *Administrative Law Review* 38 (1986): 511–33.

Gellhorn, Walter, and Seymour L. Linfield. "Politics and Labor Relations: An Appraisal of Criticisms of NLRB Procedure." *Columbia Law Review* 39 (1939): 339–95.

Gifford, Daniel J. "The *Morgan* Cases: A Retrospective View." *Administrative Law Review* 30 (1978): 237–88.

"The New Deal Regulatory Model: A History of Criticisms and Refinements." *Minnesota Law Review* 68 (1983): 299–332.

"Federal Administrative Law Judges: The Relevance of Past Choices to Future Directions." *Administrative Law Review* 49 (1997): 1–60.

Gilbert, Louis R. Comment. *Marquette Law Review* 35 (1952): 361–64.

Gilligan, John W. "Congressional Investigations." *Journal of Criminal Law and Criminology* 41 (1951): 618–38.

Ginsburg, David. "Legal Aspects of Price Control in the Defense Program." *American Bar Association Journal* 27 (1941): 527–34.

"The Emergency Price Control Act of 1942: Basic Authority and Sanctions." *Law and Contemporary Problems* 9 (1942): 22–59.

Goding, James B. "The Impact of the Administrative Procedure Act on the Administration of the Federal Food, Drug, and Cosmetic Act." *Food Drug Cosmetic Law Quarterly* 2 (1947): 139–54.

Goodbar, Joseph E. "Administrative Agency in Action." *Boston University Law Review* 25 (1945): 185–95.

Gould, Lewis L. *The Most Exclusive Club: A History of the Modern United States Senate.* New York: Basic Books, 2005.

Graham, Hugh Davis. "Legacies of the 1960s: The American 'Rights Revolution' in an Era of Divided Governance." *Journal of Policy History* 10 (1998): 267–88.

———. "Since 1964: The Paradox of American Civil Rights Regulation." In Morton Keller and R. Shep Melnick, eds., *Taking Stock: American Government in the Twentieth Century* (187–218). Cambridge: Cambridge University Press, 1999.

Greenstein, Fred I. *The Hidden-Hand Presidency: Eisenhower as Leader.* New York: Basic Books, 1982.

Griffith, Robert. "Dwight D. Eisenhower and the Corporate Commonwealth." *American Historical Review* 87 (1982): 87–122.

Grisinger, Joanna. "Law in Action: The Attorney General's Committee on Administrative Procedure." *Journal of Policy History* 20 (2008): 379–418.

Grisinger, Joanna L. "Law and the Administrative State." In Sally Hadden and Alfred L. Brophy eds., *A Companion to American Legal History.* Hoboken, NJ: Wiley-Blackwell, forthcoming.

Gross, James A. *The Making of the National Labor Relations Board: A Study in Economics, Politics, and the Law.* Vol. I 1933–1937. Albany: State University of New York Press, 1974.

———. *The Reshaping of the National Labor Relations Board: National Labor Policy in Transition, 1937–1947.* Albany: State University of New York Press, 1981.

———. *Broken Promise: The Subversion of U.S. Labor Relations Policy, 1947–1994.* Philadelphia: Temple University Press, 1995.

Gulick, Luther. "War Organization of the Federal Government." *American Political Science Review* 38 (1944): 1166–79.

Halliday, Terence C. "The Idiom of Legalism in Bar Politics: Lawyers, McCarthyism, and the Civil Rights Era." *American Bar Foundation Research Journal* 7 (1982): 911–88.

Hamilton, David E. "Building the Associative State: The Department of Agriculture and American State-Building." *Agricultural History* 64 (1990): 207–18.

Hamilton, James. *The Power to Probe: A Study of Congressional Investigations.* New York: Random House, 1976.

Harbeson, Robert W. "New Perspectives in Transport Regulation: The Cabinet Committee Report." *Northwestern University Law Review* 52 (1957): 490–513.

Hardeman, D. B., and Donald C. Bacon. *Rayburn: A Biography.* Austin: Texas Monthly Press, 1987.

Harper, Alan H. *The Politics of Loyalty: The White House and the Communist Issue, 1946–1952.* Westport, CT: Greenwood Publishing, 1969.

Harris, Douglas B. "Dwight Eisenhower and the New Deal: The Politics of Preemption." *Presidential Studies Quarterly* 27 (1997): 333–42.

Harris, Joseph P. "The Progress of Administrative Reorganization in the Seventy-Fifth Congress." *American Political Science Review* 31 (1937): 862–70.

———. "The Reorganization of Congress." *Public Administration Review* 6 (1946): 267–82.

"The Senatorial Rejection of Leland Olds: A Case Study." *American Political Science Review* 45 (1951): 674–92.

Congressional Control of Administration. Washington, DC: Brookings Institution, 1964.

Harris, Richard A. and Sidney M. Milkis. *The Politics of Regulatory Change: A Tale of Two Agencies.* 2nd ed. Oxford: Oxford University Press, 1996.

Harris, Whitney R. "The Hoover Commission Report: Improvement of Legal Services and Procedure." *American Bar Association Journal* 41 (1955): 497–500, 558–62.

"The Hoover Commission Report: Improvement of Legal Services and Procedure." *American Bar Association Journal* 41 (1955): 713–17.

Hart, James. *An Introduction to Administrative Law with Selected Cases.* 2nd ed. New York: Appleton-Century-Crofts, 1950.

Hartmann, Susan M. *Truman and the 80th Congress.* Columbia: University of Missouri Press, 1971.

Harvey, Ray, Louis W. Koenig, and Albert Somit. *Achievements in Federal Reorganization: The Contribution of the First and New Hoover Commissions.* New York: Citizens Committee for the Hoover Report, 1955.

Hawley, Ellis W. *The New Deal and the Problem of Monopoly: A Study in Economic Ambivalence.* Princeton: Princeton University Press, 1966.

"Herbert Hoover, the Commerce Secretariat, and the Vision of an 'Associative State,' 1921–1928." *Journal of American History* 61 (1974): 116–40.

"The Discovery and Study of a 'Corporate Liberalism.'" *Business History Review* 52 (1978): 309–20.

"Three Facets of Hooverian Associationalism: Lumber, Aviation and Movies, 1921–30." In Thomas K. McCraw, ed., *Regulation in Perspective: Historical Essays* (95–123). Cambridge, MA: Harvard University Press, 1981.

"The New Deal State and the Anti-Bureaucratic Tradition." In Robert Eden, ed., *The New Deal and Its Legacy: Critique and Reappraisal* (77–92). New York: Greenwood Press, 1989.

Haynes, John Earl, and Harvey Klehr. *Venona: Decoding Soviet Espionage in America.* New Haven, CT: Yale University Press, 1999.

Hays, Samuel P. *American Political History as Social Analysis.* Knoxville: University of Tennessee Press, 1980.

Heady, Ferrel. "The Operation of a Mixed Commission." *American Political Science Review* 43 (1949): 940–52.

"The New Reform Movement in Regulatory Administration." *Public Administration Review* 19 (1959): 89–100.

Heclo, Hugh. *A Government of Strangers: Executive Politics in Washington.* Washington, DC: Brookings Institution, 1977.

"Issue Networks and the Executive Establishment." In Anthony King, ed., *The New American Political System* (87–124). Washington, DC: American Enterprise Institute for Public Policy Research, 1978.

"The Sixties' False Dawn: Awakenings, Movements, and Postmodern Policy-Making." In Brian Balogh, ed., *Integrating the Sixties: The Origins, Structures, and Legitimacy of Public Policy in a Turbulent Decade* (34–63). University Park: Pennsylvania State University Press, 1996.

Hector, Louis J. "Problems of the CAB and the Independent Regulatory Commissions." *Yale Law Journal* 69 (1960): 931–64.

Heinemann, Ronald L. *Harry Byrd of Virginia.* Charlottesville: University Press of Virginia, 1996.

Heller, Francis H. "The Eisenhower White House." *Presidential Studies Quarterly* 23 (1993): 509–17.

Heller, Robert. *Strengthening the Congress, Planning Pamphlet No. 39.* Washington, DC: National Planning Association, 1945.

Henderson, Gerard C. *The Federal Trade Commission: A Study in Administrative Law and Procedure.* New Haven, CT: Yale University Press, 1924.

Henderson, Joseph W. "Making Secure 'The Blessings of Liberty.'" *Annual Report of the American Bar Association* 69 (1944): 325–43.

Henderson, Leon. "A Preface to Price Control." *Law and Contemporary Problems* 9 (1942): 3–5.

Hermanson, Judith A. "Regulatory Reform by Statute: The Implications of the Consumer Product Safety Commission's 'Offeror System.'" *Public Administration Review* 38 (1978): 151–55.

Herring, E. Pendleton. "Special Interests and the Interstate Commerce Commission." *American Political Science Review* 27 (1933): 738–51.

"Politics, Personalities, and the Federal Trade Commission, I." *American Political Science Review* 28 (1934): 1016–29.

"Politics, Personalities, and the Federal Trade Commission, II." *American Political Science Review* 29 (1935): 21–35.

Hess, Stephen. *Organizing the Presidency.* Washington, DC: Brookings Institution, 1976.

Heubel, Edward J. "Committee Resistance to Reform: The House Adopts a Code for Investigating Committees." *Midwest Journal of Political Science* 1 (1957): 313–29.

Himmelberg, Robert F. "The War Industries Board and the Antitrust Question in November 1918." *Journal of American History* 52 (1965): 59–74.

"Business, Antitrust Policy, and the Industrial Board of the Department of Commerce, 1919." *Business History Review* 42 (1968): 1–23.

Hobbs, Edward H. "The President and Administration – Eisenhower." *Public Administration Review* 18 (1958): 306–13.

Hogan, Michael J. *A Cross of Iron: Harry S. Truman and the Origins of the National Security State, 1945–1954.* Cambridge: Cambridge University Press, 1998.

Holden, Matthew, Jr. *Continuity and Disruption: Essays in Public Administration.* Pittsburgh, PA: University of Pittsburgh Press, 1996.

Holdoegel, Donald D. "The War Powers and the Emergency Price Control Act of 1942." *Iowa Law Review* 29 (1944): 454–62.

Hoogenboom, Ari Arthur, and Olive Hoogenboom. *A History of the ICC: From Panacea to Palliative.* New York: W. W. Norton & Co., 1976.

Hoover, Herbert. *The Challenge to Liberty.* New York: Charles Scribner's Sons, 1934.

Hoover, J. Edgar. "A Comment on the Article 'Loyalty among Government Employees.'" *Yale Law Journal* 58 (1949): 401–11.

"Rejoinder by Mr. Hoover." *Yale Law Journal* 58 (1949): 422–25.

"Role of the FBI in the Federal Employee Security Program." *Northwestern University Law Review* 49 (1954): 333–47.

Hopkins, Bruce. "Congressional Reform: The Clash with Tradition." *American Bar Association Journal* 54 (1968): 80–83.

Horn, Robert. "The Protection of Internal Security." *Public Administration Review* 16 (1956): 40–52.

Horwitz, Morton J. *The Transformation of American Law, 1870–1960: The Crisis of Legal Orthodoxy*. New York: Oxford University Press, 1992.

Howe, Karl J. "Legislative Changes in Scope of Judicial Review of Administrative Decisions." *Journal of Public Law* 1 (1952): 205–09.

Huard, Leo A. "Influence in Federal Agency Law-Making and Adjudicatory Proceedings – Should We Adopt a Code of Agency Ethics?" *Administrative Law Bulletin* 11 (1958): 22–26.

Hughes, Charles Evans. "Important Work of Uncle Sam's Lawyers." *American Bar Association Journal* 17 (1931): 237–39.

Huitt, Ralph K. "The Congressional Committee: A Case Study." *American Political Science Review* 48 (1954): 340–65.

Hunter, Elmo B. "The Emergency Price Control Act of 1942." *University of Kansas City Law Review* 10 (1942): 129–42.

Huntington, Samuel P. "The Marasmus of the ICC: The Commission, the Railroads, and the Public Interest." *Yale Law Journal* 61 (1952): 467–509.

Huntington, Samuel P., C. Dickerman Williams, and Charles S. Morgan. "The ICC Re-Examined: A Colloquy." *Yale Law Journal* 63 (1953): 44–63.

Hyman, Jacob D. and Nathaniel L. Nathanson. "Judicial Review of Price Control: The Battle of the Meat Regulations." *Illinois Law Review* 42 (1947): 584–634.

Imhoff, Clement. "Clifford J. Durr and the Loyalty Question: 1942–1950." *Journal of American Culture* 12 (1989): 47–54.

Irons, Peter H. *The New Deal Lawyers*. Princeton, NJ: Princeton University Press, 1982.

Jacobs, Meg. "'How About Some Meat?': The Office of Price Administration, Consumption Politics, and State Building from the Bottom Up, 1941–1946." *Journal of American History* 84 (1997): 910–41.

   Pocketbook Politics: Economic Citizenship in Twentieth-Century America. Princeton, NJ: Princeton University Press, 2005.

Jaffe, Louis L. "Invective and Investigation in Administrative Law." *Harvard Law Review* 52 (1939): 1201–45.

   "The Report of the Attorney General's Committee on Administrative Procedure." *University of Chicago Law Review* 8 (1941): 401–40.

   "The Effective Limits of the Administrative Process: A Reevaluation." *Harvard Law Review* 67 (1954): 1105–35.

   "Basic Issues: An Analysis." *New York University Law Review* 30 (1955): 1273–96.

   "James Landis and the Administrative Process." *Harvard Law Review* 78 (1964): 319–28.

Jeffries, John W. "The 'New' New Deal: FDR and American Liberalism, 1937–1945." *Political Science Quarterly* 105 (1990): 397–418.

Johnson, Cathy Marie. "New Wine in New Bottles: The Case of the Consumer Product Safety Commission." *Public Administration Review* 50 (1990): 74–81.

Johnson, David K. *The Lavender Scare: The Cold War Persecution of Gays and Lesbians in the Federal Government*. Chicago: University of Chicago Press, 2004.

Johnson, Kimberly. *Governing the American State: Congress and the New Federalism, 1877–1929*. Princeton, NJ: Princeton University Press, 2006.

Johnson, Nicholas. *How to Talk Back to Your Television Set*. Boston: Little, Brown & Co., 1970.

Johnson, Robert David. "The Government Operations Committee and Foreign Policy during the Cold War." *Political Science Quarterly* 113 (1998–99): 645–71.

Johnson, Robert L., et al. *The Temple University Survey of Federal Reorganization.* 2 vols. Philadelphia: Temple University Press, 1953.

Jones, Charles O., ed. *Preparing to Be President: The Memos of Richard E. Neustadt.* Washington, DC: AEI Press, 2000.

Jones, Harold A. "The Anomaly of the Civil Aeronautics Board in American Government." *Journal of Air Law and Commerce* 20 (1953): 140–57.

Jones, Harry W. "Department of Legislation," *American Bar Association Journal* 34 (1948): 1018–19.

"Department of Legislation." *American Bar Association Journal* 34 (1948): 726–27.

Kagan, Robert A. "Do Lawyers Cause Adversarial Legalism? A Preliminary Inquiry." *Law and Social Inquiry* 19 (1994): 1–62.

"Adversarial Legalism and American Government." In Marc K. Landy and Martin A. Levin, eds. *The New Politics of Public Policy* (88–118). Baltimore: The Johns Hopkins University Press, 1995.

Kalman, Laura. *Abe Fortas: A Biography.* New Haven, CT: Yale University Press, 1990.

Kang, Joon-Mann. "Franklin D. Roosevelt and James L. Fly: The Politics of Broadcast Regulation, 1941–1944." *Journal of American Culture* 10 (Summer 1987): 23–33.

Kaplan, H. Eliot. "Loyalty Review of Federal Employees." *New York University Law Review* 23 (1948): 437–48.

Karl, Barry D. *Executive Reorganization and Reform in the New Deal: The Genesis of Administrative Management, 1900–1939.* Cambridge, MA: Harvard University Press, 1963.

The Uneasy State: The United States from 1915 to 1945. Chicago: University of Chicago Press, 1983.

"Constitution and Central Planning: The Third New Deal Revisited." *Supreme Court Review* 1988 (1988): 163–201.

Katznelson, Ira, and Bruce Pietrykowski. "Rebuilding the American State: Evidence from the 1940s." *Studies in American Political Development* 5 (Fall 1991): 301–39.

Katznelson, Ira, Kim Geiger, and Daniel Kryder. "Limiting Liberalism: The Southern Veto in Congress, 1933–1950." *Political Science Quarterly* 108 (1993): 283–306.

Kaufman, Samuel. "Is the Administrative Process a Fifth Column?" *John Marshall Law Quarterly* 6 (1940): 1–17.

Kearney, Joseph D., and Thomas W. Merrill. "The Great Transformation of Regulated Industries Law." *Columbia Law Review* 98 (1998): 1323–409.

Kefauver, Estes. "The Need for Better Executive-Legislative Teamwork in the National Government." *American Political Science Review* 38 (1944): 317–25.

"A Code of Conduct for Congressional Investigations." *Arkansas Law Review* 8 (1954): 369–79.

Keller, Morton. *Regulating a New Economy: Public Policy and Economic Change in America, 1900–1933.* Cambridge, MA: Harvard University Press, 1990.

Regulating a New Society: Public Policy and Social Change in America, 1900–1933. Cambridge, MA: Harvard University Press, 1994.

Kennedy, Cornelius B. "Foreword: A Personal Perspective." *Administrative Law Review* 24 (1972): 371–88.

Kintner, Earl W. "The Current Ordeal of the Administrative Process: In Reply to Mr. Hector." *Yale Law Journal* 69 (1960): 965–77.

Kleps, Ralph N. Review of "First Report of the Consultants to the United States Civil Service Commission: Hearing Examiner Personnel under the Administrative

Procedure Act, Method of Rating Applicants." *California Law Review* 37 (1949): 534–37.

Kolko, Gabriel. *The Triumph of Conservatism: A Reinterpretation of American History, 1900–1916*. New York: Free Press, 1963.

Railroads and Regulation, 1877–1916. Princeton, NJ: Princeton University Press, 1965.

Kornhauser, Anne Mira. "Saving Liberalism: Political Imagination in the American Century." PhD dissertation, Columbia University, New York, 2004.

Krasnow, Erwin G., and Lawrence D. Longley. *The Politics of Broadcast Regulation*. 2nd ed. New York: St. Martin's Press, 1978.

Kravitz, Walter. "Evolution of the Senate's Committee System." *Annals of the American Academy of Political and Social Science* 411 (1974): 27–38.

"The Advent of the Modern Congress: The Legislative Reorganization Act of 1970." *Legislative Studies Quarterly* 15 (1990): 375–99.

Kutler, Stanley L. *The American Inquisition: Justice and Injustice in the Cold War*. New York: Hill and Wang, 1982.

Landis, James M. "Constitutional Limitations on the Congressional Power of Investigation." *Harvard Law Review* 40 (1926): 153–221.

The Administrative Process. New Haven, CT: Yale University Press, 1938.

"Crucial Issues in Administrative Law." *Harvard Law Review* 53 (1940): 1077–102.

Report on Regulatory Agencies to the President-Elect. Subcommittee on Administrative Practice and Procedure. Senate Judiciary Committee. 86th Cong. 2nd sess. 1960. Committee Print.

Landy, Marc K., Marc J. Roberts, and Stephen R. Thomas. *The Environmental Protection Agency: Asking the Wrong Questions from Nixon to Clinton*. Exp. ed. New York: Oxford University Press, 1994.

Lane, Chester T. Review of *Federal Examiners and the Conflict of Law and Administration* by Lloyd D. Musolf. *Columbia Law Review* 54 (1954): 1008–11.

Lane, Chester T., and Robert M. Blair-Smith, "The SEC and the 'Expeditious Settlement of Disputes.'" *Illinois Law Review* 34 (1940): 699–726.

Latham, Earl. *The Communist Controversy in Washington: From the New Deal to McCarthy*. Cambridge, MA: Harvard University Press, 1966.

Lawson, Gary. "The Rise and Rise of the Administrative State." *Harvard Law Review* 107 (1994): 1231–54.

Lederle, John W. "The Hoover Commission Reports on Federal Reorganization." *Marquette Law Review* 33 (1949): 89–98.

Lee, David D. "Herbert Hoover and the Development of Commercial Aviation, 1921–1926." *Business History Review* 58 (1984): 78–102.

Leuchtenberg, William E. *In the Shadow of FDR: From Harry Truman to Bill Clinton*. Ithaca, NY: Cornell University Press, 1993.

Leventhal, Harold. "Part II: The Role of the Price Lawyers." In Nathaniel L. Nathanson and Harold Leventhal, eds., *Problems in Price Control: Legal Phases* (49–106). Washington, DC: Government Printing Office, 1947.

Levi, Edward H. "Congressional Investigations: Foreword." *University of Chicago Law Review* 18 (1951): 421–22.

Levy, Beryl Harold. "Congressional Oversight of Administrative Agencies." *American Bar Association Journal* 36 (1950): 236–37.

Lewis, Gregory B. "Lifting the Ban on Gays in the Civil Service: Federal Policy Toward Gay and Lesbian Employees since the Cold War." *Public Administration Review* 57 (1997): 387–95.

Light, Paul Charles. *The Tides of Reform: Making Government Work, 1945–1995.* New Haven, CT: Yale University Press, 1997.

Lishman, R. W. "'Independence' in the Independent Regulatory Agencies." *Administrative Law Review* 13 (1961): 133–40.

Lore, Irving Allan. Recent Case. *Wisconsin Law Review* 12 (1937): 245–47.

Lowi, Theodore J. *The End of Liberalism: The Second Republic of the United States.* 2nd ed. New York: W. W. Norton & Co., 1979.

Mackie, David I. "The Necessity for a Federal Department of Transportation." *Journal of Public Law* 8 (1959): 1–46.

Macmahon, Arthur W. "Congressional Oversight of Administration: The Power of the Purse-I." *Political Science Quarterly* 58 (1943): 161–90.

MacNeil, Neil, and Harold W. Metz, *The Hoover Report 1953–1955: What It Means to You as Citizen and Taxpayer.* New York: Macmillan Company, 1956.

Madden, J. Warren. "Administrative Procedure: National Labor Relations Board." *West Virginia Law Quarterly* 45 (1939): 93–108.

"The National Labor Relations Act and Its Administration." *Tennessee Law Review* 18 (1943): 126–37.

Magruder, Calvert. "Administrative Procedures under the Fair Labor Standards Act." *American Bar Association Journal* 25 (1939): 688–95.

Mansfield, Harvey C. *A Short History of OPA.* Washington, DC: Government Printing Office, 1947.

"Reorganizing the Federal Executive Branch: The Limits of Institutionalization." *Law and Contemporary Problems* 35 (1970): 461–95.

Maranto, Robert. "The Administrative Strategies of Republican Presidents from Eisenhower to Reagan." *Presidential Studies Quarterly* 23 (1993): 683–97.

March, James G., and Johan P. Olson. "Organizing Political Life: What Administrative Reorganization Tells Us about Government." *American Political Science Review* 77 (1983): 281–96.

Marx, Fritz Morstein. "Congressional Investigations: Significance for the Administrative Process." *University of Chicago Law Review* 18 (1951): 503–20.

Mashaw, Jerry L. "Explaining Administrative Process: Normative, Positive, and Critical Stories of Legal Development." *Journal of Law, Economics, & Organization* 6 (Special Issue 1990): 267–98.

"Recovering American Administrative Law: Federalist Foundations, 1787–1801." *Yale Law Journal* 115 (2006): 1256–344.

"Reluctant Nationalists: Federal Administration and Administrative Law in the Republican Era, 1801–1829." *Yale Law Journal* 116 (2007): 1636–740.

"Administration and 'The Democracy': Administrative Law from Jackson to Lincoln, 1829–1861." *Yale Law Journal* 117 (2008): 1568–693.

"Federal Administration and Administrative Law in the Gilded Age." *Yale Law Journal* 119 (2010): 1362–472.

Mashaw, Jerry L., and David L. Harfst. *The Struggle for Auto Safety.* Cambridge, MA: Harvard University Press, 1990.

Mashaw, Jerry L., and Avi Perry. "Administrative Statutory Interpretation in the Antebellum Republic." *Michigan State Law Review* (2009): 7–49.

Maslow, Will. "Fair Procedure in Congressional Investigations: A Proposed Code." *Columbia Law Review* 54 (1954): 839–92.

Matthews, Donald R. "American Political Science and Congressional Reform: The American Political Science Association's Committee on Congress (1941–1945) and Study of Congress (1965–1973)." *Social Science History* 5 (1981): 91–120.

Mayhew, David R. *Divided We Govern: Party Control, Lawmaking, and Investigations, 1946–2002.* 2nd ed. New Haven, CT: Yale University Press, 2005.

McAllister, Breck P. "Administrative Adjudication and Judicial Review." *Illinois Law Review* 34 (1940): 680–98.

McCarthy, John F. "Aspects of Federal Rent Control." *Cornell Law Quarterly* 31 (1945): 68–77.

McChesney, Robert W. "Free Speech and Democracy! Louis G. Caldwell, the American Bar Association and the Debate over the Free Speech Implications of Broadcast Regulation, 1928–1938." *American Journal of Legal History* 35 (1991): 351–92.

McCraw, Thomas. "Regulation in America: A Review Article." *Business History Review* 49 (1975): 159–83.

 Prophets of Regulation: Charles Francis Adams, Louis D. Brandeis, James M. Landis, Alfred E. Kahn. Cambridge, MA: Harvard University Press, 1984.

McCubbins, Mathew D., Roger G. Noll, and Barry R. Weingast. "The Political Origins of the Administrative Procedure Act." *Journal of Law, Economics, and Organization* 15 (1999): 180–217.

McCubbins, Mathew D., and Thomas Schwartz, "Congressional Oversight Overlooked: Police Patrols versus Fire Alarms," *American Journal of Political Science* 28 (1984): 165–79.

McCulloch, Frank W. "The NLRB and Techniques for Expediting the Administrative Process." *Administrative Law Review* 14 (1961): 97–104.

McFarland, Carl. *Judicial Control of the Federal Trade Commission and the Interstate Commerce Commission, 1920–1930.* Cambridge, MA: Harvard University Press, 1933.

 "Landis' Report: The Voice of One Crying In the Wilderness." *Virginia Law Review* 47 (1961): 373–438.

McGeary, M. Nelson. "Congressional Investigations during Franklin D. Roosevelt's First Term." *American Political Science Review* 31 (1937): 680–94.

 "Congressional Investigations: Historical Development." *University of Chicago Law Review* 18 (1951): 425–39.

McQuaid, Kim. "Corporate Liberalism in the American Business Community, 1920–1940." *Business History Review* 52 (1978): 342–68.

Meader, George. "Limitations on Congressional Investigation." *Michigan Law Review* 47 (1949): 775–86.

 "Congressional Investigations: Importance of the Fact-Finding Process." *University of Chicago Law Review* 18 (1951): 449–54.

Meeds, Lloyd. "A Legislative History of OSHA." *Gonzaga Law Review* 9 (1974): 327–48.

Mehrotra, Ajay K. "Forging Fiscal Reform: Constitutional Change, Public Policy, and the Creation of Administrative Capacity in Wisconsin, 1880–1920." *Journal of Policy History* 20 (2008): 94–112.

Melnick, R. Shep. "The Politics of Partnership." *Public Administration Review* (1985): 653–60.

Merrill, Thomas W. "Capture Theory and the Courts: 1967–1983." *Chicago-Kent Law Review* 72 (1997): 1039–117.

Milazzo, Paul C. "An Oxcart in the Age of the Atom: Legislative Reorganization and the Quest for a Modern Congress." MA thesis, University of Virginia, 1994.

Milkis, Sidney M. *The President and the Parties: The Transformation of the American Party System since the New Deal.* New York: Oxford University Press, 1993.

"Remaking Government Institutions in the 1970s: Participatory Democracy and the Triumph of Administrative Politics." In David Brian Robertson, ed., *Loss of Confidence: Politics and Policy in the 1970s* (51–74). University Park: Pennsylvania State University Press, 1998.

Miller, C. A. "Impact of the Federal Administrative Procedure Act on the Procedures of the Interstate Commerce Commission." In George Warren, ed., *The Federal Administrative Procedure Act and the Administrative Agencies* (305–39). New York: New York University School of Law, 1947.

Milligan, Kelly Williams. "*Marcello v. Bonds* and *Escobar-Ruiz v. INS*: Application of the Administrative Procedure Act to Deportation Hearings." *Georgetown Immigration Law Journal* 5 (1991): 339–59.

Millis, Harry A., and Emily Clark Brown. *From the Wagner Act to Taft-Hartley: A Study of National Labor Policy and Labor Relations.* Chicago: University of Chicago Press, 1950.

Mills, Kay. *Changing Channels: The Civil Rights Case that Transformed Television.* Jackson: University Press of Mississippi, 2004.

Minow, Newton N. "Suggestions for Improvement of the Administrative Process." *Administrative Law Review* 15 (1963): 146–53.

Moe, Ronald C. *Executive Branch Reorganization: An Overview.* Washington, DC: Government Printing Office, 1978.

The Hoover Commissions Revisited. Boulder, CO: Westview Press, 1982.

Moe, Terry M. "Regulatory Performance and Presidential Administration." *American Journal of Political Science* 26 (1982): 197–224.

Monsees, Carl Henry. "Industry Advisory Committees in the War Agencies." *Public Administration Review* 3 (1943): 254–62.

Morgan, Charles S. "A Critique of 'The Marasmus of the ICC: The Commission, the Railroads, and the Public Interest.'" *Yale Law Journal* 61 (1953): 171–225.

Morgan, Iwan W. *Eisenhower versus 'The Spenders': The Eisenhower Administration, the Democrats, and the Budget, 1953–1960.* New York: St. Martin's Press, 1990.

Morgan, Robert J. "Federal Loyalty-Security Removals, 1946–1956." *Nebraska Law Review* (1957): 412–46.

Morris, Sherman O. "The Federal Aviation Act of 1958." *University of Kansas City Law Review* 28 (1959–1960): 35–40.

Morrison, Alan B. "The Administrative Procedure Act: A Living and Responsive Law." *Virginia Law Review* 72 (1986): 253–70.

Moss, David A., and Michael R. Fein. "Radio Regulation Revisited: Coase, the FCC, and the Public Interest." *Journal of Policy History* 15 (2003): 389–416.

Musolf, Lloyd. "Administrative Law Judges: A 1948 Snapshot." *Administrative Law Review* 46 (1994): 257–69.

Nathanson, Nathaniel L. "Separation of Functions within Federal Administrative Agencies." *Illinois Law Review* 35 (1941): 901–37.

"The Emergency Price Control Act of 1942: Administrative Procedure and Judicial Review." *Law and Contemporary Problems* 9 (1942): 60–76.

"Some Comments on the Administrative Procedure Act." *Illinois Law Review* 41 (1946): 368–422.

"Central Issues of American Administrative Law." *American Political Science Review* 45 (1951): 348–85.

"Law and the Future: Administrative Law." *Northwestern University Law Review* 51 (1956): 174–86.

Nathanson, Nathaniel L. and Harold Leventhal. *Problems in Price Control: Legal Phases*. Washington, DC: Government Printing Office, 1947.

Nelson, C. Roger. "Chairman's Page." *Administrative Law Review* 16 (1964): 77–79.

Nelson, James C. "Revision of National Transport Regulatory Policy: A Review Article." *American Economic Review* 45 (1955): 910–18.

Nelson, Michael. "A Short, Ironic History of American National Bureaucracy." *Journal of Politics* 44 (1982): 747–78.

Nelson, William E. *The Roots of American Bureaucracy, 1830–1900*. Cambridge, MA: Harvard University Press, 1982.

Neustadt, Richard E. "Congress and the Fair Deal: A Legislative Balance Sheet." *Public Policy* 5 (1954): 351–81.

Newman, Frank C. "The Supreme Court, Congressional Investigations, and Influence Peddling." *New York University Law Review* 33 (1958): 796–810.

Nossiter, Bernard D. *The Mythmakers: An Essay on Power and Wealth*. Boston: Houghton Mifflin Co., 1964.

Novak, William J. *The People's Welfare: Law and Regulation in Nineteenth-Century America*. Chapel Hill: University of North Carolina Press, 1996.

"The Legal Origins of the Modern American State." In Austin Sarat, Bryant Garth, and Robert A. Kagan, eds., *Looking Back at Law's Century* (249–86). Ithaca, NY: Cornell University Press, 2002.

"The Myth of the 'Weak' American State." *American Historical Review* 113 (2008): 752–72.

Nutting, Charles B. "The Administrative Court." *New York University Law Review* 30 (1955): 1384–89.

O'Brian, John Lord. "Loyalty Tests and Guilt by Association." *Harvard Law Review* 61 (1948): 592–611.

National Security and Individual Freedom. Cambridge, MA: Harvard University Press, 1955.

O'Brian, John Lord, and Manly Fleishmann. "The War Production Board Administrative Policies and Procedures." *George Washington Law Review* 13 (1944): 1–60.

O'Connor, William J., Jr. "Investigatory Powers of the House Un-American Activities Committee." *Cornell Law Quarterly* 33 (1948): 565–71.

Ogun, Morris S. *Congress Oversees the Bureaucracy*. Pittsburgh, PA: University of Pittsburgh Press, 1976.

Oleszek, Walter J. *Congressional Procedures and the Policy Process*. 5th ed. Washington, DC: CQ Press, 2001.

Orren, Karen, and Stephen Skowronek. "Regimes and Regime Building in American Government: A Review of Literature on the 1940s." *Political Science Quarterly* 113 (1998): 689–702.

Outland, George E. "Congress Still Needs Reorganization." *Western Political Quarterly* 1 (1948): 154–64.

Parker, Reginald. "The Administrative Procedure Act: A Study in Overestimation." *Yale Law Journal* 60 (1951): 581–99.

Parker, T. Nelson. "The Work of the OPA." *Tennessee Law Review* 18 (1943): 6–12.

Parrish, Michael E. *Securities Regulation and the New Deal*. New Haven, CT: Yale University Press, 1970.

Pasley, Robert S. "Legal Services in the Government: Some Thoughts on the Hoover Commission Report." *Journal of Public Law* 6 (1957): 163–93.

Patterson, James T. *Congressional Conservatism and the New Deal: The Growth of the Conservative Coalition in Congress, 1933–1939.* Lexington: University of Kentucky Press, 1967.

Grand Expectations: The United States, 1945–1974. New York: Oxford University Press, 1996.

Peck, Cornelius J. "The Atrophied Rule-Making Powers of the National Labor Relations Board." *Yale Law Journal* 70 (1961): 729–61.

"A Critique of the National Labor Relations Board's Performance in Policy Formulation: Adjudication and Rule-Making." *University of Pennsylvania Law Review* 117 (1968): 254–75.

Pedersen, William F., Jr. "Formal Records and Informal Rulemaking." *Yale Law Journal* 85 (1975): 38–88.

Pemberton, William E. *Bureaucratic Politics: Executive Reorganization during the Truman Administration.* Columbia: University of Missouri Press, 1979.

Pennock, J. Roland. *Administration and the Rule of Law.* New York: Farrar and Rinehart, 1941.

Perkins, John A. "American Government and Politics: Congressional Self-Improvement." *American Political Science Review* 38 (1944): 499–511.

Peterson, Gale E. *President Harry S. Truman and the Independent Regulatory Commissions, 1945–1952.* New York: Garland Publishing, 1985.

Phillips, Cabell B. H. *The Truman Presidency: The History of a Triumphant Succession.* New York: Macmillan, 1966.

Pierce, Richard J., Jr. "Rulemaking and the Administrative Procedure Act." *Tulsa Law Journal* 32 (1996): 185–201.

Plotke, David. "The Endurance of New Deal Liberalism." *Studies in American Political Development* 10 (1996): 415–20.

Polenberg, Richard. *Reorganizing Roosevelt's Government: The Controversy over Executive Reorganization, 1936–1939.* Cambridge, MA: Harvard University Press, 1966.

War and Society: The United States, 1941–1945. Philadelphia: Lippincott, 1972.

Polsby, Nelson W. "The Institutionalization of the U.S. House of Representatives." *American Political Science Review* 62 (1968): 144–68.

How Congress Evolves: Social Bases of Institutional Change. Oxford: Oxford University Press, 2004.

Porter, David L. *Congress and the Waning of the New Deal.* Port Washington, NY: Kennikat Press Corp., 1980.

Porter, Paul. "The Fortieth Anniversary of the Federal Communications Commission." *Federal Communications Bar Journal* 27 (1974): 109–60.

Pound, Roscoe. "The Challenge of the Administrative Process." *American Bar Association Journal* 30 (1944): 121–26.

"The Growth of Administrative Justice." *Wisconsin Law Review* 2 (1924): 321–39.

President's Advisory Committee on Management. "Improvement of Management in the Federal Government." *Public Administration Review* 13 (1953): 38–49.

Prettyman, E. Barrett. "Reducing the Delay in Administrative Hearings: Suggestions for Officers and Counsel." *American Bar Association Journal* 39 (1953): 966–70.

Trial by Agency. Charlottesville: Virginia Law Review Association, 1959.

Price, David E. *The Commerce Committees: A Study of the House and Senate Commerce Committees.* New York: Grossman Publishers, 1975.

Priest, A. J. G. "Dixon-Yates and the Public Interest." *Virginia Law Review* 41 (1955): 289–309.

Pritchett, C. Herman. "The Supreme Court and Administrative Regulation, 1941–44." *Iowa Law Review* 31 (1945): 103–28.

"The Regulatory Commissions Revisited." *American Political Science Review* 43 (1949): 978–89.

Quirk, Paul J. *Industry Influence in Federal Regulatory Agencies.* Princeton, NJ: Princeton University Press, 1981.

Rabin, Robert L. "Federal Regulation in Historical Perspective." *Stanford Law Review* 38 (1986): 1189–326.

Rao, Gautham. "The Federal *Posse Comitatus* Doctrine: Slavery, Compulsion, and Statecraft in Mid-Nineteenth-Century America." *Law and History Review* 26, (2008): 1–56.

Ratner, Mozart G. "Policy-making by the New 'Quasi-Judicial' NLRB." *University of Chicago Law Review* 23 (1955): 12–35.

Rauh, Joseph L., Jr. "Nonconfrontation in Security Cases: The Greene Decision." *Virginia Law Review* (1959): 1175–90.

Redford, E. S. "The Value of the Hoover Commission Reports to the Educator." *American Political Science Review* 44 (1950): 283–98.

Redford, Emmette S. *The President and the Regulatory Commissions.* (A Report Prepared for the President's Advisory Committee on Government Organization, 1960).

Redford, Emmette S. and Marlan Blissett. *Organizing the Executive Branch: The Johnson Presidency.* Chicago: University of Chicago Press, 1981.

Reuss, Henry S. "The Lawyer in the OPA." *American Law School Review* 10 (1942): 23–29.

Richardson, Seth W. "The Federal Employee Loyalty Program." *Columbia Law Review* 51 (1951): 546–63.

Riddick, Floyd M. "Third Session of the Seventy-sixth Congress, January 3, 1940, to January 3, 1941." *American Political Science Review* 35 (1941): 284–303.

"American Government and Politics: The First Session of the Eightieth Congress." *American Political Science Review* 42 (1948): 677–93.

"The Eighty-First Congress: First and Second Sessions." *Western Political Quarterly* 4 (1951): 48–66.

"The Eighty-Fourth Congress: First Session." *Western Political Quarterly* 8 (1955): 612–29.

Ritchie, Donald A. *James M. Landis: Dean of the Regulators.* Cambridge, MA: Harvard University Press, 1980.

"Reforming the Regulatory Process: Why James Landis Changed His Mind." *Business History Review* 54 (1980): 283–302.

Robinson, Glen O. "The Making of Administrative Policy: Another Look at Rulemaking and Adjudication and Administrative Procedure Reform." *University of Pennsylvania Law Review* 118 (1970): 485–539.

Rodgers, Daniel T. "In Search of Progressivism." *Reviews in American History* 10 (1982): 113–32.

Rodriguez, Daniel B. "Jaffe's Law: An Essay on the Intellectual Underpinnings of Modern Administrative Law Theory." *Chicago-Kent Law Review* 72 (1997): 1159–86.

Rogers, Lindsay. "Reorganization: Post Mortem Notes." *Political Science Quarterly* 53 (1938): 161–72.

"Congressional Investigations: The Problem and Its Solution." *University of Chicago Law Review* 18 (1951): 464–77.

Rohr, John A. *To Run a Constitution: The Legitimacy of the Administrative State.* Lawrence: University Press of Kansas, 1986.

Civil Servants and Their Constitutions. Lawrence: University of Kansas Press, 2002.

Roos, John. "Thinking about Reform: The World View of Congressional Reformers." *Polity* 25 (1993): 329–54.

Rosenbloom, David H. "1946: Framing a Lasting Congressional Response to the Administrative State." *Administrative Law Review* 50 (1998): 173–97.

Building a Legislative-Centered Public Administration: Congress and the Administrative State, 1946–1999. Tuscaloosa: University of Alabama Press, 2000.

"Retrofitting the Administrative State to the Constitution: Congress and the Judiciary's Twentieth-Century Progress," *Public Administration Review* 60 (2000): 39–46.

Rosenman, Samuel I., ed. *The Public Papers and Addresses of Franklin D. Roosevelt.* Vol. 1937. New York: Macmillan Company, 1941.

The Public Papers and Addresses of Franklin D. Roosevelt. Vol. 1938. New York: Macmillan Company, 1941.

The Public Papers and Addresses of Franklin D. Roosevelt. Vol. 1940. New York: Macmillan Company, 1941.

The Public Papers and Addresses of Franklin D. Roosevelt. Vol. 1942. New York: Harper & Bros. Publishers, 1950.

Rung, Margaret C. *Servants of the State: Managing Diversity & Democracy in the Federal Workforce, 1933–1953.* Athens: University of Georgia Press, 2002.

Safire, William. *Safire's Political Dictionary.* New York: Random House, 1978.

Salmond, John A. *The Conscience of a Lawyer: Clifford J. Durr and American Civil Liberties, 1899–1975.* Tuscaloosa: University of Alabama Press, 1990.

Salyer, Lucy E. *Laws Harsh as Tigers: Chinese Immigrants and the Shaping of Modern Immigration Law.* Chapel Hill: University of North Carolina Press, 1995.

Sanders, Elizabeth. *Roots of Reform: Farmers, Workers, and the American State 1877–1917.* Chicago: University of Chicago Press, 1999.

Saunders, D. A. "The Dies Committee: First Phase." *Public Opinion Quarterly* 3 (1939): 223–38.

Scalia, Antonin. "Vermont Yankee: The APA, the D.C. Circuit, and the Supreme Court." *Supreme Court Review* 1978 (1978): 345–409.

"The ALJ Fiasco – A Reprise." *University of Chicago Law Review* 47 (1979): 57–80.

Scalia, Antonin, and Frank Goodman. "Procedural Aspects of the Consumer Product Safety Act." *UCLA Law Review* 20 (1973): 899–982.

Scanlan, Alfred Long. "Judicial Review under the Administrative Procedure Act – In Which Judicial Offspring Receive a Congressional Confirmation." *Notre Dame Lawyer* 23 (1948): 501–46.

Scheele, Henry Z. "President Dwight D. Eisenhower and U.S. House Leader Charles A. Halleck: An Examination of an Executive-Legislative Relationship." *Presidential Studies Quarterly* 23 (1993): 289–99.

Scher, Seymour. "Congressional Committee Members as Independent Agency Overseers: A Case Study." *American Political Science Review* 54 (1960): 911–20.

"Regulatory Agency Control Through Appointment: The Case of the Eisenhower Administration and the NLRB." *Journal of Politics* 23 (1961): 667–88.

"The Politics of Agency Organization." *Western Political Quarterly* 15 (1962): 328–44.

"Conditions for Legislative Control." *Journal of Politics* 25 (1963): 526–51.

Schickler, Eric. *Disjointed Pluralism: Institutional Innovation and the Development of the U.S. Congress.* Princeton, NJ: Princeton University Press, 2001.

Schiller, Reuel E. "Enlarging the Administrative Polity: Administrative Law and the Changing Definition of Pluralism, 1945–1970." *Vanderbilt Law Review* 53 (2000): 1389–453.

"Rulemaking's Promise: Administrative Law and Legal Culture in the 1960s and 1970s." *Administrative Law Review* 53 (2001): 1139–88.

"Reining in the Administrative State: World War II and the Decline of Expert Administration." In Daniel R. Ernst and Victor Jew, eds., *Total War and the Law: The American Home Front in World War II* (185–206). Westport, CT: Praeger, 2002.

"'Saint George and the Dragon': Courts and the Development of the Administrative State in Twentieth-Century America." *Journal of Policy History* 17 (2005): 110–24.

"The Era of Deference: Courts, Expertise, and the Emergence of New Deal Administrative Law." *Michigan Law Review* 106 (2007): 399–441.

"The Administrative State, Front and Center: Studying Law and Administration in Postwar America." *Law and History Review* 26 (2008): 415–27.

Schlesinger, Arthur M., Jr. *The Age of Roosevelt: The Coming of the New Deal.* Boston: Houghton Mifflin, 1959.

The Age of Roosevelt: The Politics of Upheaval. Boston: Houghton Mifflin, 1960.

Schlesinger, Arthur M., Jr., and Roger Bruns, eds. *Congress Investigates: A Documented History, 1792–1974.* Vol. 4. New York: Chelsea House Publishers, 1975.

Schrecker, Ellen. *Many Are the Crimes: McCarthyism in America.* Boston: Little, Brown, 1998.

Schwartz, Bernard. "Administrative Procedure and the A.P.A." *New York University Law Quarterly Review* 24 (1949): 514–34.

"Administrative Law," *New York University Law Review* 29 (1954): 101–24.

"Administrative Justice and Its Place in the Legal Order," *New York University Law Review* 30 (1955): 1390–417.

The Professor and the Commissions. New York: Alfred A. Knopf, 1959.

Schwartz, Louis B. "Legal Restriction of Competition in the Regulated Industries: An Abdication of Judicial Responsibility." *Harvard Law Review* 67 (1954): 436–75.

Scott, Hugh, and Rufus King. "Rules for Congressional Committees: An Analysis of House Resolution 447." *Virginia Law Review* 40 (1954): 249–72.

Sears, Kenneth C. "The Morgan Case and Administrative Procedure." *George Washington Law Review* 7 (1939): 726–39.

Seasongood, Murray, and Richard L. Strecker. "The Loyalty Review Board." *University of Cincinnati Law Review* 25 (1956): 1–42.

Seidman, Harold. *Politics, Position, and Power: The Dynamics of Federal Organization.* 5th ed. New York: Oxford University Press, 1998.

Seligman, Joel. *The Transformation of Wall Street: A History of the Securities and Exchange Commission and Modern Corporate Finance.* 3rd ed. New York: Aspen Publishers, 2003.

Sellers, Ashley. "Administrative Procedure – A Suggested Classification of Procedures of Regulatory Agencies in the United States Department of Agriculture." *Washington University Law Quarterly* 25 (1940): 352–83.

"Carl McFarland – The Architect of the Federal Administrative Procedure Act." *Virginia Journal of International Law* 16 (1975): 12–18.

Shamir, Ronen. *Managing Legal Uncertainty: Elite Lawyers in the New Deal.* Durham, NC: Duke University Press, 1995.

Shapiro, David L. "The Choice of Rulemaking or Adjudication in the Development of Administrative Policy." *Harvard Law Review* 78 (1965): 921–72.

Shapiro, Martin. "APA: Past, Present, Future." *Virginia Law Review* 72 (1986): 447–92.

Who Guards the Guardians? Judicial Control of Administration. Athens: University of Georgia Press, 1998.

Shapiro, Sidney A., and Robert L. Glicksman. "Congress, the Supreme Court, and the Quiet Revolution in Administrative Law." *Duke Law Journal* 1988 (1988): 819–78.

Sharfman, I. L. *The Interstate Commerce Commission: A Study in Administrative Law and Procedure.* 4 vols. New York: Commonwealth Fund, 1931–1937.

Shepherd, George B. "Fierce Compromise: The Administrative Procedure Act Emerges from New Deal Politics." *Northwestern University Law Review* 90 (1996): 1557–683.

Shils, Edward A. "Congressional Investigations: The Legislator and His Environment." *University of Chicago Law Review* 18 (1951): 571–84.

Shull, Charles W. "The Legislative Reorganization Act of 1946." *Temple Law Quarterly* 20 (1947): 375–95.

Sklar, Martin. *The Corporate Reconstruction of American Capitalism, 1890–1916: The Market, The Law and Politics.* Cambridge: Cambridge University Press, 1988.

Skowronek, Stephen. *Building a New American State: The Expansion of National Administrative Capacities, 1877–1920.* Cambridge: Cambridge University Press, 1982.

Sloat, Robert W. "Government in the Sunshine Act: A Danger of Overexposure." *Harvard Journal on Legislation* 14 (1977): 620–50.

Slotnick, Michael C. "The Anathema of the Security Risk: Arbitrary Dismissals of Federal Government Civilian Employees and Civilian Employees of Private Contractors Doing Business with the Federal Government." *University of Miami Law Review* 17 (1962): 10–50.

Smith, Howard W. "NLRA – Abuses in Administrative Procedure." *Virginia Law Review* 27 (1941): 615–32.

"Administrative Law: A Threat to Constitutional Government?" *Virginia Law Review* 31 (1944): 1–8.

Smith, Jason Scott. *Building New Deal Liberalism: The Political Economy of Public Works, 1933–1956.* Cambridge: Cambridge University Press, 2005.

Smith, Robert A. "Administrative Law: Powers of Agencies: The Interstate Commerce Commission and Discontinuance of Railroads under the Transportation Act of 1958." *Michigan Law Review* 57 (1959): 1258–60.

Smith, Sylvester C., Jr. "Comment on Mr. Field's Reply for the OPA." *American Bar Association Journal* 30 (1944): 390–92.

Snyder, John W. "The Reorganization of the Bureau of Internal Revenue." *Public Administration Review* 12 (1952): 221–33.

Somers, Herman Miles. "The Federal Bureaucracy and the Change of Administration." *American Political Science Review* 48 (1954): 131–51.

Sparrow, Bartholomew H. *From the Outside In: World War II and the American State.* Princeton, NJ: Princeton University Press, 1996.

Sprecher, Robert A. "Price Control in the Courts." *Columbia Law Review* 44 (1944): 34–64.

Stamm, Michael. *Sound Business: Newspapers, Radio, and the Politics of New Media.* Philadelphia: University of Pennsylvania Press, 2011.

Stason, E. Blythe. "'Substantial Evidence' in Administrative Law." *University of Pennsylvania Law Review* 89 (1941): 1026–51.

Steffes, Tracy L. "Solving the 'Rural School Problem': New State Aid, Standards, and Supervision of Local Schools, 1900–1933." *History of Education Quarterly* 48 (2008): 181–220.

Stern, Robert L. "Review of Findings of Administrators, Judges and Juries: A Comparative Analysis." *Harvard Law Review* 58 (1944): 70–124

Stewart, Charles W.. Jr. Note. "The Emergency Court of Appeals: Interpretation of Procedure and Judicial Review under the Price Control Act." *Georgetown Law Journal* 32 (1943): 42–65.

Stewart, Richard B. "The Reformation of American Administrative Law." *Harvard Law Review* 88 (1975): 1667–813.

Stone, Richard D. *The Interstate Commerce Commission and the Railroad Industry: A History of Regulatory Policy.* New York: Praeger, 1991.

Storey, Robert G. "The Second Hoover Commission: Its Legal Task Force." *American Bar Association Journal* 40 (1954): 483–86 and 536–39.

Sunstein, Cass R. *After the Rights Revolution: Reconceiving the Regulatory State.* Cambridge, MA: Harvard University Press, 1990.

Taft, Robert A. "Price Fixing – A Necessary Evil." *American Bar Association Journal* 27 (1941): 534–37.

Tani, Karen M. "Flemming v. Nestor: Anticommunism, the Welfare State, and the Making of 'New Property.'" *Law and History Review* 26 (2008): 379–414.

Taylor, Telford. *Grand Inquest: The Story of Congressional Investigations.* New York: Simon and Schuster, 1955.

Theoharis, Athan. "The Escalation of the Loyalty Program." In Barton J. Bernstein, ed. *Politics and Policies of the Truman Administration* (242–68). Chicago: Quadrangle Books, 1970.

Thomas, Elbert D. "How Congress Functions Under Its Reorganization Act." *American Political Science Review* 43 (1949): 1179–89.

Thomas, Morgan. "The Selection of Federal Hearing Examiners: Pressure Groups and the Administrative Process." *Yale Law Journal* 59 (1949): 431–75.

Thompson, Francis H. *The Frustration of Politics: Truman, Congress, and the Loyalty Issue 1945–1953.* London: Associated University Presses, 1979.

Thompson, Victor A. *The Regulatory Process in OPA Rationing.* New York: King's Crown Press, 1950.

Timbers, William H., and Barry H. Garfinkel. "Examination of the Commission's Adjudicatory Process: Some Suggestions." *Virginia Law Review* 45 (1959): 817–30.

Tomlins, Christopher L. *The State and the Unions: Labor Relations, Law, and the Organized Labor Movement in America, 1880–1960.* Cambridge: Cambridge University Press, 1985.

Trachtenberg, Alan. *The Incorporation of America: Culture and Society in the Gilded Age.* New York: Hill and Wang, 1982

Troiano, M. Beth. Note. "Rulemaking or Adjudication in Administrative Policy Formation: Rock versus Hard Place?" *Duquesne Law Review* 13 (1975): 967–82.

Truman, Harry S. *Memoirs*. Garden City, NY: Doubleday & Co., 1956.

Public Papers of the Presidents of the United States: Harry S. Truman. Vol. 1946. Washington, DC: Government Printing Office, 1962.

Public Papers of the Presidents of the United States: Harry S. Truman. Vol. 1947. Washington, DC: Government Printing Office, 1963.

Public Papers of the Presidents of the United States: Harry S. Truman. Vol. 1949. Washington, DC: Government Printing Office, 1964.

Tushnet, Mark. "Administrative Law in the 1930s: The Supreme Court's Accommodation of Progressive Legal Theory." *Duke Law Journal* 60 (2011): 1565–637.

Tyack, David B., Thomas James, and Aaron Benavot. *Law and the Shaping of Public Education, 1785–1954*. Madison: University of Wisconsin Press, 1987.

Van Arkel, Gerhard P. "Administrative Law and the Taft-Hartley Act." *Oregon Law Review* 27 (1948): 171–87.

Vanderbilt, Arthur. "War Powers and Their Administration." *Annual Survey of American Law* 1943 (1943): 115–79.

Vardys, V. Stanley. "Select Committees of the House of Representatives." *Midwest Journal of Political Science* 6 (1962): 247–65.

Verkuil, Paul R. "The Emerging Concept of Administrative Procedure." *Columbia Law Review* 78 (1978): 258–329.

Vogel, David. "The 'New' Social Regulation in Historical and Comparative Perspective." In Thomas K. McCraw, ed., *Regulation in Perspective: Historical Essays* (155–85). Cambridge, MA: Harvard University Press, 1981.

Voorhis, Jerry. *Confessions of a Congressman*. Garden City, NY: Doubleday, 1947.

"Congressional Investigations: Inner Workings." *University of Chicago Law Review* 18 (1951): 455–63.

Waddell, Brian. *The War against the New Deal: World War II and American Democracy*. DeKalb: Northern Illinois University Press, 2001.

Wagner, Susan. *The Federal Trade Commission*. New York: Praeger, 1971.

Wang, Jessica. "Imagining the Administrative State: Legal Pragmatism, Securities Regulation, and New Deal Liberalism." *Journal of Policy History* 17 (2005): 257–93.

Waring, Stephen P. *Taylorism Transformed: Scientific Management Theory since 1945*. Chapel Hill: University of North Carolina Press, 1991.

Warren, George, ed. *The Federal Administrative Procedure Act and the Administrative Agencies*. New York: New York University School of Law, 1947.

Welborn, David M. "Presidents, Regulatory Commissioners and Regulatory Policy." *Journal of Public Law* 15 (1966): 3–29.

Welke, Barbara Young. *Recasting American Liberty: Gender, Race, Law, and the Railroad Revolution, 1865–1920*. Cambridge: Cambridge University Press, 2001.

Wengert, Egbert S. Review of *The Federal Loyalty-Security Program* by Eleanor Bontecou. *American Political Science Review* 48 (1954): 225–26.

Wheatley, Charles F. "A Study of Administrative Procedures – The Department of Interior." *Georgetown Law Journal* 43 (1955): 166–207.

White, G. Edward. "The Emergence of Agency Government and the Creation of Administrative Law." In *The Constitution and the New Deal* (94–127). Cambridge, MA: Harvard University Press, 2000.

Alger Hiss's Looking-Glass Wars: The Covert Life of a Soviet Spy. New York: Oxford University Press, 2004.

White, Leonard D. "Congressional Control of the Public Service." *American Political Science Review* 39 (1945): 1–11.

Wiebe, Robert H. *The Search for Order 1877–1920*. New York: Hill and Wang, 1967.

Wildavsky, Aaron B. *Dixon-Yates: A Study in Power Politics*. New Haven, CT: Yale University Press, 1962.

Wildavsky, Aaron, and Naomi Caiden. *The New Politics of the Budgetary Process*. 4th ed. New York: Addison Wesley Longman, 2001.

Williams, C. Dickerman. "Transportation Regulation and the Department of Commerce." *Yale Law Journal* 62 (1953): 563–74.

Williams, Edward B. Note. "OPA, Small Business, and the 'Due Process' Clause – A Study in Relations." *Georgetown Law Journal* 32 (1943): 76–87.

Wilson, H. H. *Congress: Corruption and Compromise*. New York: Rinehart & Company, 1951.

Wilson, Joan Hoff. "Hoover's Agricultural Policies 1921–1928." *Agricultural History* 51 (1977): 335–61.

Wise, Joseph. "*Morgan v. United States*: Administrative Hearing." *University of Cincinnati Law Review* 12 (1938): 598–605.

Wolf, Benedict. "Administrative Procedure before the National Labor Relations Board," *University of Chicago Law Review* 5 (1938): 358–82.

Woolhandler, Ann. "Judicial Deference to Administrative Action – A Revisionist History." *Administrative Law Review* 43 (1991): 197–245.

Wright, J. Skelly. "The Courts and the Rulemaking Process: The Limits of Judicial Review." *Cornell Law Review* 59 (1974): 375–97.

Young, Roland. *Congressional Politics in the Second World War*. New York: Columbia University Press, 1956.

   The American Congress. New York: Harper, 1958.

Zarkin, Kimberly A., and Michael J. Zarkin. *The Federal Communications Commission: Front Line in the Culture and Regulation Wars*. Westport, CT: Greenwood Press, 2006.

Zelizer, Julian E. *Taxing America: Wilbur D. Mills, Congress, and the State 1945–1975*. New York: Cambridge University Press, 1998.

   On Capitol Hill: The Struggle to Reform Congress and Its Consequences, 1948–2000. Cambridge: Cambridge University Press, 2004.

Zeppos, Nicholas S. "The Legal Profession and the Development of Administrative Law." *Chicago-Kent Law Review* 72 (1997): 1119–57.

Zunz, Olivier. *Making America Corporate, 1870–1920*. Chicago: University of Chicago Press, 1990.

Index

ABA. *See* American Bar Association (ABA)

Acheson, Dean, 66, 68, 155, 158, 166, 183, 189

ACLU. *See* American Civil Liberties Union (ACLU)

Adams, Sherman, 199–200, 242–243

Administrative law judges. *See* Hearing Examiners

Administrative Office of the United States Courts, 206

Administrative Procedure Act (APA) (1946), 5, 10, 11, 57–58, 59–62, 74–99, 102–103, 106, 107, 108, 109–111, 131, 139, 140, 148–149, 151–152, 171–172, 195, 196, 207, 213, 215–219, 226, 227, 233, 244, 245, 247, 250, 254, 255, 256–257

immigration and, 83–85

Advisory Committee on Management Improvement, 189, 191–192

Agricultural Adjustment Act (1938), 15

Agriculture, U.S. Department of (USDA), 9, 22–23, 31, 49, 68, 70, 74, 83, 103, 126, 165, 168, 191, 214, 217, 252

Aiken, George, 156

Aikin, Charles, 181, 182

Aitchison, Clyde, 27

Alien Registration Act (1940), 24

Alsop, Joseph, 190

Alsop, Stewart, 138

American Bar Association (ABA), 12, 21–22, 28, 56, 59–63, 65, 72, 74, 75, 80, 103, 148, 159, 195, 213, 225, 226, 227, 239, 245, 250, 256

Special Committee on Administrative Law, 21–22, 32–33, 47, 52, 62–63, 73–74

Special Committee on Legal Services and Procedure, 226–227

Special Committee on the Federal Administrative Practice Act, 244

American Civil Liberties Union (ACLU), 121, 150

American Federation of Labor, 24

American Jewish Congress, 148, 150

American Judicature Society, 66

American League for Peace and Democracy, 18

American Political Science Association (APSA) Committee on Congress, 115, 117, 128–129

Americans for Democratic Action, 150

Anti-Defamation League of B'nai B'rith, 150

APA. *See* Administrative Procedure Act (APA) (1946)

Appleby, Paul, 75–76, 181

Arnold, Fortas and Porter, 107

Arnold, Thurmond, 107, 139

Association of Interstate Commerce Practitioners, 82–83, 95, 96

Atomic Energy Commission, 165, 199, 200, 211, 252

Attorney General's Committee on Administrative Procedure, 16, 26, 27–28, 46–47, 56, 59–61, 64–74, 79, 80, 83, 91, 103, 106, 114, 156, 166, 172, 196, 205, 206, 213, 225

Bailey, Dorothy, 107

Bailey v. *Richardson*, 107

Baldwin, Roger, 121

Bar of the City of New York, 148

Special Committee on Administrative Law, 64

Bazelon, David, 98

Beard, Charles, 111, 113

Bernstein, Marver, 103, 227, 233, 235–236

Biddle, Francis, 66n24, 102, 104

Bituminous Coal Division, U.S. Department of the Interior, 71
Black, Hugo, 30, 85, 98
Board of Economic Warfare, 18
Board of Examiners, Civil Service Commission, 92–97
Board of Veterans' Appeals, 2
Bontecou, Eleanor, 105
Boren, Lyle H., 41
Bowie, Robert R., 172, 174
Bowles, Chester, 38–39, 40, 124
Bowles v. Willingham, 54–55
Brewster, Owen, 135, 145
Brookings Institution, 157, 169
Brooks, Wayland, 114
Brown, Clarence J., 208
Brown, Prentiss, 40, 42
Brownell, Herbert, 197, 209, 219, 223–224
Brownlow, Louis, 17, 139, 162
Brownlow Committee. *See* President's Committee on Administrative Management
Budget and Accounting Procedures Act (1950), 192
Bureau of Indian Affairs, 168
Bureau of Internal Revenue, 141–142. *See also* Internal Revenue Service
Bureau of the Budget, 17, 75, 129, 156, 162, 165, 171, 173, 177, 203, 224, 238
Burns, James MacGregor, 61, 182
Bush, Prescott S., 148
Byrd, Harry F., 33–35, 170. *See also* Byrd Committee
Byrd Committee (Joint Committee on Non-essential Expenditures), 33–34, 73, 132

CAB. *See* Civil Aeronautics Board (CAB)
Capehart, Homer, 115
Central Intelligence Agency (CIA), 153
Chafee, Zechariah, Jr., 102
CIO (Congress of Industrial Organizations), 18, 24, 88
Citizens Committee for the Hoover Report (first), 163–164, 182, 183–189, 191, 192, 202, 207
Citizens Committee for the Hoover Report (second), 209–210, 223, 225, 226
Civil Aeronautics Board (CAB), 95, 96–98, 125, 169, 172, 175, 176, 178, 190, 216, 227, 230–231, 233, 234, 237, 238, 240, 246, 247, 248
Civil Rights Act (1964), 252

Civil Service Commission (CSC), 63, 91–99, 106, 142, 162, 165, 170–171, 190, 203–204, 211, 216
  hearing examiner controversy and, 91–99
  Loyalty Review Board, 101–102, 104–105, 197n
Civilian Conservation Corps, 34, 73
Clark, Herbert Watson, 213
Clark, Tom C., 75, 80, 81, 82, 89, 147
Clean Air Act Amendments (1970), 252, 255, 256
Coast Guard, 169, 231
Coates, Charles B., 160–161, 163, 183, 185, 186–187, 188
Code of Ethics for Government Service, 244
Commerce, U.S. Department of, 169, 172, 182, 190, 191, 229, 231
Commission on Intergovernmental Relations, 223
Commission on Organization of the Executive Branch. *See* Hoover Commission (first), Hoover Commission (second)
Committee of Hoover Commission Task Force Members, 225–226
Committee on Department of Defense Organization, 204
Communications Act Amendments (1952), 215
Communism, 18, 99–100, 112, 130, 142–144
Conant, James B., 163
Congress, U.S. *See* Committees by name
Consumer Product Safety Act (1972), 252
Consumer Product Safety Commission, 252, 255, 256
Corcoran, Thomas, 245
Council of Economic Advisors, 165, 203
Council on Environmental Quality, 252
Covington, Burling, Rublee, Acheson & Shorb, 96
Cox, Archibald, 247–248
Cox, Eugene, 15, 114, 115, 116, 118–122, 134. *See also* Cox Committee
Cox Committee, 118–122, 145, 177, 179
Cross, Hugh, 196
CSC. *See* Civil Service Commission (CSC)
Cummings, Homer, 6, 65

Davis, Kenneth Culp, 61, 76, 79, 91, 108, 111, 222
Dawes, Charles G., 163
Defense, U.S. Department of, 189, 204, 215, 246

Democratic party
    charges of allowing Communists to infiltrate
        the federal government, 99–100
    control of Congress and, 14, 135–136
    labor unrest and economic instability in
        weakening, 86
    in 1936, 14
    in 1948 election, 160
Denham, Robert, 87, 191
Dewey, Thomas, 159, 160
Dies, Martin, Jr., 15, 18, 116–117, 148, 150.
        See also Dies Committee
Dies Committee, 18–19, 41, 99–100, 119,
        122, 145
Dirksen, Everett, 114, 126, 258–259
District of Columbia Bar Association, 244
Dixiecrats, 160
Dixon-Yates controversy, 199–200
Dodd, William E. Jr., 19
Doerfer, John C., 241
Doughton, Robert L., 34
Douglas, James Marsh, 213
Douglas, Paul H., 33, 139–142, 145, 228
Douglas, William O., 2, 54, 86, 91,
        98, 254
Dulles, John Foster, 64
Durr, Clifford J., 19, 104, 120, 179–180
Durr, Virginia, 19, 180

Eberstadt, Ferdinand, 157
Eisenhower, Dwight D., 195, 197–204, 207,
        230–233, 238, 246
    Cabinet Committee on Transport Policy and
        Organization, 229–230
    first Hoover Commission and, 163,
        202–203
    second Hoover Commission and, 223
Eisenhower, Milton, 202
Election(s)
    of 1936, 14
    of 1946, 100
    of 1948, 158, 159–161
    of 1952, 195, 197, 202
Emergency Court of Appeals, 50–54
Emergency Price Control Act (1942), 35–38,
        39–40, 42, 44–45, 49, 50–55, 56
Emerson, Thomas I., 50n
Emmerich, Herbert, 164
Employment Service, U.S., 107
Endangered Species Act (1973), 252, 255
Endangered Species Conservation Act
        (1969), 252
Environmental Protection Agency, 252, 255

Executive Office of the President, 31, 165,
        188–189, 190, 203, 232, 246
Executive Order 9835, 100–101, 104n
Executive Order 10450, 197n

Fahy, Charles, 28
Fair Labor Standards Act (1938), 15
Farley, James A., 209, 220
FCC. *See* Federal Communications
        Commission (FCC)
FCC v. Pottsville Broadcasting Co., 30
Federal Alcohol Administration, 2, 67–68
Federal Aviation Act (1958), 230
Federal Aviation Administration (FAA), 230,
        231, 246
Federal Bar Association, 150
Federal Bureau of Investigation (FBI), 19–20,
        103, 104, 197
Federal Communications Commission (FCC),
        2, 8, 9, 19–20, 23, 30, 64, 69, 70, 91,
        100, 103, 104, 125, 133–135, 172, 175,
        176, 177, 178, 179–180, 191, 196, 197,
        201, 215, 216, 234, 237–239, 240–242,
        246, 248, 250, 257
    Cox Committee investigation of, 118–122,
        145, 177, 179
    Dies Committee investigation of, 18–19
    Harness Committee investigation of,
        133–134
    House Committee on Interstate and Foreign
        Commerce and, 19, 234–235
    Senate Committee on Interstate and Foreign
        Commerce and, 134–135
Federal Deposit Insurance Corporation
        (FDIC), 214
Federal Metal and Nonmetallic Mine Safety
        Act (1966), 252
Federal Power Commission (FPC), 15, 19, 74,
        82, 112, 122, 125, 172, 190, 200, 216,
        224, 240, 245, 257
Federal Radiation Council, 252–253
Federal Register Act (1935), 77
Federal Reserve Board, 64, 172, 214, 216
Federal Rules of Civil Procedure, 206, 217
Federal Security Agency, 82, 144, 168, 190,
        191, 203
Federal Tort Claims Act (1946), 126
Federal Trade Commission (FTC), 2, 15, 63,
        74, 75, 79, 82, 125, 165, 170, 172, 176,
        179, 190, 216, 222, 224, 238, 240, 242,
        246, 247, 248
Federal Trial Examiners' Conference, 96, 98
Federal Works Agency, 18–19

Ferguson, Homer, 135
First War Powers Act (1941), 31
"Five-percenters" investigation, 137–138, 143
Flemming, Arthur S., 155, 163, 202, 208, 209, 219, 220, 230, 231
Fly, James L., 19, 119–121, 179
Food, Drug and Cosmetic Act, 82
Food and Drug Administration (FDA), 15, 214, 240
Ford Motor Co., 110
Forrestal, James V., 155
Fortas, Abe, 71, 105
Frankfurter, Felix, 30, 60, 72, 85, 90, 98
Freedom of Information Act (1965), 256–257
Freund, Paul, 36
Friendly, Henry J., 238–239, 253–254
FTC. *See* Federal Trade Commission (FTC)
Fuchs, Ralph, 66, 221, 246
Fulbright, J. William, 137–139

Galenson, Walter, 174, 179, 191
Galloway, George, 117, 125, 127–129, 131, 144
Garey, Eugene, 180
Garner, John Nance, 163
Garrison, Lloyd, 66, 103–104
Gathings, E. C., 126
Gellhorn, Walter, 65, 66
General Accounting Office, 162
General Bridge Act (1946), 126
General Electric, 41
General Motors, 204
General Services Administration, 192
George, Walter F., 34
Gilbreth, Lillian, 163
Ginsburg, David, 39
Glass, Carter, 34
Goldfine, Bernard, 242–243
Goldman Sachs, 41
Golub, William W., 177, 178, 179
Government in the Sunshine Act (1976), 258–259
Government Printing Office, 144
Griswold, Erwin, 102, 128
Groner, D. Lawrence, 66, 67, 70
Gulick, Luther H., 17

Hand, Learned, 139
Harness, Forest A., 134
Harris, Oren, 241, 245
Hart, Henry M., Jr., 66
Hatch Act (1939), 18
Health, Education and Welfare, U.S.
    Department of, 168, 192, 203, 246, 252

Hearing examiners, 11, 20–27, 31, 56, 59, 62, 68–70, 72, 74, 78, 79, 80, 82, 85, 87, 91–99, 106, 108, 135, 138, 171, 205–207, 213, 215, 216, 218, 219–220, 226, 234, 235, 238, 245, 248, 250, 259
Hecht Company department store, 40
Hector, Louis J., 227, 228, 233, 234, 235, 237
Heller, Robert, 115, 117, 123, 126
Henderson, Leon, 37, 39–40, 41
Hiss, Alger, 142, 143
Hoey, Clyde R., 136–137
Hoffman, Clare, 43–44
Holifield, Chet, 209, 220
Hollister, Solomon C., 219
Hook, Charles R., 226
Hoover Commission (first), 5, 10, 153–194, 195, 208, 209, 222, 225, 227, 228, 230, 235
    Budgeting and Accounting task force, 156
    Citizens Committee. *See* Citizens Committee for the Hoover Report
    Defense Establishment, 168
    Eisenhower and, 195, 202–203
    Federal Business Enterprise, 156, 183
    Federal Medical Services, 168
    Federal-State Relations, 156
    General Management in the Executive Branch, 164–168, 169, 192–193
    Independent Regulatory Commissions, 156, 169, 182, 213
    Personnel Management, 156, 168, 170
    Public Welfare, 157
    Public Works, 156
    Transportation, 157, 168, 169
    Truman and, 160–162, 164, 188–193
    Veterans Affairs, 156
Hoover Commission (second), 5, 12, 195, 208–226
    Budget and Accounting, 209
    Business Enterprises, 211
    Business Organization of the Department of Defense, 210
    Eisenhower and, 208, 223
    Federal Activities Competitive with Private Enterprise, 209
    Legal Services and Procedure, 195, 196, 209, 212–222, 226
    Lending, Guaranteeing, and Insurance Agencies, 211
    Medical Services, 209
    Personnel, 209
    Surplus Property, 210
    Transportation, 209, 211

Water Resources and Power, 211
Hoover Commission (third), 250
Hoover, Herbert S., 157, 195, 198, 207, 209
  and the first Hoover Commission, 153,
    156–160, 163–165, 168, 184, 186, 190,
    192, 198, 206
  and the second Hoover Commission,
    207–208, 209–210, 213, 219, 221
Hopkins, Harry, 18
House of Representatives, U.S. *See also* Joint
    committees; Senate, U.S.
  Committee on Appropriations, 19, 34,
    125, 132
  Committee on Armed Services, 132
  Committee on Education and Labor,
    87–88, 248
  Committee on Expenditures in the
    Executive Department, 118, 125, 156,
    162–163
  Committee on Government Operations,
    230, 257
  Subcommittee on Foreign Operations and
    Government Information, 256
  Committee on Interstate and Foreign
    Commerce, 19, 33, 125, 234–235, 245
  Special Subcommittee on Investigation
    of Restrictions on Brand Names and
    Newsprint, 41
  Special Subcommittee on Legislative
    Oversight, 196–197, 240–244, 247
  Committee on Rules, 150–151
  Committee on Small Business, 33, 40
  Committee on the Judiciary, 63, 121
  Committee on Un-American Activities
    Committee (HUAC), 18, 124, 133, 142,
    147, 148, 150
  Committee on Ways and Means, 34, 125
  Select Committee on Lobbying Activities, 136
  Select Committee on Small Business, 241
  Select Committee to Investigate Acts of
    Executive Agencies Beyond the Scope of
    Their Authority, 43–47
  Select Committee to Investigate
    Newsprint, 132
  Select Committee(s) to Investigate the
    Federal Communications Commission
    (Cox Committee), 118–122, 145,
    177, 179
  Select Committee to Investigate the Federal
    Communications Commission (Harness
    Committee), 133–134
  Special Committee to Investigate the
    National Labor Relations Board,
    24–26

Special Subcommittee on Government
    Information, 256
Hughes, Charles Evan, 21, 22
Huntington, Samuel, 227, 228–229, 236
Hyde, Rosel, 173

ICC. *See* Interstate Commerce Commission
    (ICC)
Ickes, Harold, 18, 162
Immigration and Naturalization Service (INS),
    83–85
Independent Regulatory Agencies Act, 244
Institute of Public Administration, 157
Interior, U.S. Department of, 9, 18, 82, 165,
    190, 211, 217, 221–222, 252, 255
Internal Revenue Service (IRS), 197
Interstate Commerce Commission (ICC), 2,
    16, 26, 27, 50, 54, 63, 69, 74, 75,
    76, 82, 83, 91, 95, 97, 125, 165, 169,
    172, 174, 175, 176, 178, 191, 193,
    196, 216, 228–230, 231, 240, 245,
    246, 248
Transportation Act of 1940, 75

Jackson, Robert H., 66, 84–85, 139, 213
Jaffe, Louis, 196, 221, 222, 227, 236, 237
Javits, Jacob, 148
Jenner, William E., 150
Jennings, John, Jr., 60
Johnson, Lyndon B., 256
Johnson, Nicholas, 258
Johnson, Robert L., 164, 183–184, 185,
    186, 187
Joint Committee on Atomic Energy, 200
Joint Committee on Foreign Economic
    Cooperation, 131
Joint Committee on Labor-Management
    Relations, 131, 132, 179
Joint Committee on Non-essential
    Expenditures (Byrd Committee),
    33–34, 132
Joint Committee on the Organization of
    Congress, 112, 114–115, 117,
    123–132
Joint Committee on the Reduction of
    Nonessential Federal Expenditures,
    33–34
Jones, Harold A., 230
Jones, Jesse, 163
Judicial Conference, 204–206
Judicial review, 5, 11, 12, 20, 21, 26, 29, 30,
    48–52, 54, 56, 59, 60–61, 65, 72, 73,
    75–76, 80–81, 83, 86, 88–90, 106–107,
    207, 214, 217–219, 224, 226, 243

Justice, U.S. Department of, 65, 83, 135, 165, 190, 197, 206, 215, 225, 243
  Attorney General's Manual on the Administrative Procedure Act, 79–81
  Office of Legal Services and Procedure, 215

Kefauver, Estes, 33, 114, 122, 145, 146, 148, 149
Kennedy, John F., 12, 238, 246–249, 258
Kennedy, Joseph P., 156, 157, 173, 208, 219, 220
Kerr Committee, 122
Kestnbaum, Meyer, 223, 225
Kieffer, Jarold, 208, 220
Kluttz, Jerry, 102
Koenig, Louis, 181, 182
Korean War, 186, 192, 202
Krock, Arthur, 14, 136

Labor, U.S. Department of, 9, 69–70, 75, 168, 184, 190
La Follette, Robert, Jr., 34, 113, 114, 116, 127, 128, 129, 130, 172
Lamb, Edward, 133
Landis, James M., 12, 16, 64, 173, 175n, 176, 213, 227, 246–249, 258
Legislative Reorganization Act (1946), 5, 10, 11, 58, 109–112, 124–131, 146–148, 151–152, 155, 195
Legislative Reorganization Act (1970), 250
Leventhal, Harold, 172
Levi, Edward, 149
Library of Congress, Legislative Reference Service, 127, 142
Lilienthal, David, 139, 170
Lockerty v. Phillips, 53
Logan, Marvel Mills, 62
Lucas, Scott, 147–148

Mack, Richard A., 241–242
Macmahon, Arthur, 112
Madden, J. Warren, 23–24, 26
Malone, Ross L., Jr., 213
Maloney, Francis, 114
Manasco, Carter, 156
Manly, Basil, 74
Mansfield, Harvey C., 52, 55
Maritime Commission, 2, 122, 138–139, 141, 169, 172, 175, 177, 178
Mayer, Louis B., 163
McCarran, Pat, 60, 75, 77, 97–98, 99, 150, 217
McCarthy, Joseph, 130, 143–144, 146, 149, 151
McClellan, John, 123, 132, 156, 208

McConnaughey, George, 242
McFarland, Carl, 66, 67, 70, 72, 73, 74, 77, 93, 96, 213, 236
Medina, Harold R., 213
Meriam, Lewis, 157
Merriam, Charles E., 17
Metz, Harold, 179
Meyers, Bennett, 143
Millis, Harry, 25, 26
Minow, Newton, 237–238, 250
Mitchell, Harry, 96
Mitchell, Sidney, 208, 219
Monroney, Mike, 110, 113, 114, 123, 132
Morgan v. United States, 22–23, 31, 53, 68, 80, 177n, 239
Morgenthau, Henry, Jr., 34
Moses, Robert, 157
Motor Carrier Act (1935), 2
Murphy, Frank, 65, 66

Nader, Ralph, 259
Nathanson, Nathaniel, 50–51, 76–77, 123–124, 234
National Aeronautics and Space Administration, 246
National Association of Hosiery Manufacturers, 42
National Association of Manufacturers, 200, 210
National Defense Advisory Commission, 31
National Environmental Policy Act (1969), 252
National Exchange Club, 185
National Grange, 182
National Highway Transportation Safety Act (1966), 252
National Highway Transportation Safety Administration, 252
National Housing Agency, 124
National Industrial Recovery Act, 38, 64
National Labor Relations Act (Wagner Act), 24, 86, 87
National Labor Relations Board (NLRB), 2, 9, 16, 20, 23–27, 28, 62, 64, 66, 69–72, 74, 75, 87, 95, 97, 114, 132, 135, 166, 172, 174, 177, 178, 179, 200, 201, 215, 222, 234, 247–248, 254
  Dies Committee investigation of, 18
  Smith Committee investigation of, 24–26, 43, 63, 69–70, 145, 179
  Taft-Hartley Act and, 62, 86–90, 108, 191, 215, 218, 247
  v. Wyman-Gordon Co., 254
National Lawyers Guild, 64

National Military Establishment, 189
National Planning Association, 115
National Recovery Administration, 8
National Resources Planning Board, 17,
    73, 172
National Retail Drygoods Association, 42
National Security Act (1947), 153, 189
National Security Council, 153, 190
National Security Resources Board, 190
National Wholesale Druggists Association, 43
National Youth Administration, 18–19, 34, 73
Navy Department, 120, 153
Nelson, Donald, 33
New Deal, 3–4, 14, 15, 18–19, 24, 34, 35, 60,
    114, 130, 142, 153, 154, 159, 198, 260,
    261, 262
Niebuhr, Reinhold, 139
Nixon, Richard M., 130
NLRB. *See* National Labor Relations Board
    (NLRB)

O'Brian, John Lord, 103n
Occupational Safety and Health Act (1970),
    252, 255
Occupational Safety and Health
    Administration, 253
Office of Defense Mobilization, 204
Office of Emergency Management, 31
Office of Federal Administrative Procedure,
    205, 225
Office of Legal Services and Procedure.
    See Justice, U.S. Department of
Office of Price Administration (OPA), 4, 8–9,
    15–16, 18, 32, 34–57, 73, 76, 124
    Byrd Committee investigation of, 34–35
    Dies Committee investigation of, 41
    Emergency Court of Appeals, 50–54
Office of Price Administration and Civilian
    Supply, 35
    Smith Committee investigation of, 43–47,
    52, 56, 73
    suspension orders, 44–49
Office of Production Management, 32
Office of Strategic Services, 142
Office of War Information, 18
Office of War Mobilization, 38
Olds, Leland, 112
OPA. *See* Office of Price Administration
    (OPA)

Pace, Frank, 189
PACGO. *See* President's Advisory Committee
    on Government Organization (PACGO)
Pearson, Drew, 119, 161

Peck, Cornelius J., 254
Pepper, Claude, 114
Perkins, Frances, 18
Perkins v. Lukens Steel Co. (1940), 30
Pittenger, William, 113, 114
Pollock, James K., 183
Post Office, 168, 185, 190
Pound, Roscoe, 21, 46, 62
President's Advisory Committee on
    Government Organization (PACGO),
    203–204, 207, 209, 223, 225,
    231–232, 234
President's Committee on Administrative
    Management, 17, 154, 156, 158, 161,
    162, 167, 173, 182, 203
President's Conference on Administrative
    Procedure (1953–55), 204–207, 225
President's Conference on Administrative
    Procedure (1961), 259
Prettyman, E. Barrett, 205
Price, Don K., 160, 164, 167
Progressive Party, 160
Public Administration Clearing House, 17, 164
Public Roads Administration, 169
Pusey, Merlo, 122, 128

Railroad Retirement Board, 2, 240
Ramspeck, Robert, 115
Rayburn, Sam, 120, 121, 240
Reconstruction Finance Corporation (RFC),
    133, 137–138, 141, 143, 191
Redford, Emmette, 181, 184, 232, 238
Rees, Edward H., 126
Remington, William, 143
Reorganization Act (1939), 161–162
Reorganization Act (1949), 189
Republican Party, 86, 130, 133, 153, 162, 195
Reston, James, 142, 198
Richardson, Seth W., 105–106
Roberts, Owen J., 54, 163
Rockefeller, Nelson, 202, 204, 223
Rogers, Lindsay, 148
Roosevelt, Franklin D., 2, 14, 15, 17–18,
    31–32, 34, 49, 59, 64–67, 110, 114,
    115, 130, 158, 161
Rowe, James H., 156, 157, 158, 161, 183
Rural Electrification Administration, 19
Russell, Richard, 114
Rutledge, Wiley B., 54

San Francisco Bar Association, 47
Sawyer, Charles, 140, 231
Schwartz, Bernard, 82, 221, 238, 240–241
Scott, Hugh, 145–146

Sears, Roebuck, 41
SEC. *See* Securities and Exchange Commission
(SEC)
Second War Powers Act, 37, 45, 48
Securities and Exchange Commission (SEC),
2, 8, 9, 16, 19, 21, 49, 69, 74, 82, 125,
138, 166, 172, 173, 175, 176, 178, 190,
200, 234, 240, 242, 246, 247, 248
Sellers, Ashley, 226
Senate, U.S. *See also* House of Representatives,
U.S.; Joint committees
Appropriations Committee, 34, 125,
132, 145
Committee on Banking and Currency, 35,
137-138
Committee on Expenditures in the Executive
Department, 125, 135, 136-137,
156, 172
Permanent Subcommittee on
Investigations, 135-136, 143-144,
146, 149
Committee on Finance, 33-34, 125
Committee on Foreign Relations, 143
Committee on Government Operations, 147
Committee on Interior, Natural Resources,
and Public Works, 124
Committee on Interstate and Foreign
Commerce, 125, 133, 134-135, 175
Committee on Labor and Public Welfare,
139-140, 228, 247
Committee on Rules and Administration,
115, 150
Committee on the District of Columbia, 125
Committee on the Judiciary, 26, 60, 72-73,
74, 77, 80, 81, 94, 97, 254
Subcommittee on Administrative Practice
and Procedure, 227, 248-249, 258
Subcommittee on Antitrust and
Monopoly, 200
Subcommittee on Internal Security, 143,
146, 150
Special Committee to Investigate the
National Defense Program, 33
Special Committee to Study the Problems
of American Small Business
Enterprises, 132
War Investigating Committee, 135, 145
Shils, Edward, 134
Shulman, Harry, 66
Smith, Edwin, 25
Smith, Harold D., 34
Smith, Howard W., 15, 43, 118, 122-123.
See also Smith Committee

Smith Committee,
House Select Committee to Investigate
Executive Agencies, 43-48, 52, 56-58,
66, 68, 73, 114
House Special Committee to Investigate
the National Labor Relations Board,
24-26, 63, 69-70, 87, 145, 179
Smithsonian Institution, 165
Social Security, 2, 198
Social Security Act, 15
Social Security Board, 79
Stans, Maurice, 231
Stason, E. Blythe, 66, 67, 70, 72, 73, 213
State, U.S. Department of, 100, 142, 165, 189
Stimson, Henry L., 157
Storey, Robert G., 213, 221
Supreme Court, 6, 20, 22, 23, 27, 28, 30,
31, 35, 49, 51, 53, 55, 56, 61, 68, 81,
83-86, 89-91, 98, 175, 216, 233, 242,
254, 257. *See also* Judicial review

Taft, Robert, 41, 188
Taft-Hartley Act (1947), 62, 86-90, 108, 153,
191, 215, 218, 247
Tariff Commission, 216
Tennessee Valley Authority (TVA), 18,
199-200
Thomas, J. Parnell, 142
Till, Irene, 176
Toots Shor (restaurant), 46
Transportation, U.S. Department of, 231, 252
Transportation Act (1940), 75
Transportation Act (1958), 230
Treasury Department, 18, 191, 211, 214, 224
Truman, Harry S., 57-58, 61, 76, 109, 127,
129, 130, 135, 138-139, 142, 147,
156, 159, 160-161, 165, 187, 197,
199, 201, 207
Fair Deal, 76, 135, 198
and the Hoover Commission, 160-162, 164,
188-192
loyalty-security program, 61, 101-108, 112
reorganization and, 161-162, 187, 190
as senator, 32, 33, 40, 118, 135, 149
Truman Committee (Senate Special Committee
to Investigate the National Defense
Program), 33, 40, 135, 149
Tuck, William Hallam, 208
Tuttle, Elbert Parr, 213

Universal Camera v. *NLRB*, 89-90, 98-99, 216
U.S. Information Service Centers, 144
U.S. Steel Corporation, 226

Vanderbilt, Arthur T., 66, 67, 70, 72, 73, 213
Vaughan, Harry, 137
Velde, Harold H., 147, 150
Veterans Administration, 2, 79, 211
Veterans of Foreign Wars, 150
Vinson, Fred, 55, 204
Voice of America, 144
Voorhis, Jerry, 57, 113, 114, 117–118,
        122, 130

Wages and Hours Act, 64
Wages and Hours Administration, 18
Wagner, Robert, 25
Wagner Act. *See* National Labor
        Relations Act
Wallace, Henry A., 22, 31, 162
Walsh-Healey Act, 30–31
Walter, Francis, 62
Walter-Logan bill, 59, 60, 62–64, 66–67,
        73–74
War Department, 67, 120, 153
War Labor Board, 32, 56, 179

War Production Board (WPB), 9, 18, 32, 33,
        34–35, 37, 40
Warren, Lindsay, 162
Watson, Goodwin, 19
Webb, James, 158, 161, 162
Weeks, Sinclair, 230
In re Weirton Steel Co., 24
Weiss, Samuel, 121
White, Leonard, 116, 170
Wiley, Alexander, 94
Williams, Ernest, 174, 227, 233–234
Wilson, Charles W., 163, 204, 230
Wong Yang Sung v. McGrath, 84
Woodrum, Clifton A., 34
Works Progress Administration (WPA), 18, 34,
        40–41, 73
WPB. *See* War Production Board (WPB)
Wyzanski, Charles, 65

Yakus v. United States, 53–55
Young, Owen D., 172
Young & Rubicam, 185

CPSIA information can be obtained
at www.ICGtesting.com
Printed in the USA
BVHW031255310719
554795BV00001B/4/P